JOHN WILLIS

SCREEN WORLD

2003

VOLUME 54

ASSOCIATE EDITOR

Barry Monush

APPLAUSE

THEATRE & CINEMA BOOKS

SCREEN WORLD
Volume 54

Art Direction: Michelle Thompson
Book Design: Kristina Rolander

ISBN (hardcover): 1-55783-528-4
ISBN (paperback): 1-55783-526-8
ISSN: 1545-9020

APPLAUSE THEATRE & CINEMA BOOKS
151 West 46th Street, 8th Floor
New York, NY 10036
PHONE: (212) 575-9265
FAX: (646) 562-5852
EMAIL: info@applausepub.com
INTERNET: www.applausepub.com

Sales & Distribution

NORTH AMERICA:
Hal Leonard Corp.
7777 West Bluemound Road
P. O. Box 13819
Milwaukee, WI 53213
PHONE: (414) 774-3630
FAX: (414) 774-3259
EMAIL: halinfo@halleonard.com
INTERNET: www.halleonard.com

UK:
Roundhouse Publishing Ltd.
Millstone, Limers Lane
Northam, North Devon EX39 2RG
PHONE: (0) 1237-474-474
FAX: (0) 1237-474-774
EMAIL: roundhouse.group@ukgateway.net

CONTENTS

EDITOR
John Willis

ASSOCIATE EDITOR
Barry Monush

ACKNOWLEDGEMENTS: Anthology Film Archives, Artistic License, Jenna Bagnini, Thomas Buxereau, Castle Hill, David Christopher, Samantha Dean, DreamWorks, Brian Durnin, The Film Forum, First Look, First Run Features, Fox Searchlight, Kino International, Leisure Time Features, Tom Lynch, Mike Maggiore, Miramax Films, David Munro, New Line Cinema / Fine Line Features, New Yorker Films, Paramount Pictures, Kristina Rolander, 7th Art Releasing, Kallie Shimek, Sony Pictures Entertainment, Sheldon Stone, Strand Releasing, Michelle Thompson, Twentieth Century Fox, Universal Pictures, Walt Disney Pictures, Zeitgeist Films

Casino Royale

Take the Money and Run

Early 1970s

Bananas

Manhattan

Stardust Memories

Zelig

Crimes and Misdemeanors

Celebrity

TO WOODY ALLEN

Whose perceptive, irreverent, often brilliantly funny views on love, death, sex and human nature have made him one of the few genuine geniuses of modern film comedy.

FILMS: *What's New Pussycat* (1965; actor, writer); *What's Up, Tiger Lily?* (1966; actor, writer, producer, footage compiler); *Casino Royale* (1967; actor, uncredited co-writer); *Take the Money and Run* (1969; actor, director, co-writer); *Bananas* (1971; actor, director, co-writer); *Play It Again, Sam* (1972; actor, writer); *Everything You Always Wanted to Know About Sex* But Were Afraid to Ask* (1972; actor, director, writer); *Sleeper* (1973; actor, director, co-writer); *Love and Death* (1975; actor, director, writer); *The Front* (1976; actor); *Annie Hall* (1977; actor, director, co-writer; Academy Award Winner for Best Director and Best Screenplay); *Interiors* (1978; director, writer; Academy Award nominations for director and screenplay); *Manhattan* (1979; actor, director, co-writer; Academy Award nomination for screenplay); *Stardust Memories* (1980; actor, director, writer); *A Midsummer Night's Sex Comedy* (1982; actor, director, writer); *Zelig* (1983; actor, director, writer); *Broadway Danny Rose* (1984; actor, director, writer; Academy Award nominations for director and screenplay); *The Purple Rose of Cairo* (1985; director, writer; Academy Award nomination for screenplay); *Hannah and Her Sisters* (1986; actor, director, writer; Academy Award Winner for Best Screenplay; Academy Award nomination for director); *Radio Days* (1987; director, writer, voice; Academy Award nomination for screenplay); *September* (1987; director, writer); *King Lear* (1988; actor); *Another Woman* (1988; director, writer); *New York Stories* (1989; actor, director, writer of "Oedipus Wrecks" segment); *Crimes and Misdemeanors* (1989; actor, director, writer; Academy Award nominations for director and screenplay); *Alice* (1990; director, writer); *Scenes from a Mall* (1991; actor); *Shadows and Fog* (1992; actor, director, writer); *Husbands and Wives* (1992; actor, director, writer; Academy Award nomination for screenplay); *Manhattan Murder Mystery* (1993; actor, director, co-writer); *Bullets Over Broadway* (1994; director, co-writer; Academy Award nominations for director and screenplay); *Mighty Aphrodite* (1995; actor, director, writer; Academy Award nomination for screenplay); *Everyone Says I Love You* (1996; actor, director, writer); *Deconstructing Harry* (1997; actor, director, writer; Academy Award nomination for screenplay); *Wild Man Blues* (1998; actor); *The Impostors* (1998; actor); *Antz* (1998; voice); *Celebrity* (1998; director, writer); *Sweet and Lowdown* (1999; actor, director, writer); *Small Time Crooks* (2000; actor, director, writer); *Company Man* (2001; actor); *The Curse of the Jade Scorpion* (2001; actor, director, writer); *Hollywood Ending* (2002; actor, director, writer); *Anything Else* (2003; actor, director, writer).

TOP BOX OFFICE STARS OF 2002

1. Tom Hanks

2. Tom Cruise

3. Mike Myers

4. Reese Witherspoon

5. Leonardo DiCaprio

6. Nicole Kidman

7. Catherine Zeta-Jones

8. Denzel Washington

9. Mel Gibson

10. Vin Diesel

DOMESTIC FILMS

2002 RELEASES

ORANGE COUNTY

(**PARAMOUNT**) Producers, Scott Rudin, Van Toffler, David Gale, Scott Aversano; Executive Producers, Herbert W. Gains, Adam Schroeder; Director, Jake Kasdan; Screenplay, Mike White; Photography, Greg Gardiner; Designer, Gary Frutkoff; Editor, Tara Timpone; Music, Michael Andrews; Music Supervisors, Manish Raval, Tom Wolfe; an MTV Films/ Scott Rudin production; Dolby; Color; Rated PG-13; 81 minutes; Release date: January 11, 2002

CAST

Shaun Brumder	Colin Hanks
Lance Brumder	Jack Black
Cindy Beugler	Catherine O'Hara
Ashley	Schuyler Fisk
Bud Brumder	John Lithgow
Don Durkett	Harold Ramis
Charlotte Cobb	Lily Tomlin
Principal Harbert	Chevy Chase
Mona	Jane Adams
Arthur Gantner	Garry Marshall
Vera Gantner	Dana Ivey
Bob Beugler	George Murdock
Krista	Leslie Mann
Arlo	Kyle Howard
Chad	RJ Knoll
Lonny Munsack	Brett Harrison
Mr. Burke	Mike White
Marcus Skinner	Kevin Kline
Firefighter	Ben Stiller
Lupe	Lillian Hurst
Dana	Olivia Rosewood
Tanya	Carly Pope

and Natasha Melnick (Katie), Manu Intiraymi (Student), Fran Kranz (Shane Brainard), Shawn Soong (Stoner), Grace Bustos (Cheerleader), Sarah Hagan (Sarah), Michael Aquino (Jake), Elsie Escobar (Rosa), Orlando Garcia (Jorge), Daniel Farber (Lucas), Carolyn Wilson (Butch Female Janitor), Brianna Shebby (Stephanie Durkett), Leslie Appleyard (Gina Durkett), Beth Gains (Mrs. Durkett), David Doty (Public Safety), Monica Keena (Gretchen), Sarah Loew, Lizzy Caplan (Party Girls), Nat Faxon (Kip)

Having decided that he's spent far too much of his life as a surfing slacker, Shaun Brumder makes it his goal to get into Stanford University and become a writer.

© Paramount Pictures

Harold Ramis, Schuyler Fisk, Colin Hanks

Brett Harrison, Kyle Howard, RJ Knoll, Colin Hanks

Colin Hanks, Lily Tomlin

Jack Black, Colin Hanks

SNOW DOGS

(**WALT DISNEY PICTURES**) Producer, Jordan Kerner; Executive Producers, Christine Whitaker, Casey Grant; Director, Brian Levant; Screenplay, Jim Kouf, Tommy Swerdlow, Michael Goldberg, Mark Gibson, Philip Halprin; Suggested by the book *Winterdance* by Gary Paulsen; Photography, Thomas Ackerman; Designer, Stephen Lineweaver; Costumes, Monique Prudhomme; Editor, Roger Bondelli; Music, John Debney; Head Animal Trainer/Coordinator, Stacy Basil; Casting, Amanda Mackey Johnson, Cathy Sandrich Gelfond; Dolby; Technicolor; Rated PG; 99 minutes; Release date: January 18, 2002

CAST

Ted Brooks	Cuba Gooding, Jr.
Thunder Jack	James Coburn
Dr. Rupert Brooks	Sisqo
Amelia Brooks	Nichelle Nichols
George	M. Emmet Walsh
Peter Yellowbear	Graham Greene
Ernie	Brian Doyle-Murray
Barb	Joanna Bacalso
Olivier	Jean-Michel Pare

and Jason Pouliotte, David Boyce (Sneed Brothers), Frank C. Turner (Nelly), Ron Small (Arthur), Alison Matthews (TV Reporter), Jascha Washington (Young Ted), Christopher Judge (Dr. Brooks), Lisa Dahling (Mrs. Yepremian), Daneille Folta Kehealy (Rollerblader with Dog), Peter "Mus" Musooli (Valet), Lossen Chambers (Receptionist), Andrea Butterfield (Patient), Oscar Goncalves (Ernesto Julio Santisto), Angela Moore (Lucy), Tracey Henderson, Randy Birch (Vets), Dave "Squatch" Ward (Taxi Driver), Donnelly Rhodes, Jay Brazeau (Race Officials), Phillip Beer, George Labelle (Chess Players), Monika Kramlik, Gwendolyn Osborne (Miami Pretty Girls), Anthony Harrison (Dentist), Shaw Madsen (Blonde Guy), Joe Maffei (Old Man), Nicole Oliver (Nurse), Veronica Shattuck, Nicola O'Shea (Chatting Women); Dogs: Fly, Dash (Nan), D.J., Cody (Demon), Floyd (Mac), Shadow (Diesel), Tika (Duchess), Speedy (Digger), Koda (Yodel), Buck (Sniff), Timber (Dog with Rollerblader), Skippy (Dog at Restaurant), Mario (Chester the Poodle); Jim Belushi (Voice of Demon), Jane Sibbett (Voice of Nana)

A Miami dentist travels to Alaska to claim an inheritance, only to discover that he has been left a team of sled dogs.

Cuba Gooding, Jr., James Coburn

Cuba Gooding, Jr.

Graham Greene, Cuba Gooding, Jr.

THE MOTHMAN PROPHECIES

(SCREEN GEMS) Producers, Tom Rosenberg, Gary Lucchesi, Gary Goldstein; Executive Producers, Ted Tannebaum, Richard S. Wright, Terry A. McKay; Director, Mark Pellington; Screenplay, Richard Hatem; Based upon the book by John A. Keel; Photography, Fred Murphy; Designer, Richard Hoover; Costumes, Susan Lyall; Editor, Brian Berdan; Music, Tomandandy; Co-Producers, Richard Hatem, James McQuaide; Casting, Sheila Jaffe; a Lakeshore Entertainment presentation of a Lakeshore Entertainment production; Dolby; Super 35 Widescreen; Color; Rated PG-13; 119 minutes; Release date: January 25, 2002

Laura Linney, Lucinda Jenney, Will Patton

CAST

John Klein	Richard Gere
Connie Parker	Laura Linney
Gordon Smallwood	Will Patton
Denise Smallwood	Lucinda Jenney
Mary Klein	Debra Messing
Dr. Alexander Leek	Alan Bates
Chief Josh Jerrett	Nesbitt Blaisdell
Kevin Mills (7 yrs.)	Clay Bunting
C.J.	Dan Callahan
Travel Lodge Clerk	Eric Cazencave
Gov. Rob McCallum	Murphy Dunne
Ed Fleischman	David Eigenberg
Dr. McElory	Yvonne Erickson
Holly	Christin Frame
Sonny	Tim Hartman
News Anchor	Doug Korstanje
Newsperson	Susan Korstanje
Indrid Cold	Bill Laing
TV Journalist	Harris Mackenzie

and Pete Handelman, Matt Miller, Josh Braun (Aides), Nick Keeley, Dixie Tymitz, Jason Billy Simmons, Bettina Rousos (Spectators), Jennifer Martin (Coffee Shop Cashier), Billy Mott (Otto), Sam Nicotero (Man on Bridge), Scott Nunnally (Orderly), Mark Pellington (Bartender), David Press (Woodrow), Dorothy Silver (Ruth), Tom Stoviak (Real Estate Agent), Rohn Thomas (Dr. Williams), Bob Tracey (Cyrus Bills), Tom Tully (Motel Manager), Betsy Zajko (Tory Pherris)

Richard Gere

Years after his wife's death in a car accident has left him numbed to life, reporter John Klein ends up in the town of Point Pleasant, West Virginia where he becomes intrigued by multiple reports of a strange apparition that seems related to his wife's final words.

© Screen Gems

Dan Callahan, Richard Gere

Debra Messing, Richard Gere

STORYTELLING

(FINE LINE FEATURES) Producers, Ted Hope, Christine Vachon; Executive Producers, David Linde, Amy Henkels, Michael De Luca; Director/Screenplay, Todd Solondz; Photography, Frederick Elmes; Designer, James Chinlund; Costumes, John Dunn; Editor, Alan Oxman; Music, Belle & Sebastian, Nathan Larson; Music Supervisor, Susan Jacobs; Line Producer, Declan Baldwin; Casting, Ann Goulder; a New Line Cinema presentation of a Killer Films/Good Machine Production; Dolby; Deluxe color; Rated R; 87 minutes; Release date: January 25, 2002

CAST

FICTION
Vi ....Selma Blair
Mr. Gary Scott ....Robert Wisdom
Marcus ....Leo Fitzpatrick
Catherine ....Aleksa Palladino
Amy ....Maria Thayer
Elli ....Angela Goethals
Lucy ....Devorah Rose
Joyce ....Nancy Ann Ridder
Melinda ....Mary Lynn Rajskub
Sue ....Tina Holmes

NONFICTION
Toby Oxman ....Paul Giamatti
Marty Livingston ....John Goodman
Consuelo ....Lupe Ontiveros
Mikey Livingston ....Jonathan Osser
Scooby Livingston ....Mark Webber
Fern Livingston ....Julie Hagerty
Brad Livingston ....Noah Fleiss
Mike ....Mike Schank
and Xander Berkeley (Mr. DeMarco), Jessica Dunphy (Cheryl), Nick Maltes (Esposito), Steve Railsback (Mr. Kirk), Crista Moore (Elizabeth St. Clair), Franka Potente (Toby's Editor), Andrew Marantz (Stanley), Conan O'Brien, Dr. Barry Jordan, Dr. Robin Goodman (Themselves), Frederick Owens (Football Coach), Eric Nieves (Dave), Marisa Redanty, Ilana Levine (Onlookers)

FICTION: A college student ends up having an affair with her creative writing professor. NONFICTION: An aspiring filmmaker talks a high school senior into allowing him to make the boy's family the subject of a documentary.

© Fine Line Features

Selma Blair

John Goodman, Julie Hagerty

Robert Wisdom

Mark Webber, Paul Giamatti, Mike Schank

A WALK TO REMEMBER

(**WARNER BROS.**) Producers, Denise Di Novi, Hunt Lowry; Executive Producers, E.K. Gaylord II, Bill Johnson, Casey La Scala, Edward L. McDonnell; Director, Adam Shankman; Screenplay, Karen Janszen; Based on the novel by Nicholas Sparks; Photography, Julio Macat; Designer/Costumes, Doug Hall; Editor, Emma E. Hickox; Music, Mervyn Warren; a Di Novi Pictures production in association with Pandora; Dolby; Super 35 Widescreen; Color; Rated PG; 101 minutes; Release date: January 25, 2002

CAST

Landon Carter	Shane West
Jamie Sullivan	Mandy Moore
Reverend Sullivan	Peter Coyote
Cynthia Carter	Daryl Hannah
Belinda	Lauren German
Dean	Clayne Crawford
Eric	Al Thompson
Tracie	Paz De La Huerta
Walker	Jonathan Parks Jordan
Clay Gephardt	Matt Lutz
Mr. Kelly	David Andrews
Dr. Carter	David Lee Smith
Luis	Xavier Hernandez
Ms. Garber	Marisa Miller

and Paula Jones (Sally), Erik Smith (Eddie Zimmerhoff), Al Butler (Security Guard), Seth Howard (Maitre d'), Julia Ann West (Church Lady), Frances E. Davis (Housekeeper), Dean Mumford (Policeman), Anne Fletcher (School Play Dancer), Mervyn Warren (Pianist), Robin Clark, Arlene Martell Martin, Elaine Caswell, Cassidy Ladden, Gordon Grody, Vivian Cherry, Nikki Gregoroff, Diva Gray, Janie Barnett, Kevin Osborne, Jason Paige (Choir Singers)

Landon Carter, an aimless, moody high schooler, finds himself falling in love with outcast Jamie Sullivan, whose independence and goodness begins to change Landon's reckless ways.

© Warner Bros.

Al Thompson, Paz De La Huerta, Clayne Crawford, Shane West, Jonathan Parks Jordan, Lauren German

Mandy Moore, Peter Coyote, Shane West

Mandy Moore, Shane West

Daryl Hannah, Shane West

A RUMOR OF ANGELS

(CINETEL) Producers, Lisa Hansen, Paul Hertzberg, Peter O'Fallon; Executive Producers, Brad Krevoy, John Hamilton; Director, Peter O'Fallon; Screenplay, James Eric, Jamie Horton, Peter O'Fallon; Based on the book *Thy Son Liveth: Messages from a Soldier to His Mother* by Grace Duffie Boylan; Co-Producer, John Paul Pettinato; Photography, Roy H. Wagner; Designer, Stephen McCabe; Costumes, Natasha Landau; Editor, Louise Rubacky; Music, Tim Simonec; Line Producer, Glenn S. Gainor; Casting, Liberman/Hirschfeld; a Motion Picture Corporation of America presentation of a Lisa Hansen/Paul Hertzberg production; Distributed by MGM; Dolby; Hawk-Scope; Deluxe color; Rated PG-13; 95 minutes; Release date: February 1, 2002.

CAST

Maddy Bennett	Vanessa Redgrave
Nathan Neubauer	Ray Liotta
Mary Neubauer	Catherine McCormack
James Neubauer	Trevor Morgan
Uncle Charlie	Ron Livingston
Dr. Sam Jenkins	George Coe
Lillian Neubauer	Michelle Grace
James as an Infant	Karsen Liotta
James as a Young Boy	Colin Rogers

A neglected 12-year-old boy, spending the summer in Maine after his mother's sudden death, befriends the local recluse, Maddy Bennett, an offbeat lady who helps the lad come to terms with his problems.

© A Rumor of Angels Inc.

Trevor Morgan, Vanessa Redgrave

Catherine McCormack, Ray Liotta

Frankie Muniz, Amanda Bynes

BIG FAT LIAR

(UNIVERSAL) Producers, Mike Tollin, Brian Robbins; Executive Producer, Michael Goldman; Director, Shawn Levy; Screenplay, Dan Schneider; Story, Dan Schneider, Brian Robbins; Photography, Jonathan Brown; Designer, Nina Ruscio; Editors, Stuart Pappé, Kimberly Ray; Co-Producer, Marie Cantin; Music, Christophe Beck; Music Supervisors, Gary Jones, Dave Jordan; Casting, Michelle Morris Gertz; a Tollin/Robbins production; Dolby; Panavision; Deluxe color; Rated PG; 87 minutes; Release date: February 8, 2002.

CAST

Jason Shepherd	Frankie Muniz
Marty Wolf	Paul Giamatti
Kaylee	Amanda Bynes
Monty Kirkham	Amanda Detmer
Frank Jackson/Kenny Trooper	Donald Faison
Mrs. Caldwell	Sandra Oh
Marcus Duncan	Russell Hornsby
Harry Shepherd	Michael Bryan French

and Christine Tucci (Carol Shepherd), Lee Majors (Vince), Sean O'Bryan (Leo), Amy Hill (Jocelyn Davis), John Cho (Dustin Wong), Matthew Frauman (Lester Golub), Don Yesso (Rocco Malone), Rebecca Corry (Astrid Barker), Sparkle (Grandma Pearl), Taran Killam (Bret Callaway), Alex Breckenridge (Janie Shepherd), Ned Brower (Rudy), John Gatins (Tow Truck Driver), Rosey Brown (Security Guard), Steven Shenbaum (Tram Guide), Jake Miner (Aaron), Ted Rooney (Boring Teacher), Marisa Petroro (Reporter), Randall Newsome (Photographer), Michelle Griffin (Shandra Duncan), Mike Smith (Limo Driver), Andrea Sevilla (Housekeeper), Pamela Paulshock (Extra), Eric Stabenau (Stunt Man), Tracey Cherelle Jones (Penny), Pat O'Brien, Jaleel White (Themselves), Brian Turk (The Masher), Sandy Gimpel (Old Lady), Tim Haldeman (Suburban Dad), Pat Falls (Chopper Stunt Man), Timmy Fitzpatrick (Darren), Corinne Reilly, Shawn Levy, Dustin Diamond, Bart Myer (Wolf Party Guests), Kenan Thompson (Party Goer), Kanan Hooker, Houston Hooker (Ninja Kids), C.J. Picerni (Party Kid)

After a chance meeting with megalomaniacal Hollywood producer Marty Wolf, teenage compulsive liar Jason Shepherd realizes that the executive has stolen his class paper and is turning it into a multimillion dollar movie.

© Universal Studios

COLLATERAL DAMAGE

(**WARNER BROS.**) Producers, Steven Reuther, David Foster; Executive Producers, Hawk Koch, Nicholas Meyer; Director, Andrew Davis; Screenplay, David Griffiths, Peter Griffiths; Story, Ronald Roose, David Griffiths, Peter Griffiths; Photography, Adam Greenberg; Designer, Philip Rosenberg; Editors, Dennis Virkler, Dov Hoenig; Music, Graeme Revell; a David Foster production, presented in association with Bel-Air Entertainment; Dolby; Associate Producers, Mitchell Dauterive, Teresa Tucker-Davies, Lowell Blank; Co-Producer, John Schimmel; Stunts, Billy Burton; Visual Effects, Flash Film Works; Visual Effects Supervisor, William Mesa; Casting, Amanda Mackey Johnson, Cathy Sandrich Gelfond; Dolby; Technicolor; Rated R; 109 minutes; Release date: February 8, 2002

Francesca Neri, Arnold Schwarzenegger

CAST

Gordy Brewer	Arnold Schwarzenegger
Selena	Francesca Neri
CIA Agent Brandt	Elias Koteas
Claudio	Cliff Curtis
Felix	John Leguizamo
Armstrong	John Turturro
Roman	Jsu Garcia
Mauro	Tyler Garcia Posey
Jack	Michael Milhoan
Ronnie	Rick Worthy
Junior	Raymond Cruz
Anne Brewer	Lindsay Frost
Matt Brewer	Ethan Dampf
Rocha	Jorge Zepeda
Phipps	Miguel Sandoval
Dray	Harry Lennix
Undersecretary Shrub	Madison Mason
Paramedic	Don Fischer
Doctor	Shelley Malil
Forensic Specialist	Jack Conley
FBI Agent	Todd Allen
CNN Anchor	Rick Garcia
Jenni Luz	Penny Griego
Ortiz	John Verea
Agent #3	Greg Collins
Brandt's Aide	Bruce Ramsay
Chairman Paul Devereaux	Michael Cavanaugh
Senator Delich	Nicholas Pryor
Rodrigo	Rodrigo Obregon
Jorge	Gerardo Albarran
Coonts	J. Kenneth Campbell
Teenage Girl	Flor Eduarda Gurrola
Fisherman	Pedro Altamirano
Peddler	Salvador Sanchez
Federale	Fernando Sarfati
Ernesto	Paul Pozos
Augustine	Ehécatl Chávez

Elias Koteas, Madison Mason

John Leguizamo, Arnold Schwarzenegger

and Victor Carpinteiro (Carlos), Natalia Traven (Lita), Enrique Munoz (Captain Miguel), Omar Ayala (Boatman), Pedro Damian (Guerilla Motorista, aka River Rat), Millie Slavin (Secretary of State), Jane Lunch (Agent Russo), Jossara Jinaro (Rosetta), Clint E. Lilley (Buzz Cut), Marianne Lewis (Agent Davis), Louis Bernstein (Hot Dog Vendor), Doralicia (Hysterical Woman), Jay Acovone (Bennie), Ronald Donahue (Bomb Squad), Robert "Bobby Z" Zajonc, Daniel H. Friedman (Helicopter Pilots), Joe Rentaria (Safe House Guerilla), Norm Compton (Brandt's Bodyguard), Esteban Cueto (Estaban)

After his wife and son are killed in a terrorist attack, L.A. firefighter Gordy Brewer sets out to track down the man responsible for the deed, a Colombian rebel leader known as The Wolf.

John Turturro, Arnold Schwarzenegger

SCOTLAND, PA.

(LOT 47) Producers, Richard Shepard, Jonathan Stern; Executive Producers, Karen Lauder, Marcus Ticotin; Co-Executive Producers, William Lauder, Andrew Farkas; Director/Screenplay, Billy Morrissette; Story, William Shakespeare; Photography, Wally Pfister; Designer, Jennifer Stewart; Costumes, David Robinson; Music, Anton Sanko; Music Supervisor, Tracy McKnight; Editor, Adam Lichtenstein; Casting, Avy Kaufman; an Abandon Pictures presentation in association with Veto Chip Productions and Paddy Wagon Productions; Dolby; Color; Rated R; 104 minutes; Release date: February 8, 2002

CAST

Joe "Mac" McBeth	James LeGros
Pat McBeth	Maura Tierney
Lt. Ernie McDuff	Christopher Walken
Anthony "Banco" Banconi	Kevin Corrigan
Norm Duncan	James Rebhorn
Malcolm Duncan	Tom Guiry
The Hippie Jesse	Andy Dick
The Hippie Stacy	Amy Smart
The Hippie Hector	Timothy "Speed" Levitch
Donald Duncan	Geoff Dunsworth
Ed the Cop	John Cariani
Robert/Richard	Nate Crawford
Frank the Pharmacist	Timothy Durkin
Lead Singer	Doug Gochman
Joey McLeary	Daniel Lillford
Mrs. Lenox	Nicola Lipman
Gyu in Band	Michael Marinoff
Joan McNulty	Rhonda McLean
Douglas McKenna	Josh Pais
Kevin "Tanman" McKane	Reed Rudy
Mrs. McGuire	Carol Sinclaira
Andy the Homeless Guy	Glenn Wadman
Jimmy McMann	David Wike
McStreaker	Richard Shepard

Caption: Timothy "Speed" Levitch, Andy Dick, Amy Smart

In this 1970s twist on Shakespeare's *Macbeth*, a fast-food restaurant employee is convinced by his scheming wife to kill his boss so that the couple can take control of the eating establishment.

© Lot 47

Christopher Walken

Geoff Dunsworth (center)

Maura Tierney, James LeGros

CROSSROADS

(PARAMOUNT) Producer, Ann Carli; Executive Producers, Clive Calder, Larry Rudolph, Johnny Wright, Van Toffler, David Gale; Director, Tamra Davis; Screenplay, Shonda Rhimes; Co-Producers, Robert Lee, Jonathan McHugh; Photography, Eric Edwards; Designer, Waldemar Kalinowski; Costumes, Wendy Schecter; Editor, Melissa Kent; Music, Trevor Jones; Music Supervisor, Daniel Carlin; Song: "I'm Not a Girl, Not Yet a Woman" by Max Martin, Rami & Dido Armstrong/performed by Britney Spears; Casting, Kim Davis-Wagner; a Zomba Films presentation in association with MTV Films; Dolby; Deluxe color; Rated PG-13; 94 minutes; Release date: February 15, 2002

Zoë Saldana, Taryn Manning, Britney Spears

CAST

Lucy	Britney Spears
Ben	Anson Mount
Kit	Zoë Saldana
Mimi	Taryn Manning
Pete	Dan Aykroyd
Caroline	Kim Cattrall
Henry	Justin Long
Kit's Mom	Beverly Johnson
Ms. Jenson	Bahni Turpin
Bar Owner	Kool Mo Dee
Dylan	Richard Voll
Dylan's Other Woman	Pippi B.
Bar Patron	David "Gruber" Allen
High School Burnout	Kyle Davis
Kurt	Branden Williams

and Celina Belizan, Shonda Farr (Kit's Friends), Bowling for Soup: Jaret Von Erich, Christopher Van Malmsteen, Erik Rodham Clinton, Gary Wiseass (Graduation Band), Ritchie Montgomery (Customer), Brandon Henschel (Guy in Bar), Janet May (Annie), The Unknowns (Audition Band), Seth Romatelli (Talent Organizer), Jesse Camp (Audition Applicant), Jamie Lynn Spears (Young Lucy), Dajne Colon (Young Kit), Crystal Milton (Young Mimi)

Following high school graduation, three estranged friends find themselves thrown back together on a cross-country trip as they rekindle the idea of making it in the music business.

© Paramount Pictures & Filmco Enterprises

Britney Spears, Kim Cattrall

Britney Spears, Anson Mount

Britney Spears, Dan Aykroyd

HART'S WAR

(MGM) Producers, David Lad, David Foster, Gregory Hoblit, Arnold Rifkin; Executive Producer, Wolfgang Glattes; Director, Gregory Hoblit; Screenplay, Billy Ray, Terry George; Based upon the novel by John Katzenbach; Photography, Alar Kivilo; Designer, Lilly Kilvert; Costumes, Elisabetta Beraldo; Editor, David Rosenbloom; Music, Rachel Portman; Casting, Deborah Aquila; a David Ladd Films, David Foster Productions, Cheyenne Enterprises production; Dolby; Super 35 Widescreen; Color; Rated R; 128 minutes; Release date: February 15, 2002

CAST

Col. William A. McNamara	Bruce Willis
Lt. Thomas W. Hart	Colin Farrell
Lt. Lincoln A. Scott	Terrence Howard
Staff Sgt. Vic W. Bedford	Cole Hauser
Col. Werner Visser	Marcel Iures
Capt. Peter A. Ross	Linus Roache
Lt. Lamar T. Archer	Vicellous Shannon
Pfc. Dennis A. Gerber	Maury Sterling
Capt. R.G. Sisk	Sam Jaeger
Cpl. Joe S. Cromin	Scott William Campbell
Sgt. Carl S. Webb	Rory Cochrane
Pvt. Bert D. "Moose" Codman	Sebastian Tillinger
Maj. Joe Clary	Rick Ravanello
Pvt. Daniel E. Abrams	Adrian Grenier
Pfc. W. Roy Potts	Michael Weston
Pvt. Lewis P. Wakely	Jonathan Brandis
Col. J.M. Lange	Joe Spano
Cpl. B.J. "Depot" Guidry	Sam Worthington

and Brad Hunt (Pvt. G.H. "Cookie" Bell), Ruaidhri Conroy (Cpl. D.F. Lisko), Tony Devlin (Pvt. Donald W. West), Michael Landes (Maj. M.F. Giannetti), David Barrass (Maj. Hans Fussel), Gary Gold (McNamara's Aide), Danny Babbington (Pvt. S.T. Engler), Holger Handtke (Maj. Johann Wirtz), Grey Williams (Pvt. R.S. Croutch), René Ifrah (Pvt. T.S. Krasner), Steve Sarossy (Lt. M.K. Adams), Rocky Marshall (Capt. Robert M. Swann), Christian Kahrmann, Jim Boeven (M.P. Sergeants), Dan Van Husen (Box Car Sergeant), Georg Vietje (Morning Guard), Lukás Kantor (Cranky Corporal), Jakub Zdenek (Delousing Private), Jan Nemejovsky (Spike Guard), Jan Marsik (Tower Sentry), Bohumil Svarc (Nighttime Appel Guard), Jiri M. Sieber (Kooler Guard), Dugald Bruce-Lockhart (Capt. Lutz), Richard Kardhordo (Barracks 27 POW), Jan Jakubec (Lowly Guard), Karel Belohradsky, Jan Tesar, Radek Kuchai, Martin Kohout, Vladimir Kulhavy, Martin Cizek (Guards), Alan T. Ward, Stephen Fisher, Daniel Fleischer-Brown (Barracks 22 Officers), Peter Varga, Jan Dostal, Vit Herzina (Russian POWs), Michael Beran (Pvt. Hugh), Joel Sugerman (Unnamed GI)

Lt. Thomas W. Hart finds himself imprisoned in a German POW camp where racial tensions lead to the murder of a bigoted sergeant.

Colin Farrell, Vicellous Shannon, Terrence Howard

Colin Farrell, Bruce Willis

Marcel Iures, Colin Farrell, Bruce Willis

Colin Farrell, Adrian Grenier, Linus Roache

Jay Chandrasekhar, Paul Soter, Steve Lemme, Erik Stolhanske, Kevin Heffernan

SUPER TROOPERS

(FOX SEARCHLIGHT) Producer, Richard Perello; Executive Producer, Peter E. Lengyel; Director, Jay Chandrasekhar; Screenplay, Broken Lizard (Jay Chandrasekhar, Kevin Heffernan, Steve Lemme, Paul Soter, Erik Stolhanske); Photography, Joaquin Baca-Asay; Designer, Ben Conable; Costumes, Melissa Bruning; Music, 38 Special; Editors, Jacob Craycroft, Jumbulingam, Kevin Heffernan; Casting, Jennifer McNamara; a Jersey Shore Pictures Production/Cataland Films/Arpad Production of a Broken Lizard Film; Dolby; Color; Rated R; 103 minutes; Release date: February 15, 2002

CAST

Thorny . . . . .Jay Chandrasekhar
Foster . . . . .Paul Soter
Rabbit . . . . .Erik Stolhanske
Mac . . . . .Steve Lemme
Farva . . . . .Kevin Heffernan
Captain O'Hagan . . . . .Brian Cox
Chief Grady . . . . .Daniel von Bargen
Officer Ursula Hanson . . . . .Marisa Coughlan
Governor Jessman . . . . .Lynda Carter
Bobbi . . . . .Amy De Lucia
Mayor Timber . . . . .John Bedford Lloyd
Larry Johnson . . . . .Jim Gaffigan
and Andre Vippolis, Joey Kern, Geoffrey Arend (College Boys), Camille Hickman (Thin Queen Bartender), Aria Alpert (Waitress), James Grace (Local Officer Rando), Michael Weaver (Local Officer Smy), Dan Fey (Local Officer Burton), Chloe Kai O'Conner (Dead Woman: Lucy Garfield), Christian Albrizio (Arlo), Jim Edwards (Complaining Fan), Jimmy Noonan (Frank Galikanokus), Philippe Brenninkmeyer (German Man), Blanchard Ryan (Casino La Fantastique Sally), Jane Heffernan, E. Michael Heffernan (Chicken Fuckers), Charlie Finn (Dimpus Burger Guy), Tracy Tobin (Governor's Aide), Rich Perello (Banquet Bartender), Trish McGettrick (Gawking Citizen), Danny Padilla (Urinatee), John Carlino (Pilot), Walt McPherson, Jerry Walsh (Foremen)

A group of hellraising, fun-loving Vermont state troopers must cope with an ongoing feud with the local cops and the possibility of the state government shutting down their operations.

RETURN TO NEVER LAND

(WALT DISNEY PICTURES) Producers, Christopher Chase, Michelle Robinson, Dan Rounds; Director, Robin Budd; Screenplay, Temple Mathews; Co-Director, Donovan Cook; Unit Director, Ian Harrowell; Voice Casting/Dialogue Director, Jamie Thomason; Music, Joel McNelly; Art Director, Wendell Luebbe; Technical Director, Charlie Luce; Editor, Anthony F. Rocco; Executive in Charge of Production, Sharon Morrill; Additional Animation Directors, Charlie Bonifacio, Keith Ingham, Ryan O'Laughlin, Larry Whitaker; Layout Supervisor, Alex Nicholas; Song: "I'll Try" written and performed by Jonatha Brooke; Distributed by Buena Vista Pictures; Dolby; Color; Rated G; 72 minutes; Release date: February 15, 2002

VOICE CAST

Jane/Young Wendy . . . . .Harriet Owen
Peter Pan . . . . .Blayne Weaver
Captain Hook . . . . .Corey Burton
Smee & Pirates . . . . .Jeff Bennett
Wendy . . . . .Kath Soucie
Danny . . . . .Andrew McDonough
Edward . . . . .Roger Rees
Cubby . . . . .Spencer Breslin
Nibs . . . . .Bradley Pierce
and Quinn Beswick (Slightly), Aaron Spann (Twins), Dan Castellaneta, Jim Cummings, Rob Paulsen, Clive Revill, Frank Welker, Wallace Winert (Additional Voices)

Peter Pan comes to the rescue of Wendy's daughter, Jane, when she is mistakenly kidnapped by the evil Captain Hook and taken to Never Land. Sequel to the 1953 Disney film *Peter Pan,* which was originally released by RKO.

Peter Pan, Captain Hook

Peter Pan, Jane

JOHN Q

(NEW LINE CINEMA) Producer, Mark Burg, Oren Koules; Executive Producers, Michael De Luca, Richard Saperstein, Avram Butch Kaplan; Director, Nick Cassavetes; Screenplay, James Kearns; Photography, Rogier Stoffers; Designer, Stefania Cella; Costumes, Beatrix Aruna Pasztor; Music, Aaron Zigman; Editor, Dede Allen; Casting, Matthew Barry, Nancy Green-Keyes; a Burg/Koules production; Dolby; Deluxe color; Rated PG-13; 118 minutes; Release date: February 15, 2002

CAST

John Q. Archibald	Denzel Washington
Lt. Frank Grimes	Robert Duvall
Dr. Turner	James Woods
Rebecca Payne	Anne Heche
Police Chief Monroe	Ray Liotta
Denise Archibald	Kimberly Elise
Lester	Eddie Griffin
Mitch	Shawn Hatosy
Mike Archibald	Daniel E. Smith
Jimmy Palumbo	David Thornton
Max	Ethan Suplee
Steve Maguire	Kevin Connolly
Tuck Lampley	Paul Johanson
Julie	Heather Wahlquist
Miriam	Troy Beyer
Sgt. Moody	Obba Babatundé

Paul Johansson, Ray Liotta

and Troy Winbush (Steve), Laura Harring (Gina Palumbo), Larissa Laskin (Dr. Klein), Dina Waters (Debby Utley), Martha Chaves (Rosa), Gabriela Oltean (Beautiful Woman), Ron Annabelle (Tow Trucker Driver), Barry G. King (Personnel Manager), Vanessa Branch (R.N.), Stephanie Moore (Admitting Nurse), James Finnerty (Reggie), Michael Jaye (Insurance Rep), Yanna McIntosh (State Employee), Linda Massad (Social Services Rep), Lester Mathews (Human Services Rep), Noam Jenkins (Medicaid Official), Allegra Fulton (Sick Girl's Mom), Darrin Brown (TV Buyer), Shera Danese (Shelby's Wife), Kirsta Teague (Dr. Turner's Asst.), Rick Sood (E.R. Doctor), Scott Bloom (Desk Guard), Carlos Diaz, Joseph Duer (Paramedics), Simon Sinn (Fong), Jeff Douglas (Computer Cop), Keram Malicki-Sanchez (Freddy B.), Philip Williams (Wally Pitoniak), Nigel Shawn Williams (News Anchor), Frank Cassavetes (Sniper), Colin Evans (Videographer), Angelo Tsarouchas (Barricade Cop), Marcia Johnson, Vijay Mehta (Medical Transplants), Andrew Schaff (U.N.O.S. Official), Malcolm Nefsky (Nick), Jay Leno, Gloria Allred, Larry King, Arianna Huffington, Ted Demme, Nas, Bill Maher (Themselves), Claire Rankin (Public Defender), Phillip Craig (Judge), Gerry Quigley (Jury Foreman)

Ray Liotta, Anne Heche, Robert Duvall, Obba Babatundé

Finding nothing but excuses, bureaucracy, and dead ends in his efforts to get medical coverage for his son's heart operation, frustrated John Archibald takes a hospital wing over at gunpoint in hopes of having his demands met.

Kimberly Elise, Daniel E. Smith, Denzel Washington

Denzel Washington

BIG BAD LOVE

(IFC FILMS) Producer, Debra Winger; Executive Producers, Manfred Wilde, Barry Navidi; Director, Arliss Howard; Screenplay, James Howard, Arliss Howard; Based on stories by Larry Brown; Co-Producers, Arliss Howard, Debra Winger; Photography, Paul Ryan; Designer, Bob Johnston; Costume Design, Patricia Norris; Editor, Jay Rabinowitz; Casting, Penny Perry; from Big Bad Love LLC, Pieface Productions, Rocking S., Sun Moon & Stars Productions; Dolby; Super 35 Widescreen; Color; Rated R; 111 minutes; Release date: February 22, 2002

CAST

Barlow . . . . .Arliss Howard
Marilyn . . . . .Debra Winger
Monroe . . . . .Paul Le Mat
Velma . . . . .Rosanna Arquette
Mrs. Barlow . . . . .Angie Dickinson
Mr. Aaron . . . . .Michael Parks
Deputy . . . . .Alex Van
Alan . . . . .Zach Moody
Alisha . . . . .Olivia Kersey
and Kevin Mitchell, Matt Mitchell (Twins), Sue Peavey (Cindy), Michael Williamson (Young Barlow), Coleman Barks (Minister), Gloria Winters (Mrs. Shepard), Kenneth Carter (Nurse), Melody Wilson (Young Mrs. Barlow), Preston Duke (Farmer), Jacob McAnally, Ian McAnally (Farmer's Sons), Bob Muse (Lost Freezer Guy), Jo Ann Robinson (One Night Stand), Cool Man, R.L. Burnside (Themselves), Kenny Brown (Boxcar Marine), Christie Jackson (Betti Deloreo), Sigourney Weaver (Voice of Betti Deloreo), Reginald Wilson (Boy Athlete), Johnny McPhail (Mop Guy), Ed Hicks (Judge), Jaymee Vowel (Rebuffing Woman), L. Jay McKinney (Geranium Drunk), Larry Brown (Mr. Barlow), Kenny Brown, Cedric Burnside (R.L.'s Band)

A failed writer tries to bring some order to his life.

© IFC Films

Debra Winger, Arliss Howard

Debra Winger, Paul Le Mat, Arliss Howard

Olivia Kersey, Arliss Howard

Debra Winger

QUEEN OF THE DAMNED

(WARNER BROS.) Producer, Jorge Saralegui; Executive Producers, Su Armstrong, Andrew Mason, Bill Gerber, Bruce Berman; Director, Michael Rymer; Screenplay, Scott Abbott, Michael Petroni; Based on *The Vampire Chronicles* by Anne Rice; Photography, Ian Baker; Designer, Graham "Grace" Walker; Costumes, Angus Strathie; Editor, Dany Cooper; Music, Richard Gibbs, Jonathan Davis; Visual Effects Supervisor, Gregory L. McMurry; Co-Producer, Channing Dungey; Casting, Kristy Sager, Greg Apps; a Material production, presented in association with Village Roadshow Pictures and NPV Entertainment; U.S.-Australian; Dolby; Panavision; Technicolor; Rated R; 101 minutes; Release date: February 22, 2002

CAST

Lestat	Stuart Townsend
Jesse	Marguerite Moreau
Akasha	Aaliyah
Marius	Vincent Perez

and Paul McGann (David Talbot), Lena Olin (Maharet), Christian Manon (Mael), Claudia Black (Pandora), Bruce Spence (Khayman), Matthew Newton (Armand), Tiriel Mora (Roger), Megan Dorman (Maudy), Johnathan Devoy (James), Robert Farnham (Alex), Conrad Standish (T.C.), Richael Tanner (Young Jesse), Christopher Kirby, Miguel Ayesha, Joe Manning (New York Vampires), Pip Mushin (Guy Being Sucked), Kat Rhodes (Vampire Girl), Christopher Connelly (Mortal Yuppie), Renee de Bondt, Renee Quast (Vampire Girls Sucking), Tayler Kane, Imogen Annesley, Daniel Schlusser (Club Vampires), Rowland S. Howard (Vampire Guitarist), Hugo Race (Vampire Bass Player), Robin Casinader (Vampire Pianist), Aimee Nash (Vampire Singer), Nicole Fantl, Alyssa McClelland (London Groupies), Marnie Reece-Wilmore (LA Groupie), Andrew L. Urban, Serena Altschul (Themselves), Jo Buckley (French Journalist), Dino Marnika (Music Journalist), Kirsty Meares (Lifestyle Journalist), Bruce Myles, Marge Downey, John Dicks (Talamascans), Fouad Harraka (Greek Father), Mandie Vieira (Young Violin Player), Bobby Bright, Darren Wilson (Sound Engineers), Russell Kiefel (Fire Marshall), Nandila Gaskell, Nalishebo Gaskell (West Indian Girls), Tamasin Ramsay (Woman Victim), Michael Azria (VW Driver), Arrowyn Lloyd (VW Passenger), Antonios Greige (Camel Driver), Nicola Paull (Flight Attendant), Peter Olsen (Enkil), Franklyn Ajaye (French Dealer), Duncan Myers, Mark O'Halloran (Rent Boys), Twapa Kapote (Prostitute), Ron Bingham (Businessman), Strawberry Fields (Girl With Businessman), Bob Halsall (Businessman With Girl), Antony Neate, Karoline Hohlweg, Rochelle Ward, Anni Finsterer, Alistair Reid (Euro Trash Vampires), Suzi Dougherty (Pale Faced Vampire), Humphrey Bower (Nigel), Pia Miranda (Jesse's Roommate), Simon Wilton (Vampire in the Park), Enrico Mammerella (Greek Fisherman), Nick Gill, Becky Thomas (Band Members), Jonathan Davis (Scalper)

Queen Akasha, the mother of all Vampires, rises from her centuries of rest to seize control of the Earth, an act that vampire Lestat must stop.

© Warner Bros.

Stuart Townsend, Aaliyah

Suzi Hofrichter, Lucinda Jenney, Kenneth Branagh, Robin Wright Penn

HOW TO KILL YOUR NEIGHBOR'S DOG

(ARTISTIC LICENSE) Producers, Michael Nozik, Nancy M. Ruff, Brad Westin; Executive Producer, Robert Redford; Co-Executive Producers, Willi Baer, Avi Lerner, Danny Dimbort, Trevor Short, John Thompson; Line Producer, Michael Potkins; Director/Screenplay, Michael Kalesniko; Photography, Hubert Taczanowski; Designer, Stephen Lineweaver; Costumes, Mary Claire Hannan; Music, David Robbins; Editor, Pamela Martin; Casting, Linda Lowy; a Millenium Films presentation in association with Cinerenta of a South Fork Pictures Production in association with Lonsdale Productions; U.S.-German, 2001; Dolby; Color; Rated R; 107 minutes; Release date: February 22, 2002

CAST

Peter McGowan	Kenneth Branagh
Melanie McGowan	Robin Wright Penn
Amy Walsh	Suzi Hofrichter
Edna	Lynn Redgrave
False Peter	Jared Harris
Larry	Peter Riegert
Brian Sellars	David Krumholtz
Adam	Jonathon Schaech
Victoria	Kaitlin Hopkins
Allana	Suzy Joachim
Janitor	Brett Rickaby
Trina Walsh	Lucinda Jenney

and Derek Kellock (Amy's Father), Stacy Hogue (Babysitter), Peri Gilpin (Debra Salhany), Tamala Jones (Laura Leeton), Benita Ha, Mark Brandon (Anchors), Brent Chapman, Markus Redmond, Mark Schooley, Mark Currie (Cops), Doug Abrahams, Ty Olsson (Detectives), Fred Ewanuick, Anthony F. Ingram (Men), Robert C. Saunders (Gynecologist), Jay Brazeau (Proctologist), Merrilyn Gann, Enuka Okuma (Nurses), Haig Sutherland (Young Man), Michael Benyaer (Father Neighbor), Sarah Cole Burnett (Teenage Neighbor), Michael Roberds (Fry Cook), Michael Kalesniko (Passerby), Banjo (Baby the Dog), Daniel Stern (Party Guest)

A cynical playwright, going through a creative dry spell while living in Los Angeles, is faced with the accusations that the character of a ten-year-old child in his latest work does not ring true, a challenge he hopes to rectify by interacting with the little girl who has just moved next door. This movie had its premiere on Starz cable network on Oct. 27, 2001.

© Artistic License

DRAGONFLY

(**UNIVERSAL**) Producers, Mark Johnson, Tom Shadyac, Roger Birnbaum, Gary Barber; Executive Producers, James D. Brubaker, Michael Bostick; Director, Tom Shadyac; Screenplay, David Seltzer, Brandon Camp, Mike Thompson; Story, Brandon Camp, Mike Thompson; Photography, Dean Semler; Designer, Linda DeScenna; Costumes, Judy Ruskin Howell; Editor, Don Zimmerman; Visual Effects Supervisor, Jon Farhat; Music, John Debney; Music Supervisor, Jeff Carson; Casting, Debra Zane, Elizabeth Marx; a Spyglass Entertainment presentation of a Gran Via/Shady Acres production; Dolby; Panavision; Deluxe color; Rated PG-13; 103 minutes; Release date: February 22, 2002

CAST

Joe Darrow	Kevin Costner
Emily Darrow	Susanna Thompson
Hugh Campbell	Joe Morton
Charlie Dickinson	Ron Rifkin
Miriam Belmont	Kathy Bates
Sister Madeine	Linda Hunt
Pilot	Jacob Vargas
Jeffrey Reardon	Robert Bailey, Jr.

and Jacob Smith (Ben), Jay Thomas (Hal), Lisa Banes (Flora), Matt Craven (Eric), Casey Biggs (Neil Darrow), Leslie Hope (Charisse Darrow), Peter Hansen (Phillip Darrow), Chea Courtney (12-Year Old Girl), Dylan Johnson (8-Year Old Boy), Anne Betancourt (A Mother), Mary Beth Fisher (Eulogist), Kim Staunton (Intake Nurse), Liza Weil (Suicide Girl), Nigel Gibbs (Paramedic), Heidi Swedberg, Jamie Sue Sherrill (Surgical Nurses), Samantha Smith (Waitress), Andy Umberger, Nicholas Cascone (Doctors), Judith Moreland, Jennifer Parsons (ICU Nurses), Oni Faida Lampley (Private Duty Nurse), L. Scott Caldwell (Head Nurse), Kent Faulcon (Paul Reardon), Deirdre O'Connell (Gwyn), Justina Machado (Oncology Desk Nurse), William Dennis Hunt (Priest), Tom Keevers, Rich Komenich (Cops), Terrell Clayton (Colleague), Lise Simms (Nephrology Desk Nurse), Joseph Will (Medical Tech), Jerome Butler (Medivac Doctor), Michael Manuel (Tough Paramedic), Henry Gerardo Cariban (Yanomami Native), Gilberto Herrera Chipiaje (Guard), Ana Garcia (Elderly Native Woman), Lina Patel (Airline Official), Meg Thalken, John Lordan, Rolanda Brigham, Gillian Vigman (Guests), Matt Champagne, Maz Jobrani, Benjamin John Parrillo, Mone Walton (Paramedics), David Doty (Hospital Chaplain), David Correia (Bus Driver)

Doctor Joe Darrow, grieving over the death of his beloved wife sixth months earlier in a freak bus accident, believes that she is trying to communicate with him through her former patients.

© Universal

Kevin Costner

Kevin Costner, Kathy Bates

Linda Hunt, Kevin Costner

WE WERE SOLDIERS

Chris Klein, Mel Gibson

(**PARAMOUNT**) Producers, Bruce Davey, Stephen McEveety, Randall Wallace; Executive Producers, Jim Lemley, Arne L. Schmidt; Director/ Screenplay, Randall Wallace; Based upon the book *We Were Soldiers Once... and Young* by Lt. Gen. Harold G. Moore (Ret) and Joseph L. Galloway; Photography, Dean Semler; Designer, Tom Sanders; Costumes, Michael T. Boyd; Editor, William Hoy; Music, Nick Glennie-Smith; Casting, Amanda Mackey Johnson, Cathy Sandrich Gelfond; an Icon Productions presentation of an Icon/Wheelhouse Entertainment production; Dolby; Panavision; Deluxe color; Rated R; 138 minutes; Release date: March 1, 2002

CAST

Lt. Col. Hal Moore	Mel Gibson
Julie Moore	Madeleine Stowe
Maj. Bruce Crandall	Greg Kinnear
Sgt. Maj. Basil Plumley	Sam Elliott
2nd Lt. Jack Geoghegan	Chris Klein
Barbara Geoghegan	Keri Russell
Joe Galloway	Barry Pepper
Lt. Col. Nguyen Huu An	Don Duong
Sgt. Ernie Savage	Ryan Hurst
1st Lt. Charlie Hastings	Robert Bagnell
2nd Lt. Henry Herrick	Marc Blucas
Spec. 4 Bob Ouellette	Josh Daugherty
Capt. Tony Nadal	Jsu Garcia
Capt. Matt Dillon	Jon Hamm
Capt. Tom Metsker	Clark Gregg
Spec. 4 Bill Beck	Desmond Harrington
Spec. 4 Galen Bungum	Blake Heron
Spec. 4 Russell Adams	Erik MacArthur
Capt. Bob Edwards	Dylan Walsh
Capt. Ed "Too Tall" Freeman	Mark McCracken
PFC Willie Godboldt	Edwin Morrow
PFC Jimmy Nakayama	Brian Tee
Cecile Moore	Sloane Momsen
Catherine Metsker	Bellamy Young
Alma Givens	Simbi Kali Williams
Maj. Gen. Harry Kinnard	Jim Grimshaw
Plt. Sgt. Carl Palmer	Forry Smith
Spec. 5 Charlie "Doc" Lose	Steven Nelson
Capt. Robert "Doc" Carrara	Vincent Angell
Col. Tim Brown	Michael Tomlinson
Diplomatic	Keith Szarabajka
Army Intelligence Officer	Tim Abell
General in Hallway	Patrick St. Espirit
Mortar Sgt.	Michael John White
Medevac Commanding Officer	Daniel Roebuck
Army Wife	Maia Lien
Cab Driver	Danny Beene
Daughter Julie Moore	Taylor Momsen
Greg Moore	Josh McLaurin
Steve Moore	Devon Wekheiser

Keri Russell, Simbi Kali Williams, Madeleine Stowe

and Luke Benward (David Moore), Billinjer C. Tran (Viet Minh Sgt.), Vien Jong (Mr. Nik), Joseph Tran (NVA Prisoner), Joseph Hieu (NVA Officer), Lam Nguyen (NVA Soldier with Bayonet), Zoë Bui (NVA Wife), Andrew Wallace (French Bugler), Nicholas Hosking (French Captain), Michael Giordani (French Lieutenant), Shep Koster, Kate Lombardi, Ingrid Semler (Repters), Jason Powell (Sgt. Robert Stokes), Doug C. Cook (Capt. Ray Lefebvre), Sean Thomas Bunch (Trooper on Fire), F. Lee Reynolds (Huey Flight Crew), Stephen Zapotoczny (Edwards' Radio Operator), Frank Kostenko, Jr. (Foxhole Trooper)

The true story of how Lt. Col. Hal Moore led the 1st Battalion, 7th Cavalry in the first major fire fight of the Vietnam War.

Sam Elliott, Mel Gibson

Shannyn Sossamon, Josh Hartnett

Paulo Costanzo, Josh Hartnett

Josh Hartnett, Monet Mazur

(MIRAMAX/UNIVERSAL) Producers, Tim Bevan, Eric Fellner, Michael London; Executive Producers, Liza Chasin, Debra Hayward; Director, Michael Lehmann; Screenplay, Robert Perez; Co-Producer, Stuart M. Besser; Photography, Elliot Davis; Designer, Sharon Seymour; Costumes, Jill Ohanneson; Editor, Nicholas C. Smith; Music, Rolfe Kent; Music Supervsior, Bonnie Greenberg-Goodman; Casting, Joseph Middleton; a Studio Canal presentation of a Working Title production; Dolby; Color; Rated R; 94 minutes; Release date: March 1, 2002

CAST

Matt Sullivan	Josh Hartnett
Erica Sutton	Shannyn Sossamon
Ryan	Paulo Costanzo
John	Adam Trese
Susie	Emmanuelle Vaugier
Diana	Lorin Heath
Waiter	Aaron Trainor
Chris	Glenn Fitzgerald
Candy	Monet Mazur
Andie	Christine Chatelain
Mandy	Keegan Connor Tracy
Bagel Guy	Michael Maronna
Nicole	Vinessa Shaw
Girl in Chinatown	Stepfanie Von Pfetten
Father Maher	Stanley Anderson
Jerry	Griffin Dunne
Duncan	Jarrad Paul
Neil	Terry Chen
Nick	Kai Lennox
Mikey	Christopher Gauthier
Dad	Barry Newman
Mom	Mary Gross

and Maggie Gyllenhaal (Sam), Alan Draven, Rueben Grundy (Computer Nerds), Dylan Neal (David), Michelle Harrison (Maureen), Jason Low (Merj), Tracy Kyser (Business Woman), Nicole Wilder (Anastasia), Lina Teal (Girl in Bed), Susan Bain (Ms. Willow), Chiara Zanni (Nun)

Following the end of a bad relationship, Matt Sullivan makes a vow to not have sex for forty days and forty nights.

© Miramax

Vinessa Shaw, Josh Hartnett

THE TIME MACHINE

(DREAMWORKS/WARNER BROS.) Producers, Walter F. Parkes, David Valdes; Executive Producers, Laurie MacDonald, Jorge Saralegui, Arnold Leibovit; Director, John Logan; Screenplay, John Logan; Based on the novel by H.G. Wells; Photography, Donald M. McAlpine; Designer, Oliver Scholl; Costumes, Bob Ringwood; Editor, Wayne Wahrman; Music, Klaus Badelt; Co-Producer, John Logan; Visual Effects Supervisor, James E. Price; Special Effects Supervisor, Matt Sweeney; Morlock Makeup Effects, Stan Winston Studio; Casting, Mindy Marin; a Parkes/MacDonald production; Dolby; Panavision; Technicolor; Rated PG-13; 96 minutes; Release date: March 8, 2002

Jeremy Irons, Guy Pearce

CAST

Alexander Hartdegen	Guy Pearce
Mara	Samantha Mumba
Uber-Morlock	Jeremy Irons
Vox	Orlando Jones
David Philby	Mark Addy
Emma	Sienna Guillory
Mrs. Watchit	Phyllida Law
Kalen	Omero Mumba
Flower Seller	Laura Kirk
Motorist	Josh Stamberg
Robber	Max Baker
Central Park Carriage Driver	Jeffrey M. Meyer
Flower Store Worker	Alan Young
Jogger	Myndy Crist

and Connie Ray (Teacher), Lennie Loftin, Thomas Corey Robinson (Soldiers), Yancey Arias (Toren), Richard Cetrone, Eddie Conna, Christopher Sayour, Jeremy Fitzgerald, Craig Davis, Grady Holder, Bryan Friday, Clint Lilley, Mark Kubr, Jeff Podgurski, Dan McCann, Bryon Weiss, Steve Upton (Hunter Morlocks), Doug Jones, Joey Anaya, Dorian Kingi, Jacob Chambers, Kevin McTurk (Spy Morlocks), Michael Chaturantabut, Jonathan Eusebio, Roel Failma, Diana Lee Inosanto, Malaea Chona Jason, Hiro Koda, Yoshio Iizuka, John Koyama, Gail Monian, R.C. Ormond, Maro Uo Richmond, Petra Sprecher, Gary Toy, Jonathan Valera (Eloi)

Samantha Mumba, Guy Pearce

On the eve of the 20th century, scientist Alexander Hartdegen invents a time travel machine that takes him 800,000 years into the future. There he discovers a division in the species, where the gentler race, the Eloi, exists to serve a terrifying breed of underground dwellers called the Morlocks. Remake of the 1960 MGM film that starred Rod Taylor, Yvette Mimieux, and Alan Young. Young makes a cameo in this version.

This film received an Oscar nomination for make-up.

Guy Pearce

Guy Pearce, Sienna Guillory

ALL ABOUT THE BENJAMINS

(NEW LINE CINEMA) Producers, Ice Cube, Matt Alvarez; Executive Producers, Toby Emmerich, Matt Moore, Claire Rudnick Polstein, Ronald Lang; Director, Kevin Bray; Screenplay, Ronald Lang, Ice Cube; Co-Producer, Douglas Curtis; Photography, Glen MacPherson; Designer, J. Mark Harrington; Costumes, Sophie de Rakoff Carbonell; Editor, Suzanne Hines; Music, John Murphy; Music Supervisor, Spring Aspers; Casting, Anne McCarthy; a Cube Vision production; Dolby; Super 35 Widescreen; Color; Rated R; 99 minutes; Release date: March 8, 2002

Ron Silver, Greta Scacchi

CAST

Bocum . . . . .Ice Cube
Reggie . . . . .Mike Epps
Williamson . . . . .Tommy Flanagan
Ursula . . . . .Carmen Chaplin
Gina . . . . .Eva Mendes
Pam . . . . .Valarie Rae Miller
Martinez . . . . .Anthony Giaimo
Mango . . . . .Jeff Chase
Julian . . . . .Roger Guenveur Smith
Mickey . . . . .Gino Salvano
TJ . . . . .Tony Ward
Roscoe . . . . .Dominic Chianese, Jr.
Lil' J . . . . .Anthony Michael Hall
and Antoni Cornacchione (Captain Briggs), Bob Carter (Mr. Barkley), Evelyn Brooks (Mr. Steinberg), Joan Turner (Mrs. Scharfenberg), Julie Ann Beres (Sharhari), Lil' Bow Wow (Kelley), Robert MacBeth (Store Owner), Barbara Baron (Mrs. Barkley), Oscar Isaac (Francesco), Jodi Wilson (Lil' J's Girlfriend), Allen Choate (Newsstand Attendant), Marianna Astakhova (Customer), Kevin Bray (Criminal)

Bocum, a Miami bounty hunter, teams with Reggie, a small-time con man, to track down some diamond thieves who have wound up with Reggie's winning lottery ticket.

Maximilian Schell, Anouk Aimée

Eva Mendes, Mike Epps, Valarie Rae Miller, Ice Cube

Ice Cube

FESTIVAL IN CANNES

(PARAMOUNT CLASSICS) Producer, John Goldstone; Director/Screenplay/Editor, Henry Jaglom; Additional Writing, Victoria Foyt; Co-Producer, Judith Wolinsky; Photography, Hanania Baer; Costumes, Jo Kissak; Music, Gaili Schoen; a Rainbow Film Company/Revere Entertainment presentation; Dolby; Color; Rated PG-13; 99 minutes; Release date: March 8, 2002

CAST

Millie Marquand . . . . .Anouk Aimée
Victor Kovner . . . . .Maximilian Schell
Alice Palmer . . . . .Greta Scacchi
Rick Yorkin . . . . .Ron Silver
Kaz Naiman . . . . .Zack Norman
Blue . . . . .Jenny Gabrielle
Barry . . . . .Alex Craig Mann
Gina . . . . .Camilla Campanale
Milo . . . . .Peter Bogdanovich
and Kim Kolarich (Libby), Rachel Bailit (Nikki), Vernon Dotcheff (Millie's Escort), Pamela Shaw (Millie's Agent), Christian Rallo (Fan in Crowd), J.C. Irondelle (General Manager Hotel du Cap), Marya Kazakova (T.V. Interviewer), Sabrina Marie Jaglom, Simon Orson Jaglom (Children Watching Blue), Louise Stratten (Milo's Girlfriend), Robert Shaye (Bert Shuster), William Shatner, Faye Dunaway, Michael White, Liam Dunaway O'Neill, John Cruikshank, Larry Fredericks (Themselves)

A diverse group of actors and filmmakers converge at the annual Cannes Film Festival, hoping to come away fulfilled and happy.

KISSING JESSICA STEIN

(FOX SEARCHLIGHT) Producers, Eden H. Wurmfeld, Brad Zions; Director, Charles Herman-Wurmfeld; Screenplay/Co-Producers, Heather Juergensen, Jennifer Westfeldt; Based on their play *Lipschtick*; Photography, Lawrence Sher; Designer, Charlotte Bourke; Editors, Kristy Jacobs Maslin, Greg Tillman; Associate Producers, Steven Firestone, Mark Pincus, Kaye Popofsky; Music, Marcelo Zarvos; Music Supervisors, Matthew Abbott, Jim Black; Casting, Susie Farris; a Brad Zions Films/Eden Wurmfeld Films production in association with Cineric and Michael Alden Productions; Dolby; Color; Rated R; 96 minutes; Release date: March 13, 2002

Tovah Feldshuh, Jennifer Westfeldt

CAST

Jessica Stein	Jennifer Westfeldt
Helen Cooper	Heather Juergensen
Josh Meyers	Scott Cohen
Joan	Jackie Hoffman
Martin	Michael Mastro
Sebastian	Carson Elrod
Judy Stein	Tovah Feldshuh
Grandma Esther	Esther Wurmfeld
Rabbi	Hillel Friedman
Himself	Ben Feldman
Sidney Stein	Robert Ari
Dan Stein	David Aaron Baker
Rachel, Dan's Fiancée	Jennifer Carta
Larry	Ben Weber
Peter	Brian Stepanek
Howard	Nick Corley
Chuck	John Cariani
Roland	Tibor Feldman
Stephen	Michael Showalter
Greg	Michael Ealy

and Christopher Berger (Malaprops Guy), Hayden Adams (Weird Smooth Guy), Kevin Sussman (Calculator Guy), Jim J. Bullock (Not-Yet-Out Gay Guy), Alysia Reiner (Schuller Gallery Artist), Naomi Sablan (Seductive Woman at Gallery), Jon Hamm (Charles), Allen Fitzpatrick (Matthew), Julie Lauren (Josh's Date), Jimmy Palumbo, Thomas Bolster (Cheesy Pick-Up Guys), Vinnie Vella (Cab Driver), Peter Hirsch (Stanley), Idina Menzel (Bridesmaid), Adele Reichman (Grandma Interrogating Helen), Amy Wilson (Bookstore Saleswoman), Ilana Levine (Helen's New Girlfriend)

Scott Cohen, Jennifer Westfeldt

Jessica Stein, feeling that she is getting nowhere dating men, decides to answer a personal ad in the "women seeking women" section and begins an affair with Helen Cooper.

© Fox Searchlight

Heather Juergensen, Jennifer Westfeldt

Heather Juergensen, Jennifer Westfeldt

SHOWTIME

(WARNER BROS.) Producers, Jorge Saralegui, Jane Rosenthal; Executive Producers, Will Smith, James Lassiter, Eric McLeod; Bruce Berman; Director, Tom Dey; Screenplay, Keith Sharon, Alfred Gough, Miles Millar; Story, Jorge Saralegui; Photography, Thomas Kloss; Designer, Jeff Mann; Costumes, Ellen Chenoweth; Editor, Billy Weber; Music, Alan Silvestri; Co-Producer, Channing Dungey; a Material production in association with Tribeca Productions; Presented in association with Village Roadshow Pictures and NPV Entertainment; Dolby; Super 35 Widescreen; Technicolor; Rated PG-13; 95 minutes; Release date: March 15, 2002

Eddie Murphy

CAST

Mitch Preston	Robert De Niro
Trey Sellars	Eddie Murphy
Chase Renzi	Rene Russo
Captain Winship	Frankie R. Faison
Himself	William Shatner
Teacher	Rachel Harris
Captain (Audition)	Zaid Farid
Casting Director	Alex Borstein
Producer	Holly Mandel
Convenience Store Owner	Marshall Manesh
Ray	Nestor Serrano
ReRun	T.J. Cross
Lazy Boy	Mos Def
Cameraman	James Roday
Vargas	Pedro Jacobson
Brad Slocum	Peter Jacobson
Annie	Drena De Niro

and Joel Hurt Jones, Chris Harrison, Perri Peltz, Amy Powell, Debra Snell, Chris Ufland (Reporters), Ewan Chung (Ping Pong Opponent), Andrew Wilson, Larry Joe Campbell, Reggie Gaskins (Locker Room Cops), Ken Campbell (Cop in Gym), Johnnie L. Cochran, Jr. (Himself), Rick Cramer (Duty Officer), Linda Hart (Waitress), Kadeem Hardison (Kyle), Joy Bryant (Lexi), Maurice Compte (Chili), Freez Luv (Freez), Merlin Santana (Hector), Julian Dulce Vida (J.J.), Jeff Sanders (Big Boy), Robert Joseph (Gangbanger #4), Judah Friedlander (Julio), Angela Rosa Alvarado (Gina Reyes), John Cariani (Charlie), Kirk Ward, Reggie Jordan (Parking Garage Police), Lucille M. Oliver (Screaming Woman), Callie Childers (Pool Girl), Tom Billett (Freddy Bouncer #2), Henry Kingi (Garbage Truck Driver), Neil Mather (Uniform), Joel Elliott, Grant Sawyer (Animal Welfare Workers), Christopher Darga (Announcer at Gun Show), Clement Blake (Gun Show Patron), Lisa Renee Pitts, Teresa DePriest (Cops), John J. Polce (Police Officer)

Rene Russo, Drena De Niro

TV executive Chase Renzi comes up with the idea of teaming real life L.A. cop Mitch Preston with aspiring actor Trey Sellars for a reality police show, a premise that irks the no-nonsense Mitch to no end.

Robert De Niro, Eddie Murphy

William Shatner, Rene Russo

ICE AGE

(20TH CENTURY FOX) Producer, Lori Forte; Executive Producer, Christopher Meledandri; Director, Chris Wedge; Co-Director, Carlos Saldanha; Screenplay, Michael Berg, Michael J. Wilson, Peter Ackerman; Story, Michael J. Wilson; Designer, Brian McEntee; Music, David Newman; Editor, John Carnochan; Character Design, Peter de Sève; Lead Layout Artist, William H. Frake III; Animation Sequence Directors, Mark Baldo, Jan Carlée; a Blue Sky production; Dolby; Deluxe color; Rated PG; 81 minutes; Release date: March 15, 2002

VOICE CAST

Manfred . . . . .Ray Romano
Sid . . . . .John Leguizamo
Diego . . . . .Denis Leary
Soto . . . . .Goran Visnjic
Zeke . . . . .Jack Black
Roshan/Start . . . . .Tara Strong
Rhinos . . . . .Cedric "The Entertainer," Stephen Root
Saber-Tooth Tiger . . . . .Diedrich Bader
Sloths . . . . .Lorri Bagley, Jane Krakowski
Dodo . . . . .P.J. Benjamin
Dodo/Glyptos . . . . .Josh Hamilton
Dodo/Scrat . . . . .Peter Wedge
Saber-Tooth Tiger/Dodo/Freaky Mammal . . . . .Alan Tudyk
Dodo/Freaky Mammal . . . . .Peter Ackerman
Glyptos . . . . .Denny Dillon, Mitzi McCall

Diego, Sid, Manfred

As the Ice Age begins, three creatures who refrained from migrating south with the others, find themselves thrown together when they try to reunite a human baby with his family.

This film received an Oscar nomination for animated feature.

Manfred, Diego

Rhino, Sid

Milla Jovovich, Michelle Rodriguez, Eric Mabius

RESIDENT EVIL

(SCREEN GEMS) Producers, Bernd Eichinger, Samuel Hadida, Jeremy Bolt, Paul W.S. Anderson; Executive Producers, Robert Kulzer, Victor Hadida, Daniel Kletzky, Yoshiki Okamoto; Director/Screenplay, Paul W.S. Anderson; Based upon Capcom's Videogame; Co-Producer, Chris Symes; Production Executive, Christine Rothe; Photography, David Johnson; Designer/Costumes, Richard Bridgland; Editor, Alexander Berner; Music, Marco Beltrami, Marilyn Manson; Music Supervisor, Liz Gallacher; Visual Effects Supervisor, Richard Yuricich; Casting, Suzanne M. Smith, Robyn Ray; a Constantin Films and Davis Films presentation of a Constantin Film/New Legacy Film/Davis Film production in association with Impact Pictures; U.S.-German-French; Dolby; Color; Rated R; 100 minutes; Release date: March 15, 2002

CAST

Alice	Milla Jovovich
Rain	Michelle Rodriguez
Matt	Eric Mabius
Spence	James Purefoy
Kaplan	Martin Crewes
One	Colin Salmon
Red Queen	Michaela Dicker
J.D.	Pasquale Aleardi
Mr. White	Stephen Billington
Dr. Green	Anna Bolt
Medic	Liz May Brice
Clarence	James Butler
Ms. Gold	Fiona Glascott
Commandos	Torsten Jerabek, Marc Logan-Black
Lisa	Heike Makatsch
Dr. Blue	Joseph May
Mr. Grey	Ryan McCluskey
Mr. Black	Indra Ové
Mr. Red	Oscar Pearce
Mr. Brown	Robert Tannion

A team of commandos enters a sealed, underground genetic research facility where a deadly virus has presumably wiped out the staff, when in fact they have been turned into zombies, which has its drawbacks.

© Screen Gems

(MIRAMAX) Producers, Ben Affleck, Matt Damon, Chris Moore; Executive Producers, Pat Peach, Michelle Sy; Director/Screenplay, Pete Jones; Co-Producer, Jeff Balis; Associate Producer, Alex Keledjian; Photography, Pete Biagi; Designer, Devorah Herbert; Editor, Gregg Featherman; Music, Danny Lux; Casting, Joseph Middleton, Michelle Morris-Gertz, Amanda Koblin; a LivePlanet production; Dolby; Color; Rated PG; 90 minutes; Release date: March 22, 2002

CAST

Joe O'Malley	Aidan Quinn
Margaret O'Malley	Bonnie Hunt
Rabbi Jacobsen	Kevin Pollak
Patrick O'Malley	Eddie Kaye Thomas
Pete O'Malley	Adi Stein
Danny Jacobsen	Mike Weinberg
Father Kelly	Brian Dennehy
Sister Leonora Mary	Peggy Roeder
Jimmy	Martin Hughes

and Ryan Kelley (Seamus O'Malley), Lindsay Light (Katie O'Malley), Will Malnati (Eddie O'Malley), Kristie Kelley (Marie O'Malley), Etel Billig (Esther), Lisa Dodson (Mrs. Jacobsen), John Connolly (Roger O'Malley), John Sierros (Jack), Howard Friedland (Jeffrey Jacobsen), Amara Balthrop-Lewis (Carly), Dana Lynne Gilhooley (Annie), David Costabile (Doctor), Frank Fowle (Bobby)

When 8-year old Pete is warned by his Catholic school teacher to clean up his act, he sets out on a mission to better his Chicago community with the help of Danny, a 7-year old Jewish boy he meets.

© Miramax

Mike Weinberg, Adi Stein

Aidan Quinn, Bonnie Hunt

33

BLADE II

(NEW LINE CINEMA) Producers, Peter Frankfurt, Wesley Snipes, Patrick Palmer; Executive Producers, Stan Lee, Avi Arad, Lynn Harris, Michael De Luca, David S. Goyer, Toby Emmerich; Director, Guillermo Del Toro; Screenplay, David S. Goyer; Blade Character Created by Marvel Comics by Marv Wolfman & Gene Colan; Co-Producers, Andrew J. Horne, Jon Divens; Photography, Gabriel Beristain; Designer, Carol Spier; Editor, Peter Amundson; Music, Marco Beltrami, Danny Saber; Music Supervisor, Happy Walters; Costumes, Wendy Partridge; Visual Effects Supervisor, Nicholas Brooks; Casting, Nancy Foy, Jeremy Zimmerman; an Amen Ra Films production in association with Peter Frankfurt; Dolby; Deluxe color; Rated R; 116 minutes; Release date: March 22, 2002

CAST

Blade	Wesley Snipes
Whistler	Kris Kristofferson
Reinhardt	Ron Perlman
Nyssa	Leonor Varela
Scud	Norman Reedus
Damaskinos	Thomas Kretschmann
Nomak	Luke Goss
Chupa	Matthew Schulze

and Danny John Jules (Asad), Donnie Yen (Snowman), Karel Roden (Kounen), Marit Velle Kile (Verlaine), Tony Curran (Priest), Daz Crawford (Lighthammer), Santiago Segura (Rush), Xuyen Tu Valdivia (Jigsaw), Marek Vasut (Golem), Pete Lee Wilson (Blood Bank Doctor/Reaper), Paul Kasey (Blood Bank Guard/Reaper), Andrea Miltner (Blood Bank Nurse), Ladislav Beran (Drug Dealer), Jiri Sieber (Blood Bank Guard), Bridge Markland (Vampire with Exposed Spine), Jamie Wilson, Stuart Luis, Ladislav Mohyla, Jan Malík, Jan Révai, Mário Wild, Tomás Böhm, Zdenek Bubák, Jan Loukota, Jan Bursa, Petr Krusalnicky, Jaroslav Misek (Reapers), Karel Vávrovec (St. Cloud), Jaroslav Peterka (Choad), Milos Kulhavy (Little G), Ivan Mares (Tea Bag), Lennox Brown (Man in London Porno Shop), André Hyde-Braithwaite (Young Blade)

Half-human, half-vampire Blade joins forces with his enemy, vampire overlord Damaskinos, to help stop a deadly super race of vampires called the Reapers. Sequel to the 1998 New Line film *Blade*, with Snipes and Kristofferson repeating their roles.

© New Line Cinema

Sarah Polley, Robert John Burke

NO SUCH THING

(UNITED ARTISTS) Producers, Fridrik Thór Fridriksson, Hal Hartley, Cecilia Kate Roque; Executive Producers, Francis Ford Coppola, Linda Reisman, Willi Baer; Director/Screenplay/Music, Hal Hartley; Photography, Michael Spiller; Designer, Árni Páll Jóhannsson; Costumes, Helga I. Stefánsdóttir; Editor, Steve Hamilton; Make-Up Effects, Mark Rappaport, Creature Effects Company; U.S.-Icelandic; Dolby; DuArt color; Rated R; 103 minutes; Release date: March 29, 2002

CAST

Beatrice	Sarah Polley
The Monster	Robert John Burke
The Boss	Helen Mirren
Dr. Anna	Julie Christie
Margaret	Annika Peterson
Fred	Paul Lazar
Dr. Artaud	Baltasar Kormakur
Rental Agent	Margarét Ákadóttir
Beautician	Julie Anderson, Miho Nikaido
Sólveig	Anna Kristín Arngrímsdóttir
Ethel	Ilene Bergelson

and Guôrún Bjarnadóttir (Marta), Bessi Bjarnason (Captain), Helgi Björnsson (Leó), Stacy Dawson (Mugger), María Ellingsen (Karlsdóttir/Gate-Manager), Anthony Giangrande (Journalist), Erica Gimpel (Judy), Pröstur Leó Gunnarsson (1st Mate), Brynhildur Guôjónsdóttir (Ticket Clerk), Baldvin Halldórsson (Jón), Björn Ingi Hilmarsson, Berger Pór Ingólfsson (Smugglers), Jón Hjartarson (Mayor), Baldur Trausti Hreinsson (Johansen), Theódór Júliusson (Borg), Sigurveig Jónsdóttir (Gréta), Björn Jörundur (Por), Kristbjörg Kjeld (Nurse Joan), Paul Lazar (Fred), Daniel C. Levine (Pissing Kid), Paul Liberti (Journalist), DJ Mendel, David Nuemann (Agents), Peter O'Hara (Tom), Abby Royle (Scientist), Bill Sage (Carlo), Ingvar Sigurôsson (Svensen), Guôrún Stephensen (Mayor's Wife), Sigurour Skúlason (Old Man), Jón Tryggvason (Guide), James Urbaniak (Concierge), Benham Valadbeygi (Cook), Wendy Walker (Journalist), Damian Young (Berger)

Beatrice, an employee on a sensationalist TV news show, discovers a genuine Monster living in the frozen north and brings him back to New York to help him find the end for his lonely, tormented existence, only to see him turned into a media curiosity.

© United Artists Films

Leonor Varela, Wesley Snipes

THE ROOKIE

Dennis Quaid, Rebecca Spicher, Rachel Griffiths, Angus T. Jones

Chad Lindberg, Brandon Garner, Rick Gonzalez, Angelo Spizziri, Jay Hernandez, Dennis Quaid, Angus T. Jones

Dennis Quaid

(**WALT DISNEY PICTURES**) Producers, Gordon Gray, Mark Ciardi, Mark Johnson; Executive Producer, Philip Steuer; Director, John Lee Hancock; Screenplay, Mike Rich; Photography, John Schwartzman; Designer, Barry Robison; Costumes, Bruce Finlayson; Music, Carter Burwell; Music Supervisor, John Bissell; Editor, Eric L. Beason; Casting, Ronna Kress; Distributed by Buena Vista Pictures; Dolby; Technicolor; Rated G; 127 minutes; Release date: March 29, 2002

CAST

Jimmy Morris . . . . .Dennis Quaid
Lorri Morris . . . . .Rachel Griffiths
Joaquin "Wack" Campos . . . . .Jay Hernandez
Jimmy's Mother . . . . .Beth Grant
Hunter Morris . . . . .Angus T. Jones
Jim Sr. . . . . .Brian Cox
Rudy Bonilla . . . . .Rick Gonzalez
Joe David West . . . . .Chad Lindberg
Joel De La Garza . . . . .Angelo Spizzirri
Henry . . . . .Royce D. Applegate
Brooks . . . . .Russell Richardson
Frank . . . . .Raynor Scheine
Cal . . . . .David Blackwell
Baseball Scout Dave Patterson . . . . .Blue Deckert
Durham Manager Mac . . . . .Daniel Kamin
Jessica . . . . .Rebecca Spicher
Janitor . . . . .Raymond Rivera
Sanchez . . . . .Marco Sanchez
Esther . . . . .Cynthia Dorn
Steve Dearborn . . . . .Robert Logan
Cory Jones . . . . .Cory Shane Harris
Owl Players . . . . .Matt Williams, Miguel Salas,
Eddie Alvarado, Brandon Garner,
Ernest Vidaure, Canuto Rey Guerrero
Tryout Catcher . . . . .Seth Spiker
Orlando Heckler . . . . .Beau Holden
Orlando Manager . . . . .Brandon Smith
Snow Covered Catcher .Chris Sheffield
Jimmy's Brother . . . . .Cameron Banfield
Student . . . . .Barbie Burke
David . . . . .Carlos A. Gonzalez
Baseball Scout . . . . .Kyle Scott Jackson
Player with Headphones .Bert Beatson
Kenny Justin . . . . .Tony Moore
Durham PR Director . . . . .Brian Shoop
Tim Stewart . . . . .Mark Ciardi
Player Behind Backstop . . . . .Matt Targac
Durham Catcher . . . . .Tiger King
Locker Room Attendant . . . . .Willie Dirden
Texas Ranger P.A. Announcer . . . . .Chuck Morgan
Texas Ranger Radio Announcer . . . . .Eric Nadel
Devils Rays Manager . . . . .Richard Dillard
Devil Rays Pitching Coach . . . . .James Fletcher
Reporters . . . . .John Wayne Shafer, Charles Sanders
Texas Oilman . . . . .Randall Wallace
and Jaime Alvarado (Wack's Sister), Quincy Wickson (Little League Umpire), Keith Mears, Tim Jackson (High School Umpires), John Williams, Jim Morris (Orlando Umpires), Gavin Forbis (Orlando Catcher), J.D. Evermore, Robert Ellis, Julio Cedillo (Relief Pitchers), Fred Osuna, Mark Baletka (Major League Umpires)

Jim Morris, a chemistry teacher and high school baseball coach, gets an unexpected chance to realize the dream he thought had vanished years earlier when a bet with his team encourages him to try out for the minor-leagues.

PANIC ROOM

(COLUMBIA) Producers, Gavin Polone, Judy Hofflund, David Koepp, Cean Chaffin; Director, David Fincher; Screenplay, David Koepp; Photography, Conrad W. Hall, Darius Khondji; Designer, Arthur Max; Costumes, Michael Kaplan; Editors, James Haygood, Angus Wall; Music, Howard Shore; Casting, Laray Mayfield; a Hofflund/Polone production of an Indelible Picture; Dolby; Super 35 Widescreen; Deluxe color; Rated R; 112 minutes; Release date: March 29, 2002

CAST

Meg Altman	Jodie Foster
Sarah Altman	Kristen Stewart
Burnham	Forest Whitaker
Raoul	Dwight Yoakam
Junior	Jared Leto
Stephen Altman	Patrick Bauchau
Lydia Lynch	Ann Magnuson
Evan Kurlander	Ian Buchanan
Sleepy Neighbor	Andrew Kevin Walker
Officer Keeney	Paul Schulze
Officer Morales	Mel Rodriguez

and Richard Conant, Paul Simon, Victor Thrash, Ken Turner (SWAT Cops), Nicole Kidman (Voice of Stephen's Girlfriend)

Meg Altman and her young daughter take refuge in their brownstone's hidden room after a group of intruders break into their home, not realizing that what they are searching for is in their hiding place.

© Columbia

Jodie Foster

Jared Leto, Jodie Foster, Kristen Stewart

Jared Leto, Forest Whitaker

Jodie Foster

Jared Leto, Dwight Yoakam, Forest Whitaker

Jodie Foster

Kristen Stewart, Jodie Foster

Jared Leto

Forest Whitaker, Dwight Yoakam

Jodie Foster, Kristen Stewart

DEATH TO SMOOCHY

(WARNER BROS.) Producers, Andrew Lazar, Peter MacGregor-Scott; Director, Danny DeVito; Screenplay, Adam Resnick; Photography, Anastas Michos; Designer, Howard Cummings; Costumes, Jane Ruhm; Editor, Jon Poll; Music, David Newman; Original Songs, David Newman, Adam Resnick; Co-Producers, Jody Hedien, Doug Davison, Jill Besnoy; Associate Producers, Joshua Levinson, Lisa Reardon, John Kreidman; Choreographer, Barry Lather; Rainbow Randolph Ice Dance Choreographer and Performer, Elvis Stojko; Visual Effects Supervisors, Jeffrey A. Okun, William Mesa; Casting, Margery Simkin; a Mad Chance production, presented in association with FilmFour and Senator Entertainment; Dolby; Technicolor; Rated R; 109 minutes; Release date: March 29, 2002

Robin Williams, Edward Norton

Catherine Keener, Edward Norton

Jon Stewart, Vincent Schiavelli

CAST

Rainbow Randolph Smiley	Robin Williams
Sheldon Mopes/Smoochy the Rhino	Edward Norton
Nora Wells	Catherine Keener
Burke Bennett	Danny DeVito
Marion Frank Stokes	Jon Stewart
Tommy Cotter	Pam Ferris
Angelo Pike	Danny Woodburn
Spinner Dunn	Michael Rispoli
Merv Green	Harvey Fierstein
Buggy Ding Dong	Vincent Schiavelli
Husband	Craig Eldridge
Wife	Judy White
Danny	Tim MacMenamin
Roy	Bruce McFee
Jimmy	Glen Cross

and Bill Lake (Bartender), Nick Taylor (Henry the Thug), Richard A. Cocchiaro, Jr. (Mitch the Thug), Tracey Walter (Ben Franks), Louis Giambalvo (Sonny Gordon), Colin Moult, Nikolai Tichtchenko, Martin Klebba, Tonya Reneé Banks, Christy Artran (Rhinette/Krinkle Kids), Philip Craig (Senator), Natasha Kinne (Smoochy's Secretary), Richard Hamilton (Old Vagrant), Shawn Byfield (Rickets), Todd Graff (Skip Kleinman), Melissa DiMarco (Tara), Dan Duran (Hunter), Michael Copeman, James Carroll, Philip Jarrett, Suzanne Leonard Feliz, Thomas Lyons, Angela Bullock, Robert M. Sussman, George Blumenthal (Reporters), Matthew Arkin (Save the Rhino Man), Hugo Jansuzian (Hispanic Dad), Silvia Rojas (Hispanic Mom), Mario Andres Torres (Hispanic Boy), Sabrina Jansuzian (Hispanic Girl), John "Cha Cha" Ciarcia (Autograph Man), Fred Peter Scialla, Adam Bryant, Richard Ziman (Men in Crowd), Frank Anello (NYPD), Samantha Cordero (Little Girl), Peter Keleghan (News Anchor), Rothaford Gray (Ellis), Dave Brown (McCall), Gerry Quigley (Ian), James Brinkley (Cop #1), Dylan Roberts (Stagehand), Vito Rezza (Lead Cop), Lou Cantres (Little Girl's Dad), John Cleland (John), Lauren Flanigan (Opera Diva), Cara Wakelin (Princess)

Randolph Smiley, fired from his job as television's top children's show host for taking bribes, plots revenge on his wholesome replacement, Smoochy the Rhino.

Danny DeVito, Harvey Fierstein

CLOCKSTOPPERS

(PARAMOUNT) Producers, Gale Ann Hurd, Julia Pistor; Director, Jonathan Frakes; Screenplay, Rob Hedden, J. David Stem, David N. Weiss; Story, Rob Hedden, Andy Hedden, J. David Stem, David N. Weiss; Executive Producer, Albie Hecht; Photography, Tim Suhrstedt; Designer, Marek Dobrowolski; Costumes, Deborah Everton; Editor, Peter E. Berger; Co-Producer, Rob Hedden; Music, Jamshied Sharifi; Executive Music Producer, Ralph Sall; Visual Effects Supervisor, Michael Fink; Visual Effects/Animation, Cinesite; Dolby; Deluxe color; Rated PG; 94 minutes; March 29, 2002

CAST

Zak Gibbs	Jesse Bradford
Dr. Earl Dopler	French Stewart
Francesca	Paula Garces
Henry Gates	Michael Biehn
George Gibbs	Robin Thomas
Meeker	Garikayi Mutambirwa
Mom (Jenny Gibbs)	Julia Sweeney
Kelly Gibbs	Lindze Letherman
Richard	Jason Winston George
Jay	Linda Kim
Agent Moore	Ken Jenkins
Ticket Agent	Esperanza Catubig
Security Officer	Jennifer Manley
Tourist Dad	Scott Thomson
Tourist Mom	Deborah Rawlings
Bright Freshman	Jodie Milks
Confused Freshman	Brad "Chip" Pope
Administrator	Tony Abatemarco

and Oanh Nguyen (Graduate Student), Andrew James Armstrong (Hot Skates Sports Boy), Rachel Arieff (Hot Skates Saleswoman), Joey Simmrin (Rick Ditmar), Finneus Egan (Ditmar's Friend), Pamela Dunlap (Vice Principal), Gina Hecht (Meter Maid), Eric Baugh (Tagger), Dwight Armstrong (Nose Ring Boy), D.J. Midas (Flavius' Opponent), Funkmaster Flex (Large Mike), D.J. Swamp (Flavius'/Ditmar Hands), Earl Barlow, Jer-Lyn Benjamin, Diana Carreno, Aisha R. Delaria, Frank Howard, Rece Jones, Alfie Lewis, Monet "Fusion" Ludlow, Clifford McGee, Kimberly Morrow, Alphonzo Rawls, Sherman Shoate, Lani Tuyor-Stanbery, Giacomo Vernice (Rave Dancers), Billy Mayo (Q.T. Agent), Jenette Goldstein (Doctor), Tom Parks (Detective), Jeff Ricketts (Officer Meyers), Melanie Mayron (Night Manager), Larry Carroll (Newscaster), Caroline Fogarty (Convention Worker), Joel Huggins, Jon Alan Lee (Convention Vendors), Colin McClean (Q.T. Security Guard), Darius Boorn, Eric Brown, Young Dopler, Miko Hughes (Q.T. Techies)

Zak Gibbs finds a magical wristwatch that allows him to freeze activity, putting him in a speeded-up version of reality, called hypertime; making his watch very desirable to evil Quantum Technologies head Henry Gates.

© Paramount

Jesse Bradford, Paula Garces

Jesse Bradford, French Stewart, Paula Garces

Jesse Bradford, Garikayi Mutambirwa

BIG TROUBLE

(TOUCHSTONE) Producers, Barry Sonnenfeld, Barry Josephson, Tom Jacobson; Executive Producer, Jim Wedaa; Co-Producer, Graham Place; Director, Barry Sonnenfeld; Screenplay, Robert Ramsey, Matthew Stone; Photography, Greg Gardiner; Designer, Garreth Stover; Costumes, Mary Vogt; Editor, Steven Weisberg; Music, James Newton Howard; Music Supervisor, Dawn Solér; Casting, Ronna Kress; a Jacobson Company and Sonnenfeld/Josephson Worldwide Entertainment production; Dolby; Technicolor; Rated PG-13; 85 minutes; Release date: April 5, 2002

Jason Lee, Sofía Vergara

Patrick Warburton, Tim Allen, Ben Foster, Rene Russo,
Zooey Deschanel

Heavy D, Omar Epps, Janeane Garofalo

CAST

Eliot Arnold	Tim Allen
Anna Herk	Rene Russo
Arthur Herk	Stanley Tucci
Snake	Tom Sizemore
Eddie	Johnny Knoxville
Henry	Dennis Farina
Leonard	Jack Kehler
Monica Romero	Janeane Garofalo
Walter Kramitz	Patrick Warburton
Matt Arnold	Ben Foster
Jenny Herk	Zooey Deschanel
Greer	Dwight "Heavy D" Myers
Seitz	Omar Epps
Puggy	Jason Lee
Nina	Sofía Vergara
Jack/Ralph Pendick	Andy Richter
Bruce	Micheal McShane
John	Daniel London
Leo	Lars Arentz Hansen
Andrew	DJ Qualls

and Cullen Douglas (Capt. Justin Hobart), Flip Schultz (Co-Pilot Jan Vigushin), Patrick Mickler, Gerald Owens, Mitchell Carrey (Cigar Buddies), Nathalie Latronico (Heather Weintraub), Jonathan Kasdan (Jack Pendick Trainee), Ian Marioles (Editorial Assistant), Philip Nolen (Deeber), David Koepp (Annoyed Sports Radio Host), Barry Sonnenfeld (Confused Sports Radio Call In Voice), Jay Rasumn, Ruben Gomez (Couriers), Antoni Cornacchione (William Spaulding), Siobhan Fallon Hogan (Fly by Air Ticket Agent), Kava Stewartson (Sour Airport Security), Gloria Kennedy (Airport X-Ray Operator), Carmen Lopez (Airport Stern Security Woman), Mark Salem (Fly by Air Baggage Handler), Renato Campilongo (Gang Leader), Marc Macaulay (Arch Ridley), James Martin Kelly (Geo Salesman), Dave Corey (Cellmate Dwight), Selma Cipes, Sid Raymond, Jody Wilson (Retirees), Mia Finnegan, Eric Geller (Aerobics Announcers), Paul Barth (Airplane Pilot)

Some Miami citizens inadvertently get involved in a plot to steal nuclear weapons.

Stanley Tucci

HIGH CRIMES

Adam Scott, Ashley Judd, Jim Caviezel, Morgan Freeman

Ashley Judd, Morgan Freeman

Jim Caviezel, Ashley Judd

(20TH CENTURY FOX) Producers, Arnon Milchan, Janet Yang, Jesse B'Franklin; Director, Carl Franklin; Screenplay, Yuri Zeltser, Cary Bickley; Based on the novel by Joseph Finder; Executive Producers, Lisa Henson, Kevin Reidy; Photography, Theo Van De Sande; Designer, Paul Peters; Costumes, Sharen Davis; Co-Producer, Naomi Despres; Editor, Carole Kravetz-Aykanian; Music, Graeme Revell; Casting, Mali Finn; a Regency Enterprises presentation of a New Regency/Mainfest Film Company/Monarch Pictures production; Dolby; Panavision; Deluxe color; Rated PG-13; 115 minutes; Release date: April 5, 2002

CAST

Claire Kubik . . . . .Ashley Judd
Charlie Grimes . . . . .Morgan Freeman
Tom Kubik . . . . .Jim Caviezel
Lt. Embry . . . . .Adam Scott
Jackie . . . . .Amanda Peet
Brig. General Marks . . . . .Bruce Davison
Mullins . . . . .Tom Bower
Major Hernandez . . . . .Juan Carlos Hernández
Major Waldron . . . . .Michael Gaston
Colonel Farrell . . . . .Jude Ciccolella
Salvadoran Man . . . . .Emilio Rivera
Abbott . . . . .Michael Shannon
Oshman . . . . .John Billingsley
Lola . . . . .Dendrie Taylor
Gracie . . . . .Paula Jai Parker
and John Apicella (Franklin), Dawn Hudson (La Pierre), Samuel Sheng (Josh), Florence Regina (Nurse), Julie Remala (Mrs. Stenstrom), Kyle T. Heffner (SF Judge), Joe Mazza (SF D.A.), Jesse B'Franklin (Ramona), Wayne Terry (Bartender), Maureen McVerry, Jakob Gentry, Anthony C. Jackson (Attorneys), Julia Mendoza (Givens), Ray Hanis, Jr. (Cook), Don Bajema (Mr. Arguer), Edith Bryson (Mrs. Arguer), Rusty Mahmood (Mahmood), Patsy Bob Rust (Pickup Truck Driver), Don J. Byron (F.B.I. Agent), Saiba Roberts (F.B.I. Swat Guy), Adam Segen (General's Aide), Eddie Santiago, Arlen Escarpeta, Lucas Ford (Guards), Andrew Wesely (Marine), Alex Nesic (Bailiff), Cynthia Shope (Court Stenographer), Stephen Jared, Randy Mulkey (Military Guards), Karen Kahn, Paul Ghiringhelli, Elaine Corral Kendall, Danny Freeman, Linda Laing (Reporters), Lee Whittaker (Student in San Salvador), Alicia Kepler (Mother Holding Baby)

High-powered lawyer Claire Kubik enlists the aide of former military attorney Charlie Grimes when her husband is accused of having murdered civilians in El Salvador during a covert military operation.

Ashley Judd, Morgan Freeman

THE SWEETEST THING

(COLUMBIA) Producer, Cathy Konrad; Executive Producers, Ricky Strauss, Stuart M. Besser; Director, Roger Kumble; Screenplay, Nancy M. Pimental; Photography, Anthony B. Richmond; Designer, Jon Gary Steele; Editors, Wendy Greene Bricmont, David Rennie; Costumes, Denise Wingate; Music, Edward Shearmur; Music Supervisor, John Houlihan; Casting, Lisa Beach; a Konrad Pictures production; Dolby; Deluxe color; Rated R; 84 minutes; Release date: April 12, 2002

CAST

Christina Walters . . . . .Cameron Diaz
Courtney Rockliffe . . . . .Christina Applegate
Peter Donahue . . . . .Thomas Jane
Jane Burns . . . . .Selma Blair
Roger Donahue . . . . .Jason Bateman
Judy Webb . . . . .Parker Posey
Aunt Frida . . . . .Lillian Adams
Geeky Guy . . . . .Bryan Anthony
Brawling Bridesmaid . . . . .Linda Asuma
Taxi Driver . . . . .Vahe Bejan
Mr. Martin . . . . .Joe Bellan
Greta . . . . .Chelsea Lee Bond
Judy's Mother . . . . .Judith Chapman
Wedding Priest . . . . .Charlie Dell
Gramps . . . . .Richard Denni
Bar Counter Guy . . . . .Timothy J. Dodge
Vera . . . . .Georgia B. Engel
and Alexander S. Chance, Damon Williams, Herbert Ankrom, Linda Stein (Wedding Guests), Manny Rodriguez, Rick Evans (San Francisco Policemen), Anne E. Fields (Valerie), Melanie H. Gassaway, Hellena Schmied, Shannon Murphy (Spinners), Jennifer Gimenez (Mariangela), Siena Goines (Tammy), Marc Goldsmith, Erik Stolhanske (Paramedics), Frank Grillo (Andy), Tria Katz (Lynne), Craig Kvinsland (Waiter), John Lehr (Ralph), Loren Lester (Mr. Mooney), Eddie James Low (Chinese Butcher), Mason Lucero (Tommy), Olivia Lucero (Susie), George Maguire (Father Flynn), Mary Mahagian (Park Ranger), James Mangold (Dr. Greg), Eddie McClintock (Michael), Johnny Messner (Todd), Jill Miller (Gina), Mitch Mullany (Craig), Philip Pavel (Room Service Waiter), John Bennett Perry (Judy's Father), Nancy Priddy (Mrs. Franklin), Andrea Sabesin (Sheila), Johnathon Schaech (Leather Coat Guy), David Nathan Schwartz (Usher), Jonathon E. Stewart (Eddie), Ted Stryker (Chuck), M. Darnell Suttles (Fireman), Sybil Temchen (Rebecca), Branden Williams (Cheeta), Don Winston (Eric the Bartender), Kristoffer Winters (Neal)

Christina Walters and her best friend Courtney take a road trip in order to track down the man Christina believes is Mr. Right.

© Columbia

Thomas Jane, Cameron Diaz

Cameron Diaz, Christina Applegate

Cameron Diaz, Selma Blair, Christina Applegate

FRAILTY

(LIONS GATE) Producers, David Kirschner, David Blocker, Corey Sienega; Executive Producers, Karen Loop, Tom Huckabee, Tom Ortenberg, Michael Paseornek; Director, Bill Paxton; Screenplay, Brent Hanley; Co-Producers, Mario Ohoven, Michael Ohoven, Eberhard Kayser; Photography, Bill Butler; Designer, Nelson Coates; Costumes, April Ferry; Editor, Arnold Glassman; Editor, Brian Tyler; Casting, Mary Gail Artz, Barbara Cohen; a David Kirschner Production in association with American Entertainment Co. and in association with Cinerenta/Cindelta; U.S.-German; Dolby; Fotokem color; Rated R; 100 minutes; Release date: April 12, 2002

Bill Paxton

CAST

Dad . . . . .Bill Paxton
Adam Meiks . . . . .Matthew McConaughey
Agent Wesley J. Doyle . . . . .Powers Boothe
Sheriff Smalls . . . . .Luke Askew
Young Adam Meiks . . . . .Jeremy Sumpter
Young Fenton Meiks . . . . .Matt O'Leary
Agent Griffin Hull . . . . .Derk Cheetwood
Becky Meiks . . . . .Melissa Crider
Fenton Meiks . . . . .Levi Kreis
Brad White . . . . .Alan Davidson
Cynthia Harbridge . . . . .Cynthia Ettinger
Edward March . . . . .Vincent Chase
Operator . . . . .Gwen McGee
The Angel . . . . .Edmond Scott Ratliff
Teacher . . . . .Rebecca Tilney
Eric . . . . .Blake King
and Brad Berryhill (Teenage Demon), Greg Serano, Edgar L. Davis, Jim Flowes, Lance E. Nichols (FBI Agents), John Paxton (Janitor in Lobby), Richard A. Bell (Curtis), Chelsea Blain Butler (Little Girl), Jennifer Drake (Teacher's Aid), Betty Gurule (Doyle's Mother)

Fenton Meiks tells FBI Agent Wesley J. Doyle the story of how his dad went insane and became a killer in the name of God, disposing of people he believed were actual demons.

© Lions Gate

Jeremy Sumpter, Matt O'Leary, Bill Paxton

Matthew McConaughey

Matt O'Leary, Bill Paxton

CHANGING LANES

(PARAMOUNT) Producer, Scott Rudin; Executive Producers, Ron Bozman, Adam Schroeder; Director, Roger Michell; Screenplay, Chap Taylor, Michael Tolkin; Story, Chap Taylor; Photography, Salvatore Totino; Designer, Kristi Zea; Costumes, Ann Roth; Editor, Christopher Tellefsen; Co-Producer, Scott Aversano; Music, David Arnold; Casting, Ellen Lewis, Marcia De Bonis; a Scott Rudin production; Dolby; Super 35 Widescreen; Deluxe color; Rated R; 98 minutes; Release date: April 12, 2002

CAST

Gavin Banek	Ben Affleck
Doyle Gipson	Samuel L. Jackson
Valerie Gipson	Kim Staunton
Michelle	Toni Collette
Stephen Delano	Sydney Pollack
Mrs. Delano	Tina Sloan
Walter Arnell	Richard Jenkins
Stephen Gipson	Akil Walker
Danny Gipson	Cole Hawkins
Ellen	Ileen Getz
Mina Dunne	Jennifer Dundas Lowe
Ron Cabot	Matt Malloy
Cynthia Banek	Amanda Peet
Judge Abarbanel	Myra Lucretia Taylor
Joe Kaufman	Bruce Altman
Judge Cosell	Joe Grifasi
Gina Gugliotta	Lisa Leguillou
Sarah Windsor	Angela Goethals
Tyler Cohen	Kevin Sussman
Sheryl Buckburg	Susan Varon
Bartender at Arlo's	Noel Wilson
Security Guards at School	Angel Caban, James Lovelett
Receptionist at AD & S	Julia Gibson
Sponsor	William Hurt
Seavers	Michael Patrick McGrath
Carlyle	John Benjamin Hickey
Finch	Dylan Baker
Willard	Ray Bokhour
Delano's Secretary	Suzanne Hevner
Kid on a Bike	Caleb Archer
Priest	Jordan Gelber
Mrs. Miller	Olga Merediz
Miss Tetley	Jayne Houdyshell
Cops at Precinct	Shabazz Richardson, Ray Anthony Thomas
Music Teacher/Conductor	Michael Pitt
Waitress	Genevieve Elam
Orchestra Children	Juan Lara, Anastasia Rojas, Nicole Wright, Clive Oliver Greenberg
Mike	Gil Williams
Orchestra Members	Sophia Guaspari, Ruben J. Seraballs
Himself	Father Bonneau
Teachers	Jewel Brimage, Katarina Kianna
Kate	Vanessa Quel
Barry	Howard I. Laniando
Office Workers	Tony Machine, Carolyn Feldschuh, Maria Alaina Mason
Author in Newsroom Interview	Harvey Waldman
Newscaster	Pamela Hart
Newsroom Writer	Neal Jones
Newsroom Producer	Susan Blackwell
Newsroom Executive Producer	Alyson Renaldo
Newsroom Associate Producer	James Soviero
Newsroom Script Supervisor	Mary Kelly

and Anthony DiGiacomo (Newsroom Associate Director), Richard Velasco (Newsroom Director), Leonard Thomas (Newsroom Reporter), Richard Kelly (AA Group Leader), Selena Blake (Insurance Broker), Harriet Rosenthal, John Kohl, Lisa Vogel (Family Court), Bob Heffernan (Simon Dunne)

Sydney Pollack, Ben Affleck

Samuel L. Jackson

Samuel L. Jackson, Ben Affleck

A self-involved, high-powered attorney finds himself in a car accident with a father on his way to an important custody hearing, an act that leads to a war between the two men who want revenge for the unexpected chaos this altercation has caused.

Amanda Peet, Ben Affleck

Samuel L. Jackson

Ben Affleck

Ben Affleck, Samuel L. Jackson

Ben Affleck, Toni Collette

Kim Staunton, Samuel L. Jackson

Samuel L. Jackson, William Hurt

MURDER BY NUMBERS

(WARNER BROS.) Producers, Barbet Schroeder, Susan Hoffman. Richard Crystal; Executive Producers, Sandra Bullock, Jeffrey Stott; Director, Barbet Schroeder; Screenplay, Tony Gayton; Photography, Luciano Tovoli; Designer, Stuart Wurtzel; Costumes, Carol Oditz; Editor, Lee Percy; Music, Clint Mansell; Co-Producer, Frank Capra III; Casting, Howard Feuer; a Castle Rock Entertainment presentation of a Schroeder/Hoffman production; Dolby; Technicolor; Rated R; 120 minutes; Release date: April 19, 2002

Ben Chaplin, Sandra Bullock

CAST

Cassie Mayweather	Sandra Bullock
Sam Kennedy	Ben Chaplin
Richard Haywood	Ryan Gosling
Justin Pendleton	Michael Pitt
Lisa Mills	Agnes Bruckner
Ray	Chris Penn
Captain Rod Cody	R.D. Call
Al Swanson	Tom Verica
Ms. Elder	Janni Brenn
Restaurant Manager	John Vickery
Mr. Chechi	Michael Canavan
Olivia Lake	Krista Carpenter
Officers in Flashback	Neal Matarrazo, Paula Scarpino
Lab Technician	Adilah Barnes
Lawyer	Jim Jansen
Parole Board Marshall	Brian Stepanek
Nurse	Sharon Madden

and John Doolittle (Fingerprint Technician), Dennis Cockrum, Eric Saiet (Criminalists at Ray's House), Nancy Osborne (Richard's Mother), Ralph Seymour (Paramedic), Christine Healy (Justin's Mother), Nick Offerman (Cop at Richard's House), Todd Leatherbury (Cop at First Crime Scene)

After the corpse of a young woman is found in the woods, homicide detective Cassie Mayweather sets out to find evidence against a pair of arrogant young men who believe they have committed the perfect crime.

© Castle Rock Entertainment

Sandra Bullock, Ryan Gosling

Agnes Bruckner, Michael Pitt

Michael Pitt, Ryan Gosling

MY BIG FAT GREEK WEDDING

(IFC FILMS) Producers, Rita Wilson, Tom Hanks, Gary Goetzman; Executive Producers, Norm Waitt, Paul Brooks, Steven Shareshian; Director, Joel Zwick; Screenplay, Nia Vardalos, based on her play; Photography, Jeffrey Jur; Designer, Gregory Keen; Costumes, Michael Clancy; Editor, Mia Goldman; Music, Chris Wilson, Alexander Janko; Casting, Liberman Patton; a Gold Circle Films presentation in association with Home Box Office and MPH Entertainment of a Playtone Picture; Dolby; Deluxe color; Rated PG; 95 minutes; Release date: April 19, 2002

CAST

Toula Portokalos . . . . .Nia Vardalos
Ian Miller . . . . .John Corbett
Gus Portokalos . . . . .Michael Constantine
Maria Portokalos . . . . .Lainie Kazan
Aunt Voula . . . . .Andrea Martin
Angelo . . . . .Joey Fatone
Nikki . . . . .Gia Carides
Nick Portokalos . . . . .Louis Mandylor
Athena . . . . .Stavroula Logothettis
Toula, aged 6 .Christina Eleusiniotis
Schoolgirl . . . . .Kaylee Vieira
Greek Teacher . . . . .John Kalangis
Toula, aged 12 . . . . .Marita Zouravlioff
Athena, aged 15 . . . . .Sarah Osman
and Petra Wildgoose, Melissa Todd (Carpool Friends), Bess Meisler (Yiayia), Gerry Mendicino (Uncle Taki), Constantine Tsapralis (Foti), Ian Gomez (Mike), Jayne Eastwood (Mrs. White), Frank Falcone, Eugene Martel, Joe Persechini, Peter Xynnis (Suitors), Fiona Reid (Harriet Miller), Bruce Gray (Rodney Miller), Anthony Kandiotis (Priest), Nick Kutsukos (Bouzouki Player), Peter Tharos (Yianni), Chrissy Paraskevopoulos (Cousin Jennie), Maria Vacratis (Aunt Frieda), Kathryn Haggis (Cousin Marianthi), Gale Zoë Garnett (Aunty Lexy), Charlene Bitzas (Aunt Nota), Chris Savides, Constantine Vardalos (Greek Chanters), Scott Khouri (Waiter), John Tsiflikis (Wedding Singer), Peter Chalkiopoulos, Peter Gogos, Spiro Milankou, Victor Politis, Jim Rouvas (Wedding Band), Arielle Sugarman (Paris)

Toula Portokalos falls in love with school teacher Ian Miller, which means she must tell her overbearing family that she plans on marrying someone who is not Greek. This film received an Oscar nomination for original screenplay.

© IFC Films

John Corbett, Nia Vardalos

Michael Constantine, Lainie Kazan, Bess Meisler

John Corbett, Nia Vardalos

Nia Vardalos, Lainie Kazan

THE SCORPION KING

(UNIVERSAL) Producers, Stephen Sommers, Sean Daniel, James Jacks, Kevin Misher; Executive Producer, Vince McMahon; Director, Chuck Russell; Screenplay, Stephen Sommers, William Osborne, David Hayter; Story, Stephen Sommers, Jonathan Hales; Photography, John R. Leonetti; Designer, Ed Verreaux; Costumes, John Bloomfield; Editors, Michael Tronick, Greg Parsons; Music, John Debney; Co-Producer, Richard Luke Rothschild; Associate Producers, Michael Tronick, Josh McLaglen; Casting, Sarah Halley Finn, Randi Hiller; an Alphaville/Stephen Sommers/Misher production, presented in association with WWF Entertainment; Dolby; Super 35 Widescreen; Fotokem color; Rated PG-13; 88 minutes; Release date: April 19, 2002

The Rock, Steven Brand

CAST

Mathayus . . . . .The Rock
Memnon . . . . .Steven Brand
Balthazar . . . . .Michael Clarke Duncan
The Sorceress . . . . .Kelly Hu
Philos . . . . .Bernard Hill
Arpid . . . . .Grant Heslov
Takmet . . . . .Peter Facinelli
Thorak . . . . .Ralf Moeller
Jesup . . . . .Branscombe Richmond
King Pheron . . . . .Roger Rees
Queen Isis . . . . .Sherri Howard
Chieftain . . . . .Conrad Roberts
Tribal Leader . . . . .Joseph Ruskin
Third Akkadian . . . . .Esteban Cueto
and Nils Allen Stewart, Scott Schwartz (Torturers), Andre Henschel (Memnon Soldier), Mike Hilow, Nick Hermz (Guards at Ant Pit), Wesley John (Guard at Gomorrah Gate), Michelle Baney (Bazaar Barmaid), Barry Kramer (Sword Merchant), Tim Iannello (Perfume Merchant), Marissa McMahon (Bird Merchant), K.D. Aubert, Sonia Vera, Angelica Castro (Harlots), Tutu Sweeney (Street Urchin), Yuki Tokuhiro, Te'Amir Sweeney (Urchins), Al Leong (Asian Training Master), Woon Young Park, Marcus Young (Asian Training Fighters), Paul Sloan (Soldier), Talani Rabb, Sole Alberti, Cristina Rodriguez, Pennelope Jimenez (Harem Girls), Sean Michael (Boy at Well), Adoni Maropis (Doubting General), Bernard White (Falconmaster), Amy Hunter, Diana Lupo, Heather Burton, Nikki Flux, Rachel Moore, Summer Altice (Warrior Women), Brandon Gonzales (Boy with Dates), Peter Quartaroli (Vision Archer), Peter Navy Tuiasosopo (Night Gate Guard), Amanda Bentley, Claudia Orellana (Courtesans), Jim Maniaci (Palace Guard), Sahnt Demirjian (Army Leader), Gus Rethwisch, Richard Cetrone (Barbarian Guards)

Trying to prevent Memnon from attaining the throne, a group of warring tribes enlist the services of Mathayus to eliminate Memnon's influential and powerful sorcerer-adviser.

© Universal

The Rock

Steven Brand (left)

Kelly Hu, The Rock

CHELSEA WALLS

(LIONS GATE) Producers, Alexis Alexanian, Pamela R. Koffler, Christine Vachon, Gary Winisk; Executive Producers, Caroline Kaplan, Jonathan Sehring, John Sloss; Director, Ethan Hawke; Screenplay, Nicole Burdette, based on her play; Photography, Tom Richmond, Richard Rutkowski; Designer, Rick Butler; Costumes, Catherine Marie Thomas; Editor, Adriana Pacheco; Music, Jeff Tweedy; Casting, Sheila Jaffe, Georgianne Walken; The Independent Film Channel Productions presentation of an InDigEnt production in association with Killer Films of an Under the Influence Film; Dolby; Color; Rated R; 112 minutes; Release date: April 19, 2002

CAST

Audrey	Rosario Dawson
Frank	Vincent D'Onofrio
Bud	Kris Kristofferson
Terry	Robert Sean Leonard
Mary	Natasha Richardson
Grace	Uma Thurman
Val	Mark Webber
Greta	Tuesday Weld
Lynny	Frank Whaley
Ross	Steve Zahn

and Bianca Bakija (Lorna Dune), Kevin Corrigan (Crutches), Paz de la Huerta (High School Girl), Mathew Del Negro (Rookie Cop), Guillermo Diaz (Kid), Paul D. Failla (Cop), Jimmy Scott (Skinny Bones), John Seitz (Dean), Heather Wattis (Ballerina), Harris Yulin (Bud's Agent), Ethan Hawke (Voice of Sam).

New York's Bohemian Chelsea Hotel plays host to a disparate group of struggling musicians, writers, and lovers.

Robert Sean Leonard

Rosario Dawson

Jay Adams

Tony Alva

DOGTOWN AND Z-BOYS

(SONY CLASSICS) Producer, Agi Orsi; Executive Producer, Jay Wilson; Co-Producers, Glen E. Friedman, Stephen Nemeth, Daniel Ostroff; Director, Stacy Peralta; Photography, Peter Pilafian; Designer, C.R. Stecyk; Editor, Paul Crowder; Music, Terry Wilson, Paul Crowder; Narrator, Sean Penn; a Vans Off the Wall Productions presentation of an AOP Production; Dolby; Color; Rated PG-13; 90 minutes; Release date: April 26, 2002. Documentary on members of the Zephyr Skateboard Team, from a section of Santa Monica and Venice called Dogtown.

WITH

Jay Adams, Tony Alva, Bob Biniak, Paul Constantineau, Shogo Kubo, Jim Muir, Peggyki, Stacy Peralta, Nathan Pratt, Wentzle Ruml, Allen Sarlo (Zephyr Skateboard Team), Jeff Ament, Skip Engblom, Glen E. Friedman, Tony Hawk, Jeff Ho, Henry Rollins, Craig Stecyk

THE SALTON SEA

Peter Sarsgaard, Adam Goldberg, Ricky Trammell, Val Kilmer

(WARNER BROS.) Producers, Frank Darabont, Eriq La Salle, Ken Aguado, Butch Robinson; Executive Producer, Jim Behnke; Director, D.J. Caruso; Screenplay, Tony Gayton; Photography, Amir Mokri; Designer, Tom Southwell; Costumes, Karyn Wagner; Editor, Jim Page; Music, Thomas Newman; Casting, Deborah Aquila; a Castle Rock Entertainment presentation of a Darkwoods/Humble Journey Films production; Dolby; Technicolor; Rated R; 103 minutes; Release date: April 26, 2002

CAST

Danny Parker/Tom Van Allen	Val Kilmer
Pooh-Bear	Vincent D'Onofrio
Kujo	Adam Goldberg
Quincy	Luis Guzman
Morgan	Doug Hutchison
Garcetti	Anthony LaPaglia
Bobby	Glenn Plummer
Jimmy the Finn	Peter Sarsgaard
Colette	Deborah Kara Unger
Liz	Chandra West
Bubba	B.D. Wong
Verne Plummer	R. Lee Ermey
Nancy	Shalom Harlow
Nancy Plummer	Shirley Knight
Bo	Meat Loaf
Teresa	Azura Skye
Big Bill	Josh Todd
Little Bill	Danny Trejo
Creeper	Ricky Trammell

and Kenji Nakamura (Kamikaze Pilot), Paula Scarpino (50s Housewife), Mike Randleman (60s Trucker), Justine Visone (Supermarket Cashier), Jerry Gauny (Freak Cook), Tanner Giles (Bobby's Daughter), Rachel Ezra (Bobby's Girlfriend), Mpho Koaho (Kid Selling Guns), Chuck Kuespert (Bar Owner), Charles Carroll (Zapruder), Lee Holmes (Oswald), Val Lauren (Third Shooter), Tom Fitzpatrick (Karaoke Man), Christian Fletcher (Stool Sample Courier), Bob Brown (Man in Salton Sea House), Dana Lynn Caruso, René Rivera, Kevin Quinn (FBI Agents), Rex Linn (Detective Bookman), Al Barker, Jr. (FBI Agent Repairing Motel Sign), Doc Duhame (Skipper)

Danny Parker, a man emotionally devastated by the brutal death of his wife at the hands of masked gunmen, finds himself adrift in the underworld of Los Angeles where he ends up serving as middle-man in a drug deal with crazed crystal meth dealer Pooh-Bear.

© Warner Bros.

Val Kilmer

Val Kilmer, Chandra West

Val Kilmer, Anthony LaPaglia, Doug Hutchison

HOLLYWOOD ENDING

(DREAMWORKS) Producer, Lety Aronson; Executive Producer, Stephen Tenenbaum; Co-Producer, Helen Robin; Co-Executive Producers, Jack Rollins, Charles H. Joffe; Director/Screenplay, Woody Allen; Photography, Wedigo von Schultzendorff; Designer, Santo Loquasto; Costumes, Melissa Toth; Editor, Alisa Lepselter; Casting, Juliet Taylor, Laura Rosenthal; Presented in association with Gravier Productions; Dolby; Color; Rated PG-13; 112 minutes; Release date: May 1, 2002

CAST

Val Waxman	Woody Allen
Ed	George Hamilton
Ellie	Téa Leoni
Lori	Debra Messing
Al	Mark Rydell
Sharon Bates	Tiffani Thiessen
Hal	Treat Williams
Galaxie Executives	Bob Dorian, Ivan Martin, Gregg Edelman
Commercial A.D.	Neal Huff
Barbeque Guests	Douglas McGrath, Stephanie Roth Haberle, Bill Gerber, Roxanne Perry
Carlyle Pianist	Barbara Carroll
Carlyle Patron	Howard Erskine
Cameraman	Lu Yu
Translator	Barney Cheng
Elio Sebastian	Isaac Mizrahi
Alexandra	Marian Seldes

and Anthony Arkin, Ramsey Faragallah (Audition Readers), Olivia Hayman (Balthazar Hostess), Peter Van Wagner, Judy Toma (Balthazar Couple), Jodie Markell (Andrea Ford), Sarah Polen, Amanda Jacobi, Steve Hurwitz, Ruth Last, Robert Lloyd Wolchok, Joel Eidelsberg (Seder Guests), Kenneth Edelson (Eye Doctor), Ted Neustadt (MRI Doctor), Peter Gerety (Psychiatrist), Reiko Takahashi (Movie Extra), Greg Mottola (Assistant Director), Fred Melamed (Pappas), Jeff Mazzola (Prop Man), Aaron Stanford (Actor), Erica Leehsen (Actress), Ray Garvey (Grip), Rochelle Oliver (Script Supervisor), Joe Rigano (Projectionist), Maurice Sonnenberg (Banquet Emcee), Mark Webber (Tony Waxman), Mary Schmidtberger (Galaxie Executive)

A once-prominent film director is given a chance at a comeback through his ex-wife's connections, only to discover that he has temporarily gone blind, an affliction he tries to hide from the studio executives while continuing to direct the film.

© Dreamworks

Woody Allen, Barney Cheng, Téa Leoni, George Hamilton

Treat Williams, Téa Leoni, Woody Allen, Debra Messing

Woody Allen

Woody Allen, Mark Rydell, Téa Leoni

SPIDER-MAN

(COLUMBIA) Producers, Laura Ziskin, Ian Bryce; Executive Producers, Avi Arad, Stan Lee; Director, Sam Raimi; Screenplay, David Koepp; Based on the Marvel Comic Book by Stan Lee and Steve Ditko; Photography, Don Burgess; Designer, Neil Spisak; Costumes, James Acheson; Editors, Bob Murawski, Arthur Coburn; Visual Effects Designer, John Dykstra; Co-Producer, Grant Curtis; Casting, Francine Maisler, Lynn Kressel; Stunts, Jeff Habberstad; a Marvel Enterprises/Laura Ziskin production; Dolby; Deluxe color; Rated PG-13; 121 minutes; Release date: May 3, 2002

Tobey Maguire

Kirsten Dunst

Tobey Maguire

CAST

Spider-Man/Peter Parker	Tobey Maguire
Green Goblin/Norman Osborn	Willem Dafoe
Mary Jane Watson	Kirsten Dunst
Harry Osborn	James Franco
Ben Parker	Cliff Robertson
May Parker	Rosemary Harris
J. Jonah Jameson	J.K. Simmons
Flash Thompson	Joe Manganiello
Maximilian Fargas	Gerry Becker
Joseph "Robbie" Robertson	Bill Nunn
Henry Balkan	Jack Betts
General Slocum	Stanley Anderson
Dr. Mendel Stromm	Ron Perkins
Simkins	K.K. Dodds
Hoffman	Ted Raimi
Ring Announcer	Bruce Campbell
Miss Brant	Elizabeth Banks
Houseman	John Paxton
Philip Watson	Tim deZarn
Madeine Watson	Taylor Gilbert
Bone Saw McGraw	Randy Savage
Wrestling Promoter	Larry Joshua
Wrestling Arena Guard	Timothy Patrick Quill
Bone-ettes	Lisa Danielle, Natalie T. Yeo, Erica D. Porter, Kristen Davidson
Flash's Crony	Jason Padgett
Teacher	Shan Omar Huey
Girl on Bus	Sally Livingstone
Doctor	Evan Arnold
Nurse	Jill Sayre
Project Coordinator	James K. Ward
Test Pilot	David Holcomb
Check-In Girl	Octavia Spencer
Heckler	Brad Grunberg
Little Billy	Shane Habberstad
Billy's Mom	Deborah Wakeham
Times Square Children	Rachael Bruce, Mackenzie Bryce, Julia Barry
Herself	Macy Gray
Cop at Fire	Myk Watford
Fireman	William Calvert
Mother at Fire	Sylvia Kelegian
Young Lady at Fire	Kristen Marie Holly
Cabbies	Ajay Mehta, Peter Appel
Marine Cop	Scott Spiegel
Cops at Carjacking	Matt Smith, Sara Ramirez
Punk Rock Girl	Lucy Lawless
Subway Guitarist	Jayce Bartok
Lady Dogwalker	Maribel Gonzalez
Office Lady	Amy Bouril
Opinionated Cop	Joseph D'Onoforio
Surly Truck Driver	Jim Norton
Chaperone on Tram	Corey Mendell Parker

and Ashley Louise Edner (Girl in Tram), William Joseph Firth, Alex Black (Boys in Tram), Laura Gray (Tram Group Mother), Joe Virzi, Michael Edward Thomas, Jeanie Fox (New Yorkers on Bridge), Robert Kerman (Tugboat Captain)

After being bitten by a genetically altered spider, mild-mannered student Peter Parker finds himself endowed with great powers, prompting him to become a daring crime fighter known as Spider-Man.

This film received Oscar nominations for sound and visual effects.

Tobey Maguire

Willem Dafoe

Cliff Robertson, Rosemary Harris

Willem Dafoe

Tobey Maguire, Kirsten Dunst

UNFAITHFUL

Diane Lane

(20TH CENTURY FOX) Producers, Adrian Lyne, G. Mac Brown; Executive Producers, Pierre-Richard Muller, Lawrence Steven Meyers; Director, Adrian Lyne; Screenplay, Alvin Sargent, William Broyles Jr.; Based upon the film *La Femme Infidèle* written and directed by Claude Chabrol; Photography, Peter Biziou; Designer, Brian Morris; Costumes, Ellen Mirojnick; Editor, Anne V. Coates; Music, Jan A.P. Kaczmarek; Casting, Billy Hopkins, Suzanne Smith, Kerry Barden, Mark Bennett; a Fox 2000 Pictures and Regency Enterprises presentation; Dolby; Deluxe color; Rated R; 124 minutes; Release date: May 8, 2002

Olivier Martinez, Diane Lane

Richard Gere, Diane Lane

Richard Gere

Diane Lane, Richard Gere

CAST

Edward Sumner . . . . .Richard Gere
Connie Sumner . . . . .Diane Lane
Paul Martel . . . . .Olivier Martinez
Bill Stone . . . . .Chad Lowe
Tracy . . . . .Kate Burton
Sally . . . . .Margaret Colin
Charlie Sumner . . . . .Erik Per Sullivan
Frank Wilson . . . . .Dominic Chianese
Detective Dean . . . . .Zeljko Ivanek
Detective Mirojnick . . . . .Gary Barasaba
Gloria . . . . .Myra Lucretia Taylor
Lindsay . . . . .Michelle Monaghan
Conductor . . . . .Joseph Badalucco, Jr.
Bob Gaylord . . . . .Erich Anderson
Other Businessman . . . . .Damon Gupton
Cafe Bartender . . . . .Marc Forget
Tim . . . . .Larry Gleason
Businessmen . . . . .George F. Miller, Paul D. Failla,
        Hal Smith-Reynolds, Tyree Michael Simpson
Grumpy Teacher . . . . .Liza Colón-Zayas
Parking Lot Attendant . . . . .Al Cayne
Other Woman . . . . .Murielle Arden
Man with Suitcase . . . . .Ludwig Salem
Passerby . . . . .William Abadie
Crying Boy . . . . .Matthew Maitland
Father of Crying Boy . . . . .Charles Glaser
Grandma . . . . .Anne Pitoniak
Aunt Rikke . . . . .Frederikke Borge
Uncle Russell . . . . .Russell Gibson
Uncle Les . . . . .Leslie Shenkel
Dry Cleaner . . . . .Sophia Wu
Beth . . . . .Lisa Emery
Josh . . . . .Michael Emerson
Jeff . . . . .Geoffrey Nauffts
Auctioneer .James Bruce-Gardyne
Cop Outside Auction . . . . .Tommy McGoldrick

Connie Sumner takes the risk of destroying her happy married life when she embarks on an affair with a younger man.

This film received an Oscar nomination for actress (Diane Lane).

© 20th Century Fox

Diane Lane, Richard Gere

Olivier Martinez

Olivier Martinez, Diane Lane

Diane Lane, Olivier Martinez

Diane Lane, Richard Gere

Natalie Portman, R2-D2, Hayden Christensen

STAR WARS EPISODE II: ATTACK OF THE CLONES

(20TH CENTURY FOX) Producer, Rick McCallum; Executive Producer/Director/Story, George Lucas; Screenplay, George Lucas, Jonathan Hales; Photography, David Tattersall; Designer, Gavin Bocquet; Editor/Sound Designer, Ben Burtt; Costumes, Trisha Biggar; Music, John Williams; Visual Effects Supervisors, John Knoll, Pablo Helman, Ben Snow, Dennis Muren; Animation Director, Rob Coleman; Casting, Robin Gurland; Lucasfilm Ltd.; Dolby; Widescreen; Color; Rated PG-13; 142 minutes; Release date: May 16, 2002

Hayden Christensen, Natalie Portman, Ewan McGregor

R2-D2, C-3PO

Ewan McGregor, Hayden Christensen

Hayden Christensen, Natalie Portman,

CAST

Obi-Wan Kenobi . . . . .Ewan McGregor
Padmé Amidala . . . . .Natalie Portman
Anakin Skywalker . . . . .Hayden Christensen
Count Dooku . . . . .Christopher Lee
Mace Windu . . . . .Samuel L. Jackson
Yoda . . . . .Frank Oz
Supreme Chancellor Palpatine . . . . .Ian McDiarmid
Shmi Skywalker . . . . .Pernilla August
Jango Fett . . . . .Temuera Morrison
Senator Bail Organa . . . . .Jimmy Smits
Cliegg Lars . . . . .Jack Thompson
Zam Wesell . . . . .Leeanna Walsman
Jar Jar Binks . . . . .Ahmed Best
Dormé . . . . .Rose Byrne
Sio Bibble . . . . .Oliver Ford Davies
Dexter Jettster . . . . .Ronald Falk
Captain Typho . . . . .Jay Laga'aia
Watto . . . . .Andrew Secombe
C-3PO . . . . .Anthony Daniels
Ki-Adi-Mundi & Nate Gunray . . . . .Silas Carson
Queen Jamillia . . . . .Ayesha Dharker
Boba Fett . . . . .Daniel Logan
Owen Lars . . . . .Joel Edgerton
Beru . . . . .Bonnie Maree Piesse
Voice of Lama Su . . . . .Anthony Phelan
Voice of Taun We . . . . .Rena Owen
Madame Jocasta Nu . . . . .Alethea McGrath
Hermione Bagwa . . . . .Susie Porter
Elan Sleazebaggano . . . . .Matt Doran
Lott Dod . . . . .Alan Ruscoe
Plo Koon . . . . .Matt Sloan
Cordé . . . . .Veronica Segura
Mas Amedda . . . . .David Bowers
Naboo Lieutenant . . . . .Steve John Shepherd
Clone Trooper . . . . .Bodie "Tihoi" Taylor
Senator Orn Free Taa . . . . .Matt Rowan
Senator Ask Aak . . . . .Steven Boyle
Kit Fisto . . . . .Zachariah Jensen
J.K. Burtola . . . . .Alex Knoll
Mari Amithest . . . . .Phoebe Yiamkiati
R2-D2 . . . . .Kenny Baker
Oppo Rancisis . . . . .Jerome Blake
Eeth Koth . . . . .Hassani Shapi
Adi Gallia . . . . .Gin
Saesee Tiin . . . . .Khan Bonfils
Even Piell . . . . .Michaela Cottrell
Depa Billaba . . . . .Dipika O'Neill Joti

David Bowers, Ian McDiarmid

Jedi knight Obi-Wan Kenobi and his apprentice, Anakin Skywalker, are assigned to protect Padmé Amidala after an attempt on her life. Fourth of the 20th Century-Fox *Star Wars* films, following *Star Wars* (1977), *The Empire Strikes Back* (1980), *Return of the Jedi* (1983), and *Star Wars Episode I: The Phantom Menace* (1999). Repeating their roles from the last are McGregor, Portman, and Jackson.

This film received an Oscar nomination for visual effects.

Daniel Logan (Right)

Ewan McGregor, Hayden Christensen

Yoda, Ewan McGregor, Samuel L. Jackson

ABOUT A BOY

(UNIVERSAL) Producers, Jane Rosenthal, Robert De Niro, Brad Epstein, Tim Bevan, Eric Fellner; Directors, Paul Weitz, Chris Weitz; Screenplay, Peter Hedges, Chris Weitz, Paul Weitz; Based on the novel by Nick Hornby; Executive Producers, Nick Hornby, Lynn Harris; Photography, Remi Adefarasin; Designer, Jim Clay; Costumes, Joanna Johnston; Editor, Nick Moore; Music, Badly Drawn Boy; Music Supervisor, Nick Angel; Song: "Santa's Super Sleigh" by Pete Brewis; Co-Producers, Debra Hayward, Liza Chasin, Hardy Justice, Nicky Kentish Barnes; Casting, Priscilla John; a StudioCanal presentation of a Tribeca/Working Title production; U.S.-British; Dolby; Super 35 Widescreen; Deluxe color; Rated PG-13; 100 minutes; Release date: May 17, 2002

Hugh Grant, Nicholas Hoult

Toni Collette

Hugh Grant, Rachel Weisz

CAST

Will Freeman	Hugh Grant
Fiona Brewer	Toni Collette
Rachel	Rachel Weisz
Marcus Brewer	Nicholas Hoult
Suzie	Victoria Smurfit
Ellie	Nat Gastiain Tena
Ali	Augustus Prew
Christine	Sharon Small
Imogen	Madison Cook, Jordan Cook
John	Nicholas Hutchison
Barney	Ryan Speechley, Joseph Speechley
Ellie's Friends	Laura Kennington, Tanika Swaby, Peter McNicholl, Christopher Webster
Lee, The Bully	Ben Ridgeway
Lee's Sidekick	Jack Warren
Maitre D'	Russell Barr
Angie	Isabel Brook
Angie's Kid	Orlando Thor Newman
Bitter Ex-Girlfriends	Paulette Williams, Fritha Goodey, Susannah Doyle, Delma Walsh
Mark	Jonathan Franklin
Nicky	John Kamal
Class Teacher	Tessa Vale
Woman in Supermarket	Lorna Dallison
Child in Supermarket	Bethany Muir
Husband in Supermarket	Bruce Alexander
Moira/SPAT	Joyce Henderson
Frances/SPAT	Jenny Galloway
Caroline/SPAT	Janine Duvitski
Additional SPAT Women	Sue Hyams, Maggie Kahal, Lynn Askew, Beverly Milward, Danielle Harvey, Anna Maria Credenzone Philip, Sarah King, Susan Ghamsary, Edna Johnson
Mothercare Shop Assistant	Frog Stone
Family in Mother Car Park	Buddy Hunter, Kristine Perrin, Nathan Perrin-Hunter, Rachael Perrin-Hunter
Suzie's Baby Megan	Amy Craven, Rebecca Craven
Park Keeper	Sidney Livingstone
Nurse	Cathy Murphy
Hairdresser	Joanne Petitt
Tom/Amnesty International Worker	Jason Salkey
Amnesty International Workers	Annabelle Apsion, Matt Wilkinson
Will's Dad	Peter Roy
Candy Throwers	Matthew Thomas, Aaron Keeling, Scott Charles
Skechers Shopgirl	Claire Harman
Cute Waitress	Sian Martin
Clive	Mark Drewry
Lindsey	Denise Stephenson
Lindsey's Mum	Rosalind Knight
New Year's Eve Party Guest	Murray Lachlan Young
Simon Cosgrove	Alex Kew
Math Teacher	Mark Heap
Def Penalty Kru	Sunanda Biswas, James Marshall-Gunn, Jamie Mayer
Mr. Chalmers, The MC	Roger Brierley
Apple Thrower	Stefan Pejic

A rich, shallow, womanizing Londoner who prides himself on not having any attachments to others, finds himself developing an unexpected friendship with a 12-year old misfit boy who is seeking help for his troubled mother.

This film received an Oscar nomination for screenplay adaptation.

Hugh Grant

Nicholas Hoult, Toni Collette, Hugh Grant

Rachel Weisz, Hugh Grant

Rachel Weisz

Hugh Grant

Hugh Grant

Nicholas Hoult

THE BELIEVER

(IDP) Producers, Susan Hoffman, Christopher Roberts; Executive Producers, Jay Firestone, Adam Haight, Daniel Diamond, Eric Sandys; Director/Screenplay, Henry Bean; Story, Henry Bean, Mark Jacobson; Photography, Jim Denault; Designer, Susan Block; Costumes, Alex Alvarez, Jennifer Newman; Music, Joel Diamond; Editors, Mayin Lo, Lee Percy; a Fireworks Pictures and Peter Hoffman presentation of a Fuller Films production, developed in association with Crannog Film Partners; Dolby; DuArt color; Rated R; 99 minutes; Release date: May 17, 2002

CAST

Danny Balint	Ryan Gosling
Carla Moebius	Summer Phoenix
Drake	Glenn Fitzgerald
Billings	Garrett Dillahunt
Carleton	Kris Eivers
O.I.	Joel Garland
Kyle	Joshua Harto
Lina Moebius	Theresa Russell
Curtis Zampf	Billy Zane

and Tommy Nohilly (Whit), Chuck Ardezzone (Chuck), Ronald Guttman (Danny's Father), Heather Goldenhersh (Linda), A.D. Miles (Guy Danielsen), Elizabeth Reaser (Miriam), Peter Meadows (Orthodox Student), Jack Drummond (Old Coot), Sig Libowitz (Rav Zingesser), James G. McCaffrey (Young Avi), Jacob Green (Young Danny), Frank Winters (Young Stuart), Ebon Moss-Bacharach (Waiter #1), Christopher Kadish (Steve), David Bailey (Judge), Lucille Patton (Mrs. Frankel), John Martin (Hate Counselor), Michael Marcus (Polish Man), Roberto Gari (Ancient Jew), Sascha Knopf (Cindy Pomerantz), Tibor Feldman (Rabbi Greenwalt), Henry Bean (Ilio Manzetti), Dean Strober (Stuart), Jordan Lage (Roger Brand), Judah Lazarus (Avi), Samantha Brody (Rosh Hashana Attendee), Michael Port (TV Reporter), Carl Fischer (Guy's Photographer), Harvey Lieberman (Man at Yom Kippur), Eileen B. Weiss (Woman at Yom Kippur)

Danny Balint, a neo-Nazi skinhead who hides his true Jewish heritage, finds himself torn between his principles when he joins a fascist group that plots to bring their message to the public through violence. This film had its premiere on Showtime cable on March 30, 2002.

Ryan Gosling

Dan Futterman, Tessa Allen, Jennifer Lopez

ENOUGH

(COLUMBIA) Producers, Irwin Winkler, Rob Cowan; Executive Producer, E. Bennett Walsh; Director, Michael Apted; Screenplay, Nicholas Kazan; Photography, Rogier Stoffers; Designer, Doug Kraner; Costumes, Shay Cunliffe; Editor, Rick Shaine; Co-Producer, Jeanney Kim; Music, David Arnold; Song: "Alive" by Jennifer Lopez, Cris Judd, Cory Rooney/performed by Jennifer Lopez; Casting, Linda Lowy, John Brace; an Irwin Winkler production; Dolby; Panavision; Deluxe color; Rated PG-13; 114 minutes; Release date: May 24, 2002

CAST

Slim Hiller	Jennifer Lopez
Mitch Hiller	Billy Campbell
Gracie Hiller	Tessa Allen
Ginny	Juliette Lewis
Joe	Dan Futterman
Robbie	Noah Wyle
Jupiter	Fred Ward
Phil	Christopher Maher
Mrs. Hiller	Janet Carroll
Jim Toller	Bill Cobbs

and Bruce A. Young (Instructor), Bruce French (Homeowner), Ruben Madera (Teddy), Michael P. Byrne (Desk Sergeant), Leif Riddell (First Cop), David Brokhim (Mustapha), Dan Martin, Jeff Kober, Brent Sexton (FBI Agents), Regan Forman (Preschool Director), Sandra Nelson Winkler (Teacher Betty), Marie Stewart (Waitress Lynne), Smadar Dishon (Receptionist), Margaret Emery (Jupiter's Blonde Girl), Victor McCay (Electronics Store Clerk), James Noah (Mr. Hiller), Nikki Bokal (Mitch's Young Blonde), John O'Brien (Front Desk Clerk), Louisa Abernathy (Bank Teller), Kerri Higuchi (Ticket Clerk), Fern Ward (Soup Server), Tanya Fishburn (Mitch's Assistant), Brett Clark (Construction Site Cop), William Barillaro (Bus Driver)

A woman tries to escape with her young daughter from her controlling, menacing husband by changing her identity and appearance, only to find that her spouse is relentlessly pursuing her.

BARTLEBY

(OUTRIDER) Producer/Director, Jonathan Parker; Co-Producer, Catherine DiNapoli; Screenplay, Jonathan Parker, Catherine DiNapoli; Based on the story *Bartleby the Scrivener* by Herman Melville; Line Producer, Debbie Brubaker; Cinematography, Wah Ho Chan; Designer, Rosario Provenza; Costumes, Morganne Newson; Editor, Rick LeCompte; Music, Seth Asarnow, Jonathan Parker; Casting, Donise L. Hardy; Parker Film Company; Dolby; Color; Rated PG-13; 82 minutes; Release date: May 24, 2002

CAST

Bartleby . . . . .Crispin Glover
The Boss . . . . .David Paymer
Vivian . . . . .Glenne Headly
Ernie . . . . .Maury Chaykin
Rocky . . . . .Joe Piscopo
Frank Waxman . . . . .Seymour Cassel
Book Publisher . . . . .Carrie Snodgress
The Mayor . . . . .Dick Martin
and Greta Danielle Newgren (Narrator's Date), Stoney Burke (Soup Kitchen Server), Ken Murakami (Landlord), Terry Allen Jones (New Tenant), Josh Kornbluth (Property Manager), Stuart Klitsner (Genetics Professor), Nick Scoggin (Street Philosopher), Pete Marvel (Repairman), Karen Argoud-Morrisey (Rocky's French Girlfriend), Victoria Smith, Catherine DiNapoli (Rocky's Girlfriends), Louis Landman (Police Officer), Robert Ernst (Shut Up Man), James Carraway, Tim Wiggins, Howie Gordon (Fighting Vagrants), Olivia Parker (Little Girl in Donut Shop), Susan Renati (Little Girl's Mother), Deanna Price (Woman in Dumpster)

A well-meaning boss is faced with a bizarre dilemma when his passive clerk suddenly refuses to do any of his duties. Earlier film version starred Paul Scofield and John McEnery and was released in the U.S. in 1972.

© Outrider

David Paymer, Crispin Glover

Maury Chaykin, Joe Piscopo, Crispin Glover

Spirit, Rain

Spirit, Little Creek

SPIRIT: STALLION OF THE CIMARRON

(DREAMWORKS) Producers, Mireille Soria, Jeffrey Katzenberg; Directors, Kelly Asbury, Lorna Cook; Screenplay, John Fusco; Music, Hans Zimmer; Songs, Bryan Adams; Supervising Editor, Nick Fletcher; Designer, Kathy Altieri; Art Directors, Luc Desmarchelier, Ronald W. Lukas; Animation Supervisor, Kristof Serrand; Artistic Supervisors: Story, Del Carmen; Layout, Lorenzo E. Martinez, Clive Hutchings; Digital Supervisor, Doug Cooper; Background, Kevin Turcotte; Supervising Character Designer, Carlos Grangel; Dolby; Digital Widescreen; Technicolor; Rated G; 82 minutes; Release date: May 24, 2002

VOICE CAST

Spirit . . . . .Matt Damon
The Colonel . . . . .James Cromwell
Little Creek . . . . .Daniel Studi
Sgt. Adams . . . . .Chopper Bernet
Murphy . . . . .Jeff LeBeau
Soldier . . . . .John Rubano
Bill . . . . .Richard McConagle
Joe . . . . .Matthew Levin
Pete . . . . .Adam Paul
Jake . . . . .Robert Cait
Roy . . . . .Charles Napier
and Meredith Wells (Little Indian Girl), Zahn McClarnon, Michael Horse (Little Creek's Friends), Jeff LeBeau (Railroad Foreman), Don Fullilove (Train Pull Foreman)

A young runaway stallion encountering humans for the first time befriends a Lakota brave named Little Creek. This film received an Oscar nomination for animated film.

INSOMNIA

(WARNER BROS.) Producers, Paul Junger Witt, Edward L. McDonnell, Broderick Johnson, Andrew A. Kosove; Executive Producers, George Clooney, Steven Soderbergh, Tony Thomas, Kim Roth, Charles J.D. Schlissel; Director, Christopher Nolan; Screenplay, Hillary Seitz; Photography, Wally Pfister; Designer, Nathan Crowley; Editor, Dody Dorn; Music, David Julyan; Casting, Marci Liroff; an Alcon Entertainment presentation of a Witt/Thomas, Section Eight production; Dolby; Panavision; Color; Rated R; 118 minutes; Release date: May 24, 2002

Al Pacino, Hilary Swank

CAST

Will Dormer	Al Pacino
Walter Finch	Robin Williams
Ellie Burr	Hilary Swank
Rachel Clement	Maura Tierney
Hap Eckhart	Martin Donovan
Fred Duggar	Nicky Katt
Chief Charles Nyback	Paul Dooley
Randy Stetz	Jonathan Jackson
Pilot	Oliver "Ole" Zemen
Farrell	Larry Holden
Francis	Jay Brazeau
Rich	Lorne Cardinal
Officers	James Hutson, Andrew Campbell
Coroner	Paula Shaw
Kay Connell	Crystal Lowe
Mrs. Connell	Tasha Simms
Principal	Malcolm Boddington
Tanya Francke	Katharine Isabelle
Trish Eckhart	Kerry Sandomirsky
Uniformed Officer	Chris Guthior
Warfield	Ian Tracey
Woman on the Road	Kate Robbins
Girl at Funeral	Emily Jane Perkins
Ticket Taker	Dean Wray

Hilary Swank

Los Angeles detective Will Dormer arrives in a desolate Alaskan town to investigate a gruesome murder, and finds himself being taunted by the killer who knows more about Will than he wants him to know. Remake of the 1997 Norweigian film of the same name.

© Insomnia Productions, LP

Al Pacino

Robin Williams

Al Pacino, Robin Williams

Al Pacino, Jonathan Jackson

Hilary Swank

Robin Williams, Al Pacino

Robin Williams, Al Pacino

Al Pacino

Matthew McConaughey, Alan Arkin

Barbara Sukowa, John Turturro

THIRTEEN CONVERSATIONS ABOUT ONE THING

(SONY CLASSICS) Producers, Beni Atoori, Gina Resnick; Executive Producers, Sandy Stern, Michael Stipe, Doug Mankoff, Andrew Spaulding, Peter Wetherell, James Burke, Heidi Crane; Director, Jill Sprecher; Screenplay, Karen Sprecher, Jill Sprecher; Co-Producers, Colin Bates, Sabrina Atoori, Andrew Fierberg, Amy Hobby; Photography, Dick Pope; Designer, Mark Ricker; Costumes, Kasia Walicka Maimone; Editor, Stephen Mirrione; Music, Alex Wurman; Line Producer, Stacy Plavoukos; Casting, Adrienne Stein; a Stonelock Pictures and Echo Lake Productions presentation in association with Single Cell Pictures of a Gina Resnick/ Beni Atoori Production with Double A Films and Entitled Entertainment; Dolby; Color; Rated R; 103 minutes; Release date: May 24, 2002

CAST

THE ATTORNEYS
Troy . . . . .Matthew McConaughey
Owen . . . . .David Connolly
and Joseph Siravo (Bureau Chief), A.D. Miles (Co-Worker), Sig Libowitz (Assistant Attorney), James Yaegashi (Legal Assistant), Dion Graham (Defense Attorney), Fernando Lopez (Defendant), Brian Smiar (Judge), Paul Austin (Bartender), Allie Woods (Cab Driver)

THE ACADEMICS
Walker . . . . .John Turturro
Patricia . . . . .Amy Irving
Helen . . . . .Barbara Sukowa
and Rob McElhenney (Aspiring Medical Student), Avery Glymph (Intelligent Student), Elizabeth Reaser (Young Woman in Class), Deirdre Lovejoy (Student Teacher), Barbara Andres (Neighbor), William Severs (Doctor), Joel Garland (Mover)

THE HOUSEKEEPERS
Beatrice . . . . .Clea DuVall
Dorrie . . . . .Tia Texada
Bea's Mother . . . . .Peggy Gormley
and Malcolm Gets (Architect), Miles Thompson (Neighborhood Boy), Robert Carricart (Pastor)

THE CLAIMS ADJUSTORS
Gene . . . . .Alan Arkin
Dick Lacey . . . . .Frankie Faison
Wade Bowman . . . . .William Wise
and Shawn Elliot (Mickey Wheeler), Alex Burns (Bonnie), James Murtaugh (Lew Kincannon), Richard E. Council (Del Strickland), Walt MacPherson (Donald), Leo V. Finnie III (Pete), Daryl Edwards (Glenn), Charlie Schroeder (Young Finance Manager), Robert Colston (Sales Manager), Gammy Singer (Gene's Secretary), Melissa Maxwell (Del's Receptionist), Eliza Pryor Nagel (Ronnie's Roommate), Jeff Robins (Freeloader), Victor Truro (Coffee Shop Counterman), Paul Klementowicz (Public Defender), Phyllis Bash (Judge), Peter McCabe (Court Clerk), Christan Pabon (Teenager on Subway)

A seemingly disparate group of disenchanted people have an unknowing effect on one another's lives.

© Sony Pictures

Tia Texada, Clea DuVall

John Turturro, Amy Irving

UNDERCOVER BROTHER

(**UNIVERSAL**) Producers, Brian Grazer, Michael Jenkinson, Damon Lee; Executive Producers, John Ridley, Bill Carraro, Kim Roth; Director, Malcolm D. Lee; Screenplay, John Ridley, Michael McCullers; Story, John Ridley, based on his Internet Series; Photography, Tom Priestley; Designer, William Elliott; Costumes, Danielle Hollowell; Editor, William Kerr; Music Supervisor, Bonnie Greenberg; Music, Stanley Clarke; Stunts, Steve Lucescu; Casting, Robi Reed-Humes; an Imagine Entertainment presentation; Dolby; Color Rated PG-13; 84 minutes; Release date: May 31, 2002

CAST

Undercover Brother	Eddie Griffin
Mr. Feather	Chris Kattan
White She Devil	Denise Richards
Sistah Girl	Aunjanue Ellis
Conspiracy Brother	Dave Chappelle
The Chief	Chi McBride
Lance	Neil Patrick Harris
Brother	Gary Anthony Williams
General Boutwell	Billy Dee Williams
Mr. Elias	Jack Noseworthy
The Man	Robert Trumbull
Narrator	J.D. Hall
Roscoe	William Taylor
Wendy	Shauna McDonald
Chuck	Ron Pardo
Bonnie	Susie Spear
Chad	Jim O'Connor

and Dave Pearce, Liz West, Enid-Raye Adams (Reporters), Divine Earth Essence, Jenni Burke, Keisha T. Fraser (GFC Singers), James C. Mathis III (GFC Announcer), Troy Taylor (Li'l UB), Robert Townsend (Mr. UB), Gina Sorrell (Multinational Receptionist), James Brown (Himself), Simon Reynolds, Kenner Ames (Golfers), Lee Smart, David Sparrow (Golf Cart Guards), Randy Butcher, Bryan Thomas (Bank Security Guards), Tig Fong, Darrin McGuire (White She Devil's Enforcers), Marvin Kaye, LJ Vasilantonakis, Paul Rapovski, Layton Morrison, Marco Bianco, Nick Alachiotis, Peter Szkoda, Wayne Downer, Bryan Renfro (Fortress Security)

Funky crime fighter Undercover Brother is called on to stop a sinister underground movement from unleashing a psycho-hallucinogenic drug that will control the world population.

© Universal

Chris Kattan, Eddie Griffin

Dave Chappelle, Eddie Griffin

Denise Richards, Aunjanue Ellis

Neil Patrick Harris

THE SUM OF ALL FEARS

(PARAMOUNT) Producer, Mace Neufeld; Executive Producers, Tom Clancy, Stratton Leopold; Director, Phil Alden Robinson; Screenplay, Paul Attanasio, Daniel Pyne; Based on the novel by Tom Clancy; Photography, John Lindley; Designer, Jeannine Oppewall; Costumes, Marie-Sylvie Deveau; Editor, Neil Travis; Music, Jerry Goldsmith; Casting, Mindy Marin; a Mace Neufeld production; Dolby; Panavision; Deluxe color; Rated PG-13; 124 minutes; Release date: May 31, 2002

CAST

Jack Ryan	Ben Affleck
William Cabot	Morgan Freeman
President Fowler	James Cromwell
John Clark	Liev Schreiber
Richard Dressler	Alan Bates
Defense Secretary Becker	Philip Baker Hall
Secretary of State Owens	Ron Rifkin
National Security Advisor Revell	Bruce McGill
President Nemerov	Ciarán Hinds
Dr. Cathy Muller	Bridget Moynahan
Syrian Radar Operator	Ian Mongrain
Israeli Pilot	Russell Bobbitt
Admiral Pollack	Ken Jenkins
General Lasseter	John Beasley
US STRATCOM Colonel	Al Vandercruys
Mt. Weather General	Richard Cohee
President's Military Aide	Philip Pretten
Fowler's Aide	Alison Darcy
President Zorkin	Richard Marner
Zorkin's Translator	Ostap Soroka
Zorkin's Interviewer	Robert Martin Robinson
Rudy	Dale Godboldo
Mary Pat Foley	Lee Garlington
Dillon	Jamie Harrold
Arab Gravedigger	Stefan Kalipha
Ghazi	Nabil Elouahabi
Zorkin's Aide	Maria Monakhova
CIA Wardrobe Guy	Francoise Bryon
Senator Jessup	Josef Sommer
Dr. Rita Russell	Pragna Desai
Olson	Colm Feore

and Michel "Gish" Abou-Samah (Olson's Translator), Edward Zinoviev (Nemerov's Aide), Sheena Larkin "La Brie" (Pam Lathrop), Frank Fontaine (General Rand), Andre Cornellier (Kremlin Photographer), Maxime Opadtchii (Kremlin Photographer's Assistant), Mariusz Sibiga (Nemerov's Translator), Michael Byrne (Anatoli Grushkov), Norm Berketa (American Scientist), Lev Prygounov (General Saratkin), Mace Neufeld (WHCA Dinner Chairman), Jennifer Seguin (President's Aide), Josh Kimmel (White House Mess Waiter), Eugene Lazarev (General Dubinin), Sven-Ole Thorsen (Haft), Heinar Piller, Arthur Holden (Dressler's Associates), Marcel Sabourin (Monsieur Monceau), Vie Nystrom (Dressler's Secretary), Joel Bissonnette (Jared Mason), Kwasi Songui (Dockyard Navy Veteran), Marina Lapina (Nemerov's Wife), Victoria Reuter (Russian Nurse), France Arbour (Spassky's Mother), Lubomir Mykytiuk (Spassky), Vladimir Radian (Orlov), Gregory Hlady (Milinov), Valeri Koudriavtsev, Victor Pedtchenko (Ukranian Guards), Willie Gault, Gary Gelfand (Sportscasters), Arnold McCuller (National Anthem Singer), Craig Hosking (Helicopter Pilot), Jerry Markbreit (Referee), John Eaves (Secret Service Agent), JJ Carle (Hospital Physician), Msgt. David Vazquez (Marine Rescuer), David Schaap (US STRATCOM Colonel), Lisagay Hamilton (Capt. Lorna Shiro), Kirk Taylor (AFRAT Specialist Wesson), Jason Antoon (AFRAT Specialist Stubbs), Lisa Bronwyn Moore (NAOC Hotline Operator), Alexander Belyavsky (Admiral Ivanov), Jason Winer, Antonio David Lyons (Aircraft Carrier Petty Officers), Lennie Loftin (Aircraft Carrier Duty Officer), Mike McDougal (Russian Pilot),

Morgan Freeman, Ben Affleck

Constantine Gregory, Ciarán Hinds, Mariusz Sibiga

Bridget Moynahan, Ben Affleck

Matt Holland (Pickup Truck Driver), Roger Tonry (F-16 Pilot), Oleg Belkin (Russian Defense Minister), Constantine Gregory (General Bulgakov), Griffith Brewer (Burn Victim), Jacklyn St. Pierre, Mariah Inger (Baltimore Nurses), Mark Anthony Krupa (US STRATCOM Captain), Joseph Antaki (Arab Doctor), Marcel Jeanin (Baltimore Cop), Gerry Wood (AF Lt. Colonel), Conrad Pla (Pentagon Security Guard), Philip Akin (General Wilkes), Henri Pardo (Pentagon NCO), Irwin Dillion (Pentagon Mo-Link Operator), Real Auger, Gilles Marsolais (Dubinin's Killers), Eric Steibi (Dressler's Aide)

CIA Analyst Jack Ryan uncovers a plot to detonate a nuclear weapon on American soil, an event certain to cause a rift between the U.S. and the Soviet Union. Fourth in the Jack Ryan series of films distributed by Paramount, following *The Hunt for Red October* (1990; with Alec Baldwin as Ryan), *Patriot Games* (1992; with Harrison Ford), and *Clear and Present Danger* (1994; Ford).

BAD COMPANY

(TOUCHSTONE) Producers, Jerry Bruckheimer, Mike Stenson; Executive Producers, Chad Oman, Clayton Townsend, Lary Simpson, Gary Goodman; Director, Joel Schumacher; Screenplay, Jason Richman, Michael Browning; Story, Gary Goodman, David Himmelstein; Photography, Darius Wolski; Designer, Jan Roelfs; Costumes, Beatrix Pasztor; Editor, Mark Goldblatt; Music, Trevor Rabin; Music Supervisors, Kathy Nelson, Bob Badami; Stunts, Ken Bates; Casting, Victoria Thomas; a Jerry Bruckheimer Films presentation; Dolby; Panavision; Technicolor; Rated PG-13; 116 minutes; Release date: June 7, 2002

CAST

Gaylord Oakes	Anthony Hopkins
Jake Hayes/Kevin Pope	Chris Rock
Dragan Adjanic	Matthew Marsh
Agent Seale	Gabriel Macht
Julie	Kerry Washington
Jarma	Adoni Maropis
Nicole	Garcelle Beauvais-Nilon
Adrik Vas	Peter Stormare
Michelle Petrov	Dragan Micanovic
Roland Yates	John Slattery
Officer Swanson	Brooke Smith
Officer Carew	Daniel Sunjata
Officer Parish	Devone Lawson, Jr.
Officer McCain	Willis Robbins
Andre	Marek Vasut
Mrs. Banks	Irma P. Hall
Darius	Petr Jakl

and Adoni Maropis, Majed Ibrahim, Peter Macdissi, Fuman Dar (Dragan Henchmen), Dan Ziskie (Officer Dempsey), John Aylward (Officer Ferren), John Fink (Officer Fink), Joseph Edward (Club Owner), Deborah Rush (Mrs. Patterson), David Fisher (Young Valet), Jan Nemejovsky (Hotel Manager), Winter Uhlarik, Elin Spidlova, Magdalena Souskova (Manicurists), Michael Ealy (G-Mo), T.J. Cross (Cool Bean), Peter Davies (Doorman Tim), Lanette Ware (Pam), Ammar Daraiseh (Assassin), Jiri Simbersky (Ivan), Mikulas Kren (Hotel Clerk), Eddie Yansick (Bad Eddie), Philip Buch (Businessman), Steve Fisher (CIA Officer), Milos Kulhavy (Intruder #1), Peter Vlasak, Viktor Cervenka, Dusan Hyska (Thugs), P.I. Noccio (Military Interpreter), Minna Pyyhkala (Concierge), Kurt Bryant, Pavel Kratky, Frantisek Deak, Muslim Tagirov (Hotel Intruders), Brad Harper (NYTA Officer), Jeff Mantel (General), Bill Massoff (SWAT Team Leader), Shabazz Richardson (SWAT Guy), Joel Sugarman (Spo), Chris Best, Matthew Zolan (Henchmen), Dale Wyatt, Clare Britton (Tourists), Peter Von Berg (Manager), Philippe Vonlanthen (Desk Clerk)

Veteran CIA agent Gaylord Oakes is given nine days to transform street wise Jake Hayes into a savvy spy in order to replace his murdered identical twin brother.

© Touchstone Pictures/Jerry Bruckheimer Inc.

Anthony Hopkins, Gabriel Macht, Chris Rock

Tim Blake Nelson, Robin Tunney

CHERISH

(FINE LINE FEATURES) Producers, Johnny Wow, Mark Burton; Executive Producers, Jeffery Boortz, John Sideropoulos, Steven Siebert; Director/Screenplay, Finn Taylor; Photography, Barry Stone; Designer, Don Day; Costumes, Amy Brownson Donato; Editor, Rick LeCompte; Music, Mark De Gli Antoni; Music Supervisor, Charles Raggio; Casting, Joseph Middleton; a Concrete Pictures presentation in association with Wonderfilms; Dolby; Color; Rated R; 102 minutes; Release date: June 7, 2002

CAST

Zoe Adler	Robin Tunney
Deputy Bill Daly	Tim Blake Nelson
DJ	Brad Hunt
Brynn	Liz Phair
Andrew	Jason Priestley
Bell	Nora Dunn
Therapist	Lindsay Crouse
Max	Ricardo Gil
Officer Yee	Kelvin Han Yee
Woman in Bar	Karen Davis
Officer Ruiz	Scott Breitenstein
Officer Griffin	Tim Griffin
Head Prison Guard	Kathleen Stefano
Joyce	Stephen Polk
Yung	Kenny Kwong
Kids	Alex Gonzalez, Kellan Patrick
Jimmy	Adam Del Rio
Wife	Nina Du Val
Husband	Daniel DeShara

and Sumalee G. Montano (Officer Montano), Bill Ferrell (Heavier Officer), Phil LaMarr (Yoga Instructor), Jeremy Toback (Record Store Owner), Veronica Brown (Woman in Apartment), Tim Wiggins (Motorist), Michael Vaughn Breitenstein (Officer "Hand Bitten"), Banks McClintock (Engineer), Matt King (Young Man on Train), Mary Saudargas (Woman), Sophia Sharp (New Waitress), Todd Stoneman (Hustler), Matte Finish (Woman Behind Bars), Beth Daly (Computer Voice)

Zoe Adler, a jittery, fantasy prone woman, is unjustly accused of a cop's death, forcing her to be placed under house arrest where she becomes the object of obsession of the county deputy.

© Fine Line Features

DIVINE SECRETS OF THE YA-YA SISTERHOOD

Ellen Burstyn, Maggie Smith, Fionnula Flanagan, Shirley Knight

Katy Selverstone, Kiersten Warren, Ashley Judd

Angus MacFadyen, Sandra Bullock

(WARNER BROS.) Producers, Bonnie Bruckheimer, Hunt Lowry; Executive Producers, Bette Midler, Mary McLaglen, E.K. Gaylord II, Lisa Stewart; Director/Screenplay, Callie Khouri; Adaptation, Mark Andrus; Based on the novels *Divine Secrets of the Ya-Ya Sisterhood* and *Little Altars Everywhere* by Rebecca Wells; Photography, John Bailey; Designer, David J. Bomba; Editor, Andrew Marcus; Music, T Bone Burnett, David Mansfield; Costumes, Gary Jones; Casting, Avy Kaufman; an All Girl Production, presented in association with Gaylord Films; Dolby; Panavision; Technicolor; Rated PG-13; 116 minutes; Release date: June 7, 2002

CAST

Sidda Lee Walker . . . . .Sandra Bullock
Vivi Walker . . . . .Ellen Burstyn
Teensy . . . . .Fionnula Flanagan
Shep Walker . . . . .James Garner
Buggy . . . . .Cherry Jones
Young Vivi . . . . .Ashley Judd
Necie . . . . .Shirley Knight
Connor . . . . .Angus MacFadyen
Caro . . . . .Maggie Smith
Younger Teensy .Jacqueline McKenzie
Younger Caro . . . . .Katy Selverstone
Younger Necie . . . . .Kiersten Warren
Younger Shep Walker . . . . .David Lee Smith
Genevieve . . . . .Gina McKee
Jack . . . . .Matthew Settle
Taylor Abbott . . . . .David Rasche
and Leslie Silva (Willetta), Ron Dortch (Chaney), Fred Koehler (Pete Abbott), Allison Bertoino (Little Sidda), Austin R. Cooper (Little Shep Jr.), Sarah Huck (Lulu), Alex Cooper (Baylor), Caitlin Wachs (Little Vivi), Alyssa May Gold (Little Teensy), Mary Katherine Weiss (Little Caro), Nicki Tschudi (Little Necie), Deborah Hobart (Aunt Louise), Clint Lienau (James Jr.), David Bridgewater (Dr. Beau Poche), Sarallen (Older Willetta), Veda Wilson (Shirley), Mark Joy (Mr. Whitman), Michael Mattison (Officer Roscoe Jenkins), Gil Johnson (Younger Chick), Boyd Kestner (Adult Shep Jr.), Barbara Weetman (Interviewer), Suellen Yates (Stage Manager), Don Baker (Confessional Priest), E. Michael Hewett (Airplane Man), Robert Longstreet (Pilot), Mark Jeffrey Miller (Lyle Johnson), Nina Repeta (Lady at Gas Station), Michael Moyer (Pawn Broker), Taj Mahal (Swing Band Singer), Ann Savoy (Chanteuse)

Sidda Lee Walker's unflattering comments about her mother Vivi Walker's eccentric behavior are printed in *Time* magazine, causing a rift between the two women that Vivi's lifelong friends, the Ya-Ya Sisterhood, hope to mend.

© Warner Bros.

Sandra Bullock, James Garner

SWIMMING

(OCEANSIDE) Producers, Linda Moran, Robert J. Siegel; Director, Robert J. Siegel; Screenplay, Lisa Bazadona, Robert J. Siegel, Grace Woodard; Photography, John Leuba; Designer, Charlotte Bourke; Costumes, Laura Sewrey; Co-Producers, Ciro Silva, Grace Woodard; Line Producer, Valerie Romer; Editor, Frank Reynolds; Casting, Judy Henderson; Dolby; Color; Rated R; 98 minutes; Release date: June 14, 2002

CAST

Frankie Wheeler . . . . .Lauren Ambrose
Josee . . . . .Joelle Carter
Nicola Jenrette . . . . .Jennifer Dundas Lowe
Heath . . . . .Jamie Harrold
Lance . . . . .Joshua Harto
Neil Wheeler . . . . .Josh Pais
Phil Dunlop . . . . .Joe Roseto
Kalani . . . . .Anthony Ruivivar
Marianne Wheeler . . . . .Sharon Scruggs
and Summer Still (Guard), James Villemaire (Brad), Jeffrey Ware (Buzz)

During summer at Myrtle Beach, SC, restless teenager Frankie Wheeler finds herself intrigued by a drifter who sells tie-dyed T-shirts from his van and by a manipulative new waitress.

© Oceanside

Joelle Carter, Jennifer Dundas Lowe, Lauren Ambrose

Lauren Ambrose

Linda Cardellini, Freddie Prinze, Jr., Scooby-Doo

SCOOBY-DOO

(WARNER BROS.) Producers, Charles Roven, Richard Suckle; Executive Producers, Robert Engelman, Andrew Mason, Kelley Smith-Wait, William Hanna, Joseph Barbera; Director, Raja Gosnell; Screenplay, James Gunn; Story, Craig Tilley, James Gunn; Based on characters created by Hanna-Barbera Productions; Photography, David Eggby; Designer, Bill Boes; Costumes, Leesa Evans; Editor, Kent Beyda; Music, David Newman; Music Supervisor, Laura Z. Wasserman; Visual Effects Supervisor, Peter Crosman; Second Unit/Stunts, Guy Norris; Casting, Mary Vernieu; a Mosaic Media Group production; Dolby; Technicolor; Rated PG; 86 minutes; Release date: June 14, 2002

CAST

Fred . . . . .Freddie Prinze, Jr.
Daphne . . . . .Sarah Michelle Gellar
Shaggy . . . . .Matthew Lillard
Velma . . . . .Linda Cardellini
Mondavarious . . . . .Rowan Atkinson
Mary Jane . . . . .Isla Fisher
Voodoo Maestro . . . . .Miguel A. Nunez, Jr.
N'Goo Tuana . . . . .Steven Grives
Sugar Ray . . . . .Stan Frazier, DJ Homicide,
            Murphy Karges, Mark McGrath, Rodney Sheppard
Zarkos . . . . .Sam Greco
Velma's Friend . . . . .Charles Cousins
and Kristian Schmid (Erad), Nicholas Hope (Old Man Smithers), Neil Fanning (Scooby Voice), Scott Innes (Scrappy Voice), J.P. Manoux (Scrappy Rex Voice), Christ Cruickshanks (Tiny Henchman), Alex Ruiz, Sheryl Benko (Reporters), Rio Nugara (Island Emissary), David Vallon (Bartender, Dead Mike's), Troy MacKinder (Guy in the Vat), Michala Banas (Carol), Holly Ann Brisley (Training Video Woman), Robert Diaz, Remi Broadway (Training Video Guys), Martin Broome (Melvin Doo), Simone Dumbleton (Co-Ed), Jonathan Coffey (Fitzgibbon), Michael Caffrey (Coast Guard #2), Kyas Sherriff (Airport Attendant), Celeste Gosnell, Bradley Gosnell, Cayley Gosnell, Audrey Gosnell (Airport Family), Kurt Duval (Spooky Hotel Bartender), Janis McGavin (Co-Ed Hottie), Emily Gosnell, Marea Lambert Barker, Kym Jackson, Danielle Starkey (Autograph Seekers), Andrew Bryniarski (Cavern Henchman), Craig Behenna, Keith Bullock (Henchmen), Jess Harnell, Frank Welker (Creature Voices), Stephen Colyer, Ashley Evans, Mark Hodge, Steve Holford, Matt Lee, Michael Montgomery, Deon Nuku, Robert Ricks, Rodney Syaranamual, Ashley Wallen, Andrew Waters, Adam Williams (Dancers)

Four crime-solving friends and their animated great Dane arrive at Spooky Island to investigate a series of paranormal incidents. Based on the animated TV series *Scooby-Doo, Where Are You?* that premiered on CBS in 1969, and the later *Scooby-Doo* series on the Cartoon Network.

© Warner Bros.

WINDTALKERS

(**MGM**) Producers, John Woo, Terence Chang, Tracie Graham, Alison Rosenzweig; Executive Producer, C.O. Erickson; Director, John Woo; Screenplay, John Rice, Joe Batteer; Photography, Jeffrey L. Kimball; Designer, Holger Gross; Line Producers, John J. Smith, Richard Stenta; Co-Producers, Caroline Macaulay, Arthur Anderson; Editors, Steven Kemper, Jeff Gullo, Tom Rolf; Music, James Horner; Casting, Mindy Marin; a Lion Rock production; Dolby; Super 35 Widescreen; Deluxe color; Rated R; 134 minutes; Release date: June 14, 2002

CAST

Joe Enders	Nicolas Cage
Ben Yahzee	Adam Beach
Hjelmstad	Peter Stormare
Chick	Noah Emmerich
Pappas	Mark Ruffalo
Harrigan	Brian Van Holt
Nellie	Martin Henderson
Charlie Whitehorse	Roger Willie
Rita	Frances O'Connor
Ox Henderson	Christian Slater
Major Mellitz	Jason Isaacs
Fortino	William Morts
Mertens	Cameron Thor
Ear Doctor	Kevin Cooney

and Holmes Osborne (Colonel Hollings), Keith Campbell (Kittring), Clayton Barber (Hasby), Scott Atkinson (Camp Tarawa Staff Sergeant), Jeremy Davidson (Marine), Brian F. Maynard (Corpsman), Albert Smith (Navajo Man), James Dever (Field Hospital Colonel), Vincent Whipple (Navajo Instructor), Jim Morse (Marine Recruit), Chris Devlin (Sgt. Code Instructor), Jeff Davis (Tech Sgt.), Glen Begay (Radio Codetalker), Ross Lasi Tanoai (Eddie the Bartender), Brian Kasai (Japanese Intelligence Officer), Hiroshi "Rosh" Mori (Japanese Radio Operator), John Takeshi Ichikawa (Japanese Bunker Commander), Christopher T. Yamamoto (Japanese Bunker Gunner), Marc McClellan (Marine Artillery Commander), Steve Tanizaki (Japanese Artillery Officer), Malcolm Dohi (Battleship Codetalker), Darrel Guilbeau (Battleship Petty Officer), Aaron Yamagata (Tanapag Boy), Victoria Chen (Tanapag Mother), Jon Michael Souza (N.C.O. Officer), Carissa Jung (Tanapag Girl), Wataru Yoshida (Japanese Artillery), Junya Oishi (Japanese Artillery Sighter), Jiro Koga (Japanese Artillery Gunner), Lynn Kawailele Allen, Ilima Pumphrey, Tina Leialoha Gube, Lena Savalinaea, Alewa T. Olotoa, Kaliko Scott (Hula Dancers)

During the World War II Battle of Saipan, two Marines, Joe Enders and Ox Henderson, are assigned the task of protecting two Navajo codetalkers, soldiers who hold a secret military code based on their native language.

© MGM

Roger Willie, Christian Slater

Nicolas Cage, Mark Ruffalo, Martin Henderson, Noah Emmerich

Nicolas Cage, Adam Beach

Adam Beach

THE BOURNE IDENTITY

(UNIVERSAL) Producers, Doug Liman, Patrick Crowley, Richard N. Gladstein; Executive Producers, Frank Marshall, Robert Ludlum; Director, Doug Liman; Screenplay, Tony Gilroy, William Blake Herron; Based on the novel by Robert Ludlum; Photography, Oliver Wood; Designer, Dan Weil; Costumes, Pierre-Yves Gayraud; Editor, Saar Klein; Music, John Powell; Music Supervisor, Julianne Jordan; Visual Effects Supervisor, Peter Donen; Stunts, Nicholas Powell; Casting, Joseph Middleton, Kate Dowd; a Kennedy/Marshall—Hypnotic production; Dolby; Panavision; Deluxe color; Rated PG-13; 118 minutes; Release date: June 14, 2002

Clive Owen

CAST

Jason Bourne . . . . .Matt Damon
Marie Kreutz . . . . .Franka Potente
Ted Conklin . . . . .Chris Cooper
The Professor . . . . .Clive Owen
Ward Abbott . . . . .Brian Cox
Nykwana Wombosi . . . . .Adewale Akinnuoye-Agbaje
Zorn . . . . .Gabriel Mann
Research Techs . . . . .Walton Goggins, Josh Hamilton
Nicolette . . . . .Julia Stiles
Giancarlo . . . . .Orso Maria-Guerrini
Eamon . . . . .Tim Dutton
Picot . . . . .Dennis Braccini
Castel . . . . .Nicky Naude
Marshall . . . . .David Selburg
Com Tech . . . . .Demetri Goritsas
Manheim . . . . .Russel Levy
Security Chief . . . . .Anthony Green
Morgue Boss .Hubert Saint Macary
Consulate Clerk . . . . .David Bamber
and Gwenaël Clause (Deauvage), Manu Booz (Taxi Driver), Philippe Durand (Morgue Attendant), Vincent Franklin (Rawlins), Paulette Frantz (Concierge), Thierry Ashanti (Wombosi Counselor), Roger Frost (Apfel), David Gasman (Deputy DCM), Harry Gilbert (Alain), Delphine Lanson (Alliance Secretary), William Cagnard (Davies), Kait Denison (Bank Receptionist), Joseph Beddelin, Rainer Werner (Zurich Cops), Katie Thynne (Claudia), Aaron Lilly, Ronald Benefield, Bradley Goode, Troy Lenhardt, Joshua McNew, Joe Montana, John Pawlikwoski, Michael Rix, Brad Rizer, Andrew Webster, Houston Williams (Marines), Alain Grellier (Salvi), Arnaud Henriet, Jean-Yves Billien, Daniel Erskine Nartay, Elvin "Chopper" David (Wombosi Bodyguards)

Matt Damon, Franka Potente

An amnesiac, rescued at sea, does not realize that he is a secret agent whom the CIA want killed because he has failed his mission.

© Universal

Matt Damon

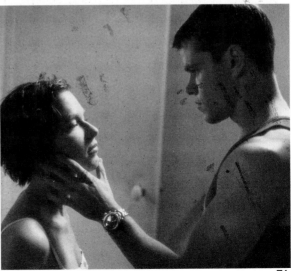

Franka Potente, Matt Damon

THE DANGEROUS LIVES OF ALTAR BOYS

(THINKFILM) Producers, Meg Lefauve, Jay Shapiro, Jodie Foster; Executive Producers, Graham King, David A. Jones, John Watson, Pen Densham; Director, Peter Care; Screenplay, Jeff Stockwell, Michael Petroni; Based upon the book by Chris Fuhrman; Co-Producer, Tim Harbert; Photography, Lance Acord; Designer, Gideon Ponte; Costumes, Marie France; Music, Marco Beltrami; Additional Music, Joshua Homme; Editor, Chris Peppe; Animation Producers, Todd McFarlane, Terry Fitzgerald; Casting, Laray Mayfield; an Initial Entertainment Group presentation of an Egg Pictures production in association with Trilogy Entertainment Group; Dolby; Color; Rated R; 104 minutes; Release date: June 14, 2002

CAST

Tim Sullivan	Kieran Culkin
Margie Flynn	Jena Malone
Francis Doyle	Emile Hirsch
Father Casey	Vincent D'Onofrio
Sister Assumpta	Jodie Foster
Wade Scalisi	Jake Richardson
Joey Anderson	Tyler Long
Donny Flynn	Arthur Bridges
Newsie	Scott Simpson
Mrs. Doyle	Melissa McBride
Mr. Doyle	Mike Harding
Naturalist	Chandler McIntyre
Professor Sullivan	Jeffrey West
Mrs. Sullivan	Yvonne Erickson
Colin Gibbney	Nicky Olson
Jay Flynn	Carson Pigott

In the 1970s, two irreverent, comic book-loving Catholic high school boys confront the mysteries of adolescence, the opposite sex, and the nun they have deemed their arch enemy while devising a series of outlandish pranks.

© ThinkFilm

Emile Hirsch, Jena Malone

Jena Malone, Emile Hirsch, Kieran Culkin

Emile Hirsch, Kieran Culkin

Jodie Foster, Kieran Culkin

SUNSHINE STATE

(SONY CLASSICS) Producer, Maggie Renzi; Director/Screenplay/Editor, John Sayles; Photography, Patrick Cady; Designer, Mark Ricker; Costumes, Mayes C. Rubeo; Music, Mason Daring; Casting, John and Ros Hubbard; presented in association with Anarchists' Convention; Dolby; Color; Rated R; 141 minutes; Release date: June 21, 2002

CAST

Delia Temple	Jane Alexander
Eunice Stokes	Mary Alice
Desiree Perry	Angela Bassett
Earl Pickney	Gordon Clapp
Dr. Lloyd	Bill Cobbs
Marly Temple	Edie Falco
Lester	Miguel Ferrer
Jack Meadows	Timothy Hutton
Murray Silver	Alan King
Reggie Perry	James McDaniel
Francine Pickney	Mary Steenburgen
Furman Temple	Ralph Waite
Flash Phillips	Tom Wright
Scotty Duvbal	Marc Blucas
Terrellbernard	Alexander Lewis
Todd Northupsam	Sam McMurray
Greg	Perry Lang
Loretta	Charlayne Woodard
Buster Bidwell	Clifton James
Jefferson Cash	Cullen Douglas
Silent Sam	Eliot Asinof
Steve Tregaskis	Richard Edson
Billy Trucks	Michael Greyeyes

The possibility of a lucrative redevelopment of the town of Delrona Beach, FL, sparks various reactions from the locals.

© Sony Pictures

Mary Steenburgen

Edie Falco, Timothy Hutton

James McDaniel, Angela Bassett

Miguel Ferrer

73

MINORITY REPORT

(20TH CENTURY FOX/DREAMWORKS) Producers, Gerald R. Molen, Bonnie Curtis, Walter F. Parkes, Jan De Bont; Director, Steven Spielberg; Screenplay, Scott Frank, Jon Cohen; Based on the short story by Philip K. Dick; Photography, Janusz Kaminski; Designer, Alex McDowell; Costumes, Deborah L. Scott; Editor, Michael Kahn; Music, John Williams; Special Animation and Visual Effects, Industrial Light & Magic; Visual Effects Supervisor, Scott Farrar; Associate Producers, Sergio Mimica-Gezzan, Michael Doven; Stunts, Brian Smrz; Casting, Denise Chamian; a Cruise/Wagner/Blue Tulip/Ronald Shusett/Gary Goldman production; Dolby; Panavision; Technicolor; Rated PG-13; 144 minutes; Release date: June 21, 2002

CAST

PRE-CRIME
Chief Paul Anderton . . . . .Tom Cruise
Director Lamar Burgess .Max von Sydow
Jad . . . . .Steve Harris
Fletcher . . . . .Neal McDonough
Knott . . . . .Patrick Kilpatrick
Evanna . . . . .Jessica Capshaw
and Richard Coca, Keith Campbell, Kirk B.R. Woller, Klea Scott, Frank Grillo (Pre-Crime Cops), Anna Maria Horsford (Casey), Sarah Simmons (Lamar Burgess' Secretary), Eugene Osment (Jad's Technician), James Henderson, Vene Arcoraci (Office Workers), Erica Ford (Employee), Keith Flippen (Tour Guide), Nathan Taylor (Kid Tourist), Radmar Agana Jao, Karina Logue, Elizabeth Anne Smith, Victoria Kelleher, Jim Rash (Technicians)
FBI
Danny Witwer . . . . .Colin Farrell
Jucket—Agent #1 . . . . .Stephen Ramsey
Paymen—Agent #2 . . . . .Tom Choi
Price—Agent #3 . . . . .Tom Whitenight
Foley—Agent #4 . . . . .Billy Morts
PRE-COG CHAMBER
Agatha . . . . .Samantha Morton
Wally the Caretaker . . . . .Daniel London
Arthur . . . . .Michael Dickman
Dashiell . . . . .Matthew Dickman
THE GREENHOUSE
Dr. Iris Hineman . . . . .Lois Smith
DEPARTMENT OF CONTAINMENT
Gideon . . . . .Tim Blake Nelson
PRE-CRIME WITNESSES
Chief Justice Pollard . . . . .George D. Wallace
Dr. Katherine James . . . . .Ann Ryerson
ANDERTON'S FAMILY
Lara Clarke . . . . .Kathryn Morris
Sean at Nine . . . . .Spencer Treat Clark
Sean at Six . . . . .Tyler Patrick Jones
Sean at Four . . . . .Dominic Scott Kay
Sean at Two . . . . .Brennen Means
VICTIMS & KILLERS
Howard Marks . . . . .Arye Gross
Sarah Marks . . . . .Ashley Crow
Leo Crow . . . . .Mike Binder
Donald Doobin . . . . .Joel Gretsch
Anne Lively . . . . .Jessica Harper
John Doe . . . . .Bertell Lawrence
and THE MALL: Jason Antoon (Rufus Riley at Cyber Parlor), William Mesnik (Cyber Parlor Customer), Scott Frank (Conceited Customer), Severin Wunderman (Skiing Customer), Max Trumpower (Bum); THE CHASE: Allie Raye (Hamburger Mom), Rocael Rueda, Sr. (Hamburger Dad), Nicholas Edwin Barb (Homework Boy), Catfish Bates (Tenement Snitch); OPERATING ROOM & TENEMENT BLDG.: Peter Stormare

(Dr. Solomon Eddie), Caroline Lagerfelt (Greta van Eyck), Danny Lopes (Man), Vanessa Cedotal (Woman), Katy Boyer (Mother), Adrianna Kamosa, Elizabeth Kamosa, Laurel Kamosa, Kari Gordon, Raquel Gordon (Children), Fiona Hale (Old Woman), Pamela Roberts (Violent Wife), Clement E. Blake (Husband), Jerry Perchesky (Grandfather); THE BALLROOM: Victor Raider-Wexler (Attorney General Nash), Nancy Linehan Charles (Celeste Burgess), Nadia Axakowsky, Tony Hill, Dude Walker, Drakeel Burns (Reporters); and William Mapother (Hotel Clerk), Paul Wasilewski (Nathan with Bicycle), Morgan Hasson (Paperboy), Andrew Sandler (Marks' Son), Kimiko Gelman (Mother on Metro), Caitlin Mao (Girl on Metro), Bonnie Morgan (Contortionist), Kathi Copeland, Lucille M. Oliver, Ana Maria Quintana, Gene Wheeler (Murder Bystanders), Payman Kayvanfar (Card Player), Tonya Ivey (Gap Girl), David Stifel (Lycon-seller of Black Inhalers), Kurt Sinclair, Rebecca Ritz, Beverly Morgan, John Bennett, Maureen Dunn, Ron Ulstad (Adulations), Blake Bashoff, David Doty, Gina Gallego, David Hornsby, Anne Judson-Yager, Meredith Monroe, Benita Krista Nall, Shannon O'Hurley, Jorge-Luis Pallo, Elizabeth Penn Payne (Pre-Crime Public Service Announcers); COMMERCIALS: Ethan Sherman (Revo Sunglass Model), Jarah (AMEX Polynesian Woman), Miles Dinsmoor (Guinness Man)

In the year 2054, the Justice Department's Pre-Crime unit has made it possible to stop criminal acts *before* they are committed, a system that seems infallible until the organization's top man, Chief John Anderton, finds himself accused of a future murder.

This film received an Oscar nomination for sound editing.

Tom Cruise

Tom Cruise, Samantha Morton

Tom Cruise

Tom Cruise

Tom Cruise, Samantha Morton

Neal McDonough, Tom Cruise

Tom Cruise

Tom Cruise

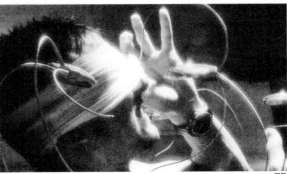
Tom Cruise

LILO & STITCH

(WALT DISNEY PICTURES) Producer, Clark Spencer; Directors/ Screenplay, Chris Sanders, Dean Deblois; Based on an original idea by Chris Sanders; Editor, Darren Holmes; Associate Producer, Lisa M. Poole; Art Director, Ric Sluiter; Music, Alan Silvestri; Artistic Coordinator, Jeff Dutton; Production Designer, Paul Felix; Layout Supervisor, Arden Chan; Background Supervisor, Robert E. Stanton; Clean-Up Supervisors, Philip S. Boyd, Christine Lawrence-Finney; Visual Effects Supervisor, Joseph F. Gilland; Computer Animation Supervisor, Eric Guaglione; Songs: "He Mele No Lilo" and "Hawaiian Roller Coast Ride" by Alan Silvestri and Mark Keali'i Ho'Omalu/performed by Mark Keali'i Ho'Omalu; Distributed by Buena Vista Pictures; Dolby; Technicolor; Rated PG 85 minutes; Release date: June 21, 2002

VOICE CAST

Lilo . . . . .Daveigh Chase
Stitch . . . . .Christopher Michael Sanders
Nani . . . . .Tia Carrere
Jumba . . . . .David Ogden Stiers
Pleakley . . . . .Kevin McDonald
Cobra Bubbles . . . . .Ving Rhames
Grand Councilwoman . . . . .Zoe Caldwell
David Kawena . . . . .Jason Scott Lee
Captain Gantu . . . . .Kevin Michael Richardson
Rescue Lady . . . . .Susan Hegarty
Mrs. Hasagawa . . . . .Amy Hill
and Steve Alterman, Emily Anderson, Jack Angel, Bill Asing, Eric Beck, Robert Bergen, Steven Jay Blum, Rodger Bumpass, Catherine Cavadini, Jennifer Darling, Alexandra Deary, John DeMita, Judi Durand, Greg Finley, Jeff Fischer, Valerie Flueger, Jess Harnell, T. Aszur Hill, Barbara Iley, Daamen Krall, Todd Kurosawa, Chloe Looper, Mickie McGowan, Kunewa Mook, Courtney Mun, Mary-Linda Phillips, Patrick Pinney, Paige Pollack, David Randolph, Noreen Reardon, Debra Jean Rogers, Susan Silo, Kath Soucie, Melanie Spore, Doug Store, Drew Lexi Thomas, Miranda Walls, Karle Warren, Ruth Zalduondo (Additional Voices)

An out-of-control genetic experiment from another galaxy ends up on Earth where he is befriended by Lilo, a lonely Hawaiian girl.

This film received an Oscar nomination for animated feature.

© Disney Enterprises

Stitch, Nani, Lilo

Lilo, Stitch

The Grand Councilwoman (center)

Cobra Bubbles, Nani

Stitch, Lilo

Jumba, Pleakley

Lilo, Stitch

Stitch, Nani, Lilo

Nani, Lilo, David Kawena

Stitch

LOVELY & AMAZING

Emily Mortimer

Dermot Mulroney, Emily Mortimer

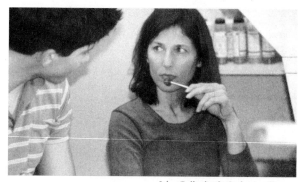

Jake Gyllenhaal, Catherine Keener

Brenda Blethyn, Raven Goodwin

(LIONS GATE) Producers, Anthony Bregman, Eric D'Arbeloff, Ted Hope; Executive Producers, Jason Kliot, Joana Vicente, Michael Kafka; Director/Screenplay, Nicole Holofcener; Photography, Harlan Bosmajian; Designer, Devorah Herbert; Costumes, Vanessa Vogel; Music, Craig Richey; Music Supervisor, Amy Rosen; Edutirm Rivert Frazen; Co-Executive Producers, Charles Rusbasan, Judith Zarin, Mike Escott; Co-Producer, Debra Grieco; Casting, Jeanne McCarthy; a Blow Up Pictures presentation of a Good Machine production in association with Roadside Attractions; Dolby; Color; Rated R; 89 minutes; Release date: June 28, 2002

CAST

Michelle Marks	Catherine Keener
Jane Marks	Brenda Blethyn
Elizabeth Marks	Emily Mortimer
Kevin McCabe	Dermot Mulroney
Jordan	Jake Gyllenhaal
Paul	James LeGros
Annie Marks	Raven Goodwin
Photographer	Tray Ruptash
Saleswomen	Ileen Getz, Kristen Dalton
Romy Rosemont	Debbie Waldman
Lorraine	Aunjanue Ellis
Pool Administrator	Brooke Allison
Teased Girl	Jennifer Zehnder
Maddy	Ashlynn Rose
Bill	Clark Gregg
Donna	Dreya Weber
Dr. Crane	Michael Nouri

and Christine Mourad (Cindy), Mariah O'Brien (Kevin's TV Co-Star), Jeanne McCarthy (Casting Director), Evan Miranda (Director), Ivy Strohaimer (Jessie), Spencer Garrett (Willy), Branden Williams (Teenage Boy), Nate Richert (Other Teenage Boy), Cory Joffe (Customer), Dawn Saucier (Bartender), Stacy Jorgensen (Lorraine's Pool Friend), Tennison Hightower (Baldasaro Salesgirl), Lee Garrington (Jordan's Mom), John Srednicki, Madeline Moskowitz, Mark Beltzman (Premiere Guest), Jeremy Kramer (Premiere Photographer), Eric Wizenreid (Parking Attendant), Greer Goodman (ER Doctor), Jerome Butler (Policeman), Scott Adsit (Young Man at Phone), Ryan Wolfe (McDonald's Clerk), Alan Naggar (McDonald's Customer), Elayn Taylor (Jane's Nurse)

Two sisters, whose mother is about to subject herself to a liposuction operation, begin to question their own lives, one being an actress obsessed with maintaining her looks, the other a restless, failing artist who finds herself having an affair with a 16-year-old.

© Lions Gate

James LeGros, Emily Mortimer

MR. DEEDS

(COLUMBIA/NEW LINE CINEMA) Producers, Sid Ganis, Jack Giarraputo; Executive Producers, Adam Sandler, Joseph M. Caracciolo; Director, Steven Brill; Screenplay, Tim Herlihy; Adapted from the film *Mr. Deeds Goes to Town*, directed by Frank Capra, screenplay by Robert Riskin, based on the story *Opera Hat* by Clarence Budington Kelland; Photography, Peter Lyons Collister; Designer, Perry Andelin Blake; Costumes, Ellen Lutter; Editor, Jeff Gourson; Music, Teddy Castellucci; Music Supervisor, Michael Dilbeck; Co-Producer, Alex Siskin; Casting, Roger Mussenden; a Happy Madison Production in association with Out of the Blue Entertainment; Dolby; Deluxe color; Rated PG-13; 96 minutes; Release date: June 28, 2002

CAST

Longfellow Deeds	Adam Sandler
Babe Bennett	Winona Ryder
Emilio Lopez	John Turturro
Marty	Allen Covert
Chuck Cedar	Peter Gallagher
Mac McGrath	Jared Harris
Cecil Anderson	Erick Avari
Murph	Peter Dante
Jan	Conchata Ferrell
Preston Blake	Harve Presnell
Crazy Eyes	Steve Buscemi

and Blake Clark (Buddy Ward), John McEnroe, Radioman, Rev. Al Sharpton (Themselves), JB Smoove (Reuben), Tom McNulty (Red Parka Man), Buddy Bolton (Cameraman), Angelito Bautista (Sherpa), Scott Thompson Baker (News Anchor), Robert Frank Telfer (Business Anchor), Elizabeth Owens (Kitty), Florence Anglin (Jane), Sylvia Kauders (Sue), Henry Hayward (Mr. Wetherley), Frank Weller (Old Farmer), Karen Nation (Lucy), Bruce French (Pilot), Ken Forsgren (Co-Pilot), Earl Schuman (Valet), Marijan Zoric (Chef), Irina Davidoff (Russian Maid), William Brady (Chauffeur), Brandon Molale (Kevin Ward), Derek Hughes (Waiter), Walter Williamson (Kurt), Roark Critchlow (William), Billy St. John (George), Kevin Grady, Dru Homer (Anniversary Couple), Frank Montella (Bishop), Alfred Dennis (Old Timer), Margie Loomis (Martha), Alex Buck (Gum Chewer), Tyler Roche (Young Kid), Lauren Mieske (Little Sister), Steele Hunter (Children's Father), George Wallace (NAACP Administrator), Gabriel Williams (Mailroom Clerk), Dianne Crawford (Secretary), John Kirk (Bartender), Aloma Wright (Cat Lady), J.D. Donaruma (Fake Cop), Carter Edwards (Yelling Cop), Steven Golebiowski (Yelling Fireman), Tim Herlihy (Fireman), Ked McFarlane Jimenez (Heroic Dog), Chloé Hult (Waitress), Randolph LeRoi (Afro Man), Jeremy Chu, Gideon Jacobs (Bike Riding Kids), Gina Gallego (Consuela Lopez), Dion Anderson, Susan Bjurman, Tony Chu, Andy Kreiss, Ramesh Pandey, Maurice G. Smith (Shareholders), Jennifer Tisdale, Toshi Toda (Card Readers), Rob Schneider (Nazo)

Longfellow Deeds, a simple small-town pizzeria owner, arrives in New York City after inheriting $40 billion, only to find himself the target of corrupt outside parties looking to exploit him and get a piece of his wealth. Remake of the 1936 Columbia film *Mr. Deeds Goes to Town,* which starred Gary Cooper and Jean Arthur.

© Columbia/New Line Cinema

John Turturro, Adam Sandler

Peter Dante, Conchata Ferrell

Winona Ryder, Jared Harris

Adam Sandler

THE POWERPUFF GIRLS

(WARNER BROS.) Producer, Donna Castricone; Supervising Producer, Jennifer Pelphrey; Executive Producers, Craig McCracken, Brian A. Miller; Co-Executive Producers, Mike Lazzo, Linda Simensky, Mark Norman; Director, Craig McCracken; Screenplay/Storyboards, Charlie Bean, Lauren Faust, Craig McCracken, Paul Rudish, Don Shank; Art Director, Mike Moon; Animation Director, Gennedy Tartakovsky; Music, James L. Venable; Editor, Rob DeSales; Development/Character Design, Craig Kellman; Casting and Voice Direction, Collette Bennett Sunderman; a Cartoon Network production; Dolby; Technicolor; Rated PG; 74 minutes; Release date: July 3, 2002

VOICE CAST

Blossom . . . . .Catherine Cavadini
Bubbles . . . . .Tara Strong
Buttercup . . . . .E.G. Daily
Mojo Jojo . . . . .Roger L. Jackson
Professor Utonium . . . . .Tom Kane
Mayor/Narrator . . . . .Tom Kenny
Ms. Keane . . . . .Jennifer Hale
Sara Bellum . . . . .Jennifer Martin
and Jeff Glen Bennett (Ace/Big Billy/Grubber), Greg DeLisle (Linda/Woman at Zoo), Phil LaMarr (I.P. Host/Local Anchor), Rob Paulsen (Hota Wata/Killa Drilla), Kevin Michael Richardson (Rocko Socko/Ojo Tango), Frank Welker (Whole Lotta Monkeys)

The Powerpuff Girls, feeling unappreciated by their town, are convinced by the evil Mojo Jojo to help him build a Help-the-Town-and-Make-It-a-Better-Place Machine, unaware that he is planning to use the device for his own nefarious purposes. Based on *The Powerpuff Girls* series that made its debut on the Cartoon Network in 1998.

© Warner Bros.

Bubbles, Professor Utonium, Blossom, Buttercup

Mojo Jojo, Blossom, Buttercup, Bubbles

Will Smith, Tommy Lee Jones

MEN IN BLACK II

(COLUMBIA) Producers, Walter F. Parkes, Laurie MacDonald; Executive Producer, Steven Spielberg; Director, Barry Sonnenfeld; Screenplay, Robert Gordon, Barry Fanaro; Story, Robert Gordon; Based on the Malibu Comic by Lowell Cunningham; Co-Producer, Graham Place; Photography, Greg Gardiner; Designer, Bo Welch; Costumes, Mary E. Vogt; Editors, Steven Weisberg, Richard Pearson; Music, Danny Elfman; Alien Make-Up Effects, Rick Baker; Visual Effects Supervisor, John Berton; Casting, Ronna Kress; an Amblin Entertainment Production in association with MacDonald/Parkes Productions; Dolby; Deluxe color; Rated PG-13; 88 minutes; Release date: July 3, 2002

CAST

Kay . . . . .Tommy Lee Jones
Jay . . . . .Will Smith
Zed . . . . .Rip Torn
Serleena . . . . .Lara Flynn Boyle
Scrad/Charlie . . . . .Johnny Knoxville
Laura Vasquez . . . . .Rosario Dawson
and Tony Shalhoub (Jeebs), Patrick Warburton (Agent Tee), Jack Kehler (Ben), David Cross (Newton), Colombe Jacobsen (Hailey), Peter Spellos (Motorman), Michael Rivkin (Man with Dog), Michael Bailey Smith (Creepy), Lenny Venito, Howard Spiegel (New York Guys), Alpheus Merchant (MIB Guard), Jay Johnston, Joel McKinnon Miller (Agents), Derek Cecil (Repairman Agent), Sean Rouse (MIB Agent), Peter Spruyt, Kevin Cotteleer, Marty Belafsky (MIB Customs Agents), Rick Baker (MIB Passport Control Agent), Martha Stewart (Herself), Michael Jackson (Agent M), Sid Garza-Hillman (Agent Gee), Tom Whitenight (Agent C), Nick Cannon (MIB Autopsy Agent), Andre Blair (Central Park Agent), Jeremy Howard (Bird Guy Alien/Postal Sorting Alien), Mary Stein (Bird Lady Alien), Marty Klebba (Family Child Alien), John Alexander (Jarra/Family Dad Alien), Denise Cheshire (Family Mom/Locker Alien), Ernie Grunwald (Young Postal Employee), Chloe Sonnenfeld (Young Girl at Post Office), John Berton (Split Alien Guy), William E. Jackson (Eye Guy), Doug Jones (Joey), Peter Graves (Himself), Linda Kim (Ambassador Lauranna), Paige Brooks ("Mysteries in History" Lauranna), Stephanie Kemp (Neuralyzed Mother), Barry Sonnenfeld (Neuralyzed Father), Victoria Jones (Neuralyzed Daughter), Michael Garvey (Corn Face), Michael Dahlen (Flesh Balls), Kevin Grevioux (Pineal Eye), Derek Mears (Mosh Tendrils), Sonny Tipton (Dog Poop), John Richardson (Postman), Philip Goodwin (Diner Guy), Tony Urbano (Puppet Master), Tim Blaney (Voice of Frank the Pug); The Worm Guys Voices: Greg Ballora (Sleeble), Carl J. Johnson (Gleeble), Thom Fountain (Neeble), Brad Abrell (Mannix), Richard Pearson (Gordy)

Alien hunters Jay and Kay try to stop Serleena, a deadly extraterrestrial who has taken female human form, from tracking down a device that will give her the power to destroy the world. Sequel to the 1997 Columbia film with Jones, Smith, Torn, and Shalhoub repeating their roles.

© Columbia

Margaret Cho

NOTORIOUS C.H.O.

(WELLSPRING) Producer/Director/Editor, Lorene Machado; Executive Producers, Margaret Cho, Karen Taussig; Screenplay, Margaret Cho; Photography, Kirk Miller; Designer, Kristin Zavorska; Associate Producer, Ran Barker; Music, Greg Burns, Jeff Burns, Andrea Bensmiller, Eve Buigues; a Cho Taussig production; Color; Not rated; 95 minutes; Release date: July 3, 2002; Comedian Margaret Cho in concert.

© Wellspring

Lil' Bow Wow, Jason Kidd

Morris Chestnut, Eugene Levy

LIKE MIKE

(20TH CENTURY FOX) Producers, Barry Josephson, Peter Heller; Executive Producers, Adam Silver, Gregg Winik; Director, John Schultz; Screenplay, Michael Elliot, Jordan Moffet; Story, Michael Elliot; Photography, Shawn Maurer; Designer, Arlan Jay Vetter; Costumes, Mary Jane Fort; Editors, Peter Berger, John Pace; Music, Richard Gibbs; Executive Music Producers, Jermaine Dupri, Michael Mauldin; Co-Producer, Garrett Grant; Stunts, Tierre Turner; Casting, Risa Bramon Garcia, Brennan du Fresne; a Heller Highwater/Josephson Entertainment production, presented in association with NBA Entertainment; Dolby; Deluxe color; Rated PG; 99 minutes; Release date: July 3, 2002

CAST

Calvin Cambridge	Lil' Bow Wow
Tracey Reynolds	Morris Chestnut
Murph	Jonathan Lipnicki
Reg Stevens	Brenda Strong
Ox	Jesse Plemons
Marlon	Julius Charles Ritter
Stan Bittleman	Crispin Glover
Sister Theresa	Anne Meara
Coach Wagner	Robert Forster
Frank Bernard	Eugene Levy
Marvin Joad	Roger Morrissey
Henderson	Timon Kyle
Smith	Stephen Thompson
Krivov	Alex Krilov
Jones	David Brown
Sloan	Peter Moret
Segretti	Josef Canon
Ngudu	Kingsley Nwekenbia
Coltrain	Jesse Justice Smith, Jr.

and Gregory L. Hall (Schultz), Laurent Crawford (Grant), Pat Croce, Michael Finley, Lethon Flowers III, Steve Francis, Allen E. Iverson, Jason Kidd, Tracy McGrady, Alonzo Mourning, Steve Nash, Dirk Nowitski, Gary Payton, Jason Richardson, David M. Robinson, Takeo Spikes, John Robert Thompson, Rasheed Wallace, Gerald Wallis, Chris Webber (Themselves), Reggie Theus (Interviewer), Reginald Veljohnson (Mr. Boyd), Valarie Pettiford (Mrs. Boyd), Roqui Theus (Young Boyd Daughter), Sandra Prosper (Janet), Doug MacMillan (Security Guard), Vanessa Williams (Pharmacist), Basil Wallace (Drill Sgt. Dad), Courtney Black (Drill Sgt. Mom), Christine Mitges (Musical Theatre Mom), Stephen Holland (Musical Theatre Dad), Susan Chuang (Hallmark Mom), Craig Tsuyumine (Hallmark Dad), Fred Armisen (New Age Dad), Nona D. Simpson (Trucker's Wife), Sterfon Demings (Potential Parent), Keiann Collins (Rasta Woman), Julie Brown (New Age Mother), Tucker Smallwood (Mr. Reynolds), James McManus (Mr. Williams), Rick Ducommun (Dad Outside Arena), Miles Koules (Miles), Arielle Peterson, April Peterson (Kids with Dad), Daniel Stone (Fan "Coach Sucks"), Geoff Witcher (Announcer), Sybil Azur, Kimi Bateman, Diana Carreno, Faune A. Chambers, Karen Elmore, Staci Flood, Stacey Harper, Sandra McCoy, Udee McGeoy, Sarah Smith, Addie Yungmee, Hayley Zelniker (Cheerleaders), Bobby Pappas (Moving Man at Tracy's), Amissa Miller (Ice Cream Waitress), Sarah Whalen (Daisy Daye), Jimmy Kimmel (Client in Commercial), Lance Barber (Director in Commercial), Ryan Thomas (Ryan), Robert Morris, Jr. (Robert), Jon Edwin Wright, Dwayne Foster, Tyrone Merriweather (Coaches), Sloan Fischer, Coltrane Isaac Marcus (Young Orphans), Bobby Hall, Curtis McCoy (Trainers), Joe Crawford, James R. Platt (Referees), Wayne "Spoon" Witherspoon (Tarmac Supervisor), Corey Holcomb (Trucker Dad), Tyler T. Romary, Sunni Ali Powell (TV Delivery Men), Charlie Schultz (Cab Driver)

A fourteen-year-old basketball fan realizes his dream of becoming an NBA superstar after he puts on a pair of magical sneakers that give him the power to play like a pro.

© 20th Century Fox

ROAD TO PERDITION

Tyler Hoechlin, Tom Hanks

Jude Law

Jennifer Jason Leigh, Liam Aiken

(DREAMWORKS/20TH CENTURY FOX) Producers, Richard D. Zanuck, Dean Zanuck, Sam Mendes; Executive Producers, Walter F. Parkes, Joan Bradshaw; Director, Sam Mendes; Screenplay, David Self; Based upon the graphic novel by Max Allan Collins, and illustrated by Richard Piers Rayner; Photography, Conrad L. Hall; Designer, Dennis Gassner; Costumes, Albert Wolsky; Editor, Jill Billcock; Music, Thomas Newman; Associate Producers, Cherylanne Martin, Tara B. Cook; Casting, Debra Zane; a Zanuck Company production; Dolby; Super 35 Widescreen; Technicolor; Rated R; 119 minutes; Release date: July 12, 2002

CAST

Michael Sullivan	Tom Hanks
John Rooney	Paul Newman
Maguire	Jude Law
Annie Sullivan	Jennifer Jason Leigh
Frank Nitti	Stanley Tucci
Connor Rooney	Daniel Craig
Michael Sullivan, Jr.	Tyler Hoechlin
Peter Sullivan	Liam Aiken
Finn McGovern	Ciarán Hinds
Jack Kelly	David Darlow
Alexander Rance	Dylan Baker
Drugstore Owner	Rob Maxey
Boy Michael Fights	Nicholas Cade
Michael's Teacher	Maureen Gallagher
Frank the Bouncer	Kevin Chamberlin
Brothel Maid	Juanita Wilson
Calvino	Doug Spinuzza
Secretary	Lee Roy Rogers
Tenement Murderer	Kurt Naebig
Crime Scene Policeman	Lance Baker
Living Corpse	Monte
Father Callaway	Duane Sharp
Aunt Sarah	Diane Dorsey
Motel Manager	Michael Sassone
Cop at Diner	John Sterchi
Farmer at Diner	Robert Jones
Ruby the Waitress	Lara Phillips
Mr. McDougal	Harry Groener
Betty the Waitress	Mina Badie
Young Bank Manager	Ed Kross
Prostitute	Heidi Jayne Netzley
Hotel Manager	Phil Ridarelli
Farmer Virginia	Peggy Roeder
Farmer Bill	James Greene
Finn McGovern's Henchmen	Stephen Dunn, Paul Turner
Nitti's Henchmen	Roderick Peeples, Keith Kupferer
Irish Musicians	Kathleen Keane, Brendan McKinney, Jackie Moran, Kieran O'Hare
Rooney's Business Associates	John Sierros, Jon Sattler, Michael Brockman, John Judd, Christian Stolte, Jack Callahan
Bankers	Jobe Cerny, Lawrence MacGowan, Timothy Hendrickson, Marty Higginbotham

When his young son unwittingly witnesses his father's involvement in a gangland murder, hit man Michael Sullivan and the boy find themselves on the run from the mob's vengeance.

2002 Academy Award winner for Best Cinematography. This film received additional Oscar nominations for supporting actor (Paul Newman), art direction, original score, sound, and sound editing.

Stanley Tucci

Tyler Hoechlin

Daniel Craig

Jude Law

Tom Hanks

Tom Hanks, Tyler Hoechlin

Paul Newman

STUART LITTLE 2

(COLUMBIA) Producers, Lucy Fisher, Douglas Wick; Executive Producers, Jeff Franklin, Steve Waterman, Rob Minkoff, Gail Lyon, Jason Clark; Director, Rob Minkoff; Screenplay, Bruce Joel Rubin; Story, Douglas Wick, Bruce Joel Rubin; Based upon characters from the book *Stuart Little* by E.B. White; Photography, Steven Poster; Designer, Bill Brzeski; Editor, Priscilla Nedd Friendly; Music, Alan Silvestri; Music Supervision, Bonnie Greenberg-Goodman; Costumes, Mona May; Visual Effects Supervisor, Jerome Chen; Supervising Animation Puppeteer, David Barclay; Casting, Francine Maisler; a Douglas Wick/Lucy Fisher production, a Franklin/Waterman production; Dolby; Deluxe color; Rated PG; 72 minutes; Release date: July 19, 2002

CAST

Voice of Stuart Little	Michael J. Fox
Mrs. Little	Geena Davis
Mr. Little	Hugh Laurie
George Little	Jonathan Lipnicki
Martha Little	Anna Hoelck, Ashley Hoelck
Voice of Snowbell	Nathan Lane
Voice of Margalo	Melanie Griffith
Voice of Falcon	James Woods
Voice of Monty	Steve Zahn
Will	Marc John Jefferies
Wallace	Angelo Massagli
Coach	Jim Doughan
Plumber	Brad Garrett
Referee	Conan McCarty
Teacher	Maria Bamford
Student	Daniel Hansen
Irwin	Kevin Johnson Olson
Kid	Dyllan Christopher

and Bobby Walsh (Tony), Michael C. Fuchs (Mark), Raymond Ma (Chef), Amelia Marshall (Will's Mom), Ronobir Lahiri (Cab Driver), Connie Roderick (Nun), David Tabatsky (Balloon Man), Frank Aquilino, Salvatore Pate (Onlookers), David Shiner (Clown), Rachael Harris (Additional Voices)

New York mouse Stuart Little teams with his former nemesis, Snowbell the cat, in order to rescue a little bird who has been kidnapped by a villainous falcon. Sequel to the 1999 Columbia film with most of the performers repeating their roles.

© Columbia

Margalo, Stuart Little

Aaron Stanford, Sigourney Weaver

Bebe Neuwirth, Aaron Stanford

TADPOLE

(MIRAMAX) Producers, Alexis Alexanian, Dolly Hall, Gary Winick; Executive Producers, Caroline Kaplan, Jonathan Sehring, John Sloss; Director, Gary Winick; Screenplay, Heather McGowan, Niels Mueller; Story, Heather McGowan, Niels Mueller, Gary Winick; Photography, Hubert Taczanowski; Designer, Anthony Gasparro; Costumes, Suzanne Schwarzer; Editor, Susan Littenberg; Music, Renaud Pion; Casting, Marcia DeBonis, Jennifer Euston, Ellen Lewis; Dolly Hall Productions, IFC Productions, InDigEnt; Dolby; Color; Rated PG-13; 78 minutes; Release date: July 19, 2002

CAST

Oscar Grubman	Aaron Stanford
Eve Grubman	Sigourney Weaver
Stanley Grubman	John Ritter
Diane	Bebe Neuwirth
Charlie	Robert Iler
Miranda Spear	Kate Mara
Jimmy	Peter Appel
Professor Tisch	Ron Rifkin
Daphne Tisch	Alicia Van Couvering

and Paul Butler (Prof. Sherman), Adam LeFevre (Phil), Hope Chernov (Samantha), Debbon Ayer (Jean), Michael W. Connors (Man in Bar), Theo Kogan (Woman in Bar), Harry Kellerman (Tea Waiter), Reade Kelly (Mr. Smith), Danielle Di Vecchio (Danielle Divecchio), John Feltch (Mr. Spear), Henry Haile (Le Gardin Waiter), Lee Brock (Charlie's Mom), Giselle Berk, Steven Dismomma, Charles Fombrun, Joyce Grodinsky, Joan Roland, Lou Vitale, Penny Winick (Thanksgiving Party Guests)

Fifteen-year-old Oscar Grubman returns from boarding school to spend Thanksgiving with his family, only to find himself facing the dilemma of being in love with his stepmother, while carrying on with her best friend.

© Miramax

K-19: THE WIDOWMAKER

Ingvar Sigurdsson, Harrison Ford, Liam Neeson

(PARAMOUNT) Producers, Kathryn Bigelow, Joni Sighvatsson, Christine Whitaker, Edward S. Feldman; Executive Producers, Harrison Ford, Nigel Sinclair, Moritz Borman, Guy East; Director, Kathryn Bigelow; Screenplay, Christopher Kyle; Story, Louis Nowra; Photography, Jeff Cronenweth; Designers, Karl Juliusson, Michael Novotny; Costumes, Marit Allen; Editor, Walter Murch; Music, Klaus Bladet; Executive Music Producer, Joel Sill; Co-Producers, Steven-Charles Jaffe, Basil Iwanyk; Visual Effects Supervisors, Bruce Jones, John Nelson; Casting, Mali Finn, Mary Selway; Stunts, Mickey Giacomazzi, Jamie Jones; an Intermedia Films presentation of a National Geographic/Palomar Pictures/First Light/IMF production; Dolby; Panavision; Deluxe color; Rated PG-13; 138 minutes; Release date: July 19, 2002

CAST

Captain Alexei Vostrikov	Harrison Ford
Captain Mikhail Polenin	Liam Neeson
Reactor Office Vadim Radtchenko	Peter Sarsgaard
Pavel Loktev	Christian Camargo
Marshal Zelentstov	Joss Ackland
Admiral Bratyeev	John Shrapnel
Dr. Savran	Donald Sumpter
Patronov	Tim Woodward
Demichev	Steve Nicholson
Suslov	Ravil Isyanov
Dmitri	Sam Spruell
Kuryshev	Peter Stebbings
Lapnish	Roman Podhora
Vasily	Sam Redford
Kornilov	Lex Shrapnel
Leonid	Shaun Benson
Anton	Kristen Holden-Ried
Sergei	Dmitry Chepovetsky
Kikiidze	Christopher Redman
Maxim	Tygh Runyan
Konstantin	George Anton
Anatoly	James Ginty

and Peter Graham (Danya Yashin), Shawn Mathieson (Stepan), Jacob Pitts (Grigori), Christopher Routh (Oleg), Lubomir Mykytiuk (Dr. Gabril), Michael J.X. Gladis (Yevgeny), Natalia Vintilova (Kataya), Steve Cumyn (Arseni), Augustin Strugnell (Yakov Raktin), Arsenty Sydelnykov (Seymon "Syoma" Dydik), JJ Feild (Andrei), Peter Oldring (Vanya), Joshua Close (Viktor), Ingvar Sigurdsson (Gorelov), Gerrit Vooren (Voslensky), Lev Prygunov (Ivan Vershinin), Jeremy Akerman (Fyodor Tsetkov), Lee J. Campbell (Judge)

During the Cold War, Captain Alexei Vostrikov is ordered to take command of the nuclear missile submarine K-19 finding his crew in peril when a reactor malfunctions.

© Paramount

K-19

Christian Carmago, Peter Sarsgaard

Peter Sarsgaard, Harrison Ford, James Ginty, Ravil Isyanov

AUSTIN POWERS IN GOLDMEMBER

(NEW LINE CINEMA) Producers, Suzanne Todd, Jennifer Todd, Demi Moore, Eric McLeod, John Lyons, Mike Myers; Executive Producers, Toby Emmerich, Richard Brener; Director, Jay Roach; Screenplay, Mike Myers, Michael McCullers; Photography, Peter Deming; Designer, Rusty Smith; Costumes, Deena Appel; Editors, Jon Poll, Greg Hayden; Music, George S. Clinton; Choreography, Marguerite Derricks; Co-Producer, Gregg Taylor; Associate Producers, Katherine E. Beyda, Marco Schnabel; Visual Effects Supervisor, David D. Johnson; Visual Effects, Pacific Vision Productions; a Gratitude International, Team Todd/Moving Pictures production; Dolby; Super 35 Panavision; Deluxe color; Rated PG-13; 95 minutes; Release date: July 26, 2002

Michael Caine, Beyoncé Knowles, Mike Myers

Mike Myers (center)

Michael Caine

CAST

Austin Powers/Dr. Evil/Goldmember/Fat Bastard	Mike Myers
Foxxy Cleopatra	Beyoncé Knowles
Scott Evil	Seth Green
Basil Exposition	Michael York
Number Two	Robert Wagner
Frau Farbissina	Mindy Sterling
Mini Me	Verne Troyer
Nigel Powers	Michael Caine
Number Three	Fred Savage
Fook Mi	Diane Mizota
Fook Yu	Carrie Ann Inaba
Mr. Roboto	Nobu Matsuhisa
Young Austin	Aaron Himelstein
Young Evil	Josh Zuckerman
Young Basil	Eddie Adams
Young Number Two	Evan Farmer
Physician	Neil Mullarkey
Henchman Sailor	Eric Winzenried
Prisoner #2	Tommy "Tiny" Lister
French Teacher	Nicole Hiltz
Headmaster	Jimmy Piddock
Judge	Esther Scott
Anchor Woman	Leyna Nguyen
The Queen	Jeanette Charles
Japanese Pedestrians	Brian Tee, Masi Oka
General Clark	Kevin Cooney
Johnson	Clint Howard
Royal Guard	Michael McDonald
Vendors	Donna D'Errico-Sixx, Fred Stoller
Shirtless Fan A	Brad Grunberg
Shirtless Fan T	Greg Grunberg
Sumo Referee	Ren Urano
Sumo Wrestler	Nate K. Kange
Austin's Mom	Kinga Phillips
Young Nigel	Scott Aukerman
Toothless Gardener	John Donovan

Themselves . . . . .Tom Cruise, Danny DeVito, Quincy Jones, Ozzy Osbourne, Gwyneth Paltrow, Kevin Spacey, Steven Spielberg, Britney Spears, John Travolta and Masa Kanome (Fountain Security Guard), Hideo Kimura, Hiroshi Otaguro (Japanese Surveillance Guards), Kevin Stea (Austinpussy Assistant Director), Linda Kim (Geisha Secretary), Anna Marie Goddard, Nina Kaczorowski, Tammy Vanderpool, Nikki Ziering (Henchwomen), Sybil Azur, Nicole Humphries (Foxxy's Backup Dancers), Susanna Hoffs (Jillian Shagwell, Ming Tea Member), Stuart Johnson (Trevor Eggberth, Ming Tea Member), Matthew Sweet (Syd Belvedere, Ming Tea Member), Christopher Ward (Manny Sticksman, Ming Tea Member), Patrice Fisher, Timothy G. Anderson, Faune A. Chambers, Kelly Cooper, R.J. Durell, Shaun Earl, Michelle Elkin, Jennifer Hamilton, Hunter Hamilton, Michael Higgins, Mark Meismer, Mandy Moore, Ayesha Orange, Nathan Prevost, Liz Ramos, Shealan Spencer, Kevin Stea, Becca Sweitzer, Salvatore Vassallo, Robert Vinson (Dancers), Annie Barsky, Linda Chmiel, Sharon Ferguson, Trey Knight, Angela Meryl, Brian Richardson, Kimberlee Suerth, Lakisha Swift (Skaters)

Secret Agent Austin Powers travels back in time to 1975 in order to save his father who has been kidnapped by the evil Goldmember. The third *Austin Powers* film from New Line Cinema, following *Austin Powers: International Man of Mystery* (1997), and *Austin Powers: The Spy Who Shagged Me* (1999), with Myers, Wagner, Green, Sterling, and York repeating their roles from both films, and Troyer returning for the second time.

© New Line Cinema

Beyoncé Knowles, Mike Myers

Seth Green

Mindy Sterling

Michael York

Verne Troyer, Mike Myers

Verne Troyer

Mike Myers

Zeb Zoober, Beary

THE COUNTRY BEARS

(WALT DISNEY PICTURES) Producers, Andrew Gunn, Jeffrey Chernov; Director, Peter Hastings; Screenplay, Mark Perez; Based on Walt Disney's Country Bear Jamboree; Photography, C. Mitchell Amundsen; Designer, Dan Bishop; Costumes, Genevieve Tyrrell; Editors, George Bowers, Seth Flaum; Music, Christopher Young; Music Supervisor, Nora Felder; Original Songs, John Hiatt; Animatronic Bears Designed and Built by Jim Henson's Creature Shop; Choreographers, Marguerite Derricks, Peggy Holmes; Puppeteer Coordinator, Michelan Sisti; Casting, Ruth Lambert; Dolby; Panavision; Technicolor; Rated G; 88 minutes; Release date: July 26, 2002

CAST

Reed Thimple . . . . .Christopher Walken
Norbert Barrington . . . . .Stephen Tobolowsky
Officer Hamm . . . . .Daryl "Chill" Mitchell
Roadie . . . . .M.C. Gainey
Officer Cheets/Voice of Ted . . . . .Diedrich Bader
Rip Holland . . . . .Alex Rocco
Mrs. Barrington . . . . .Meagen Fay
Dex Barrington . . . . .Eli Marienthal
Cha-Cha . . . . .Queen Latifah
Voice of Beary . . . . .Haley Joel Osment
and Chip Chinery (Tom Tamina), Carolyn Almos (Tina Tamina), Marcus Knight (Chef), Michael Lawrence Morgan (Benny Bogswaggle), Alpheus Merchant (Elderly Black Man), Daniel Escobar (Store Manager), Christopher Darga (Mr. Slamboni), Jess Harnell (Long-Haired Dude), Ann Hastings (Elderly Woman), Paul Rugg (TV Reporter), Dennis E. O'Donnell, Michael R. Hastings, Peter Leinheiser, Art Repola (Wedding Band Members), Betty Weiss (Cashier), Jennifer S. Paige (Waitress), Josh Quirk (Fry Cook), Sean O'Connell (Grip), Larry Burke (Video Roadie), Krystal Marie Harris, Don Henley, Wyclef Jean, Elton John, Willie Nelson, Bonnie Raitt, Brian Setzer, Don Was, Xzibit (Themselves); VOICES: Candy Ford (Trixie), James Gammon (Big Al), Brad Garrett (Fred), Toby Huss (Tennessee), Kevin Michael Richardson (Henry), Stephen Root (Zeb)

An 11-year-old bear, feeling it is time to move on from his human family, sets out to reunite the members of his favorite band, the Country Bears, to hold a benefit concert to save Country Bear Hall.

THE KID STAYS IN THE PICTURE

(FOCUS FEATURES) Producers, Brett Morgen, Nanette Burstein, Graydon Carter; Directors, Brett Morgen, Nanette Burstein; Adapted for the screen by Brett Morgen; Based on the book by Robert Evans; Co-Producers, Kate Driver, Chris Garrett, Sara Marks; Associate Producer, Christopher Keene; Photography, John Bailey; Editor, Jun Diaz; Music, Jeff Danna; a Highway Films and Ministry of Propaganda Films production; Dolby; Color; Rated R: 93 minutes; Release date: July 26, 2002. Documentary on Robert Evans' rise from failed actor to successful film producer, and his inevitable downfall, featuring Robert Evans and Dustin Hoffman

© USA Films

Ali MacGraw, Robert Evans

Robert Evans

Blair Underwood, Julia Roberts

FULL FRONTAL

(MIRAMAX) Producers, Scott Kramer, Gregory Jacobs; Director, Steven Soderbergh; Screenplay, Coleman Hough; Photography, Peter Andrews (Steven Soderbergh); Editor, Sarah Flack; Casting, Debra Zane; Dolby; Digital Video; Color; Rated R; 101 minutes; Release date: August 2, 2002

CAST

Bill/Gus	David Duchovny
Hitler	Nicky Katt
Lee	Catherine Keener
Linda	Mary McCormack
Carl	David Hyde Pierce
Catherine/Francesca	Julia Roberts
Nicholas/Calvin	Blair Underwood
Arty/Ed	Enrico Colantoni
Lucy	Erika Alexander
Heather	Tracy Vilar

and Brandon Keener (Francesca's Assistant), Jeff Garlin (Harvey), David Alan Basche (Nicholas' Agent), Nancy Lenehan (Woman on Plane), Brad Rowe (Sam Osbourne), David Fincher (Film Director), Jerry Weintraub (Jerry), Rainn Wilson, Dina Waters, Sandra Oh (Fired Employees), Eddie McClintock (David), Justina Machado (Linda's Friend in Kitchen), Meagan Fay (Diane), Joe Chrest, Wayne Pére (Sex Shop Men), January Jones (Tracy), Mike Malone (Mike), Anthony Powers (Message Client), Alison Ebbert (Hitler Girlfriend), Jennifer Brusciano (Hitler Hitchhiker), Cole Andersen (Freud), Al Ahlf (Hitler Guard), Lacy Livingston (Miramax Receptionist), Patrick Fischer (Harvey, Probably's Assistant), Nathalie Seaver (Clothing Store Owner), Soledad St. Hilaire (Soledad), Roger Garcia (Vampire Neighbor), Lauren Schwaar (Concierge), Maria Rogers (Woman in Bed), Dawn Suggs (Hotel Hostess), Charlotte Puckett (Hotel Waitress), Chance Robertson (Biker), Monica Lee Burland, Keen Wood (Theater Patrons), Cynthia Gibb (Pregnant Woman), Andrew Connolly, Karen Woodley-Connolly, Chris DeRose, Randy Lowell, Pliny Porter, Coleman Hough (Partygoers), Terence Stamp (Man on Man/Himself), Brad Pitt (Himself), Camille Wainwright (Daphne)

A glimpse at a seemingly disparate group of Los Angeles inhabitants over a 24-hour period, including those working on a Hollywood opus called "Rendezvous."

THE MASTER OF DISGUISE

(COLUMBIA) Producers, Sid Ganis, Alex Siskin, Barry Bernardi, Todd Garner; Executive Producers, Adam Sandler, Jack Giarraputo; Director, Perry Andelin Blake; Screenplay, Dana Carvey, Harris Goldberg; Photography, Peter Lyons Collister; Designer, Alan Au; Costumes, Mona May; Editors, Peck Prior, Sandy Solowitz; Music, Marc Ellis; Music Supervisor, Michael Dilbeck; Special Makeup Effects Creator, Kevin Yagher; Casting, Roger Mussenden, Elizabeth Torres; a Revolution Studios presentation of a Happy Madison production in association with Out of the Blue Entertainment; Dolby; Deluxe color; Rated PG; 80 minutes; Release date: August 2, 2002

CAST

Pistachio Disguisey	Dana Carvey
Jennifer	Jennifer Esposito
Grandfather Disguisey	Harold Gould
Frabbrizio Disguisey	James Brolin
Devlin Bowman	Brent Spiner
Mother Disguisey	Edie McClurg

and Austin Wolff (Barney), Maria Canals (Sophia), Robert Machary (Texas Man), Rachel Lederman (Texas Wife), Mark Devine (Trent), Jay Johnston (Rex), Michael Bailey Smith, Vincent Riverside, Mark Ginther, Carrick O'Quinn, Mitch Silpa, John Tenn (Henchmen), Virginia Hawkins (Interview Woman), Jessica Simpson, Michael Johnson, Bo Derek, Kenan Thompson, Jesse Ventura, Paula Abdul (Themselves), Jonathan Loughran, Ted Rooney (Security Guards), Brandon Molale (Doorman), Erick Avari (Cigar Maker), Phil Jones, Michael DeLuise, Larry Cedar (Businessmen), Andrew Shaifer (Liberty Bell Security Guard), Vincent Castellanos (Art Dealer), Roger Mussenden (Waiter), Al Goto, Simon Rhee (Ninja Warriors), Kevin Nealon (White Collar Executive), Bill Cho Lee (Mongolian Elder), Chao-Li Chi (Mongolian), Steve Gormley (German Businessman), Christel Smith (German Businesswoman), Ava Metz (Another German), Barry Bernardi (Bernardo), Brian Catalano (Italian Officer), Gabriel Pimentel (Boxing Dummy), Martha Del Rio (Puerto Rican Housekeeper), Guelmari Oppenheimer (Waitress), Tracy E. Wilson (Partygoer), Patricia De Leon (Waitress), Phillip Fischer (Bully), Steven Hack (Chemistry Teacher), Dane Morris, Cole Mitchell Sprouse, Dylan Thomas Sprouse (Young Pistachio), Bryan Jefrey Price (Jock), Andy Morrow, Naya Rivera, Julius Ritter, Brighton Hertzford (Captain America Kids), Sandra Lindqvist (Bartender), Eugene C. Palmer (Chef), Leland Crooke (Appraiser), Mike Johnson, Michael Lee Phillips, Jr. (Constitution Security Guards), Buddy Bolton (Abe Lincoln), Stuart Quan, Spencer Sano, Hiro Hoda, Johnny Nguyen, Yoshio Izuka, Ronn Surels, Andy Cheng, Steven Ho (Ninjas), Tony Wilde (Doug), Burgland Icey, Leasi Andrews, Anna-Marie Simone Goddard, Theresa Madelin Lin (Big Bottom Girls), Adrian Armas, Gustavo Vargas, Jessica Keller, Paul Benshoof, Oscar Orosco, Andrea Bogart, Paulette Maxwell (Group Dancers), Kevin Nealon (White Collar Executive)

After his parents are kidnapped by a nefarious criminal master mind, mild-mannered waiter Pistachio Disguisey is told of his inherited family talent for morphing into a wide range of different personalities, a gift he uses to help him save the day.

Dana Carvey, Jennifer Esposito

SIGNS

(TOUCHSTONE) Producers, M. Night Shyamalan, Frank Marshall, Sam Mercer; Director/Screenplay, M. Night Shyamalan; Executive Producer, Kathleen Kennedy; Photography, Tak Fujimoto; Designer, Larry Fulton; Editor, Barbara Tulliver; Costumes, Ann Roth; Visual Effects and Animation, Industrial Light & Magic; Music, James Newton Howard; Casting, Douglas Aibel; a Blinding Edge Pictures/Kennedy/Marshall production; Dolby; DuArt color; Rated PG-13; 107 minutes; Release date: August 2, 2002

Mel Gibson, Rory Culkin

CAST

Graham Hess	Mel Gibson
Merrill Hess	Joaquin Phoenix
Morgan Hess	Rory Culkin
Bo Hess	Abigail Breslin
Officer Paski	Cherry Jones
Ray Reddy	M. Night Shyamalan
Colleen Hess	Patricia Kalember
SFC Cunningham	Ted Sutton
Tracey Abernathy	Merritt Weaver
Mr. Nathan	Lanny Flaherty
Mrs. Nathan	Marion McCorry
Lionel Prichard	Michael Showalter
Brazilian Birthday Boy	Kevin Pires
Columbia University Professor	Clifford David
Sarah Hughes	Rhonda Overby
TV Anchor	Greg Wood

and Paul Nolan (Voice of Mexico City Reporter), Ukee Washington (Off Screen TV Anchor), Babita Hariani (Car Radio Voice), Adam Way (Radio Eye Witness), Angela Eckert (Soda Commercial Girl), Jose L. Rodriguez (Radio Host), Paul Wilson, Thomas Griffin (Soda Commercial Singers), Caseline T. Kunene, Ambition Sandamela (Sound Effects Voices)

Widowed farmer Graham Hess discovers a series of mysterious crop circles on his land, leading to the speculation that visitors from another world might be planning a confrontation with Earth.

© Touchstone

Rory Culkin, Mel Gibson, Abigail Breslin   Rory Culkin, Mel Gibson, Abigail Breslin, Joaquin Phoenix

Joaquin Phoenix, Mel Gibson, Rory Culkin, Cherry Jones

Mel Gibson

Mel Gibson

Mel Gibson, Joaquin Phoenix

Joaquin Phoenix, Mel Gibson

THE GOOD GIRL

(FOX SEARCHLIGHT) Producer, Matthew Greenfield; Executive Producers, Kirk D'Amico, Philip von Alvensleben, Carol Baum; Director, Miguel Arteta; Screenplay, Mike White; Co-Producers, Shelly Glasser, Gina Kwon; Photography, Enrique Chediak; Designer, Daniel Bradford; Costumes, Nancy Steiner; Music, Joey Waronker, Tony Maxwell, James O'Brien, Mark Orton; Casting, Joanne Colbert; a Myriad Pictures presentation, in association with In-Motion AG, WMF V and Hungry Eye Lowland Pictures, of a Flan de Coco Film; Dolby; Color; Rated R; 124 minutes; Release date: August 7, 2002

CAST

Justine Last	Jennifer Aniston
Cheryl	Zooey Deschanel
Holden Worther	Jake Gyllenhaal
Bubba	Tim Blake Nelson
Phil Last	John C. Reilly
Gwen Jackson	Deborah Rush
Corny	Mike White
Jack Field, Your Store Manager	John Carroll Lynch
Heavy Set Woman	Jacquie Barnbrook
Haggard Woman	Annie O'Donnell
Mr. Worther	John Doe
Mrs. Worther	Roxanne Hart
Lester	Jonathan Shere
Big Haired Woman	Alice Amter
Old Woman	Jean Rhodes
Nurse	Aimee Garcia
Blackberry Vendor	Lalo Guerrero
Floberta	Michael Hyatt
Reporter	Ken Rudulph

Zooey Deschanel, Jennifer Aniston

Unfulfilled Justine Last, hoping to find some variation in her dead-end existence in a small Texas town, begins a heated affair with a young, sensitive co-worker.

© Fox Searchlight

John C. Reilly, Jennifer Aniston

Jennifer Aniston, Jake Gyllenhaal

Jake Gyllenhaal

SPY KIDS 2: THE ISLAND OF LOST DREAMS

(DIMENSION) Producers, Elizabeth Avellan, Robert Rodriguez; Executive Producers, Bob Weinstein, Harvey Weinstein; Director/Screenplay/Editor/Director of Digital Photography/Designer, Robert Rodriguez; Costumes, Graciela Mazon; Music, Robert Rodriguez, John Debney; Visual Effects Supervisors, Robert Rodriguez, Daniel Leduc; Casting, Mary Vernieu; a Troublemaker Studios production; Distributed by Miramax Films; Dolby; Deluxe color; Rated PG; 100 minutes; Release date: August 7, 2002

CAST

Gregorio Cortez	Antonio Banderas
Ingrid Cortez	Carla Gugino
Carmen Cortez	Alexa Vega
Juni Cortez	Daryl Sabara
Donnagon Giggles	Mike Judge
Grandfather	Ricardo Montalban
Grandmother	Holland Taylor
President of the USA	Christopher McDonald
Machete	Danny Trejo
Fegan Floop	Alan Cumming
Alexander Minion	Tony Shalhoub
Gary Giggles	Matt O'Leary
Alexandra, President's Daughter	Taylor Momsen
Gerti Giggles	Emily Osment
Felix Gumm	Cheech Marin
Romero	Steve Buscemi

and Dale Dudley (Head Magna Man), Troy Robinson (Magna Man/Waiter), Ron Hayden (Main Secret Service Agent), Brian Thornton, Mark Turner (Secret Service Agents), Bill Paxton (Dinky Winks, Theme Park Owner), Angela Lanza (Park Public Relations), Felix Sabates, Lynda Sabates, Alexandra Sabates, Victoria Sabates (Test Family), Jasmine Marin (Spy Girl)

Juni and Carmen Cortez, the children of spies Gregorio and Ingrid Cortez, head for a remote island to find out who is responsible for the theft of the Transmooker, a device that can disable the world's electricity. Sequel to the 2001 Dimension release *Spy Kids*, with many of the principals repeating their roles.

© Dimension

Daryl Sabara, Alexa Vega

Sylvie Testud

Paul Rudd, Romany Malco

THE CHÂTEAU

(IFC FILMS) Producers, Scott Macaulay, Robin O'Hara; Executive Producers, John Penotti, Fisher Stevens, Bradley Yonover, Dolly Hall; Director, Jesse Peretz; Based on a concept by Jesse Peretz, Thomas Bidegain; Line Producer, Amalric de Pancharra; Photography, Tom Richmond; Designer, Christian Marti; Costumes, Nathalie de Roscoat; Editors, James Lyons, Steve Hamilton; Music, Nathan Larson, Patrik Bartosh; Casting, Antoinette Boulat; a GreeneStreet Films presentation of a Forensic Films production in association with Crossroads Films; Dolby; Color; Rated R; 91 minutes; Release date: August 9, 2002

CAST

Graham Granville	Paul Rudd
Allen Granville	Romany Malco
Jean	Didier Flamand
Isabelle	Sylvie Testud
Pierre	Philippe Nahon
Sabine	Maria Verdi
Sonny	Donal Logue

and Nathalie Jouen (Real Estate Agent), Marie Girard (Blonde Girl), Estelle Sobelman (Estelle Kirsner), Jim Lyons, Pierre Michaud, Christian Marti (Buyers)

Having unexpectedly inherited a French château from their great-uncle, brothers Graham and Allen Granville show up at the site with the intention of making an easy transaction, only to discover that the building is a shambles and inhabited by a staff that refuses to vacate the premises.

© IFC Films

XXX

Asia Argento, Vin Diesel

Samuel L. Jackson, Vin Diesel (on screen)

(COLUMBIA) Producer, Neal H. Moritz; Executive Producers, Vin Diesel, George Zakk, Arne L. Schmidt, Todd Garner; Director, Rob Cohen; Screenplay, Rich Wilkes; Photography, Dean Semler; Designer, Gavin Bocquet; Costumes, Sanja Milkovic Hays; Editors, Chris Lebenzon, Paul Rubell, Joel Negron; Co-Producers, Creighton Bellinger, Derek Dauchy; Music, Randy Edelman; Music Supervisor, Kathy Nelson; Visual Effects Supervisor, Joel Hynek; Casting, Ronna Kress, Kate Dowd; Stunts, Lance Gilbert, James Arnett, Pavel Cajzl; a Revolution Studios presentation of a Neal H. Moritz production; Dolby; Panavision; Deluxe color; Rated PG-13; 124 minutes; Release date: August 9, 2002

CAST

Xander Cage . . . . .Vin Diesel
Yelena . . . . .Asia Argento
Yorgi . . . . .Marton Csokas
Agent Augustus Gibbons .Samuel L. Jackson
Toby Lee Shavers . . . . .Michael Roof
Milan Sova . . . . .Richy Müller
Kirill . . . . .Werner Daehn
Kolya . . . . .Petr Jakl
Viktor . . . . .Jan Filipensky
Senator Dick Hotchkiss . . . . .Tom Everett
El Jefe . . . . .Danny Trejo
Agent Jim McGrath .Thomas Ian Griffith
J.J. . . . . .Eve
Jordan King . . . . .Leila Arcieri
Agent Roger Donnan . . . . .William Hope
James Tannick . . . . .Ted Maynard
Virg . . . . .Joe Bucaro
and Chris Gann (T.J.), Martin Hub (Ivan Podrov), Radek Tomecka (Ivan Pedgrag), Mary-Pat Green (Waitress), Tanner Gill (Trucker), Scott Waugh (Stock Broker), Vaclav Chalupa (Nervous Hacker), Martina Smukova (Czech Cop), Teejay Boyce (Bimbo Intern), Tony Hawk (Caddy Driver), Mat Hoffman, Brian Deegan (Extreme Guys), Mike Vallely (Skater), Mike Escamilla (Ramp Truck Passenger), Rob Wells (Hillside Video Shooter), Rick Thorne, Cary Hart (Caddy Passengers), Colin McKay (Van Driver), Jason Ellis (Van Video Shooter), Marek Vasut (Czech General), Lubos Pospisil (Czech Major), Ivo Niederle (Head Chemist), Vitezslav Bouchner (Head Technician), Esteban Cueto (Gold Tooth Narco), Martin Barta, Martina Bauerova (Opera Singers), Rich Wilkes (Tall Guy), F. Valentino Morales (Short Order Cook/NSA Agent), Leonard Thomas (NSA Agent), Ivan Rueda, Joshua Montero (Child Field Workers), Armando Cantina (Field Worker), Roman Matrka (Czech Agent), Alena Cihalikova (Xander's Bedroom Dancer), Rammstein, Orbital (Themselves), Michal Muller (Zither Player)

Xander Cage, an extreme sports enthusiast, is recruited to be a secret agent in order to infiltrate a dangerous gang of European criminals bent on unleashing a series of biological attacks on various world cities.

© Columbia

Vin Diesel

Vin Diesel

BLOOD WORK

Clint Eastwood, Anjelica Huston

Wanda De Jesus

(WARNER BROS.) Producer/Director, Clint Eastwood; Executive Producer, Robert Lorenz; Screenplay, Brian Helgeland, based on the novel by Michael Connelly; Co-Producer, Judie G. Hoyt; Photography, Tom Stern; Designer, Henry Bumstead; Music, Lennie Niehaus; Costumes, Deborah Hopper; Editor, Joel Cox; Casting, Phyllis Huffman; a Malpaso Production; Dolby; Panavision; Technicolor; Rated R; 111 minutes; Release date: August 9, 2002

CAST

Terry McCaleb . . . . .Clint Eastwood
Buddy Noone . . . . .Jeff Daniels
Dr. Bonnie Fox . . . . .Anjelica Huston
Graciella Rivers . . . . .Wanda De Jesús
Jaye Winston . . . . .Tina Lifford
Detective Ronaldo Arrango . . . . .Paul Rodriguez
Detective John Waller . . . . .Dylan Walsh
Raymond . . . . .Mason Lucero
Mr. Toliver . . . . .Gerry Becker
James Lockridge . . . . .Rick Hoffman
Mrs. Cordell . . . . .Alix Koromzay
Bolotov . . . . .Igor Jijikine
Reporters . . . . .Dina Eastwood, Beverly Leech
Mrs. Kang . . . . .June Kyoko Lu
Mr. Kang . . . . Chao-Li Chi
Captain . . . . .Glenn Morshower
Restaurant Manager . . . . .Robert Harvey
Young Detective . . . . .Matt Huffman
James Cordell . . . . .Mark Thomason
Gloria Torres . . . . .Maria Quiban
and Brent Hinkley (Cab Driver), Natalia Ongaro (Receptionist), Amanda Carlin (Officer Manager), Ted Rooney, P.J. Byrne (Forensics), Sam Jaeger (Deputy), Derric Nugent (L.A.P.D. Officer)

When retired FBI profiler Terry McCaleb discovers that his life-saving heart transplant was made possible by the victim of an unsolved homicide, he sets out to find the link between that killing and a series of other murders.

© Warner Bros.

Dylan Walsh, Paul Rodriguez

Clint Eastwood, Jeff Daniels

BLUE CRUSH

Mika Boorem, Michelle Rodriguez, Kate Bosworth, Sanoe Lake

Kate Bosworth, Keala Kennelly

Matthew Davis

Matthew Davis, Kate Bosworth

(UNIVERSAL) Producers, Brian Grazer, Karen Kehela; Executive Producers, Buffy Shutt, Kathy Jones, Louis G. Friedman; Director, John Stockwell; Screenplay, Lizzy Weiss, John Stockwell; Based on the magazine article "Surf Girls of Maui" by Susan Orlean; Co-Producer, Rick Dallago; Photography, David Hennings; Designer, Tom Meyer; Costumes, Susan Matheson; Editor, Emma E. Hickox; Music, Paul Haslinger; Music Supervisor, Dana Sano; 2nd Unit/Stunts, Gregory J. Barnett; Casting, Randi Hiller, Sarah Halley Finn; an Imagine Entertainment presentation of a Brian Grazer production; Dolby; Color; Rated PG-13; 104 minutes; Release date: August 16, 2002

CAST

Anne Marie . . . . .Kate Bosworth
Matt . . . . .Matthew Davis
Eden . . . . .Michelle Rodriguez
Lena . . . . .Sanoe Lake
Penny . . . . .Mika Boorem
Drew . . . . .Chris Taloa
Kala . . . . .Kala Alexander
JJ . . . . .Ruben Tejada
Kaupena . . . . .Kaupena Miranda
Asa . . . . .Asa Aquino
Leslie . . . . .Faizon Love
Fiji . . . . .George Veikoso
Omar . . . . .Shaun Robinson
Paul . . . . .Paul Hatter
Tamayo . . . . .Tamayo Perry
Mr. Pukui . . . . .James Grant Benton
Mrs. Milari . . . . .Blossom Lam
and Paul Chicoine (Hotel Manager), Deniese Bee (Cashier), Alana Mock (Girls at Gas Station), Fredrick Patacchia, Jr. (Ben), Jason Castillo (Jimmy), Kimo Kahoano (Luau MC), Jenn Boneza (Marisa), Kim Chipman (Pam), Tara Sweatt (Devon), Donna Perry (Denise), Sonny Miller (Contest Announcer), Carol Anne Philips (Event Coordinator), Keala Kennelly, Kate Skarratt, Rochelle Ballard, Layne Beachley, Megan Abubo (Themselves), Brian L. Keaulana, Kai Garcia, Daryl Stant (Lifeguards), Chad Lerma (Chiropractor), Daren Crawford (Surf Magazine Reporter), Todd Messick (Surf Photographer), Zandi Eguires, Sage Erickson (Girls on Beach), Jessica Trent Nicols (Billabong Rep), Jenn Marr (Surf Rep), Braden Dias, Tom Carroll, Jaime O'Brien, Rico Jimenez, Bruce Irons, Larry Rios, Kalani Robb, Perry Danes, Makua Rothman, Gavin Sutherland (Surfers), Coco Ho (Young Anne Marie)

Anne Marie arrives in Hawaii to compete in the dangerous, male-dominated Pipe Masters surf competition on the North Shore of Oahu.

© Universal

Kate Bosworth

POSSESSION

Gwyneth Paltrow, Aaron Eckhart

Gwyneth Paltrow, Aaron Eckhart

(FOCUS FEATURES/WARNER BROS.) Producers, Paula Weinstein, Barry Levinson; Executive Producers, David Barron, Len Amato; Director, Neil LaBute; Screenplay, David Henry Hwang, Laura Jones, Neil LaBute; Based on the novel by A.S. Byatt; Co-Producer, Stephen Pevner; Photography, Jean-Yves Escoffier; Designer, Luciana Arrighi; Costumes, Jenny Beavan; Editor, Claire Simpson; Music, Gabriel Yared; Casting, Mary Selway; a Baltimore/Spring Creek Pictures production in association with Contagious Films; Dolby; Panavision; Color; Rated PG-13; 103 minutes; Release date: August 16, 2002

CAST

Maud Bailey . . . . .Gwyneth Paltrow
Roland Michell . . . . .Aaron Eckhart
Randolph Henry Ash . . . . .Jeremy Northam
Christabel LaMotte . . . . .Jennifer Ehle
Blanche Glover . . . . .Lena Headey
Ellen Ash . . . . .Holly Aird
Fergus Wolfe . . . . .Toby Stephens
Cropper . . . . .Trevor Eve
Blackadder . . . . .Tom Hickey
Paola . . . . .Georgia Mackenzie
Euan . . . . .Tom Hollander
Sir George . . . . .Graham Crowden
Lady Bailey . . . . .Anna Massey
Hildebrand . . . . .Craig Crosbie
Crabb-Robinson . . . . .Christopher Good
Sabine . . . . .Elodie Frenck
Woman in Hotel . . . . .Victoria Bensted
Candi . . . . .Shelley Conn
Shop Owner . . . . .Jonty Stephens
Auction Director .Alexi Kaye Campbell
Librarian . . . . .Hugh Simon
and Richard Heffer (Lord Lytton), Felicity Brangan (Ash's Maid), Holly Earl (May Bailey), Kate O'Toole (Mrs. Jameson), Meg Wynn Owen (Mrs. Lees), Roger Hammond (Professor Spear), Jeanne Marine (University Secretary)

Maud and Roland, a pair of scholars, team to research the relationship between two poets of the Victorian era after discovering a cache of love letters that appear to be correspondences between their subjects.

© Focus Features

Jennifer Ehle, Jeremy Northam

Jennifer Ehle, Jeremy Northam

Robin Williams

Connie Nielsen, Dylan Smith, Michael Vartan

Robin Williams, Connie Nielsen

(FOX SEARCHLIGHT) Producers, Christine Vachon, Pamela Koffler, Stan Wlodkowski; Executive Producers, Robert B. Sturm, Jeremy W. Barber, John Wells; Director/Screenplay, Mark Romanek; Photography, Jeff Cronenweth; Designer, Tom Foden; Costumes, Arianne Philipps; Editor, Jeffrey Ford; Music, Reinhold Heil, Johnny Klimek; Music Supervisor, Chris Douridas; Casting, Deborah Aquila, Tricia Wood; a Killer Films/Laughlin Park Pictures production, presented in association with Catch 23 Entertainment; Dolby; Deluxe color; Rated R; 96 minutes; Release date: August 21, 2002

CAST

Seymour "Sy" Parrish . . . . .Robin Williams
Nina Yorkin . . . . .Connie Nielsen
Will Yorkin . . . . .Michael Vartan
Jakob Yorkin . . . . .Dylan Smith
Maya Burson . . . . .Erin Daniels
Yoshi Araki . . . . .Paul Hansen Kim
Waitress . . . . .Lee Garlington
Bill Owens . . . . .Gary Cole
Mrs. Von Unwerth . . . . .Marion Calvert
Mr. Siskind . . . . .David Moreland
Young Father . . . . .Shaun P. O'Hagan
Amateur Porn Guy . . . . .Jim Rash
Repairman . . . . .Nick Searcy
Sav-Mart Clerk . . . . .Dave Engfer
Soccer Coach . . . . .Jimmy Shubert
Det. James Van Der Zee .Eriq La Salle
Det. Paul Outerbridge . . . . .Clark Gregg
Officer Lyon . . . . .Andrew A. Rolfes
Officer Bravo . . . . .Carmen Mormino
Superintendent . . . . .Izrel Katz
and Peter Mackenzie (Hotel Desk Manager), Andy Comeau (Duane), Robert Clotworthy (Eye Surgeon), Wayne Wilderson (Booking Clerk), Jeana Wilson (Nurse), Megan Corletto (Risa Owens)

A lonely photo developer, who takes a special interest in the lives of his customers, becomes obsessed with the Yorkins, whom he believes are the perfect family.

© Fox Searchlight

Robin Williams

UNDISPUTED

Ving Rhames, Wesley Snipes

Ving Rhames

(MIRAMAX) Producers, David Giler, Walter Hill, Brad Krevoy, Andrew Sugerman; Executive Producers, Avi Lerner, Sandra Schulberg, Rudolf Wiesmeier, Danny Dimbort, Trevor Short, Boaz Davidson, John Thompson, Wesley Snipes; Director, Walter Hill; Screenplay, David Giler, Walter Hill; Photography, Lloyd Ahern; Designer, Maria Caso; Costumes, Barbara Inglehart; Editor, Freeman Davies; Music, Stanley Clarke; Stunts/Fight Coordinator, Cole S. McKay; Casting, Ruben Cannon; a David Giler production, presented in association with Millennium Films in association with Hollywood Partners and Amen Ra Films and Motion Picture Corporation of America; Dolby; Panavision; CFI Color; Rated R; 94 minutes; Release date: August 23, 2002

CAST

Monroe Hutchens	Wesley Snipes
Iceman Chambers	Ving Rhames
Mendy Ripstein	Peter Falk
A.J. Mercker	Michael Rooker
Jesus "Chuy" Campos	Jon Seda
Mingo Pace	Wes Studi
Ratbag Dolan	Fisher Stevens
Yank Lewis	Dayton Callie
Al	Johnny Williams
Vinnie	Joe D'Angerio
Vern Van Zandt	Nils Allen Stewart
Warden Lipscom	Denis Arndt
Himself	Jim Lampley
Marvin Bonds	Ed Lover
Barry Pearl	Nicholas Cascone
Charles Soward	Bruce A. Young
Saladin	Byron Minns

and Master P, Silkk the Shocker, C-Murder, Boz (Rappers), Taylor Young (Emily Byrne), Susan Dalian (Jonelle), Johnathan Wesley Wallace (Antoine Bonét), J.W. Smith (Mess Guard), John David Jackson (Man), Michael Bailey Smith (Skinhead), Peter Jason (Oakland TV Announcer), Steve Heinze (Carlos), Ken Medlock (Guard #1), George Grigas (Tower Guard 1), Chris Wynne (Central Security Guard), George Christy, Jim Hensz, John D. Harrington (Reporters), Toby Gibson (Referee), Daren Libonatt (Ref), Rose Rollins (Tawnee Rawlins), Maureen O'Boyle (CNOX Interviewer), Elaine Kagan (Lady Judge), Sandra Vidal (Fight Fan)

Arrogant heavyweight fighter Iceman Chambers is sent to prison where an incarcerated gangster arranges a fight between Chambers and the lock-up's undefeated champ, Monroe Hutchens.

© Miramax

Peter Falk, Ving Rhames

Wesley Snipes

SIMONE

Al Pacino, Catherine Keener

Al Pacino, Rachel Roberts (on screen)

(NEW LINE CINEMA) Producer/Director/Screenplay, Andrew Niccol; Executive Producers, Bradley Cramp, Lynn Harris, Michael De Luca; Photography, Daniel Lupi; Designer, Jan Roelfs; Costumes, Elisabetta Beraldo; Music, Carter Burwell; Editor, Paul Rubell; Special Visual Effects, CIS Hollywood; Casting, Francine Maisler, Jon Stroheide; a Niccols Films production; Dolby; Panavision; Deluxe color; Rated PG-13; 118 minutes; Release date: August 23, 2002

CAST

Viktor Tarnasky	Al Pacino
Elaine Christian	Catherine Keener
Max Sayer	Pruitt Taylor Vince
Hal Sinclair	Jay Mohr
Milton	Jason Schwartzman
Frank Brand	Stanley Anderson
Lainey Christian	Evan Rachel Wood
Chief Detective	Daniel von Bargen
Simone	Rachel Roberts
Personal Assistant	Benjamin Salisbury
Nicola Anders	Winona Ryder
Hank Aleno	Elias Koteas
Studio Exectuives	Darnell Williams, Jim Rash, Ron Perkins
Kent	Jeffrey Pierce
Man in Suit	Jeff Williams

and Mitzi Martin, Carol Androsky, Christopher Neiman, Julie Jenkins, Derrex Brady, Lisa Cerasoli, Darin Heames, Patrick Dancy, Adrian R'Mante (Premiere Audience), David Doty (Theatre Owner), Maureen Mueller (Entertainment Reporter), Barry Papick (Security Guard), James Gleason, Andi Carnick, Richard Saxton, Vincent Boling, Mark Thompson, Keith MacKechnie (Reporters), Alan Loayza (Valet Manager), Chris Coppola (*Echo* Photographer), Lombardo Boyar (Paparazzi Photographer), Jenni Blong (Jane), Susan Chuang (Lotus), Robert Musgrove (Mac), Deborah Rawlings (Corel), Christina Rydell (Claris), Rod Simmons (Hewlett), Hal Ozsan (Hotel Concierge), Jaehne Moebius (Drunk Woman), Claudia Jordan (Simone Lookalike), Henry D. Zapata (Studio Executive), Christopher Comes (Concert Promoter), Chip Pope, Gordon Simmons (Concert Technician), Teresa Parente, Bill A. Jones (Talk Show Hosts), Daniel Do (Monk), Clyde Tull (Priest), Moss Mossberg (Rabbi), Ronnie W. Elliot Sr. (Arresting Officer), Charles Noland (Detective), Christopher Marley (Diver), Sean Cullen (Lawyer), Alec Murdock (VBC Anchor), Rebecca Romijn-Stamos (Faith)

When his temperamental star walks off his latest project, Viktor Tarnasky, a once promising director, comes up with the idea of creating his own computer generated actress to fill the role, a ruse he keeps from the public who fall madly in love with the new star.

Rachel Roberts

Pruitt Taylor Vince, Jason Schwartzman

CITY BY THE SEA

(WARNER BROS.) Producers, Brad Grey, Elie Samaha, Michael Caton-Jones, Matthew Baer; Executive Producers, Andrew Stevens, Dan Klores, Don Carmody, Roger Paradiso; Director, Michael Caton-Jones; Screenplay, Ken Hixon; Based on the *Esquire* article "Mark of a Murderer" by Michael McAlary; Photography, Karl Walter Lindenlaub; Designer, Jane Musky; Costumes, Richard Owings; Editor, Jim Clark; Music, John Murphy; Co-Producer, Laura Viederman; Casting, Amanda Mackey Johnson, Cathy Sandrich Gelfond; a Franchise Pictures presentation of a Brad Grey Pictures production; Dolby; Super 35 Widescreen; Deluxe color; Rated R; 108 minutes; Release date: September 6, 2002

CAST

Vincent LaMarca . . . . .Robert De Niro
Michelle . . . . .Frances McDormand
Joey LaMarca . . . . .James Franco
Gina . . . . .Eliza Dushku
Spyder . . . . .William Forsythe
Reg Duffy . . . . .George Dzundza
Maggie . . . . .Patti LuPone
Dave Simon . . . . .Anson Mount
Henderson . . . . .John Doman
Snake . . . . .Brian Tarantina
Vanessa Hansen . . . . .Drena De Niro
Herb . . . . .Michael P. Moran
Rossi . . . . .Nestor Serrano
Arnie . . . . .Matthew Cowles
Margery . . . . .Linda Emond
Carl . . . . .Cyrus Farmer
Picasso . . . . .Jay Boryea
Lieutenant Katt . . . . .Leo Burmester
A.P.C. Johnson . . . . .Gregg Edelman
and Jason Winther (Jason), Orlando Pabjoy (Will), Leslie Cohen (Jean), Michelle Daimer (Terry), Stephi Lineberg (Bree), Mark La Mura (Mayor Jackson), Jill Marie Lawrence (Evelyn), Teresa Kelsey (Reporter Laura), Teresa Woods (Reporter Carol), Michael Dellafemina (Angelo LaMarca), Jim Marcus (Medical Examiner), Joanne Lamstein (Screaming Teenager), Dominick Angelo Cangro, Pasquale Enrico Cangro (Baby Angelo)

New York City detective Vincent LaMarca comes home to the ruins of the shore town of Long Beach to investigate a murder, the chief suspect being his estranged, drug addicted son Joey.

© Warner Bros.

Anson Mount, George Dzundza, Robert De Niro

James Franco, Robert De Niro

Eliza Dushku

Frances McDormand, Robert De Niro

SWIMFAN

(20TH CENTURY FOX) Producers, John Penotti, Allison Lyon Segan, Joe Caracciolo, Jr.; Executive Producers, Fisher Stevens, Tim Williams; Director, John Polson; Screenplay, Charles Bohl, Phillip Schneider; Photography, Giles Nuttgens; Designer, Kalina Ivanov; Costumes, Arjun Bhasin; Co-Producers, Marcy Drogin, Jamie Gordon, Bradley Yonover; Music, Louis Febre; Music Themes, John Debney; Executive Music Producer, Alex Steyermark; Casting, Mindy Marin, Amanda Harding; a GreenStreet Films/Cobalt Media Group/Further Films production; Dolby; J-D-C Scope; Deluxe color; Rated PG-13; 85 minutes; Release date: September 6, 2002.

CAST

Ben Cronin	Jesse Bradford
Madison Bell	Erika Christensen
Amy Miller	Shiri Appleby
Carla	Kate Burton
Josh	Clayne Crawford
Randy	Jason Ritter
Rene	Kia Joy Goodwin
Coach Simkins	Dan Hedaya
Mr. Tillman	Michael Higgins
Detective John Zabel	Nick Sandow
Mrs. Egan	Pamela Isaacs

and James Debello (Dante), Phyllis Somerville (Aunt Gretchen), Tom Cappadona (Janitor), Malcolm Barrett (Jock), Ken Triwush (Big Man), Peter Hermann (ER Doctor), John Knox (ER Guard), Amy Mapother (Petite Nurse), Patricia Rae (Jake's Nurse), Ben Epps (Passenger Cop), Dan Fountain (Police Officer), Max Rosmarin (Music Nerd), Chris Fischer (Parking Garage Cop), Christopher Rivera (Party Guy), Kevin Payne (Priest), Monroe Mann (Jake Donnelly)

High school swimming star Ben Cronin finds his life falling apart after a new girl makes it her goal to seduce and destroy him.

© 20th Century Fox

Jesse Bradford, Clayne Crawford

Jesse Bradford

Jesse Bradford, Erika Christensen

Jesse Bradford, Shiri Appleby

IGBY GOES DOWN

(UNITED ARTISTS) Producers, Lisa Tornell, Marco Weber; Executive Producer, Fran Lucci, David Rubin, Lee Solomon, Helen Beadleston; Director/Screenplay, Burr Steers; Photography, Wedigo von Schultzendorff; Designer, Kevin Thompson; Costumes, Sarah Edwards; Editor, William Anderson; Music, Uwe Fahrenkrog-Petersen; Music Supervisor, Nic Harcourt; Co-Producers, Trish Hofmann/Miggel; Casting, Ronnie Yeskel, Richard Hicks; an Atlantic Streamline presentation in association with Crossroads Films of a Marco Weber/Lisa Tornell production; Dolby; Super 35 Widescreen; Color; Rated R; 98 minutes; Release date: September 13, 2002

CAST

Igby Slocum	Kieran Culkin
Sookie Sapperstein	Claire Danes
D.H.	Jeff Goldblum
Russel	Jared Harris
Rachel	Amanda Peet
Oliver Slocum	Ryan Phillippe
Jason Slocum	Bill Pullman
Mimi Slocum	Susan Sarandon
10-year-old Igby	Rory Culkin
13-year-old Oliver	Peter Tambakis
Lt. Smith	Bill Irwin
Ida	Kathleen Gati
Little Cadet	Gannon Forrester
Bunny	Celia Weston
Lisa Fiedler	Elizabeth Jagger
Suit	Nick Wyman
Girl	Amber Gross
Hockey Players	Cassidy Ladden, Erin Fritch
Hotel Manager	Jim Gaffigan
Front Desk Clerk	Arnie Burton
Mr. Nice Guy	Eric Bogosian
Mrs. Piggee	Cynthia Nixon

and Michael Formica Jones (Peeka), Glenn Fitzgerald (Surfer), Reg Rogers (Therapist), Danny Tamberelli (Turtle), David Arrow (Waiter), Ronobir Lahiri (Intern)

Igby Slocum, an angry, sarcastic, well-to-do teenager trying to cope with his self-absorbed mother and his schizophrenic father, skips out of military school and winds up having an affair with his godfather's mistress.

Kieran Culkin, Claire Danes

Ryan Phillippe, Susan Sarandon, Jeff Goldblum

Jared Harris, Amanda Peet

Susan Sarandon

BARBERSHOP

(MGM) Producers, Robert Teitel, George Tillman, Jr., Mark Brown; Executive Producers, Matt Alvarez, Larry Kennar; Director, Tim Story; Screenplay, Mark Brown, Don D. Scott, Marshall Todd; Story, Mark Brown; Photography, Tom Priestley; Designer, Roger Fortune; Costumes, Devon P.F. Patterson; Music, Terence Blanchard; Editor, John Carter; Line Producer, Thomas J. Busch; Casting, Mary Vernieu, Felicia Fasano; a State Street Pictures/Cube Vision production; Dolby; Deluxe color; Rated PG-13; 102 minutes; Release date: September 13, 2002

Ice Cube, Keith David

Anthony Anderson, Lahmard Tate

Sean Patrick Thomas, Michael Ealy, Eve, Ice Cube, Troy Garity, Cedric the Entertainer, Leonard Earl Howze

CAST

Calvin Palmer	Ice Cube
JD	Anthony Anderson
Eddie	Cedric the Entertainer
Jimmy James	Sean Patrick Thomas
Terri Jones	Eve
Isaac Rosenberg	Troy Garity
Ricky Nash	Michael Ealy
Dinka	Leonard Earl Howze
Lester	Keith David
Jennifer Palmer	Jazsmin Lewis
Billy	Lahmard Tate
Detective Williams	Tom Wright
Kevin	Jason George
Hustle Guy	DeRay Davis
Janelle	Sonya Eddy

and Saralynne Crittenden (Big Mamma), Jasmine Randle (Gabby), Naomi Young Armstrong (Grandma), Marcia Wright (Angry Woman), Lorenzo Clemons (Bank Manager), Frank Townsend (Terri's Customer), Scott Dent (Boy), Carl Wright (Checkers Fred), Laura E. Walls (Church Lady); Customers: Woody Bolar (Artis), Deon Cole (Darrel), Marshall Titus (Joe), Clifford T. Frazier (Kwame), J. David Shanks (Lamar), Leon S. Rogers, Jr. (Larry), Jam (Lloyd), Eric Lane (Rodney), Norm Van Lier (Sam), Ray Thompson (Tyrone), Mark Simmons (Rob), Vince Green (Waiting Customer); Cassandra Lewis (Young Mom), Janina Gavankar (Fine Woman), Olumiji Olawumi (Jay), Satya Lee (Korean Woman), Kevin Morrow (Monk), Teara Hill Willborn, Ebboney Wilson (Little Kids), Chester Clay McSwain (Mailman), Steven Simoncic (Officer with Photo), Matt Orlando, Willie B. Goodson (Officers), Cynthia Maddox (Prison Guard), Montina Woods (Rhonda Watts), Llou Johnson (Salesman), Dana Min Goodman (Cashier), Parvesh Chenna (Samir), Pat "Soul" Scaggs (Motel Manager), Dev Kennedy (Det. Williams' Partner), Malik S. Middleton (Construction Worker), Kwame Amoaku (Stair Guy), Toyiah Marquis (Samir's Wife), Cerall Duncan (Kevin's Other Woman), Eddie Bo Smith, Jr. (Crazy Inmate), Maestro Harrell (Customer Tillman), Rhonda Bobo (Ricky's Girlfriend), Jalen Rose (Himself), Tiffany S. Gaji (Cop)

During one day of business, Calvin wrestles with the prospect of selling the struggling barbershop he inherited from his dad, knowing that it has become a make-shift community center for the neighborhood.

Eve, Jason George

© MGM

THE BANGER SISTERS

(FOX SEARCHLIGHT) Producer, Mark Johnson, Elizabeth Cantillon; Executive Producer, David Bushell; Director/Screenplay, Bob Dolman; Photography, Karl Walter Lindenlaub; Designer, Maia Javan; Costumes, Jacqueline West; Editor, Aram Nigoghossian; Music, Trevor Rabin; Music Supervisors, Maureen Crowe, John Bissell; Casting, Sheila Jaffe, Georgianne Walken; a Gran Via/Elizabeth Cantillon production; Dolby; Panavision; Deluxe color; Rated R; 98 minutes; Release date: September 20, 2002

CAST
Suzette	Goldie Hawn
Lavinia	Susan Sarandon
Harry	Geoffrey Rush
Hannah	Erika Christensen
Raymond	Robin Thomas
Ginger	Eva Amurri
Jules	Matthew Carey
Jake the Bartender	Andre Ware
Club Owner	Adam Tomei
Pump Attendant	Sal Lopez
Hotel Clerk	Kohl Sudduth
Prom Girl	Tinsley Grimes
Man in Bar	Larry Krask
Young Groupie	Marlayna Garrett

and Buckcherry: Josh Todd, Yugomir Lonich, Keith Nelson, Devon Glenn, Jonathan Brightman, Ben Skorstad, Eliza Coleman (L.A. Band)

Suzette, a former rock groupie, way past her prime and fired from her bartending job, seeks out her one-time partner, Lavinia, only to discover that the latter has become a prim and respectable suburban mom who does not want to be reminded of the wild lifestyle she once led.

© Fox Searchlight

Goldie Hawn, Geoffrey Rush, Susan Sarandon

Erika Christensen, Robin Thomas, Susan Sarandon, Eva Amurri, Goldie Hawn

Goldie Hawn

Susan Sarandon, Goldie Hawn

TRAPPED

(COLUMBIA) formerly *24 Hours*; Producers, Mimi Polk Gitlin, Luis Mandoki; Executive Producers, Mark Canton, Hanno Huth, Neil Canton, Glen Ballard, Rick Hess; Director, Luis Mandoki; Screenplay, Greg Iles, based upon his novel *24 Hours;* Photography, Frederick Elmes, Piotr Sobocinski; Designer, Richard Sylbert; Costumes, Michael Kaplan; Editor, Jerry Greenberg; Music, John Ottman; Co-Producers, Carsten Lorenz, Nathan Kahane, Michael McDonnell; Casting, Louis DiGiaimo; a Mandolin Entertainment/Propaganda Films production, presented in association with Senator Entertainment and the Canton Company; Dolby; Deluxe color; Rated R; 105 minutes; Release date: September 20, 2002

CAST

Karen Jennings	Charlize Theron
Cheryl Hickey	Courtney Love
Will Jennings	Stuart Townsend
Joe Hickey	Kevin Bacon
Marvin	Pruitt Taylor Vince
Abby Jennings	Dakota Fanning
Hank Ferris	Steve Rankin
Agent Chalmers	Garry Chalk
Mary McDill	Jodie Markell
Peter McDill	Matt Koby
Dr. Stein	Gerry Becker
Holden	Andrew Airlie
Hotel Operator	Randi Lynne
Joan Evans	Colleen Camp
Gray Davidson	J.B. Bivens
SWAT Leader	John Scott
Heins	Gregory Bennett
Helicopter Pilot	Jim Filippone
Violent Man	Brent Woolsey

Charlize Theron, Kevin Bacon

Three kidnappers keep Karen Jennings, her husband, and their six-year-old daughter hostage in three separate locations, giving them twenty-four hours to come up with the ransom money.

© Columbia

Courtney Love, Charlize Theron

Stuart Townsend, Charlize Theron

Kevin Bacon, Charlize Theron

THE FOUR FEATHERS

(PARAMOUNT/MIRAMAX) Producers, Stanley R. Jaffe, Robert D. Jaffe, Marty Katz, Paul Feldscher; Executive Producers, Allon Reich, Julie Goldstein; Director, Shekhar Kapur; Screenplay, Michael Schiffer, Hossein Amini; Based on the novel by A.E.W. Mason; Photography, Robert Richardson; Designer, Allan Cameron; Costumes, Ruth Myers; Music, James Horner; Casting, Ros and John Hubbard; Stunts, Jorge Casares; a Jaffilms production; Dolby; Panavision; Deluxe color; Rated PG-13; 130 minutes; Release date: September 20, 2002

CAST

Harry Feversham	Heath Ledger
Jack Durrance	Wes Bentley
Ethne	Kate Hudson
Abou Fatma	Djimon Hounsou
Trench	Michael Sheen
Colonel Hamilton	Alex Jennings
Willoughby	Rupert Penry-Jones
General Feversham	Tim Pigott-Smith
Sudanese Storyteller	Mohamed Bouich
Dervish Ansar	Campbell Brown
Gustave	Daniel Caltagirone
Col. Sutch	James Cosmo
Colonel, Other Regiment	Andy Coumbe
Aunt Mary	Angela Douglas
Egyptian Orderlies	Karim Doukkali, Mark Tonderai, Alex Zorbas
Isabelle	Lucy Gordon
Millie	Megan Hall
Drunken Corporal	James Hillier
British Lion	Nick Holder
Woman in Red Veil	Alexandra Kabi Saadi
	Julio Lewis

and Craig McDonald (Wounded Captain), Lionel Mahop (Dervish Captain), Richard Manlove (British Corporal), Kris Marshall (Castleton), Manar Mohamed (Youssef), Marouazi Mohammed (Dervish Sniper), Nider Mohamed (Mullah), Anna Diafe Ndiaye, Thioumbe Samb (Dinka Slavegirls), Medoune Ndiaye (Gentle Faced Porter), Deobia Oparei (Idris-Es-Saier), Medhi Ouzzani (Hassan), Charles Pemberton (Impressario), Mohammed Quatib (Ibrahim), Laila Rouass (Sudanese Girl), Hugh Ross (Regimental Priest), Alek Wek (Aquol).

When Harry Feversham's regiment is assigned to active duty in North Africa to fight the Sudanese rebels, he resigns his commission, causing friends and family to brand him a coward. Previous film versions include those made in 1929 (Paramount) and starring Richard Arlen (Harry), Fay Wray (Ethne), and William Powell (Trench), and a British production released here by UA in 1939 and starring John Clements (Harry), Ralph Richardson (Jack), and June Duprez (Ethne).

Djimon Hounsou, Heath Ledger

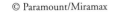

Heath Ledger, Kate Hudson

Heath Ledger, Wes Bentley

SECRETARY

James Spader, Maggie Gyllenhaal

Maggie Gyllenhaal

James Spader, Maggie Gyllenhaal

(LIONS GATE) Producers, Andrew Fierberg, Amy Hobby; Executive Producers, Jamie Beardsley, Joel Posner, P.J. Posner, Michael Roban; Director, Steven Shainberg; Screenplay, Erin Cressida; Adapted by Steven Shainberg, Erin Cressida Wilson from the short story by Mary Gaitskill; Photography, Steven Fierberg; Designer, Amy Danger; Costumes, Marjorie Bowers; Editor, Pam Wise; Music, Angelo Badalamenti; Casting, Ellen Parks; from Double A Films, Slough Pond, Two Pound Bag Productions; Dolby; Color; Rated R; 104 minutes; Release date: September 20, 2002

CAST

Mr. Grey	James Spader
Lee Holloway	Maggie Gyllenhaal
Peter	Jeremy Davies
Joan Holloway	Lesley Ann Warren
Burt Holloway	Stephen McHattie
Dr. Twardon	Patrick Bauchau
Tricia O'Connor	Jessica Tuck
Jonathan	Oz Perkins
Lee's Sister	Amy Locane
Sylvia	Mary Joy
Stewart	Michael Mantell
Paralegal	Lily Knight
Allison	Sabrina Grdevich
Louisa	Lacey Kohl
Jessica	Julene Renee

and Lauren Cohn (First Secretary), Ezra Buzzington (Typing Teacher), Kyle Colerider-Krugh (Mr. Garvey), Steven Fierberg (First Date), Russel Harper (Second Date), David Wiater (Tomato Date), Shannon Convery (New Secretary), Alison Tatlock (TV Reporter)

A masochistic young woman finds her perfect job when her seemingly stoic boss starts demeaning her and asking her to accept his sadistic physical treatment of her.

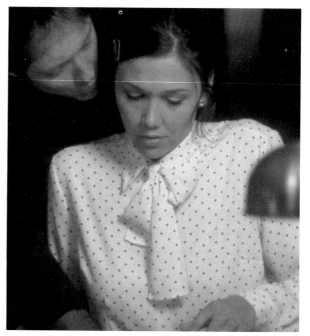

James Spader, Maggie Gyllenhaal

THE TUXEDO

(DREAMWORKS) Producers, John H. Williams, Adam Schroeder; Executive Producers, Walter F. Parkes, Laurie MacDonald, Williams S. Beasley; Director, Kevin Donovan; Screenplay, Michael J. Wilson, Michael Leeson; Story, Phil Hay, Matt Manfredi, Michael J. Wilson; Photography, Stephen F. Windon; Designers, Paul Denham Austerberry, Monte Fay Hallis; Costumes, Erica Edell Phillips; Editor, Craig P. Herring; Music, Christophe Beck, John Debney; Casting, Lisa Beach; Stunts, Rick Forsayeth, Chung Chi Li; a Vanguard Films production, a Parkes/ MacDonald production; Dolby; Technicolor; Rated PG-13; 98 minutes; Release date: September 27, 2002.

CAST

Jimmy Tong . . . . .Jackie Chan
Del Blaine . . . . .Jennifer Love Hewitt
Clark Devlin . . . . .Jason Isaacs
Steena . . . . .Debi Mazar
Diedrich Banning . . . . .Ritchie Coster
Dr. Simms . . . . .Peter Stormare
Cheryl . . . . .Mia Cottet
Mitch . . . . .Romany Malco
Rogers . . . . .Daniel Kash
Kells . . . . .Jody Racicot
Vic . . . . .Boyd Banks
and Scott Wickware (CSA Agent Wallace), Christian Potenza (CSA Agent Joel), Karen Glave (CSA Agent Randa), Scott Yaphe (CSA Agent Gabe), Paul Bates (Lundeen), Noah Danby (Bike Messenger), Cecile Cristobal (Girl in Gallery), Colin Mochrie (Gallery Owner), Kim Roberts (ER Nurse), Fred Rutherford (Banning Party Bouncer), Jordan Madley (Fast Food Girl), Phoenix Gonzalez (De L'Air Saleswoman), Craig Eldridge (Doran), Stacey DePass (Woman in Park), Ron Gabriel (Frank Rollins), Marcia Bennett, Michael Ayoub, Brian Rhodes, Frank T. Nakashima, Ruby Webb, Reg Dreger (Water Executives), Diana C. Weng (Flower Shop CSA Op), Mike Nahrgang (Homeless CSA Op), Paul Braunstein (Sewer CSA Op), John Catucci, Robert Tinkler (CSA Firing Range Ops), Daniel Aiken (Bogus CSA Op), Bayo Akinfemi (S.W.A.T. CSA Op), Allen Stewart-Coates (Concert Maitre'D), Lawrence Kamikawaji (Assistant Maitre'D), Paul Huggett, Daveed Louza (Banning Lab Workers), Gavin Stephens (Hotel Security Guard), Michael Panucci (Security Guard #2), Ian Downie (Banning Party Guest), Jamie Jones (Banning Guard), Perry Perlmutar (Guy in Toilet), William Lynn (Doorman), Jean Green (Elderly Woman), Jack Duffy (Elderly Man), Fred Lee, Peter Yip (Poultry Employees), Jim Davis, Marion Dressler, Naomi (Hospital Patrons), Poi Wong (Hospital Patient), Lisa Levy (Nurse #2), Peter Gail Williams (Backstage Fan), Rafael Brown (Drunk Fan), James Brown (Himself)

Chauffeur Jimmy Tong disobeys the warning to never put on his boss's prized tuxedo and finds himself capable of amazing feats, thrusting him into the world of espionage with rookie Del Blaine as his partner.

© Dreamworks

Henry Kissinger

THE TRIALS OF HENRY KISSINGER

(FIRST RUN FEATURES) Producers, Alex Gibney, Eugene Jarecki; Executive Producer, Roy Ackerman; Director, Eugene Jarecki; Screenplay, Alex Gibney; Editor, Simon Barker; Music, Peter Nashel; Co-Producer, Susan Motamed; Associate Producer, Jennie Amias; Film Researchers, Salimah El-Amin, Melinda Shopsin; Narrator, Brian Cox; a Think Tank and Jigsaw production for the BBC in association with Diverse Limited; Produced in association with ARTE-Zeta Prods., History Television, SBS Television, Australia and TV 2 Denmark; U.S.-U.K.; Color; Not rated; 127 minutes; Release date: September 20, 2002. Documentary questioning whether Henry Kissinger's involvement with such countries as Chile, Cambodia, and Indonesia has resulted in needless deaths.

WITH

Christopher Hitchens, William Safire, Gen. Alexander Haig, Gen. Brent Scowcroft, Seymour Hersch, Daniel Davidson, Roger Morris, William Shawcross, Walter Isaacson, Michael Tigar, Amy Goodman.

© First Run Features

Jason Isaacs, Jackie Chan

MOONLIGHT MILE

(TOUCHSTONE) Producers, Mark Johnson, Brad Silbering; Executive Producers, Patricia Whitcher, Susan Sarandon, Asok Amritraj, David Hoberman; Director/Screenplay, Brad Silbering; Photography, Phedon Papamichael; Designer, Missy Stewart; Costumes, Mary Zophres; Editor, Lisa Zeno Churgin; Music, Mark Isham; Music Supervisor, Dawn Solér; Casting, Avy Kaufman; a Hyde Park Entertainment presentation of a Reveal Entertainment/Gran Via/Punch production; Dolby; Panavision; Technicolor; Rated PG-13; 117 minutes; Release date: September 27, 2002

Jake Gyllenhaal, Ellen Pompeo

CAST

Joe Nast	Jake Gyllenhaal
Ben Floss	Dustin Hoffman
JoJo Floss	Susan Sarandon
Asst. D.A. Mona Camp	Holly Hunter
Bertie Knox	Ellen Pompeo
Ty	Richard T. Jones
Stan Michaels	Allan Corduner
Mike Mulcahey	Dabney Coleman
Cheryl	Aleksia Landeau
Rabbi	Richard Messing
Cantor	Lev Friedman
Servers	Robert Clendenin, Jim Fyfe
Mrs. Meyerson	Mary Ellen Trainor
Mr. Meyerson	Richard Fancy
Fashion Plate	Marcia Mitzman Gaven
Diana Floss	Careena Melia
Speedwalker	Gary Hetzler
Photographer	Ed Lachman
Tanner	Gordon Clapp
Caroline	Mary Catherine Garrison
Audrey Anders	Audrey Marie Anderson
Patty	Colombe Jacobsen

and Virginia Newcomb, Elizabeth Janas (Cheryl's Friends), Richard T. Jones (Ty), Lenny Clarke (Gordy), Robert Wahlberg (Pinky), J. Tom Carey (Baxter), Dee Nelson (Waitress), McNally Sagal (Mrs. Tippet), Roxanne Hart (June Mulcahey), Lisa Anne Hillman (Jillian Mulcahey), Rachel Singer (Rhonda Ketch), John Balma (Walter Ketch), Paul Perri (Public Defender), Tom Dahlgren (Judge), Mark Lotito (Diner Manger), David Wheeler (Diner Grandfather), Alexandra Hoffman (Diner Granddaughter)

After his fiancee is tragically killed, Joe Nast feels obligated to play the role of loyal and dutiful surrogate son to the girl's grieving parents.

© Touchstone Pictures

Holly Hunter, Jake Gyllenhaal

Jake Gyllenhaal, Dustin Hoffman

Dustin Hoffman, Susan Sarandon

THE MAN FROM ELYSIAN FIELDS

(GOLDWYN) Producers, Andrew Pfeffer, Donald Zuckerman, Andy Garcia; Executive Producers, Norm Waitt, Paul Brooks, Larry Katz, Morris Ruskin, Vicky Pike; Director, George Hickenlooper; Screenplay, Philip Jayson Lasker; Photography, Kramer Morgenthau; Designer, Franckie Diago; Costumes, Matthew Jacobsen; Editor, Michael Brown; Music, Anthony Marinelli; Music Supervisor, Randy Gerston; Co-Producers, Tony Vitale, Glenn S. Gainor, Dara Weintraub; Associate Producer, Josie Wechsler; Casting, Heidi Levitt; a Fireworks Pictures and Gold Circle Films in association with Shoreline Entertainment presentation of a Donald Zuckerman/Pfilmco/Cineson production; Dolby; Color; Rated R; 105 minutes; Release date: September 27, 2002

CAST

Byron Tiller	Andy Garcia
Dena Tiller	Julianna Margulies
Andrea Alcott	Olivia Williams
Tobias Alcott	James Coburn
Luther Fox	Mick Jagger
Jennifer Adler	Anjelica Huston
Greg	Michael Des Barres
Domenico	Joe Santos
Book Store Clerk	Maureen McCormick
Woman	Laura Meshell
Man	Kerry Li
Edward Rodgers	Richard Bradford
Customer	Rosalind Chao
Joey	Eddie Santiago
Virgil Koster	Xander Berkeley
Lottie	Elisa Gallay
Bartender	Tracey Walter
Street Car Vendor	Tommy Perna
Paul Pearson	Sherman Howard

and Asha Siewkumar (Receptionist), J.B. White (Waiter), Marianne Muelerleile (Woman #3), Joseph Della Sorte (Valet), Michael Hughes (Car Valet), Ezra Buzzington (Driver), Hannah Sim, Mark Steger (Performance Artists), Christopher & Killian Shreenan (Nathaniel Tiller), Julian Fleischer (Jazz Singer), Joseph Paur (Opera Singer), Yasmin D'Mello, Sonia Sanz (Women), Jan Triska (Marcus)

Struggling author Byron Tiller reluctantly agrees to become a gigolo, bringing him into contact with famed writer Tobias Alcott, who is facing his own mortality.

© Samuel Goldwyn Film/Fireworks Pictures

Julianna Margulies, Andy Garcia

Anjelica Huston, Mick Jagger

Andy Garcia, James Coburn

Andy Garcia

SWEET HOME ALABAMA

(TOUCHSTONE) Producers, Neal H. Moritz, Stokely Chaffin; Executive Producers, Jon Jashni, Wink Mordaunt, Michael Fottrell; Director, Andy Tennant; Screenplay, C. Jay Cox; Story, Douglas J. Eboch; Photography, Andrew Dunn; Designer, Clay A. Griffith; Costumes, Sophie De Rakoff Carbonell; Editors, Troy Takaki, Tracey Wadmore-Smith; Music, George Fenton; Music Supervisors, Dawn Solér, Laura Z. Wasserman; Casting, Juel Bestrop, Jeanne McCarthy, Kathleen Chopin; a Neal H. Moritz production; Dolby; Super 35 Widescreen; Technicolor; Rated PG-13; 108 minutes; Release date: September 27, 2002

Nathan Lee Graham, Reese Witherspoon, Rhona Mitra

Reese Witherspoon

Reese Witherspoon, Patrick Dempsey, Candice Bergen

Patrick Dempsey, Reese Witherspoon, Josh Lucas

CAST

Melanie Carmichael	Reese Witherspoon
Jake	Josh Lucas
Andrew	Patrick Dempsey
Kate	Candice Bergen
Pearl	Mary Kay Place
Earl	Fred Ward
Stella Kay	Jean Smart
Bobby Ray	Ethan Embry
Lurlynn	Melanie Lynskey
Wade	Courtney Gains
Dorothea	Mary Lynn Rajskub
Tabatha	Rhona Mitra
Frederick	Nathan Lee Graham
Eldon	Sean Bridgers
Clinton	Fleet Cooper
Barry	Kevin Sussman
Young Jake	Thomas Curtis
Young Melanie	Dakota Fanning
Bruno	Mark Skinner
Pan	Michelle Krusiec
Pablo	Phil Cater
Devin	Michael Snow
Wallace Buford	Bob Penny
Tom Darovsic	Mark Matkevich
Eugene the Guard	Lee Roy Giles
Jimmy Lee	Afemo Omilami
Jimmy the Driver	Kevin Hagan
Reporters	Dennis Ryan, Jim O'Connor, Leslie Hendrix
Gentleman	Tony Rizzoli
Bartender	Bob Seel
Carrie Lee	Kesley Lowenthal
Starr	Jen Apgar
Dix	Sarah Baker
Sherma	Deborah Calloway Duke
Colonel Murphy	Ted Manson
Virgie	Sharon Blackwood
Shirleen	Suzi Bass
Old Dead Soldier	Don Young
Guard #2	Mark Oliver
Press Secretary	Deide Deionne

and Doug Johnson-Killen, Emily Furman, Pete Talton (Catfish Festival Dancers), Kelli Franklin, Keni Thomas, Jeanne Arnold, Osjha Anderson (Catfish Festival Singers), Charlotte Pierrepont, Traci Ann Wolfe, Jana Lynn Schoep, Eddy Donno (Models)

Successful New York fashion designer Melanie Carmichael, who has left behind her Southern roots, reluctantly returns to her home town in Alabama to get her estranged husband to sign divorce papers so Melanie can marry the mayor's son.

Patrick Dempsey, Reese Witherspoon

Josh Lucas, Reese Witherspoon

Reese Witherspoon, Nathan Lee Graham

Jean Smart, Reese Witherspoon

Fred Ward, Candice Bergen, Mary Kay Place

WELCOME TO COLLINWOOD

(WARNER BROS.) Producers, George Clooney, Steven Soderbergh; Executive Producers, Hunt Lowry, Casey La Scala, Hendrik Hey, Ben Cosgrove; Director/Screenplay, Anthony & Joe Russo; Based on the film *I Solti Ignoti (Big Deal on Madonna Street)* by Suso Cecchi d'Amico, Mario Monicelli, Agenore Incrocci, Furio Scarpelli; Photography, Lisa Rinzler, Charles Minsky; Designer, Tom Meyer; Costumes, Juliet Polcsa; Music, Mark Mothersbaugh; Editor, Amy E. Duddleston; Co-Producer, Scott Shiffman; Associate Producer, James Henney; Casting, Christine Sheaks; a Section Eight production, presented in association with Pandora and H585 Media AG; Dolby; Super 35 Widescreen; CFI Color; Rated R; 85 minutes; Release date: October 4, 2002

CAST

Riley	William H. Macy
Leon	Isaiah Washington
Pero	Sam Rockwell
Toto	Michael Jeter
Cosimo	Luis Guzmán
Old Man in Prison	John Buck, Jr.
Rosalind	Patricia Clarkson
Basil	Brett C. Leonard
Mickey	Frank O'Donnell
Referee	Peter Veneziano
Judge	Bernard Canepari
Corrections Officer	Art Oughton
Oswald	Ray Calabrese
Jerzy	George Clooney

and Annie Kitral, Lissy Gulick, Dorothy Silver (Nuns), Maryanne Nagel (Mrs. Antwerp), David Warshofsky (Babitch), Jennifer Esposito (Carmela), Gabrielle Union (Michele), June Lang (Old Purse Women), Basil Russo (Funeral Home Director), Angela Russo (Arguing Woman), Wayne S. Turney (Arguing Man), Rohn Thomas (Janitor)

A group of second-rate safecrackers hope to pull off a sure thing to solve their various problems only to end up bungling every possible aspect of the heist.

© Warner Bros.

William H. Macy, Sam Rockwell, Isaiah Washington

Khalil, Whale

Archibald the Asparagus, Reginald

JONAH: A VEGGIETALES MOVIE

(ARTISAN/FHE PICTURES) Producer, Ameake Owens; Executive Producers, Terry Botwick, Dan Philps, Phil Vischer; Directors/Screenplay, Mike Nawrocki, Phil Vischer; Art Director, Joe Sapulich; Visual Development, Dennis Bredow; Editor, John Wahba; Music, David Mullen; Songs, Kurt Heinecke, Phil Vischer, David Mullen, Mike Nawrocki; Director of Technology, Visual Effects, Henry Vera; Dolby; Color; Rated G; 82 minutes; Release date: October 4, 2002

VOICE CAST

Archibald Asparagus ("Jonah"/"Twippo")/Bob the Tomato/Mr. Lunt ("Pirate Lunt")/Percy Pea/Phillipe Pea/Pa Grape ("Pirate Pa")/Nezzer/King Twistomer/Cockney Pea #2 . . . . .Phil Vischer
Larry the Cucumber ("Pirate Larry")/Jean Claude Pea/Cockney Pea #1/Self-Help Tape Voice/Jerry Gourd/Whooping BBQ Pea . . . . .Mike Nawrocki

Khalil	Tim Hodge
Junior Asparagus	Lisa Vischer
Dad Asparagus	Dan Anderson
Laura Carrot	Kristin Blegen
Annie	Shelby Vischer

and Jim Poole (Scooter/Townsperson), Ron Smith (City Official/Crazy Jopponian), Sarah Catherine Brooks, Paige Craig, Adam Frick, Chris Geiger, Mike Harrison, Amy Howard, Tracy Johnson, Paul Kaiser, Bob Landon, Joshua Lindsay, Rebekah Litfin, Shari Martin, Laura Richey, Jon Reich, Brian Roberts, Ellen Silvestri, Christy Sumner, John Trauscht, Nathan Tungseth, Elizabeth West (Message from the Lord Choir)

Archibald, an asparagus who serves as a messenger of God, is ordered to take his word of the Lord to the sinful city of Nineveh.

© Artisan/FHE Pictures

RED DRAGON

(UNIVERSAL) Producers, Dino De Laurentiis, Martha De Laurentiis; Executive Producer, Andrew Z. Davis; Director, Brett Ratner; Screenplay, Ted Tally; Based on the novel by Thomas Harris; Photography, Dante Spinotti; Designer, Kristi Zea; Costumes, Betsy Heimann; Editor, Mark Helfrich; Music, Danny Elfman; Casting, Francine Maisler; a Dino De Laurentiis presentation in association with Metro-Goldwyn-Mayer Pictures; Dolby; Panavision; Deluxe color; Rated R; 126 minutes; Release date: October 4, 2002

Philip Seymour Hoffman, Harvey Keitel, Edward Norton

Anthony Hopkins, Edward Norton

Tyler Patrick Jones, Mary-Louise Parker

CAST

Hannibal Lecter . . . . .Anthony Hopkins
Will Graham . . . . .Edward Norton
Francis Dolarhyde . . . . .Ralph Fiennes
Jack Crawford . . . . .Harvey Keitel
Reba McClane . . . . .Emily Watson
Molly Graham . . . . .Mary-Louise Parker
Freddy Lounds .Philip Seymour Hoffman
Dr. Chilton . . . . .Anthony Heald
Lloyd Bowman . . . . .Ken Leung
Barney . . . . .Frankie Faison
Josh Graham . . . . .Tyler Patrick Jones
Conductor . . . . .Lalo Schifrin
Flautist . . . . .Tim Wheater
Charles Leeds . . . . .Tom Verica
Valerie Leeds . . . . .Marguerite MacIntyre
Billy Leeds . . . . .Tommy Curtis
Sean Leeds . . . . .Jordan Gruber
Susie Leeds . . . . .Morgan Gruber
Forensic Dentist . . . . .Michael Cavanaugh
Police Commissioner . . . . .Madison Mason
Detective . . . . .Katie Rich
and John Rubinstein, David Doty, Brenda Strong, Robert Curtis Brown, Mary Anne McGarry, Marc Abraham, Veronica De Laurentiis (Dinner Guests), Cliff Dorfman, Philip B. Fahey (Cops), Elizabeth Dennehy (Beverly), Stanley Anderson (Jimmy), Richard Pelzman (Locksmith), Dwier Brown (Mr. Jacobi), Grace Stephens, Lucy Stephens, Kevin Bashor (Jacobi Children), Azura Skye (Bookseller), William Lucking (Byron Metaclf), Alex D. Linz (Voice of Young Dolarhyde), Ellen Burstyn (Voice of Dolarhyde's Mother), Mary Beth Hurt (Museum Curator), Frank Whaley (Ralph Mandy), Lisa Thornhill (Mrs. Sherman), Andreana Weiner (Dr. Bloom's Secretary), Jeanine Jackson (Dr. Hassler), Mark Moses (Father in Video), Kyra Helfrich (Child in Video), Alex Berliner (Photographer), Gianni Russo (Newsie), Al Brown (Tattler Guard), Christopher Curry (Mr. Fisk), Tanya Newbould (Chromalux Secretary), Edward Nickerson (FBI Agent), Terence Rowley (Superintendent), Frank Bruynbroek (Chef), Hillary Straney (Museum Secretary), Conrad E. Palmisano (Deputy in Car)

FBI Investigator Will Graham turns to incarcerated psychiatrist-turned-killer Hannibal Lecter to help him solve a grisly string of murders.
Remake of the 1986 film *Manhunter* (DEG), which starred William H. Peterson (Will Graham), Brian Cox (Hannibal Lecter), and Tom Noonan (Dolarhyde).

This is the third Lecter film to star Anthony Hopkins in the role, following *The Silence of the Lambs* (Orion, 1991) and *Hannibal* (MGM/Univ, 2001). Frankie Faison plays Barney for the third time and Anthony Heald repeats his role as Dr. Chilton from *Lambs*.

Ralph Fiennes, Emily Watson

TUCK EVERLASTING

(WALT DISNEY PICTURES) Producers, Jane Startz, Marc Abraham; Executive Producers, Armyan Bernstein, Thomas A. Bliss, Deborah Forte, Max Wong, William Teitler; Director, Jay Russell; Screenplay, Jeffrey Lieber, James V. Hart; Based on the book by Natalie Babbitt; Photography, James L. Carter; Designer, Tony Burrough; Costumes, Carol Ramsey; Editor, Jay Cassidy; Music, William Ross; Casting, Mary Gail Artz, Barbara Cohen; a Beacon Pictures/Scholastic Entertainment/Jane Startz production; Dolby; Panavision; Technicolor; Rated PG; 90 minutes; Release date: October 11, 2002

Alexis Bledel, Jonathan Jackson

CAST

Winnie Foster . . . . Alexis Bledel
Angus Tuck . . . . William Hurt
Mae Tuck . . . . Sissy Spacek
Jesse Tuck . . . . Jonathan Jackson
Miles Tuck . . . . Scott Bairstow
Man in the Yellow Suit . . . . Ben Kingsley
Mother Foster . . . . Amy Irving
Robert Foster . . . . Victor Garber
Miles' Wife . . . . Kosha Engler
Constable . . . . Richard Pilcher
Lead Mill Boy . . . . Bradley Coryell
Baker . . . . John Badila
Sally Hannaway . . . . Julia Hurt
Beatrice Ruston . . . . Naomi Kline
Mrs. Hannaway . . . . Kathryn Kelley
Mrs. Ruston . . . . Brigid Cleary
Young Pastor . . . . Sean Pratt
Sore Loser . . . . Kyle Prue
and Neal Moran (Lounge Tender), Irving Jacobs (Old Timer), Robert Logan (Night Deputy), Jean Schertler (Grandmother Foster), Dominic Angellella (Bernard Price), Theresa Flynn (Mrs. Price), Elizabeth McNamara (Maid), Steve Walker (Card Player), Maurice Philogene (Bouncer), Kelly McDaniel (Young Anna, age 8), Reeny Eul (Young Anna, age 11), Jordan McDaniel (Young Anna, 14), Beau Russell (Beau, age 3), Dillion Gardner (Beau, age 8), Charlie Cooper (Beau, age 11), Lester Horn (Driver at Croquet Game), Cynthia Webb-Manly (Cook/Maid), Stephen Szibler, Sam De Crispino, Tom McNutt, Helene McNutt, Megan Cooper, Mac McLure, Matthew Staley, Tamara Carter (Dinner Guests), Elisabeth Shue (Narrator)

Jonathan Jackson, Scott Bairstow, Sissy Spacek, William Hurt

Young Winnie Foster, longing to break away from her mother's iron grip, wanders into the woods where she meets Jesse Tuck who introduces her to his unconventional family, who harbor a great secret.

© Disney Enterprises

Alexis Bledel, Amy Irving, Ben Kingsley

Alexis Bledel, Jonathan Jackson

COMEDIAN

Jerry Seinfeld

Jerry Seinfeld

Jerry Seinfeld

Jerry Seinfeld

(MIRAMAX) Producer, Gary Streiner; Executive Producer, Jerry Seinfeld; Director, Christian Charles; Photography, Christian Charles, Mark Lumber, Gary Streiner; Editor, Chris Franklin; a Bridgnorth Films, New Material production; Dolby; Color; Rated R; 82 minutes; Release date: October 11, 2002.

WITH

Jerry Seinfeld, Orny Adams, Bill Cosby, Mario Joyner, Robert Klein, Jay Leno, Kevin Nealon, Colin Quinn, Chris Rock, Ray Romano, Paul Schorsch, Garry Shandling, George Shapiro, George Wallace

Documentary on comedian Jerry Seinfeld, as he returns to the nightclub circuit to perfect his stand-up act, and a look at up-and-coming comic Orny Adams

© Miramax

Jerry Seinfeld

Jerry Seinfeld, George Shapiro

PUNCH-DRUNK LOVE

(COLUMBIA) Producers, Joanne Sellar, Daniel Lupi, Paul Thomas Anderson; Director/Screenplay, Paul Thomas Anderson; Photography, Robert Elswitt; Designer, William Arnold; Costumes, Mark Bridges; Editor, Leslie Jones; Artwork, Jeremy Blake; Music, Jon Brion; Casting, Cassandra Kulukundis; a Revolution Studios presentation of a Joanne Sellar/Ghoulardi Film Company production; Dolby; Panavision; Color; Rated R; 97 minutes; Release date: October 11, 2002

CAST

Barry Egan . . . . Adam Sandler
Lena Leonard . . . . Emily Watson
Dean Trumbell . . . . Philip Seymour Hoffman
Lance . . . . Luis Guzmán
Elizabeth . . . . Mary Lynn Rajskub

THE SISTERS:
Susan . . . . Lisa Spector
Kathleen . . . . Julie Hermelin
Anna . . . . Karen Hermelin
Rhonda . . . . Hazel Mailloux
Nicole . . . . Nicole Gelbard
Gilda . . . . Mia Weinberg

THE BROTHERS:
David . . . . David Stevens
Jim . . . . Jimmy Stevens
Nate . . . . Nathan Stevens
Mike D. . . . . Mike D. Stevens

Phone Sex Sister . . . . Ashley Clark
Walter the Dentist . . . . Robert Smigel
and Jason Andrews (Voice of Operator Carter), Don McManus (Plastic's Voice), David Schrempf, Seann Conway (Customers), Rico Bueno (Rico), Karen Kilgariff (Anna's Voice on Phone), Salvador Curiel (Sal), Jorge Barahona (Jorge), Ernesto Quintero (Ernesto), Julius Steuer (Mechanic), Larry Ring (Steve, Brother-in-Law), Kerry Gelbard (Richard, Brother-in-Law), Alan Parry, John E. Beck, Eddie Wayne Howell, Taylor J. Thomas (After Eden Band), Bobby Bluehouse (After Eden Sound Man), Carol Mirelez, June Sepulveda (Phone Sex Girls, Utah), Andrew Higgs (Restaurant Manager), Rogerlyn Kanealii Wakinekona (Lena's Apartment Receptionist), Catherine L. Cooley (Flight Attendant), Michael Immel (Flight Attendant), Ross Lasi Tanoai (Cab Driver), Jonathan Loughran (Wrong Number), Kaila, Ku'Ulei (Ladies K Band), Sissy Lake (Hula Dancer), Marie Irwin (Lena's Nurse), Esther Imade Balogun (Receptionist Nurse), Tom Bornt (Dean's Employee), Mary Kilmartin (D & D Matress Customer)

Barry, a lonely, anti-social wholesaler whose shyness hides a violent temper, begins a very tenuous, awkward courtship with divorcee Lena.

© Revolution Studios

Mary Lynn Rajskub, Emily Watson, Adam Sandler

Luis Guzmán, Adam Sandler

Adam Sandler

Philip Seymour Hoffman

BROWN SUGAR

(FOX SEARCHLIGHT) Producer, Peter Heller; Executive Producer, Earvin "Magic" Johnson; Director, Rick Famuyima; Screenplay, Michael Elliott, Rick Famuyima; Story, Michael Elliott; Photography, Enrique Chediak; Designer, Kalina Ivanov; Costumes, Darryle Johnson; Editor, Dirk Westervelt; Co-Producer, Trish Hofmann; Music, Robert Hurst; Music Supervisors, Barry Cole, Christopher Covert; Casting, Alexa L. Fogel; a Heller Highwater/Magic Johnson Entertainment production; Dolby; Deluxe color; Rated PG-13; 98 minutes; Release date: October 11, 2002

CAST

Dre	Taye Diggs
Sidney	Sanaa Lathan
Chris	Mos Def
Reese	Nicole Ari Parker
Kelby	Boris Kodjoe
Francine	Queen Latifah
Simon	Wendell Pierce
Ren	Erik Weiner
Ten	Reggi Wyns
Meghan	Melissa Martinez
Young Sidney	Aaliyyah Hill
Young Dre	Marc John Jefferies
Older Woman	Venida Evans
Trish Hofmann	Rosalyn Coleman

and Breece Wilson, Brett Taylor, Donna Duplanter (Women), Robin T. Kirksey, Wyking Jones (Bartenders), Sterling K. Brown (Co-Worker), Kofi Boakye (Host), Dena Atlantic (Hot 97 Assistant), Gerry Pinzon (Instructor), Sam McPherson (Iridium Waiter), Big Daddy Kane, Black Thought, Ahmir "?uestlove" Thompson, Kool G Rap, Angie Martinez, Dana Dane, Doug E. Fresh, Slick Rick, Jermaine Dupri, Pete Rock, Trugoy the Dove, Plugwon Posdnuos, Vincent L. Mason, Kimora Lee Simmons, Beanie Sigel, Talib Kweli, Common (Themselves), Helmar Augustus Cooper (Reverend), Keith Tisdell (Richard), Toks Olagundoye (Sidney's LA Assistant), Opal Alladin (Crafts Vendor), Hadley Martin Fisher (Backstage Bartender), D.J. Jus (Kid in the Park), Liza Lapira (Hot 97 Receptionist)

Dre and Sidney, lifelong friends whose love of hip-hop has landed them positions in the music industry, begin to question the intensity of their friendship when they plan on marrying others.

© Fox Searchlight

Sanaa Lathan, Taye Diggs

Boris Kodjoe, Nicole Ari Parker, Reggi Wyns, Erik Weiner, Taye Diggs, Sanaa Lathan

Nicole Ari Parker, Sanaa Lathan

Queen Latifah, Mos Def

119

THE RULES OF ATTRACTION

(LIONS GATE) Producer, Greg Shapiro; Executive Producers, Michael Paseornek, Marc Butan, Tom Ortenberg, Jeremiah Samuels, Samuel Hadida, James Deutch, Marsha Oglesby, Roger Avary; Director/ Screenplay, Roger Avary; Based on the novel by Brett Easton Ellis; Photography, Robert Brinkmann; Designer, Sharon Seymour; Costumes, Louise Frogley; Editor, Sharon Rutter; Music, Tomandandy; Casting, Rick Montgomery; a Kingsate Films production in association with Roger Avary Filmproduktion GmbH; U.S.-German; Dolby; Color; Rated R; 110 minutes; Release date: October 11, 2002

CAST

Sean Bateman . . . . .James Van Der Beek
Lauren Hynde . . . . .Shannyn Sossamon
Victor Johnson . . . . .Kip Pardue
Laura Holleran . . . . .Jessica Biel
Paul Denton . . . . .Ian Somerhalder
Rupert Guest . . . . .Clifton Collins, Jr.
Mitchell Allen . . . . .Thomas Ian Nicholas
Mrs. Mimi Jared . . . . .Swoosie Kurtz
Mrs. Eve Denton . . . . .Faye Dunaway
Kelly . . . . .Kate Bosworth
Mr. Lance Lawson . . . . .Eric Stoltz
Claudia . . . . .Hayley Keenan
Richard "Dick" Jared . . . . .Russell Sams

Shannyn Sossamon, Jessica Biel

and Eric Szmanda (NYU Film Student), Holly Hollywood, Alaina, Amber Smith, Trisha Upton (Undressed to Get Screwed), Curtis Andersen (Guy Rolling Keg), Charlie Babcock (Party Guy), Colin Bain (Donald), Jay Baruchel (Harry), Noelle Evans (Crack Whore), Quincy Evans (Dicky), Malcolm Galt (Hacky Sack Guy), Anderson Goncalves (Bertrand), Chase Hampton (Townie), Jesse Heiman (Lucky Party Goer), Ron Jeremy (At the Player Piano), Clare Kramer (Candice), Matthew Lang (Getch), Joel Michaely (Raymond), Lucille M. Oliver (Young Nurse), Michael Ralph (Bumba Clot), Kavan Reece (Steve the Handsome Dunce), Fred Savage (A Junkie Named Marc), Katja Schuurman (Herself), Skyler Stone (Quinlivan), Theresa Wayman (Food Service Girl), Cheyenne Wilbur (Maitre d'), Paul Williams (Dr. Phibes, Waiting Room Doctor), Drew Wood (Jim from Dartmouth)

A diverse group of college students freely explore drugs and sex in their seemingly hopeless pursuit of love.

© Lions Gate

Kip Pardue

Ian Somerhalder

Clifton Collins, Jr., James Van Der Beek

WHITE OLEANDER

(**WARNER BROS.**) Producers, John Wells, Hunt Lowry; Executive Producers, Kristin Harms, Stacy Cohen, E.K. Gaylord II, Patrick Markey; Director, Peter Kosminsky; Screenplay, Mary Agnes Donoghue; Based on the novel by Janet Fitch; Photography, Elliot Davis; Designer, Donald Graham Burt; Costumes, Susie De Santo; Music, Thomas Newman; Editor, Chris Ridsdale; Casting, Ellen Lewis; a John Wells production, presented in association with Pandora; Dolby; Color; Rated PG-13; 109 minutes; Release date: October 11, 2002

CAST

Astrid Magnusson . . . . .Alison Lohman
Starr . . . . .Robin Wright Penn
Ingrid Magnusson . . . . .Michelle Pfeiffer
Claire Richards . . . . .Renée Zellweger
Barry . . . . .Billy Connolly
Rena Grushenka . . . . .Svetlana Efremova
Paul Trout . . . . .Patrick Fugit
Ray . . . . .Cole Hauser
Mark Richards . . . . .Noah Wyle
Miss Martinez . . . . .Amy Aquino
Girl in Fight . . . . .Elisa Bocanegra
Prisoner . . . . .Darlene Bohorquez
Guards . . . . .Solomon Burke, Jr., Vernon Haas
Bill Greenway . . . . .Scott Allan Campbell
Teacher . . . . .Sam Catlin
and John Billingsley, Melissa McCarthy (Paramedics), Debra Christofferson (Marlena), Marc Donato (Davey Thomas), Sean Happy (Dirt Bike Boyfriend), Leila Kenzle (Ann Greenway), Cathy Ladman (Swap Meet Mother), Drinda La Lumia (Patty), Myra Lamar (Detective), James Lashly (Reverend Daniels), James W. Lee (Prison Visitor), Daniel Mandehr (Dad at Induction Area), DeVonda Manghane (Guard at X-ray Machine), Taryn Manning (Niki), Melissa Marsala (Julie), Roger McIntyre (Police Officer), Dallas McKinney (Owen), Brian Mulligan (Bailiff), Allison Munn (Hannah), Kali Rocha (Susan Valeris), Stephen Root (Michael), Jennifer Saxon (Swap Meet Daughter), Samantha Shelton (Yvonne), Mark Soper (Patrick), Liz Stauber (Carolee), Carl Sundstrom (Police Officer), Kimo Wills (Comic Book Store Clerk), Biff Yeager (Judge)

After her mother is jailed for murdering her lover, young Astrid is shuttled through a series of foster homes where she comes into contact with a variety of emotionally damaged women.

© Warner Bros.

Cole Hauser, Alison Lohman

Patrick Fugit, Alison Lohman

Renée Zellweger, Michelle Pfeiffer

Robin Wright Penn, Alison Lohman

BELOW

(DIMENSION) Producers, Sue Baden-Powell, Darren Aronofsky, Eric Watson; Executive Producers, Bob Weinstein, Harvey Weinstein, Andrew Rona; Co-Producers, Mark Indig, Michael Zoumas; Director, David Twohy; Screenplay, Lucas Sussman, Darren Aronofsky, David Twohy; Photography, Ian Wilson; Designer, Charles Lee; Costumes, Elizabeth Waller; Editor, Martin Hunter; Music, Graeme Revell; Visual Effects Supervisor, Peter Chiang; Visual Effects, Double Negativew; Casting, Mary Vernieu, Anne McCarthy, Felicia Fasano, Daniel Hubbard; a Protozoa Pictures production; Distributed by Miramax Films; Dolby; Deluxe color; Rated R; 105 minutes; Release date: October 11, 2002

CAST

Ensign O'Dell . . . . .Matt Davis
Lt. Brice . . . . .Bruce Greenwood
Claire Paige . . . . .Olivia Williams
Lt. Loomis . . . . .Holt McCallany
Coors . . . . .Scott Foley
Weird Wally . . . . .Zach Galifianakis
Stumbo . . . . .Jason Flemyng
Kingsley . . . . .Dexter Fletcher
Chief . . . . .Nick Chinlund
and Andrew Howard (Hoag), Christopher Fairbank (Pappy), Chuck Ellsworth (Navy Pilot), Crispin Layfield (Navy Lookout), Jonathan Hartman (Schillings), Sebastian Knapp (Sonar), Max Casali (Air Manifold), Alexis Conran (Helmsman), Matthew Leitch (Zap), Gary Broadway (Mess Steward), Tim Plester (Motomac), Craig Blake (Steward), Mitchell Barnett (Bow Planesman), Nick Hobbs (Captain Winters), Chris Bridgeman (Stern Planesman), David Twohy (British Captain)

During World War II, a U.S. submarine picks up three survivors of a sunken hospital ship, after which a series of unfortunate events start taking place.

© Miramax/Dimension

Bruce Greenwood

Matthew Davis, Jason Flemyng

David Arquette

THE GREY ZONE

(LIONS GATE) Producers, Pamela Koffler, Christine Vachon, Tim Blake Nelson, Avi Lerner, Danny Lerner; Director/Screenplay, Tim Blake Nelson; Based on the play *The Grey Zone* by Tim Blake Nelson and based in part on the book *Auschwitz: A Doctor's Eyewitness Account* by Dr. Miklos Nyiszli; Executive Producers, Danny Dimbort, Trevor Short, Brad Weston, John Wells, Harvey Keitel, Peggy Gormley; Co-Producer, David Varod; Line Producer, Trish Hofmann; Photography, Russell Lee Fine; Designer, Maria Djurkovic; Costumes, Marina Draghici; Editors, Tim Blake Nelson, Michelle Botticelli; Music, Jeff Danna; Casting, Bernard Telsey, David Vaccari; a Millennium Films presentation of a Killer Films production, in association with The Goatsingers; Dolby; Color; Rated R; 108 minutes; Release date: October 18, 2002

CAST

Hoffman . . . . .David Arquette
Schlermer . . . . .Daniel Benzali
Abramowics . . . . .Steve Buscemi
Rosenthal . . . . .David Chandler
Dr. Nyiszli . . . . .Allan Corduner
Muhsfeldt . . . . .Harvey Keitel
Rosa . . . . .Natasha Lyonne
Dina . . . . .Mira Sorvino
Anja . . . . .Lisa Benavides-Nelson
Moll . . . . .Velizar Binev
and Michael Stuhlberg (Cohen), George Zlatarev (Lowy), Dimitar Ivanov (Old Man), Henry Stram (Megele), Kamelia Grigorova (Girl), Shirly Brener (Inmate), Dafina Katzarraska, Rumena Trifonova, Ioana Christova (Inmates), Donka Avramova (Young Woman), Simeon Vladov (Guard), Mariana Stanisheva (Girl's Mother), Oncho Alexanyan (Rivkin), Georgi Kalchev, Dobrin Dosev (SS Officers), Lee Wilkof (Man with Watch), Jessica Hecht (Man's Wife), Brian O'Byrne (Interrogator), Valentin Ganev (Torturer), Steve Ubels (Hauptman), Vladimir Velev (KS Man), Victor Kalev (Kahn), Hristo Shopov (Halivni), Mark Wing-Davey (Schott), Harry Anichkin (Kaminski), Portia Ranier (Voice of Young Girl)

The true story of how a unit of Jewish prisoners planned a revolt against their Nazi captors at Auschwitz.

© Lions Gate

REAL WOMEN HAVE CURVES

(NEWMARKET FILMS) Producers, George LaVoo, Effie T. Brown; Director, Patricia Cardoso; Screenplay, George LaVoo, Josefina Lopez; Based on play by Josefina Lopez; Photography, Jim Denault; Designer, Brigitte Broch; Costumes, Elaine Montalvo; Editor, Sloane Klevin; Music, Heitor Pereira; Casting, Ellyn Long Marshall, Maria E. Nelson; an HBO Films presentation; a LaVoo production; Dolby; Color; Rated PG-13; 86 minutes; Release date: October 18, 2002

CAST

Ana Garcia	America Ferrera
Carmen Garcia	Lupe Ontiveros
Estela Garcia	Ingrid Oliu
Mr. Guzman	George Lopez
Jimmy	Brian Sites
Pancha	Soledad St. Hilaire
Rosali	Lourdes Perez
Raúl Garcia	Jorge Cervera, Jr.
Grandfather	Felipe De Alba
Juan José	José Gerardo Zamora, Jr.
Juan Martin	Edgar Lujan
Norma	Lina Acosta
Glitz Receptionist	Celina Belazin
Singing Woman	Ramona Garcia Coronado
Mrs. Glass	Marlene Forte
Landlord	Jimmy Ishida
Dr. Lopez	Pete Leal
Veronica	Josefina Lopez

and Esmerelda Mcquillan (Pharmacy Attendant), Jose Tolentino (Mariachi), Sandie Torres (Doña Carlota), Dale Turner (Policeman), Julia Vera (Doña Gorgonia), Lisa Guzman, Lackey Bevis, Michelle Moretti (Girls)

Following high school graduation, Ana finds herself in conflict with her strict mother over working in a dress factory run by her sister and Ana's ambition to apply for a scholarship and continue her education.

© Newmarket Films

America Ferrera, Ingrid Oliu

America Ferrera, Lupe Ontiveros

America Ferrera

THE RING

(DREAMWORKS) Producers, Walter F. Parkes, Laurie MacDonald; Executive Producers, Mike Macari, Roy Lee, Michele Weisler; Director, Gore Verbinski; Screenplay, Ehren Kruger; Based on the novel by Koji Suzuki, and on the motion picture *The Ring* by The Ring/Spiral Production Group; Photography, Bojan Bazelli; Designer, Tom Duffield; Costumes, Julie Weiss; Editor, Craig Wood; Music, Hans Zimmer; Special Make-up Effects, Rick Baker; Visual Effects Supervisor, Charles Gibson; Co-Executive Producer, Neal Edelstein; Casting, Denise Chamian; a MacDonald/Parkes production; Dolby; Technicolor; Rated PG-13; 115 minutes; Release date: October 18, 2002

Amber Tamblyn, Rachel Bella

CAST

Rachel Keller	Naomi Watts
Noah	Martin Henderson
Aidan	David Dorfman
Richard Morgan	Brian Cox
Dr. Grasnik	Jane Alexander
Ruth	Lindsay Frost
Katie	Amber Tamblyn
Becca	Rachael Bella
Samara	Daveigh Chase
Anna Morgan	Shannon Cochran
Teacher	Sandra Thigpen
Innkeeper	Richard Lineback
Girl Teens	Sasha Barrese, Tess Hall
Teen	Adam Brody
Harvey	Alan Blumenfeld
Beth	Pauley Perrette
Doctor	Joe Chrest
Library Clerk	Ronald William Lawrence
Donna	Stephanie Erb
Babysitter	Sara Rue

and Lindsey Stoddart (Grad Student), Joe Sabatino (Orderly), Joanna Lin Black (Cashier), Maura McNamara (Girl on Ferry), David Proval (Girl's Father), Keith Campbell (Ship's Mate), Chuck Hicks (Ferry Worker), Michael Spound (Dave), Gary Cervantes (Painter), Aixa Clemente (Nurse), Art Frankel (Cal), Billy Lloyd (Darby), Coleen Malone, Catherine Paolone (Mourners)

Reporter Rachel Keller gets hold of a deadly video tape that has reportedly been responsible for the deaths of various viewers, watches it and realizes that she has only seven days in which to unravel its mystery before she herself will supposedly die.

© Dreamworks

Naomi Watts

Martin Henderson, Naomi Watts

Naomi Watts, Daveigh Chase

AUTO FOCUS

(SONY CLASSICS) Producers, Scott Alexander, Larry Karaszweski, Todd Rosken, Pat Dollard, Alicia Allain; Executive Producers, Trevor Macy, Rick Hess, James Schamus; Director, Paul Schrader; Screenplay, Michael Gerbosi; Based on the book *The Murder of Bob Crane* by Robert Graysmith; Photography, Fred Murphy; Designer, James Chinlund; Costumes, Julie Weiss; Editor, Kristina Boden; Music, Angelo Badalamenti; Casting, Wendy Kurtzman; Presented in association with Propaganda Films and Good Machine; Dolby; Color; Rated R; 105 minutes; Release date: October 18, 2002

CAST

Bob Crane	Greg Kinnear
John Carpenter	Willem Dafoe
Anne Crane	Rita Wilson
Patricia Crane	Maria Bello
Lenny	Ron Leibman
Feldman, Hogan's Producer	Bruce Solomon
Richard Dawson	Michael Rodgers
Werner Klemperer ("Klink")	Kurt Fuller
Robert Clary ("LeBeau")	Christopher Neiman
John Banner ("Schultz")	Lyle Kanouse
Mel Rosen	Ed Begley, Jr.
Video Executive	Michael McKean
Mistress Victoria	Donnamarie Recco
Emily	Alex Meneses
Elaine	Cassie Townsend
Cynthia Lynn	Cheryl Lynn Bowers
Priest	Don McManus
Victoria Berry	Sarah Ulrich
Press Party Waitress	Amanda Niles
Dawson's Blonde	Kelly Packard
Armand	Jeff Harlan
Hogan's AD	Kevin Beard
Salome's Announcer	Joe Grifasi

and Vyto Ruginis (Nickie D), Amber Griebel (Jill), Nikita Ager (Julie), Bob Crane, Jr. (Interviewer), Arden Myrin (Hippie Girl), Joseph D. Reitman (Hippie Boy), Kitana Baker (Girl at Hippie Party), Gibby Brandt (Judge), Katie Lohmann (Dallas Girl), Roderick McCarthy (Bartender), Catherine Dent (Seattle Secretary), John Kapelos (Bruno Gerussi), Shawn Reaves (Bob Crane, Jr. at 20), Michael Tachovsky (Bob Crane, Jr. at 12), Bruce Bauer (Talk Show Host), Marieh Delfino (Bobby's Girlfriend), Hannah Felder-Shaw (Judy), Kitten De Ville Aka Teri (Dancer, Miss Kitty), Geary (Dancer, Angela), Jade Ruggiero (Classic Cat Dancer)

The true story of how television actor Bob Crane's obsession with sex led to his brutal murder.

© Sony Pictures

Donnamarie Recco, Willem Dafoe

Greg Kinnear, Michael Rodgers, Willem Dafoe

Ron Leibman, Greg Kinnear

Rita Wilson, Greg Kinnear

FRIDA

(MIRAMAX) Producers, Sarah Green, Salma Hayek, Jay Polstein, Lizz Speed, Nancy Hardin, Lindsay Flickinger, Roberto Sneider; Executive Producers, Margaret Rose Perenchio, Brian Gibson, Mark Amin, Mark Gill, Jill Sobel Messic, Amy Slotnick; Director, Julie Taymor; Screenplay, Clancy Sigal, Diane Lake, Gregory Nava, Anna Thomas; Based on the book by Hayden Herrera; Photography, Rodrigo Prieto; Designer, Felipe Fernández del Paso; Costumes, Julie Weiss; Editor, Françoise Bonnot; Music, Elliot Goldenthal; Song: "Burn It Blue" by Elliot Goldenthal, Julie Taymor; Frida/Diego's Painting Teams: Head Artists, Mariano Grimaldo, Dionisio Ceballos; Visual Effects Supervisors, Jeremy Dawson, Dan Shrecker; Casting, Claudia Becker; a Ventanarosa production in association with Lions Gate Films, presented in association with Margaret Rose Perenchio; Dolby; Color; Rated R; 123 minutes; Release date: October 25, 2002

Alfred Molina

Salma Hayek

CAST

Frida Kahlo	Salma Hayek
Diego Rivera	Alfred Molina
Lupe Marín	Valeria Golino
Cristina Kahlo	Mía Maestro
Guillermo Kahlo	Roger Rees
Alejandro "Alex" Gómez Arias	Diego Luna
Matilde Kahlo	Patricia Reyes Spíndola
Natalie Sedova Trotsky	Margarita Sanz
Leon Trotsky	Geoffrey Rush
Maid	Amelia Zapata
Professor	Alejandro Usigli
Auditorium Model	Lucía Bravo
Nanny	Loló Navarro
Painter on Bus	Fermín Martínez
Dr. Farril	Roberto Medina
Tina Modotti	Ashley Judd
David Alfaro Siqueiros	Antonio Banderas
Tango Singer	Lila Downs
Women at Wedding	Martha Claudia Moreno, Maria Inés Pintado
Lupe's Maid	Aida López
Chapingo Chapel Model	Ivana Sejenovich
Pulquería Singer	Diego Espinozaé
Drunk Young Man	Ehécatl Chávez
Voice of Newsreel Reporter	Elliot Goldenthal
Nelson Rockefeller	Edward Norton
Gracie	Saffron Burrows
Waitress	Didi Conn
NY Reporter	Julian Sedgwik
Priest at Funeral	Jorge Guerrero
Isolda	Mary Luz Palacio
André Breton	Omar Rodríguez
Trotsky's Armed Sentries	Antony Alvarez, Enoc Leaño
Paris Chanteuse	Karine Plantadit-Bageot
Death "La Pelona"	Chavela Vargas
Detective	Jorge Zepeda

The true story of visionary Mexican artist Frida Kahlo, her ever-present struggle with physical pain after her accident as a teenager, her stormy marriage to painter Diego Rivera, and the eventual acclaim for her work.

2002 Academy Award winner for Best Original Score and Best Makeup. This film received additional Oscar nominations for actress (Salma Hayek), costume design, original song ("Burn It Blue"), and art direction.

Antonio Banderas, Salma Hayek, Ashley Judd, Alfred Molina

© Miramax

Ashley Judd, Salma Hayek

Salma Hayek, Alfred Molina

Alfred Molina, Salma Hayek

127

GHOST SHIP

(WARNER BROS.) Producers, Joel Silver, Robert Zemeckis, Gilbert Adler; Executive Producers, Bruce Berman, Steve Richards; Director, Steve Beck; Screenplay, Mark Hanlon, John Pogue; Story, Mark Hanlon; Photography, Gale Tattersall; Designer, Graham "Grace" Walker; Co-Producers, Richard Mirisch, Susan Levin; Editor, Roger Barton; Music, John Frizzell; Visual Effects Supervisor, Dale Duguid; a Dark Castle Entertainment production, presented in association with Village Roadshow Pictures and NPV Entertainment; Dolby; Technicolor; Rated R; 91 minutes; Release date: October 25, 2002

CAST

Captain Sean Murphy . . . . .Gabriel Byrne
Maureen Epps . . . . .Julianna Margulies
Dodge . . . . .Ron Eldard
Jack Ferriman . . . . .Desmond Harrington
Greer . . . . .Isaiah Washington
Santos . . . . .Alex Dimitriades
Munder . . . . .Karl Urban
Katie . . . . .Emily Browning
Francesa . . . . .Francesca Rettondini
and Boris Brkic (Chief Steward), Robert Buggiero (Captain), Iain Gardiner (Purser), Adam Bieshaar (First Officer), Cameron Watt (Second Officer), Jamie Giddens (Friendly Officer)

A salvage crew comes across the remains of a fabeled ocean liner, thought lost at sea for over 40 years, but are shocked to find that something horrifying and deadly lurks aboard the seemingly deserted vessel.

© Warner Bros.

Wood Harris, Mekhi Phifer, Cam'ron

PAID IN FULL

(DIMENSION) Producers, Damon Dash, Shawn Carter, Brett Ratner; Executive Producers, Ron Rotholz, Jesse Berdinka; Director, Charles Stone III; Screenplay, Matthew Cirulnick, Thulani Davis; Photography, Paul Sarossy; Designer, Maher Ahmad; Costumes, Abram Waterhouse, Suzette Daigle; Editors, Bill Pankow, Patricia Bowers; Music, Vernon Reid, Frank Fitzpatrick; Casting, Billy Hopkins, Suzanne Smith, Kerry Barden; a presentation of a Roc-a-Fella Films production in association with Rat Entertainment/Loud Films; Distributed by Miramax Films; Dolby; Deluxe color; Rated R; 97 minutes; Release date: October 25, 2002

CAST

Ace . . . . .Wood Harris
Mitch . . . . .Mekhi Phifer
Calvin . . . . .Kevin Carroll
Lulu . . . . .Esai Morales
Pip . . . . .Chi McBride
Rico . . . . .Cam'ron
Sonny . . . . .Remo Green
Dora . . . . .Cynthia Martells
Aunt Jane . . . . .Elise Neal
Kiesha . . . . .Regina Hall
and Joyce Walker Joseph (Janet Woods), Ron Cephas Jones (Ice), Nelson Tynes (Wedge), Karen Andrew (Cakes), Pedro Salvin, Ramon Marroquin (Colombian Men), Bruce Robinson (The World Famous Bruce B), Jonas Chernick (Detective/Surgeon), Wes "Maestro" Williams (Mitch's Friend), Rufus Crawford (Tommy), Jason Burke (Street Runner), Chris Collins, Geoffrey Antoine (Kids), Arnold Pinnock (Wiry Man), Tyson Hall (Customer), Flash, Martin Roach (D.C.s), Noreaga, Tobias Truvillion (Runner), Jesse Gibbons (Antoine), Rohan Waugh (Andre), Raven Dauda (Donna), Eduardo Gomez (Colombian #3), Anthony Clark, Michael Pope (Rico's Buddies), Busy Bee, Doug E. Fresh (Themselves), Khalida Outlaw (Homegirl on the Street), Terrance Telfair (Neutral Kid), Derrick Simmons (Taunting Guy), Angela Martinez (Girl in Car), Jamie Hector (Dunn), Hassan Johnson (Accomplice), Jermaine Lloyd (Money Counter), Clarence Ford (Dancer), Hakan Coskuner (Laz)

A young Harlem deliveryman, seeing his associates live high from dealing crack cocaine, finds himself seduced into this life of crime.

© Miramax

Julianna Margulies

THE TRUTH ABOUT CHARLIE

(UNIVERSAL) Producers, Jonathan Demme, Peter Saraf, Edward Saxon; Executive Producer, Ilona Herzberg; Director, Jonathan Demme; Screenplay, Jonathan Demme, Steve Schmidt, Peter Joshua, Jessica Bendinger; Based on the motion picture *Charade*, screenplay by Peter Stone; Photography, Tak Fujimoto; Designer, Hugo Luczyc-Wyhowski; Costumes, Catherine Leterrier; Editor, Carol Littleton; Co-Producers, Neda Armian, Mishka Cheyko; Music, Rachel Portman; Music Supervisor, Deva Anderson; Casting, Françoise Combardière Stern; a Clinica Estetico production; Dolby; Panavision; Color; Rated PG-13; 104 minutes; Release date: October 25, 2002

CAST

Joshua Peters	Mark Wahlberg
Regina Lambert	Thandie Newton
Mr. Bartholomew	Tim Robbins
Il-Sang Lee	Joong-Hoon Park
Emil Zatapec	Ted Levine
Lola Jansco	Lisa Gay Hamilton
Commandant Dominque	Christine Boisson
Charles Lambert	Stephen Dillane
Lieutenant Dessalines	Simon Abkarian
Madame du Lac	Frédérique Meininger
Himself	Charles Aznavour
Karina	Anna Karina
Woman in Black	Magali Noël
Sylvia	Sakina Jaffrey
The Widow Hyppolite	Agnès Varda

Saïan Supa Crew ....Feniksi, Leeroy Kesiah, Sir Samuel, Sly the Mic Buddah, Specta, Vicelow and Olga Sékulic (Junior Military Officer), Françoise Bertin (Woman on Train), Cassius Kumar Wilkinson (Hecules), Christophe Salengro (Morgue Attendant), Philippe Fretun, Loeïza Jacq (Evident Handlers), Raphaelle Gallizzi (Romantic Taxi Driver), Michel Crémadès (Amiable Desk Clerk), Denis Jousselin (Hotel Barman), Christian Wojtowicz (Lonely Clown), Marine Danaux (Hotel Langlois Chambermaid), Olivier Broche ("Aznavour Fan" Desk Clerk), Wilfred Benaïche (Toy Store Manager), Catherine Chevron (Toy Store Salesgirl), Lionel Elie (African Dignitary), Tony Amoni, Eric Aufèvre (Undercover ODC), Hubert Ravel, Pascal Parmentier, Cheikna Sankare, Mustapha Bensittu, Chantal Banlier, Patrice Keller (Undercover Cops), Benjamin Euvrard (Ticket Agent), Jean-Marc Bihour (Café Waiter), Philippe Duquesne (Café Cook), Manno Charlemagne (Chez Josephine Maitre D'), Philippe Katerine (Karina Fan), Pierre Carré (Bistro Singer), René Comte (Shouting Waiter), Kate Castle, Robert Castle (Flea Market Bargain Hunters), Kenneth Utt (The Late Monsieur Hyppolite), Sotigui Kouyaté (Dealer Prophète), Georges Trillat (Angry Man on Metro), Ramona Demme (Young Girl with Pug), Paula Moore (Ms. Hoskins), Natacha Atalas (Spirit Voice)

Regina Lambert enlists the help of Joshua Peters to find out why her husband was murdered and what those three men following her are looking for. Remake of the 1963 Universal film *Charade* (Cary Grant, Audrey Hepburn, Walter Matthau).

© Universal

Christine Boisson

Stephen Dillane

Thandie Newton, Mark Wahlberg

Thandie Newton, Tim Robbins

129

ROGER DODGER

(ARTISAN) Producers, Anne Chaisson, Dylan Kidd, George Van Buskirk; Executive Producers, Martin Garvey, David Newman, Campbell Scott, Bruce Cowan, Michael Lauer; Director/Screenplay, Dylan Kidd; Photography, Joaquin Baca-Asay; Designer, Stephen Beatrice; Costumes, Amy Westcott; Music, Craig Wedren; Music Supervisor, Jonathan McHugh; Co-Producer, Per Melita; Casting, Laylee Olfat, Marcia Turner; Rated R; 104 minutes; Release date: October 25, 2002

CAST

Roger	Campbell Scott
Nick	Jesse Eisenberg
Joyce	Isabella Rossellini
Andrea	Elizabeth Berkley
Sophie	Jennifer Beals
Donna	Mina Badie
Donovan	Ben Shenkman
Chris	Chris Stack
Girl in Bar	Morena Bacarin
Woman in Bar	Lisa Emery
Young Working Woman	Flora Diaz
Angela	Stephanie Gatschet
Angus	Colin Fickes
Darren	Tommy Savas
Felix	Gabriel Millman
Patricia	Libby Larson
Susan	Courtney Sherman
Alert Doorman	Peter Apel
Bouncer	Ato Essandoh
Waitress	Michelle Six
Tired Woman	Juliet Morgan

An arrogant, womanizing New York copywriter, recently dumped by his lover, takes his impressionable nephew on the town in hopes of relieving the lad of his virginity.

© Artisan

Jesse Eisenberg, Mina Badie, Campbell Scott

Campbell Scott, Jesse Eisenberg

Jennifer Beals, Jesse Eisenberg, Elizabeth Berkley

Catherine McCormack, Elizabeth Hurley

Sean Penn, Josh Lucas

THE WEIGHT OF WATER

(LIONS GATE) Producers, Janet Yang, Sigurjon Sighvatsson, A. Kitman Ho; Executive Producers, Lisa Henson, Steven-Charles Jaffe; Director, Kathryn Bigelow; Screenplay, Alice Arlen, Christopher Kyle; Based on the novel by Anita Shreve; Photography, Adrian Biddle; Designer, Karl Juliusson; Costumes, Marti Allen; Music, David Hirschfelder; Editor, Howard E. Smith; Casting, Mali Finn; a Studio Canal presentation of a Manifest Film Company/Sixty Six Degrees North/Miracle Pictures production; U.S.-French-Canadian; Dolby; Deluxe color; Rated R; 113 minutes; Release date: November 1, 2002

CAST

Adaline Gunne . . . . .Elizabeth Hurley
Jean Janes . . . . .Catherine McCormack
Thomas Janes . . . . .Sean Penn
Maren Hontvedt . . . . .Sarah Polley
Rich Janes . . . . .Josh Lucas
Louis Wagner . . . . .Ciarán Hinds
John Hontvedt . . . . .Ulrich Thomsen
Evan Christenson . . . . .Anders W. Berthelsen
Karen Christenson . . . . .Katrin Cartlidge
Anethe Christenson . . . . .Vinessa Shaw

The psychological tensions between four people aboard a sailboat off of New Hampshire, is contrasted with a gruesome 19th-century double murder being investigated by a photographer who believes a third party may have been involved in the crime.

© Lions Gate

TULLY

(SMALL PLANET PICTURES) formerly *The Truth About Tully*; Producers, Anne Sundberg, Hilary Birmingham; Line Producer, Debi Zelko; Director, Hilary Birmingham; Screenplay, Matt Drake, Hilary Birmingham; Based upon the short story by Tom McNeal; Photography, John Foster; Designer, Mark White; Costumes, Christine Volmer; Music, Marcelo Zarvos; Editor, Affonso Goncalves; Casting, Ellen Parks; Presented in association with Telltale Films; Dolby; Color; Not rated; 102 minutes; Release date: November 1, 2002

CAST

Tully Coates, Jr. . . . . .Anson Mount
Ella Smalley . . . . .Julianne Nicholson
Earl Coates . . . . .Glenn Fitzgerald
April Reece . . . . .Catherine Kellner
Claire . . . . .Natalie Canerday
Mal "Mac" MacAvoy . . . . .John Diehl
Tully Coates, Sr. . . . . .Bob Burrus
Burt Hodges . . . . .V. Craig Heidenreich
and Delaney Driscoll (Mrs. Smalley), Tim Driscoll (Clarence Heiting), Andy Signore (Pete Heiting), Kristopher Kling (Dexter), Aaron Zavitz (Chuck), Harry Gibbs (Mr. Sullivan), Kathryn Gayner (Irene Duffy, in photos), John Durbin (Marshall), Michael McCormack (Fred Robertson), Laura Walker (Wendy Adams), Joe Smalley (Brad), Richard Hansen (Charlie), Justin Hyde (Deodorant Boy), Mellisa Bryson (Jeannie), Vivek Kumar (Essa)

Tully, a handsome womanizing farmer, is faced with the possible loss of the family property, a crisis prompted by his father having led his two sons to believe that their mother had passed away.

© Small Planet Pictures

Anson Mount

Anson Mount, Julianne Nicholson

I SPY

(COLUMBIA) Producers, Jenno Topping, Betty Thomas, Mario Kassar, Andy Vajna; Executive Producers, Warren Carr, Marc Toberoff, David R. Ginsburg; Director, Betty Thomas; Screenplay, Marianne Wibberley, Cormac Wibberley, Jay Scherick, David Ronn; Story, Marianne Wibberley, Cormac Wibberley; Photography, Oliver Wood; Designer, Marcia Hinds-Johnson; Costumes, Ruth Carter; Editor, Peter Teschner; Music, Richard Gibbs; Music Supervisor, Elliot Lurie; Special Visual Effects, Sony Pictures Imageworks Inc.; Visual Effects Supervisor, Carey Villegas; Stunts, Brent Woolsey, Gabor Piroch; Fight Coordinator, Darrell Foster; a Tall Trees/C-2 Pictures production in association with Sheldon Leonard productions; Dolby; Deluxe color; Rated PG-13; 96 minutes; Release date: November 1, 2002

Owen Wilson

Owen Wilson, Eddie Murphy

Malcolm McDowell, Eddie Murphy, Owen Wilson

Famke Janssen

CAST

Kelly Robinson . . . . .Eddie Murphy
Alex Scott . . . . .Owen Wilson
Rachel Wright . . . . .Famke Janssen
Arnold Gundars . . . . .Malcolm McDowell
Carlos . . . . .Gary Cole
Jerry . . . . .Phil Lewis
T.J. . . . . .Viv Leacock
Lunchbox . . . . .Keith Dallas
Lieutenant Percy . . . . .Tate Taylor
Edna . . . . .Lynda Boyd
McIntyre . . . . .Bill Mondy
Vegas Commentators . . . . .Larry Merchant, Sugar Ray Leonard
Vegas Ring Announcer . . . . .Jimmy Lennon, Jr.
Vegas Referee . . . . .Joe Cortez
Europe Referee . . . . .Gordon Racette
Europe Announcers .Steve Albert, Bobby Cyze
Cedric Mills . . . . .Darren Shahlavi
Himself . . . . .Blake "The Blade" Lirette
Zhu Tam . . . . .Dana Lee
and Edmond Wong (Zhu Tam's Pilot), Gus Lynch (General Elmo Tucker), Malik McCall (Kelly's Pilot), Ray Galletti (BNS Man), Mike Dopud (Jim), Aleks Paunovic (Bob), Kendall Saunders, Crystal Lowe (Beautiful Girls), Peter Vida (Vespa Guy), J.B. Bivens (BNS Equipment Technician), Steve Lesko (Massage Patron), Zinaid Memisevic (Tent Chef), John Scott, Norman Edge (Spa Patrons), Peter Linka (Master of Ceremonies), Bernard J. Manuel (Abi), Mihaly Tabanyi (Hungarian Violinist), Csaba Szocs, Yaroslav Poverlo (Hungarian Cops), Eric Bryson, Glenn Ennis, George Josef, Roger Lewis, Tony Morelli, Layton Morrison, Mike Roselli, Kevin Rushton (Gundars' Posse), Simone Bailly, Kylea Beil, Ocean Bloom, Jade Boragno, Kristene Keward, Deborah Macatumpag, Colette Perry, Angela Uyeda (Vegas Showgirls)

Special agent Alex Scott and boxer Kelly Robinson are teamed to help recover a state-of-the-art reconnaissance aircraft that has been hijacked by arms dealer Arnold Gundars. Based on the TV series that ran on NBC from 1965 to 1968 and starred Robert Culp (Kelly Robinson) and Bill Cosby (Alexander Scott).

THE SANTA CLAUSE 2

(WALT DISNEY PICTURES) Producers, Brian Reilly, Bobby Newmyer, Jeffrey Silver; Executive Producers, William W. Wilson III, Rick Messina, Richard Baker, James Miller; Director, Michael Lembeck; Screenplay, Don Rhymer, Cinco Paul, Ken Daurio, Ed Decter, John J. Strauss; Story, Leo Benvenuti, Steve Rudnick, based on their characters; Photography, Adam Greenberg; Designer, Tony Burrough; Costumes, Ingrid Ferrin; Editor, David Finfer; Special Character Effects Designers/Creators, Alec Gillis, Tom Woodruff, Jr.; Music, George S. Clinton; Music Supervisor, Frankie Pine; Casting, Jackie Burch; an Outlaw Productions/Boxing Cat Films production; Dolby; Technicolor; Rated G; 104 minutes; Release date: November 1, 2002

CAST

Scott Calvin/Santa/Toy Santa	Tim Allen
Carol Newman	Elizabeth Mitchell
Bernard	David Krumholtz
Charlie Calvin	Eric Lloyd
Neil Miller	Judge Reinhold
Laura Miller	Wendy Crewson
Curtis	Spencer Breslin
Lucy Miller	Liliana Mumy
Abby	Danielle Woodman
Tooth Fairy	Art LaFleur
Mother Nature	Aisha Tyler
Cupid	Kevin Pollak
Easter Bunny	Jay Thomas
Sandman	Michael Dorn

and Christopher Attadia, Bryce Hodgson (Engineer Elves), Curtis Butchart (Elf Center), Jamal Allen (Elf Quarterback), Alexander Pollock (Richie/Elf Tight End), Molly Shannon (Tracy), Carmen Aquirre (Spanish Teacher), Leanne Adachi (Grace), Blu Mankuma (John Pierce), Andrew Stone (Picardo), Kenya Jo Kennedy (Pamela), Janne Mortil (Pamela's Mother), Alexandra Purvis (Danielle), Fred Keating (Security Guard), Fred Ewanuick (Seismic Interpreter), Dan Joffre (C-130 Pilot), J.B. Bivens (Engineer), Alexander Hoy (Elf With Kangaroo), Bart Anderson (Hangdog Teacher), Beverly Elliott, D. Neil Mark, Ted Cole, Nicole Leroux, Beatrice Zeilinger, Michael P. Northey, Alejandro Abellon, June B. Wilde-Eremico, Charles Payne, Gary Jones (Teachers), Victor Brandt (Reindeer), Kath Soucie (Voice of Chet), Bob Bergen (Voice of Comet)

The newest Santa Clause, Scott Calvin, realizes that if he doesn't get married by Christmas Eve he'll stop being Santa forever. Sequel to the 1994 Walt Disney film *The Santa Clause* with many of the principals repeating their roles.

Liliana Mumy, Comet, Tim Allen

Molly Shannon, Tim Allen

Spencer Breslin, David Krumholtz, Tim Allen

Elizabeth Mitchell, Tim Allen

8 MILE

(UNIVERSAL) Producers, Brian Grazer, Curtis Hanson, Jimmy Iovine; Executive Producers, Carol Fenelon, James Whitaker, Gregory Goodman, Paul Rosenberg; Director, Curtis Hanson; Screenplay, Scott Silver; Photography, Rodrigo Prieto; Designer, Philip Messina; Costumes, Mark Bridges; Editors, Jay Rabinowitz, Craig Kitson; Music, Eminem; Song: "Lose Yourself" by Eminem, Jeff Bass, and Luis Resto; Casting, Mali Finn; an Imagine Entertainment presentation of a Brian Grazer/Curtis Hanson production; Dolby; Super 35 Widescreen; Deluxe color; Rated R; 110 minutes; Release date: November 8, 2002

Eminem

Brittany Murphy, Eminem

CAST

Jimmy Smith, Jr.	Eminem
Stephanie	Kim Basinger
Future	Mekhi Phifer
Alex	Brittany Murphy
Cheddar Bob	Evan Jones
Sol George	Omar Benson Miller
DJ Iz	De'Angelo Wilson
Wink	Eugene Byrd
Janeane	Taryn Manning
THE SHELTER	
Bouncer	Larry Hudson
Lil' Tic	Proof
Shorty Mike	Mike Bell
Battle DJ	DJ Head
THE TRAILER PARK	
Greg Buehl	Michael Shannon
Lily	Chloe Greenfield
Mrs. Helgeland	Mary Hannigan
THE FREE WORLD	
Papa Doc	Anthony Mackie
Lyckety-Splyt	Strike
Lotto	Nashawn "Ox" Breedlove
Papa Doc's Girl	Na'Keya Snoddy
Moochie	Malik Barnhardt
Day	Day Golfin
Omar	Allen Adams
THE CHIN TIKI	
Parking Lot Rappers	Hom, Obie Trice, Njeri Earth
Willing Girl	Jennifer Kitchen
Alex's Friend	Kyla Womack
Christine	Melissa Zaglanikzny
Rocky	Rockey Black
NEW DETROIT STAMPING	
Paul	Craig Chandler
Manny	Paul Bates
Lunch Truck Rappers	Miz-Korona, Xzibit
Joe Lee Patton	Abdul Salaam El Razzac
Plant Worker	Steven Monroe
WJLB	
Lobby Security Guard	John Smith, Jr.
WJLB Receptionist	Venice Foreman
Big O	Waverly W. Alford II
WJLB Disc Jockey	Bushman
Roy Darucher	Adam Brook

Jimmy Smith, Jr. hopes to escape his dead-end existence in Detroit's slums by making his name in the city's hip-hop scene.

2002 Academy Award winner for Best Song ("Lose Yourself").

Eugene Byrd, Eminem

Eminem, Kim Basinger

Eminem

Chloe Greenfield, Kim Basinger

De'Angelo Wilson, Evan Jones, Omar Benson Miller

Mekhi Phifer, Eminem, Evan Jones, De'Angelo Wilson

Evan Jones, Eminem, De'Angelo Wilson

Nashawn Breedlove, Eminem

135

FAR FROM HEAVEN

Dennis Quaid, Julianne Moore

Olivia Birkelund, Barbara Garrick, Patricia Clarkson,
Julianne Moore

(FOCUS FEATURES) Producers, Christine Vachon, Jody Patton; Executive Producers, Steven Soderbergh, George Clooney, John Wells, Eric Robison, Tracy Brimm, John Sloss; Director/Screenplay, Todd Haynes; Co-Producers, Bradford Simpson, Declan Baldwin; Photography, Edward Lachman; Designer, Mark Friedberg; Costumes, Sandy Powell; Editor, James Lyons; Music, Elmer Bernstein; Associate Producers, Didier Sapault, Jean Charles Lévy; Casting, Laura Rosenthal; a Vulcan Productions presentation of a Killer Films/John Wells/Section Eight production; Dolby; Color; Rated PG-13; 107 minutes; Release date: November 8, 2002

CAST

Cathy Whitaker . . . . .Julianne Moore
Frank Whitaker . . . . .Dennis Quaid
Raymond Deagan . . . . .Dennis Haysbert
Eleanor Fine . . . . .Patricia Clarkson
Sybil . . . . .Viola Davis
Dr. Bowman . . . . .James Rebhorn
Mrs. Leacock . . . . .Bette Henritze
Stan Fine . . . . .Michael Gaston
David Whitaker . . . . .Ryan Ward
Janice Whitaker .Lindsay Andretta
Sarah Deagan . . . . .Jordan Puryear
Billy Hutchinson . . . . .Kylle Smith
Mona Lauder . . . . .Celia Weston
Doreen . . . . .Barbara Garrick
Nancy . . . . .Olivia Birkelund
Dick Dawson .Stevie Ray Dallimore
Esther . . . . .Mylika Davis
Photographer . . . . .Jason Franklin
Reginald Carter . . . . .Gregory Marlow
Marlene . . . . .C.C. Loveheart
Elderly Woman . . . . .June Squibb
Man with Mustache . . . . .Laurent Giroux
Spanish Bartender . . . . .Alex Santoriello
Red-Faced Man . . . . .Matt Malloy
Farnsworth . . . . .J.B. Adams
Soda Jerk . . . . .Kevin Carrigan
Tallman . . . . .Chance Kelly
Officers . . . . .Declan Baldwin, Brian Delate
Kitty . . . . .Pamela Evans
Hotel Waiter . . . . .Joe Holt
Hutch's Friend . . . . .Ben Moss
Receptionist . . . . .Susan Willis
Conductor . . . . .Karl Schroeder
Bail Clerk . . . . .Lance Olds
Blond Boy . . . . .Nicholas Joy
Blond Boy's Father . . . . .Virl Andrick
Staff Member #1 . . . . .Jonathan McClain
Hooker . . . . .Jezebel Montero
Woman at Party . . . . .Geraldine Bartlett
Glaring Man . . . . .Ernest Rayford III
Jake . . . . .Duane McLaughlin
and Betsy Aidem (Pool Mother), Mary Anna Klindtworth (Pool Daughter), Ted Neustadt (Ron), Thomas Torres (Band Leader), Blondell Cooper (Hostess)

In 1950s Connecticut, Cathy Whitaker's seemingly idyllic suburban life is shattered by the revelation of her husband's hidden lifestyle, prompting her to turn to her black gardener for sympathy, an act that sets tongues wagging in her narrow-minded community.

This film received Oscar nominations for actress (Julianne Moore), original screenplay, cinematography, and original score.

Julianne Moore, Dennis Haysbert

Dennis Quaid, Viola Davis, Julianne Moore,
Lindsay Andretta, Ryan Ward

Julianne Moore, Dennis Quaid

Dennis Haysbert

Julianne Moore

Patricia Clarkson

Dennis Quaid, Julianne Moore

137

HARRY POTTER AND THE CHAMBER OF SECRETS

(WARNER BROS.) Producer, David Heyman; Executive Producers, Chris Columbus, Mark Radcliffe, Michael Barnathan, David Barron; Director, Chris Columbus; Screenplay, Steve Kloves; Based on the novel by J.K. Rowling; Photography, Roger Pratt; Designer, Stuart Craig; Costumes, Lindy Hemming; Editor, Peter Honess; Music, John Williams; Co-Producer, Tanya Seghatchian; Casting, Karen Lindsay-Stewart; Visual Effects, Industrial Light & Magic, Mill Film, The Moving Picture Company, Framestore CFC, Cinesite (Europe) Ltd.; Visual Effects Supervisors, Jim Mitchell, Nick Davis; Creature Make-up Effects Designer, Nick Dudman; a Heyday Films/1492 Pictures production; Dolby; Super 35 Widescreen; Technicolor; Rated PG; 161 minutes; Release date: November 15, 2002

Emma Watson, Daniel Radcliffe

Kenneth Branagh, Rupert Grint, Daniel Radcliffe

Daniel Radcliffe, David Bradley

CAST

Harry Potter	Daniel Radcliffe
Ron Weasley	Rupert Grint
Hermione Granger	Emma Watson
Gilderoy Lockhart	Kenneth Branagh
Nearly Headless Nick	John Cleese
Rubeus Hagrid	Robbie Coltrane
Professor Flitwick	Warwick Davis
Uncle Vernon Dursley	Richard Griffiths
Albus Dumbledore	Richard Harris
Lucius Malfoy	Jason Isaacs
Professor Snape	Alan Rickman
Aunt Petunia Dursley	Fiona Shaw
Professor Minerva McGonagall	Maggie Smith
Mrs. Weasley	Julie Walters
Moaning Myrtle	Shirley Henderson
Madam Pomfrey, School Nurse	Gemma Jones
Professor Sprout	Miriam Margolyes
Mr. Weasley	Mark Williams
Dudley Dursley	Harry Melling
Voice of Dobby the House Elf	Toby Jones
Mr. Mason	Jim Norton
Mrs. Mason	Veronica Clifford
Fred Weasley	James Phelps
George Weasley	Oliver Phelps
Ginny Weasley	Bonnie Wright
Percy Weasley	Chris Rankin
Draco Malfoy	Tom Felton
Mr. Borgin	Edward Tudor Pole
Aged Witch	Jenny Tarren
Mr. Granger	Tom Knight
Mrs. Granger	Heather Bleasdale
Girl in Bookshop	Isabella Columbus
Daily Prophet Photographer	Peter O'Farrell
Angus, Diagon Boy	Ben Borowiecki
Station Guard	Harry Taylor
Neville Longbottom	Matthew Lewis
Seamus Finnegan	Devon Murray

and David Bradley (Mr. Argus Filch, School Caretaker), Jamie Waylett (Crabbe), Josh Herman (Goyle), Gemma Padley (Penelope Clearwater), Hugh Mitchell (Colin Creavey, Boy with Camera), Alfred Enoch (Dean Thomas), Eleanor Columbus (Susan Bones), Sean Biggerstaff (Oliver Wood), Rochelle Douglas (Alicia Spinnet), Emily Dale (Katie Bell), Angelina Johnson (Danielle Tabor), Marcus Flint (Jamie Yeats), Vilet Columbus (Girl with Flowers), Peter Taylor (Man in Moving Picture), Luke Youngblood (Lee Jordan), Scott Fearn (Adrian Pucey), David Holmes, David Massam, Tony Christian (Slyth Beaters), David Churchyard (Slyth Keeper), Edward Randell (Justin Finch-Fletchley), Sally Moretemore (Madam Pince), Louis Doyle (Ernie MacMillan), Charlotte Skeoch (Hannah Hufflepuff), Brendan Columbus, Robert Ayres (Boys in Study Hall), Alfred Burke (Professor Dippet), Leslie Phillips (Voice of the Sorting Hat), Helen Stuart (Millicent Bulstrode), Daisy Bates (Brunette Lady in Moving Picture), David Tysall (Count in Moving Picture), Christian Coulson (Tom Marvolo/Lord Voldemort), Martin Bayfield (Young Hagrid), Robert Hardy (Cornelius Fudge, Minister for Magic), Julian Glover (Voice of Aragog the Giant Spider), Les Bubb (Reader)

During his second year at Hogwarts School of Witchcraft and Wizardy, Harry Potter and his friends try to find out how the Chamber of Secrets being opened has lead to the petrification of several staff members and students. The second *Harry Potter* film from Warner Bros. following the 2001 release *Harry Potter and the Sorcerer's Stone*, with most of the cast principals repeating their roles here.

Maggie Smith, Miriam Margolyes, Richard Harris, Alan Rickman

Rupert Grint, Daniel Radcliffe

Robbie Coltrane

Daniel Radcliffe, John Cleese

Richard Harris, Daniel Radcliffe

Dobby

Daniel Radcliffe, Emma Watson, Rupert Grint

Alan Rickman, Tom Felton, Daniel Radcliffe

Funk Brothers: Joe Messina, Johnny Griffith, Joe Hunter, Bob Babbit, Richard "Pistol" Allen

STANDING IN THE SHADOWS OF MOTOWN

(ARTISAN) Producers, Sandy Passman, Allan Slutsky, Paul Justman; Executive Producers, Paul Elliott, David Scott; Director, Paul Justman; Narrration Writers, Walter Dallas, Ntozake Shange; Inspired by the book by Allan "Dr. Licks" Slutsky; Co-Producer, Mary Petryshyn; Consulting Producer, Jonathan Dana; Associate Producers, Keith Benson, Richard Adler, Janice Ginsberg, Michael Q. Martin; Music Supervisor, Allan Slutsky; Photography, Doug Milsome, Lon Stratton; Editor, Anne Erikson; Narrator, Andre Braugher; an Elliott Scott/Rimshot production; Dolby; Color; Rated PG; 116 minutes; Release date: November 15, 2002. Documentary on unsung Motown backup band The Funk Brothers, Benny "Papa Zita" Benjamin, Eddie "Bongo" Brown, James "Igor" Jamerson, Earl "Chunk of Funk" Van Dyke, Robert White

WITH

Richard "Pistol" Allen, Jack "Black Jack" Ashford, Bob Babbitt, Johnny Griffith, Joe Hunter, Uriel Jones, Joe Messina, Eddie "Chank" Willis (The Funk Brothers) and Alex Alexander (Young Marvin Gaye), Donald Becks, Jr. (Young Uriel Jones), Gary Bosek (Young Bob Babbitt), Michael Ellison (Young Benny Benjamin), Otis Lockhart (Young Robert White), Brian Marable (Young James Jamerson), Antonie McKay (Young Jack Ashford), Mark Mutafian (Young Jack Brokensha), Antonio Ramirez (Young Eddie Willis), Kevin Smith (Young Joe Hunter), Lynch Travis (Young Earl Van Dyke), Tom Ventimiglio (Young Joe Messina), Joe Wheeler (Young Richard "Pistol" Allan), Paul Burt (Funeral Director), Lamont Witcher (Executive), Aubree Gaston (Older Country Girl), Deseray Teague (Young Country Girl), Tyler Blakely (Country Boy with Fishing Pole), William Stockdale (James Jamerson as Child), James Herron (Eddie Willis as Child), Patti Willis (Bootsy Dancer), Rashid Mausi (Interviewer), Michael Ellison (Interviewer Voice), Leo Brown, Katie Chonacas, Teedra Cryer, Peter Dale, Maciek Dolata, Andrea Horvath, Pili Jamal, Laytonya Jordan, Benjamin Keysaer, Kelly McCormick, Jennifer Meier, Kathryn "Kat" Roy, Pradeep Suri, Ezar Thomas, Earl Wenk (Interview Subjects), Bootsy Collins, Ben Harper, Montell Jordan, Chaka Khan, Gerald Levert, Meshell Ndegeocello, Joan Osborne, Tom Scott (Themselves)

© Artisan

FRIDAY AFTER NEXT

(NEW LINE CINEMA) Producers, Ice Cube, Matt Alvarez; Executive Producers, Toby Emmerich, Matt Moore, Douglas Curtis; Director, Marcus Raboy; Screenplay, Ice Cube; Based on characters created by Ice Cube and DJ Pooh; Photography, Glen MacPherson; Designer, Amy B. Ancona; Costumes, Dana Campbell; Associate Producer, Ronn Riser-Muhammad; Music, John Murphy; Music Supervisor, Spring Aspers; Editor, Suzanne Hines; a Cube Vision production; Dolby; Deluxe color; Rated R; 85 minutes; Release date: November 22, 2002

CAST

Craig .... Ice Cube
Day-Day .... Mike Epps
Mr. Jones .... John Witherspoon
Uncle Elroy .... Don "DC" Curry
Mrs. Jones .... Anna Maria Horsford
Pinky .... Clifton Powell
Donna .... K.D. Aubert
Ms. Pearly .... BeBe Drake
Money Mike .... Katt Williams
Santa Claus .... Rickey Smiley
Damon .... Terry Crews
Moly .... Maz Jobrani
and Reggie Gaskins (Officer Dix), Joel McKinnon Miller (Officer Hole), Brian Stepanek (Officer #3), Angela Bowie (Tasha), Dolores Sheen (Grandma Jones), Sommore (Cookie), Gerry Bednob (Moly's Father), Starletta Dupois (Sister Sarah/Old Woman at Fridge), Frances Dee Gray, Jennifer Echols (Church Ladies), Lileé Anderson (Girl Driver), Donald Campbell (Bishop Magic Juan), Chris Williams (Broadway Bill), Erica Vittina Phillips (Booster Pat), Jovun Fox (Thugged Out Boy), Khleo "Khaleed" Thomas, Dan Curtis Lee (Bad Boys), Quentin Prescott Price, Darryl Graves, Allen Maldonado (Juveniles), Terence L. Washington, Kelly "K-Mac" Garmon, Wayne King, Jr., Malieek Straughter (Crime Brothers), Crystal Mattison (Mo'Wet), Tekla Ruchi (Cinnamon), Nikki Davis (Lollipop), Traci L. Nelson, Amber Stuart (Apartment Girls), Mike Epps (Old Man with Shotgun), John Gipson (Old Man at Fridge), Lendell "Kebo" Keeble (C.W.)

When Craig and Day-Day have their rent money stolen by a ghetto Santa, they are forced to make some quick cash by working as security guards. Sequel to the New Line films *Friday* (1995) and *Next Friday* (2000).

© New Line Cinema

Mike Epps, John Witherspoon, Ice Cube

THE EMPEROR'S CLUB

(UNIVERSAL) Producers, Andrew Karsch, Marc Abraham; Executive Producers, Sean Bailey, Cooper Layne, Armyan Bernstein, Thomas A. Bliss, Sidney Kimmel, Eric Newman; Director, Michael Hoffman; Screenplay, Neil Tolkin; Based upon the short story "The Palace Thief" by Ethan Canin; Photography, Lajos Koltai; Designer, Patrizia von Brandenstein; Costumes, Cynthia Flynt; Music, James Newton Howard; Co-Producer, Lisa Bruce; Casting, Sheila Jaffe, Georgianne Walken; a Sidney Kimmel Entertainment/Longfellow Pictures and LivePlanet production; Dolby; Deluxe color; Rated PG-13; 109 minutes; Release date: November 22, 2002

Kevin Kline, Emile Hirsch, Jesse Eisenberg, Rishi Mehta, Paul Dano

Kevin Kline

Rishi Mehta, Emile Hirsch, Jesse Eisenberg, Paul Dano

CAST

William Hundert	Kevin Kline
Sedgewick Bell	Emile Hirsch
Elizabeth	Embeth Davidtz
James Ellerby	Rob Morrow
Headmaster Woodbridge	Edward Herrmann
Senator Hyram Bell	Harris Yulin
Martin Blythe	Paul Dano
Deepak Mehta	Rishi Mehta
Louis Masoudi	Jesse Eisenberg
Older Martin Blythe	Steven Culp
Older Fred Masoudi	Patrick Dempsey
Older Sedgewick Bell	Joel Gretsch
Older Deepak Mehta	Rahul Khanna
Robert Brewster	Gabe Millman
Eugene Field	Chris Morales
Copeland Gray	Luca Bigini
Russell Hall	Michael Coppola
Mr. Harris	Sean Fredericks
The Nun	Katherine O'Sullivan

and Melissa Brown (Blonde Girl), Sophie Wise (Brunette), Emily Dara Doubilet (Redhead), Michelle Foody (Real Redhead), Caitlin O'Heaney (Mrs. Woodbridge), Charu R. Mehta (Deepak's Mom), Pamela Wehner (Senator Bell's Wife), Molly Regan (Miss Peters), Roger Rees (Mr. Castle), Helen Carey (Miss Johnston), Matthew Douglas (Well Wisher/Good Luck Boy), Charles McConnell (Third Form Boy), Allan M. Care (Other Student), Jimmy Walsh (Robert Bell), Elizabeth Hobgood (Victoria Bell), Purva Bedi (Anna Mehta), Deirdre Lorenz (Dr. Kelly Ryan), Anthony Vincent Bova (Older Robert Brewster), Mark Nichols (Older Copeland Gray), George Miller (Old Eugene Field), David C. Hatch (Older Deibel), Tom Bloom (Maitre 'D), Matthew Clark (Waiter), James Shanklin (Valet), Denis Gawley (Sound Board Mixer), Nick Hagelin (Martin Blythe, the 4th), Henry Glovinsky (William Simon), Duane McLaughlin (George Duncan), Jessica Brooks Grant (Kathryn Scott), Charles Estes (Howard Hollander), Dominique Devereau (Tawana Carter), Ben Levin (Steven Wong), Jase Blankfort (Alec Matthews)

Classics professor William Hundert looks back on the fall of '72 when he found himself in a battle of wills with insolent student Sedgewick Bell.

© Universal

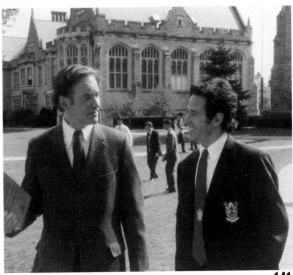

Kevin Kline, Rob Morrow

THE QUIET AMERICAN

Michael Caine

(MIRAMAX) Producers, William Horberg, Staffan Ahrenberg; Executive Producers, Sydney Pollack, Anthony Minghella, Guy East, Nigel Sinclair, Moritz Borman, Chris Sievernich, Director, Phillip Noyce; Screenplay, Christopher Hampton, Robert Schenkkan; Based on the novel by Graham Greene; Photography, Christopher Doyle; Designer, Roger Ford; Costumes, Norma Moriceau; Editor, John Scott; Music, Craig Armstrong; Line Producer, Antonia Barnard; Casting, Christine King; an Intermedia Films presentation of a Mirage Enterprises/Saga Pictures/IMF production; U.S.-German; Dolby; Color; Rated R; 101 minutes; Release date: November 22, 2002

CAST

Thomas Fowler	Michael Caine
Alden Pyle	Brendan Fraser
Phuong	Do Thi Hai Yen
Inspector Vigot	Rade Sherbedgia
Hinh	Tzi Ma
Joe Tunney	Robert Stanton
Bill Granger	Holmes Osbourne
General Thé	Quang Hai
Mr. Muoi	Ferdinand Hoang
Phuong's Sister	Pham Thi Mai Hoa
French Captain	Mathias Miekuz
Watch Tower Soldier	Lap Phan

and Tim Bennett (American Photographer), Jeff Truman (Dancing American), Hong Nhung (House of 500 Girls Singer), Nguyen Ha Phong (Muoi's Henchman), Navia Nguyen (House of 500 Woman), Lucia Noyce, Hilary Douglas (American Women at Continental Hotel), Daniel Hung, Nguyen Kim Hoan, Nguyen Trinh Mal, Pham Trong (Assassins), Tran Do Luc (Vietnamese Policeman), Nguyen Cong-Ly (Vietnamese Guard at General Thé's), George Mangos (French Soldier), Natasha Hunter, Martine Monroe (French Singers at L'arc en Ciel), José de la Vega (Hotel Continental Maitre d'), Roland Rohrer (Vieux Moulin Maitre d'), Susan Parry (French Woman), Nguyen Anh Dung (Mechanic in Muoi's Garage), Peter Holdsworth (Pyle's Bodyguard), Ngoc Tuan Joang, Trece Lambatan, Erwin Abarico, Jun Javier, Nguyen Van Phuoc, Mark Szeto, Askar Nurlanov, Douglas Gallagher, Nicholas Parry, Vov Dylan (L'arc en Ciel Band)

In 1952 Saigon, British journalist Thomas Fowler's seemingly comfortable existence with his Vietnamese lover, Phuong, is disrupted by the appearance of American economic-aid officer Alden Pyle, and the massacre of civilian villagers by the French colonial troops. Previous film version was released in 1958 by United Artists and starred Michael Redgrave (Fowler) and Audie Murphy (Pyle).

© Miramax

Brendan Fraser, Michael Caine

Tzi Ma, Michael Caine

Michael Caine

PERSONAL VELOCITY

(UNITED ARTISTS) Producers, Lemore Syvan, Gary Winick, Alexis Alexanian; Executive Producers, Jonathan Sehring, Caroline Kaplan, John Sloss; Director/Screenplay, Rebecca Miller, based on her book of short stories; Photography, Ellen Kuras; Designer, Judy Becker; Costumes, Marie Abma; Music, Michael Rohatyn; Music Supervisor, Linda Cohen; Executive Music Producer, Alex Steyermark; Line Producers, Jenny Schweitzer, Brian Bell; Casting, Cindy Tolan; an IFC Productions presentation of an InDigEnt production in association with Goldheart/Blue Magic Pictures; Dolby; Color; Rated R; 86 minutes; Release date: November 22, 2002

Parker Posey, Tim Guinee

Kyra Sedgwick, Leo Fitzpatrick

Parker Posey

CAST

Delia Shunt	Kyra Sedgwick
Greta Herskovitz	Parker Posey
Paula	Fairuza Balk
Narrator	John Ventimiglia
Avram Herskovitz	Ron Leibman
Aaron Gelb	Wallace Shawn
Kurt Wurtzle	David Warshofsky
Mylert	Leo Fitzpatrick
Lee Schneeweiss	Tim Guinee
Celia	Patti D'Arbanville
Max	Ben Shenkman
Thavi Matola	Joel de la Fuente
Pam	Marceline Hugot
Peter Shunt	Brian Tarantina
Vincent	Seth Gilliam
Oscar	Josh Philip Weinstein
Kevin	Lou Taylor Pucci
Fay	Mara Hobel
Peter	David Patrick Kelly

and Nick Cubbler (John Wurtzle), Nicole Murphy (May Wurtzle), Sarah Morf (Claire Wurtzle), Laura Finelli (Young Delia), Dean Strange (Norweigan Man), Michi Barall (Felicia Wong), Tim Hopper (Mr. Brown, The Adventist), Maria Elena Ramirez (News Reporter), Christopher Fitzgerald (Greg), Susan Blommaert (Mrs. Toron), Angela Trento (Lola), Danielle Tagger (Marla), Peter Galman (Man in His 50s), Tony Osso (Waiter), Monica Paskiewicz (Mimi), Quentin Mare (Darius), Brian Bell (Playwright), Kaluska Poventud (Maroushka), Francis Akins (Jesse), Bill Burns (Court Steps Reporter), Jennifer Lent (Young Fay), Lynne Anne Hart (Mylert's Mother), Eileen Stancage (Old Woman), Corinne Brownsell (Dunkin Donuts Cashier)

Three separate stories of three women trying to escape from men who confine their personal freedom: Delia, stuck in a relationship with her abusive husband Kurt; Greta, an ambitious editor struggling to stay faithful to her dull husband Lee; and Paula, who, after a near-death experience, picks up a hitchhiker who helps her discover a new sense of spirit.

© United Artists

Lou Taylor Pucci, Fairuza Balk

ADAM SANDLER'S EIGHT CRAZY NIGHTS

(COLUMBIA) Producers, Allen Covert, Jack Giarraputo, Adam Sandler; Executive Producer, Ken Tsumura; Director, Seth Kearsley; Screenplay, Brooks Arthur, Allen Covert, Brad Isaacs, Adam Sandler; Co-Producer, Brooks Arthur; Designer, Perry Andelin Blake; Editor, Amy Budden; Music, Ray Ellis, Marc Ellis, Teddy Castellucci; Art Director/Layout Supervisor, Philip A. Cruden; a Happy Madison production; Dolby; Deluxe color; Rated PG-13; 86 minutes; Release date: November 27, 2002

VOICE CAST

Davey Stone/Whitey Duvall/Eleanore Duvall/Deer . . . . .Adam Sandler
Jennifer . . . . .Jackie Titone
Benjamin . . . . .Austin Stout
Mayor . . . . .Kevin Nealon
Chinese Waiter/Narrator . . . . .Rob Schneider
Judge . . . . .Norm Crosby
Tom Baltezor . . . . .Jon Lovitz
Victoria's Secret Gown . . . . .Tyra Banks
and Cole Sprouse, Dylan Sprouse (K-B Toy Soldiers), Blake Clark (Radio Shack Walkie-Talkie), Peter Dante (Footlocker Guy), Elnne Albertini Dow (See's Candies Box), Kevin Farley (Panda Express Panda), Lari Friedman (Coffee Bean and Tea Leaf Cup), Tom Kenny (Sharper Image Chair), Carl Weathers (GNC Guy), Jamie Alcroft (Eli Wolstan), Brooks Arthur (Rabbi Fliegel), James Barbour (Singing Mayor), Allen Covert (Old Lady/Bus Driver/Mayor's Wife), J.D. Donaruma (Cop #3/Worker #3), Kelly Dugan (Fat Kid/Telephone Kid), Sharon Dugan (Mrs. Selman), John Farley (Cop #2), Carmen Filip (Homeless Guy), Kevin Grady (Cop #4/Worker #1), Archie Hahn (TV Announcer), Betsy Hammer (Phone Sex Lady), Ali Hoffman (Young Jennifer), Max Hoffman (Donald Hardy), Todd Holland (Brill), Jason Housman (Singing Benjamin), Lainie Kazan (Singing Old Woman), Seth Kearsley (Brill's Teammate), Hunter Kitagawa (Basketball Kid), Alison Krauss (Singing Jennifer), Chance Langton (Singing Mr. Thompson), Jonathan Loughran (Cop #1), Richard Page (Singing Dad), Denise Pleune (Concession Stand Worker), Jana Sandler (Victoria's Secret Customer), Jared Sandler, Jillian Sandler (Dreidel Kids), Judith Sandler (Davey's Mom), Stan Sandler (Davey's Dad), Josh Uhler (Young Davey), Ann Wilson (Singing Mom)

Davey Stone, a rude, holiday-hating troublemaker, is taken under the wing of basketball ref Whitey Duvall, who tries to show him the good in the world.

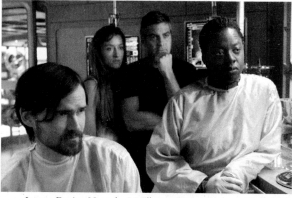

Jeremy Davies, Natascha McElhone, George Clooney, Viola Davis

George Clooney, Natascha McElhone

SOLARIS

(20TH CENTURY FOX) Producers, James Cameron, Rae Sanchini, Jon Landau; Executive Producer, Gregory Jacobs; Director/Screenplay, Steven Soderbergh; Based on the book by Stanislaw Lem; Photography, Peter Andrews; Designer, Philip Messina; Costumes, Milena Canonero; Editor, Mary Ann Bernard; Music, Cliff Martinez; Co-Producers, Michael Polaire, Charles V. Bender; Visual Effects and Animation, Cinesite; a Lightstorm Entertainment production; Dolby; Panavision; Deluxe color; Rated PG-13; 98 minutes; Release date: November 27, 2002

CAST

Dr. Chris Kelvin . . . . .George Clooney
Rheya . . . . .Natascha McElhone
Gordon . . . . .Viola Davis
Snow . . . . .Jeremy Davies
Gibarian . . . . .Ulrich Tukur
Suited Professionals . . . . .John Cho, Morgan Rusler
Young Boy/Gibarian's Son . . . . .Shane Skelton
Mrs. Gibarian . . . . .Donna Kimball
Friends . . . . .Michael Ensign, Elpidia Carrillo
Patients . . . . .Kent Faulcon, Lauren Cohn

Dr. Chris Kelvin, sent to investigate the unexplained events on the space station Prometheus, finds himself making contact with his deceased wife. Remake of the 1972 Russian film.

Davey Stone

TREASURE PLANET

(WALT DISNEY PICTURES) Producers, Roy Conli, John Musker, Ron Clements; Directors, John Musker, Ron Clements; Screenplay, Ron Clements, John Musker, Rob Edwards; Adapted from the novel *Treasure Island* by Robert Louis Stevenson; Animation Story, Ron Clements, John Musker, Ted Elliott, Terry Rossio; Music, James Newton Howard; Original Songs Written and Performed by John Rzeznik; Associate Producer, Peter Del Vecho; Editor, Michael Kelly; Art Director, Andy Gaskill; Associate Art Directors, Ian Gooding; Artistic Supervisors: Story, Barry Johnson; Layout, Rasoul Azadani; Background, Dan Cooper; Clean-Up, Vera Pacheco; Visual Effects, Dave Tidgwell; Computer Graphics Imagery, Kyle Odermatt; Production Designers, Steven Olds, Frank Nissen; Casting, Ruth Lambert, Mary Hidalgo, Matthew Jon Beck; Dolby; Technicolor; Rated PG; 94 minutes; Release date: November 27, 2002

VOICE CAST

Mr. Arrow . . . . .Roscoe Lee Browne
Onus . . . . .Corey Burton
Morph . . . . .Dane A. Davis
Jim Hawkins . . . . .Joseph Gordon-Levitt
Narrator . . . . .Tony Jay
Young Jim . . . . .Austin Majors
Billy Bones . . . . .Patrick McGoohan
Hands . . . . .Micheal McShane
Sarah . . . . .Laurie Metcalf
John Silver . . . . .Brian Murray
Doctor Doppler . . . . .David Hyde Pierce
B.E.N. . . . . .Martin Short
Captain Amelia . . . . .Emma Thompson
Scroop . . . . .Michael Wincott
and Jack Angel, Bob Bergen, Rodger Bumpass, Jane Carr, John Cygan, Jennifer Darling, Paul Eiding, Sherry Lynn, Mona Marshall, Mickie McGowan, Patrick Pinney, Phil Proctor, Jeremy Suarez, Jim Ward (Additional Voices)

After being given a treasure map by the crazed Billy Bones, 15-year-old Jim Hawkins sets out with Captain Amelia and her crew for Treasure Planet, where the ship's galley cook, John Silver, has other plans for the precious trove. Previous versions of *Treasure Island* include those made by MGM in 1934 (Wallace Beery, Jackie Cooper), Disney in 1950 (Robert Newton, Bobby Driscoll), and Paramount in 1972 (Orson Welles, Kim Burfield).

This film received an Oscar nomination for animated feature.

© Disney Enterprises

John Silver, Jim Hawkins

Doctor Doppler, Jim Hawkins, Captain Amelia

Morph, Jim Hawkins, B.E.N.

Jim Hawkins

EMPIRE

(UNIVERSAL) Producers, Daniel Bigel, Michael Mailer; Executive Producer, Robert B. Campbell; Co-Executive Producers, Evan Lamberg, Steven C. Beer; Co-Producers, John Leguizamo, Jill Footlick; Director/Screenplay, Franc Reyes; Photography, Kramer Morgenthau; Designer, Ted Glass; Costumes, Jacki Roach; Editor, Peter C. Frank; Music, Ruben Blades; Music Supervisor, Kathy Nelson; Casting, Sig De Miguel; an Arenas Entertainment presentation of a Daniel Bigel/Michael Mailer production; Dolby; Super 35 Widescreen; Color; Rated R; 90 minutes; Release date: December 6, 2002.

Christian Bale

CAST

Victor Rosa	John Leguizamo
Jack Wimmer	Peter Sarsgaard
Trish	Denise Richards
Jimmy	Vincent Laresca
La Colombiana	Isabella Rossellini
Iris	Sonia Braga
Carmen	Delilah Cotto
Rafael Menendez	Nestor Serrano
Chedda	Treach
Jay	Rafael Baez
Tito Severe	Fat Joe (Joseph Cartagena)
Hector	Carlos Leon

and Felix Solis (Jose), Omar Bastran (Jason), Rob B. Campbell (Det. O'Brien), Granville Adams (Det. Jones), Jean Luke Figueroa (Little Boy), Nicole Fisher (Waitress), Maritza Morgado (Maria), Sam Coppola (Bobby Gold), Karina Arroyave (Cheena), Mike Figueroa (Mark), Marta Vidal (Aunt), Andre De Leon (Teenager), Monica Steuer (Receptionist), Teo Castellanos (Raul), Tanya Byers (Cleo), Giovanna Gomez (Bartender), Jaime Velez (Thug), Rosanne C. Lucarelli (Nurse), Sally Simone Dealy (Angelina), Christina Benitan (Sandy), Edward Rosado (Lil' Vic), Tom York (Taylor), Dashia Lopez (Waitress), Luis Ganell ("G"), Tim Gallin (Doorman), Elliot Santiago, Tony Rhune, Derrick Simmons (Tito's Boys), Stracy Diaz (Gina), Kidada Jones (Sasha), Keith Hochstin (Hoc), George Whipple, Gigi Stone, Robert B. Campbell (Themselves)

Bronx heroin dealer Victor Rosa thinks he has found his ticket out of the criminal lifestyle when investment banker Jack Wimmer offers him a substantial return on a stock deal.

© Universal

EQUILIBRIUM

(DIMENSION) Producers, Jan De Bont, Lucas Foster; Executive Producers, Bob Weinstein, Harvey Weinstein, Andrew Rona; Director/Screenplay, Kurt Wimmer; Co-Producer, Sue Baden-Powell; Photography, Dion Beebe; Designer, Wolf Kroeger; Costumes, Joseph Porro; Editors, Tom Rolf, William Yeh; Music, Klaus Badelt; Digital Cityscapes Created by Digital Firepower, Inc., Hollywood; Associate Producer, Ninon Tantet; Casting, Juel Bestrop, Jeanne McCarthy, Lucinda Syson (European); Stunts/Fight Choreographer, Jim Vickers; a Blue Tulip Inc. production; Distributed by Miramax Films; Dolby; Super 35 Widescreen; Color; Rated R; 107 minutes; Release date: December 6, 2002.

CAST

John Preston	Christian Bale
Mary O'Brien	Emily Watson
Brandt	Taye Diggs
Dupont	Angus MacFadyen
Partridge	Sean Bean
Robbie Preston	Matthew Harbour
Jurgen	William Fichtner
Seamus	Dominic Purcell
Proctor	David Hemmings

and Christian Kahrmann (Office in Charge), John Keogh (Chemist), Sean Pertwee (Father), David Barrash (Evidentiary Storage Officer), Dirk Martens (Gate Guard), Maria Pia Calzone (Preston's Wife), Emily Siewert (Lisa Preston), Mike Smith (Enforcement Commander), Florian Fitz (Gate Guard), Daniel Lee (Lead Sweeper), Francesco Calabras (Rebel Leader), Kurt Wimmer (Rebel Victim), Anatole Taubmann (Crematory Technician), Brian Connelly (Reading Room Proprietor), Alexa Summer (Viviana Preston), Brian Cook (Dupont's Secretary), Mehmet Kurtulus (Search Coordinator), Klaus Schindler (Interrogator), Oliver Brandl (Polygraph Technician)

In the distant future, when all display of emotion has been outlawed, John Preston, a law-enforcement officer, fails to take his daily dose of anti-feeling drug, and begins to wonder if perhaps the oppression of feeling is something to rebel against.

John Leguizamo, Vincent Laresca

© Dimension

ANALYZE THAT

(WARNER BROS.) Producers, Paula Weinstein, Jane Rosenthal; Executive Producers, Billy Crystal, Barry Levinson, Chris Brigham, Len Amato, Bruce Berman; Director, Harold Ramis; Screenplay, Peter Steinfeld, Harold Ramis, Peter Tolan; Photography, Ellen Kuras; Designer, Wynn Thomas; Editor, Andrew Mondshein; Co-Producer, Suzanne Herrington; Music, David Holmes; Costumes, Aude Bronson-Howard; Casting, Ellen Chenoweth; a Baltimore/Spring Creek Pictures/Face/Tribeca production, presented in association with Village Roadshow Pictures and NPV Entertainment; Dolby; Technicolor; Rated R; 95 minutes; Release date: December 6, 2002.

Joe Viterelli, Robert De Niro

Billy Crystal, Lisa Kudrow

Robert De Niro, Anthony LaPaglia

CAST

Paul Vitti	Robert De Niro
Ben Sobel	Billy Crystal
Laura Sobel	Lisa Kudrow
Jelly	Joe Viterelli
Patti LoPresti	Cathy Moriarty-Gentile
Little Caesar Star	Anthony LaPaglia
Ducks	Joey "Coco" Diaz
Convict	Jerome Le Page
Wiseguy	Joseph Bono
Earl	Brian Rogalski
Coyote	Thomas Rosales, Jr.
Prisoner	Patrick Marcune
Prison Guards	John F. Gooding, Henry Morales-Ballet, Scotty Dillin
Rabbi	Ted Neustadt
Michael Sobel	Kyle Sabihy
Ben's Mother	Rebecca Schull
Agent Miller	James Biberi
Agent Cerrone	Callie Thorne

and Dr. Joyce Brothers, Joe Torre, Michael Torre (Themselves), Firdous Bamji (Dr. Kassam), John Finn (Richard Chapin), David Fonteno (Davis), Donnamaire Recco (Sheila), Sylvia Kauders (Aunt Esther), Kendall Pettygrove, Bea Super (Brunch Guests), Raymond Franza (Eddie DeVol), Stephen Kampann (Mr. Macinerny), Susie Gilder Hayes (Mrs. Macinerny), Tom Papa (Boyfriend), Sunny Chae (Fiance), Sal Cecere (20 Minute Man), Richard Brennan (Steakhouse Patron), Paul Herman (Joey Boots), Charles A. Gargano (Maitre'D), Dino Van Simco (Dino), Seth Isler (Businessman), Reg Rogers (Raoul Berman), Anita Durst (Raoul's Girlfriend), Joseph D'Onofrio (Rigazzi Gunman), David Salerno (Rigazzi Soldier), Vinny Vella, Sr. (Mello), Alfred Sauchelli, Jr. (Mo-Mo), Frank Pietrangeolare (Tuna), Frank Aquilino (Eddie "Cokes"), Chris Tardio (Enormous Bobby), William DeMeo ("Al Pacino"), Joe Columbo, Angelo Natoli, Anthony Krosinski, Nick Massi, Jr., Frank Bonsangue, Ralph Cefarello (LoPresti Soldiers), Joseph Marzella, Phil Campanella, Louis Fattell, Michael Zotto, Tony Vitucci, Paul John Cicero, Gene Di Silvio, Gaetano LoGiudice, Rino Vitucci (Vitti Crew), Joseph Reidy (1st AD), Richard Maldone (Rigazzi Driver), Leif Riddell (*Little Caesar* Soundman), Suzanne Herrington (Drive-Thru Bank Teller), Demitri Martin (P.A.), Michael Jannetta (Lieutenant), Robert Cea (Captain), Annika Pergament (Newscaster, V.O.), Bart Tangredi (Vitti Father)

Fearing that he is being targeted for death, mob boss Paul Vitti fakes insanity to be let out of prison, and is handed into the custody of therapist Ben Sobel. Sequel to the 1999 Warner Bros. film *Analyze This*, with several of the principals repeating their roles.

© Warner Bros.

Cathy Moriarty-Gentile, Robert De Niro

147

ADAPTATION.

(COLUMBIA) Producers, Edward Saxon, Vincent Landay, Jonathan Demme; Executive Producers, Charlie Kaufman, Peter Saraf; Director, Spike Jonze; Screenplay, Charlie Kaufman, Donald Kaufman; Based on the book *The Orchid Thief* by Susan Orlean; Photography, Lance Acord; Designer, K.K. Barrett; Costumes, Casey Storm; Editor, Eric Zumbrunnen; Music, Carter Burwell; Visual Effects Supervisor, Gray Marshall; Casting, Justine Baddeley, Kim Davis-Wagner; a Magnet/Clinica Estetico production, presented in association with Intermedia Films; Dolby; Deluxe color; Rated R; 114 minutes; Release date: December 6, 2002

Chris Cooper

Maggie Gyllenhaal, Nicolas Cage, Nicolas Cage

Nicolas Cage

Nicolas Cage, Brian Cox

CAST

Charlie Kaufman/Donald Kaufman	Nicolas Cage
Susan Orlean	Meryl Streep
John Laroche	Chris Cooper
Valerie	Tilda Swinton
Amelia	Cara Seymour
Robert McKee	Brian Cox
Alice the Waitress	Judy Greer
Caroline	Maggie Gyllenhaal
Marty	Ron Livingston
Matthew Osceola	Jay Tavare
Russell	G. Paul Davis
Randy	Roger Willie
Ranger Tony	Jim Beaver
Augustus Margary	Doug Jones
Ranger Steve Neely	Stephen Tobolowsky
Buster Baxley	Gary Farmer
Defense Attorney	Peter Jason
Prosecutor	Gregory Itzin
Orlean's Husband	Curtis Hanson
David	Bob Stephenson
Charlie Darwin	Bob Yerkes
Laroche's Dad	Lynn Court
Laroche's Mom	Sandra Gimpel
Laroche's Wife	Caron Colvett
EMT	Larry Krask
McKee Lecture Attendee	John Etter
Police Officer	Ray Berrios
Kaufman's Mother	Nancy Lenehan

Orlean Dinner Guests . . . . Agnes Badoo, Paul Fortune, Paul Jasmin, Lisa Love, Wendy Mogel, David O. Russell
Themselves . . . . John Malkovich, John Cusack, Catherine Keener

Screenwriter Charlie Kaufman, struggling to adapt Susan Orlean's book *The Orchid Thief* into a film, finds himself confronting his own feelings of inadequacy, his ambitious twin brother's efforts to become a script writer, and the bizarre life of the book's subject, poacher John Laroche.

2002 Academy Award winner for Best Supporting Actor (Chris Cooper). This film received additional Oscar nominations for actor (Nicolas Cage), supporting actress (Meryl Streep), and screenplay-adaptation.

Meryl Streep

Chris Cooper, Meryl Streep

Nicolas Cage, Nicolas Cage

Nicolas Cage, Nicolas Cage

Maggie Gyllenhaal, Nicolas Cage

Meryl Streep

DRUMLINE

(20TH CENTURY FOX) Producers, Wendy Finerman, Timothy M. Bourne, Jody Gerson; Executive Producers, Dallas Austin, Greg Mooradian; Director, Charles Stone III; Screenplay, Tina Gordon Chism, Shawn Schepps; Story, Shawn Schepps; Photography, Shane Hurlbut; Designer, Charles C. Bennett; Costumes, Salvador Perez; Editors, Bill Pankow, Patricia Bowers; Music, John Powell; Executive Music Producer, Dallas Austin; Casting, Aleta Chappelle; Dolby; Super 35 Widescreen; Deluxe color; Rated PG-13; 118 minutes; Release date: December 13, 2002

CAST

Devon Miles	Nick Cannon
Laila	Zoe Saldana
Dr. Lee	Orlando Jones
Sean Taylor	Leonard Roberts
Jayson	GQ
Ernest	Jason Weaver
Charles	Earl C. Poitier
Diedre	Candance Carey
Big Rob	Shay Rountree
Trey	Miguel A. Gaetan
Mr. Wade	J. Anthony Brown
President Wagner	Afemo Omilami
Dorothy	Angela E. Gibbs
Henry	Tyrese Burnett
Buck Wild	Brandon Hirsch

and O'Mar J. Dorsey (James), Al Wiggins (Principal), Nicholas B. Thomas (Pooh Bear), Petey Pablo (Himself), Stuart Scott (Fox Sports Commentator), Courtney Stewart (Student #1), Von Coulter (Devon Miles, Sr.), James Sims-Prewitt (Trumpet Section Leader), Gary Yates (Coach Ellison), Rob Cleveland (Music Professor), Enoch King (Tuba Section Leader), AJ Calloway, Free (BET Announcers), Reggie Gay (Morris Brown Announcer), Ryan Cameron (A &T Announcer), Blu Cantrell (National Anthem Singer), Erin Brantley, Kiara Nicole Ely, Stacey A. Fann, Christy Gamble, Brianne Landry, Pauline S. Lewis, Glenda Morton, Shamea Morton, Jenear Wimbley (Dancers)

Talented but undisciplined and individualistic drummer Devon Miles earns a scholarship to Atlanta A&T where he becomes part of the school's show-style marching band.

© 20th Century Fox

Zoe Saldana, Nick Cannon

Nick Cannon

Orlando Jones

Candace Carey, Nick Cannon (center)

MAID IN MANHATTAN

(COLUMBIA) Producers, Elaine Goldsmith-Thomas, Deborah Schindler, Paul Schiff; Executive Producers, Charles Newirth, Benny Medina; Director, Wayne Wang; Screenplay, Kevin Wade; Story, Edmond Dantès (John Hughes); Photography, Karl Walter Lindenlaub; Designer, Jane Musky; Costumes, Albert Wolsky; Music, Alan Silvestri; Music Supervisor, Randall Poster, Editor, Craig McKay; a Revolution Studios presentation of a Red Om Films production; Dolby; Panavision; Deluxe color; Rated PG-13; 105 minutes; Release date: December 13, 2002

Amy Sedaris, Natasha Richardson, Jennifer Lopez

Tyler Garcia Posey, Jennifer Lopez

Bob Hoskins, Jennifer Lopez

Ralph Fiennes, Stanley Tucci

CAST

Marisa Ventura	Jennifer Lopez
Christopher Marshall	Ralph Fiennes
Caroline Lane	Natasha Richardson
Jerry Siegel	Stanley Tucci
Ty Ventura	Tyler Garcia Posey
Paula Burns	Frances Conroy
John Bextrum	Chris Eigeman
Rachel Hoffberg	Amy Sedaris
Stephanie Kehoe	Marissa Matrone
Veronica Ventura	Priscilla Lopez
Lionel Bloch	Bob Hoskins
Cora	Lisa Roberts Gillan
Leezette	Maddie Corman
Clarice	Sharon Wilkins
Carmen	Jayne Houdyshell
Barb	Marilyn Torres
Keef Townsend	Lou Ferguson
Lily Kim	Di Quon
Anouk Guedj	Liliane Thomas
Monique Guedj	Raquel Shapiro

and Ton Voogt (Pilates Instructor), Ray Aranha (Bus Driver), Emma Thaler (Tiana), Becky Veduccio (Ty's Teacher), Gayle Scott (Frances), Michelle Thomas (Michelle), Jeff Hephner (Harold the Room Service Waiter), Beth Dodye Bass,Catherine Anne Hayes (Telephone Operators), Millie Tirelli (Miss V.), Shaun Powell, Thomas M. Sullivan (Paparazzi), Michelle Vicidomini-Serdaros (Neta), Larry Fleischman (Full Monty), Nick Wyman (Concierge), Richie Karron (Harry Schiff), Dave Rosenberg, Eric Michael Gillet, Joel Marsh Garland, Mark Fairchild, Jay Edwards, Bill Edwards, Amy Redford, Gil Williams, Bethann Schebece, Patricia Lavery (Reporters), Margaret Harth (Roosevelt Maid), Tom O'Rourke (Maddox), Tobias Maendel, Kenneth Goodstein (Bellmen), Javier Picayo (Ninth Grade Boy), Glenn Lewis (Lead Singer), Mirjana Jokovic, Saundra McClain, Kae Shimizu (Maids), Daniella van Graas (Fiancee), Donna Karger, Annika Pergament (NY1 Reporters), Emily Frances (WPIX Reporter), Paul Messina (Journalist), Richard E. Hirschfeld (Security Man), Larry Pine (Mr. Lefferts), Hillary B. Smith (Mrs. Lefferts), Crystal Allen (Mr. Lefferts' Girlfriend), Seth William Meier, Stephanie Langhoff, Daniel A. Thomas (Christopher Marshall's Aides), Joseph Siravo (Delgado), Gloria Colonnello, Minna Rose, Maja Niles, Brigitte Barnett (Shoppers), Amber Gristak (Autograph Girl), Patrick Anderson (Roosevelt Manager), Mike Morris (News Commentator), Anthony Caforio (Power Politican), Cole Razzano (Political Supporter), Lizza Oliver (Roosevelt Food Manager), Carla Duren, Rachel Hollingsworth (Singers), Jeffrey Dinowitz (Congressman Grey), Sylvia Gottlieb (Congressman Grey's Wife), Rufus Thomas (Rufus the Dog)

Aspiring senator Christopher Marshall finds himself falling in love with Marisa Ventura, not realizing that she is a maid at the hotel where he is staying.

Jack Nicholson

Kathy Bates

ABOUT SCHMIDT

(NEW LINE CINEMA) Producers, Harry Gittes, Michael Besman; Executive Producers, Bill Badalato, Rachel Horowitz; Director, Alexander Payne; Screenplay, Alexander Payne, Jim Taylor; Based on the novel by Louis Begley; Photography, James Glennon; Designer, Jane Ann Stewart; Costumes, Wendy Chuck; Editor, Kevin Tent; Music, Rolfe Kent; Casting, Lisa Beach, Sarah Katzman; a Michael Besman/Harry Gittes production; Dolby; Deluxe color; Rated R; 125 minutes; Release date: December 13, 2002

CAST

Warren Schmidt	Jack Nicholson
Jeannie Schmidt	Hope Davis
Randall Hertzel	Dermot Mulroney
Ray Nichols	Len Cariou
Larry Hertzel	Howard Hesseman
Roberta Hertzel	Kathy Bates
Helen Schmidt	June Squibb
Gary Nordin, Warren's Replacement	Matt Winston
John Rusk	Harry Groener
Vicki Rusk	Connie Ray
Randall's Best Man	James Micheal Connor
Duncan Hertzel	Mark Venhuizen
Saundra	Cheryl Hamada
Bridesmaid Reading St. Paul	Jill Anderson
Man Mourning Helen	Vaughan Wenzel
Woman Mourning Helen	Judith Kathryn Hart
Neighbor Lady	Marilyn Tipp
Priest in Omaha	Reverend Robert Kem
Dairy Queen Employee	Melissa Hanna
Frat Kids	Tung Ha, James J. Crawley
Bartender	Mary Beth Nelson
Tire Store Employee	Stephen Heller
Native American Cashier	Lester Kills Crow
Funeral Director	Thomas Michael Belford
6-year-old Jeannie	McKenna Gibson
12-year-old Jeannie	Stephanie Curtis
Wedding Singers	Beth Heimann, Linda Wilmot

Newly retired Warren Schmidt, facing an uncertain future, heads west for his daughter's wedding, questioning his place in the world and trying to find some meaning to the relatively uneventful life he has lead.

This film received Oscar nominations for actor (Jack Nicholson) and supporting actress (Kathy Bates).

© New Line Productions

Hope Davis

Dermot Mulroney, Hope Davis, Jack Nicholson

Jack Nicholson

Kathy Bates

Harry Groener, Connie Ray, Jack Nicholson

Kathy Bates, Cheryl Hamada, Howard Hesseman,
Mark Venhuizen, Jack Nicholson

Dermot Mulroney

THE HOT CHICK

(TOUCHSTONE) Producers, John Schneider, Carr D'Angelo; Executive Producers, Adam Sandler, Jack Giarraputo, Guy Riedel; Director, Tom Brady; Screenplay, Tom Brady, Rob Schneider; Photography, Tim Suhrstedt; Designer, Marc Fisichella; Costumes, Alix Friedberg; Editor, Peck Prior; Music, John Debney; Music Supervisor, Peter Afterman; Co-Producers, Nathan T. Reimann, Ian Maxtone-Graham; Casting, Marcia Ross, Donna Morong, Gail Goldberg; a Happy Madison production; Dolby; Panavision; Technicolor; Rated PG-13; 105 minutes; Release date: December 13, 2002

CAST

Jessica	Rob Schneider
April	Anna Faris
Billy	Matthew Lawrence
Jake	Eric Christian Olsen
Stan	Robert Davi
Carol	Melora Hardin
Lulu	Alexandra Holden

and Rachel McAdams (Jessica), Maritza Murray (Keecia), Fay Hauser (Mrs. Thomas), Jodi Long (Korean Mother), Tia Mowry (Venetia), Tamera Mowry (Sissy), Lee Garlington (Vice Principal Bernard), Angie Stone (Madam Mambuza), Matt Weinberg (Booger), Leila Kenzle (Julie), Michelle Branch (DJ), Michael O'Keefe (Richie), Samia Doumit (Eden), Megan Kuhlmann (Hildenberg), Ashlee Simpson (Monique), Melissa Lawner (Sasha), Nicko Mariolis (Grotesque Groom), Tony Wilde (Spinozi), Steven Kravitz (Ben Feingold), Shazia (Princess Nawa), Osman Soykut (King), Vivian Corado (Servant Girl), Jeremy Kramer (Yogurt Boss), Adam Del Rio (Yogurt Guy), Maria-Elena Laas (Bianca), Jake Iannarino (Bonesy), Mane Rich Andrew (Marlon), Chase Penny (Long-Haired Jock), Dick Gregory (Bathroom Attendant), Pilar Schneider, Lisa Brady (Judges), Wiley Roberts (Keecia's Dad), Jason Tobin, Sean Meagher (Jocks), Wes Takahashi (Reporter), Scott Dolezal (Night Club Bartender), Clark Taylor (Fitzi), Katie Lohmann (Pole Cat Stripper), Icey Berglind (Stripper), Bob Rubin (Pole Cat Bouncer), Louis Lombardi (Pole Cat Bar Patron), Giselle Fernandez (Newscaster), Carmit Bachar, Michael Anthony Bean, Staci Flood, Kimberly Morrow, Lisette Bustamante, Lisa Joann Thompson, Jesse Santos, Ronnie Willis, Chris Moss, Robert Vinson (Hip Hop Dancers), Paul Benshoof, Teresa Espinosa, Earl Wright (Hip Hop Freestyle Dancers), Chonique Sneed (Freestyle Dancer), Melanie Benz, Rebecca Lin, Madine Ellis, Vergi Rodriguez (Palace Girls), Katie Wiersema, Paige Peterson, Kim Green, Michelle Heitzler, Joslin Marie De Diego, Nicole Albright, Sandra McCoy (Jessica Cheer Girls), Rhonda Roberts, Erin Hernandez, Maria Carmen, Denise Marie Jerome, Jolene Walker, Christine Herrera, Monica Soto, Leilani Rios, Jenna Stewart, Jenna Dewan (Bianca Salsa Girls), Adam Sandler (Drum Player)

Because of a magical curse, a gorgeous, self-involved high school girl finds herself trading bodies with a 30-year-old male criminal.

© Touchstone

154 Anna Faris, Rachel McAdams, Rob Schneider, Maritza Murray

Anthony LaPaglia, Sigourney Weaver

Sigourney Weaver, Anthony LaPaglia

THE GUYS

(FOCUS) Producers, Joana Vicente, Jason Kliot; Executive Producers, Edward R. Pressman, John Schmidt, Bonnie Timmermann; Director, Jim Simpson; Screenplay, Anne Nelson, Jim Simpson; Based on the play by Anne Nelson; Photography, Maryse Alberti; Designer, Susan Block; Costumes, Sarah Beers; Editor, Sarah Flack; Music, Mychael Danna; Music Supervisor, Tracy McKnight; Co-Producer, Gretchen McGowan; a Content Film presentation of an Open City Films production; Dolby; Color; Rated PG; 85 minutes; Release date: December 13, 2002

CAST

Joan	Sigourney Weaver
Nick	Anthony LaPaglia
Joan's Sister	Irene Walsh
Joan's Husband	Jim Simpson
Joan's Daughter	Charlotte Simpson
Joan's Son	Julian Trompeter
Sister's Daughter	Katharine Schreiber
Sister's Son	Lucas Debassac
Sister's Infant	Joshua Ross
Masseuse	Shelita Birchett
Joan's Friend	Ron Dortch
Diner's Cashier	Alfredo Narciso
Acolytes	Julia Nelson Black, David Nelson Black

In the days following the September 11, 2001 terrorists attacks on New York, a journalist is given the task of helping a fire captain write the eulogies for his fallen men. Weaver and LaPaglia repeat their performances from the original 2001 Off-Broadway play.

© Focus

STAR TREK: NEMESIS

(PARAMOUNT) Producer, Rick Berman; Executive Producer, Marty Hornstein; Director, Stuart Baird; Screenplay, John Logan; Story, John Logan, Rick Berman, Brent Spiner; Based upon *Star Trek* created by Gene Roddenberry; Photography, Jeffrey L. Kimball; Designer, Herman Zimmerman; Costumes, Bob Ringwood; Editor, Dallas Puett; Co-Producer, Peter Lauritson; Music, Jerry Goldsmith; Casting, Amanda Mackey Johnson, Cathy Sandrich Gelfond; a Rick Berman production; Dolby; Panavision; Deluxe color; Rated PG-13; 117 minutes; Release date: December 13, 2002

Brent Spiner, Brent Spiner

CAST

Captain Jean-Luc Picard	Patrick Stewart
Commander William Riker	Jonathan Frakes
Lieutenant Commander Data/Story	Brent Spiner
Lieutenant Commander Geordi La Forge	LeVar Burton
Lieutenant Commander Worf	Michael Dorn
Dr. Beverly Crusher	Gates McFadden
Commander Deanna Troi	Marina Sirtis
Shinzon	Tom Hardy
Viceroy	Ron Perlman
Senator Tal'aura	Shannon Cochran
Commander Donatra	Dina Meyer
Commander Suran	Jude Ciccolella
Praetor Hiren	Alan Dale
Senator	John Berg
Helm Officer Branson	Michael Owen
Captain Kathryn Janeway	Kate Mulgrew
Reman Officer	Robertson Dean
Commanders	David Ralphie, J. Patrick McCormack
Wesley Crusher	Wil Wheaton
Computer Voice	Majel Barrett Roddenberry
Guinan	Whoopi Goldberg

The crew of the *Enterprise* agrees to discuss a possible peace treaty with the Romulans only to find out that their new leader is a Remus native who is a human replica of Jean-Luc Picard, bio-engineered by the Romulans to be substituted for the Captain as a weapon against the Federation. The fourth Paramount feature based on the series "Star Trek: The Next Generation," following *Star Trek: Generations* (1994), *Star Trek: First Contact* (1996), and *Star Trek: Insurrection*, with the same cast principals from those films appearing here as well.

© Paramount

Tom Hardy, Ron Perlman

Jonathan Frakes, Marina Sirtis, Gates McFadden

Patrick Stewart, Tom Hardy

155

THE LORD OF THE RINGS: THE TWO TOWERS

(NEW LINE CINEMA) Producers, Barrie M. Osborne, Fran Walsh, Peter Jackson; Executive Producers, Robert Shaye, Michael Lynne, Mark Ordesky, Bob Weinstein, Harvey Weinstein; Director, Peter Jackson; Screenplay, Fran Walsh, Philippa Boyens, Stephen Sinclair, Peter Jackson; Based on the book by J.R.R. Tolkien; Co-Producers, Rick Porras, Jamie Selkirk; Photography, Andrew Lesnie; Designer, Grant Major; Costumes, Ngila Dickson, Richard Taylor; Editor, Michael Horton; Music, Howard Shore; Visual Effects Supervisor, Jim Rygiel; Special Make-up, Creature, Miniature and Digital Effects, Weta Ltd., NZ; Casting, Victoria Burrows (US), John Hubbard, Amy MacLean (UK); a Wingnut Films production; Dolby; Super 35 Widescreen; Deluxe color; Rated PG-13; 179 minutes; Release date: December 18, 2002

Elijah Wood, Sean Astin

Viggo Mortensen, Liv Tyler

Viggo Mortensen, Orlando Bloom, Ian McKellen

CAST

Frodo Baggins	Elijah Wood
Gandalf the White	Ian McKellen
Arwen	Liv Tyler
Aragorn	Viggo Mortensen
Samwise Gamgee	Sean Astin
Galadriel	Cate Blanchett
Gimli/Voice of Treebeard	John Rhys-Davies
Pippin (Peregrin Took)	Billy Boyd
Merry (Meriadoc Brandbuck)	Dominic Monaghan
Legolas	Orlando Bloom
Saruman	Christopher Lee
Elrond	Hugo Weaving
Eowyn of Rohan	Miranda Otto
King Theoden of Rohan	Bernard Hill
Grima Wormtongue	Brad Dourif
Gollum/Smeagol	Andy Serkis
Faramir	David Wenham
Eomer	Karl Urban
Gamling	Bruce Hopkins
Aldor	Bruce Allpress
Madril	John Bach
Man Flesh Uruk	Sala Baker
Sharku/Snaga	Jed Brophy
Eothain	Sam Comery
Haleth	Calum Gittins
Theodred	Paris Howe Strewe
Ugluk	Nathaniel Lees
Hama	John Leigh
Mauhur	Robbie Magasiva
Morwen	Robyn Malcolm
Haldir	Craig Parker
Rohan Soldier	Bruce Phillips
Mordorc Orc	Robert Pollock
Freda	Olivia Tennet
Bereg	Ray Trickett
Grishnakh	Stephen Ure

Hobbits Frodo and Sam are joined by Gollum who promises to guide them to the Black Gates of Mordor. Meanwhile Aragorn, Legolas, and Gimli help the besieged kingdom of Rohan prepare for battle with the evil Saruman's forces. Second installment of New Line's *The Lord of the Rings* trilogy, following *The Lord of the Rings: The Fellowship of the Ring* (2001), and preceding *The Lord of the Rings: The Return of the King* (2003).

2002 Academy Award winner for Best Visual Effects and Best Sound Editing. This film received additional Oscar nominations for picture, editing, sound, and art direction.

Brad Dourif, Christopher Lee

Elijah Wood

Liv Tyler

Ian McKellen

Hugo Weaving, Liv Tyler

Karl Urban

Viggo Mortensen

Billy Boyd, Dominic Monaghan

25TH HOUR

Rosario Dawson, Barry Pepper

Barry Pepper, Philip Seymour Hoffman, Edward Norton

(TOUCHSTONE) Producers, Tobey Maguire, Julia Chasman; Executive Producer, Nick Wechsler; Director, Spike Lee; Screenplay, David Benioff, based on his book; Photography, Rodrigo Prieto; Designer, James Chinlund; Costumes, Sandra Hernandez; Editor, Barry Alexander Brown; Music, Terence Blanchard; Casting, Aisha Coley; a 40 Acres and a Mule Filmworks/Industry Entertainment/Gamut Films production; Dolby; Super 35 Widescreen; Technicolor; Rated R; 134 minutes; Release date: December 19, 2002

CAST

Monty Brogan	Edward Norton
Jacob Elinsky	Philip Seymour Hoffman
Francis Xavier Slaughtery	Barry Pepper
Naturelle Riviera	Rosario Dawson
Mary D'Annuzio	Anna Paquin
James Brogan	Brian Cox
Kostya Novotny	Tony Siragusa
Uncle Nikolai	Levani
Senka Valghobek	Misha Kuznetsov
Agent Flood	Isiah Whitlock, Jr.
Agent Cunningham	Michael Genet
Khari	Patrice Oneal
Salvatore Dominick	Al Palagonia
Marcuse	Aaron Stanford
Schutlz	Marc H. Simon
Phelan	Armando Riesco

and Brad Williams, Bear Jackson (Traders), Keith Nobbs (Luke), Felicia Finley (Jody), Radu Spinghel (Zakharov), Dania (Daphne), Oleg Aleksandrovich Prudius, Igor Zhivotovsky (Russian Hoods), Paul Diomede (Simon), Cynthia Darlow (Ruth), Michole Briana White (Coventry Administrator), Vanessa Ferlito (Lindsay Jamison), Coati Mundi (Louis Volandes), Larissa Drekonja (Dasha), Christine Pepe (Jogger), Lawrence Bullock, Patrick Illig (Chelsea Men), Maja Niles (Woman on Park Avenue), Daniel R. Reton (Wall Street Guy #1), Ed Rubeo (Hasidic Jeweler), Peter James Kelsch (Panhandler), Al McCoy (Squeegee Man), R.L. Brazil (Bouncer), Howard Crowns (Tattoo Parlor Worker), DJ Cipha Sounds (DJ Dusk), Jamil Mullen (Lady With Baby), Rescue 5: FDNY: Capt. Louis Modafferi, FF. Alan Taraseiwicz, FF. Nicholas Rossomodo, FF. Jeffrey Palazzo, FF. Douglas Miller, FF. Mike Fiore, FF. Andre Fletcher, FF. Carl Bini, FF. Joseph Mascall, FF. John Bergen (Brogan's Bar Patrons)

Monty Brogan spends one final day of freedom before he must serve a seven-year prison term for dealing drugs.

© Touchstone

Edward Norton

Brian Cox, Edward Norton

ANTWONE FISHER

(FOX SEARCHLIGHT) Producers, Todd Black, Randa Haines, Denzel Washington; Executive Producer, Nancy Paloian-Breznikar; Director, Denzel Washington; Screenplay, Antwone Fisher; Photography, Philippe Rousselot; Designer, Nelson Coates; Costumes, Sharen Davis; Co-Producers, Antwone Fisher, Chris Smith; Editor, Conrad Buff; Music, Mychael Danna; Casting, Robi Reed-Humes; a Mundy Lane/Todd Black production; Dolby; Panavision; Deluxe color; Rated PG-13; 120 minutes; Release date: December 19, 2002

A volatile navy man, Antwone Fisher, is ordered to see a pyschiatrist, who helps him delve into the past to seek the reason behind his behavior. This film marked the directorial debut of actor Denzel Washington.

© Fox Searchlight

Derek Luke, Denzel Washington

Derek Luke, Joy Bryant

Derek Luke

Derek Luke, Denzel Washington

GANGS OF NEW YORK

(MIRAMAX) Producers, Alberto Grimaldi, Harvey Weinstein; Executive Producers, Michael Hausman, Maurizio Grimaldi, Michael Ovitz, Bob Weinstein, Rick Yorn; Director, Martin Scorsese; Screenplay, Jay Cocks, Steven Zaillian, Kenneth Lonergan; Story, Jay Cocks; Co-Producers, Joe Reidy, Laura Fattori; Co-Executive Producers, Rick Schwartz, Colin Vaines, Graham King; Photography, Michael Ballhaus; Designer, Dante Ferretti; Costumes, Sandy Powell; Editor, Thelma Schoonmaker; Music, Howard Shore: Song: "The Hands That Built America" written and performed by U2; Executive Music Producer, Robbie Robertson; Special Visual Effects, Industrial Light & Magic; Casting, Ellen Lewis; Dolby; Super 35 Widescreen; Technicolor; Rated R; 168 minutes; Release date: December 20, 2002

CAST

Amsterdam Vallon	Leonardo DiCaprio
Bill "The Butcher" Cutting	Daniel Day-Lewis
Jenny Everdeane	Cameron Diaz
Boss Tweed	Jim Broadbent
Happy Jack	John C. Reilly
Johnny Sirocco	Henry Thomas
Walter "Monk" McGinn	Brendan Gleeson
McGloin	Gary Lewis
Shang	Stephen Graham
Killoran	Eddie Marsan
Reverend Raleigh	Alec McCowen
Mr. Schermerhorn	David Hemmings
Jimmy Spoils	Larry Gilliard, Jr.
Hell Cat Maggie	Cara Seymour
P.T. Barnum	Roger Ashton-Griffiths
Priest Vallon	Liam Neeson
Young Amsterdam	Cian McCormack
One-Armed Priest	Peter Hugo Daly
Young Johnny	Andrew Gallagher

and Philip Kirk (O'Connell Guard Leader), Rab Affleck (Plug Uglies Leader), Bill Barclay (Shirt Tails Leader), Nick Bartlett (Chichesters Leader), Robert Goodman (Forty Thieves Leader), Tim Pigott-Smith (Calvinist Minister), Liam Carney, Gary McCormack, David McBlain (Bill the Butcher's Gang), Dick Holland (True Blue American Speaker), Katherine Wallach, Carmen Hanlon, Ilaria D'Elia (Jenny's Girls), Laurie Ventruy (Resident Woman), Ford Kiernan (Black Joke Chief), Alec McMahon (Resident Man), Nevan Finegan, Dominique Vandenberg (Dead Rabbit Gang Members), Stuart Ong (Chinese at Sparrow's Pagoda), Basil Chung (Elderly Chinese at Pagoda), Finbar Furey (Satan's Circus Singer), Sean Gilder (Rat Pit Game Master), Richard Graham (Harvey, Card Player), Richard Strange (Undertaker), Douglas Plasse (Medical Student), Bruce Steinheimer (Army Recruiter), David Bamber (Passenger on Omnibus), Barbara Bouchet (Mrs. Schermerhorn), Michael Byrne (Horace Greeley), Lucy Davenport (Miss Schermerhorn), Maura

Cameron Diaz

O'Connell (Street Singer), Alex Howden (Assistant Hangman), James Ramsay (Arthur, Condemned Man), Iain McColl (Seamus, Condemned Man), Louis Brownsell (Legless Soldier), Gennaro Condemi (She-He), Kiernan Hurley (Recruiter), John Sessions (Harry Watkins/Lincoln), Michael H. Billingsley (Uncle Tom), Steven C. Matthews (Mr. Shelby), Giovanni Lombardo Radice (Mr. Legree), Alexia J. Murray (Topsy), Flaminia Fegarotti (Miss Eliza), Bronco McLoughlin (Assassin), Channing Cook Holmes (Tap Dancer), Elaine Chappuis (Chinese Whore), Roberta Quaresima, Marta Pilato (Whores), Su Jian (Chinese Acrobat), Cao Man (Chinese General), Kathy Shao-Lin Lee (Chinese Dancer), Alexander Deng (Chinese Boy Singer), Peter Berling (Knife Act Caller), Patrick Gordon (Surgeon), Brendan White (Archbishop), Brendan Dempsey (Provost Marshal Registrar), Taddeo Harbutt (Unruly Man), Nazzareno Natale (Don Whiskerandos), Colin Hill (Nativist Candidate), Robert Linge (One-Armed Veteran), Richard Syms (Drunken Repeater), Christian Burgess (The Mayor), Gerry Robert Byrne (Draft Official), Dave Nicholls (O'Connell Guard Leader), Tim Faraday (Plug Uglies Leader), Sean McGinley (Forty Thieves Leader), John Anthony Murphy (Kerryonians Leader), Terry O'Neill (Chichesters Leader), Vincent Pickering (American Guard Leader), Nick Miles (Atlantic Guard Leader), Ian Pirie (Slaughter Housers Leader), John McGlynn (Bowery Boys Leader), Larry Kaplan (Bloodied Bureaucrat), Leo Burmeister, Justin Brennan, Brian Mallon (Telegraph Operator Voices), Joseph Reidy (Police Chief), Joel Strachan (Telegraph Operator), Bill Murdoch (Robbert on Dock), Angela Pleasence (Accomplice), Ian Agnew (General Wool), Michael Hausman (Gunboat Captain), Bob Colletti (Soldier in Mist), Martin Scorsese (Head of Rich Household)

Sixteen years after his father was slain by Native American gang leader Bill "the Butcher" Cutting, Amsterdam Vallon returns to New York's rowdy and dangerous Five Points seeking vengeance.

This film received Oscar nominations for picture, actor (Daniel Day-Lewis), director, original screenplay, cinematography, art direction, editing, sound, costume design, and song ("The Hands That Built America").

© Miramax

Daniel Day-Lewis and the Native Americans

Jim Broadbent

Leonardo DiCaprio, Gary Lewis

Daniel Day-Lewis, Cameron Diaz, Leonardo DiCaprio

Daniel Day-Lewis, Leonardo DiCaprio

Leonardo DiCaprio

Cameron Diaz, Leonardo DiCaprio

Cara Seymour, John C. Reilly, Liam Neeson,
Brendan Gleeson, Gary Lewis

NARC

Ray Liotta, Jason Patric

(PARAMOUNT/LIONS GATE) Producers, Diane Nabatoff, Ray Liotta, Michelle Grace, Julius R. Nasso; Executive Producers, Randall Emmett, George Furla, Peter Block, Michael Z. Gordon, Jeff G. Waxman, Adam Stone, Tom Cruise, Paula Wagner, David C. Glasser; Director/Screenplay, Joe Carnahan; Photography, Alex Nepomniaschy; Designer, Greg Beale; Costumes, Gersha Phillips; Editor, John Gilroy; Music, Cliff Martinez; Music Supervisor, Brian Ross; Co-Executive Producers, Carol Gillson, Brian R. Keathley, Andy Emilio, Jed Baron, Michael S. Grayson; Line Producer, Tony Grazia; Casting, Mary Vernieu, Felicia Fasano, Clare Walker; a Cruise/Wagner production in association with Splendid Pictures, Emmett Furla Films, of a Julius R. Nasso production and Tiara Blu Films; Dolby; Deluxe color; Rated R; 105 minutes; Release date: December 20, 2002

CAST

Nick Tellis	Jason Patric
Henry Oak	Ray Liotta
Darnell "Big D Love" Beery	Busta Rhymes
Captain Cheevers	Chi McBride
Audrey Tellis	Krista Bridges
Elvin Dowd	Dan Leis
Walter Dandridge	Lloyd Adams
Little Girl	Meagan Issa
Jeanine Mueller	Lina Felice
Freeman Franks	Alan C. Peterson
Liz Detmer	Karen Robinson
Cecil Mitchum	Booth Savage
Michael Calvess	Alan Van Sprang
Tellis' Infant Son	Gavyn Donaldson, Myles Donaldson
Officer Marcotte	Thomas Patrice
Biker	Garry Robbins
Strung Out Woman	Lilette Wiens
Crackhead Junkie	Omar Samuels
Strung Out Man	Mauricio Rodas
Drug Dealer	Darren John
Porn Shop Dude	Steve Hunt

and Paulino Nunes (Officer Ellis Breaves), Marilo Nunez (Ruiz' Smoldering Squeeze), John Ortiz (Octavio Ruiz), Tony DeSantis (Medical Examiner, Art Harlan), Carson Durven (Leonard "Leo Lee" Leflore), Donna Croce (Oak's Wife), Kevin Rushton (Meth Dealer), Stacey Farber (Young Kathryn), Anne Openshaw (Kathryn Calvess), Mallory Mahoney (Calvess' Daughter), Carly Marie Alves (Lilian Rose Calvess), Bishop (Eugene "Deacon" Sheps), Richard Chevolleau (Latroy Steeds)

Undercover narc Nick Tellis, hoping to give up the field and settle into a desk job, is reluctantly teamed with volatile Henry Oak for one last case, to find out who is responsible for killing Oak's former partner.

© Paramount/Lions Gate

Ray Liotta, Jason Patric

John Ortiz, Jason Patric

John Ortiz, Busta Rhymes, Ray Liotta

Nigel, Eliza, Marianne

THE WILD THORNBERRYS MOVIE

(PARAMOUNT) Producers, Arlene Klasky, Gabor Csupo; Executive Producers, Albie Hecht, Julia Pistor, Eryk Casmerio, Hal Waite; Directors, Jeff McGrath, Cathy Malkasian; Screenplay, Kate Boutilier; Based on characters created by Arlene Klasky, Gabor Csupo, Steve Pepoon, David Silverman, Stephen Sustarsic; Co-Producers, Tracy Kramer, Terry Thoren, Norton Virgien, Sean Lurie; Production Designer, Dima Malanitchev; Music, Drew Neumann; Additional Music, Randy Kerber; Song: "Father and Daughter" written/performed and produced by Paul Simon; Executive Music Producer, George Acogny; Lead Character Design, Patrick J. Dene; Character Designers, Steve Fellner, Bill Schwab; Casting, Barbara Wright; a Nickelodeon Movies presentation of a Klasky Csupo production; Dolby; Widescreen; Deluxe color; Rated PG; 85 minutes; Release date: December 20, 2002

VOICE CAST

Mrs. Fairgood	Brenda Blethyn
Sloan Blackburn	Rupert Everett
Cordelia Thornberry	Lynn Redgrave
Bree Blackburn	Marisa Tomei
Akela, the Mother Cheetah	Alfre Woodard
Donnie	Flea (Michael Balzary)
Marianne Thornberry	Jodi Carlisle
Eliza Thornberry	Lacey Chabert
Nigel Thornberry	Tim Curry
Debbie	Danielle Harris
Darwin	Tom Kane
Boko	Obba Babatundé
Jomo	Brock Peters

and Cree Summer (Phaedra, Elephant), Crystal Scales (Cheetah Cubs), Kimberly Brooks (Tally, Cheetah Cub), Melissa Greenspan (Sarah Wellington), Alexandra Boyd (Victoria), Moira Quirk (Jane), Tara Strong, Hynden Walch, Mae Whitman (Schoolgirls), Roger L. Jackson (Reggie the Squirrel/Thunder), John Kassir, Charles Shaughnessy (Squirrels), Kevin Michael Richardson (Shaman Mnyambo), Billy Brown (Rhino), Jeff Coopwood (Tim, Park Ranger), Didier M. Ngole, Anthony Okungbowa (Rangers), James Brown Orleans (Zebu), Michael Chinyamurindi (Cart Owner), Earl Boen (Gorilla), Molanga Casquelourd (BoAka Leader), Alu Amina, Didier M. Ngole, Nsaka Kaninda, B. Didio Tshimanga, Camille Ntoto, Colette Elimo, Lunkeba Texo, Jeanne Kilimi, Inousca Kayombo, Mata Mokowala (BoAka Villagers), Keith Szarabajka (Poacher)

12-year-old Eliza Thornberry, who can secretly communicate with animals, tries to stop a group of poachers who are endangering the lives of some African creatures. Based on the Nickleodeon series *The Wild Thornberrys*.

This film received an Oscar nomination for song ("Father and Daughter").

TWO WEEKS NOTICE

(WARNER BROS.) Producer, Sandra Bullock; Executive Producers, Mary McLaglen, Bruce Berman; Director/Screenplay, Marc Lawrence; Photography, Laszlo Kovacs; Designer, Peter Larkin; Costumes, Gary Jones; Editor, Susan E. Morse; Music, John Powell; Music Supervisor, Laura Wasserman; Associate Producer, Scott Elias; Casting, Ilene Starger; a Castle Rock Entertainment presentation in association with Village Roadshow Pictures and NPV Entertainment; Dolby; Technicolor; Rated PG-13; 100 minutes; Release date: December 20, 2002

CAST

Lucy Kelson	Sandra Bullock
George Wade	Hugh Grant
June Carter	Alicia Witt
Ruth Kelson	Dana Ivey
Larry Kelson	Robert Klein
Meryl Brooks	Heather Burns
Howard Wade	David Haig
Tony	Dorian Missick

and Joseph Badalucco (Construction Foreman), Jonathan Dokuchitz (Tom), Veanne Cox (Melanie Corman), Janine LaManna (Elaine Cominsky), Iraida Polanco (Rosario), Charlotte Maier (Helen Wade), Katheryn Winnick (Tiffany), Jason Antoon (Norman), Rocco Musacchia (Fisherman), Wynter Kullman (Tyler), Francie Swift (Lauren Wade), Adam Grupper (Ex-Mrs. Wade's Lawyer), Johnny Dee (Homeless Man), John Cunningham (Justice of the Peace), Mark Feuerstein (Rich Beck), David Aaron Baker (Man Getting Into Cab), Teagle F. Bougere (Willie the Bellboy), Mandy Siegfried (Hana the Hostess), Mark Zeisler (Mr. Lowell), Nadine Mozon (Ms. Gonzales), Tim Kang (Paul the Attorney), Libby West (Masseuse), Sharon Wilkins (Polly St. Clair), Mike Piazza, Donald Trump, Norah Jones (Themselves), Shannon Fiedler (Cookie Girl), Becky Ann Baker (RV Woman), Adam LeFevre (RV Man), Sebastian R. Rand, George Gearhart King III (RV Sons), Bill Bowers (Dance Floor Mime), William Thourlby (Man in Elevator), Elizabeth Owens (Woman in Elevator), Dori Kancher (Farewell Party Girl), Marina Lutz (Lucy's Assistant), Jose Ramon Rosario (Assemblyman Perez)

Attorney and environmental advocate Lucy Kelson reluctantly agrees to serve as chief counsel for a real estate developer she blames for destroying most of the city's valuable property, under the condition that he will refrain from demolishing the Community Center in her neighborhood.

Hugh Grant, Sandra Bullock

CATCH ME IF YOU CAN

(DREAMWORKS) Producers, Steven Spielberg, Walter F. Parkes; Executive Producers, Barry Kemp, Laurie MacDonald, Michel Shane, Tony Romano; Co-Executive Producer, Daniel Lupi; Director, Steven Spielberg; Screenplay, Jeff Nathanson; Based upon the book by Frank W. Abagnale, with Stan Redding; Photography, Janusz Kaminski; Designer, Jeannine Oppewall; Costumes, Mary Zophres; Editor, Michael Kahn; Music, John Williams; Co-Producer, Devorah Moos-Hankin; Titles, Kuntzel + Deygas; Casting, Debra Zane; a Kemp Company and Splendid Pictures production, a Parkes/MacDonald production; Dolby; Technicolor; Rated PG-13; 141 minutes; Release date: December 25, 2002

Tom Hanks, Leonardo DiCaprio

Leonardo DiCaprio, Amy Adams

CAST

Frank Abagnale, Jr.	Leonardo DiCaprio
Carl Hanratty	Tom Hanks
Frank Abagnale	Christopher Walken
Roger Strong	Martin Sheen
Paula Abagnale	Nathalie Baye
Brenda Strong	Amy Adams
Jack Barnes	James Brolin
Tom Fox	Brian Howe
Earl Amdursky	Frank John Hughes
Paul Morgan	Steve Eastin
Special Agent Wilkins	Chris Ellis
Assistant Director Marsh	John Finn
Cheryl Ann	Jennifer Garner
Carol Strong	Nancy Lenehan
Marci	Ellen Pompeo
Lucy	Elizabeth Banks
Warden Garren	Guy Thauvette
Darcy	Candice Azzara
Loan Officer	Matthew Kimbrough
Football Player	Joshua Boyd
Joanna	Kaitlin Doubleday
Girl #1	Kelly McNair
Student #1	Jonathan Dankner
Teacher	Maggie Mellin
Principal Evans	Thomas Kopache

and Margaret Travolta (Ms. Davenport), Jimmie F. Skaggs (Bartender), Alex Hyde-White (Mr. Kesner), Lilyan Chauvin (Mrs. Lavalier), Eugene Fleming (Ticket Clerk), Robert Ruth (Hotel Manager), Jennifer Manley (Ashley), James Morrison (Pilot), Robert Symonds (Mr. Rosen), Jennifer Kan (Bank Teller), Robert Curtis Brown (Front Desk Clerk), Kelly Hutchinson (Young Teller), Steve Witting (Manager), Wendy Worthington (Receptionist), Jane Bodle (TWA Ticket Agent), J. Patrick McCormack (Auctioneer), Brian Goodman (Motel Owner), Ray Proscia (Salesman), Sarah Lancaster, Jill Matson (Riverbend Women), Mike Baldridge (Terry), Joel Ewing (Party Guy), Ritchie Montgomery (Young Doctor), Jim Antonio (Victor Griffith), Angela Sorensen (Party Girl), Jonathan Brent (Dr. Ashland), Benita Krista Nall (Emergency Nurse), Shane Edelman (Doctor Harris), Andrew Meeks (Young Patient), Morgan Rusler (FBI Agent), Jane Edith Wilson (Bar Examiner), Dave Hager (Judge), Kyle Davis (Kid), Patrick T. O'Brien (Mr. Hendricks), Jamie Ray Newman (Monica), Deborah Kellner (Debra Jo), Mercedes Cornett (Heather), Amy Acker (Miggy), Robert Peters, James Dumont, Thomas Crawford (FBI Agents), Sarah Rush (Secretary), Malachi Throne (Abe Penner), Alfred Dennis (Ira Penner), Max J. Kerstein (Penner Brother), Donna Kimball (TWA Stewardess), Jan Munroe (Captain Oliver), Stephen Dunham, Brandon Keener (Pilots), Jasmine Jessica Anthony (Little Girl), Anthony Powers (NY Savings Bank Manager), Lauren Cohn (Teller), Jeremy Howard (Teen Waiter), Jack Knight (Man #3), Jamie Anderson (Ilene), Kam Heskin (Candy), Ana Maria Quintana (Hotel Maid), Gerald Molen (FBI Agent), Celine Du Tertre (Little Girl on Street), Stan Bly (Blind Man), Jamie Moss (Young Man), Jessica Collins (Peggy), Frank W. Abagnale (French Policeman), Roger Léger (Prison Guard), Jean-François Blanchard (French Police Captain), Mathieu Gaudreault, Guy Daniel Tremblay, Alexandre Bisping, Patrick Dussault (French Police), Paul Todd (Maitre D'), Jake Wagner (Kid), Ashley Cohen, Kelly Cohen (Party Twins), Ellis Hall (Piano Player/Singer), Steven Meizler (Piano Player), Fred Datig (Co-Pilot)

The true story of how Frank Abagnale Jr. passed himself off as various people, including an airline pilot and a doctor, while he was still a teenager.

This film received Oscar nominations for supporting actor (Christopher Walken) and original score.

Leonardo DiCaprio (center)

Tom Hanks

Martin Sheen

Leonardo DiCaprio, Jennifer Garner

Christopher Walken, Leonardo DiCaprio

Leonardo DiCaprio (center)

Nathalie Baye

THE HOURS

Meryl Streep

Jack Rovello, Julianne Moore

(PARAMOUNT/MIRAMAX) Producers, Scott Rudin, Robert Fox; Executive Producer, Mark Huffam; Director, Stephen Daldry; Screenplay, David Hare; Based upon the novel by Michael Cunningham; Photography, Seamus McGarvey; Designer, Maria Djurkovic; Costumes, Ann Roth; Editor, Peter Boyle; Music, Philip Glass; Casting, Daniel Swee, Patsy Pollock; a Scott Rudin/Robert Fox production; Dolby; Deluxe color; Rated PG-13; 114 minutes; Release date: December 27, 2002

CAST

Virginia Woolf	Nicole Kidman
Laura Brown	Julianne Moore
Clarissa Vaughan	Meryl Streep

1923

Leonard Woolf	Stephen Dillane
Vanessa Bell	Miranda Richardson
Quentin Bell	George Loftus
Julian Bell	Charley Ramm
Angelica Bell	Sophie Wyburd
Lottie Hope	Lyndsay Marshal
Nelly Boxall	Linda Bassett
Ralph Partridge	Christian Coulson
Doctor	Michael Culkin

1951

Dan Brown	John C. Reilly
Richie Brown	Jack Rovello
Kitty Barlowe	Toni Collette
Mrs. Latch	Margo Martindale
Hotel Clerk	Colin Stinton

2001

Richard Brown	Ed Harris
Sally Lester	Allison Janney
Julia Vaughan	Claire Danes
Louis Waters	Jeff Daniels
Barbara in the Flower Shop	Eileen Atkins
Clarissa's Neighbor	Carmen De Lavallade
Rodney	Daniel Brocklebank

Three different women in three different eras: author Virginia Woolf, battling insanity as she begins to write her classic novel *Mrs. Dalloway;* 1950s housewife Laura Brown, questioning her staid existence, as she reads the same book; and modern day Clarissa Vaughan as she prepares a party in celebration of her dying friend, in a story paralleling the character in Woolf's book.

2002 Academy Award winner for Best Actress (Nicole Kidman). This film received additional Oscar nominations for picture, supporting actor (Ed Harris), supporting actress (Julianne Moore), director, screenplay adaptation, editing, costume design, and original score.

© Paramount/Miramax

Nicole Kidman

Nicole Kidman, Miranda Richardson

Claire Danes, Allison Janney

Sophie Wyburd, Nicole Kidman

Toni Collette, Julianne Moore

Julianne Moore

Stephen Dillane

John C. Reilly

Meryl Streep, Jeff Daniels

167

NICHOLAS NICKLEBY

(UNITED ARTISTS) Producers, Simon Channing Williams, John N. Hart, Jeffrey Sharp; Executive Producers, Gail Egan, Robert Kessel, Michael Hogan; Director/Screenplay, Douglas McGrath; Based on the novel by Charles Dickens; Photography, Dick Pope; Designer, Eve Stewart; Costumes, Ruth Myers; Editor, Lesley Walker; Music, Rachel Portman; Line Producer, Robert How; Hair Designer, Simon Thompson; Make-up Designer, Sarah Monzani; Casting, Lina Todd, Nina Gold; a Harp Entertainment production in association with Cloud Nine Films; Distributed by MGM Distribution Co.; Dolby; Super 35 Widescreen; Color; Rated PG; 132 minutes; Release date: December 27, 2002

CAST

Smike	Jamie Bell
Wackford Squeers	Jim Broadbent
Newman Noggs	Tom Courtenay
Mr. Folair	Alan Cumming
Sir Mulberry Hawk	Edward Fox
Kate Nickleby	Romola Garai
Madeline Bray	Anne Hathaway
Mrs. Crummles/Mr. Leadville	Barry Humphries (Dame Edna Everage)
Nicholas Nickleby	Charlie Hunnam
Vincent Crummles	Nathan Lane
Ralph Nickleby	Christopher Plummer
Charles Cheeryble	Timothy Spall
Mrs. Squeers	Juliet Stevenson
Bray	David Bradley
Brooker	Phil Davis
Ned Cheeryble	Gerard Horan
John Browdie	Kevin McKidd
Lord Verisopht	Nicholas Rowe
Miss Lacreevy	Sophie Thompson
Mrs. Nickleby	Stella Gonet
Mr. Nickleby	Andrew Havill
Child Nicholas Nickleby	Henry McGrath
Boy Nicholas Nickleby	Hugh Mitchell
Child Kate Nickleby	Poppy Rogers
Young Kate Nickleby	Jessie Lou Roberts

and Angela Curran (Parent), Bruce Cook (Little Wackford Squeers), Greg Sheffield (Bolder), Alex Graham (Cobbery), Jordan Calvert, Joel Pitts (Boys), Billy Hill (Tomkins), Heather Goldenhersh (Fanny Squeers), Lucy Davies (Maid), Helen Coker (Tilda), Angus Wright (Mr. Pluck), Eileen Walsh (The Infant Phenomenon), Alfred Harmsworth (Young Smike), Mark Wells (Romeo), Daisy Haggard (Juliet), Jacob Engleberg (Boy Messenger), Lisa Martin (Ribbon Girl), William Ash (Frank), Celia Henebury (Mrs. Bray), Edward Hogg (Young Mr. Bray), Roger Ashton-Griffiths (Doctor), Diana Morrison (Bray's Maid), Amber Batty (Mrs. Ralph Nickleby), Mark Dexter (Young Ralph Nickleby), Mark Meadows (Lone Soldier)

When the Nickleby family ends up penniless following their father's death, Nicholas and his sister are left at the mercy of his heartless Uncle Ralph, who splits the family apart, sending Nicholas to work at the orphanage run by the abusive Wackford Squeers. Earlier version was the 1947 British film that starred Derek Bond (Nicholas), Cedric Hardwicke (Ralph), Sally Ann Howes (Kate), Jill Balcon (Madeline), and Aubrey Woods (Smike).

© United Artists

Charlie Hunnam, Jamie Bell

Christopher Plummer

Nathan Lane, Barry Humphries

Charlie Hunnam, Tom Courtenay

LOVE LIZA

Jack Kehler, Philip Seymour Hoffman

Philip Seymour Hoffman, Sarah Koskoff

Philip Seymour Hoffman

(SONY CLASSICS) Producers, Ruth Charny, Chris Hanley, Jeff Roda, Fernando Sulichin; Executive Producers, Jim Czarnecki, Daniel Guckau, Rainer Kolmel; Director, Todd Louiso; Screenplay, Gordy Hoffman; Photography, Lisa Rinzler; Designer, Stephen Beatrice; Costumes, Jill Newell; Editor, Anne Stein Katz; Music, Jim O'Rourke; Casting, Monika Mikkelsen, Rita VanderWaal, Mark Bennett, Lisa Mae Fincannon; a Kinowelt Filmprouktion GmbH and Wild Bunch presentation in association with Studio Canal, a Muse/Blacklist production in association with Ruth Charny and Jeff Roda; U.S.-French; Dolby; Color; Rated R; 90 minutes; Release date: December 30, 2002

CAST

Wilson Joel	Philip Seymour Hoffman
Denny	Jack Kehler
Maura Haas	Sarah Koskoff
Tom Bailey	Stephen Tobolowsky
Mary Ann Bankhead	Kathy Bates
Brenda	Erika Alexander
Bern	J.D. Walsh
Pad	Jimm Raskin
Waiter with Drunk	Mark Hannibal
Bland Man	Jim Wise
Bland Woman	Trace Turville
Cashier, Gas Station #1	Wayne Duvall
Jim	Kevin Breznahan
Lynne	Jennifer Keddy
Hobbytown USA Clerk	David Lenthal
Zoo	Pauline Boyd
Trucker	Ernest Perry, Jr.

and Cullen Douglas (Cashier at Pancake House), Joanne Pankow (Grandma Clerk), Dan Klaas (Officer Escort Out of Town), Chris Ellis (Patriot Hobby), George Mills (Pickup Truck Drivers), Julia LaShae (Breakfast Woman), Terry O'Deen (Parking Lot Date), Don Hood (Good Morning Man)

Wilson Joel, shattered by the unexpected suicide of his wife Liza, refuses to open the note she left behind for fear that its contents will destroy his memory of what he felt was a perfect relationship.

© Sony Pictures

Philip Seymour Hoffman, Kathy Bates

CONFESSIONS OF A DANGEROUS MIND

(MIRAMAX) Producer, Andrew Lazar; Executive Producers, Steven Soderbergh, Rand Ravich, Bob Weinstein, Harvey Weinstein, Jon Gordon, Stephen Evans; Director, George Clooney; Screenplay, Charlie Kaufman; Based on the book by Chuck Barris; Co-Producer, Jeffrey Sudzin; Co-Executive Producer, Far Shariat; Associate Producers, Amy Minda Cohen, Gym Hinderer; Photography, Newton Thomas Sigel; Designer, James D. Bissell; Costumes, Renée April; Music, Alex Wurman; Editor, Stephen Mirrione; Casting, Ellen Chenoweth; a Mad Chance Production in association with Section Eight; Dolby; Super 35 Widescreen; Color; Rated R; 113 minutes; Release date: December 31, 2002

George Clooney, Sam Rockwell

Drew Barrymore, Sam Rockwell

Drew Barrymore, Sam Rockwell

CAST

Chuck Barris	Sam Rockwell
Jim Byrd	George Clooney
Penny	Drew Barrymore
Patricia	Julia Roberts
Keeler	Rutger Hauer
Debbie	Maggie Gyllenhaal
Themselves	Dick Clark, Jaye P. Morgan, Jim Lange
Housekeeper	Michelle Sweeney
Tuvia (8 years)	Chelsea Ceci
Chuck (8 & 11 years)	Michael Céra
Chuck's Dates	Aimee Rose Ambroziak, Isabelle Blais, Melissa Carter
Georgia	Jennifer Hall
Georgia's Girlfriend	Ilona Elkin
Barfly	Sean Tucker
Freddie Cannon	David Hirsh
Larry Goldberg	Jerry Weintraub
ABC Executive	Frank Fontaine
Tuvia (25 years)	Rachelle Lefevre
Actual Gene Gene	Gene Gene Patton
Instructor Jenkins	Robert John Burke
Renda	Daniel Zacapa
Benitez	Emilio Rivera
Brazioni	Carlos Carrasco
Woman in Veil	Barbara Bacci
Blonde Bachelorette	Janet Lane
Beanpole Bachelor	Shaun Balbar
Frizzy Hair Bachelor	Jeff Lefebvre
Handsome Bachelor	Michael Filipowich
Black Bachelorette	Samantha Banton
Black Bachelor	Christian Paul
Loretta	Kristen Wilson
Dating Game Director	Steve Adams
Stud Bachelorette	Maria Bertrand
Stud Bachelor	John Todd Anderson
Bachelor Brad	Brad Pitt
Bachelor Matt	Matt Damon
Actual Unknown Comic	Murray Langston
Woman in Pub	Marlida Ferreira
English Man	Jerome Tiberghien
Simon Oliver	Michael Ensign
Chuck's Father	Martin Kevan
Chuck's Mother	Claudia Besso
Amana Girl	Isabelle Juneau
Bachelorette Winner	Nathalie Morin
Bachelor Winner	Tony Zanca
Shaving Man	Sergei Priselkov
Colbert	Norman Roy
Casting Executives	Marlene Fisher, Richard Kind

Asian Folksingers ....Suyan Kim, Shulan Noma and Andre Minicozzi, Richard Beaudet, Ron Di Lauro, Peter N. Wilson, Bruce Pepper, Francois St-Pierre (Gong Show Band), Cheryl Murphy (Little Person), Krista Allen (Pretty Woman), George Randolph (Gene Gene), Pascale De Vigne (Critic), Carlo Berardinucci (Waiter), Tanya Anthony (Prostitute), Andrée-Anne Quesnel (Gong Show Model), Keshav Patel (Elvis Singer), James Urbaniak (Rod Flexner), Leslie Cottle (L.A. Bar Woman), Dino Tosques (L.A. Bartender), Joe Cobden (Unknown Comic), Ethan Thomas C. Dempster (Chuck, 3 years), Tommy Hinkley (Hambone Man), Bill Corday (Justice of the Peace), Chuck Barris (Actual Barris)

The story of television game show creator Chuck Barris, dramatizing his claim that he led a double life during his career in the show business spotlight working as an assassin for the CIA.

Sam Rockwell, George Clooney

Drew Barrymore, Sam Rockwell

George Clooney, Sam Rockwell

IMPOSTOR

(DIMENSION) Producers, Gary Fleder, Gary Sinise, Marty Katz, Daniel Lupi; Executive Producer, Michasel Phillips; Co-Executive Producers, Bob Weinstein, Harvey Weinstein; Co-Producers, Gary Granat, Andrew Rona, Michael Zoumas; Director, Gary Fleder; Screenplay, Caroline Case, Ehren Kruger, David Twohy; Based on the story by Philip K. Dick; Adapation, Scott Rosenberg; Photography, Robert Elswit; Designer, Nelson Coates; Costumes, Abigail Murray; Editors, Armen Minasian, Bob Ducsay; Music, Mark Isham; Visual Effects, Industrial Light & Magic; Casting, Heidi Levitt, John Papsidera; a Marty Katz production in association with Mojo Films; Distributed by Miramax Films; Dolby; Color; Rated PG-13; 96 minutes; Release date: January 4, 2002. CAST: Gary Sinise (Spencer Olham), Madeleine Stowe (Dr. Maya Olham), Vincent D'Onofrio (Hathaway), Tony Shalhoub (Nelson Gittes), Mekhi Phifer (Cale), Gary Dourdan (Capt. Burke), Tim Guinee (Dr. Carone), Lindsay Crouse (Chancellor), Elizabeth Pena (Midwife), Tracey Walter (Mr. Siegel), Greg Serand, Jason Beck (Gang Boys), Judy Jean Berns (Disgruntled Woman), Veena Bidasha (Frowning Nurse), Ellen Bradley (Nursing Mother), Shane Brolly (Lt. Burrows), Golden Brooks (Cale's Sister), Brian Brophy (Military Official), Scott Burkholder (Jack Stoller), and Erica Gimpel, Arly Jover, Burt Bulos (Newscasters), Morty Coyle (Kissing Couple Man), Yvette Ocampo Coyle (Kissing Couple Woman), Adam Rodriguez, Cristos, Giovanni Sirchia (Troopers), Una Damon (Local Newscaster), John Gatins (Patient—Soldier), Bayani Ison (Squad Leader), Elizabeth Kate (Maya Lookalike), Jonell Kennedy, Malea McGuinness (Screaming Nurses), Ted King (RMR Operator), Rachel Luttrell (Scan Room Nurse), Ivana Milicevic (Gang Girl), Diane Mizota (Receptionist), Melinda Ramos (Reporter), Shannon Saint Ryan (Zoner), Kimberly Scott (Comms Officer), Mac Sinise (Young Spence), Julie Vitz (Typox Child)

E-DREAMS

(SEVENTH ART) Producer/Director/Editor, Wonsuk Chin; Executive Producer, Sam Pai; Photography, Joia Speciale; Color; Not rated; 93 minutes; Release date: January 11, 2002. Documentary about the rise and fall of Kozmo.com, an internet company that delivered goods ordered online faster than any other company. Featuring Joseph Park, Yong Kang.

Gary Sinise in *Impostor* © Dimension

STATE PROPERTY

(LIONS GATE) Producer, Damon Dash; Executive Producers, Ron Rothholz, Phyllis Cedar; Line Producer, Robert Khristov; Director, Abdul Malik Abbott; Screenplay, Tron Anderson, Abdul Malik Abbott; Story, Tron Anderson; Costumes, Chasia Kwane, Natalie Johnson; Editors, Paul Frank, Tim French, Justine Harari; Dolby; Color; Rated R; 88 minutes; Release date: January 18, 2002. CAST: Beanie Sigel (Beans), Omilio Sparks (Baby Boy), Memphis Bleek (Blizz), Damon Dash ("Boss" Dame), Sundy Carter (Aisha), Tyran "Ty-Ty" Smith (Shareef), Oskeeno (D-Nice), Jay-Z ("Untouchable J"), Brother Newz (P-Nut), Randolph Curtis Rand (Saul Weisberg), Nicole Madeo (Leslie Tucci), Leslie Pilgrim (Aja), Kyndra Monet (Selena), Pain in Da Ass (Mario), Dee Lee (Poochie), Rell (Butter), Leah Leatherbury (Tonya), Reb (Snoop), Rashie Constantine (Mel), Steven "X" Baker (Bruce), Willie Esco (Papi Wil'), Cousin Ervan ("E"), Andrea Videla (Nina), Constanza Casas (Leila), James "Murda" Smith (Murda), Burt Bazin (Timmy), Christina Morales (Waitress), Larry "Tron" Quarrels (Futch), Tatiana Vujoshevich (TV Reporter), Devin "DeMarco" Ramos (Tone), Walter "DeMiggs" Patterson (Malik), Garvin Stewart (Chedda), G. Roberson (Manny), Chris Eric Williams (C-Zer), Bobby Dash (Bob), Big Skane (Skane), Robert Burke (Bob), Jennifer Cordero (Dana), Derren Fuentes (Det. Jenkins), Tim House (Det. Mason), Oria Rodriguez (Sahsa), Arda "Muggs" Henderson (Bartender), Jennifer Pan (Club Waitress), Letisha Wilson (Tisha), Christopher Reis (Ricky), Hanif "Neef" Muhammed (Troy), AMIL (Boss' Assassin), DJ Clue (Boss Informant), Greg "M&M" Werts, Big Shon (Mario's Henchmen), Richard Bravo (Ramon), Dave Sierra (Benito), Jacob "The Jeweler" (Eli), Raouf Simmons (Brother UF), Kevin Nunan (Sergeant Kev), Giovanni Laws (Det. Ashley), J. Diamond, Frank Minerva (Medics), Gabina Cordero (P-Nut's Girl), Slice (Slice), Lenny Santiago (Len)

E-Dreams © Seventh Art

Jay-Z in *State Property* © Lions Gate

Keesha Sharp, Paolo Montalban in *American Adobo* © Outrider

AMERICAN ADOBO

(OUTRIDER PICTURES) Producer, Tony Gloria, Vincent R. Nebrida, Steve Grenyo; Executive Producers, Charo Santos-Concio, Kevin J. Foxe; Director, Laurice Guillen; Screenplay, Vincent R. Nebrida; Photography, Lee Meily; Designer, Fiel Corrales Zabat; Editor, Efren Jarlego; an ABS-CBN Entertainment and Unitel Pictures in association with Magic Adobo Productions presentation; Color; Rated R; 102 minutes; Release date: January 25, 2002. CAST: Christopher De Leon (Mike), Dina Bonnevie (Marissa), Ricky Davao (Gerry), Cherry Pie Picache (Tere), Paolo Montalban (Raul), Randy Becker (Sam), Gloria Romero (Gerry's Mom), Keesha Sharp (Debbie), Sandy Andolong (Emma), Susan Valdez-LeGoff (Gigi), Sol Oca (Lorna), Wayne Waugans (Chris), Traci Ann Wolfe (Denise), Martha Millan (Candy), Lorli Villanueva (Lydia), Jojo Gonzalez (Frank), Luis Pedron (Nonong), Jason Verdadero (Mark), James Burns (Fireman), Marcel Simoneau (Sal), Stan Carp (Irish Tenant)

WANNABES

(PINNACLE FILMWORKS) Producers, A. Charles Addessi, Charles A. Addessi, Nicole Craig, William DeMeo; Directors, A. Charles Addessi, Charles A. Addessi, William DeMeo; Screenplay, William DeMeo; Costumes, Mildred Brignoni; Casting, Kim Eva Matuka; Color; Rated R; 110 minutes; Release date: January 25, 2002. CAST: William DeMeo (Angelo), Conor Dubin (Paulie), Ray Serra (Uncle Tommy), Daniel Margotta (Pete), John Palumbo (Dom), Joe Viterelli (Santo), Joseph D'Onofrio (Vinny), John Glenn Hoyt (John Hoyt), Vinny Vella (Carmine), Joseph Daleo, Jr. (Lenny), Joseph Carl Dibitetto (Pino), Michael Caldera (Matty), Robert Costanzo (Mr. Letto), Billy Knight (Mario), Anthony T. Donofrio III (Carlos), Raymond Cassar (Caesar), Sascha Knopf (Tammy), Mario Macalus (Tammy's Boyfriend), Lenny N. Rizzo (Obnoxious Customer), Madonna Guzzardo (Mario's Friend's Girlfriend), Lenny Ligotti (Freddie), Leslie Cottle (Loretta), Nelson Vasquez (Hector), Nicola Diamond (Hector's Girl), Richard Maldone (Bruno), Joe D'Alessio (Kid in Store), Angelo DeRossi (Harry the Bird), Barry Gold (Harry's Friend), Michelle Otto (Lisa), Daniel Baker (Yuppie #1), Dyanne Mercante (Monica), Danny Frank Depasquale (Lace Club Owner), Patrick Cooley (Touchy Customer), Desiree Russo (Lace Waitress), Frank Morano (Frankie), Aesha Waks (Stephanie), Philip Ligotte (Victor), Joseph Daleo III (Angelo, 10 years old), Anthony Prianti, Jr. (Angel, 5 years old), Charles Addessi II (Paulie, 7 years old), Daniel Dryer (Paulie, 3 years old), Andrew Marchisello (Dom, 7 years old), Michael Salvatore (Angelo and Paulie's Father), Barbara Teti (Angelo and Paulie's Mother), Ranjit Bhogal (Singh)

KUNG POW: ENTER THE FIST

(20TH CENTURY FOX) Producers, Paul Marshal, Tom Koranda, Steve Oedekerk; Director/Screenplay, Steve Oedekerk; Photography, John J. Connor; Designer, Héctor Vélez; Costumes, Shawnelle Cherry; Editor, Paul Marshal; Music, Robert Folk; Stunts/Fight Coordinator, Todd Bryant; Casting, Linda Francis; an O Entertainment production; Dolby; Panavision; Deluxe color; Rated PG-13; 81 minutes; Release date: January 25, 2002. CAST: Steve Oedekerk (Chosen One/Dubbed Voices), Lung Fai (Master Pain—Betty), Leo Lee (Young Master Pain), Tse Ling Ling (Ling), Yan Lin (Dying Ling), Lau Kar Wing (Wimp Lo), Chen Hui Lou (Master Tang), Ma Chi (Master Doe), Jennifer Tung (Whoa), Escobar Tongue (Tonguey), Ming Lo (Father), Peggy Lu (Mother), Tad Horino (Chew Fat Lip), Tori Tran (Peasant Woman), Simon Rhee, Joon B. Kim (Young Master Pain's Henchmen), Philip Tan (Grilled Face Fight), Nasty Nes (Boom Box Henchman), Chad Stahelski (Masked Fighter), Michael Li, Jen Sung Outerbridge, Al Goto, Will Leong (Stick Fighters), Woon (Lone Fighter), Hiro Koda, Ron Yuan, David Wald, John Koyama, Johnny Eusebio (Gang Fighters), Marcus Young (Gang Fighter with Hole in Stomach), Elsa Cancino (Bikini Fighter), James Wing Woo, Charles Park, Cary Y. Mizobe (Martial Arts Masters), Alejandro Olazabal (Chosen One Baby), Paulina Guerrero (Chosen One's Sister), Emanuel Kohakura (Chosen One's Brother), Ivan Nakamura, Oscar Carrillo (Crane Students) (Note: This motion picture contains footage from the 1976 Hong Kong film *Hu He Shuang Xiang/Tiger & Crane Fists*)

Steve Oedekerk (right) in *Kung Pow: Enter the Fist* © 20th Century Fox

HOMETOWN LEGEND

(JENKINS ENTERTAINMENT) Producer, Dallas Jenkins; Executive Producers, Robert Abramoff, Ron Booth, Jerry B. Jenkins, Leslie McRay; Director, James Anderson; Screenplay, Shawn Hoffman, Michael Patwin; Photography, Mark Petersen; Designer, Alice Baker; Costumes, Liz Staub; Music, Dan Haseltine, Joe Hogue; Editor, Daniel Cahn; Casting, Cathy Henderson, Dori Zuckerman; a Miracle Network Group production; Color; Rated PG; 108 minutes; Release date: January 25, 2002. CAST: Terry O'Quinn (Buster Schuler), Lacey Chabert (Rachel Sawyer), Nick Cornish (Elvis Jackson), Kirk B.R. Woller (Cal Sawyer), Ian Bohen (Brian Schuler), Mary Pat Gleason (Tee Naters), Mark McLachlan (Sherman Naters), Daniel Franzese (Abel), Kelli Garner (Josie), Jay Hastings, Pablo (Painted Face Redneck Fans), Dallas Jenkins (Jack Schuler), Chris Lumpkin (Stupid Snitch), F.X. Vitolo (Shazam), Sewell Whitney (Robert), Greg Bond, Brian Collins (Football Players)

James King, Jason Schwartzman in *Slackers* © Screen Gems

DOMESTIC VIOLENCE

(ZIPPORAH FILMS) Producer/Director/Editor, Frederick Wiseman; Photography, John Davey; Color; Not rated; 196 minutes; Release date: January 30, 2002. Documentary on the devastating effects of domestic violence in America and the efforts to help abused women and children by the staff of The Spring, a shelter in Tampa, FL.

THE SINGLES WARD

(HALESTORM) Producer, Dave Hunter; Director, Kurt Hale; Screenplay, Kurt Hale, John E. Moyer; Photography, Ryan Little; Music, Cody Hale; Editor, Wynn Hougaard; Casting, Michelle Wright; a Halestorm Entertainment, LDS Singles Online, Linger Longer production; Dolby; Color; Rated PG; 110 minutes; Release date: January 30, 2002. CAST: Will Swenson (Jonathan Jordan), Connie Young (Cammie), Daryn Tufts (Eldon), Kirby Heyborne (Dallen), Michael Birkeland (Hyrum), Robert Swenson (Zak), Lincoln Hoppe (DeVerl), Tarance Edwards (Troy), Michelle Ainge (Allyson), Gretchen Whalley (Stacie), Sedra Santos (Laura), Wally Joyner, Danny Ainge (Sunbeam Teacher), Richard Dutcher (West the Neighbor), Shawn Bradley (A Mechanic), Kim Wares (Sarah), Gordon Jump (An Airline Passenger), Jimmy Chunga (Phat Cop), Kerry Jackson (Skinny Cop), LaVell Edwards (The Golfer), Ron McBride (Brother Giles), Steve Young (Brother Niner), Johnny Biscuit (A TV Salesman), Thurl Bailey (A Traveler), Mitch English (Star Wars Guy), Julie Stoffer (Real World Actress), Scott Christopher (Chicken Guy), Ali Durham (Michelle), Jeremy Elliott (Sam), Joy Gardner (Sister Missionary), Coz Green (Video Store Customer), Ruth Hale (Old Woman), Adam Johnson (Acorn)

SLACKERS

(SCREEN GEMS) Producers, Neal H. Moritz, Erik Feig; Executive Producer, Patrice Theroux; Co-Executive Producers, Brad Jenkel, Mark Morgan; Director, Dewey Nicks; Screenplay, David H. Steinberg; Photography, James Bagdonas; Designer, William Arnold; Costumes, Jennifer Levy; Editor, Tara Timpone; Music Supervisor, Amanda Scheer-Demme; Co-rpdocuer, Louis G. Friedman; Casting, John Papsidera; a Neal H. Moritz production in association with Erik Feig productions, presented in association with Alliance Atlantis; Dolby; Color; Rated R; 87 minutes; Release date: February 1, 2002. CAST: Devon Sawa (Dave), Jason Schwartzman (Ethan), James King (Angela), Jason Segel (Sam), Michael C. Maronna (Jeff), Laura Prepon (Reanna), Mamie Van Doren (Mrs. Van Graaf), Sam Anderson (Charles Patton), Japhet "J.P" Coe (Phillip), Travis Davis (Airborne Driver), Charles Dougherty (Astronomy Professor), Shelley Dowdy (Shelley), Rick Dubov (Security Guard), Margaret Easley (Receptionist), Mary Faulkner, Wesley Mann (Executives), Nat Faxon (Karl), Joe Flaherty (Mr. Leonard), Jason Garner (Singing Waiter), Todd Giebenhain (Stoned Testtaker), Jonathan Kasdan (Barry), Heidi Kramer, Alissa Kramer (Hotties), Robert B. Martin, Jr. (The Gimp), Michael McDonald (Economics Professor), Don Michaelson (Professor Markoe), Melanie Deanne Moore (Pissed Off Co-Ed), Howard Mungo (Doctor), Jim Rash (Head T.A.), Retta (Office Manger), Joanna Sanchez (Nurse), Marilyn Staley (Singing Waitress), Kim Stanwood (Dave's Mom), Michael Swiney (Homeless Guy), Leigh Taylor Young (Valerie Patton), Gedde Watanabe (Japanese Proctor)

Domestic Violence © Zipporah Films

LL Cool J in *Rollerball* © MGM

ROLLERBALL

(MGM) Producers, Charles Roven, Beau St. Clair, John McTiernan; Executive Producer, Michael Tadross; Director, John McTiernan; Screenplay, Larry Ferguson, John Pogue; Based on the short story and screenplay by William Harrison; Photography, Steve Mason; Designer, Norman Garwood; Costumes, Kate Harrington; Editor, John Wright; Music, Eric Serra; Visual Effects Supervisor, John Sullivan; Casting, Pat McCorkle; Stunts, Jamie Jones; Presented in association with Mosaic Media Group; Dolby; Deluxe color; Rated PG-13; 98 minutes; Release date: February 7, 2002. CAST: Chris Klein (Jonathan Cross), Jean Reno (Petrovich), LL Cool J (Marcus Ridley), Rebecca Romijn-Stamos (Aurora), Naveen Andrews (Sanjay), Oleg Taktarov (Denekin), David Hemblen (Serokin), Janet Wright (Coach Olga), Andrew Bryniarski (Halloran), Kata Dobo (Katya); Red Team: Alice Poon (#7), Lucia Rijker (#9), Melissa Stubbs (#12), Paul Wu (U-Chow, #16), Yolanda Hughes-Heying (#28), Jay Mahin (Toba, #39), Simon Girard (Rabbit, #68), Kevin Rushton (Tom Farr), Anatoly Zinoviev (Eitan Kramer), Ruth Chiang (Victor Callender), Shawn Stewart (Mike Dopud), Pink, Slipknot (Themselves), Toshiro Ito (Japanese Announcer), Michael Tadross (Starter), Amy Whitmore (Photographer), Shaun Austin-Olsen (Foreign Guest), Flint Tecumseh Eagle (Eskimo), Steve P. Park (Gold Team Thug), Eugene Lipinski (Yuri Kotlev), Susan Cannon (Club Bartender), Kim Cannon, George Christy (Club VIPs), Mischa Hausserman (Gold Coach), Frank Ferrara (Asst. Gold Coach), Peter Kosaka (German Guest), Gabor Zsigovics (Herzen), Vitali Makarov (Komo), Tony Palermo (Toll), Oleg Ferdman (Miner), Philippe Soucy (Ally), Paulino Nunes (Borges), Peter von Berg (Chwoler), Eugene Geylik (Chwoler's Asst.), Barry Shurchin (Director), Ivan Smith (Tahli), Shane McMahon (American Media Mogul), Ola Sturik (Russian Translator), Norman Yap (Mandarin Translator), Kes Kwansa (African Sports Announcer), George Ghali (Arabic Sports Announcer), Luoyong Wang (Chinese Sports Announcer), Paul Heyman (English Sports Announcer), Jean Brassard (French Sports Announcer), Peter Blake (German Sports Announcer), Ismail Bashey (Indian Sports Announcer), Angelo Pedari (Italian Sports Announcer), Slava Schoot, Guy Ale (Russian Sports Announcer), Damir Andrei (Serbo-Croatian Sports Announcer), Pedro Salvin (Spanish Sports Announcer), Alice Benjamin (Russian Doctor), Ghiziane & Dalila Alini (Club Galore Twins), Michelle Leblanc (Petrovich's Girlfriend), Richard Zeman (Petrovich's Heavy), Scott Taylor, Eddy Salim, Richard Labelle, John Kesler (Petrovich's Bodyguards), François Paquette (VIP), Nick Sita (Italian VIP), Tom Karle (VIP Booth Judge), Richard Orlando (Patriarch), Zhi Xu (English Announcer's Asst.), Léopold Boisvert, Jitka Svecova (Technicians), Debbie-Ann Champagne (Cigarette Girl), Lilly He, Florence Situ, Zoran Krzisnik, Vsevolod Malamud (Journalists), Tony Xinkang (Asian Director), Bruno Mourani (Arabic Man), Claudine Robitaille (Production Asst.), Isabelle Landreville (Stewardess), Ahmet Salihu (Hot Dog Vendor), Hassan Hakmoun, Azam Ali, Jamshied Sharifi, Miyuki Sakamoto, Tristan Avakian, Tsutomu Takeishi, Benjamin Wittman (Home Band)

THE LAST MAN

(CASTLE HILL) Producers, Tamara Hernandez, Jessica Rains, Harry Ralston; Executive Producer, Roger Avary; Director/Screenplay, Harry Ralston; Photography, Michael Grady; Designer, John Grant; Costumes, C.T. DeNelli; Editor, Tony Miller; Music, Woody Jackson, Ivan Knight; Co-Executive Producer, Ash Shah; Co-Producer, Doug Ryan; an ID Films Motion Picture; Dolby; Color; Rated R; 95 minutes; Release date: February 15, 2002. CAST: David Arnott (Alan), Dan Montgomery (Raphael), Jeri Ryan (Sarah)

WENDIGO

(MAGNOLIA) Producer, Jeffrey Levy-Hinte; Director/Screenplay/Editor, Larry Fessenden; Photography, Terry Stacey; Designer, Stephen Beatrice; Music, Michelle Dibucci; Special Effects Producer, Dayton Taylor; Casting, Sheila Jaffe, Georgianne Walken, Mary-Clay Boland; Stunts, Mary Siverio; a Content Film presentation; DuArt color; Rated R; 90 minutes; Release date: February 15, 2002. CAST: Patricia Clarkson (Kim), Jake Weber (George), Erik Per Sullivan (Miles), John Speredakos (Otis), Christopher Wynkoop (Sheriff), Lloyd E. Oxendine (Elder), Brian Delate (Everett), Daniel Stuart Sherman (Billy), Jennifer Wiltsie (Martha), Maxx Stratton (Brandon), Richard Stratton (Earl), Dash Stratton (Earl), Dwane Navara (Mechanic), Shelley Bolding (Store Owner), Susan Pellegrino (Nurse), James Godwin (Wendigo)

Dan Montgomery, Jeri Ryan, David Arnott in *The Last Man* © Castle Hill

Erik Per Sullivan in *Wendigo* © Magnolia

175

SCRATCH

(PALM PICTURES/MAGIC LAMP RELEASING) Producers, Brad Blondheim, Ernest Meza, Esq.; Director/Editor, Doug Pray; Story Structure Writer, Brad Blondheim; Co-Producer, Heidi Addison; Executive Producers, The Hughes Brothers; Associate Producer, John Carluccio; Photography, Robert Bennett; a Ridgeway Entertainment presentation of a Firewalk Films production; Color; Rated R; 92 minutes; Release date: February 15, 2002. Documentary exploring the world of hip-hop and those who scratch vinyl for the cause; featuring Granwizzard Theodore, Afrika Bambaataa, Jazzy Jay, Grandmixer DXT, Steinski, Mix Master Mike, Qbert and the Invisible Skratch Piklz, DJ Shadow, Rob Swift and the X-Ecutioners, DJ Babu and the Beat Junkies, DJ Faust and Shortee, DJ Craze and the Allies, Steve Dee, Cut Chemist and Numark of Jurassic 5, DJ Premier, Z-Trip, DJ Relm and DJ Streak of Supernatural Turntable Artists, DJ Krush, The Bullet Proof Scratch Hamsters, DJ Swamp, Almight Kaygee, Dot a Rock, Kevie Kev, Billy Jam and Dave Paul, Naut Humon, John Carluccio, Christie Z, Pabon, The DMC Battle, Mark Herlihy, Doze Green

MARYAM

(STREETLIGHT FILMS) Producer, Shauna Lyon; Director/Screenplay, Ramin Serry; Co-Producers, Jonathan Shoemaker, Derrick Tseng; Photography, Harlan Bosmajian; Designer, Petra Barchi; Costumes, Nancy Brous; Editor, Gary Levy; Music, Ahrin Mishan; Color; Not rated; 87 minutes; Release date: February 22, 2002. CAST: Mariam Parris (Mary Armin), David Ackert (Ali Armin), Shaun Toub (Dr. Armin), Shohreh Aghdashloo (Mrs. Armin), Maziyar Jobrani (Reza), Sabine Singh (Jill), Victor Jory (Jamie), Michael Blieden (Pete), Jason Nash (Joel)

REVOLUTION OS

(7TH ART) Producer/Director/Screenplay/Photography/Editor, J.T.S. Moore; Music, Christopher Anderson-Bazzoli; Wonderview Productions; Narrator, Susan Egan; Not rated; 85 minutes; Release date: February 22, 2002. Documentary, feautring Linus Torvalds, Richard Stallman, Eric Raymond, Bruce Perens, Larry Augustin, Michael Tiemann, Brian Behlendorf, Frank Hecker, Chris DiBona, Nick Moffitt, Rob Malda, Donnie Barnes, Marc Merlin, Terry Egan, Lisa Corsetti, David Ljung, Jose Medeiros, Russ Emerson, Patrick Devine, The GNU/Stallmans

DJ Qbert, DXT in *Scratch* © Palm Pictures/Magic Lamp Releasing

THE GENTLEMAN BANDIT

(PATHFINDER) a.k.a. *Gentleman B.*; Producers, Douglas Hunter, Meta Puttkammer, Charlie Mattera, Jordan Alan; Executive Producer, Alfred Joyal; Director/Photography, Jordan Alan; Screenplay, Charlie Mattera, Mark Petracca; Designer, Nathan Vane; Costumes, Billy Ray McKenna; Editors, Paul O'Brien, Brett Smith; Music, Lawrence Nash Groupe; a Terminal Bliss Pictures presentation in association with 47 Prods. of an Alfred Joyal production; Dolby; Ultravision widescreen; CFI color; Not rated; 89 minutes; Release date: Feb. 22, 2002. CAST: Ed Lauter (Harry Koslow), Peter Greene (Manny Breen), Justine Micelli (Maria DeRazio), Charlie Mattera (Nick Vincent), Kristina Malota (Ally), Phil Fondacaro (Sleazy Hotel Manager), Zack Rau (Delivery Boy), Patric Stillman (Rabbi), Ryan O'Neal, Todd Newman, Maria Cina

RAM DASS FIERCE GRACE

(LEMLE PICTURES) Producer/Director, Mickey Lemle; Photography, Buddy Squires; Associate Producer, Linda K. Moroney; Editors, Aaron Vega, Mickey Lemle, Jacob Craycroft; Music, Teese Gohl; Co-Producers, Jessica Brackman, Buddy Squires; Color; Not rated; 93 minutes; Release date: February 27, 2002. Documentary on spiritual leader, author, and lecturer Ram Dass (formerly Richard Alpert), and his study of the nature of consciousness over a 45-year period.

MISS WONTON

(DREAMCHAMBER) Producer, Dave Johnson; Director/Screenplay/Editor, Meng Ong; Photography, Tsuyoshi Kimoto; Designer, Charlotte Bourke; Costumes, Bryan Wang; Co-Producer, Hisami Kuroiwa; Music, Evan Evans; Color; Not rated; 87 minutes; Release date: March 8, 2002. CAST: Amy Ting (Ah Na), Ben Wang (Chung), James C. Burns (Jack), Chyna Ng (Ling), Sakura Teng (Mrs. Sum), Scott Chan (Kang), Shen Han Ying (Mother), Victoria Rong (Lily), Claire Peng (Fang), Yang Liu (May), Cornel Chang (Uncle Wang), Lynne Otis (Susan), Tienne Vu (Madam Lan), Elene Chung (Ex-Worker), ShingKa (Peng), Jeannie Ng, Elisa Lam (Golden Palace Girls), Rich Dita (Golden Palace Meatloaf), Eliot Sash (Golden Palace Casserole), Elizabeth Chiang (Flashback Wonton)

Victor Jory, Mariam Parris in *Maryam* © Streetlight Films

THE MAKING AND MEANING OF "WE ARE FAMILY"

(INDEPENDENT) Director, Danny Schecter; No other credits available; Color; Not rated; 64 minutes; Release date: March 8, 2002. CAST: Laurie Anderson, Afrika Bambaataa, Stephen Bishop, Jackson Browne, Bebe Buell, Macaulay Culkin, Roberta Flack, Joel Grey, Milla Jovovich, Angélique Kidjo, Eartha Kitt, Patti LaBelle, Spike Lee, John McEnroe, Joan Osborne, Rosie Perez, Bernadette Peters, Maury Povich, Joan Rivers, Nile Rodgers, Diana Ross, Phoebe Snow, Angie Stone, Luther Vandross, Dionne Warwick, Montel Williams (Themselves)

YUGOSLAVIA: THE AVOIDABLE WAR

(HARGROVE ENTERTAINMENT) Producers, George Bogdanich, Martin Lettmayer; Director/Screenplay, George Bogdanich; Photography, Predrag Bambic, Joe Friendly, Dragan Milinkovic; Music, Chris Rea; Editor, Mary Patierno; Color; Not rated; 165 minutes; Release date: March 15, 2002. Documentary about the events that led to the breakup of Yugoslavia in 1991.

RACE TO SPACE

(LIONS GATE) Producers, David Brookwell, Glenn Greene, Sean McNamara; Executive Producers, Glenn Greene, Peter Lambert, Al Lapin, Jr., Neil P. White; Director, Sean McNamara; Screenplay, Eric Gardner, Steven H. Wilson; Photography, Christian Sebaldt; Designer, Dawn R. Ferry; Costumes, Kristin M. Burke; Editor, Greg Hobson; Music, John Coda; Casting, Sarah Dalton, Joey Paul; a Brookwell-McNamara Entertainment, Century Entertainment, Telepool production; U.S.-German; Dolby; Color; Rated PG; 104 minutes; Release date: March 15, 2002. CAST: James Woods (Dr. Wilhelm Von Huber), Annabeth Gish (Donni McGuinness), Alex D. Linz (Billy Von Huber), Patrick Richwood (Dieter), William Devane (Roger Thornhill), Mark Moses (Alan Shepard), William Atherton (Ralph Stanton), Michael Tylo (Guidance Technician), Scott Thompson Baker (Telemetry Technician), Michael Jeffrey Woods (Dexterity Technician), T.J. Beacom (Ed the Bully), James Benson (Gertz), Jack McGee (Fielding), Marc Kittay (Rat Patrol #1), Denae Adams (Stephanie), Pam Baumann (Mrs. Gallagher), Tim Goodwin (Principal Turner), John O'Hurley (Barnett, PR Official), Jim Wise (Air Policeman), Barry Corbin (Earl Vestal), Brendan O'Brien (Centrifuge Technician), Barry James (Guard #1), John H. Johnson (Class Technician), Jason Savage (NASA Guard in School), Richard Horvitz (Keith), John Nielsen, Tom Dugan (Reporters), Patrick Ecclesine (Vet Technician), Kristian Truelsen (Baldy), Chris Doyle (Chopper Pilot), Joan Fagan (Mother on Beach), Holland Hayes (Deporter), Ben Rawnsley (News Anchor), Thomas Stearns (OSI Agent), Kim Morgan Greene (Thornhill Asst.), Dawn Ferry (Sgt.), Austin Joseph Schwartz (Little Kid), Robin McWilliams (Billy's Mom), Tony Jay (Narrator)

SORORITY BOYS

(TOUCHSTONE) Producers, Larry Brezner, Walter Hamada; Executive Producer, Michael Fottrell; Director, Wally Wolodarsky; Screenplay, Joe Jarvis, Greg Coolidge; Photography, Michael D. O'Shea; Designer, Edward T. McAvoy; Costumes, Melinda Eshelman; Editor, Richard Halsey; Music, Mark Mothersbaugh; Casting, John Papsidera; a Morra-Brezner-Steinberg-Tenebaum production; Dolby; Panavision; Technicolor; Rated R; 94 minutes; Release date: March 22, 2002. CAST: Barry Watson (Dave), Michael Rosenbaum (Adam), Harland Williams (Doofer), Melissa Sagemiller (Leah), Tony Denman (Jimmy), Brad Beyer (Spence), Kathryn Stockwood (Patty), Heather Matarazzo (Katie), Yvonne Scio (Frederique), Kerri Higuchi (Susie), Dublin James (Littlest Pledge), Omar Benson Miller (Big Johnson), Mike Beaver (Big Fat Frat), Rich Ronat, Brian Gross (Frats), Christopher Leps (Crazed Frat), Daniel Farber (Naked Pledge), Phyllis Lyons (Polly), Peter Scolari (Louis), Bree Turner (Tiffany), Monica Staggs, Lydia Hull, Nikki Matin, Jessica Kiper (Tri Pis), James Daughton (Dave's Dad), Mark Metcalf (John Kloss), Stephen Furst (The Alum), Johnny A. Sanchez (The Littlest Alum), Brad Grunberg (Drunk Alumni), Bruce French (Dean Blevins), Wendie Jo Sperber (Prof. Bendler), Cristin Coppen, Vanessa Evigan (Hot Girls), Samantha Shelton (Waitress), Brian Posehn (Haggard Alum), Stuart Stone (Valet), Greg Coolidge (Pete), Jessica Morrison (Sorority Girl), Anthony Natale, Allen Neece (Deaf Students), John Vernon (Old Man), Susie Spear (Talk Show Host)

Harland Williams, Barry Watson, Michael Rosenbaum in *Sorority Boys* © Touchstone

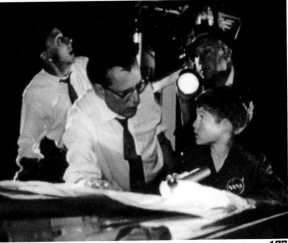

Amy Ting (right) in *Miss Wonton* © Dreamchamber

James Woods, Alex D. Linz in Race to *Space* © Lions Gate

177

JIM BROWN: ALL-AMERICAN

(40 ACRES AND A MULE FILMWORKS) Producer/Director, Spike Lee; Executive Producers, Ross Greenburg, Rick Bernstein; Co-Producers, Mike Ellis, Sam Pollard; Photography, Ellen Kuras; Supervising Editor, Sam Pollard; Editor, Mark Fason; Music Supervisor, Alex Steyermark; an HBO Sports production; Color; Not rated; 130 minutes; Release date: March 22, 2002. Documentary on football player-turned-actor Jim Brown; featuring Jim Brown, Art Modell, John Wooten, Joe Frazier, Hank Aaron, Ralph Wiley, Stuart Scott, Karen Brown Ward, Kim Brown, Jim N. Brown Jr., Amber Ward, Brandon Well, Ian Ward, Sea Island Singers, Chief Oren Lyons, Manny Breland, Roy Simmons, Ed Walsh, Al Dawson, Dr. Walter Beach, Arias Dallas Brown, Monique Brown, Kevin Brown, Richard Johnson, Aqeela Sherrills, Daude Sherrills, Bo Taylor, Twilight Bey, Rudolph "Rockhead" Johnson, Raquel Welch, Willie Davis, Oliver Stone, Bernie Casey, Sheila Frazier, Phil Gersh, Willis Edwards, Fred "The Hammer" Williamson, Stella Stevens, Leon Isaac Kennedy, Bobby Mitchell, William C. Rhoden, Paul Warfield, James Toback, Pat Callan, Mike Francesa, Ed Corley, David Skinner, Michael Wilbon, Sam Oakley, Senator Dick Schafrath, Johnnie L. Cochran Jr., Bert Sugar, Melvin Van Peebles, Donald Bogle, Bill Russell

Jim Brown, Spike Lee in *Jim Brown: All-American*
© 40 Acres and a Mule Filmworks

MARGARITA HAPPY HOUR

(PASSPORT PICTURES) Producers, Michael Ellenbogen, Susan Leber; Director/Screenplay, Ilya Chaiken; Photography, Gordon Chou; Designer/Costumes, Bridget Evans; Music, Max Lichtenstein; Editors, Ilya Chaiken, Meg Reticker; Casting, David Leslie; a presentation of Little Z Productions, Susie Q Productions; Dolby; Color; Not rated; 98 minutes; Release date: March 22, 2002. CAST: Elenor Hutchins (Zelda), Larry Fessenden (Max), Holly Ramos (Natali), Barbara Sicuranza (Graziella), Amanda Vogel (Raquel), Macha Ross (Sofia), Kristin Di Spaltro (Marie), Jonah Leland, Tippitina Horowitz, Theodora Horowitz (Little Z), George Schnore, Katherine Gange (Little S), Arthur Crockett (Little M), Viva Ruiz, Kelly Webb (Flashback Friends), Will Keenan (Lester), Greg Zuccalo (Jimmy), Maura Naughton (Francie), Ruby Evans Leary (New Born Z), Lucy Knight, Tara Lee Hergenham, Lora Marie Williams (Roommates), Michael Buscemi (The Pornographer), David Turley (Barker), Cherry Brodbeck (Crucified Woman), Julie Spodek (Trapeze Woman), Lisa Ludwig (Miss Tall Tanny Puppet), Matthew Gellert, Lucas Cooper (Moneky Boys), Sandra Trevilcock (Aretha), Isabel Robayo (Bianca), Rik Giannola, Greg Siebel (Party Boys), Verna Hampton (Medicaid Interviewer), Janet Ninatanta (Spanish Speaker), George Crooks (Man with List), Margarita Santiago (Confrontational Woman), Tony Navarro (Confrontational Man), Michael Fegley (Potato Chip Man), Carol Todes (Magie), Sophia Alexis (Bakery Lady), Margaret Elizabeth Mann (Counter Girl), David Leslie (Bicyclist), Steve Vassi (Harrassing Man), Ezra Venetos (Fighting Man), Jay Evans, Todd Carlstrom (Waiter), Elizabeth Cummings, Michael Vacco (Bartenders), Jerrie Swanson (Can Lady), Michael Schmidt, Michael Goduti, John B. Davila (Attackers)

Elenor Hutchins in *Margarita Happy Hour* © Passport Pictures

SHOT IN THE HEART

(HBO FILMS) Producer, Nina Kostroff Noble; Executive Producers, Barry Levinson, Tom Fontana, Jim Finnerty; Director, Agnieszka Holland; Screenplay, Frank Pugliese; Based on the book by Mikal Gilmore; Photography, Jacek Petrycki; Color; Not rated; 98 minutes; Release date: March 27, 2002. CAST: Giovanni Ribisi (Mikal Gilmore), Elias Koteas (Gary Gilmore), Lee Tergesen (Frank Gilmore, Jr.), Amy Madigan (Bessie Gilmore), Eric Bogosian (Larry Schiller), Sam Shepard (Frank Gilmore, Sr.), Kim Abunuwara (Melissa Brown), Matthew Armstrong (Frank Jr, age 17-24), Al Brown (Counter Man), Robert Randolph Caton (Courtroom Visitor), Evyn Clark (Bessie, age 12), Tom Cleary, Alex Kozushin (Reporter), Ashley Edwards (Alta Brown), Brett Fleisher (Gaylen Gilmore), Trevor Gosden (Mikal, age 5-12), Naomi Kline (Bessie, age 29), Evan Knapp (Frank Jr., age 7), Rosemary Knower (Aunt Ida), Reid Sasser, Mark Bernier, Michael Gabel, David Parker (Guards), Arthur Laupus (Warden), Lance Lewman (Moody), Rick Macy (Will Brown), Robby Ost (Gary, age 5), Jim Page (Prison Guard), Pete Papageorge (Tower Guard), Anne Kathryn Parma (Wanda Brown), Kimberly Perfetto (Nicole), Richard Pilcher (Judge), Tom Quinn (Uncle Vern), Doug Roberts (Chief of Security), Craig Sechler (Interviewer), Mets Subert (Man with Food), Christopher Crutchfield Walker (Stranger), Paul Wasilewski (Gary, age 15-22), Joseph M. West, Jr. (Bar Patron), William Zielinski (Bobby Gene) (This film had its premiere on HBO on October 13, 2001).

Lee Tergesen, Giovanni Ribisi in
Shot in the Heart © HBO Films

George Wendt, Kurtwood Smith, Henry Gibson in
Teddy Bears' Picnic © Magnolia

PRESUMED GUILTY:
TALES OF THE PUBLIC DEFENDERS

(SKYLIGHT PICTURES) Producers, Peter Kinoy, Pamela Yeats; Director, Pamela Yeats; Photography, Paul Mailman; Editor, Peter Kinoy; Music, Douglas J. Cuomo; Color; Not rated; 116 minutes; Release date: March 29, 2002. Documentary on public defenders, featuring Jeff Adachi, Michele Forrar, Will Maas, Phoenix Streets

TEDDY BEARS' PICNIC

(MAGNOLIA) Producer, Marc Ambrose; Director/Screenplay, Harry Shearer; Executive Producers, John Bard Manulis, Harry Shearer, Michael Kastenbaum; Photography, Jaime Reynoso; Designer, Cliff Spencer; Costumes, Anne Gray Attwood; Editor, Jeff Ford; Casting, Michael Donovan & Jeff Hardwick; a Visionbox Pictures Production in association with Century of Progress Productions; Color; Not rated; 80 minutes; Release date: March 29, 2002. CAST: Bob Einstein (Dom Molinari), Henry Gibson (Clifford Sloane), Annabelle Gurwitch (Jennifer Gersh), Howard Hesseman (Ted Frye), John Michael Higgins (Whittaker "Whit" Summers), Justin Kirk (Damien Pritzker), Robert Mandan (Stanton Vandermint), Kenneth Mars (Gene Molinari), Michael McKean (Porterfield "Porty" Pendleton), Ming-Na (Katy Woo), David Rasche (Elliot Chevron), Thom Sharp (James Neal), Harry Shearer (Joey Lavin), Alan Thicke, Peter Marshall (Themselves), George Wendt (Gen. Edison "Pete" Gerberding), Fred Willard (Sen. Roger Dickey), Brenda Strong (Jackie Sloane Chevron), Judith Owen (Nancy McMahan), Gilley Grey (Guard), Julie Payne (Lila Claypool), Morgan Fairchild (Courtney Vandermint), Travis Wester (Denny O'Leary), John O'Hurley (Earle Hansen), Richard Israel (Ad Agency Guy), Delaune Michel (Ruby), Joyce Hyser (Rita D'Onofrio), Darron Johnson (Malcolm the Bartender), Burt Bulos (Billy the Driver), Kurtwood Smith (Sec. of Transportation William Easler), John Marrott (County Sheriff), Dale E. Turner (Maurice the Driver), Kiran Rao (Yeti)

NATIONAL LAMPOON'S VAN WILDER

(ARTISAN) Producers, Robert L. Levy, Peter Abrams, Andrew Panay, Jonathon Komack Martin; Executive Producers, Kirk D'Amico, Philip von Alvensleben, Lucas Foster; Director, Walt Becker; Screenplay, Brent Goldberg, David T. Wagner; Photography, James Bagdonas; Designer, Rachel Kamerman; Costumes, Alexis Scott; Editor, Dennis M. Hill; Music, David Lawrence; Music Supervisor, Chris Violette; Co-Producers, Ari Newman, Peter Nelson; a Myriad Pictures presentation in association with In-Motion AG and WMF V of a Tapestry Films production; Dolby; Color; Rated R; 95 minutes; Release date: April 5, 2002. CAST: Ryan Reynolds (Van Wilder), Tara Reid (Gwen Pearson), Tim Matheson (Vance Wilder, Sr.), Kal Penn (Taj Mahal Badalandabad), Teck Holmes (Hutch), Daniel Cosgrove (Richard Bagg), Deon Richmond (Mini Cochran), Alex Burns (Gordon), Emily Rutherford (Jeannie), Paul Gleason (Prof. McDoogle), Erik Estrada, Dr. Joyce Brothers (Themselves), Curtis Armstrong (Campus Cop), Jason Winer (Panos Patakos), Chris Owen (Suicidal Freshman), Simon Helberg (Vernon), Aaron Paul (Wasted Guy), Ivana Bozilovic (Naomi), Kim Smith (Casey), Teresa Hill (Hot Doctor), Megan Gallagher (Holyoke Hottie), Jason Hopkins (Sick Boy), Lydia Hull (Lindsey), Mark Chaet (Business Manager), Michael Waltman (Coach Ken Massey), Cynthia Fancher (Ms. Haver), Michael Olowokandi (Leron), Darius Miles (Darius), Quentin Richardson (Quentin), Lamar Odom (Coolidge Chickadee Player), Nick Puga (Pimply Faced Freshman), Joshua Swanson (Annoyingly Peppy Freshman), Jenny Leone (Desiree), Ronald Hunter (Gus), Jeremy Phillips (Overweight Freshman), Darcy Shean (Gwen's Mom), Harry Danner (Dr. Beeverman), Tom Howard (Gwen's Dad), John Colton (Dr. Henke), Sophia Bush (Sally), J. Patrick McCormack (Dean Mooney), Gregg Daniel (English Professor), Lauren Birkell (Cheesy TV Announcer), Teesha Lobo (Hot Indian Girl), Cheryl Bricker (Mrs. Henke), Chris Sowers (Thin Pledge), Colin Campbell (Archive Guy), Willie Latimore (Ming Impersonator), Sean Marquette (Little Kid), Sterling Rice (Little Girl), Albert Owens (Another Doctor), Anderson Goncalves (Dorky Brother), Anne Varnishung (Gorgeous Secretary), Erik Aude (Martial Arts Freshman), Sarah Fairfax (Mrs. Seay), Travis McKenna (Milty), Lou Beatty, Jr. (Library Man), Andrew Bilgore (Party Busting Cop), Alexia Chiaromonte (Stunning Co-ed Freshman), Brent Goldberg, David Wagner (Freshman Interviewees), Chad Evans (Stoner Freshman), Brandon Kessel (College Kid), Ryan Carlberg (Worried Preppy Freshman), Matthew Newton (Sophmore), Edie McClurg (Campus Tour Guide), Shaina Fewell (Hot Senior), Megan Litwin (Hotter Friend), Sarah Paul (Terri), Michelle Thomas (Sherri), Sirin Suprasert (Suk Mee), Tom Everett Scott (Elliot Grebb)

AMERICAN CHAI

(MAGIC LAMP) Producer, Taylor MacCrae; Executive Producers, Kathy Perone, Sapna Shah, Ashish Shah, Victoria Dingman; Director/Screenplay, Anurag Mehta; Photography, John Matkowsky; Designer, Cecile Thalmann; Costumes, Kristen Couchot; Editor, Ann E. Holbrook; Music, Aalok Mehta, Jack Bowden Faulkner, for Melody Vision; Line Producer, Patrick Sheedy; Associate Producer, Andrew Suhl; a Dream Merchant Pictures production, presented in association wtih Wildcard Releasing and Praveen Bhutani; Color; Rated R; 92 minutes; Release date: April 5, 2002. CAST: Aalok Mehta (Sureel), Sheetal Sheth (Maya), Aasif Mandvi (Engineering Sam), Josh Ackerman (Toby), Ajay Naidu (Hari), Paresh Rawal (Sureel's Dad), Bharti Desai (Sureel's Mom), Akshay Oberoi (Neel), Rajiv Reddy (Young Sureel), Jamie Hurley (Jen), Reena Shah (Sejal), Anand Chulani (Raju), Jill Anderson (Lisa), Kyle Koehl (Young Boy), Marlee Kattler (Young Girl), Lanre Olibisi (Harvest Moon MC), Monir Hossain (Tabla Player), Bernadette Healy (American Chai Groupie), Oak Porcelli (Frat Boy), Niti Chhaya, Niru Dixit, Sharad Mehta, A.D. Bhatt, Ranjit Daphtary, Sanjay Bardwaj (Parents at Party), Vini Malhotra, Priti Tanna (South Asian Confernce Speaker), Michael J. Beahm (Battle of Bands MC), Jon Cole, Herb Detres, Jeremy Dyen, Jay Horvath, Rico Joseph, Pete Keenan, Christopher Mottershead (Fathead Band Members), Charles Amos, Charles Megules, Christopher Millan, Aaron Protocny (American Chai Band)

Jason Winer, Teck Holmes, Ryan Reynolds, Kal Penn in
National Lampoon's Van Wilder © Artisan

ASTORIA

(MENEMSHA/MAREVAN) Producers, Athena Efter, Jamie Dakoyannis; Executive Producers, Paul S. Mezey, Marisa Nicole Stefatos; Director/Screenplay, Nick Efteriades; Photography, Elia Lyssy; Designer, Jody Asnes; Costumes, Eden Miller; Music, Nikos Papazoglou; Editor, Stuart Emanuel; Casting, Judy Henderson; an Astoria Partners production; Color; Rated R; 103 minutes; Release date: April 5, 2002. CAST: Paige Turco (Elena), Rick Stears (Alex), Ed Setrakian (Demo), Joseph D'Onofrio (Theo), Geraldine Librandi (Soula), Steven J. Christofer (Lakis), Yanni Sfinias (Mitsos), Gregory Sims (George), Stelio Savante (Nick), Chelsea Altman (Betty), James Dukas (Kostas), George Morafetis (Nikos), Nia Hatsopoulos (Lisa), Elsa Tsartsidou (Katina), Kleanthis Bakalis, Nicholas Belleas, Chris Koron (Cardplayers), Ajay Mehta (Lawyer), Zoe Bournelis (Airport Ticket Agent), Ierotheos Markopoulos (Priest REV), Ahmed Nazir (Demo's Buyer), Athena Efter (Waitress at Cafe), Despina Koumis, Eleftheria Christopoulos, Helen Drivas (Dancing Girls at Club), Martha Kyriakides (Waitress at Social Club)

30 YEARS TO LIFE

(KEYSTONE) Producer, Gingi Rochelle; Executive Producers, Vanessa Middleton, Timbaland; Director/Screenplay, Vanessa Middleton; Photography, Cliff Charles; Designer, Liba Daniels; Editor, Gershon Hinkson; Music, Timbaland; Casting, Winsome Sinclair & Assoc.; an Exodus Entertainment presentation in association with Keystone Entertainment & Turtles Crossing; Color; Rated R; 110 minutes; Release date: April 5, 2002. CAST: Erika Alexander (Joy), Melissa De Sousa (Natalie), Tracy Morgan (Troy), Paula Jai Parker (Stephanie), Allen Payne (Malik), T.E. Russell (Leland), Kadeem Hardison (Bruce), Eddie Brill (Lenny), Janet Hubert (Joy's Mother), Laz Alonso (Richard), Dominique, Wil Slyvince, Godfrey (Comedians)

HARD LUCK

(FILM KITCHEN) Executive Producer, Annemarie Curry; Director, Jack Rubio; Screenplay, Kirk Harris; Music, Evan Evans; a Film Kitchen, Rogue Arts production; Color; Rated R; 98 minutes; Release date: April 5, 2002. CAST: Kirk Harris (Lucky O'Donnell), Renée Humphrey (Sheryl Billings), Matthew Faber (Eric Billings), Karen Black (Aunt Judy), Ron Gilbert (Lou Billings), Darrell Bryan (Matt), Gareth Williams (Raymond), Tony Longo (Bobby), Joanne Baron (Gretchen), Luca Bercovici (Chris), Jon Jacobs (Jeff), Matt Clifford (Jason)

ECHOES

(ARROW) Director/Screenplay/Editor, Atsushi Funahashi; Photography, Eric Van Den Brulle; Village Productions; U.S.-Japanese; Black and white/color; Not rated; 72 minutes; Release date: April 10, 2002. CAST: Eden Roundtree (Leslie), Paolo Pagiacolo (Marko), Joe Marino (Luca), Bobby Sobel (Nick), Allison Wright (Anna), Travis J. Meinolf (Travis), Elizabeth Valerio (Leslie's Roommate), Edward Winrow (Uncle Jeff), Joseph Maysonet (Guy 1), Shelley Dague (Isabelle), Rodney Jackson (Jack), James Sabo, Bruce Saunders (Bartender), Nanu (Busboy)

THE EARTH WILL SWALLOW YOU

(HANSON) Producers/Directors, Geoff Hanson, Chris Hanson; No other credits available; Color; Not rated; 100 minutes; Release date: April 12, 2002. Widespread Panic in concert, with Jorma Kaukonen, Taj Mahal, Jerry Joseph, Vic Chestnutt.

OUTTA TIME

(ARTISAN) Producer, Mark Roberts; Executive Producers, Larry Crowder, John Powell, David M. Grey; Co-Producer, Mario Lopez; Director, Lorena David; Screenplay, Scott Duncan, Ned Kerwin; Photography, Lisa Wiegand; Music, Scott Gilman; Editor, Allan Spencer Wall; Casting, Katy Wallin-Sandalis; a Roberts/David Production, presented in association with Filmstar Productions and Silverstar Productions; Color; Rated R; 94 minutes; Release date: April 12, 2002. CAST: Mario Lopez (David Morales), Tava Smiley (Emma Cross), Carlos Mencia (Juancho), Ali Landry (Bella), Nancy O'Dell (Dr. Drake), Dyana Ortelli (Gloriana), John Saxon (Prof. Jonas Darabont), Richard Lynch (Franco), George Lopez (Felix), Richard Cox (Taylor), Gary Cervantes (Watts), Fritz Greve (Businessman), Marcus Lavoi (Riker), Tim Sitarz (Brock), Edgar Martinez (T-Shirt Vendor), Al Septien (Last Checkpoint Guard), Chantille Field (Student), Kimberly Wallis (Secretary), Mark Chaet (Professor), Christopher Durand (Superintendent), Mikko D. Sperber (Security Guard), Steve Sandalis (Sergeant), Dennis Gubbins (Pizza Guy), Ken Merckx (Patrolman), Carlos Compean, Annie Hinton (Detectives), Cade McNown (Policeman), Gena Landry (Clerk), Craig Patton (Father), Christina Cameron Mitchell (CHP), Christina Crowder (Girl on Scooter), Taylor Lawrence (Girl in Park), Linda Medina (Nurse), Tony Gorodeckas (FBI Agent), Robert Arevalo (Rico), Nick Hernz (Slow Coyote), Lorenzo Rodriguez (Tijuana Cop)

Mario Lopez, Ali Landry in *Outta Time* © Artisan

Allen Payne, Melissa DeSousa, Tracy Morgan, Paula Jai Parker, Erika Alexander, T.E. Russell in *30 Years to Life* © Keystone

Widespread Panic in *The Earth Will Swallow You* © Hanson

Beanie Andrew, Gorilla in *Mule Skinner Blues* © Steel Carrot

MULE SKINNER BLUES

(STEEL CARROT) Producers, Victoria Ford, Stephen Earnhart; Executive Producers, Gavin O'Connor, Greg O'Connor; Director, Stephen Earnhart; Photography, Victoria Ford; Music, John M. Davis; Editor, Ellen Goldwasser; a Solaris presentation of a Steel Carrot production in association with Bean-Tyle Prods.; Color; Not rated; 93 minutes; Release date: April 12, 2002. Documentary on how alcoholic Beanie Andrew rallies his fellow trailer park denizens to help him make a "B" horror movie in the local junkyard; featuring Beanie Andrew, Steve Walker, Miss Jeannie, Larry Parrot, Ricky Lix, Annabelle Lea Usher

NEW BEST FRIEND

(TRISTAR) Producer, Frank Mancuso, Jr.; Director, Zoe Clarke-Williams; Screenplay, Victoria Strouse; Photography, Tom Priestley; Designer, Burton Rencher; Costumes, Patsy C. Rainey; Editors, Norman Buckley, Leo Trombetta; Music, David A. Hughes, John Murphy; Casting, Amanda Mackey Johnson, Cathy Sandrich; FGM Entertainment; Dolby; Color; Rated R; 91 minutes; Release date: April 12, 2002. CAST: Mia Kirshner (Alicia), Meredith Monroe (Hadley), Dominique Swain (Sidney), Scott Bairstow (Trevor), Rachel True (Julianne), Taye Diggs (Artie), Glynnis O'Connor (Glynnis O'Connor), Joanna Canton (Sarah), Eric Michael Cole (Warren), Oliver Hudson (Josh), Dean James (Max), J. Michael Hunter (Charlie), Edmund J. Kearney (Dean), Don Henderson Baker (Haas), Shawn Michelle Cosby (Joanie), Ralph Price (Eddie), Lynda Clark (Interviewer), Ben Epps (Dexter), Dale Frye (Trainer), Scott Miles (Bartender), Sandi Shackelford (Hadley's Nurse), Mark Jeffrey Miller (Orderly), Christopher Stokes (Dion), Ed Grady (Alicia's Doctor), Michael Mattison (Bud), Cordelia G. McArtor (Sister Devore), Melissa Kuulei (Townie Girl), Robert Pentz (ER Nurse), Melissa L. Bitto, Marie C. Hooks (Nurses), Chad Brandon (Trevor's Friend), Jennifer Barnes (Student)

FOR DA LOVE OF MONEY

(URBANWORLD) Producers, Pierre, Taj Lewis; Director/Screenplay, Pierre; Photography, David Fox; Costumes, Terri Middleton; Color; Rated R; 97 minutes; Release date: April 12, 2002. CAST: Pierre (Dre Mitchell), Reynaldo Rey (Pops), Christian Keiber (Det. Clay Parker), Sacha Kemp (Tasha), Maurice Patton (Boom), Tanya Boyd (Ms. Anderson), Cherry Lynn, Princess Maggay (Popsicle Girls), Ralphie May (Otis), Tommy Franklin (Too Sweet), Honest John (Mrs. Tibbs), Willie Tyler & Lester (Themselves), Stevie Johnson (Det. Lewis), Brian Anthony Wilson (Kelvin)

HARVARD MAN

(COWBOY) Producers, Daniel Bigel, Michael Mailer; Executive Producers, Edward R. Pressman, Michael Burns, Jeff Sackman, Peter Locke, Donald Kushner; DIrector/Screenplay, James Toback; Photography, David Ferrara; Designer, Rupert Lazarus; Costumes, Maxyne Baker; Music, Stomy Bugsy, Ryan Shore; Editor, Suzy Elmiger; Co-Producer, J. Miles Dale; Casting, Felicia Fasano, Anne McCarthy, Mary Vernieu; from Bigel/Mailer Films; Dolby; Super 35 Widescreen; Color; Rated R; 100 minutes; Release date: April 12, 2002. CAST: Adrian Grenier (Alan Jensen), Sarah Michelle Gellar (Cindy Bandolini), Joey Lauren Adams (Chesney Cort), Eric Stoltz (Teddy Carter), Rebecca Gayheart (Kelly Morgan), Gianni Russo (Andrew Bandolini), Ray Allen (Marcus Blake), Michael Aparo (Russell), Scottie Epstein (Mario), John Neville (Dr. Reese), Polly Shannon (Juliet), Phillip Jarrett (Coach Preston), Adam Bloch (Kenner), Lauren Collis (Connie), Landy Cannon (Butch), Clé Bennett (Hal), Chantal Cousineau (Sandy), Maria Ricossa (Charlotte Jensen), Booth Savage (Steve Jensen), Mung Ling Tsui (Reporter), Brendan Ryder (Jonathan), Kelly Ryder (Jonathan's Mother), Kristi Angus (Bartender), Tara Samuel (Waitress), Ayanna Sealey, Jamie Holmes (Coeds), Al Franken (Himself), Thomasin Franken (Al Franken's Daughter), Peter Menash (Cyril the Butler), Joe Pingue (Joe), J. Miles Dale (Howie), Nicholas Bacon (Seth), Kate Crowley (Kate), Kimberly Pullis (Kimberly), Brian Schulz, Chris Wolfe (Harvard Radio Broadcasters)

Sarah Michelle Gellar, Rebecca Gayheart in *Harvard Man* © Cowboy

Dominique Swain, Meredith Monroe, Mia Kirshner, Rachel True in *New Best Friend* © TriStar

Billy Crudup in *World Traveler* © Thinkfilm

WORLD TRAVELER

(THINKFILM) Producers, Tim Perell, Bart Freundlich; Executive Producers, Jonathan Sehring, Caroline Kaplan; Director/Screenplay, Bart Freundlich; Photography, Terry Stacey; Designer, Kevin Thompson; Costumes, Victoria Farrell; Editor, Kate Sanford; Music, Clint Mansell; Casting, Douglas Aibel; an Independent Film Channel Productions presentation of a Process production; U.S.-Canadian; Dolby; Color; Rated R; 104 minutes; Release date: April 12, 2002. CAST: Billy Crudup (Cal), Julianne Moore (Dulcie), Cleavant Derricks (Carl), Liane Baliban (Meg), David Keith (Richard), Mary McCormack (Margaret), Karen Allen (Delores), James LeGros (Jack), Francie Swift (Joanie), Nicolas Suresky (Leo), Richie Dye (Local Bar Bartender), Kaili Vernoff (Andrea), Margaret Devine (Andrea's Friend), John Forman (Dakota Customer), Bert Miller (Dakota Bartender), Patricia French (Dakota Waitress), Shontelle Thrash (Dakota Mom), Isis Faust (Dakota Girl), BJ Mitchell (Dakota Boy), Mark Gray (Ficus Lounge Host), Josie Lawson (Sadie), Elijah Saucier (Imaginary Carl)

JOSHUA

(CRUSADER ENTERTAINMENT) Producers, Howard Baldwin, Karen Baldwin, Paul Pompian; Director, John Purdy; Screenplay, Brad Mirman, Keith Giglio, based on the novel by Joseph Girzone; Photography, Bruce Surtees; Designer, Brian Eatwell; Music, Michael W. Smith; Casting, Monika Mikkelsen, Jane Alderman; an Epiphany Films production; Dolby; Deluxe color; Rated G; 90 minutes; Release date: April 19, 2002. CAST: Tony Goldwyn (Joshua), F. Murray Abraham (Father Tardone), Kurt Fuller (Father Pat Hayes), Stacy Edwards (Maggie), Colleen Camp (Joan Casey), Giancarlo Giannini (The Pope), Jordan Allen (Michael Reed), Tom Brainard (Young Pastor), Alec De Rosa (Evangelist Kid)

MUTANT ALIENS

(ALPHA CINE) Producer/Director/Screenplay/Animator, Bill Plympton; Photography, John Donnelly; Music, Hank Bones, Maureen McElheron; Editor, Anthony Arcidi; produced by Plymptoons; Dolby; Color; Not rated; 81 minutes; Release date: April 19, 2002. VOICE CAST: Dan McComas (Earl Jensen), Francine Lobis (Josie), George Casden (Dr. Frubar/President), Matthew Brown (Darby/Tomkins), Jay Cavanaugh (Boris), Amy Allison (Secretary), Christopher Schukai (Guard), Kevin Kolack (Preacher), Vera Beren (Repter)

DIVORCE: THE MUSICAL

(STE INC.) Producers, Tim Counihan, Steven Dworman, Eric M. Galler, Rebecca Ross; Director/Screenplay, Steven Dworman; Photography, Isidore Mankofsky; Music, Alan O'Day, Don Peake; Editor, Rebecca Ross; Color; Not rated; 86 minutes; Release date: April 19, 2002. CAST: Steven Dworman (Bob Weber), Amy Lyndon (Jane), Kehli O'Byrne (Tanya Levy), Heidi Krämer (Sara Wasterman), Kevin Sateri (Teenage Bob Weber)

SPOOKY HOUSE

(ENTERTAINMENT HIGHWAY) Producers, Anthony Esposito, William Sachs; Executive Producers, Anthony Esposito, Kirk Friedman, Richard Houghton; Director, William Sachs; Screenplay, Margaret Sachs, William Sachs; Photography, Thomas Burstyn; Designer, Ian Thomas; Costumes, Trish Keating; Music, Garry Schyman; Editor, Jeremy Presner; Casting, Elissa Meyers, Paul Fouquet; a Spooky House Entertainment production; Dolby; Color; Rated PG; 107 minutes; Release date: April 19, 2002. CAST: Ben Kingsley (The Great Zamboni), Mercedes Ruehl (Boss), Matt Weinberg (Max), Jason Fuchs (Yuri), Ronald Joshua Scott (Beans), Simon Baker (Prescott), Myles Ferguson (Mike the Mouth), Katharine Isabelle (Mona), Kyle Labine (Dumb Dave), Chaz Monet (Zoe), Carmen Moore (Dawn Starr), Yanna McIntosh (Nicole), Stephen Dimopoulos (Boris), David "Squatch" Ward (Cigar Van Driver), Carolyn Tweedle (Neighbor), Benz Antoine (Police Officer), Danny McKinnon (Orphanage Boy), Joey Shea, Neil Denis (Audience Kids), Gary Savard (Assistant), Marnie Connolly, Melissa Chew (Theatre Assistants), Mike Weinberg (Halloween Kid)

Tony Goldwyn (with log) in
Joshua © Crusader Entertainment

Matt Weinberg, Ben Kingsley in *Spooky House*
© Entertainment Highway

LIFE OR SOMETHING LIKE IT

(20TH CENTURY FOX) Producers, Arnon Milchan, John Davis, Chi-Li Wong, Toby Jaffe; Executive Producers, Ric Kidney, Ken Atchity, Teddy Zee; Director, Stephen Herek; Screenplay, John Scott Shepherd, Dana Stevens; Story, John Scott Shepherd; Photography, Stephen Burum; Designer, Bill Groom; Costumes, Aggie Rodgers; Editor, Trudy Ship; Music, David Newman; Executive Music Producer, Budd Carr; Casting, Sharon Bialy; a Regency Enterprises presentation of a David Entertainment/New Regency production; Dolby; Panavision; Color; Rated PG-13; 103 minutes; Release date: April 26, 2002. CAST: Angelina Jolie (Lainie Kerrigan), Edward Burns (Pete), Tony Shalhoub (Prophet Jack), Christian Kane (Cal), James Gammon (Lanie's Father), Melissa Errico (Andrea), Stockard Channing (Deborah Connors), Lisa Thornhill (Gwen), Greg Itzin (Dennis), Max Baker (Vin), Andromeda Dunker (Mo), Jesse James Rutherford (Tommy), Veena Sood (Doctor), Eric Snellman (George), Theron Zahn (Steve), Paul Morgan Stetler (Limo Driver), David Dunard (Striker Bob), Johnny "Sugar Bear" Willis, Tawnya Pettiford-Wates (Strikers), Vincent Fluck, P.J. Prinsloo (Club Kids), Tony Doupe, Jamie Moss (Men in Sports Bar), Barry Michael Greene (Maitre D'), Pamela Martin (KQMO Anchorwoman), Jill Krop (Strike News Anchor), Jonathan Brownlee (Morning Show Host), Catherine Lough Haggquist (Morning Show Hostess), Amanda Tapping (Carrie Maddox), Dan Lewis (Jake Manning), Margo Myers (Lori Ruben), Christopher Shyer (Mark Laughlin), Steve Pool (Weatherman Sam), Michelle Esteban (Hope Carmichael), Suleka Mathew (Airline Attendant), Marika Anuik (Lanie—10 years old), Ashlyn Morgan Williams (Lanie—5 years old), Kasey Stevens (Gwen—15 years old), Sean Watson (High School Teenager), John C. Havens (Plaza Doorman), Shannon Powell (Lanie's Mother), Kristine Beuerleine (Gwen's Daughter), Scott Beuerleine (Gwen's Son), Bruce Dawson (Gwen's Husband), Blake Willet (NYC Cop), James Owen (KQMO News Director), George Catalano (Control Room Tech), Patrick McEnroe (Rick), Appollonia Vanova (Stewardess), Shawn Bordoff (Frightened Flyer), Angela Moore (Airport Guard), Dick Henley (Plaza Bell Man), Alexander Kalugin (Russian Driver), Rick Tae (Fan), Peter Kelamis (AMUSA Producer), Berend McKenzie (Makeup Guy), Eileen Pedde (Stage Manager), Victoria Deschanel (Woman at Cafe), Henry O. Watson (Man at Cafe), Tim Watters (Bill Clinton), Brent Mendenhall (George Bush), Tracy Trueman (Pete's Ex-Wife), Jack Heptonstall (Farmer Hubbard), Lyle Campbell (Man on Plane), Riley Cantner (Kid with Cold), Ken Whelan, Michael Arthur (Police Officers), Peter Epstein (New York Gunman), Heidi Hoppenfeld (Exec. Assist.), Gary Lindsay, Natasha Smith, John Sharify, Tracy Vedder, Mike James (Reporters)

Angelina Jolie, Edward Burns in *Life or Something Like It*
© 20th Century Fox

SEX WITH STRANGERS

(VIEW FILM, INC.) Producers/Directors, Joe Gantz, Harry Gantz; Photography, Kary D'Alessandro, Mike Roth; Editor, Alysha Cohen; Music, Eric Avery, Larry Cohn; Color; Not rated; 105 minutes; Release date: April 26, 2002. Documentary about three couples who are into a "swinging" sexually open lifestyle of multiple partners, featuring James and Theresa, Calvin and Sara, Shannon and Gerard.

CIRCUIT

(JOUR DE FÊTE) Producers, Steven J. Wolfe, Michael J. Roth, Gregory Hinton; Director, Dirk Shafer; Screenplay, Gregory Hinton, Dirk Shafer; Photography, Joaquin Sedillo; Designer, John De Meo; Costumes, Katy Welch; Editor, Glen Richardson; Music, Tony Moran; from Sneak Preview Entertainment; Dolby; Color; Not rated; 130 minutes; Release date: April 26, 2002. CAST: Jonathan Wade-Drahos (John), Andre Khabazzi (Hector), Kiersten Warren (Nina), Brian Lane Green (Gill), Daniel Kukan (Tad), Jim J. Bullock (Mark), Darryl Stephens (Julian), Bruce Vilanch (MC), Randall Kleiser (Bobby's Doctor), Stanton Schnepp (Andy French), China Cat & Jeremy Hirst (Blue Party Band), Paul Lekakis (Bobby), William Katt (Gino), Nancy Allen (Louise), Michael Bailey Smith (Mike), Brian Beacock (Suspect/Drag Queen), Michael Keenan (Police Captain), Santo Ragno (Man-ette), Lauren Foster (Door Girl), Bill Leyton (Drag Comic), Chris Lugo, Eric Lee, Gabriel Byer, Ashley Holbrook, Deven Michaels ("Eat Well" Guys), Ant, Dan Castle, Woody Schultz, Glenn Soukesian, Todd Williams (Video Circuit Men), James Matusky (White Party Stagehand), Zoe "Joshua Tree" Logan (White Party Barback), Craig Chester (White Party Customer), Eddie Caldwell (Fire Marshal), Paul Seidler (Hotel Detective), Hilde Garcia (Hysterical Maid), Boris Gorovatsky, Ellia Gorovatsky (White Party Twins), Scott Helsop (Bobby's Dancer), Eddie Jamison (Shirtless Jogger), Derrek Cameron (Boy in Window), Mike Stevens (Man in Alley), Robert Musselman (Guy in Cadillac), Nicholas Downs (Overdosing Circuit Boy)

Andre Khabazzi in *Circuit* © Jour de Fête

Peter Menash, Kane Hodder in *Jason X* © New Line

JASON X

(NEW LINE) Producer, Noel J. Cunningham; Executive Producer, Sean S. Cunningham; Director/Co-Producer, Jim Isaac; Screenplay, Todd Farmer; Photography, Derick Underschultz; Designer, John Dondertman; Costumes, Maxyne Baker; Editor, David Handman; Music, Harry Manfredini; Casting, Robin D. Cook; Digital Film & Visual Effects, Toybox; Visual Effects Supervisor, Kelly Lepowsky; a Crystal Lake presentation of a Sean S. Cunningham production; Dolby; Deluxe color; Rated R; 93 minutes; Release date: April 26, 2002. CAST: Kane Hodder (Jason Voorhees/Uber Jason), Lexa Doig (Rowan), Lisa Ryder (KAY-EM 14), Chuck Campbell (Tsunaron), Jonathan Potts (Professor Lowe), Peter Menash (Sgt. Brodski), Melyssa Ade (Janessa), Dov Tiefenbach (Azrael), Melody Johnson (Kinsa), Derwin Jordan (Waylander), David Cronenberg (Dr. Wimmer), Jeff Geddis (Johnson, Soldier #1), Marcus Parilo (Sgt. Marcus), Boyd Banks (Fat Lou), Barna Moricz (Kicker), Dylan Bierk (Briggs), Todd Farmer (Dallas), Phillip Williams (Crutch), Kristi Angus (Adrienne), Yani Gellman (Stoney), Robert A. Silverman (Dieter Perez), Steve Lucescu (Condor), Thomas Seniuk (Sven), Amanda Brugel (Geko), Roman Podhora (Rescue Pilot), Kaye Penaflor, Tania Maro (VR Teen Girls), Mika Ward, David Cook (Campfire Teens)

NIGHT AT THE GOLDEN EAGLE

(KEYSTONE) Producers, Steve Bing, Adam Rifkin; Executive Producers, Mindy Marin, Morgan Sackett; Co-Producers, Lisa Perkins, Peter Schink; Director/Screenplay, Adam Rifkin; Photography, Francesco Varese; Designer, Sherman Williams; Costumes, Mynka Draper; Music, Tyler Bates; Editor, Peter Schink; Casting, Mindy Marin; from Shangri-La Entertainment; Super 35 Widescreen; Color; Rated R; 87 minutes; Release date: April 26, 2002. CAST: Vinnie Jones (Rodan), Donnie Montemarano (Tommy), Vinny Argiro (Mic), James Caan (Prison Warden), Natasha Lyonne (Amber), Ann Magnuson (Sally), Fayard Nicholas (Mr. Maynard), Sam Moore (Sylvester), Kitten Natividad (Ruby), Nicole Jacobs (Loirann), Miles Douglas (Desk Clerk), Badja Djola (Gabriel)

SOME BODY

(LOT 47) Producers, Henry Barrial, Stephanie Bennett, Geoffrey Pepos; Executive Producer, Peter Broderick; Director, Henry Barrial; Screenplay, Henry Barrial, Stephanie Bennett; Photography/Editor/Music, Geoffrey Pepos; Associate Producer, Mark Stolaroff; a Rhythm + Films and Cubano Films production; Color; Not rated; 77 minutes; Release date: April 26, 2002. CAST: Stephanie Bennett (Samantha), Jeramy Guillory (Anthony), Billy Ray Gallion (Billy), Tom Vitorino (Tony T.), Laura Katz (Eve), Sean Michael Allen (Bobby), Marnie Shelton (Leann), Matt Casado (Matt), Richie Magallanes (Richie), Niklaus Lange (Nickie), Ringo Hayden (Ringo), Liam Lockhart (Billy's Friend), Lyndon Johnson (Leann's date), Faleena Hopkins (Bobby's New Girl), Jay Webster (Bartender), Kaye Moore (Sam's Mom), Terry Chisholm (Sam's Aunt), John Chisholm (Sam's Uncle), Jonas Barrish (Leann's Date's Friend), Gerald Katzman, James Franco, Val Lauren, Christian Olave (Apartment Guys)

VULGAR

(LIONS GATE) Producer, Monica Hampton; Executive Producers, Scott Mosier, Kevin Smith; Director/Screenplay, Bryan Johnson; Photography, David Klein; Designer, Lisa Beth Mareiniss; Music, Ryan Shore; Casting, Paris Petrick; Color; Not rated; 97 minutes; Release date: April 26, 2002. CAST: Brian Christopher O'Halloran (Will Carlson/Vulgar), Bryan Johnson (Syd), Jerry Lewkowitz (Ed Fanelli), Ethan Suplee (Frankie Fanelli), Matt Maher (Gino Fanelli), Jay Petrick (Wilma Carlson), Jason Mewes (Tuott the Basehead), Dave Klein (Cinnamon), Bob Hawk (Old Man), Scott Schiaffo (Travis), Kevin Smith (Martan), Don Gentile (Sleepy Bum), Michael Tierney (Sknny Bum), Thom Leidner (Large Bum), Susanna Jolly (Jill), Ceton Tate (Ashley), Bob Farley (Barron), Edgar Johnson (Diaper Boy), Scott Mosier (Scotty), Diane Devlin (Sultry Audience), Soby (Beggar), Gertrude Johnson (Old Lady), Darin Johnson, Brian Hartsgrove (Boys), Michael Dinigris (Sam Mosier), David Gilbert, Eric Johnson (Delinquents), Jill Robertson (Shongo), Jamie Schutz, Aaron Hakeem (Cops), Paris Petrick (Nurse), Debbie Karr (Mother #1), Walt Flanagan (Caddy), Brian Quinn (Traffic Cop), Kiven Wiedmyer (Irate Motorist), Joe Mullins (Joe-Joe), Tim Miller (Gillian), Deanna Le'shell Rowe (Jennifer), Melissa Rayworth (Kelly), Sean Marquis (Dirty Junkie), Tobias Carroll (Toby)

Brian O'Halloran in *Vulgar* © Lions Gate

Vinnie Jones, Nicole Jacobs in *Night at the Golden Eagle* © Keystone

FRANK MCCLUSKY, C.I.

(TOUCHSTONE) Producer, Robert Simonds; Executive Producer, Tracey Trench; Director, Arlene Sanford; Screenplay, Mark Perez; Story, David Sheridan, Mark Perez; Photography, Tim Suhrstedt; Designer, Victoria Paul; Costumes, Tom Bronson; Music, Randy Edelman; Editor, Alan Cody; from Robert Simonds Productions; Dolby; Color; Rated PG-13; 82 minutes; Release date: April 26, 2002. CAST: David Sheridan (Frank McClusky), Kevin P. Farley (Jimmy), Cameron Richardson (Sharon Webber), Enrico Colantoni (Scout Bayou), Dolly Parton (Mrs. McCluskey), Randy Quaid (Mr. McCluskey), Orson Bean (Mr. Gafty), Joanie Laurer (Freeda), Kevin Pollak (Ronnie Rosengold), Tracy Morgan (Reggie Rosengold), Andy Richter (Herb), Josh Jacobson (Darryl McKlusky), Joseph Patrick Cranshaw (The Old Man), Adam Carolla, George Lopez (Detectives), Molly Sims (Injured Girl), Scott Baio, Lou Ferrigno, Issac Hanson, Jordan Taylor Hanson, Zac Hanson, Emmanuel Lewis, Pat O'Brien, Gary Owens (Themselves), Valerie Ianniello (Vicki), Eric Lichtenberg (Annoying Raceway Fan), Dominique Moceanu (Sports Commentator), Eric Moyer (Bar Patron), Ramona Oprea (Irza Topnizki), Matthew Parrott (Large Baio Fan), R. Lee Ermey (Jockey Master)

Freshmen © Pathfinder

FRESHMEN

(PATHFINDER) Producer/Director/Screenplay, Tom Huang; Photography, Brian Harding; Art Director, Andrea Pocaccini; Casting, Tina Gee, Amy Laundin, Mac Libanao; Editors, Tom Huang, Monina Verano; Color; Rated PG; 121 minutes; Release date: April 26, 2002. CAST: N.D. Brown (Tonisha), ToHuang (San), Kurt Kohler (Rick), Margaret Scarborough (Judy), Wendy Speake (Dana), Mary Chen (Grace), Ricahrd Guiton (Marc), Jake White (Jack), Sonya Leslie (Prof. Miller), Patrick Gorman (Prof. Palin), Deborah Kellar (Tonisha's Mom), Billee Thomas (Byron), Kim Robinson (Judy's Mom), Lowell Dean (Judy's Dad), Brenda Liu (San's Mom), Ming Lo (San's Dad), Eugene Lo (San's Grandfather), Stephen Owsley (Rick's Dad), Kelly McGowan (Britta), Ian Simeoneon (Seth), Kal Penn (Ajay), Steve Callaghan (Patrick), Ed Matz (Chris)

THE OTHER BROTHER

(XENON) Producer/Director/Screenplay, Mandel Holland; Photography, Matthew Clark; Designer, Milady D. JB Hartmann; Costumes, Mildred Brignoni; Editor, Anna Celada; Co-Prodcuers, Beverley Gordon, Lisa Pitt, Carrie Specht; Music Supervisors, J.C. McCoy, Dennis Poore; Casting, Susan Shopmaker; Dolby; Color; Rated R; 94 minutes; Release date: April 26, 2002. CAST: Mekhi Phifer (Martin), Andre Blake (Junnie), Michele Morgan (Bobbi), Tangi Miller (Paula), Ebony Jo-Ann (Mother Pearl), Sandra Prosper (Didi), O.L. Duke (Londel), Tammi Katherine Jones (Simone), Angela Nirvana (Carmen), Collette Wilson (Joy), Sally Reeves (Lips), Odell Holland (Tony), Jasmine Avilez (Cheryl), Candace Carter (Whitney), Mandel Holland (Big T), Regina Hall (Vicki), Aiesha Turman (Simone's Lover), Gerald Kelly (Joe), Cole Murray (Monique), Tony West (Guy in Bar), Mike Hodge (Mr. Simmons), Timmy Kimbro (Lemonade Vendor), Karen Hamilton (Mrs. Clark), Arlene McGruder (Mrs. Fincher), J.C. McCoy (Sweets), Camen de Lavallade (Cris Vincent), Gail Hall (Mrs. Younge), Thoundia Bickham (Cop), Norman Bullard (Cheap Shoes Guy), Teele Lewis (Girl in Purple)

GREEN DRAGON

(SILVER NITRATE) Producers, Elie Samaha, Andrew Stevens, Tony Bui, Tajamika Paxton; Director/Screenplay, Timothy Linh Bui; Story, Timothy Linh Bui, Tony Bui; Executive Producers, Forest Whitaker, Alison Semenza; Photography, Kramer Morgenthau; Designer, Jerry Fleming; Costumes, Ghia Fam; Editor, Leo Trombetta; Line Producer, William B. Steakley; Music, Jeff Danna, Mychael Danna; Casting, Rene Hayes; a Franchise Classics presentation of a Spirit Dance Entertainment production in association with Rickshaw Filmworks; Dolby; Color; Rated PG-13; 115 minutes; Release date: May 1, 2002. CAST: Patrick Swayze (Jim Lance), Forest Whitaker (Addie), Don Duong (Tia Tan), Hiep Thi Le (Thuy Hoa), Billinjer Tran (Duc), Long Nguyen (Q. Hai), Phuoc Quan Nguyen (Loi), Catherine Ai (Hien), Phu Cuong (Old Man), Jennifer Tran (Anh), Trung Nguyen (Minh Pham), Kieu Chinh (Kieu)

Tangi Miller, Mekhi Phifer in *The Other Brother* © Xenon

Don Duong, Patrick Swayze in *Green Dragon*
© Silver Nitrate

185

James Franco, Brad Renfro, Alex City, Stephen Dorff, Ronnie Marmo, Danny Cistone, Shamus Murphy in *Deuces Wild* © UA

DEUCES WILD

(UA) Producers, Michael Cerenzie, Willi Baer, Fred Caruso, Paul Kimatian; Executive Producers, Mario Ohoven, Ederhard Kayser, Marc Sferrazza; Director, Scott Kalvert; Screenplay, Paul Kimatian, Christopher Gambale; Co-Producers, Melissa Barrett, Charlie Loventhal, Scott Valentine; Photography, John A. Alonzo; Designer, David L. Snyder; Costumes, Marianna Åström-DeFina; Editor, Michael R. Miller; Music, Stewart Copeland; a Cinerenta-Cinewild and Unity Productions presentation in association with Presto Productions and the Antonia Company; Distributed by MGM Distribution Co.; Dolby; Panavision; FotoKem Color; Rated R; 97 minutes; Release date: May 3, 2002. CAST: Stephen Dorff (Leon), Brad Renfro (Bobby), Fairuza Balk (Annie), Norman Reedus (Marco), Max Perlich (Freddie), Drea de Matteo (Betsy), Vincent Pastore (Father Aldo), Frankie Muniz (Scooch), Balthazar Getty (Jimmy Pockets), Nancy Cassaro (Esther), Matt Dillon (Fritzy), Deborah Harry (Wendy), James Franco (Tino), Josh Leonard (Punch), Alba Albanese (Brenda), Danny Cistone (Little Jack), Louis Lombardi (Philly Babe), Johnny Knoxville (Vinnie Fish), Melvin Rodriguez (Big Dom), Robert Miranda (Gino), Shamus Murphy (Patty Cugire), Ronnie Marmo (Moof), Paul Sampson (Joey Pants), Maurice Compte (Maurice), George Georgiadis (Willie), Jackie Tohn (Mary Ann), George Palermo (Stevie Olives), Steve Picerni (Jerry), Marc Alexander Sferrazza (Young Boy at Pool), Blake Bashoff (Allie Boy), Larry Moss (Pops), Alex Watson (Sal), Alex City (Stretch), Stephanie Stenta (Marco's Babe), Clayton Barber (Top Hat), Michael Endoso (Louie), Lee Whitaker, Christopher Lep (Vipers), Norman Panto, Frank Panto, Tony Doria, Tony Giaimo (Italian Band), Albert Joby, Jeffrey Clark (Cops), Ian Quinn (Alley Cop), Joe Campana (Feast Barker), Eric Prescott (Carnival Patron)

HOME MOVIE

(COWBOY) Producers, Barbara Laffey, Susane Preissler; Executive Producers, Stuart Wolff, John Shirley, Richard Siegel; Director, Chris Smith; Photography, Hubert Taczanowski; Editor, Jun Diaz; Color; Not rated; 60 minutes; Release date: May 3, 2002. Documentary looking at five idiosyncratic households in America, featuring Bill Tregle, Ben Skora, Darlene Santrinano, Ed Peden, Diana Peden, Bob Walker, Francis Mooney, Linda Beech

A SHOT AT GLORY

(MAC RELEASING) Producers, Rob Carliner, Michael Corrente, Robert Duvall; Executive Producers, Steven Bowman, Billy Heinzerling, Denis O'Neill; Co-Producer, Marisa Polvino; Director, Michael Corrente; Screenplay, Denis O'Neill; Photography, Alex Thomson; Designer, Andy Harris; Costumes, Trisha Biggar; Editor, David Ray; Music, Mark Knopfler; Casting, John Hubbard, Ros Hubbard; Revere Pictures; Dolby; Panavision; Color; Rated R; 115 minutes; Release date: May 3, 2002. CAST: Robert Duvall (Gordon McLeod), Michael Keaton (Peter Cameron), Ally McCoist (Jackie McQuillan), Libby Langdon (Annie), Brian Cox (Martin Smith), Cole Hauser (Kelsey), Morag Hood (Irene), Kirsty Mitchell (Kate McGullan), Owen Coyle, Elaine M. Ellis, Alex Ferguson, Peter Hearthersont, John McViegh, Claudio Reyna, Andy Smith

Ally McCoist, Robert Duvall in *A Shot At Glory* © MAC Releasing

Linda Beech in *Home Movie* © Cowboy

HYBRID

(INDICAN) Producer/Director/Photography/Music, Monteith McCollum; Editor, Ariana Gerstein; Vagrant Films; Dolby; Black and white; Not rated; 92 minutes; Release date: May 10, 2002. Documentary on Milford Beeghly who, in the 1930s, pioneered the process of genetically enhanced crops.

THE COCKETTES

(STRAND) Producer, David Weissman; Directors, Bill Weber, David Weissman; Photography, Marsha Kahm; Editor, Bill Weber; Co-Producer, Roger Klorese; Associate Producer, Robert Croonquist; Music, Richard "Scrumbly" Koldewyn; Color; Not rated; 100 minutes; Release date: May 10, 2002. Documentary about a group of San Francisco drag performers from the "psychedlic" era, the Cockettes, featuring Dusty Dawn, Anton "Reggie" Dunnigan, John Flowers, Goldie Glitters, Fayette Hauser, Richard "Scrumbly" Koldewyn, Marshall Olds, Ocean Michael Moon, Kreemah Ritz, Rumi, Sweet Pam (The Cockettes), Larry Brinkin, Denise Hale, Ann Harris, Sal Innocencio, Jilala, Michael Kalmen, Sylvia Miles, Peter Mintun, Maureen Orth, Ralph, Sebastian, Cara Vida, John Waters, Errol Wetson, Holly Woodlawn

Eddie Griffin, DJ Qualls in *The New Guy* © Columbia

THE NEW GUY

(COLUMBIA) Producers, Todd Garner, Gordon Gray, Mark Ciardi; Executive Producers, John J. Strauss, Ed Decter, Michael Fottrell, Greg Silverman; Director, Ed Decter; Screenplay, David Kendall; Photography, Michael D. O'Shea; Designer, Dina Lipton; Costumes, Susie DeSanto; Editor, David Rennie; Music, Ralph Sall; Executive Music Producer, Ralph Sall; a Revolution Studios presentation; Dolby; Deluxe color; Rated PG-13; 89 minutes; Release date: May 10, 2002. CAST: DJ Qualls (Gil Harris "Dizzy"), Eliza Dushku (Danielle), Zooey Deschanel (Nora), Jerod Mixon (Kirk), Parry Shen (Glen), Lyle Lovett (Bear), Eddie Griffin (Luther), Sunny Mabrey (Courtney), Ross Patterson (Conner), Matt Gogin (Ed Liggett), Horatio Sanz (Dance Instructor), Tony Hawk, David Hasselhoff, Tommy Lee (Themselves), Geoffrey Lewis (Principal Zaylor), Charlie O'Connell (Charlie), Gene Simmons (Reverend), Kool Mo Dee (Ted), Jermaine D. Mauldin (Jermaine), Josh Todd (Rudy), Henry Rollins (Warden), Illeana Douglas (Kiki Pierce), Kurt Fuller (Mr. Undine), Julius Carry (Coach), M.C. Gainey (Clem), Hans Stroble (Dave), Charles Hutchison (Lonnie), Avery Waddell (Pete), Mike Erwin (Travis), Brian Schaible (Mark), Jesse Castillo (Gordon), Rachael E. Stevens (Tina), Laura Clifton (Emily), Conrad Goode (Billy Ray), Jai Rodriguez (Jose), Robert C. Anthony (Damian), Matthew Lee Pelosi (Young Dizzy), Ryan Waller (Announcer), Kina Cosper (Estelle), Robert Van Winkle (Music Store Employee), Bill Wolkoff (Music Store Manager), Mike Wachs (Henry), Pride Grinn (Redneck), Kyle Gass (Mr. Luberoff), Valente Rodriguez (Mrs. Whitman), Billy F. Harden (Choir Member), Joy Hadnott (Carmen), Christie Abbott (Christie), Meredith May, Andrea Ulmer, Saudia Rashed, Shana McClendon, Camille Chen, Jessica Hale, Kelly Bright, Kristen Anderson, Kellye Cunningham (Cheerleaders)

THE BUSINESS OF FANCYDANCING

(OUTRIDER) Producers, Larry Estes, Scott M. Rosenfelt; Executive Producers, John Benear, Bradford Bond; Line Producer, Craig Markey; Director/Screenplay, Sherman Alexie; Photography/Editor, Holly Taylor; Art Director, Jonathon Saturen; FallsApart Productions; Dolby; Color; Not rated; 103 minutes; Release date: May 10, 2002. CAST: Evan Adams (Seymour Polatkin), Michelle St. John (Agnes Roth), Gene Tagaban (Aristotle Joseph), Swil Kanim (Mouse), Rebecca Carroll (The Interviewer), Cynthia Geary (Teresa), Leo Rossi (Mr. Williams), Kevin Phillip (Steven), Elaine Miles (Kim), Arthur Tulee (Junior One), Jim Boyd (Junior Two), Jennifer Kreisberg (Salmon Girl), Ron Otis (White Motorist), William Joseph Elk III (Tavern Father)

STANDING BY YOURSELF

(CHEAPO FILMS) Producer/Director/Editor/Photography, Josh Koury; Color; Not rated; 65 minutes; Release date: May 15, 2002. CAST: Josh Siegfried, Adam Koury, Helen Koury, Roselyn Siegfried, Richard Koury Jr., Richard Koury Sr., Brandon Shorey

The Cockettes in *The Cockettes* © Strand

Josh Siegfried in *Standing by Yourself* © Cheapo Films

CREMASTER 3

(GLACIER FIELD LLC) Producers, Matthew Barney, Barbara Gladstone; Director/Screenplay, Matthew Barney; Photography, Peter Streitmann; Designers, Hal McFeely III, Matthew D. Ryle; Costumes, Linda LaBelle; Music, Jonathan Bepler; Visual Effects Supervisor, Matthew Wallin; Dolby; Color; Not rated; 182 minutes; Release date: May 15, 2002. Cast: Richard Serra, Mike Bocchetti, David Edward Campbell, James Pantoleon, Jim Tooey (Grand Masters), Matthew Barney (The Entered Apprentice), Aimee Mullins (The Entered Novitiate/Oonagh MacCumhail), Paul Brady (Cloud Club Maitre D'), Terry Gillespie (Cloud Club Barman), Peter D. Badalamenti (Fionn MacCumhail), The Mighty Biggs (Fingal)

CQ

(UNITED ARTISTS) Producer, Gary Marcus; Executive Producers, Francis Ford Coppola, Georgia Kacandes, Willi Baer; Director/Screenplay, Roman Coppola; Co-Producers, Jimmy De Brabant, Michael Polaire; Photography, Robert D. Yeoman; Designer, Dean Tavoularis; Costumes, Judy Shrewsbury; Music, Roger Neill; Editor, Leslie Jones; Casting, Blythe Cappello, Béatrice Kruger, Juliette Ménager; an American Zoetrope production, Delux Productions in association with Film Fund Luxembourg; Distributed by MGM; U.S.-Luxembourg-French; Dolby; Color; Rated R; 91 minutes; Release date: May 24, 2002. Cast: Jeremy Davies (Paul), Angela Lindvall (Dragonfly/Valentine), Elodie Bouchez (Marlene), Gerard Depardieu (Andrezej), Giancarlo Giannini (Enzo), Massimo Ghini (Fabrizio), John Phillip Law (Chairman), Jason Schwartzman (Felix DeMarco), Dean Stockwell (Dr. Ballard), Billy Zane (Mr. E), Silvio Muccino (Pippo), Natalia Codianova (Brigit), Bernard Verley (Trailer Voiceover), L.M. Kit Carson, Chris Bearne, Jean-Paul Scrapitta, Nicolas Saada, Remi Fourquin, Jean-Claude Schlim, Sacha Levy, Jacques Deglas, Gilles Soeder (Fantasy Critics), Julian Nest, Greta Seacat Kafuman, Barbara Sarafian (Festival Critics), Les Woodhall, Jean-Baptiste Kremer (Board Members), Franck Sasonoff (Angry Man at Riots), Jean-Francois Wolff (Party Man), Eric Connor (Long Haired Actor at Party), Diana Gartner (Cute Model at Party), Stéphane Gesnel (Actress at Party), Frédéric de Brabant (Steward), Shawn Mortensen, Matthieu Tonetti (Revolutionary Guards), Ann Maes, Giantare Parulyte, Caroline Lies, Stokyanka Tanya Gospodinova, Magali Dahan, Natalie Broker, Wanda Perdelwitz (Vampire Actresses), Mark Ashworth (Lead Goul), Pieter Riemens (Asst. Director), Frederica Citarella (Talkative Girl), Andrea Comaci (Soldier Boy), Corinne Terenzi (Teen Lover), Sofia Coppola (Enzo's Mistress), Emidio La Vella (Italian Actor), Massimo Schina (Friendly Guy at Party), Caroline Colombini (Girl in Miniskirt), Rosa Pianeta (Woman in Fiat), Christophe Chrompin (Jealous Boyfriend), Romain Duris (Hippie Filmmaker)

Jacqueline Bisset, Seymour Cassel in *The Sleepy Time Gal* © Antarctic

THE MAD SONGS OF FERNANDA HUSSEIN

(TRAVELING LIGHT PRODS.) Producer/Director/Screenplay, John Gianvito; Photography, Ulli Bonnekamp; Music, Johannes Ammon, Jakov Jakoulov, Igor Tkachenko; Color; Not rated; 168 minutes; Release date: May 31, 2002. Cast: Thia Gonzalez (Fernanda), Robert Perrea (Carlos), Dustin Scott (Raphael Sinclair), Sherri Goen, Elizabeth Pilar, Carlos Stevens

THE SLEEPY TIME GAL

(ANTARCTIC) Producers, Christopher Münch, Ruth Charny; Co-Producers, Jim McKay, Michael Stipe; Director, Christopher Münch; Screenplay, Christopher Münch, Alice Elliott Dark; Photography, Marco Fargnoli, Rob Sweeney; Art Directors, Jody Asnes, Jesse Epstein, Melissa Frankel, Bryan Hodge; Costumes, Kristen Anacker; Editors, Annette Davey, Dody Dorn, Christopher Münch; Casting, Kerry Barden, Mark Bennett, Billy Hopkins, Suzanne Smith; C-Hundred Film Corp./Münch-Charny productions; Color/Black and white; Rated R; 94 minutes; Release date: May 31, 2002. Cast: Jacqueline Bisset (Frances), Martha Plimpton (Rebecca), Nick Stahl (Morgan), Amy Madigan (Maggie), Frankie R. Faison (Jimmy Dupree), Carmen Zapata (Anna), Peggy Gormley (Betty), Seymour Cassel (Bob), Molly Price (Rebecca's Colleague), Kate McGregor-Stewart (Miriam), Clara Bellar (Mushroom Girl), Justin Theroux (Rebecca's Boyfriend), Mark Tymchyshyn (Larry Mosher), Anibal O. Lleras (Mr. Vega), Phyllis Somerville (Rebecca's Adoptive Mother), Robert Hogan (Rebecca's Adoptive Father), Lola Pashalinski (Adoption Agency Director), Robin Weigert (Hospital Records), John Arkoosh (Naked Boy), Rain Phoenix (WROD Receptionist), Jessica Brooks Grant (Frances, ages 10 and 14), Louise Fernandez (Frances, age 3), E. Hernandez (Frances's Father), Kimberly Scott (Emergency Room Nurse), Sarah Lassez (Frances, age 25), Aaron Amara Davis (Jimmy, age 25), Pepe Altramontes (La Llorona Guitarist) (This film had its premiere on cable television)

Jeremy Davies, Angela Lindvall in *CQ* © United Artists

THE NEXT BIG THING

(CASTLE HILL) Producers, P.J. Posner, Joel Posner, Andrew Fierberg, Amy Hobby; Director, P.J. Posner; Screenplay, Joel Posner, P.J. Posner; Co-Producers, Anthony Katagas, Callum Greene; Photography, Oliver Bokelberg; Designer, Deana Sidney; Costumes, Luca Mosca, Marco Cattoretti; Editor, David Zieff; Music, Ferdinand Jay Smith, Casey Fillaci, Jay Smith IV; Music Supervisor, Doug Bernheim; Casting, Adrienne Stern; a Curb Entertainment presentation of a Twopoundbag Production in association with Double A Films; Dolby; Color; Rated R; 87 minutes; Release date: May 31, 2002. CAST: Chris Eigeman (Gus Bishop), Jamie Harris (Deech Scumble), Connie Britton (Kate Crowley), Janet Zarish (Florence Rubin), Mike Starr (Walter Sznitken), Farley Granger (Arthur Pomposello), Marin Hinkle (Shari Lampkin), Peter Giles (Roger), Dechen Thurman (Damian Spire), John Seitz (Mr. Chesnick), Ileen Getz (Trish Kane), Ed Hyland (Museum Director), Gerta Grunen (Bernice Chesick), Samia Shoaib (Varda Abromowitz), Doug Stone (Mr. Willard), Joel Posner (Destitute Passenger), Summer Mahoney (Pomposello Receptionist), Rahsa Mella ("Nihilistic" Woman), Martin Moran ("Solipsism" Man), Tibor Feldman ("Weltanschauung" Man), Catherine Curtin ("Weltanschauung" Woman), Johann Carlo ("Absolutist" Woman), Andrew Fierberg (Wan Man), Robert J. Epstein (Mr. Rubin), George A. Williams, Jr. (Mr. Kulak), Katalin Pota (Marjana), Delora Whitney (Gus's Supervisor), Andrew Palermo (Aspiring Novelist), PJ Posner (Art Instructor), Abiola Wendy Abrams (Hip Bistro Hostess), Cara Leigh (Hip Bistro Blonde), Perry Wolberg ("Cheese" Artiste at Bar), Daniel Dresner, Rohan Quine (Artistes at Bar), Chelsea Lagos, Alice Liu (Dance Floor Girls), Eric Riley (Dance Floor Guy), Mitch Greene (Pickpocketed Straphanger), Christine Rogers (Biennial Attendant), Tony Rossi (Biennial Guard), Shelley Kirk (Biennial Patron), Anthony Katagas, John Denatale (Gallery Guys), Jill Johnson (Gallery Girl), Richard Gallela (Club Doorman), Yves Rene (Florence's Chauffeur), Greg Orvis (Fantasy Geoffrey), Kim Merritt (Studio Model), Richard L. Smith (Voice of Talk Show Host), Myrtle & Glen (Endora)

KAATERSKILL FALLS

(WHISKEY OUTPOST PRODS.) Directors, Josh Apter, Peter Olsen; Screenplay, Josh Apter, Hilary Howard, Anthony Leslie, Peter Olsen, Mitchell Riggs; Photography, Peter Olsen; Editor, Josh Apter; Lo-Fi Pictures; Color; Not rated; 86 minutes; Release date: June 5, 2002. CAST: Hilary Howard (Ren), Anthony Leslie (Lyle), Mitchell Riggs (Mitchell)

Lisa Enos, Danny Huston, Peter Weller in
Ivansxtc. © Artistic License

Clint Jordan in *Virgil Bliss* © First Run Features

IVANSXTC.

(ARTISTIC LICENSE) Producer, Lisa Enos; Director, Bernard Rose; Screenplay, Bernard Rose, Lisa Enos; Based on the novel *The Death of Ivan Ilyich* by Leon Tolstoy; Photography, Bernard Rose, Ron Forsythe; Color; Rated R; 93 minutes; Release date: June 7, 2002. CAST: Danny Huston (Ivan Beckman), Peter Weller (Don West), Jay Itzkowitz (Joe), Lisa Enos (Charlotte White), Lisa Henson (Margaret Mead), Hal Lieberman (Lloyd Hall), James Merendino (Danny McTeague), Adam Krentzman (Barry Oaks), Dan Ireland (Ted Zimblest), Caroleen Feeney (Rosemary Kramer), Sarah Goldberg (Naomi), Morgan Vukovic (Lucy Lawrence), Carol Rose (Judy Tarzana), Steve Dickman (Melvin), Wendy Rhoads (Missy), Kate Connor (Avery), Ken Stephens (Ken), Julia Verdin (Mary), Alex Butler (Brad East), Ruby Rose (Vicky West), Boris Gorbis, Ira Newborn (Rabbis), Marcia Beckman (Joanne Duckman), Sid Beckman (Robert Graham), Heidi Jo Markel (Francesca Knight), Alison Taylor (Nurse Jackie), Tiffani-Amber Thiessen (Marie Stein), Pierre Tisserand (Reporter), Marilyn Heston (Bonnie Shane), Valeria Golino (Constanza Vero), Angela Featherstone (Amanda Hill), Bobby Bell (Derek), Vladimir Tuchinsky (Dr. Gold), Victoria Silvstedt (Melanie), Ken Enos (Bad Bobby), Crystal Atkins (Jessie), Sofia Eng (Anita), Courtney Kling (Kimmi), Sam Lingenfelter (AAA Man), Mike Gold (Ira Reuther), Megan Carson (Cashier), Pria Chattergee (Mrs. Mrinalini), Tommy Harris, Jerry Kaona (Cops), Todd Williams (Paramedic), Sharon Hall (Slim), Dino DeConcini (Dr. Meyer), Camille Alick (Hilda)

VIRGIL BLISS

(FIRST RUN FEATURES) Producers, Joe Maggio, John Maggio; Executive Producers, Matthew Myers, Thierry Cagianut; Director/ Screenplay, Joe Maggio; Photography, Harlan Bosmajian; Music, Greta Gaines, Clint Jordan, Anthony Gorman; Color; Not rated; 94 minutes; Release date: June 12, 2002. CAST: Clint Jordan (Virgil Bliss), Kirsten Russell (Ruby), Anthony Gorman (Manny), Marc Romeo (Devo), Greg Amici (Gillette), Tom Brangle (Prison Captain), Rich Bierman (Prison Guard)

John Leguizamo, Sam Jones III in *Zigzag* © Silver Nitrate

Rudy Burckhardt in *Not Nude Though:
A Portrait of Rudy Burckhardt* © Two Boots

ZIGZAG

(SILVER NITRATE) Producers, Elie Samaha, Andrew Stevens; Executive Producer, Tracee Stanley; Director/Screenplay, David S. Goyer; Based on the novel by Landon J. Napoleon; Co-Producers, James A. Holt, Alison Semenza; Photography, James L. Carter; Designer, Philip Toolin; Music, Grant Lee Philips; Mariachi Songs, Herman Beeftink; Editor, Conrad Smart; Casting, Richard Hicks, Ronnie Yeskel; a Epsilon, Franchise Pictures production; Dolby; Color; Rated R; 101 minutes; Release date: June 14, 2002. CAST: John Leguizamo (Singer), Wesley Snipes (Fletcher), Oliver Platt (Toad), Natasha Lyonne (Jenna), Luke Goss (Cadillac Tom), Sam Jones III (ZigZag), Sherman Augustus (Hawke), Michael Greyeyes (Dale), Julian Dulce Vida (Ramon), Ivan Basso (Javier), Abraham Benrubi (Hector), Warren G. Hall (Wayne), Daniel Louis Rivas (Rico), Roberta Valderrama (Tawny), Eddie Perez (Eddie), Elizabeth Peña (Ms. Tate), Stephanie Chao (Jordan), Miguel A. Nuñez, Jr. (Bentley), Mary Randle (Diane), Lynette Du Pre (Hooker), Kathleen Gati (Doctor), Patton Oswalt (Shelly), Ronny Rosemont (Sara), Ernest Hardin, Jr. (Nurse), Valerie Ianniello, Regina Russell (Dancers)

NOT NUDE THOUGH:
A PORTRAIT OF RUDY BURCKHARDT

(TWO BOOTS) Producer/Director, Doris Kornish; Photography, Gary Steele, Mike Stiller, Joel Schlemowitz; Editor, Joel Schlemowitz; Music, Various; Color; Not rated; 88 minutes; Release date: June 19, 2002. Documentary on visual artist Rudy Burckhardt, featuring George Schneeman, Yoshiko Chuma, Alex Katz, Mimi Gross, Tom Burckhardt, Lucas Burckhardt, Michael Scholnick, Lorna Smedman, Gabriella Lanser, Christopher Sweet, Greg Masters, Eric Holtzman, Bob Holman, Jacob Burckhardt

WAR PHOTOGRAPHER

(FIRST RUN/ICARUS) Producer/Director/Editor, Christian Frei; Photographs/Microcam Cinematography, James Nachtwey; Digital Betacam Cinematography, Peter Ingergand; Music, Eleni Karaindrou, Arvo Part, David Darling; Dolby; Color; Not rated; 96 minutes; Release date: June 19, 2002. Documentary on war photographer James Nachtwey, featuring James Nachtwey, Christiane Amanpour, Hans-Hermann Klare, Christiane Breustedt, Des Wright, Denis O'Neill

JUWANNA MANN

(WARNER BROS.) Producer, James G. Robinson, Bill Gerber, Steve Oedekerk; Director, Jesse Vaughan; Screenplay, Bradley Allenstein; Executive Producers, Jonathan A. Zimbert, Ralph Singleton; Photography, Reynaldo Villalobos; Designer, Eve Cauley Turner; Costumes, Peggy Farrell; Editor, Seth Flaum; Music, Wendy Melvoin, Lisa Coleman; Co-Producer, David C. Robinson; Casting, Pam Dixon Mickelson; a James G. Robinson presentation of a Morgan Creek production; Dolby; Technicolor; Rated PG-13; 91 minutes; Release date: June 21, 2002. CAST: Miguel A. Nuñez (Jamal Jefferies/Juwanna Mann), Vivica A. Fox (Michelle Langford), Kevin Pollak (Lorne Daniels), Tommy Davidson (Puff Smokey Smoke), Kim Wayans (Latisha Jansen), Jenifer Lewis (Aunt Ruby), Ginuwine (Romeo), Kimberly "Lil' Kim" Jones (Tina Parker), Annie Corley (Coach Rivers), Tammi Reiss (Vickie Sanchez), Heather Quella (Magda Rowonowitch), Angela Cossey (Natalie Kemper), Itoro Coleman (Debbie Scruggs), Terry Loughlin (Commissioner), Bonnie Johnson (Lorne's Secretary), Deanna Davis (Carla), Carol Mitchell (Betty), Deborah Calloway Duke (Mable), Pearl Jones (Esther), Tyrone "Mugsy" Bogues (Andrew Stewart), Dikembe Mutombo (Arch Player Coyner), Rasheed Wallace (Beat Player Whitley), Vlade Divac (Beat Player Morse), Jeanne Zelasko, Chris Myers, Roy Firestone, Kenny Albert, Kevin Frazier, Cynthia Cooper, Katy Steding, Teresa Weatherspoon, Jay Leno (Themselves), Reginald Coles III (Beat Player Kerns), Ric Reitz (Beat Coach), J. Don Ferguson (UBA Referee), Mark Allan Stewart (City Cop), Omar Dorsey (Rickey), Andrew Kenny (Autograph Kid), Brittani Warrick (Young Girl), Mert Hatfield (Arbitrator), Elliott Street (Doctor), Judy Simpson Cook (Nurse), Jaclyn Dahm, Erica Dahm, Nicole Dahm (Triplets), Lance Krall (Asian Guy), Eddie Rouse, Jr. (Moving Man), Michael Drake (Waiter), Everett Summers (WUBA Referee)

James Nachtwey in *War Photographer* © First Run/Icarus

Miguel A. Nunez in *Juwanna Mann* © Warner Bros.

BOBBY G. CAN'T SWIM

(GABRIEL FILM GROUP) Producers, Gill Holland, Michael Pilgram; Executive Producers, Matoni Bros, Adriana Chiesa, Julia Coppola, Michael Morley, Kevin Chinoy; Director/Screenplay, John-Luke Montias; Photography, George Gibson; Editor, Michael Pilgram; Music, Ed Tomney; a cinéBlast! production; Color; Rated R; 85 minutes; Release date: June 21, 2002. CAST: John-Luke Montias (Bobby G), Susan Mitchell (Lucy), Paul Maged (Mike), Andrew Rein (Andy), Michael Gnat (Tim), Vincent Vega (Coco), Norman Middleton (Popeet), Donna Sonkin (Gina), Caesar DeLeon (Ricky), Carlos Rafart (Domingo), Herbert Rogers (Jackson), Bill Golodner (Det. Smith), Tom Flanagan (Det. Nuzzo), Rick Poli (Dollar Bill), Anthony Caso (Tony Zino), Steve Heinze (Astro), Nora King (Cora), Gene Ruffini (Alex), Gilbert Brown (Jimmy), Wil Townsend (Hooch Dealer), Veronica Bero (His Girl), Derrick Roberts (Shooter), Lynrod Douglas (Driver), Michael Pilgram (Helmut), Amro Salama (Hafiz), Michael Donovan (Tough Guy), Mike Taylor (His Buddy), Araceli Baulete (Girl), Irene Shea (Woman in Street), Mark Heimann (Club Bartender), John Boyle (Man with Lucy), Wilhelmina Garcia (Brenda), Gene Wynn (Irish Bartender), Robert Stevens (Bobby's Customer), Carolyn Thomas, Melissa Cavan (Coco's Nieces), Katrina Ferguson (Woman at Church), Carly Weil (Girl at Church), Martha Elliot (Homeless Woman), Burnett Lingister (Man on Dock), Fouad Boutiba (Guy Who Gets Peed On), Tom McQuaid (Guy Who Tosses Bobby Out)

John-Luke Montias, Susan Mitchell in
Bobby G. Can't Swim © Gabriel Film Group

DAHMER

(PENINSULA FILMS) Producer, Larry Rattner; Executive Producers, Timothy Swain, Leonard Shapiro; Director/Screenplay, David Jacobson; Co-Producer, Susan R. Rodgers; Photography, Chris Manley; Designer, Eric J. Larson; Costumes, Dana Hart; Music, Christina Agamanolis, Mariana Bernoski, Willow Williamson; Casting, Ricki G. Maslar; an Infinityland Productions, LLC Film; Dolby; Color; Rated R; 102 minutes; Release date: June 21, 2002. CAST: Jeremy Renner (Jeffrey Dahmer), Bruce Davison (Lionel Dahmer), Artel Kayaru (Rodney), Matt Newton (Lance Bell), Dion Basco (Khamtay), Kate Williamson (Grandma), Christina Payano (Letitia), Tom'ya Bowden (Shawna), Sean Blakemore (Corliss), Mickey Swenson (Officer Phillips), Julius Branca (Officer Powell), Pierson Blaetz (Officer Martin), Vincent Zangari (Ohio Officer), Xavier Lawrence (Young Man in Bar), David Manis (Shop Steward), Lily Knight (Mother), Steve Keyes (New Guy), Daniel McInterney (Bartender), Archie J. Howard II, Damian Forester (Bouncers), Christopher Louis (Corpse), Edgar Allen (Bird)

Jeremy Renner, Dion Basco in *Dahmer* © Peninsula Films

MR. SMITH GETS A HUSTLER

(OUTRIDER) Director, Ian McCrudden; Screenplay, Matthew Swan; Photography, Matthew Swan; No other credits available; Mr. Smith Productions; Dolby; Color; Not rated; 91 minutes; Release date: June 21, 2002. CAST: Larry Pine (Mr. Smith), Alex Feldman (Bobby), J.D. Williams (Abe), Benjamin Hendrickson (Mr. Lapp), Thomas Hildreth (Jack), Anna Thomson (Doreen), Jodie Baker (Sheila), Antonio Rodriguez (Angel), Eddy Hudson, Phil McGlaston (Collectors), Jim Sherigon, Alexander Scott (Johns)

MONEY BUYS HAPPINESS

(WIGGLY WORLD STUDIOS) Producers/Editors, Jamie Hook, Gregg Lachow; Director/Screenplay, Gregg Lachow; Photography, Jamie Hook; Art Directors, Blake Hellman, Adam Roffman; Costumes, Nina Moser; Music, Jim Ragland; Casting, Rachel Parks; a Start-to-Finish project; Stereo; Color; Not rated; 104 minutes; Release date: June 26, 2002. CAST: Megan Murphy (Georgia), Jeff Weatherford (Money), John Holyoke (Peter), Cynthia Whalen (Jane), Cathy Sutherland (Carla), Michael Chick (Vincent), Caveh Zahedi (Steve)

Jeff Weatherford, Megan Murphy in
Money Buys Happiness © Wiggly World Studios

PUMPKIN

(UNITED ARTISTS) Producers, Karen Barber, Christina Ricci, Andrea Sperling, Albert Berger, Ron Yerxa; Executive Producers, Francis Ford Coppola, Linda Reisman, Willi Baer; an American Zoetrope production; Directors, Adam Larson Broder, Tony R. Abrams; Screenplay, Adam Larson Broder; Photography, Tim Suhrstedt; Designer, Richard Sherman; Costumes, Edi Giguere; Music, John Ottoman; Editors, Sloane Klevin, Richard Halsey; Music Supervisors, Mary Ramos, Michelle Kuzentsky; Line Producer, Betsy Danbury; Casting, Mary Vernieu, Anne McCarthy, Felicia Fasano, Rita VanderWaal; an American Zoetrope production; Distributed by MGM; Dolby; Color; Rated R; 113 minutes; Release date: June 28, 2002. CAST: Christina Ricci (Carolyn McDuffy), Hank Harris (Pumpkin Romanoff), Brenda Blethyn (Judy Romanoff), Dominique Swain (Jeanine Kryszinsky), Marisa Coughlan (Julie Thurber), Sam Ball (Kent Woodlands), Harry Lennix (Robert Meary), Nina Foch (Betsy Collander), Caroline Aaron (Claudia Prinsinger), Lisa Banes (Chippy McDuffy), Julio Oscar Mechoso (Dr. Frederico Cruz), Phil Reeves (Burt Wohlfert), Tait Smith (Hansie Prisinger), Michael Bacall (Casey Whitner), Erinn Bartlett (Corinne), Michelle Krusiec (Ann Chung), Melissa McCarthy (Cici Pinkus), Marisa Parker (Courtney Burke), Amy Adams (Alex), Ginny Schreiber (Diana), Shaun Weiss (Randy Suskind), Julia Vera (Ramona Ramirez), Shane Johnson (Jeremy), Elsie Escobar (Sascha Santiago), John Henry Binder (Newscaster), Margaret Travolta (Vera Whitner)

Hank Harris, Christina Ricci in *Pumpkin* © United Artists

HEY ARNOLD! THE MOVIE

(PARAMOUNT) Producers, Albie Hecht, Craig Bartlett; Executive Producers, Marjorie Cohn, Julia Pistor; Director, Tuck Tucker; Screenplay, Craig Bartlett, Steve Viksten; Based on characters created by Craig Bartlett; Co-Executive Producer, Steve Vikstein; Music, Jim Lang; Co-Producer, Joe Purdy; Animation Directors, Christine Kolosov, Frank Weiss; Editor, Christopher Hink; Art Director, Christine Kolosov; Sequence Directors, Tim Parsons, Carson Kugler, Chris Robertson, Aldin Baroza; Original Character Designer, Craig Bartlett; Casting, Joey Paul; Dolby; Deluxe color; Rated PG; 76 minutes; Release date: June 28, 2002. VOICE CAST: Spencer Klein (Arnold), Francesca Marie Smith (Helga/Deep Voice), Jamil Smith (Gerald/Rasta Guy), Dan Castellaneta (Grandpa/Nick Vermicelli), Tress MacNeille (Grandma/Mayor Dixie/Red), Paul Sorvino (Scheck), Jennifer Jason Leigh (Bridget), Christopher Lloyd (Coronoer), Vincent Schiavelli (Mr. Bailey), Maurice LaMarche (Big Bob/Head of Security), Kath E. Soucie (Miriam/Mona/Reporter), Christopher P. Walberg (Stinky), Sam Gifaldi (Sid), Justin Shenkarow (Harold), Blake Ewing (Eugene), Olivia Hack (Rhonda), Anndi McAfee (Phoebe), James Keane (Mr. Green/Riot Cop), Elizabeth Ashley (Mrs. Vitello), Michael Levin (Ray Doppel), Steve Viksten (Oskar), Dom Irrera (Ernie), Baoan Coleman (Mr. Hyunh), Craig Bartlett (Brainy/Murray/Grubby/Monkeyman)

THE FIRST $20 MILLION IS ALWAYS THE HARDEST

(20TH CENTURY FOX) Producer, Trevor Albert; Executive Producers, Harold Ramis, Neil Machlis; Director, Mick Jackson; Screenplay, Jon Favreau, Gary Tieche; Based on the novel by Po Bronson; Photography, Ron Garcia; Designer, William Sandell; Costumes, Jill Ohanneson; Editor, Don Brochu; Co-Producer, Michele Imperator Stabile; Associate Producer, Kym Bye; Music, Marco Beltrami; Music Supervisor, Sharon Boyle; Casting, Mindy Marin; a Trevor Albert/Ocean Pictures production; Dolby; Deluxe color; Rated PG-13; 105 minutes; Release date: June 28, 2002. CAST: Adam Garcia (Andy Caspar), Rosario Dawson (Alisa), Jake Busey (Darrell), Enrico Colantoni (Francis), Ethan Suplee (Tiny), Anjul Nigam (Salman), Gregory Jbara (Hank), Dan Butler (Lloyd), Linda Hart (Mrs. "B"), Shiva Rose (Terse), Chandra West (Robin), Robert Patrick Benedit (Willy), Heather Paige Kent (Claudia Goss), Stoney Westmoreland (Link), John M. Rothman (Ben), Andy Berman (Old Man), Reggie Lee (Suit), Brent Hinkley (Security Guard), Amy Van Horne (Blonde Money Honey), Dagney Kerr (Janie Hickenlocker), Jerry M. Haleva (Hologram Saddam), Victoria Kelleher (Woman with Pictures), Jonathan Klein (Dental Patient), Christopher Pérez (Passing Guy), Jerrod Cornish (Busboy), Chris B. Harrison (Wake-Up Newscaster), Gonzalo Menendez (Security Guard #2), Alice Davis, Katie Lohmann (Hottubbers), Laurel Ward, Nancy Honaker (Frisbee Girls), Paul McKinney (Griff), Diana Terranova (Screen Saver Stripper)

Gerald, Arnold in *Hey Arnold! The Movie* © Paramount

Adam Garcia, Jake Busey, Anjul Nigam, Ethan Suplee in *The First $20 Million Is Always the Hardest* © 20th Century Fox

S. Ann Hall, Nomy Lamm in *Group* © Artistic License

NEVER AGAIN

(FOCUS FEATURES) Producers, Eric Schaeffer, Terence Michael, Dawn Wolfrom, Bob Kravitz; Director/Screenplay, Eric Schaeffer; Photography, Tom Ostrowski; Designer, John Nyomarkay; Costumes, Eden Miller; Co-Producers, Noel Ashman, Brenda Kravitz; Line Producer, Annetta Marion; Music, Amanda Kravat; Casting, Adrienne Stern; a Five Minutes Before the Miracle production, presented in association with Amy Robinson Productions; Dolby; Color; Rated R; 97 minutes; Release date: July 12, 2002. CAST: Jeffrey Tambor (Christopher), Jill Clayburgh (Grace), Caroline Aaron (Elaine), Bill Duke (Earl), Sandy Duncan (Natasha), Michael McKean (Alex), Suzanne Shepherd (Mother), Lily Rabe (Tess), Dan'l Linehan (Leather Go-Go Boy), Bill Weeden (Mr. Speedy), Eric Axen (College Girl-Boy), David Bailey (Chad), Trazana Beverley (Night Nurse), Tom Cappadona, Charles Schroeder (Waiters), Caitlin Clarke (Allison), India Cooper (Nurse), Peter Dinklage (Harry Appleton), Jenny Kravat (Big Sister), Kasia Ostlun (College Girl), Douglas Ladnier (Craig), Meredith Lauren (Waitress/Body Double), Rachel Marteen (Carrie), Melissa Maxwell (Doctor), Dolores MacDougal (Mrs. Fienstein), Abigail Morgan, Anne Marie Leighton (Girls), Ebon Moss-Bacharach (Andy), James Noonan (Muscular Waiter), Peter Reardon (Runner), Manuel Santiago (Doorman), Eric Scott (Arthur), Edward Steele (Handicapped Man), Victor Truro (Sex Shop Clerk)

GROUP

(ARTISTIC LICENSE) Producers, Anne de Marcken, Marilyn Freeman; Director, Marilyn Freeman; Story, Anne de Marcken, Marilyn Freeman, in collaboration with the cast; Photography/Designer, Anne de Marcken; Editor, Tim Jenson; a Movie production; Color; Not rated; 90 minutes; Release date: July 5, 2002. CAST: Carrie Brownstein (Grace), Kari Fillipi (Clare), S. Ann Hall (Tody), Vicki Hollenberg (Violet), Tracy Kirkpatrick (Rachel), Nomy Lamm (Pipi), Ruby Martin (Ruby), Lola Rick N' Rolla (Rita), Tony Wilkerson (Clansey)

ELVIRA'S HAUNTED HILLS

(ELVIRA FILMS) Producer, Mark Pierson; Director, Sam Irvin; Screenplay, Cassandra Peterson, John Paragon; Photography, Viorel Sergovici; Designer, Radu Corciova; Costumes, Radu Corciova, Jerry Jackson; Music, Eric Allaman; Editor, Stephen R. Myers; Casting, Florin Chevorchian; Mediapro Pictures; Dolby; Color; Rated PG-13; 90 minutes; Release date: July 5, 2002. CAST: Cassandra Peterson (Elvira, Mistress of the Dark/Lady Elura Hessubus), Richard O'Brien (Lord Vladimere Hellsubus), Mary Scheer (Lady Ema Hellsubus, The Adultress), Scott Atkinson (Dr. Bradley Bradley, The Charlatan), Heather Hopper (Lady Roxana Hellsubus, Catalepsy Poster Child), Mary Jo Smith (Zou Zou), Gabi Andronache (Adran, Stable Stud), Lucia Maier (The Maid), Mark Pierson (The Butler), Theodor Danetti (The Innkeeper), Constantin Cotimanis (The Coachman), Remus Cernat (Nicholai Hellsubus), Jerry Jackson (The English Gentleman), Robert Dornhelm (Emissary), Rob Paulsen (Voice of Adrian)

LAST DANCE

(FIRST RUN FEATURES) Producers, Mirra Bank, Vic Losick; Director, Mirra Bank; Photography, Vic Losick; Associate Producer, Nancy Rosenthal; Editors, Mirra Bank, Axuce Espinosa; a Vic Losick Inc. & Nobody's Girls Inc. production; Color; Not rated; 84 minutes; Release date: July 12, 2002. Documentary on the collaboration between the dance company Pilobolus and author-illustrator Maurice Sendak, resulting in the work *A Selection;* featuring Maurice Sendak, Arthur Yorinks (The Night Kitchen Theater Artistic Directors), Robby Barnett, Michael Tracy, Jonathan Wolken (Pilobolus Dance Theatre Artistic Directors), Rebecca Anderson, Otis Cook, Josie Coyoc, Matt Kent, Gaspard Louis, Benjamin Pring (Pilobolus Dancers)

Jeffrey Tambor, Jill Clayburgh in *Never Again* © Focus Features

Mary Jo Smith, Cassandra Peterson in *Elvira's Haunted Hills* © Elvira Films

Last Dance © First Run Features

193

Jamie Lee Curtis in *Halloween: Resurrection* © Dimension

CHOICE OF WEAPONS

(OUTRIDER PICTURES) Producer/Director/Photography/Editor, Chris Dalrymple; Music, George Small; Color; not rated; 75 minutes; Release date: July 12, 2002. Documentary on five African-Americna competitive fencers, featuring Herby Raynaud, Peter Westbrook, Keeth Smart, Erinn Smart, Akhnaten Spencer-El, Harvey Miller, Ivan Lee, Mikail Sankora

HALLOWEEN: RESURRECTION

(DIMENSION) Producer, Paul Freeman; Executive Producer, Moustapha Akkad; Director, Rick Rosenthal; Screenplay, Larry Brand, Sean Hood; Story, Larry Brand; Based on characters created by John Carpenter; Co-Executive Producers, Bob Weinstein, Harvey Weinstein, Louis Spiegler, H. Daniel Gross; Photography, David Geddes; Designer, Troy Hansen; Costumes, Brad Gough; Music, Danny Lux; *Halloween* Theme, John Carpenter; Editor, Robert A. Ferretti; Visual Effects Supervisor, Jamison Goei; Casting, Ross Brown, Mary West, Robin Nassif, Patrick Baca; a Moustapha Akkad presentation of a Nightfall production; Distributed by Miramax Films; Dolby; Super 35 Widescreen; Color; Rated R; 89 minutes; Release date: July 12, 2002. CAST: Jamie Lee Curtis (Lauire Strode), Brad Loree (Michael Myers), Busta Rhymes (Freddie Harris), Bianca Kajlich (Sara Moyer), Sean Patrick Thomas (Rudy), Daisy McCrackin (Donna), Katee Sackhoff (Jen), Luke Kirby (Jim), Thomas Ian Nicholas (Bill), Ryan Merriman (Myles Barton), Tyra Banks (Nora), Billy Kay (Scott), Gus Lynch (Harold), Lorena Gale (Nurse Wells), Marisa Rudiak (Nurse Phillips), Brent Chapman (Franklin), Dan Joffre (Willie), Haig Sutherland (Aron), Brad Sihvon (Charley), Kelly Nielson, Gary Tunnicliffe (Officers), Ryan McDonald (Letter Sweater Guy), Charisse Baker (Teen Girl #2), Natassia Malthe (French Maid), Kyle Labine (Teen Party Guy), Rick Rosenthal (Professor), David Lewis (Bob Green), Chris Edwards (Fireman), Michael McCartney (Orderly), Ananda Thorson (Coroner)

DON'T ASK DON'T TELL

(CLICK IV ENTERTAINMENT) Producers, Tex Hauser, Jackie Eagan, Doug Miles; Director, Doug Miles; Conceived and Written by Tex Hauser, using the original 1954 RKO film *Killers from Space,* directed by W. Lee Wilder, written by Bill Raynor; Photography, George Gibson; Editor, Jackie Eagan; Music, Bruce Engler, Raj Halder, Spencer Miles; Wizzer D. and the Sophisticuffs; Black and white; Not rated; 73 minutes; Release date: July 12, 2002. A redubbed version of *Killers from Space*, which starred Peter Graves, Barbara Bestar, James Seay, Steve Pendleton, Frank Gerstle; VOICES: Lloyd Floyd, Rosa Rugosa, Erik Frandsen, Mike McCurry, Greg Roman.

EIGHT LEGGED FREAKS

(WARNER BROS.) Producers, Dean Devlin, Bruce Berman; Executive Producers, Roland Emmerich, Peter Winther, William Fay; Director, Ellory Elkayem; Screenplay, Jesse Alexander, Ellory Elkayem; Story, Ellory Elkayem, Randy Kornfield; Photography, John Bartley; Designer, Charles Breen; Costumes, Alix Friedberg; Editor, David J. Siegel; Co-Producer, Kelly Van Horn; Music, John Ottoman; Visual Effects Supervisors, Karen E. Goulekas, Thomas Dadras; Casting, April Webster, Paula Rosenberg; an Electric Entertainment production, presented in association with Village Roadshow Pictures and NPV Entertainment; Dolby; Super 35 Widescreen; Technicolor; Rated PG-13; 100 minutes; Release date: July 17, 2002. CAST: David Arquette (Chris McCormick), Kari Wuhrer (Sheriff Sam Parker), Scott Terra (Mike Parker), Scarlett Johansson (Ashley Parker), Doug E. Doug (Harlan Griffith), Rick Overton (Deputy Pete Willis), Leon Rippy (Mayor Wade), Matt Czuchry (Bret), Jay Arlen Jones (Leon), Eileen Ryan (Gladys), Riley Smith (Randy), Matt Holwick (Larry), Jane Edith Wilson (Emma), Jack Moore (Amos, the Truck Driver), Roy Gaintner (Floyd), Don Champlin (Leroy), John Christopher Storey (Mark), David "Earl" Waterman (Norman), Randi Klein, Terey Summers (Waitresses), John Ennis, Ryan C. Benson (Cops), Bruiser (Himself), Tom Noonan (Josh, Spider Farmer)

Dancing Aliens in *Don't Ask Don't Tell* © Click IV Entertainment

Eileen Ryan, David Arquette in *Eight Legged Freaks* © Warner Bros.

Bach, Tweedy, Stirratt, Kotche in
I Am Trying to Break Your Heart © Cowboy

Portia de Rossi, Christian Slater in
Who Is Cletis Tout? © Paramount Classics

BEING CLAUDINE

(FIRST GENERATION PRODS.) Produer/Director, I-fan Quirk; Co-Producer, Jackie Stolfi; Screenplay, I-fan Quirk, Justin Lichtman; Photography, Matthew Brookman; Designer, Greg Park; Music, Christopher McGlumphy; Editor, Mary Martin Torras; Color; Not rated; 85 minutes; Release date: July 19, 2002. CAST: Justine Lichtman (Claudine Bloomberg), Mushashi Alexander (Jack), James Bowman (Hans), Jordan Cael (Violet), Rose Arrick, Russ Vigilante, Reggi Wyns

I AM TRYING TO BREAK YOUR HEART

(COWBOY) Producers, Peter Abraham, Sam Jones; Executive Producer, Gary Hustwit; Director/Photography, Sam Jones; Co-Executive Producers, Albert Berger, Ron Yerxa; Editor, Erin Nordstrom; Music Supervisor, Tracy McKnight; Color; Not rated; 92 minutes; Release date: July 26, 2002. Documentary about the recording of the Chicago-based rock group Wilco's fourth album, *Yankee Hotel Foxtrot*, featuring Jeff Tweedy, John Stirratt, Leroy Bach, Glenn Kotche, Jay Bennett (Wilco); Greg Kot, Tony Margherita, Jonathan Parker, Fred Armisen, Daniel Herbst, Fred Longberg Holm, Christ Brickley, Ron Lowe, Jim O'Rourke, Jason Tobias, Bill Bentley, Wes Orshoski, Howie Klein, David Fricke, Miiri Kotche, Chris Green, Lin Brehmer, Marty Lennartz, Jonathan Valania, Josh Greir, Sam Tweedy, Susan Miller Tweedy, Spencer Tweedy, David Bither

WHO IS CLETIS TOUT?

(PARAMOUNT CLASSICS) Producers, Matthew Grimaldi, Robert Snukal, Daniel Grodnik, Jay Firestone, Adam Haight; Executive Producer, Daniel Diamond; Co-Producers, Dennis Murphy, Mary Jo Slater, Tony Thatcher, Michael Philip, Eric Sandys; Director/Screenplay, Chris Ver Wiel; Photography, Jerzy Zielinski; Designer, Charles Rosen; Costumes, Betsy Cox; Editor, Roger Bondelli; Music, Randy Edelman; a Fireworks Pictures and Peter Hoffman presentation of a Fireworks Entertainment/Itasca Pictures Production in association with Nichol Moon Films; U.S.-Canadian, 2001; Dolby; Super 35 Widescreen; Color; Rated R; 92 minutes; Release date: July 26, 2002. CAST: Christian Slater (Trevor Allen Finch), Tim Allen (Critical Jim), Portia de Rossi (Tess Donnelly), Richard Dreyfuss (Micah Donnelly), Billy Connolly (Dr. Savian), Peter MacNeil (Detective Tripp), Elias Zarou (Det. Delaney), Richard Chevolleau (Det. Horst), RuPaul (Ginger Markum), Joseph Scoren (Rowdy Virago), Eugene Lipinski (Falco), Shawn Doyle (Crow Gollotti), Louis Di Bianco (Nimble), Tony Nappo (Fife), Tim Progosh (Young Micah), Alan Peterson (Henry Flatt), Danny Lima (Cletis Tout), Kay Tremblay (Old Mrs. Stanton), Rachel Grodnik (Young Tess), Tannis Burnett (Nun), Michael Filipowich (Dodger Blue), B.J. McQueen (Yard Prison Guard), Kevin Rushton (Road Work Prison Guard), Rick Demas (Cell Block Prison Guard), Quancetia Hamilton (Receptionist), Corinne Jenner (Merrill Candide), Mauricio Rodas (Tough No. 1), Diego Fuentes (Big Tough)

GAZA STRIP

(INDEPENDENT) Producer/Director/Editor/Music, James Longley; Photography, James Longley, Abed Shana; Little Red Button productions; Dolby; Super 35 Widescreen; Color; Not rated; 74 minutes; Release date: August 1, 2002. Documentary on the Israeli Defence Force and their methods of combating Palestinians.

MARTIN LAWRENCE LIVE: RUNTELDAT

(PARAMOUNT) Producers, Michael Hubbard, Beth Hubbard, David Gale, Loretha Jones; Executive Producers, Martin Lawrence, Robert Lawrence, Van Toffler; Director, David Raynr; Co-Producers, Michael Cole, Momita Sengupta; Photography, Daryn Okada; Designer, Richard Hoover; Editor, Nicholas Eliopoulos; Associate Producer, Sean Lampkin; Dolby; Color; Rated R; 104 minutes; Release date: August 2, 2002. Comedian Martin Lawrence in concert.

Martin Lawrence in *Martin Lawrence Live: Runteldat*
© Paramount

STRIPPED

(VISION FILMS/DYLAN PRODS.) Producers, Jill Morley, Nelson Ryland; Director/Screenplay, Jill Morley; Photography, Peter Klusman, Josh Horowitz, Valerie Barnes, John Rosenblatt, John Petrocelli, Rob Klug, Jill Morley; Editor, Nelson Ryland; Color; Not rated; 74 minutes; Release date: August 9, 2002. Documentary on strippers, with Billie, Vicki, Angela, and Susan.

THE ADVENTURES OF PLUTO NASH

(WARNER BROS.) Producers, Martin Bregman, Michael Bregman, Louis A. Stroller; Executive Producer, Bruce Berman; Director, Ron Underwood; Screenplay, Neil Cuthbert; Photography, Oliver Wood; Designer, Bill Brzeski; Costumes, Ha Nguyen; Editors, Paul Hirsch, Alan Heim; Music, John Powell; Visual Effects Supervisor, Nick Davis; Co-Producers, Frank Capra III, Michael Klawitter; a Castle Rock Entertainment presentation in association with Village Roadshow Pictures and NPV Entertainment of a Bregman production; Dolby; Technicolor; Rated PG-13; 95 minutes; Release date: August 16, 2002. CAST: Eddie Murphy (Pluto Nash), Randy Quaid (Bruno), Rosario Dawson (Dina Lake), Joe Pantoliano (Mogan), Jay Mohr (Tony Francis), Luis Guzman (Felix Laraga), James Rebhorn (Belcher), Peter Boyle (Rowland), Burt Young (Gino), Miguel A. Nunez, Jr. (Miguel), Pam Grier (Flura Nash), John Cleese (James), Victor Varnado (Kelp), Illeana Douglas (Dr. Mona Zimmer), Jacynthe René (Babette), Alissa Kramer (Filomina Francis), Lillo Brancato (Larry), Alex Sol (Tommy), Doug Spinozza (Doug), Andrée Fafard (Holographic Spokesmodel), Stu "Large" Riley (Club Pluto Bouncer), Roc Lafortune (Jimmy), Russell Yuen (Oliver), Bill Corday (Roy), Angela Perzow (Robot Maid), Ezra Franklyn (Robot Thug), Don Jordan (Reporter), Lorca Simons (Pretty Reporter), Eric Hoziel (Johnson), Christopher Bregman (Michalak), Marlon Long (Lindsey), Mary Hammett (Holographic Nurse), Serge Houde (FBI Agent), Jonathan Stark (Desk Clerk), Terry Haig (Security Guard), Roger Reid (Pit Boss), Michael Rudder (Croupier), Alexandre Bisping (Ted Jefferies), Cornelia Sharpe Bregman (Tony Francis Fan), Mark Camacho (Robot Holding Cell Clerk), Lana Underwood (Sexy Robot), Alec Baldwin (M.C.M.)

BOXHEAD REVOLUTION

(FINDARTFILMS.COM) Producer/Director/Photography/Designer/Editor, Mark Christensen; Screenplay, Mark Christensen, Brian Hamill; Music, Ant Man Bee; Special Effects, Josh Beaneatte; Black and white; Not rated; 76 minutes; Release date: August 21, 2002. CAST: Adam Cooper (Grit), Jenny Kim (Brythle), Amy Davenport (Mom), Dan Farren (Dad), Heather Watson (Humie), Mark Christensen (Villain), James Berry (Tin), Susan Warner, Brian Hamill (Voices)

Stripped © Vision Films/Dylan Prods.

Rosario Dawson, Randy Quaid, Eddie Murphy in
The Adventures of Pluto Nash © Warner Bros.

SERVING SARA

(PARAMOUNT) Producer, Dan Halsted; Executive Producer, Dan Kolsrud; Director, Reginald Hudlin; Screenplay, Jay Scherick, David Ronn; Photography, Robert Brinkmann; Designer, Rusty Smith; Costumes, Francine Jamison-Tanchuck; Editor, Jim Miller; Music, Marcus Miller; Casting, Heidi Levitt, Monika Mikkelsen; a Mandalay Pictures presentation of an Illusion/Halsted Pictures production; Dolby; Deluxe color; Rated PG-13; 100 minutes; Release date: August 23, 2002. CAST: Matthew Perry (Joe Tyler), Elizabeth Hurley (Sara Moore), Vincent Pastore (Tony), Bruce Campbell (Gordon Moore), Cedric the Entertainer (Ray Harris), Amy Adams (Kate), Terry Crews (Vernon), Jerry Stiller (Milton the Cop), Marshall Bell (Warren Cebron), Derek Southers (Bouncer), Alan Ackles (Man in Elevator), Robin McGee (Jimmy the Elevator Operator), Brent Duncan (Blackjack Dealer), Eli Jacques (Woman at Blackjack Table), John Wayne Shafer (Pit Boss), Joe Viterelli (Fat Charlie), Vince Cecere (Aldo), Tony Longo (Petey), Roderick Watson (Kid with Walkie Talkie), Georgia Foy (Ray's Secretary), Marie Miranda (Elderly Woman in Elevator), Alaina Kalanj (Spa Receptionist), Heather Hunt (Swamp Thing at Spa), Melinda Ramos Renna (Saleswoman in Boutique), Maria Arita (Reservations Clerk), Mary Lyons (Amanda), Jim Wikley (Bus Driver), Hal Rawley (Judge), Coati Mundi (Miami Cab Driver), Julio Cedillo (Marriott Hotel Clerk), Andrew Wilson (Mr. Andrews), John Rawley (Moore Company Employee), Robert D. McTeer (Moore Company Executive), Ouida White (Doris), Paul Schulte (Man in Wheelchair), Kelley Saunders (Denise the Ticket Agent), Cheryl Akemi Toma (Japanese Interpreter), Paul Fujimoto (Japanese Businessman), Don Piri, Wally Welch, Toby Metcalf (Cowboys), Ramsey Williams (Nurse), Ruth Osuna (Maria), Libby Villari (Cowgirl Waitress), Amanda Denton (Tony's Flight Attendant), Court Young (Arena Ticket Collector), David Scott Heck (Rusty the Scoreboard Guy), Rick Morrow (Man in Crowd), Nikki Ziering (Gordon's Trainer), Mike Judge (Motel Clerk)

Jenny Kim, Adam Cooper in *Boxhead Revolution*
© Findartfilms.com

LITTLE SECRETS

(TRISTAR/GOLDWYN) Producers, Don Schain, Blair Treu, Jessica Baronides; Director, Blair Treu: Screenplay, Jessica Baronides; Photography, Brian Sullivan; Designer, Gary Griffin Constable; Costumes, Lanny Sikes; Editor, Jerry Stayner; Music, Sam Cardon; Dolby; Color; Rated PG; 107 minutes; Release date: August 23, 2002. CAST: Evan Rachel Wood (Emily), Michael Angarano (Philip), David Gallagher (David), Vivica A. Fox (Pauline), Jan Broberg Felt (Caroline), Rick Macy (Eddie), Paul Kiernan (Don), Tayva Pattch (Elaine), Micah Schow (Gregoray), Caitlin Meyer (Isabelle), Landon Kunzelman (Mikey), Danielle Chuchran (Lea), Haley McCormick (Jenny), Rudee Lipscomb (Laurel), Carli Treu, Erica Angarano (Girls), Matthew Grace (Harold), Joey Miyashima (Dr. Mezzie), Janice Knickrehm (Mrs. Neiderhoffer), Wayne Brennan (Gump's Secretary), Elizabeth Grand (Greenbacks Saleswoman), Micaela Nelligan (Gregory's Mother), Dustin Harding (Jordan), Clara Susan Morey III (Bohemian Woman), Carlton Bluford (Oboe Player), Robin Ballard (Elderly Woman), Tracy Scott (Doctor), Christy Summerhays, Queenie Aydelott (Nurses)

Michael Angarano, Evan Rachel Wood, David Gallagher in *Little Secrets* © TriStar/Goldwyn

AMY'S ORGASM

(MAGIC LAMP) Producers, Julie Davis, Fred Kramer; Executive Producers, Scott Mandell, David Straus; Co-Executive Producers, Jeanette Volturno, Trey Wilkins; Line Producer, Gary Kout; Director/Screenplay/Editor, Julie Davis; Photography, Mark Mervis; Music, Miriam Cutler; Casting, Nancy Nayor; a Serious Dan presentation in association with Without a Box and Catchlight Films; Dolby; Color; Not rated; 87 minutes; Release date: August 23, 2002. CAST: Julie Davis (Amy Mandell), Nick Chinlund (Matthew Starr), Caroline Aaron (Janet Gaines), Mitchell Whitfield (Don), Jennifer Bransford (Elizabeth), Jeff Cesario (Priest), Mary Ellen Trainor (Amy's Mom), Charles Cioffi (Amy's Dad), Tina Lifford (Irene Barris), Michael Harris (Jerry Hegeman), Vincent Castellanos (Hans), Kira Reed (Shannon Steele), Mark Brown (Mike), Nell Balaban (Tina), Wally Kurth (Beautiful Guy), Andrea Bendewald (Beautiful Girl), Cirri Nottage (Cherry Goldstein), Steve O'Connor (Kirk), Jackie Debatin (Susan), Carrie Genzel (Michelle), Julie Bowen (Nikki), Bette Hurwitz (Belle), Sara Van Horn (Supportive Fan), J.R. Smith (Angry Fan), Emily Wagner (Prim Girl), Bob Harvey (Interviewer), David Malek (Sleazy Controller), Bob Riley (Masturbating Man), Lori Rozman (Masturbating Woman), Dave Noonan (Fantasy Priest), Jerry Penacoli (Himself), Patrick Egan (Michael Hendricks), Marissa Jaret Winokur (Radio P.A.), Don Bloomfield (Radio Host), Joe Neulight (Angry Caller), Robbin Wood (Radio Slut), Stephen Polk (Bill)

Julie Davis, Nick Chinlund in *Amy's Orgasm* © Magic Lamp

Nelly in *Snipes* © Innovation Film Group

SNIPES

(INNOVATION FILM GROUP) Producer, Rich Murray; Executive Producer, Chris Schwartz; Director, Rich Murray; Screenplay, Rob Wiser, Rich Murray; Photography, Alexander Buono; Designer, David Barnes; Costumes, Fontella Boone; Music, Nelly; Editor, Seth Anderson; Line Producer, Michael J. Zampino; a Ruff Nation Films production; Dolby; Color; Rated R; 113 minutes; Release date: September 4, 2002. CAST: Sam Jones III (Erik), Nelly (Prolifik/Clarence), Zoe Saldana (Cheryl), Dean Winters (Bobby Starr), Rashaan Nall (Floyd), Schooly D. (Tony), Joel Garland (Ceaser), J.D. Williams (J.D.), Mpho Koaho (Malik), Victor Togunde (Midas), Carlo Alban (Bugsy), Rich Heidelberg (Donnie), Charli Baltimore (Trix), Frank Vincent (Johnni Marandino), Johnnie Hobbs, Jr. (Mr. Triggs), Ophelia M. Turner (Grandmother), Jessica Rodriguez (Receptionist), Heather Hunter (Lucinda), Larry Mendte (TV Anchor), Kevin Anthony (Motel Clerk), Andy Ranley (Egineer), Sal Darigo (Jimmy Bones)

Elizabeth Hurley, Matthew Perry in *Serving Sara* © Paramount

THE BURNING SENSATION

(E FILM STUDIOS) Producers, Alex Nohe, Alan Roberts; Director, Alex Nohe; Co-Producer, Travis Harrod; Associate Producers, Chuck Cirino, Duane Weaver; Photography, Alex Nohe, Pilar Otero, David Smith, Chris Strong, Ted Trost; Editors, James Frisa, Cassandra Marshall; Music Supervisor, Charles Raggio; Color; Not rated; 75 minutes; Release date: September 6, 2002. Documentary on the 2001 "Burning Man" experience, when some 20,000 people made a pilgrimage to the Black Rock Desert for this ritual of self-expression.

HEARTBREAK HOSPITAL

(SEVENTH ART) Producers, Ram Bergman, Lemore Syvan Ruedi Gerber, Dana Lustig; Director, Ruedi Gerber; Screenplay, Henry Slesar, Ruedi Gerber; Photography, Wolfgang Held; Art Director, Shawn Carol; Music, John Davis; Editor, Sabine Krayenbühl; a Bergman Lustig Productions, Goldheart Pictures and ZAS Films presentation; Technicolor; Not rated; 91 minutes; Release date: September 6, 2002. CAST: Chelsea Altman (Nelly Kendall), Patricia Clarkson (Lottie Ohrwasher), Diane Venora (Sunday Tyler/Andrea Harmon), John Shea (Milo Derringer/Dr. Jonathan), Demian Bichir (Tonio), Robert LuPone (Hal), Annie Meisels (Susan), Samantha Buck (Sandy), Lou Martini, Jr. (Restaurant Manager), Michael Hannon (Theater Director), Gilberto Gonzalez (Street Vendor), Kate Blumberg (Young Actress), Erik Jensen (HH Producer), Kevin Draine (HH Director), Jeffrey Ross (Norman Radcliff), LaChanze (Lisa), Jared Ryan (Evan the PA), Michael Watson (Chris, Wardrobe), Phyllis Meryl (Sopa Fan), Mario Bosco (Little Boy Fan), Bob Greenberg (Security Guard, Reception), Scott Roberson (Police Officer #1), Cynthia Webb-Manly (Nurse), Malachy Cleary (Lt. Cobb), Harrison Lee (Detective Grady), Robert Bogue (Newscaster), Nick Gregory (David, Studio Executive), Paulette Rubinstein (Cleaning Woman), Howard Spiegel (Minister), Michael Bourne (Radio Announcer)

The Book Man in *The Burning Sensation* © E Film Studios

John Shea, Chelsea Altman in
Heartbreak Hospital © Seventh Art

Wanda Jean Allen in *The Execution of Wanda Jean* © Seventh Art

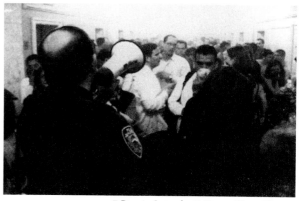

7 Days in September © CameraPlanet Pictures

THE EXECUTION OF WANDA JEAN

(SEVENTH ART) Producers, Liz Garbus, Rory Kennedy; Director, Liz Garbus; Photography, Tony Hardmon; Editor, Mary Manhardt; Music, Wendy Blackstone; Line Producer, Julie Gaither; Color; 87 minutes; Release date: September 6, 2002. Documentary focusing on the last three months in the life of Wanda Jean Allen, who was executed in Oklahoma in January of 2001, almost 12 years after she shot her lover.

7 DAYS IN SEPTEMBER

(CAMERAPLANET PICTURES) Producer/Director, Steven Rosenbaum; Executive Producers, Steve Carlis, Steven Rosenbaum; Co-Producers, Lori Fechter, Dave Goldberg, Pamela Yoder; Supervising Producer, Bruce Kennedy; Editor, Marc Senter; Segment Editor, Mustafa Bhagat; Color; Not rated; September 6, 2002. Documentary looking at the events of September 11, 2001, and the week following the aftermath of the terrorist attacks on New York City, as covered by the following filmmakers: Justin Adler, Bruce Cotler, Mike Cunga, Peter Dipilato, Brian Gately, Jim Goetz, Sumner Glimcher, Dmitry Kibrik, Harry Lapham, Robert Lieblein, Kyle McCabe, King Molapo, Seamus Mills, Roy Nelson, Gary Pollard, Michael Rey, Max Rosenbaum, Alan Roth, Rob Santana, Jennifer Spell, Jenny Tolan, Brian Tunney, Scott Vandervoort, Sherwin Winick.

LOW HEIGHTS

(INDEPENDENT) Producer, Manouchehr Mohammadi; Director/Screenplay, Ebrahim Hatamikia; Photography, Hassan Pouya; Music, Mohammad Rez Aliqoli; Editor, Haydeh Safiyari; Iranian; Dolby; Color; Not rated; 115 minutes; American release date: September 12, 2002. CAST: Hamid Farokhnezad (Ghasem), Leila Hatami (Narges), Gohar Kheirandish (Atieh), Ahmad Kavari, Mehdi Saki

STEALING HARVARD

(COLUMBIA) Producer, Susan Cavan; Executive Producers, Howard Lapides, Chris Brancato, Albert J. Salke, Maureen Peyrot; Director, Bruce McCulloch; Screenplay, Peter Tolan; Story, Martin Hynes, Peter Tolan; Photography, Ueli Steiger; Designer, Gregory Keen; Editor, Malcolm Campbell; a Revolution Studios and Imagine Entertainment presentation; Dolby; Color; Deluxe color; Rated PG-13; 83 minutes; Release date: September 13, 2002. CAST: Jason Lee (John Plummer), Tom Green (Duff), Leslie Mann (Elaine), Megan Mullally (Patty), Dennis Farina (Mr. Warner), Tammy Blanchard (Noreen), Richard Jenkins (Mr. Cook), Chris Penn (David Loach), John C. McGinley (Det. Charles), Seymour Cassel (Uncle Jack), Zeus (Rex the Dog), Ken Magee (Butcher), Martin Starr (Liquor Store Kid), Mary Gillis (Duff's Mom), Bruce McCulloch (Fidio the Lawyer), Ashlynn Rose (Younger Noreen), Lorna Scott (Aunt Jean), Bobby Harwell (Uncle Dave), Jeanette Miller (Grandma), Gabe Laskin, Ashley Bishop (Underage Kids), Pamela Gordon (Loretta), Tracy Ryan (Toy Store Salesperson), Marshall Manesh (Toy Store Manager), Nick Offerman, Paul Feig (Electricians), Shane Wayton (Kid in Tree), Vinnie Curto, Don Wilson (Loach's Friends), Gilbert Rosales, Thomas Rosales (Loach's Bandits), Steffiana Dela Cruz (Coach's Girlfriend), Ernie Grunwald (Lineup Man), Channing Chase (Neighbor Lady), Brian Galyean, Susan Solari, Courtney Black (Phone Sales), Terita Jackson (Noreen's Harvard Roommate), Frank Welker (Special Vocal Effects)

THE DOGWALKER

(OUTRIDER) Producer, Vera Anderson; Executive Producers, Lon Bender, Wylie Stateman; Co-Producers, Roderick Spencer, Stacy Leah Winkler; Director/Screenplay, Paul Duran; Photography, Dean Lent; Designer, Teri Whitaker; Editor, Julie Rogers; Music, Joseph L. Altruda; Casting, Jennifer Fishman; a production of Rita Films; Dolby; Color; Not rated; 105 minutes; Release date: September 13, 2002. CAST: Will Stewart (Jerry), Stepfanie Kramer (Helene), Tony Todd (Mones), John Randolph (Ike), Cress Williams (K.C.), Walter Jones (Blonde), Carol Gustafson (Alma), Nicki Lynn Aycox (Susan), Allan Rich (Sam), Stacey Williams (Darlene), Murray Leaward (Abe), Tony Carreiro (Don), Gabe Dell (The Musician)

Jason Lee, Leslie Mann in *Stealing Harvard* © Columbia

TED BUNDY

(TARTAN/OVERSEAS FILMGROUP) a.k.a. *Bundy*; Producers, Hamish McAlpine, Michael Muscal; Co-Producer, Françoise Gillard; Photography, Sonja Rom; Designer, Chris Anthony Miller; Costumes, Elena Baranova, Kristin Persson; Music, Kennard Ramsey; Editor, Paul Heiman; Special Make-up Effects, Tom Savini; Casting, Johanna Ray; Color; Rated R; 99 minutes; Release date: September 13, 2002. CAST: Michael Reilly Burke (Ted Bundy), Boti Ann Bliss (Lee), Julianna McCarthy (Professor), Jennifer Tisdale (Pretty Girl), Michael Santos (Man at the Window), Anna Lee Wooster (Girl Attacked in the Street), Steffani Brass (Julie), Tricia Dickson (Vincennes), Meadow Sisto (Welch), Eric Dare, Melissa Schmidt (Partygoers), Deborah Offner (Beverly), Zarah Little (Garber), Alison West (Randall), Matt Hoffman (Arnie), Renee Madison Cole (Cutler), Orly Tepper (Dead Girl in Woods), Jason Collins (Washington Cop), Michael Keeley (Washington Detective), Diana Kaufmann (Fitz), Zak Ruben, Laura Robb, Emily Stofle, Susan Featherly (Bundy Victims), Tiffany Shepis (Gambler), Katrina Miller (Gilcrest), Rachel Rowan (Bell), J. Marvin Campbell (Utah Highway Trooper), Tom Savini (Salt Lake City Detective), Gary Walton (Guard), Marina Black (Kate), Sharon McWilliams (Aspen Deputy), Alexa Jago (Betty), Michael Meredith (Garfield Guard), Carol Mansell (Mrs. Myers), Rachael MacKenna (Cassidy), Brigett Butler (Davidson), Holly Towne (Lopez), Phoebe Dollar (Richardson), Deanna Dylan (Chi Omega Victim), Natasha Goodman (Moore), J. Ray (Bruster), Bobby King (Florida State Trooper), Randy Polk (Minister), David Schroeder (Warden), Joseph McDouglas (Florida Guard "Joe"), Wayne Morse (Florida Guard "Bob"), Steven Whelan (Florida Guard "Smiley"), Danielle Parris (Executioner), Jim Kundig (Lee's Husband), Jesse James Rutherford, Oliver Kindred, Timothy Deeters, Alexa Nikolas ("I'm Ted" Kids)

FILM #18, MAHAGONNY

(ANTHOLOGY FILM ARCHIVES/HARRY SMITH ARCHIVES) Producer/Director/Photography/Editor, Harry Smith; Music, Kurt Weill; Libretto, Bertolt Brecht; Performed by the North German Radio Chorus, starring Lotte Lenya; Color; Not rated; 141 minutes; Release date: September 13, 2002. An experimental feature of images set to the music of the Brecht-Weill opera *The Rise and Fall of the City of Mahagonny*.

CIAO AMERICA

(MAVEX PRODUCTIONS) Producer, Roger Marino; Executive Producers, Conchita Airoldi, Dino Di Dionisio; Director, Frank Ciota; Screenplay, Joseph A. Ciota; Photography, Giulio Pietromarchi; Designer, Enrico Serafini; Music, Andrea Morricone; Editor, Tia Schellstede; Casting, Sheila Jaffe, Shaila Rubin, Georgianne Walken; a co-production of Urania Pictures, Revere Productions; Dolby; Color; Rated R; 100 minutes; Release date: September 20, 2002. CAST: Eddie Malavarca (Lorenzo Primavera), Maurizio Nichetti (Giulio Fellini), Violante Placido (Paola Angelini), Nathaniel Marston (Skip Cromwell), Anthony DeSando (Frank Mantovani), Giancarlo Giannini (Zi' Felice), Paul Sorvino (Antonio Primavera), Reynolds "Rene" Alexander (Referee), Vittorio Amandola (Professor Angelini), Vincenzo Amato (Bongo), Giancarlo Baldini (Lamberto), Marco Basile (Giova), Michele Bertelli (Massimo Ferrarese), Primo Boarin (Man Knocked Off Bike), Vanni Borghi (Train Conductor), Marco Calura (Enzo), Eleanora Carpanelli (Chiara), Franco Casoni (Borghetti), Riccardo Cervellati (Romano), Anthony Di Nanno (Young Lorenzo), Elena Felloni, Daniele Landini, Luca Landini, Vincenzo Li Volzi, Anthony "Ando" Meoli (Referees), Giacomo Ferrari (Baby Mantovani), Umberto Franchini (Ruzzi), Lorenzo Greghi (Bologna Coach), Pierpaolo Lovino (Alex Guio), Roger Marino (Head Referee), Lorenza Mazzetti (Paola's Mother), Emanuele Morandi (Casone), Claudia Gamberini Moretti (Isabella), Paolo Napizia (Morandi), Elisa Soffritti (Alessia), Michele Ventorre (Zuffi)

Lucy Liu, Antonio Banderas in *Ballistic: Ecks vs. Sever* © Warner Bros.

THE MESMERIST

(SEVENTH ART) Producers, Terry Dougas, Peter Raskin; Executive Producer, Barbara De Fina; Co-Producers, Jack Ernades, Michael Feifer, Kostas Sommer; Director, Gil Cates, Jr.; Screenplay, Michael A. Goorjian, Ron Marasco; Photography, Tom Harting; Designer, Aaron Osborne; Costumes, Mimi Maxmen; Music, Brahm Wenger; Casting, Barbara Fiorentino; a Roxbury Films production; Color; Not rated; 95 minutes; Release date: September 20, 2002. CAST: Neil Patrick Harris (Benjamin), Jessica Capshaw (Daisy), Howard Hesseman (Mr. Valdemar), Jason Carter (Dr. Pretory), Jo Champa (Consuela), George Wyner (Dr. Hoffler), Galina Jovovich (Mother), Michael A. Goorjian, Richmond Arquette (Coroners)

BALLISTIC: ECKS VS. SEVER

(WARNER BROS.) Producers, Elie Samaha, Chris Lee, Kaos; Executive Producers, Andrew Stevens, Tarak Ben Ammar, Tracee Stanley; Director, Kaos (Wych Kaosayananda); Screenplay, Alan McElroy; Photography, Julio Macat; Designer, Doug Higgins; Costumes, Magali Guidasci; Editors, Jay Cassidy, Caroline Ross; Co-Producers, James Holt, Peter M. Lenkov; Line Poruder, Andrew Sugerman; Music, Don Davis; Music Supervisor, Michael Lloyd; Casting, Jeff Gerard; Stunts, Joel J. Kramer, Melissa R. Stubbs; Fight Choreographer, Philip Tan; a Chris Lee/Franchise Pictures production; U.S.-German; Dolby; Super 35 Widescreen; Technicolor; Rated R; 91 minutes; Release date: September 20, 2002. CAST: Antonio Banderas (Jeremiah Ecks), Lucy Liu (Sever), Gregg Henry (Gant/Clark), Ray Park (Ross), Talisa Soto (Vinn/Rayne), Miguel Sandoval (Julio Martin), Terry Chen (Harry), Roger R. Cross (Zane), Sandrine Holt (Agent Bennett), Steve Bacic (Agent Fleming), Aidan Drummond (Michael), Eric Breker (Agent Curtis), Tony Alcantar (Edgar Moore), David Parker (Dark Suit #1), Josephine Jacob (Pretty Girl), David Palffy (Sleazy Man), David Allan Pearson (VPD Officer, Sc. 73), John McConnach (Escort Agent, Sc. 111), Norm Sherry (Ross Sniper), Brian Drummond (VPD Officer, Sc. 116), Ashley Kobayashi (Mali), Lenora Wong (Harry's Wife), Joel J. Kramer (Bus Driver), John De Santis (Bus Guard #2), Charles Andre (Agent Addis), Mike Dopud (DIA Agent, Sc. 36, 154), Scott Leva (Lone Sniper), Jim Filippone (DIA Pilot)

Graham Greene in *Skins* © First Look Pictures

DAYDREAM BELIEVER

(IN THE RAW PRODS.) Producer/Director/Screenplay/Photography/Editor, Debra Eisenstadt; Music, Jennifer Jackson; Associate Producer, Sybil Kempson; Color; Not rated; 79 minutes; Release date: September 25, 2002. CAST: Sybil Kempson (Valerie Woodbury), Gladden Schrock (Boyd), Wendy Lawrence (Wendy), Louis Puopolo (Kent Black), Andrew Hernon (Carl), Jacqueline Knapp (Margot), Sherri Parker Lee (Pamella), Tom McWilliams (Marty), Gail Blobner (Mother), Jacqueline Cohen (Agent), Jodi Melnick (Photographer), Suzanne Griffin (Temp Agent), Heather Beckett (Jackie), Jason Eksuzian (Tom), Steve MacKinney (Mini-Storage Man), Rayme Lyn Cornell (Party Woman), Phil Nelson (Party Man), John Savilove, Eddie Reagan (Temp Talent Show Flirtations)

CHARLY

(EXCEL ENTERTAINMENT GROUP) Producers, Micah Merrill, Lance C. Williams; Executive Producer, Herbert Christensen; Director, Adam Thomas Anderegg; Screenplay, Janine Whetton Gilbert; Based on the novel by Jack Weyland; Photography, Bengt Jan Jonsson; Designer, Kee Miller; Editor, M. William Merrill; Music, Aaron Merrill; a Cinergy Films, in association with Kaleidoscope Pictures and Focused Light Films presentation; Color; Rated PG; 103 minutes; Release date: September 27, 2002. CAST: Heather Beers (Charlene "Charly" Riley), Gary Neilson (Edward Riley), Lisa McCammon (Claire Riley), Jackie Winterrose-Fullerup (Ena Riley), Jeremy Elliott (Sam Roberts), Randy King (Frank Roberts), Diana Dunkley (JoEllen Roberts), Adam Johnson (Mark Randolph), Bernie Diamond (Rafferty)

Jeremy Elliott, Heather Beers in *Charly* © Excel Entertainment Group

SKINS

(FIRST LOOK PICTURES) Producer, Jon Kilik; Executive Producers, Dave Pomier, Chris Cooney, Jeff Cooney; Director, Chris Eyre; Screenplay, Jennifer D. Lyne; Based on the novel by Adrian C. Louis; Co-Producers, Chris Eyre, Jennifer D. Lyne, Eugene Mazzola; Photography, Stephen Kazmierski; Designer, Debbie Devilla; Costumes, Ronald Leamon; Music, BC Smith; Editor, Paul Trejo; Casting, René Haynes; a Starz Encore Entertainment, Aboriginal Peoples Television Network and Jon Kilik presentation of a a Grandview Pictures production; Dolby; Color; Rated R; 87 minutes; Release date: September 27, 2002. CAST: Graham Greene (Mogie Yellow Lodge), Eric Schweig (Rudy Yellow Lodge), Joseph American Horse (Panhandler), Nathaniel Arcand (Teen Mogie), Wilda Asimont (Neighbor), David Bald Eagle (Old Soldier), Bruce Bennett (Medical Examiner), Robert A. Bennett (Officer Comes Running), Gil Birmingham (Sonny Yellow Lodge), Joe Black Elk (Drill Team Member #2), Kato Buss (ER Doctor), Jenny Cheng (Anchor Woman), Gerald Tokala Clifford (Black Lodge Boy), Dale Cooks With Lightning, Jr. (Young Storks), Chris Eyre (Cop), Gary Farmer (Verdell Weasel Tail), Larry Dean Fuss (FBI Agent), Leonard George (Captain Eagleman), James Hatzell (Hardware Clerk), Jacob Hjorten (Liquor Store Clerk), Gansler Janis, Charles White Elk (Drill Team Members), Tina Keeper (Dr. Fitzgerald), Zahn McClarnon (Elton Blue Cloud), Elaine Miles (Rondella Roubaix), Renae Morriseau (Evangeline Yellow Lodge), Dillon Nelson (Young Mogie), Canku One Star (Young Rudy), Yellow Pony Pettibone (Corky Red Tail), Lois Red Elk (Aunt Helen), Myrton Running Wolf (Ed Little Bald Eagle), Michael Spears (Mr. Green Laces), Chaske Spencer (Teen Rudy), Larry Swalley (Shift Commander), Michelle Thrush (Stella), Misty Upham (Mrs. Blue Cloud), Markus J. Volimas (Wally Roubaix), Noah Watts (Herbie Yellow Lodge), Lisa White Face (Wallina Four Strikes)

CRAZY AS HELL

(ARTISTIC LICENSE) Producers, Ken Aguado, D.J. Caruso, Michael Huens, Eriq La Salle, Butch Robinson; Director, Eriq La Salle; Screenplay, Jeremy Leven, Erik Jendresen; Based on the novel *Satan* by Jeremy Leven; Photography, George Mooradian; Designer, Charles Lagola; Art Director, David Blass; Costumes, Donna Berwick; Music, Billy Childs; Editor, Troy Takaki; Casting, Lynn Kressel; a Humble Journey Films, Loose Screw Films production; Dolby; Deluxe color; Rated R; 113 minutes; Release date: September 27, 2002. CAST: Eriq La Salle (The Man), Michael Beach (Dr. Ty Adams), Ronny Cox (Dr. Delazo), John C. McGinley (Parker), Sinbad (Orderly), Tia Texada (Lupa), Tracy Pettit (Cheryl), William Bassett (Mr. Brennan), Twink Caplan (Suzanne), Tom Everett (Mansell), Roberta Haze (Ms. Aslee), Khylan Jones (Brianna), J.P. Manoux (Arnie), Jim Ortlieb (Mr. Tobin), Shelly Robertson (Veda), Ray Xifo (Selden), Chris Gann (Shirtless Man)

Eriq LaSalle in *Crazy as Hell* © Artistic License

Marisa Tomei, Ron Eldard, Kyra Sedgwick in
Just a Kiss © Paramount Classics

THE OPERA LOVER

(OUTRIDER) Producers, Ed Amaya, Tom Bastounes; Directors, Ron Lazzeretti, Venturino Liberatore; Screenplay, Tom Bastounes, Ron Lazzeretti; No other credits available; Color; Not rated; 93 minutes; Release date: September 27, 2002. CAST: Robert Altman (Marty), Dean Bastounes (Dean), Nick Bastounes (Gus), Tom Bastounes (George), Megan Moore Burns (Jill), Pat Healy (Al), Melanie Deanne Moore (Bibi), Jim Ortlieb (Emcee), Karen Vaccaro (Lil), Monica Zaffarano (Gina)

PANDORA'S BOX

(RAINFOREST) Producer, William Packer; Director, Rob Hardy; Screenplay, Gregory Anderson, Rob Hardy; Photography, Matt MacCarthy; Designer, Korey Michael Washington; Costumes, Sybil Pennix; Editor, Brian Cavanaugh; Music, Steven Gutheinz; Co-Producer, Gregory Anderson; Casting, Ayo Davis; a Will Power production; Dolby; Color; Rated R; 103 minutes; Release date: September 27, 2002. CAST: Michael Jai White (Hampton), Monica Calhoun (Mia DuBois), Kristoff St. John (Victor DuBois), Chrystale Wilson (Tammy Racine), Joseph Lawrence (Detective Anderson), Tyson Beckford (Lance Racine), Marvin Dixon (Patron), Beauty Jackson

JUST A KISS

(PARAMOUNT CLASSICS) Producer, Matthew H. Rowland; Executive Producers, Dolly Hall, John Penotti, Tim Williams, Bradley Yonover; Line Producer, Carolin Jaczko; Director, Fisher Stevens; Screenplay, Patrick Breen; Photography, Terry Stacey; Designer, Happy Massee; Costumes, Arjun Bhasin; Music, Sean Dinsmore; Editor, Gary Levy; GreeneStreet Films Inc.; Dolby; Color; Rated R; 89 minutes; Release date: September 27, 2002. CAST: Ron Eldard (Dag Hammerskjold), Patrick Breen (Peter), Kyra Sedgwick (Halley), Marley Shelton (Rebecca), Marisa Tomei (Paula), Taye Diggs (Andre), Sarita Choudhury (Colleen), Zoe Caldwell (Jessica), Ron Rifkin (Dr. Fauci), Kelly Cole (Jimmy), Idina Menzel (Linda), Peter Dinklage (Dink), Bruno Amato (Joe), Billy Strong (Sal the Flight Attendant), Zofia Borucka (Flight Attendant), Upendran Panicker, Hollis Granville (Cabbies), Donna Hanover (Newscaster), Daryl Dismond (Paramedic), Sean Meenan (Police), Venida Evans (Nurse), Melissa Kemlitz (Vacationer)

HELL HOUSE

(SEVENTH ART) Producers, Zachary Mortensen, Selina Lewis Davidson, George Ratliff; Executive Producer, Paige West; Director, George Ratliff; Photography, Jawad Metni; Editor, Michael LaHaie; Music, Bubba Kadane, Matthew Kadane; a Mixed Greens presentation of a Cantina Pictures production; Color; Not rated; 85 minutes; Release date: October 4, 2002. Documentary about an annual Halloween ritual in which a Dallas Pentecostal church tries to scare kids into coming to services.

PIPE DREAM

(CASTLE HILL) Producers, Sally Roy, Carole Curb Nemoy, Mike Curb; Director, John C. Walsh; Screenplay, John C. Walsh, Cynthia Kaplan; Executive Producer, Michael Zilkha; Photography, Peter Nelson; Designer, Paul Avery; Costumes, Elizabeth Shelton; Editor, Malcolm Jamieson; Music, Alexander Lasarenko; Casting, Brett Goldstein, Susie Farris; from Curb Entertainment; Dolby; Color; Rated R; 91 minutes; Release date: October 4, 2002. CAST: Martin Donovan (David Kulovic), Mary-Louise Parker (Toni Edelman), Rebecca Gayheart (Marliss Funt), Anthony Arkin (Cousin Mike), Marla Sucharetza (Lorna Hufflitz), Kevin Carroll (RJ Martling), Kevin Sussman (James), Natalie B. Pyper (Melanie Phillips), Joel Horwitz (Lloyd Hernandez), Kelley Harron (Fran), Spencer Kayden (Waitress), Jonathan M. Woodward (Reporter), Michaela Conlin (Reporter), Guinevere Turner (Diane Beltrami), Peter Jacobson (Arnie Hufflitz), Cynthia Kaplan (Charlotte), Jack Merrill (Rich Glover), Laura Cahill (Anya), Kevin Seal (Ned Kurland), Tim Hopper (Mitch Farcus), Susan Misner (Onica), Jill Hennessy (Marina Peck), Jim Simpson (Louis Marisco), Sue Jing Song (Jen Sue), Ritchie Coster (Pascal), Jacob Pitts (Autumn), Anton Capone (Camera Assistant), George T. Odom (Maintenance Man), Kelly De Martino, Mitch Roberson (Extras), Adina Porter (Lauren Gunther), E.J. Carroll (Tow Guy), Michael Kaycheck (Manny)

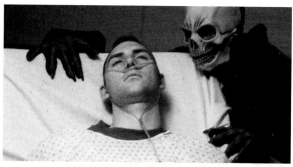

Hell House © Seventh Art

Mary-Louise Parker, Martin Donovan in
Pipe Dream © Castle Hill

Ray Johnson in *How to Draw a Bunny* © Mr. Mudd

Kathleen Bremner in *Family Fundamentals* © DeepFocus Prods.

HOW TO DRAW A BUNNY

(MR. MUDD) Producer/Photography, Andrew Moore; Director/Editor, John Walter; Executive Producers, Lianne Halfon, John Malkovich, Russell Smith, Stephen Apicella, Rocky Collins; Music, Max Roach; Ray Johnson's Letters Read by Judith Malina; a Moticos Motion Pictures/ Elevator Pictures production; Color; Not rated; 90 minutes; Release date: October 9, 2002. Documentary on New York artist Ray Johnson; featuring Gerald Ayres, Frances Beatty, Christo and Jeanne-Claude, Buster Cleavland, Chuck Close, Richard Feigen, Janet Giffra, Coco Gordon, Eric Granros, Chief Joseph Iliacci, Morton Janklow, Roy Lichtenstein, Dorothy Lichtenstein, Richard Lippold, Judith Malina, Nick Maravell, Billy Name, Clive Philpot, Ed Plunkett, James Rosenquist, Malka Saffro, Peter Schyuff, Dennis Selby, Normon Solomon

FAMILY FUNDAMENTALS

(DEEPFOCUS PRODS.) Producer/Director/Screenplay/ Photography/ Editor, Arthur Dong; Music, Mark Adler; Dolby; Color; Not rated; 75 minutes; Release date: October 11, 2002. Documentary on three fundamentalist Christian families who produced homosexual children, featuring Susan Jester, Kathleen Bremner, David Jester, Brett Mathews, Brian Bennett, Bob Dornan.

ASH WEDNESDAY

(IFC) Producers, Margot Bridger, Edward Burns; Executive Producers, Glen Basner, Caroline Kaplan, Jonathan Sehring; Co-Producer, Aaron Lubin; Line Producer, William Perkins; Director/Screenplay, Edward Burns; Photography, Russell Lee Fine; Designer, Susan Block; Costumes, Catherine Marie Thomas; Music, David Shire; Editor, David Greenwald; Casting, Ali Farrell, Laura Rosenthal; IFC Productions and Marlboro Road Gang; Dolby; Technicolor; Rated R; 98 minutes; Release date: October 11, 2002. CAST: Edward Burns (Francis Sullivan), Elijah Wood (Sean Sullivan), Rosario Dawson (Grace Quinonez), Oliver Platt (Moran), Malachy McCourt (Whitey), James Handy (Father Mahoney), Julie Hale (Maggie Shea), Pat McNamara (Murph), James Burke (Red Kelly), Michael Leydon Campbell (Jimmy Burke), Michael Mulheren (Det. Pulaski), Brian Burns (Cousin Mike Moran), Vincent Rubino (Vinny Boombata), James Cummings (J.C.), John DiResta (Pete at the Bar), Christopher McGovern (Whitey's Driver), Peter Gerety (Uncle Handy), Stephen Murphy (Whitey's Man), Brian Delate (Crazy George Cullen), Teresa Yenque (Mrs. Diaz), Kathleen Doyle (Mrs. Flanagan), Marina Durell (Mrs. Quinonez), Dara Coleman (John Coleman), Penny Balfour (Callie), Kevin Kash (Paulie Numbers), Gregg Bello (Larossa), Joe Lisi (Wiseguy), Matty Delia (Brooklyn Barkeep), Jack DeFuria (Little Sean)

KWIK STOP

(KWIK STOP LLC) Producer, Rachel Tenner; Executive Producers, Fern Baker, Scott Casty; Co-Producers, Bob Fagan, Paul Marcus; Director/Screenplay, Michael Gilio; Photography, David Blood; Art Directors, Tricia O'Connell, Rebekah Wiest; Costumes, Stacy Ellen Rich; Editor, Chris McKay; Casting, Mickie Paskal, Rachel Tenner; Color; Not rated; 110 minutes; Release date: October 11, 2002. CAST: Michael Gilio (Mike), Lara Phillips (Didi), Rich Komenich (Emil), Karin Anglin (Ruthie), Kris Wolff, Doug Steckel (Clerks), Guy Barile (Ticket Teller), Eric Curtis Johnson (Dr. Milk), Bob Rokos (Bar Thug), Sunny Seigel (Sunny)

KNOCKAROUND GUYS

(NEW LINE CINEMA) Producers, Lawrence Bender, Brian Koppelman, David Levien; Executive Producers, Michael De Luca, Brian Witten, Stan Wlodkowski; Directors/Screenplay, Brian Koppelman, David Levien; Photography, Tom Richmond; Designer, Lester Cohen; Costumes, Beth Pasternak; Editor, David Moritz; Music, Clint Mansell; Special Effects, Martin Malivoire, Bob Munroe; Casting, Laurel Smith; Stunts, Steve Lucescu; Lawrence Bender Productions, Levien Koppelman Films; Dolby; Super 35 Widescreen; Color; Rated R; 92 minutes; Release date: October 11, 2002. CAST: Barry Pepper (Matty Demeret), Andrew Davoli (Chris Scarpa), Seth Green (Johnny Marbles), Vin Diesel (Taylor Reese), John Malkovich (Teddy Deserve), Arthur Nascarella (Billy Clueless), Tom Noonan (Sheriff Decker), Nicholas Pasco (Freddy the Watch), Shawn Doyle (Deputy Ward), Kevin Gage (Brucker), Dennis Hopper (Benny Chains), Andrew Francis (Matty at 13), John Liddle (Heslep the Barkeep), Kris Lemche (Decker), Dov Tiefenbach (Teeze), Catherine Fitch (Louise), Ceciley Jenkins (Claire the Waitress), Jennifer Baxter (Terri the Waitress), Josh Mostel (Mac McCreadle), Mike Starr (Bobby Boulevard), Allan Havey (Dean the Greenskeeper), Bruce McFee (Devin the Bartender), Boyd Banks (Bar Patron), Angela White (Bernadette the Waitress), James Barrett (Wilkes), Joe Pingue (Klanderud), Silvio Oliviero (Noriega), Kim Kopyl, Hayley Verlyn (Blondes), Tony Nappo (Tony the Waiter), Robert Hilton (Cloutier the Clerk), George Buza (Earl at the Gunshop), Marty Antonioni (Airport Mechanic), Catherine Burdon (Sleepy Girl in Bed), Julian Reed (Georgie Yarkas), Frank Pellegrino (Joey Hook), Moira Dunphy (Mary the Desk Clerk), Lawrence Bender (Bar Patron), Lester Cohen, Doug Pepper (Waiters), Jennifer Deathe (Sandy), Peter Natalizio (Peter the Croupier), Brian Koppelman (Animatronic Cowboy)

Edward Burns, Elijah Wood in *Ash Wednesday* © IFC

Dennis Hopper, John Malkovich, Barry Pepper in *Knockaround Guys* © New Line Cinema

A CUBAN LEGEND

(FIRST RUN FEATURES) Producers, Lech Kowalski, Bette Wanderman; Executive Producer, Alan Boss; Director, Bette Wanderman; Photography, Aleksandar Jovanovic, Lech Kowalski, Philippe La Beau, Bette Wanderman; Editors, Sasa Jocik, Bette Wanderman; from KW Filmworks, Legends Productions; Black and white/color; Not rated; 79 minutes; Release date: October 11, 2002. Documentary on Cuban moralist Salvador Gonzalez.

BLINK OF AN EYE

(ARRIVAL) a.k.a. *Urban Jungle*; Producer, Jo Marr; Director, Van Fischer; Screenplay, Chris Ver Wiel; Designer, Jennifer Cinader; Costumes, Terri Middleton; Editor, Mike Murphy; Music, Steve Bauman, Nick Nolan; Van Fischer Films; Dolby; Color; Not rated; 92 minutes; Release date: October 16, 2002. CAST: Frank John Hughes (Tommy), Seidy Lopez (Sophia), Joseph Bologna (Renfro), Lombardo Boyar (Guillermo), Castulo Guerra (Father Chavez), Richard C. Sarafin (Erlik), Cory Buck (Tommy, age 8), Travis Lowen (Tommy, age 13), Pat Asanti (The Fat Man), August Amarino (Mauricio), Ryan Browning (Drug Boy), Loyda Ramos (Guillermo's Mother), Carlos Alvarado (Gangmember), Richard Riehle (Main Prison Guard), Anthony Albano (Prison Guard), Dana Ashbrook (Mikey), Gabriel Koloyan (Street Kid), Scott Loughran (Artie), Rachel Martin (Landlord), Cristos (Gangleader)

STEALING THE FIRE

(CINEMA NATION) Producer, John S. Friedman, Eric Nadler; Executive Producer, Hamilton Fish; Co-Producer, Jeffrey Levy-Hinte; Directors, John S. Friedman, Eric Nadler; Photography, Slawomir Grunberg; Editor, Susanne Rostock; Music, Hahn Rowe; Associate Producers, Frank Greenberg, Judith Greenberg, Herta Schuster, Joseph Coplan; a Hamilton Fish and Friedman-Nadler prods. presentation in association with Blue Planet Entertainment, ARD/Radio Bremen, SWR, and Antidote Films Intl.; U.S.-German; Color; Not rated; 95 minutes; Release date: October 16, 2002. Documentary on Iraq's secret atomic bomb project and how Karl-Heinz Schaab, a German nuclear technician, was charged with treason for selling the blueprints of a powerful weapon to Saddam Hussein.

WHITE BOY

(PATHFINDER) Producer, Spencer Thornton; Executive Producer, Johnny Ciarcia; Director, John Marino; Screenplay, Johnny Green, John Marino; Photography, Lon Magdich; a Banned in America Films presentation; Color; Not rated; 93 minutes; Release date: October 18, 2002. CAST: Johnny Green (Brian Lovero), Allen Garfield (Mr. Rosen), David Proval (Jim Lovero), Lysa Flores (Carla), Jonathan Avildsen (Cole), Paris (Stevie Robinson), James Andronica (Vinny Tarantino), Alison Lohman (Amy), Jan-Michael Vincent (Ron Masters), Merced Bacon (T-Bone), Romany Malco (Mike Robinson), Terence Tierney (Sean), Mike Tierney

Frank John Hughes, Seidy Lopez in *Blink of an Eye* © Arrival

Fidel Castro, in *Fidel* © First Run Features

Taylor Momsen, Jacob Smith in *Hansel & Gretel* © Innovation Film Group

FIDEL

(FIRST RUN FEATURES) Producers, Alan Fountain, Silvia Steven; Executive Producers, Ernesto Bravo, David Frankel; Director, Estella Bravo; Photography, Roberto Chile, Kevin Keating; Music, Frank Fernandez; Editors, Davey Frankel, Fermín González, Monica Henriquez, Felipe Lacerda; a Bravo Films, Four Point Entertainment production; Dolby; Black and white/color; Not rated; 91 minutes; Release date: October 18, 2002. Documentary on Cuban President Fidel Castro and forty years of the Cuban Revolution.

HANSEL & GRETEL

(INNOVATION FILM GROUP) Producers, Steve Austin, Jonathan Bogner; Director, Gary J. Tunnicliffe; Screenplay, Jonathan Bogner, Timothy Dolan, Gary J. Tunnicliffe; Photography, Brian Baugh; Designers, Deborah Raymond, Dorian Vernacchio; Costumes, Julia Schklair; Music, Rusty Andrews, Bob Mothersbaugh; Editor, Andrew Cohen; Casting, Janet Hirshenson, Jane Jenkins; a Steve Austin and Jonathan Bogner presentation of a Tag Entertainment in association with Majestic Film Partners IV; Dolby; Arriscope; Color; Rated PG; 88 minutes; Release date: October 18, 2002. CAST: Taylor Momsen (Gretel), Jacob Smith (Hansel), Delta Burke (Stepmother), Howie Mandel (Sandman), Gerald McRaney (Father), Lynn Redgrave (Woman/Witch), Alana Austin (Wood Faerie), Dan Roebuck (Dad), Thomas Curtis (Andrew), Dakota Fanning (Katie); VOICES: Tom Arnold (Boogeyman), Bob Goldthwait (Troll), Sinbad (Raven)

NAQOYQATSI

(MIRAMAX) Producers, Joe Beirne, Godfrey Reggio, Lawrence Taub; Executive Producer, Steven Soderbergh; Co-Producer, Mel Lawrence; Line Producer, Federico Negri; Director, Godfrey Reggio; Screenplay, Philip Glass, Godfrey Reggio; Photography, Russell Lee Fine; Music, Philip Glass; Editor, Jon Kane; Visual Effects and Image Reanimation, Manuel Gaulot; Original CGI Animators, Cameron Hickey, Zachary David Medow; Qatsi Productions; Dolby; Color; Rated PG; 89 minutes; Release date: October 18, 2002. A visual montage of today's world as dominated by technology.

ABANDON

(PARAMOUNT) Producers, Lynda Obst, Edward Zwick, Roger Birnbaum, Gary Barber; Director/Screenplay, Stephen Gaghan; Suggested by the book *Adam's Fall* by Sean Desmond; Executive Producer, Richard Vane; Photography, Matthew Libatique; Designer, Gideon Ponte; Costumes, Louise Frogley; Editor, Mark Warner; Music, Clint Mansell; Casting, Juel Bestrop, Jeanne McCarthy, Kathleen Chopin; a Spyglass Entertainment presentation of a Lynda Obst production; Dolby; Super 35 Widescreen; Deluxe color; Rated PG-13; 99 minutes; Release date: October 18, 2002. CAST: Katie Holmes (Katie Burke), Benjamin Bratt (Wade Handler), Charlie Hunnam (Embry Larkin), Zooey Deschanel (Samantha Harper), Mark Feuerstein (Robert Hanson), Fred Ward (Lt. Bill Stayton), Melanie Jayne Lynskey (Mousy Julie), Philip Bosco (Prof. Jergensen), Gabriel Mann (Harrison Hobart), Will McCormack (August), Gabrielle Union (Amanda Luttrell), Greg Kramer (Andre), Gillian Ferrabee (Susan), Barry Julien (Ted), Tony Goldwyn (Dr. David Schaffer), Scott Faulconbridge (Jed), Vanessa Petch, Victoria Petch (Young Katies), Kevin Ryder (Regular Guy), Rachelle Lefevre, Paul Lemelin (Eager Beavers), Simon Peacock (Tech Recruiter), Howard Bilerman (Venture Capitalist), Mark Camacho (Det. Rigney), Mike Tsar (Det. Kanter), Rob Burns (Archivist), Kim Lambert (Interviewee), Alicia Westelman, Jay Lavallée (Campus Security Officers), Arthur Holden (Frank Peabody), Brett Watson (Recovering Alcoholic College Student), Noel Burton (Bill), Bill Rowat (Harrison Hobart, Sr.), Liz MacRae (Mrs. Harrison Hobart), Richard McConomy (Cabbie), Bill Corday (Homeless Guy), Gian Paolo Venuta (Research Assistant), Sheena Larkin (Mogul), Ivan Smith (Professor), Mike Paterson (Russian Bear), Samir Mallal (Indian Guy), David Gow (Passerby Outside Plum), Tim Petch (Katie's Father), Ryan Wilner (Student in Cafeteria), Charles Doucet, Charles Papasoff, Andrea Sadler, Christian Paul (Recovering Alcoholic Members), Joan McBride (Library Assistant), Iwan Edwards (Choir Conductor); Trip Hop Inferno: Shawn Baichoo (Virgil), Ryan Kennedy, Philip Lemaistre (Tortured Souls), Giancarlo Caltabiano (Dante), Joseph Baugniet, Bryanne Hastings (Performer), John Fallon (Mime), Daniel Lee (Wolf), Malcolm Travis (Minos)

DERRIDA

(ZEITGEIST) Producer, Amy Ziering Kofman; Directors, Kirby Dick, Amy Ziering Kofman; Photography, Kirsten Johnson; Editors, Kirby Dick, Matt Clarke; Music, Ryuichi Sakamoto; U.S.-French; Color; Not rated; 85 minutes; Release date: October 23, 2002. Documentary on French philosopher Jacques Derrida, the founder of Deconstructionism.

MANNA FROM HEAVEN

(FIVE SISTERS PRODS.) Producers, Maria Burton, Jennifer Burton, Ursula Burton, Gabrielle C. Burton, Charity Burton; Co-Producers, Gabrielle B. Burton, Roger Burton; Directors, Gabrielle C. Burton, Maria Burton; Screenplay, Gabrielle B. Burton; Photography, Ed Slattery; Designer, Linda Louise Sheets; Costumes, Geraldine Duskin; Editors, Andy Peterson, Robert Tate; Dolby; Color; Rated PG; 119 minutes; Release date: October 25, 2002. CAST: Seymour Cassel (Stanley Stanley), Shelley Duvall (Det. Dubrinski), Jill Eikenberry (Dottie), Louise Fletcher (Mother Superior), Frank Gorshin (Ed Burns), Faye Grant (Rita Annunciata), Harry Groener (Tony Annunciata), Shirley Jones (Bunny Burns), Cloris Leachman (Helen Madden), Wendie Malick (Inez), Austin Pendleton (2-Digit Doyle), Maria Burton (Ramona Annunciata), Ursula Burton (Theresa Annunciata), Vincent O'Neill (Monsignor Dailey), Steven J. Tasker (Buffalo Bills Football Player), Phil Lamarr (Smary John, Casino Manager), Maureen Porter (Rosalie Annunciata), Gabrielle C. Burton (Young Bunny), Jennifer Burton (Young Helen), Buddy Bolton (Young Ed), Tamera Gindlesperger (Young Dottie), Kate LoConti (Young Inez), Abby Royle (Young Rita), Neal Moeller (Young Tony), Hallee Hirsch (Young Theresa), Amy Wieczorek (Mrs. MacNamara), Kathleen Bestko Yale (Poor Woman), Carolyn Ferrini, Michael Dugan (First Dance Couple), Gabrielle B. Burton, Roger Burton (Second Dance Couple), Drew Pillsbury (Mac/Bake), Al Dinneen (Casino Manager, Winnemucca & Buffalo), Eric Ronis (Homeless Man), Aniruddh Patel (Print Shop Manager), Charity Burton (Runaway Teen), Paul Todaro (Freddy, Freddy's Fresh Fish), Joey Giambra (Clifford), Cameron Watson (Patrick), Susan Rossetti (Battered Woman), Kristen Gasser (Annie MacNamara), Mayor Anthony Masiello (Himself), Jerry Orbach (Waltz Contest Announcer)

Naqoyqatsi © Miramax

Jacques Derrida in *Derrida* © Zeitgeist

Katie Holmes, Charlie Hunnam in *Abandon* © Paramount

BY HOOK OR BY CROOK

(ARTISTIC LICENSE) Producers, Steak House, Silas Howard, Harry Dodge; Directors/Screenplay/Editors, Harry Dodge, Silas Howard, Stanya Kahn; Consulting Producers, Annie Imhoff, Jenni Olson; Photography, Ann T. Rossetti; Designer, Samara Halperin; Music, Carla Bozulich; Color; Not rated; 98 minutes; Release date: October 25, 2002. CAST: Silas Howard (Shy), Harry Dodge (Valentine), Stanya Kahn (Billie), Carina Gia (Isabelle), Cash Askew (Little Shy), Misha Klein (Shy's Dad), Miracle Malone (Reporter), Joan Jett (News Intervieweee), Tina Marie (Ms. Red), Kris Kovick (Crazy Nut in Park), Machiko Saito (Gun Store Clerk), James Cotner (Attacker), Nancy Stone (Lucky Penny Waitress), Jimmy Broustis (Hardware Store Clerk), Carmen White (Singer), Sunny Haire (Bartender), Samuel Sheng (Tired Cop), Josh Zinn (Morose Cop)

LOOKING THROUGH LILIAN

(PATHFINDER) Producers, Nelson Bartolome, Chris Dobbs, Darin Kuhlmann, Jake Torem; Line Producer, Laszlo Bene; Director, Jake Torem; Screenplay, Jade Henham, Jake Torem; Photography, Glen Ade Brown; Designer, Margaret M. Miles; Costumes, Elaine Montalvo; Music, Stefan Schulzki; Editor, Shannon Mitchell; Casting, Akua Campanella, Patrick S. Cunningham; a Mad Sun Films, Penelope Pictures production; Dolby; Color; Not rated; 98 minutes; Release date: October 25, 2002. CAST: Sam Bottoms (Gene), Jade Henham (Lilly), Robert Glen Keith (Luke), Essence Atkins (Andrea), Edward Lee Johnson (Mick), Hedia Anvar (Hot Girl in Bar), Susan Barnes (Helen)

Harry Dodge, Stanya Kahn, Silas Howard in *By Hook or by Crook* © Artistic License

Jade Henham in *Looking Through Lillian* © Pathfinder Pictures

Johnny Knoxville, Bam Margera in *Jackass: The Movie* © Paramount

JACKASS: THE MOVIE

(PARAMOUNT) Producers, Jeff Tremaine, Spike Jonze, Johnny Knoxville; Executive Producers, Trip Taylor, John Miller, David Gale; Director, Jeff Tremaine; Co-Executive Producers, Michelle Klepper, Jessica Swirnoff; Co-Producers, Sean Cliver, Dimitry Elyashkevich; Photography, Dimitry Elyashkevich; Music Supervisor, Karen Galuber; a MTV Films presentation a Dick House production in association with Lynch Siderow productions; Dolby; Color; Rated R; 87 minutes; Release date: October 25, 2002. CAST: Johnny Knoxville, Bam Margera, Chris Pontius, Steve-O, Dave England, Ryan Dunn, Jason "Wee Man" Acuña, Preston Lacy, Ehren McGhehey (Themselves)

13TH CHILD

(ALEX MENDOZA & ASSOCS.) Producers, Michael T. Murphy, Patricia M. Reider; Executive Producers, Michael Maryk, Larry Solari; Director, Steven Stockage; Screenplay, Michael Maryk, Cliff Robertson; Photography, Howard Krupa; Creature Design, Thomas Ashley; Editor, Thomas Ashley; from Painted Zebra Productions; Color; Rated R; 98 minutes; Release date: October 25, 2002. CAST: Cliff Robertson (Mr. Shroud), Robert Guillaume (Riley), Lesley-Anne Down (District Attorney Murphy), Wesley Duncan (Brandon Hunter), Christopher Atkins (Ron), Gano Grills (Mitch), Michelle Maryk (Kathryn), John Otis (Piney Hunter), John Wesley (Jones), Peter Jason (Coroner)

TIME CHANGER

(8X ENTERTAINMENT) Producers, Rich Christiano, Kevin Downes; Executive Producer, Paul Crouch; Co-Producer, Bobby Downes, Geoff Ludlow; Director/Screenplay, Rich Christiano; Photography, Philip Hurn; Designer, Laird Pulver; Costumes, Rebecca Smith-Serna; Editor, Jeffrey Lee Hollis; Music, Jasper Randall; Visual Effects Supervisor, Phillip Moses; a Christiano Film Group production; Color; Rated PG; 95 minutes; Release date: October 25, 2002. CAST: D. David Morin (Russell Carlisle), Gavin MacLeod (Norris Anderson), Hal Linden (The Dean), Jennifer O'Neill (Michelle Bain), Paul Rodriguez (Eddie Martinez), Richard Riehle (Dr. Wiseman), John Valdetero (Tom Sharp), Brad Heller (Salesman), Ruben Madera (Bellhop), Kevin Downes (Greg), Paige Peterson (Cindy), Alana Curry (Kelly), Chip Lowell (Guy)

WAKING UP IN RENO

(MIRAMAX) Producers, Ben Myron, Robert Salerno, Dwight Yoakam; Executive Producers, Bob Weinstein, Harvey Weinstein, Jonathan Gordon, Jeremy Kramer; Co-Producer, Bruce Heller; Director, Jonathan Brady; Screenplay, Brent Briscoe, Mark Fauser; Photography, William A. Fraker; Designer, Jeannine Oppewall; Costumes, Doug Hall; Music, Marty Stuart; Editor, Lisa Zeno Churgin; Casting, Emily Schweber; a Ben Myron/Crossfire Sound & Pictures; Dolby; Deluxe color; Rated R; 91 minutes; Release date: October 25, 2002. CAST: Billy Bob Thornton (Lonnie Earl Dodd), Charlize Theron (Candy Kirkendall), Natasha Richardson (Darlene Dodd), Holmes Osborne (Doc Tuley), Chelcie Ross (Fred Bush), Penelope Cruz (Brenda), Brent Briscoe (Officer Russell Whitehead), Elizabeth Karsell (Lonnie III's Girlfriend), George "Buck" Flower (Buster), Wayne Federman (Ronnie), David Koechner (Bellhop), Billy O'Sullivan (Lonnie III), Mark Fauser (Boyd)

DAUGHTER FROM DANANG

(BALCONY/COWBOY) Producer, Gail Dolgin; Directors, Gail Dolgin, Vicente Franco; Photography, Vicente Franco; Editor, Kim Roberts; Music, B. Quincy Griffin, Hector Pérez; Associate Producer, Sunshine Ludder; Presented by the American Experience and Independent Television Service (ITVS) in association with the National Asian American Telecommunications Association (NAATA); Color; Not rated; 80 minutes; Release date: November 1, 2002. Documentary on how, in 1975, 7-year-old Ameriasian Heidi was brought from Danang as part of Operation Babylift, a program to find adoptive parents for Vietnamese orphans, when in fact Heidi's mother had been forced to give her daughter up; featuring Heidi Bub (a.k.a. Mai Thi Hiep), Mai Thi Kim, Tran Tuong Nhu, John Bub, Brenda Lewis, Do Trong Tinh, Do Thi Thu Hien, Do Thi Hong Lien, Do Huu Vinh, Tom Miller, Jessica Bub, Kaitlin Bub, Royce Hughes

Mai Thi Kim, Heidi Bub in *Daughter from Danang* © Balcony/Cowboy

Gavin MacLeod, D. David Morin in *Time Changer*
© 8X Entertainment

Patrick Swayze, Billy Bob Thornton in *Waking Up in Reno* © Miramax

Steve Buscemi, Malcolm Gets in *Love in the Time of Money* © Thinkfilm

LOVE IN THE TIME OF MONEY

(THINKFILM) Producers, Lisa Bellomo, Jason Kliot, Gretchen McGowan, Joana Vicente; Executive Producers, Michael Kafka, Michael Nozik, Robert Redford; Line Producer, Allen Bain; Co-Producer, Yves Chevalier; Director/Screenplay, Peter Mattei; Photography, Stephen Kazmierski; Designer, Susan Block; Costumes, Catherine George; Music, Theodore Shapiro; Editor, Myron I. Kerstein; Casting, Katharine Eggman, Sheila Jaffe, Georgianne Walken; a Blow Up Pictures, Open City Films, Sagittaire Films, South Fork Pictures production; Dolby; Color; Rated R; 90 minutes; Release date: November 1, 2002. CAST: Steve Buscemi (Martin Kunkle), Jill Hennessy (Ellen Walker), Michael Imperioli (Will), Rosario Dawson (Anna), Adrian Grenier (Nick), Malcolm Gets (Robert Walker), Carol Kane (Joey), Vera Farmiga (Greta), Domenick Lombardozzi (Eddie Iovine), Nahanni Johnstone (Marianne Jones), John Ottavio (Mark Jones), Ross Gibby (Jack), Alexa Fischer (Elaine), Tamara Jenkins (Susan Kopit)

BESOTTED

(ARTISTIC LICENSE) Producer/Director/Screenplay, Holly Angell Hardman; Co-Producers, Amy Jelenko, Isen Robbins; Photography, Howard Krupa, T.W. Li, Stephen Treadway; Designers, Charlotte Bourke, Tina Manfredi, Sue Ellen Stroum; Costumes, Martha Greusch; Editor, Youna Kwak; Music, Big Stick, John Gill, Yanna Trance; Casting, Liz Lewis, Robyn Todd; a Surf n Turf Films production; Dolby; Color; Not rated; 92 minutes; Release date: November 1, 2002. CAST: Jim Chiros (Shep), Susan Gibney (Vicky), Holly Angell Hardman (The Sorceress), Liam Waite (Damien), Amy Wright (Mona), Gary Ray (Harris), Cole Murray (Nicole), Richard Cox (Raymond), Dawn Lolos (Ashley), John Doman (Cap'n Dave), Kirby Mitchell (Phil), Diane McBain (Mrs. Buell), Ray Michael Karl (Nathan), Xander Skye (Scott), Marni Lustig (Kristen), Peter Linari (Brass Anchor Bartender), Henry Stolow (Toad), Steven M. Brisco (Randy), Kelly Varley (Yvonne), Buck Berk (Buck), Greta Watson (Fannie), Seamus Frawley (Video Game Player), Bruce Peters (Moorehead), Rachel Kaliti, Hannah Kaliti (Berry Pickers), Bill Galvin (Sentinel Editor), Stacy Arnost (Happy Paddy's Bartender)

STRANGE FRUIT

(CALIFORNIA NEWSREEL) Producer/Director/Editor, Joel Katz; Coordinating Producer, Prudence Hill; Photography, John Miglietta, Thomas Torres; Narrator, Dorothy Thigpen; Music, Don Byron; Color; Not rated; 60 minutes; Release date: November 6, 2002. Documentary on the origins of the anti-lynching song "Strange Fruit;" featuring Amiri Baraka, Don Byron, Abbey Lincoln, Pete Seeger, Cassandra Wilson, Michael Meeropol, Robert Meeropol.

Justifiable Homicide © Reality Films/Gabriel Films

JUSTIFIABLE HOMICIDE

(REALITY FILMS/GABRIEL FILMS) Producers/Directors, Jon Osman, Jonathan Stack; Co-Producer, Simon Nasht; Photography, Teymoore Nabili, Jon Osman; Editors, Frank Kauredren, David Moore, Jon Osman; Music, Wendy Blackstone; Color; Not rated; 85 minutes; Release date: November 6, 2002. Documentary about the 1995 Bronx police shooting of three Puerto Rican men.

THE RISING PLACE

(FLATLAND PICTURES) Producers, Tom Rice, Tracy A. Ford, Marshall Peck; Director/Screenplay, Tom Rice; Based on the novel by David Armstrong; Photography, Jim Dollarhide; Designer, William J. Blanchard; Costumes, Mark Horton; Editor, Mary Morrisey; Music, Conrad Pope; Original Songs Written and Performed by Jennifer Holliday; Dolby; Color; Rated PG-13; 92 minutes; Release date: November 8, 2002. CAST: Laurel Holloman (Emily Hodge), Elise Neal (Wilma Watson), Mark Webber (Will Bacon), Liam Aiken (Emmett Wilder), Billy Campbell (Streete Wilder), Gary Cole (Avery Hodge), Alice Drummond (Millie Hodge/Older Emily), Frances Fisher (Virginia Wilder), Mason Gamble (Franklin Pou), Beth Grant (Melvina Pou), Tess Harper (Rebecca Hodge), S. Epatha Merkerson (Lessie Watson), Scott Openshaw (Eddie Scruggs), Frances Sternhagen (Ruth Wilder), Jennifer Holliday (Sadie), Jackie Bateman (Emily Hodge, age 10), Courtney Campbell (Wilma Watson, age 10), Janie Story (Young Ruth, age 8), Jackson Walker (Harry C. Devening), Eddie Cotton, Jr. (Walter Malone), Debra Heitman (Mary Beth Dearing), Paul Davis (Franklin Pou, age 8), James Smith (Young Private), Julia Lawshae (Army Dance Crooner), Judy Rice (Mrs. Moseley), Nate Bynum (Brother Isaac), Margo St. John (Defense Attorney), Tommy Rice (Judge), John Maxwell (Funeral Director)

Holly Angell Hardman in *Besotted* © Artistic License

Laurel Holloman, Mark Webber in
The Rising Place © Flatland Pictures

THE BREAD, MY SWEET

(PANORAMA) Producers, Melissa Martin, William C. Hulley; Executive Producer, William C. Hulley; Director/Screenplay, Melissa Martin; Photography, Mark Knobil; Costumes, Montie Cholmeley-Jon; Music, Susan Hartford; Editor, Chuck Aikman; Casting, Adrienne Stern; Who Know Productions; Color; Not rated; 105 minutes; Release date: November 8, 2002. CAST: Scott Baio (Dominic), John Seitz (Massimo), Kim Martin (Customer), Billy Mott (Eddie), Shuler Hensley (Pino), Jennie Martin (Maude), Rose Bray (Rose), John Bechtol (Jeffrey), Rosemary Prinz (Bella), Jody O'Donnell (Preston), Marty Sheets (Liz), Bingo O'Malley (CEO), Nick Tallo (Bomba), Dan Stafford (Boardroom Guy), Philip Winters (Dr. Wahl), John Amplas (Jimmy), Fred Lehman (Lorenzo), Katherine McKenna (Coffee Shop Regular), Rachel McCartney (Street Musician), Nardi Novak (Nancy the Cop), Adrienne Wehr (Tamela), Manik Bhojwani (Boardroom Drone), Daniel Catanro (Priest), Barbara Thomas (Donna the Cop), Kristin Minter (Lucca), Kevin Lageman (Len), Nancy Bach (2nd Doctor), Paula Carroll (Bibi), Mary Harvey (Sister Grace)

THE FLIP SIDE

(PURO PINOY) Producer/Director/Screenplay, Rod Pulido; Associate Producer, Rudy Pulido; No other credits available; Color; Not rated; 81 minutes; Release date: November 8, 2002. CAST: Verwin Gatpandan (Darius Delacruz), Jose Saenz (Davis Delacruz), Ronalee Par (Marivic Delacruz), Manong Peping Baclig (Grandpa Delacruz), Ester Pulido (Mrs. Delacruz), Abe Pagtama (Mr. Delacruz)

LEELA

(CINEBELLA ENTERTAINMENT) Producers, Anjalika Mathur, Kavita Munjal; Executive Producers, Raj Singh, Harkishan Vasa; Director/Screenplay, Somnath Sen; Photography, Steven Douglas Smith; Designer, Aradhana Seth; Costumes, Celeste Hines; Editors, Peggy Davis, Suresh Pai; Music, Jagjit Singh; Casting, Jeff Golomb; a Lemon Tree Films production; Dolby; Kodak color; Not rated; 97 minutes; Release date: November 8, 2002. CAST: Dimple Kapadia (Leela), Vinod Khanna (Nashaad), Deepti Naval (Chaitali), Amol Mhatre (Kris/Krishna), Gulshan Grover (Jai), Brendan Hughes (Summer), Kelly Gunning (JC), Garrett Devereux (Chip), Kyle Erby (Jamaal), Michelle Van Wagner (Jennifer), Sarayu Rao (Mira), Partha Dey (Shantanu), Sandeep Walia (Harsh), Delna Rustomjee (Joya Chatterjee), Gargi Sen (Maheed), Sulekha Naidu (Restma), Sameea Thakur (Zatar), Sushmita Sen (Guari), Shaleha Sen (Guari), Rajnish Sinha (Activist), Dana Duff (Airline Clerk), Doug James (Pool Player), Polly Ahluwalia, Punita Khankha, Anisha Pattamaic (Party Women)

'R XMAS

(PATHFINDER) Producer, Pierre Kalfon; Executive Producers, Barry Amato, Stefano Celesti; Co-Producers, Frank DeCurtis, Denis Héraud, Richard Klug; Director, Abel Ferrara; Screenplay, Abel Ferrara, Scott Pardo; Story, Cassandra DeJesus; Photography, Ken Kelsch; Designer, Frank DeCurtis; Costumes, Debra Tennenbaum; Editors, Patricia Bowers, Bill Pankow, Suzanne Pillsbury; Music, Schooly-D; a Valence Films, Barnholtz Entertainment production; U.S.-French; Dolby; 2001; Dolby; Color; Rated R; 83 minutes; Release date: November 8, 2002. CAST: Drea de Matteo (The Wife), Lillo Brancato, Jr. (The Husband), Lisa Valens (Lisa, the Daughter), Ice-T (Kidnapper), Victor Argo (Louie), Denia Brache (Louie's Wife), Gloria Irizarry (Aunt), Naomi Morales (The Niece), Nelson Vasquez (Niece's Husband), Andy Fiscella, Thomas Murray, Edwin Martinez (Accomplices), Janis Corsair, Anne Ackerman (Shoppers), Frank Antonio "Anthony" Cuervo (Bike Pick Up Man), John R. Tramatola III (Child Scrooge), Meredith Ostrom (Elf No. 2), Dan Sweeney (Santa Claus), Andrew Lasky (Security Guard), Bersalde Vega (Toy Store Manager), James R. Bilz (High Rise Doorman), Raymond "Voodoo Ray" Ultarte (Parking Attendant), Luis Santos (Tio), Orran Farmer (Sucio), Jamal "Redrum" Simmons (Trey), Oscar S. Tevez (Gypsy Cab Driver), Rosa Nino (Gypsy Cab Driver's Wife), Clarence Dorsey (Bronx Dealer No. 1), Roman Rivera (Felipe), Javier "Java" Núñez (Felipe's Brother), Jay "J-Dog" Dog (Felipe's Bodyguard), Anthony "Dust" Ortiz (Latino Dealer No. 1), Benny Nieves (Priest), Victor Pagan (Needy P.R. Husband), Yolanda Nieto (Needy P.R. Wife), Louise Colon (Neighbor), Petra Quinones (Stash Pad Old Lady), Jose "Pepe" Castillo (Guitarist), Antoine Pagan (Swag Shop Owner), Carlos Leon (Husband's Friend)

HALF PAST DEAD

(SCREEN GEMS) Producers, Andrew Stevens, Elie Samaha, Steven Seagal; Executive Producers, Christopher Eberts, Uwe Schott, Randall Emmett, George Furla; Director/Screenplay, Don Michael Paul; Co-Producers, Phil Goldfine, James Holt; Photography, Michael Slovis; Designer, Albrecht Konrad; Editor, Vanick Moradian; Music, Tyler Bates; Music Supervisor, Michael Lloyd; Line Producer, Alison Semenza; Casting, Jeff Gerrard; a Franchise Pictures presentation; Dolby; Color; Rated PG-13; 98 minutes; Release date: November 15, 2002. CAST: Steven Seagal (Sascha Petrosevitch), Morris Chestnut (Donny/49er One), Ja Rule (Nick Frazier), Nia Peeples (49er Six), Tony Plana (El Fuego), Kurupt (Twitch), Matt Battaglia (49er Three), William T. Bowers (Alcatraz Guard), Richard Bremmer (Sonny Eckvall), Stephen J. Cannell (Hubbard), Claudia Christian (E.Z. Williams), Yasmina Filali-Bohnen (Sophia), Hannes Jaenicke (Agent Hartmann), Alexandra Kamp (Reporter), Ross King (FBI Agent), Michael McGrady (Bad Ass Guard), Mo'Nique (Twitch's Girl), Don Michael Paul (SWAT Captain), Eva-Maria Schoenecker (The Priest), Jed Sutton (Air 49er), Michael "Bear" Taliferro (Little Joe), Linda Thorson (Justice Jane McPherson), Bruce Weitz (Lester)

Steven Seagal, Ja Rule in *Half Past Dead* © Screen Gems

Ice-T, Drea de Matteo in *'R Xmas* © Pathfinder

209

INTERVIEW WITH THE ASSASSIN

(MAGNOLIA) Producers, Brian Koppelman, David Levien; Executive Producer, Tom Tucker; Director/Screenplay, Neil Burger; Photography, Richard Rutkowski; Designer, Greg Finnin; Costumes, Jenny Gering; Editor, Brad Fuller; Casting, Nicole Arbusto, Joy Dixon; Dolby; Color; Not rated; 88 minutes; Release date: November 15, 2002. CAST: Raymond J. Barry (Walter Ohlinger), Dylan Haggerty (Ron Kobeleski), Renee Faia (Karen Kobeleski), Kelsey Kemper (Sharon Kobeleski), Dennis J. Lau (Steven Wu), Jared McVay (Jimmy Jones), Christel Khalil (Babysitter), Lillias White (Nurse), Kate Williamson (Walter's Ex-Wife), Jack Tate (John Seymour, Jr.), Nick Mize (Gary Deetz), James Hiser (Alan Delvecchio), Mike Wood (Marine Guard), Darrell Sandeen (John Seymour, Sr.), Evan O'Meara, Robert Samuel Thompson (Secret Service Agents), Jimmy Burke (DC Cop)

REVOLUTION #9

(EXILE PRODUCTIONS) Producers, Shannon Goldman, Tim McCann, Michael Risley; Executive Producers, Adolfo Vargas, Gill Holland; Director/Screenplay/Photography, Tim McCann; Line Producer, Jennifer Carter; Designer, Elise Bennett; Costumes, Nives Spaleta; Editors, Tim McCann, Shannon Goldman; Music, Douglas J. Cuomo; Casting, Vince Liebhart, Tom Alberg; Dolby; Color; Not rated; 91 minutes; Release date: November 15, 2002. CAST: Michael Risley (James Jackson), Adrienne Shelly (Kim Kelly), Spalding Gray (Scooter McCrae), Callie Thorne (Stephanie), Michael Rodrick (Joe Kelly), Sakina Jaffrey (Dr. Ray), Jase Blankfort (Tommy Kelly), Kristin Griffith (Gale), Jonathan Hogan (Dr. Phil Karlson), Ted Sutton (Dr. Fred Lang), Jim Burton (Therapist Fuller), David Deblinger (Bar Manager), Claire Beckman (Sarah McCrae), Armand Shultz (John Ford), Phyllis Sommerville (Judge Hathaway), Mark Zeisler (Hospital Attorney), Mary Elaine Monti (Patient Attorney), Tony Arkin (Boss), Frank Olivier (Superintendent), William Severs (Mr. Kelly), Tanny McDonald (Mrs. Kelly), Retheal Bean (Henry Jackson), Ross Benjamin (Randolph), Kim Winter (Salesgirl), Missy Hargraves (Laurie Kelly), Stephanie Gatshet (Young Model), Yvette McLarty (Secretary), Chad Coleman (Night Nurse)

BETTER HOUSEKEEPING

(MODERNICA PICTURES) Producer, Mark G. Mathis; Director/Screenplay, Frank Novak; Photography, Alex Vendler; Designer, Elizabeth M. Burhop; Costumes, Kate Meehan; Editor, Fritz Feick; Dolby; Color; Rated R; 90 minutes; Release date: November 20, 2002. CAST: Bob Jay Mills (Don), Al Schuermann (Joe), Zia (Chuck), Tacey Adams (Marion), Andrew Eichner (Don, Jr.), Jerry O'Conner (Mike), Scooter Stephan (Barry), Petra Westen (Donatella)

Adrienne Shelley, Michael Risley in *Revolution #9* © Exile Productions

Georg Grosskurth, Robert Havemann in
The Burning Wall © Films Transit International

THE BURNING WALL

(FILMS TRANSIT INTERNATIONAL) Producer/Director/Screenplay, Hava Kohav Beller; Photography, Christoph Lerch, Judith Kaufmann, Harald Klix; Editors, Markus Akira Peters, Lawrence Silk; Narrator, John Dildine; USA-German; Color; Not rated; 116 minutes; Release date: November 20, 2002. Documentary on the techniques used by the Stasi, a secret police force, to monitor and destroy the lives of those who opposed the communist regime in East Germany from 1949–1989.

THE 4TH TENOR

(WINE WOMEN & SONG FILMS) Producer, Joseph Merhi; Director, Harry Basil; Screenplay, Rodney Dangerfield, Harry Basil; Photography, Ken Blakey; Designer, Jacqueline Masson; Costumes, Nicole L. Schroud; Music, Christopher Lennertz; Editor, Tony Lombardo; Casting, Allison Cowitt, Mike Fenton; Dolby; Color; Rated PG-13; 97 minutes; Release date: November 22, 2002. CAST: Rodney Dangerfield (Lupo), Robert Davi (Ierra), Annabelle Gurwitch (Gina), Anita De Simone (Rosa), Charles Fleischer (Alphonse), Richard Libertini (Vincenzo), Dom Irrera (Petey), Vincent Schiavelli (Marcello), Patrick Cupo (Nunzio), Joe Vassallo (Cop #2)

Raymond J. Barry in *Interview with the Assassin*
© Magnolia

THEY

(DIMENSION) Producers, Scott Kroopf, Tom Engelman; Executive Producers, Ted Field, David Linde; Director, Robert Harmon; Screenplay, Brendan William Hood; Photography, Rene Ohashi; Designer, Douglas Higgins; Costumes, Karen Matthews; Editor, Chris Peppe; Music, Elia Cmiral; Co-Producers, Barbara Kelly, Tony Blain; Creature Designer/Supervisor, Patrick Tatopoulos; Casting, Jennifer Fishman Pate, Amy McIntyre Britt, Anya Colloff; a Focus Features presentation of a Radar Pictures production; Presented by Wes Craven; Distributed by Miramax Films; Dolby; Super 35 Widescreen; Color; Rated PG-13; 89 minutes; Release date: November 27, 2002. CAST: Laura Regan (Julia), Marc Blucas (Paul), Ethan Embry (Sam), Dagmara Dominczyk (Terry), Jon Abrahams (Billy), Alexander Gould (Young Billy), Desiree Zurowski (Mary Parks), Mark Hildreth (Troy), Jonathan Cherry (Darren), Peter Lacroix (David Parks), Jessica Amlee (Young Julia), Jay Brazeau (Dr. Booth), L. Harvey Gold (Prof. Crawley), David Abbott (Prof. Adkins), Jodelle Micah Ferland (Sarah), Mark Brandon (Newscaster #1), Colin Foo (Chinese Chef), Claire Riley, Tamara Taggart (Newscasters), Wendy Morrow Donaldson (Waitress), Bob Wilde (Ghoulish Man), Bill Waters (Priest), Ken Roberts (Tenant), John Hainsworth (Old Man), Henry O. Watson (Subway Engineer)

TO END ALL WARS

(ARGYLL FILM PARTNERS) Producer, David L. Cunningham, Jack Hafer, Nava Levin; Executive Producers, Greg Newman, John Quested, Scott Walchek; Director, David L. Cunningham; Screenplay, Brian Godawa; Based on the book by Ernest Gordon; Photography, Greg Gardiner; Designer, Paul Sylbert; Costumes, Tamara More, Rina Ramon; Editor, Tim Silano; Music, John Cameron; Casting, Allison Cowitt, Mike Fenton, Celestia Fox; a Gumshoe Productions, Integrity Partners, Pray for Rain Pictures Inc. production; U.S.-Thai-British; Dolby; Color; Rated R; 117 minutes; Release date: December 6, 2002. CAST: Robert Carlyle (Campbell), Kiefer Sutherland (Reardon), Ciarán McMenamin (Ernest Gordon), Mark Strong (Dusty), Sakae Kimura (Ito), Masayuki Yui (Noguchi), James Cosmo (McLean), John Gregg (Dr. Coates), Shu Nakajima (Nagatomo), Yugo Saso (Takashi Nagase), Pip Torrens (Foxworth), Adam Sinclair (Jocko), Winton Nicholson (Duncan), Greg Ellis (Primrose), James McCarthy (Norman), Brendan Cowell (Wallace Hamilton), Tracy Anderson (Crazy Man), Duff Armour (Jan), Sergio Alarcon (Irishman), Jonathon Chapman (Server), Christopher White (Cockney), Jeremy Pippin (Young Dutch), Dennis Ihara (Tool Shed Guard), Robert Jobe (Lars), Richard Lafond, Jr. (American Soldier), Robert Lee (Paratrooper), Daryl Bonilla (Young P.O.W.), Clyde Yamashita (Japanese NCO), Joji Yoshida (Guard #1), Ernest Gordon, Takashi Nagase (Themselves), Richard Joseph Lafond, Jr. (American Soldier)

SOAP GIRL

(LEAP FROG PRODS.) Producer, Dennis James Lee; Executive Producers, Tomiko Lee, Edwin A. Santos; Director/Editor, Young Man Kang; Screenplay, Tony T.L. Young; Photography, Henryk Cymerman; Costumes, Natalie Lander; Music, Matt Walsh; Dolby; Color; Not rated; 90 minutes; Release date: December 6, 2002. CAST: Luciano Saber (Harry), Kerry Liu (Maya), Tomiko Lee (Mamasan), Gina Hiraizumi (Asia), Kate Holliday (Sammy), Hiromi Nishiyama (Jenna), Dennis James Lee (Teddy Song), Derek Kim (Undercover Cop), Rosco Karzas (Fat Man), Jesse Pate (Effeminate Male), Edwin A. Santos (Frustrated Boyfriend), Justin Born (Mr. Jones), Lea Downey (Karin), Tommy Le (Bartender), Erin Marie Moore (Sofia), Julie Della Ripa (Janis), Jasmine Jong Ok Kang (Sooki), Kazumi Aihara (Kimi), Tony T.L. Young (Poetry Host), David Mersault (Eric), Mari Tanaka (Yuko)

BOOM: THE SOUND OF EVICTION

(MOUNTAIN EYE MEDIA) Producers, Francine Cavanaugh, A. Mark Liiv, Jeff Taylor, Adams Wood; Directors/Editors, Francine Cavanaugh, A. Mark Liiv, Adams Wood; Photography, Francine Cavanaugh, A. Mark Liiv, Jeff Taylor, Adams Wood; a Whispered Media production; Color; Not rated; 96 minutes; Release date: December 13, 2002. Documentary about how the dotcom boom of the 1990s forced many long-time tenants out of San Francisco's Mission District.

Luciano Saber (center) in *Soap Girl* © Leap Frog Prods.

Laura Regan in *They* © Dimension

Robert Carlyle in *To End All Wars* © Argyll Film Partners

In Shifting Sands © Independent

SONNY

(SAMUEL GOLDWYN FILMS) Producers, Nicolas Cage, Norm Golightly, Paul Brooks; Executive Producer, Norm Waitt; Director, Nicolas Cage; Screenplay, John Carlen; Photography, Barry Markowitz; Designer, Monroe Kelly; Costumes, Shawn-Holly Cookson; Music, Clint Mansell; Music Supervisor, Randy Gerston; Co-Executive Producer, Norm Waitt; Associate Producer, Debra L. Gainor; Casting, Jeffery Passero, Elizabeth Hayden-Passero; a Gold Circle Films presentation of a Saturn Films Production; Dolby; Color; Rated R; 110 minutes; Release date: December 27, 2002. CAST: James Franco (Sonny), Brenda Blethyn (Jewel), Harry Dean Stanton (Henry), Mena Suvari (Carol), Seymour Cassel (Albert), Brenda Vaccaro (Meg), Josie Davis (Gretchen), Willie Metcalf (Cal), Janet Shea (Wealthy Woman), Cary Wilmot Alden (Catherine), Nicolas Cage (Acid Yellow), Scott Caan (Jesse), Graham Timbes (Troy), Wallace Merck (Scott), Doug Barden (Maitre'D), Katherine Randolph (Dagmar), Bernard Hocke (Clerk), David E. Jensen (Mr. Penn), Karen Kaia Livers (Mattie), Don Yesso, Thomas Williams (Waiters), Mark W. Davison (Acid Yellow's Thug), Marc Coppola (Jimmy at Mattie's), Norm Golightly (Man at Party with Tie), Houston Parker (Lilly White), Shelby Rachel Griggs, Sarah Allison Griggs (Girls), Natasha Mince (Hooker), Delisha Prince (Mattie's Girl), Monica L. Monica (Party Lady), Robert Burton (Man at Door), Michael James Dukes, Kyle Hand, Ben Jones, Andrew Miller, Nick Paoletti (Boys)

THE JIMMY SHOW

(FIRST LOOK) Producers, Beni Tadd Atoori, Mary Jane Skalski; Executive Producer, Heidi Crane; Co-Producers, Sabrina Atoori, Colin Bates; Line Producer, Per Melita; Director/Screenplay, Frank Whaley; Based on the play *Veins and Thumbtacks* by Jonathan Marc Sherman; Photography, Michael Mayers; Designer, Judy Becker; Costumes, Dawn Weisberg; Editor, Miran Miosic; Music, Robert Whaley, Tony Grimaldi; Casting, James Calleri; a Stonelock Pictures production; Dolby; Color; Rated R; 96 minutes; Release date: December 13, 2002. CAST: Frank Whaley (Jimmy O'Brien), Carla Gugino (Annie), Ethan Hawke (Ray), Lynn Cohen (Ruth), Jillian Stacom (Wendy), Spelman M. Beaubrun (Claude), Mark Birch (Track Coach), Jefferson Breland, George Demas, William Peden (Men in Club), Heather Bucha (Hostess), Frankie Dellarosa, Jeff Wells (Jersey Guys), John Elsen (Tony), Mitchell Greenberg (Dr. Schull), Laura Jordan, Lynn Pesce (Jersey Girls), Ruth Kulerman (Keema Woman), Matthew Lawler (Dr. Burke), Bunny Levine (Fireplace Woman), Joanna Merlin (Emily), Edgar Oliver (Mulligatawny Man), Bill Rowley (Fireplace Man), Raynor Scheine (Pharmacist), Rachel Stern (Nurse Allen), Sam Stone (Jimmy at 5), Robert Whaley (Mr. Slocum)

IN SHIFTING SANDS:
THE TRUTH ABOUT UNSCOM AND THE DISARMING OF IRAQ

(INDEPENDENT) Director, Scott Ritter; Screenplay, Alex Cohn, Scott Ritter, Scott Rosann; Narrator, Scott Rosann; No other credits available; Color; Not rated; 92 minutes; Release date: December 27, 2002. Documentary about how U.N. weapons inspectors were betrayed by Iraq, the U.N., and the United States, featuring Rolf Ekeus, Tim Trevan, Lt. Gen. Amer Rashid, Lt. Gen. Amer al-Sa'adi, Tariq Aziz

Brenda Blethyn, James Franco, Harry Dean Stanton in *Sonny* © Samuel Goldwyn Films

Carla Gugino, Frank Whaley in *The Jimmy Show* © First Look

PROMISING
NEW ACTORS

Alexis Bledel of *Tuck Everlasting*

Gael García Bernal of *Y Tu Mamá También, El Crimen del Padre Amaro*

Kevin Bishop of *Food of Love*

Zooey Deschanel of *Abandon, Big Trouble, The Good Girl, The New Guy*

America Ferrera of *Real Women Have Curves*

Ryan Gosling of *The Believer, Murder by Numbers*

Emile Hirsch of *The Dangerous Lives of Altar Boys, The Emperor's Club*

Alison Lohman of *White Oleander, White Boy*

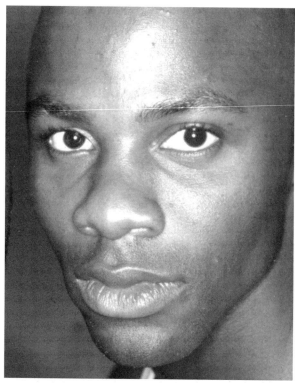

Derek Luke of *Antwone Fisher*

Mandy Moore of *A Walk to Remember*

Jennifer Westfeldt of *Kissing Jessica Stein*

Aaron Stanford of *Tadpole, Hollywood Ending, 25th Hour*

ACADEMY AWARD
WINNERS & NOMINEES

BEST PICTURE OF 2002

CHICAGO

(MIRAMAX) Producer, Martin Richards; Executive Producers, Harvey Weinstein, Meryl Poster, Julie Goldstein, Jennifer Berman, Bob Weinstein, Sam Crothers, Craig Zadan, Neil Meron; Director/Choreographer, Rob Marshall; Screenplay, Bill Condon; Based on the musical play with book by Bob Fosse and Fred Ebb, based on the play by Maurine Dallas Watkins; Music, John Kander; Lyrics, Fred Ebb; Photography, Dion Beebe; Designer, John Myhre; Costumes, Colleen Atwood; Co-Producer, Don Carmody; Original Music Score, Danny Elfman; Music Supervisor/Conductor, Paul Bogaev; Music Supervisor, Maureen Crowe; Editor, Martin Walsh; Casting, Laura Rosenthal, Ali Farrell; a Producer Circle Co. production, a Zadan/Meron production; Dolby; Deluxe color; Rated PG-13; 113 minutes; Release date: December 27, 2002

Catherine Zeta-Jones, Renée Zellweger

Renée Zellweger

Catherine Zeta-Jones

John C. Reilly

Renée Zellweger

CAST

Roxie Hart . . . . Renée Zellweger
Velma Kelly . . . . Catherine Zeta-Jones
Billy Flynn . . . . Richard Gere
Matron Mama Morton . . . . Queen Latifah
Amos Hart . . . . John C. Reilly
Kitty Baxter . . . . Lucy Liu
Bandleader . . . . Taye Diggs
Martin Harrison . . . . Colm Feore
Mary Sunshine . . . . Christine Baranski
Fred Casely . . . . Dominic West
Mona . . . . Mýa Harrison
June . . . . Deidre Goodwin
Annie . . . . Denise Faye
Hunyak (Katalin Helinszki) . . . . Ekaterina Chtchelkanova
Liz . . . . Susan Misner
Stage Manager . . . . Cliff Saunders
Mrs. Borusewicz . . . . Jayne Eastwood
Police Photographer . . . . Bruce Beaton
Sergeant Fogarty . . . . Roman Podhora
Newspaper Photographer . . . . Rob Smith
Reporter . . . . Sean Wayne Doyle
Prison Clerk . . . . Steve Behal
Prison Guard . . . . Robbie Rox
Nickie . . . . Chita Rivera
Bernie . . . . Joey Pizzi
Ezekial Young . . . . Scott Wise
Wilbur . . . . Ken Ard
Hunyak's Husband . . . . Marc Calamia
and Niki Wray (Veronica), Greg Mitchell (Charlie), Sebastian LaCause (Al Lipschitz), Brendan Wall (Billy's Assistant), Cleve Asbury, Rick Negron, Shaun Amyot (Gun Reporters/Dancers), Eve Crawford (Billy's Secretary), Bill Corsair (Newsreel Announcer), Bill Britt (Auctioneer), Gerry Fiorini (Sailor), Elizabeth Law (Perfume Lady), Joseph Scoren (Harry), Monique Ganderton, April Morgan (Bare Women), Martin Moreau (Groin Reporter), Conrad Dunn, Cleve Asbury (Doctors), Jonathan Whittaker (Bailiff), Rod Campbell (Jury Foreman), Brett Caruso (Harrison's Assistant), Sean McCann (Judge), Jeff Clarke (Court Clerk), Patrick Salvagna (Newsboy), Kathryn Zenna (Shooter), Jeff Purstil (Club Owner), Roxanne Barlow, Joey Dowling, Melanie Gage, Michelle Johnston, Charley King, Mary Ann Lamb, Vicky Lambert, Tara Nicole, Cynthia Onrubia, Karine Plantadit-Bageot, Jennifer Savelli, Natalie Willes, Karen Andrew, Kelsey Chace, Catherine Ghiarelli, Theresa Coombe, Lisa Ferguson, Melissa Flerangile, Michelle Galati, Sheri Godfrey, Brittany Gray, Karen Holness, Amber-Kelly Mackereth, Jodi-Lynn McFadden, Faye Rauw, Rhonda Roberts, Leigh Torlage, Robyn Wong, Ken Ard, Cleve Asbury, Ted Banfalvi, Harrison Beal, Paul Becker, Marc Calamia, Jean-Luke Coté, Scott Fowler, Edgar Godineaux, Billy Hartung, Darren Lee, Troy Liddell, Blake McGrath, Robert Montano, Sean Palmer, Desmond Richardson, Martin Samuel, Jason Sermonia, Jeff Sibert, Sergio Trujillo (Dancers), Stacy Clark Baisley, Megan Fehlberg, Rachel Jacobs, Rebecca Leonard, Erin Michie, Danielle Rueda-Watts (Acrobats)

Show business hopeful Roxie Hart finds herself getting attention at last after she murders her lover, taking the spotlight away from Velma Kelly, whose own crime of passion has recently turned her into an instant celebrity as well. Previous film versions of the original play were *Chicago* (Pathe, 1927) starring Phyllis Haver as Roxie, and *Roxie Hart* (20th, 1942) starring Ginger Rogers.

Richard Gere, Catherine Zeta-Jones

2002 Academy Award winner for Best Picture, Best Supporting Actress (Catherine Zeta-Jones), Best Editing, Best Sound, Best Costume Design, and Best Art Direction. This film received additional Oscar nominations for actress (Renée Zellweger), supporting actor (John C. Reilly), supporting actress (Queen Latifah), director, screenplay adaptation, song ("I Move On"), cinematography.

© Miramax

Queen Latifah

Richard Gere

BEST DOCUMENTARY OF 2002

BOWLING FOR COLUMBINE

Michael Moore

Michael Moore (right)

(UNITED ARTISTS) Producers, Michael Moore, Kathleen Glynn, Jim Czarnecki, Charles Bishop, Michael Donovan; Director/Screenplay, Michael Moore; Executive Producer, Wolfram Tichy; Co-Executive Producer, Kurt Engfehr; Line Porudcer, Siobhan Oldham; Coordinating Producer, Rehya Young; Supervising Producer, Tia Lessin; Photography, Brian Danitz, Michael McDonough; Music, Jeff Gibbs; Animation, Harold Moss; Associate Editor, T. Woody Richman; Chief Archivist, Carl Deal; an Alliance Atlantis presentation of a Salter Street Films, VIF 2, and Dog Eat Dog Films production; Dolby; DuArt color; Rated R; 119 minutes; Release date: October 11, 2002. Documentary in which the horrifying school shootings at Columbine High School prompt filmmaker Michael Moore to investigate America's obsession with violence and firearms.

WITH

Michael Moore, Richard Castaldo, Dick Clark, Barry Glassner, Charlton Heston, Marilyn Manson, James Nichols, Matt Stone

2002 Academy Award winner for Best Documentary Feature.

© United Artists

Matt Stone, Michael Moore

Michael Moore

Shelby the dog

Mark Taylor, Michael Moore

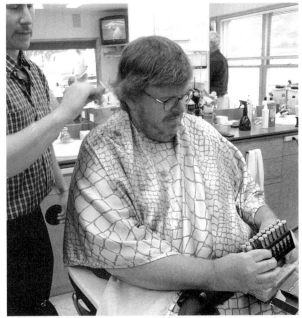

Chip Smith, Michael Moore

Barry Glassner, Michael Moore

Principal Hughes, Michael Moore

Amanda Duncan, Michael Moore

BEST ANIMATED FEATURE OF 2002

Chihiro, Haku

No-Face, Chihiro, Zeniba

SPIRITED AWAY

(WALT DISNEY PICTURES) Chief Executive Producer, Yasuyoshi Tokuma; Director/Screenplay, Hayao Miyazaki; Executive Producers, Takeyoshi Matsushita, Seiichiro Ujiie, Yutaka Narita, Koji Hoshino, Banjiro Uemura, Hironori Aihara; Music, Joe Hisaishi; Supervising Animators, Masashi Ando, Kitaro Kosaka, Megumi Kagawa; U.S. Production: Director, Kirk Wise; Producer, Donald W. Ernst; Executive Producer, John Lasseter; English Language Adaptation, Cindy Davis Hewitt, Donald H. Hewitt; Associate Producer, Lori Korngiebel; Voice Casting, Jamie Thomason, David Wright; a Tokuma Shoten, Studio Ghibli, Nippon Television Network, Dentsu, Buena Vista Home Entertainment, Tohoku Shinsha Film and Mitsubishi presentation; Japanese; Dolby; Color; Rated PG; 125 minutes; American release date: September 20, 2002

VOICE CAST

Chihiro . . . . .Daveigh Chase
Yubaba/Zeniba . . . . .Suzanne Pleshette
Haku . . . . .Jason Marsden
Lin . . . . .Susan Egan
Kamaji . . . . .David Ogden Stiers
Chihiro's Mother . . . . .Lauren Holly
Chihiro's Father . . . . .Michael Chiklis
Assistant Manager . . . . .John Ratzenberger
Boh (Baby) . . . . .Tara Strong
and Mickie McGowan, Sherry Lynn, Jack Angel, Mona Marshall, Bob Bergen, Candi Milo, Rodger Bumpass, Colleen O'Shaughnessey, Jennifer Darling, Phil Proctor, Paul Eiding, Jim Ward (Additional Voices)

A ten-year old girl is taken away to a fantasy world where she is taught to overcome her fears in order to save her parents and herself.

2002 Academy Award winner for Best Animated Feature.

© Walt Disney Pictures

Chihiro, No-Face

Chihiro, Lin

Haku, Chihiro

Assistant Manager, Frog Foreman

Chihiro

Chihiro, No-Face

Boh, Chihiro

ADRIEN BRODY in *The Pianist*

NICOLE KIDMAN in *The Hours*

CHRIS COOPER in *Adaptation*.

ACADEMY AWARD FOR BEST SUPPORTING ACTRESS 2002

CATHERINE ZETA-JONES in *Chicago*

ACADEMY AWARD NOMINEES FOR BEST ACTOR

Nicolas Cage in *Adaptation.*

Michael Caine in *The Quiet American*

Daniel Day-Lewis in *Gangs of New York*

Jack Nicholson in *About Schmidt*

ACADEMY AWARD NOMINEES FOR BEST ACTRESS

Salma Hayek in *Frida*

Diane Lane in *Unfaithful*

Julianne Moore in *Far from Heaven*

Renée Zellweger in *Chicago*

ACADEMY AWARD NOMINEES FOR BEST SUPPORTING ACTOR

Ed Harris in *The Hours*

Paul Newman in *Road to Perdition*

John C. Reilly in *Chicago*

Christopher Walken in *Catch Me If You Can*

ACADEMY AWARD NOMINEES FOR BEST SUPPORTING ACTRESS

Kathy Bates in *About Schmidt*

Queen Latifah in *Chicago*

Julianne Moore in *The Hours*

Meryl Streep in *Adaptation.*

TOP 100 BOX OFFICE FILMS OF 2002

1. Spider-Man (Col) $405,150,000
2. The Lord of Rings: The Two Towers (NL) $339,760,000
3. Star Wars Episode II: Attack of the Clones (20th) $310,620,000
4. Harry Potter and the Chamber of Secrets (WB) $261,840,000
5. My Big Fat Greek Wedding (IFC) $241,430,000
6. Signs (BV) $227,860,000
7. Austin Powers in Goldmember (NL) $213,120,000
8. Men in Black II (Col) $189,510,000
9. Ice Age (20th) $176,370,000
10. Chicago (Miramax) $170,690,000
11. Catch Me If You Can (DW) $163,790,000
12. Die Another Day (UA) $158,630,000
13. Scooby-Doo (WB) $152,910,000
14. Lilo & Stitch (BV) $145,240,000
15. XXX (Col) $139,810,000
16. The Santa Clause 2 (BV) $138,140,000
17. Minority Report (20th/DW) $131,720,000
18. The Ring (DW) $128,290,000
19. Sweet Home Alabama (BV) $127,220,000
20. Mr. Deeds (Col) $126,100,000
21. The Bourne Identity (Univ) $121,410,000
22. The Sum of All Fears (Par) $118,230,000
23. 8 Mile (Univ) $116,730,000
24. Road to Perdition (DW/20th) $103,560,000
25. Panic Room (Col) $95,310,000
26. Maid in Manhattan (Col) $93,820,000
27. Two Weeks Notice (WB) $93,140,000
28. Red Dragon (Univ) $92,960,000

Jack Nicholson in *About Schmidt*

Leonardo DiCaprio in *Catch Me If You Can*

29. The Scorpion King (Univ) $90,350,000
30. Spy Kids 2: The Island of Lost Dreams (Mir) $84,500,000
31. Snow Dogs (BV) $81,140,000
32. Blade II (New Line) $80,100,000
33. We Were Soldiers (Par) $78,100,000
34. Gangs of New York (Mir) $77,700,000
35. The Rookie (BV) $75,600,000
36. Barbershop (MGM) $75,230,000
37. Spirit: Stallion of the Cimarron (DW) $73,220,000
38. John Q (New Line) $70,620,000
39. Divine Secrets of the Ya-Ya Sisterhood (WB) $69,550,000
40. Insomnia (WB) $67,100,000
41. Changing Lanes (Par) $66,750,000
42. About Schmidt (NL) $64,970,000
43. Jackass: The Movie (Par) $64,100,000
44. Stuart Little 2 (Col) $63,740,000
45. The Time Machine (DW/WB) $56,570,000
46. Drumline (20th) $56,270,000
47. The Count of Monte Cristo (BV) $54,220,000
48. Unfaithful (20th) $52,660,000
49. Like Mike (20th) $51,420,000
50. The Tuxedo (DW) $50,100,000
51. Return to Never Land (BV) $48,250,000
52. Big Fat Liar (Univ) $47,200,000
53. Star Trek: Nemesis (Par) $43,120,000
54. Reign of Fire (BV) $43,000,000

Tobey Maguire, Kirsten Dunst in *Spider-Man*

Paul Newman, Tom Hanks in *Road to Perdition*

55. The Hours (Par/Mir) $41,610,000
56. High Crimes (20th) $41,340,000
57. A Walk to Remember (WB) $41,110,000
58. Orange County (Par) $41,100,000
59. The Master of Disguise (Col) $40,170,000
60. Windtalkers (MGM) $40,150,000
61. Blue Crush (Univ) $40,120,000
62. Collateral Damage (WB) $39,790,000
63. The Wild Thornberrys Movie (Par) $39,770,000
64. Resident Evil (Screen Gems) $39,540,000
65. Enough (Col) $39,100,000
66. About a Boy (Univ) $38,920,000
67. 40 Days and 40 Nights (Mir) $37,890,000
68. Showtime (WB) $37,840,000
69. Treasure Planet (BV) $37,490,000
70. Undercover Brother (Univ) $37,360,000
71. Crossroads (Par) $37,100,000
72. Clockstoppers (Par) $36,710,000
73. The Mothman Prophecies (Screen Gems) $35,170,000
74. E.T.: The Extra-Terrestrial (reissue) (Univ) $35,150,000
75. K-19: The Widowmaker (Par) $35,110,000
76. The Hot Chick (BV) $35,100,000
77. I Spy (Col) $33,100,000
78. Friday After Next (NL) $32,870,000
79. The Pianist (Focus) $32,550,000
80. Analyze That (WB) $32,130,000
81. Murder by Numbers (WB) $31,800,000
82. One Hour Photo (Fox Searchlight) $31,530,000

Nicole Kidman in *The Hours*

Robin Williams in *One Hour Photo*

Harrison Ford, Ingvar Sigurdsson in *K-19: The Widowmaker*

83. Queen of the Damned (WB) $30,310,000
84. The Banger Sisters (Fox Searchlight) $30,270,000
85. Ghost Ship (WB) $30,110,000
86. Halloween: Resurrection (Mir) $30,100,000
87. Bad Company (BV) $29,730,000
88. Dragonfly (Univ) $29,460,000
89. The New Guy (Col) $28,830,000
90. Swimfan (20th) $28,570,000
91. The Crocodile Hunter: Collision Course (MGM) $28,440,000
92. Brown Sugar (Fox Searchlight) $27,270,000
93. Blood Work (WB) $26,000,000
94. Jonah: A VeggieTales Movie (Artisan) $25,490,000
95. Frida (Mir) $25,400,000
96. All About the Benjamins (NL) $25,390,000
97. The Transporter (20th) $25,270,000
98. Beauty and the Beast (reissue)(BV) $25,170,000
99. The Sweetest Thing (Col) $24,100,000
100. Adam Sandler's Eight Crazy Nights (Col) $23,350,000

Clint Eastwood, Wanda De Jesus in *Blood Work*

FOREIGN FILMS

RELEASED IN THE U.S. IN 2002

BROTHERHOOD OF THE WOLF (LE PACTE DES LOUPS)

(UNIVERSAL) Producers, Richard Grandpierre, Samuel Hadida; Director, Christophe Gans; Screenplay, Stéphane Cabel; Adaptation, Stéphane Cabel, Christophe Gans; Photography, Dan Laustsen; Designer, Guy-Claude François; Costumes, Dominique Borg; Music, Joseph Lo Duca; Editors, Sébastien Prangère, David Wu, Xavier Loutreuil; Special Digital Effects, Duran; Beast Special Effects, Jim Henson's Creature Shop; Casting, Nathalie Chéron, Brigitte Moidon, Bernard Savin Pascaud; a Samuel Hadida and Richard Grandpierre presentation of a Davis Film/ Eskwad/Studio Canal production in co-production with TF1 Films Productions with the participation of Canal+ in assocation with Soficas, Natexis Banques, Populaires Images and Studio Images; French, 2001; Dolby; Super 35 Widescreen; Color; Rated R; 142 minutes; American release date: January 11, 2002

Vincent Cassel

Monica Bellucci

Jérémie Rénier, Samuel Le Bihan

CAST

Grégoire de Fronsac	Samuel Le Bihan
Jean François de Morangias	Vincent Cassel
Marianne de Morangias	Émilie Dequenne
Sylvia	Monica Bellucci
Thomas d'Apcher	Jérémie Rénier
Mani	Mark Dacascos
Count de Morangias	Jean Yanne
Henri Sardis	Jean-François Stévenin
Old Thomas	Jacques Perrin
Beauterne	Johan Leysen
Laffont	Bernard Farcy
Mme. de Morangias	Edith Scob
Marquis d'Apcher	Hans Meyer
Loudmouth Woman	Virginie Darmon
Jean Chastel	Philippe Nahon
Captain Duhamel	Éric Prat
Duke de Moncan	Jean-Loup Wolff
Mercier	Bernard Fresson
Old Thomas' Servant	Christian Marc
Shepherdess on Hillside	Karin Kristöm
Soldier	Vincent Cespedes
Father Georges	Jean-Paul Farré
Jacques	Pierre Lavit
Bishop de Mende	Michel Puterflam
Maxime des Forëts	Nicolas Vaude
Old Noblemen	Max Delor, Christian Adam
Nobleman at Dinner	Jean-Pierre Jackson
La Felure	Nicky Naude
Blond Man	Daniel Herroin
La Loutre	Gaëlle Cohen
La Pintade	Virginie Arnaud
Valet at Teissier	Charles Maquignon
Madame Teissier	Franckie Pain
Brunette Prostitute	Isabelle Le Nouvel
Prostitutes at Teissier	Albane Fioretti, Clarice Plasteig dit Cassou
Valentine	Delphine Hivernet

and Juliette Lamboley (Cécile), Gaspad Ulliel (Louis), Pierre Castagné (Cécile's Father), Stéphane Pioffet (Peasant), Eric Laffitte (A Villager), Eric Delcourt (Beauterne's Assistant), André Penvern (Buffon), Christelle Droy (Shepherdess with Goat), Andres Fuentes (Peasant Who Gives Directions), Nadine Marcovici (Jeanne, Marianne's Nanny), Jean-Claude Braquet (Pierre), David Bogino (Knife Thrower), Emmanuel Booz (Officer Bucher), François Hadji Lazaro (Machemort), Pascal Laugier (Machemort's Assistant)

Grégoire de Fronsac and Mani arrive in the town of Gevaudin in 1766 France in order to kill a mysterious and deadly beast that is stalking the land.

Samuel Le Bihan

WHAT TIME IS IT THERE?

(WELLSPRING) *Et la-bas, quelle heure est-il?*; Producer, Bruno Pesery; Director, Tsai Ming-Liang; Screenplay, Tsai Ming-Liang, Yang Pi-Ying; Photography, Benoît Delhomme; Designer, Yip Kam Tim; Editor, Chen Sheng-Chang; Associate Producer, Chinlin Hsieh; Taiwanese-French, 2001; Dolby; Color; Not rated; 116 minutes; American release date: January 11, 2002

CAST

Hsiao Kang	Lee Kang-Sheng
Shiang-Chyi	Chen Shiang-Chyi
Mother	Lu Yi-Ching
Father	Miao Tien
Woman in Paris	Cecilia Yip
Man in Subway Station	Chen Chao-Jung
Prostitute	Tsai Guei
Man at Phone Booth	Arthur Nauzyciel
Man at Restaurant	David Ganansia
Man at the Cemetery	Jean-Pierre Léaud

A young man and his grieving mother react to the death of the family patriarch in obsessive ways.

© Winstar Cinema

Aki Avni, Edan Alterman

Lee Kang-Sheng

Amnon Wolf, Aki Avni

TIME OF FAVOR

(KINO) Producers, David Mandil, Eyal Shiray; Director/Screenplay, Joseph Cedar; Photography, Ofer Inov; Designers, Yair Greenberg, Ofer Rachanim; Costumes, Etti Lugassi; Editor, Tova Asher; Music, Yonatan Bar-Giora; Casting, Galit Eshkol; an Israel Film Fund, Yes and Cinema Factory co-production; Israeli, 2000; Dolby; Color; Not rated; 98 minutes; American release date: January 18, 2002

CAST

Menachem	Aki Avni
Michal	Tinkerbell
Pini	Edan Alterman
Rabbi Meltzer	Assi Dayan
Itamar	Micha Selektar
Mookie	Amnon Wolf
Benny	Shimon Mimram
Sivan	Uri Klausner
Doron	Shemuel Kalderon

West Bank army officer Menachem falls in love with the daughter of the rabbi despite the fact that she is promised to Menachem's best friend, Pini, who reacts to this betrayal with an act of vengeance.

© Kino

Jean-Pierre Léaud, Chen Shiang-Chyi

ITALIAN FOR BEGINNERS

(MIRAMAX) Producer, Ib Tardini; Director/Screenplay, Lone Scherfig; Photography, Jørgen Johansson; Editor, Gerd Tjur; a Zentropa Entertainments presentation of Dogme XII with support from DR V/ Marianne Mortizen and the Danish Film Institute V/Vinca Wiedeman and Gert Duve Skovlund; Danish, 2000; Dolby; Color; Rated R; 99 minutes; American release date: January 18, 2002

CAST

Andreas . . . . .Anders W. Berthelsen
Olympia . . . . .Anette Støvelbæk
Jørgen Mortensen . . . . .Peter Gantzler
Karen . . . . .Ann Eleonora Jørgensen
Halvfinn . . . . .Lars Kaalund
Real Estate Dealer .Karen-Lise Mynster
Nurse . . . . .Rikki Wölck
Kirketjener . . . . .Elsebeth Steentoft
Giulia . . . . .Sara Indrio Jensen
Reverend Wredmann . . . . .Bent Mejding
Klaus Graversen . . . . .Claus Gerving
Olympia's Father . . . . .Jesper Christensen
Marcello . . . . .Carlo Barsotti
Karen's Mother . . . . .Lene Tiemroth
and Alex Nyborg Madsen, Steen Svare Hansen (Sports Men/Church Singers), Susanne Oldenburg (Lady), Martin Brygmann (Night School Teacher)

Six thirty-something singles find their lives changed for the better when they sign up for an introductory Italian class to get them through the bleak Copenhagen winter.

Ann Eleonora Jørgensen

Sara Indrio Jensen

Peter Gantzler, Sara Indrio Jensen, Lars Kaalund, Anette Støvelbæk, Ann Eleonora Jørgensen, Karen-Lise Mynster, Rikki Wölck, Elsebeth Steentoft, Anders W. Berthelsen

Peter Gantzler, Lars Kaalund

Peter Gantzler, Lars Kaalund

BEIJING BICYCLE

(SONY CLASSICS) Producers, Peggy Chiao, Hsu Hsiao-Ming, Han Sangping; Executive Producer, Hsu Bing-Shi; Director, Wang Xiaoshuai; Screenplay, Wang Xiaoshuai, Tang Danian, Peggy Chiao, Hsu Hsiao-Ming; Photography, Liu Jie; Art Directors, Tsai Chao-Yi, Cao Anjun; Costumes, Pang Yan; Editor, Liao Ching-Song; Associate Producer, Fabienne Vonier; Music, Wang Feng; a Pyramide Productions and Arc Light Films presentation; Taiwanese-Chinese, 2001; Dolby; Color; Rated PG-13; 113 minutes; American release date: January 25, 2002

Zhou Xun, Li Mengnan

CAST

Guei	Cui Lin
Jian	Li Bin
Qin	Zhou Xun
Xiao	Gao Yuanyuahn
Da Huan	Li Shuang
Father	Zhao Yiwei
Mother	Pang Yan
Rong Rong	Zhou Fangfei
Manager	Xie Jian
Accountant	Ma Yuhong
Mantis	Liu Lei
Qui Sheng	Li Mengnan

and Li Jian, Zhang Yang, Wang Yuzhong, Hui Wei (Classmates of Jian), Ji Hua, Ren Hougang, Zhang Yu (Bikers), Zhang Lei, Chang Jiayin, Wang Yan (Classmates of Xiao), Liu Jingyi, Zhuang Qingning, Huang Bo, Chen Fanghan, Fu Peng, Li Zhenhua (Others)

Just when he has almost finished paying for his new silver mountain bike, which he uses for his job as delivery boy, Guei has it stolen, the vehicle ending up in the possession of a young man whose life has now been changed by it.

© Sony Classics

Cui Lin, Li Bin

Cui Lin

Li Bin, Gao Yuanyuahn

ALEXANDRE DUMAS'
THE COUNT OF MONTE CRISTO

(TOUCHSTONE) Producers, Roger Birnbaum, Gary Barber, Jonathan Glickman; Executive Producer, Chris Brigham; Director, Kevin Reynolds; Screenplay, Jay Wolpert; Based on the novel by Alexandre Dumas; Photography, Andrew Dunn; Designer, Mark Geraghty; Costumes, Tom Rand; Editors, Stephen Semel, Chris Womack; Music, Edward Shearmur; Co-Producer, Morgan O'Sullivan; Casting, Priscilla John (U.K.), Marcia Ross (U.S.); Stunts, Paul Weston; a Spyglass Entertainment presentation of a Birnbaum/Barber production; British-Irish; Dolby; Super 35 Widescreen; Technicolor; Rated PG-13; 131 minutes; Release date: January 25, 2002

James Frain, Helen McCrory, Jim Caviezel

CAST

Edmond Dantes	Jim Caviezel
Fernand Mondego	Guy Pearce
Mercedes	Dagmara Dominczyk
Abbe Faria	Richard Harris
Jacopo	Luis Guzman
Villefort	James Frain
Albert Mondego	Henry Cavill
Danglars	Albie Woodington
Dorleac	Michael Wincott
Napoleon Bonaparte	Alex Norton
Maurice	Christopher Adamson
Luigi	JB Blanc
Mansion Owner	Guy Carleton
Old Dantes	Barry Cassin
Casino Prostitute	Briana Corrigan
Viscount	Brendan Costello
Morrell	Patrick Godfrey
Julianne	Katherine Holme
Col. Villefort	Freddie Jones

Jim Caviezel, Richard Harris

and Maireid Devlin, Stella Feeley, Joe Hanley (Partygoers), Joseph Kelly (Gardener), Ivan Kennedy (Outrider), Alvaro Lucchesi (Claude), Helen McCrory (Valentina Villefort), Karl O'Neill (Marchand), Robert Price (Pascal), Derek Reid (Banker), Eric Stovell (Nobleman Duellist), Jude Sweeney (Mondego Servant), Brian Thunder (Militia—Gendarme—Officer), Gregor Truter (Lt. Graypool), Andrew Woodall (Gendarmes Captain)

After sailor Edmond Dantes is unjustly sent to prison on charges concocted by his jealous friend Fernand, he plots his escape from the island hellhole with the intention of exacting vengeance on those responsible for his misfortune. Previous motion picture versions include those made in the U.S. (*Monte Cristo*, 1922, with John Gilbert; 1934, with Robert Donat), and France (1955, with Jean Marais; 1961, with Louis Jourdan).

© Spyglass Entertainment Group

Jim Caviezel, Dagmara Dominczyk

Guy Pearce, Jim Caviezel

THE SON'S ROOM

(MIRAMAX) Producers, Angelo Barbagallo, Nanni Moretti; Director, Nanni Moretti; Screenplay, Linda Ferri, Nanni Moretti, Heidrun Schleef; Based on an original idea by Nanni Moretti; Photography, Giuseppe Lanci; Set Designer, Giancarlo Basili; Music, Nicola Piovani; Editor, Esmeralda Calbria; Costumes, Maria Rita Barbera; a Sacher Film (Rome), BAC Films, Studio Canal (Paris) co-production with the collaboration of RAI Cinema and Tele+; Italian-French, 2001; Dolby; Color; Not rated; 87 minutes; American release date: January 25, 2002

CAST

Giovanni	Nanni Moretti
Paola	Laura Morante
Irene	Jasmine Trinca
Andrea	Giuseppe Sanfelice
The Patients	Stefano Abbati, Stefano Accorsi, Toni Bertorelli, Dario Cantarelli, Eleonora Danco, Claudia Della Seta, Luisa De Santis, Silvio Orlando
Arianna	Sofia Vigliar
Headmast	Renato Scarpa
Priest	Roberto Nobile
Luciano's Father	Paolo De Vita
Record Store Clerk	Robert De Francesco

and Claudio Santamaria (Dive Shop Clerk), Antonio Petrocelli (Errnico), Lorenzo Alessandri (Filippo's Father), Alessandro Infusini (Matteo), Silvia Bonucci (Carla), Marcello Bernacchini (Luciano), Alessandro Ascoli (Stefano), Emanuele Lo Nardo (Filippo)

A small town psychiatrist finds his seemingly perfect life shattered when his beloved son is killed in a scuba-diving accident.

© Miramax

Giuseppe Sanfelice, Nanni Moretti

Laura Morante, Giuseppe Sanfelice, Jasmine Trinca, Nanni Moretti

Laura Morante, Giuseppe Sanfelice

Laura Morante, Nanni Moretti

BIRTHDAY GIRL

Vincent Cassel, Nicole Kidman

Nicole Kidman, Mathieu Kassovitz

Ben Chaplin

(MIRAMAX) Producers, Steve Butterworth, Diana Phillips; Executive Producers, Paul Webster, Julie Goldstein, Colin Leventhal, Sydney Pollack; Director, Jez Butterworth; Screenplay, Tom Butterworth, Jez Butterworth; Photography, Oliver Stapleton; Designer, Hugo Luczyc-Wyhowski; Costumes, Phoebe De Gaye; Editor, Christopher Tellefsen; Music, Stephen Warbeck; Music Supervisor, Bob Last; Song: "Something Stupid" by C Carson Parks/performed by Robbie Williams and Nicole Kidman; Casting, Jina Jay; a FilmFour in association with Mirage Enterprises presentation; British-U.S.; Dolby; Super 35 Widescreen; Color; Rated R; 93 minutes; American release date: February 1, 2002

CAST

Nadia	Nicole Kidman
John Buckingham	Ben Chaplin
Alexei	Vincent Cassel
Yuri	Mathieu Kassovitz
Clare	Kate Evans
Bank Manager	Stephen Mangan
Robert Moseley	Xander Armstrong
Karen	Sally Phillips
Waitress	Jo McInnes
Concierge	Ben Miller
D.I. O'Fetiger	Jonathan Aris
Young Sophia	Katya Barton-Chapple
Bank Collegues	Rebecca Clarke, Raj Ghatak, David Mark, Jack Pierce
Tim	Mark Gatiss
Woman with Lost Hat	Sue Maund
Duty Sergeant	Steve Pemberton
Porter	Reece Shearsmith
Passport Official	Alan Stocks
Policeman #2	J.J. Toba

A mild-mannered bank employee sends for a Russian bride over the Internet and gets more than he bargained for when the woman's unsavory "friends" eventually show up.

© Miramax

Ben Chaplin, Nicole Kidman

MONSOON WEDDING

Lillete Dubey, Naseeruddin Shah

(USA FILMS) Producers, Caroline Baron, Mira Nair; Executive Producers, Jonathan Sehring, Caroline Kaplan; Director, Mira Nair; Screenplay, Sabrina Dhawan; Photography, Declan Quinn; Designer, Stephanie Carroll; Costumes, Arjun Bhasin; Editor, Allyson C. Johnson; Music, Mychael Danna; Line Producers, Shernaz Italia, Freny Khoadiji; Casting, Loveleen Tandan, Uma da Cunha, Dileep Shankar; an IFC Productions presentation in association with Key Films, Pandora Films, and Paradis Films of a Mirabai Films production; Indian-U.S.; Dolby; Color; Rated R; 114 minutes; American release date: February 22, 2002

CAST

Lalit Verma . . . . .Naseeruddin Shah
Pimmi Verma . . . . .Lillete Dubey
Ria Verma . . . . .Shefali Shetty
P.K. Dube . . . . .Vijay Raaz
Alice . . . . .Tilotama Shome
Aditi Verma . . . . .Vasundhara Das
Hemant Rai . . . . .Parvin Dabas
C.L. Chadha . . . . .Kamini Khanna
Tej Puri . . . . .Rajat Kapoor
Ayesha Verma . . . . .Neha Dubey
Aliya Verma . . . . .Kemaya Kidwai
Varun Verma . . . . .Ishaan Nair
and Randeep Hooda (Rahul Chadha), Roshan Seth (Mohan Rai), Soni Razdan (Saroj Rai), Sameer Arya (Vikram Mehta), Rahul Vohra (Uday Verma), Natasha Rastogi (Sona Verma), Vimla Bhushan (Veena Verma), Ira Pandey (Vijaya Puri), Dibyendu Bhattacharya (Lottery), Deepak Kumar Bandhu (Tameez-Ud-Din), Pankaj Jha (Yadav), Mohini Mathur (Old Mother), Sharda Desohras (P.K. Dube's Mother), Rumaan Kidwai (Jibesh), Sahira Nair (Vandana), Urvashi Nair (Leena), Ram Kapoor (Shelly), Jas Arora (Umang Chadha), Rajiv Gupta, Shubro Bhattacharya (Cops), Rajeev Suri, Vikram Nair, Rajeev Bal (Golfers), Raman Chawla, Milan Moudgill, Himani Dehlvi (Talk Show Panelists), Nishi Singh Bhadli (Dubbist), Neelu Khanna (Talk Show Assistant), Motilal Khare (Sari Salesman), Paritosh Sand (Jai Chand), Ambar B. Capoor (Photographer), Renuka (Woman in the Rain), Inderjit & Reena Singh (Foxtrotting Couple), Madan Bala Sindhu (Featured Punjabi Singer), Rekha (Featured Solo Singer)

Members of a Punjabi family from all over the world converge on New Delhi for the arranged wedding of the Verma's young daughter Aditi.

© USA Films

Parvin Dabas, Naseeruddin Shah

Vasundhara Das, Shefali Shetty

Vasundhara Das, Parvin Dabas

Alan Bates, Charlotte Rampling

THE CHERRY ORCHARD

(KINO) Producer/Director/Screenplay, Michael Cacoyannis; Based on the play by Anton Chekhov; Photography, Aris Stavrou; Designer, Dionysis Fotopoulos; Costumes, Jane Hamilton; Music, Piotr Ilyich Tchaikovsky; Executive Producers, Yannoulla Wakefield, Alexander Metodiev; Editors, Michael Cacoyannis, Takis Hadzis; Casting, Bruce H. Newberg, Slater & Associates Casting; a Melinda Film Productions, Amanda Productions, Films De L'Astre co-production; Greek-French, 1999; Dolby; Color; Not rated; 137 minutes; American release date: February 22, 2002

CAST

Lyubov Andreyevna (Ranevskaya)	Charlotte Rampling
Gaev (Leonid Andreyevich)	Alan Bates
Varya (Varvava Mihailovna)	Katrin Cartlidge
Lopahin (Yermolai Alexeyevich)	Owen Teale
Anya	Tushka Bergen
Epihodov	Xander Berkeley
Yasha	Gerard Butler
Trofimov (Pyotr Sergeyevich)	Andrew Howard
Dunyasha	Melinda Lynskey
Pishchik (Semyon Semyonovich)	Ian McNeice
Charlotta (Ivanova)	Frances De La Tour
Feers	Michael Gough

Madame Lyubov returns to the Ranevsky Estate after years of mourning for her drowned son, only to find that the family's fortune has dwindled.

© Kino

ESTHER KAHN

(EMPIRE) Producers, Pascal Caucheteux, Grégoire Sorlat, Chris Curling; Director, Arnaud Desplechin; Screenplay, Arnaud Desplechin, Emmanuel Bourdieu; Based on the story by Arthur Symons; Photography, Eric Gautier; Designer, Jon Henson; Costumes, Nathalie Duerinckx; Music, Howard Shore; Editors, Hervé de Luze, Martine Giordano; Line Producers, Oury Milshtein, Waldo Roeg; Casting, Leo Davis, Wendy Brazington; a Why Not Productions/Les Films Alain Sarde/France 3 Cinéma/France 2 Cinéma/Zephyr Films co-production in association with the Arts Council of England with the participation of Canal+, BSkyB & British Screen; French-British, 2000; Dolby; Color; Not rated; 145 minutes; American release date: March 1, 2002

CAST

Esther Kahn	Summer Phoenix
Nathan Quellen	Ian Holm
Rivka Kahn	Frances Barber
Ythzok Kahn	Laszlo Szabo
Philip Haygard	Fabrice Desplechin
Trish	Kika Markham
Italian Girl	Emmanuelle Devos
Sean	Anton Lesser

and Hilary Sesta (Sophie, Grandmother), Berna Raif (Becky Kahn), Claudia Solti (Mina Kahn), Akbar Kurtha (Samuel Kahn), Ian Bartholomew (Norton), Paul Regan (Joel), Philadelphia Deda (Esther as a Child), Sef Naaktgeboren (Rebtchick), Yusuf Altin (Samuel as a Child), Marwa Zahri (Mina as a Child), Tina Nichols (Becky as a Child), Kyri Kambanis (Doctor), Claire Lubert (Colleague in the Match Factory), Arnold Brown (Rabbi), Leon Lissek (Theatre Manager), Christopher Logan (Assistant at the 2nd Theatre), Jackie Skarvellis (Friend in the Market), Ralph Nossek (Manager), Jon Rumney (Prompter), Samuel Lavelle (Christel), Loizos Loizou (Bookseller), Claudine Thomas (Young Woman in the Pub), Monty Ogus (Barber), Paul Ritter (Alman, Photographer), Tony Vogel (Dodo), Maurice Kanareck (Banker), Theresa Boden (Kathryn, Make-up Girl), Maggie McCarthy (Vivian, Dresser), Derek Smee (Cashier), Zita Sattar (Asst. Make-up Girl), Tony Brace (Nurse), David Thomson (Shy Stagehand), Ranin Gray (The Narrator); The Daughter of Love: Gregory Gudgen (Khayim), Natasha Pollard (Kave), Anita Leaf (Hinde);Wages of Sin: Allison Gaudion (Daughter), Rupert Fawcett (Fiance), Kenneth Hazeldine (Father); Rouge et Noir: Adrian Hammond (The Kisser of Mature Years); Hedda Gabler: Crispin Letts (Brian "Tesman"), Ann Firbank (Sarah "Aunt Julia"), Deidre Doone (Margaret "Berta"), Samantha Holland (Johanna "Mrs. Elvsted"), Michael Müller (David "Lovborg")

Esther Kahn, a detached Jewish immigrant living in 19th-century London, decides to pursue her dream to become an actress.

© Empire

Summer Phoenix

BORSTAL BOY

(STRAND) Producers, Pat Moylan, Arthur Lappin; Executive Producers, Jim Sheridan, Nye Heron; Director, Peter Sheridan; Screenplay, Nye Heron, Peter Sheridan; Inspired by the book by Brendan Behan; Photography, Ciaran Tanham; Designer, Crispian Sallis; Costumes, Marie Tierney; Editor, Stephen O'Connell; Music, Stephen McKeon; Co-Producer, Judy Counihan; Line Producer, Paul Myler; Casting, Maureen Hughes; a co-production of BSkyB, British Screen, Bórd Scannán na Éireann, Dakota Films, Full Schilling Investments, Hell's Kitchen Films, Radio Teilifís Eireann (RTE), British-Irish, 2000; Dolby; Color; Not rated; 91 minutes; American release date: March 1, 2002

CAST

Brendan Behan	Shawn Hatosy
Charlie Milwall	Danny Dyer
Dale	Lee Ingleby
Jock	Robin Laing
Liz Joyce	Eva Birthistle
Joyce	Michael York
Mac	Mark Huberman
Parson	Jim Byrne
Borstal Boys	Garret Deady, Darren Donohue, William Fitzpatrick, Keith Murtaugh
Customs Man	Ronnie Drew
Miller	Luke Griffin
Soldier	Tervor Hanly
Hassel	Klaus Hassel
Alex	Luke Hayden
Landlady	Patricia Levento
Verreker	Ina McElhinney
Jerzy	Viko Nikci
Republican in Court	Jer O'Leary
Whitbread	John O'Toole
Librarian	Arthur Riordan
Albert	Owen Sharpe
James	Eoin Slattery

In 1942, Brendan Behan, a sixteen-year-old Irish republican caught smuggling explosives into Liverpool, finds himself incarcerated in a British reform institution where he forms a special bond with fellow inmate Charlie Milwall.

© Strand

Shawn Hatosy

Michael York, Eva Birthistle

Robin Laing, Danny Dyer, Shawn Hatosy

Danny Dyer, Shawn Hatosy

HARRISON'S FLOWERS

(**UNIVERSAL FOCUS**) Producers, Elie Chouraqui, Albert Cohen; Director, Elie Chouraqui; Screenplay, Elie Chouraqui, Didier Le Pecheur, Isabel Ellsen, Michael Katims; Based on the book by Isabel Ellsen; Photography, Nicola Pecorni; Designer, Giantito Burchiellaro; Costumes, Mimi Lempicka; Music, Cliff Eidelman; Editors, Emmanuelle Castro, Jacques Witta; Casting, Amanda Mackey Johnson, Cathy Sandrich; Produced by 7 Films Cinéma, Studio Canal, France 2 Cinéma, with the participation of Canal+; French, 2001; Dolby; Super 35 Widescreen; Color; Rated R; 130 minutes; American release date: March 15, 2002

CAST

Sarah Lloyd . . . . .Andie MacDowell
Yeager Pollack . . . . .Elias Koteas
Marc Stevenson . . . . .Brendan Gleeson
Kyle Morris . . . . .Adrien Brody
Harrison Lloyd . . . . .David Strathairn
Samuel Brubeck . . . . .Alun Armstrong
Cesar Lloyd . . . . .Scott Michael Anton
Chetnik . . . . .Dragan Antonic
Mary Francis . . . . .Diane Baker
Austrian Woman . . . . .Marie-Béatrice Bernert
Doctor in Vukovar . . . . .Predrag Bjelac
Freddy . . . . .Antony Boehm
Chris Kumac . . . . .Gerard Butler
Jeff . . . . .Christian Charmetant
David . . . . .Christopher Clarke
and Kurt Cramer (CNN Journalist), Rich Gold, Gregory Linington, Deborah Michaels, Nicole Estabrooks (Journalists), Simon Francis (Layout Technician), Milan Gargula (Katzman), Caroline Goodall (Johanna Pollack), Bela Grushka (Nina Portnoy), Jessica Horvathova (HTV Interviewer), Amy Huck (Cybil), Corey Johnson (Peter Francis), Joel Kirby (Michael), Rianne Kooiman (Newsweek Journalist), Liliana Krstic (Old Woman), Mirko Medenica (Croatian Officer), Slobodan Milovanovic (Base Commander), Sasa Nikolitch (Chtiomac), Zivko Petrov (Nustar Peasant), Dragan Radivojevic (Sniper), Michael Rogers (Canadian Cameraman), Quinn Shepherd (Margaux Lloyd), Bruce Soloman (Rabbi), Joel Sugarman (Nelson), Marie Trintignant (Cathy), Dale Wyatt (Mistress of Ceremony)

When her husband Harrison is presumed dead, Sarah Lloyd teams up with a group of photojournalists to search war-torn Yugoslavia, determined to find him, dead or alive.

© Universal Pictures

Andie MacDowell, Elias Koteas

Andie MacDowell, David Strathairn

David Strathairn, Andie MacDowell

Adrien Brody, Brendan Gleeson

247

Y TU MAMÁ TAMBIÉN

(IFC FILMS) Producers, Jorge Vergara, Alfonso Cuarón; Executive Producers, Sergio Agüero, David Linde, Amy Kaufman; Director, Alfonso Cuarón; Screenplay, Carlos Cuarón, Alfonso Cuarón; Photography, Emmanuel Lubezki; Designer, Miguel Angel Álvarez; Costumes, Gabriela Diaque; Editors, Alfonso Cuarón, Alex Rodríguez; Music Supervisors, Liza Richardson, Annette Fradera; Casting, Manuel Teil; a Jorge Vergara, Producciones Anhelo presentation; Mexican, 2001; Dolby; DuArt color; Not rated; 106 minutes; American release date: March 15, 2002

Gael García Bernal, Maribel Verdú, Diego Luna

Gael García Bernal

Diego Luna, Gael García Bernal

Gael García Bernal, Maribel Verdú

CAST

Luisa Cortés	Maribel Verdú
Julio Zapata	Gael García Bernal
Tenoch Iturbide	Diego Luna
Enriqueta "Queta" Allende	Marta Aura
Silvia Allende de Iturbide	Diana Bracho
Miguel Iturbide	Emilio Echevarría
María Eugenia Calles de Huerta	Verónica Langer
Esteban Morelos	Arturo Rios
Ana Morelos	Ana López Mercado
Manuel Huerta	Nathan Grinberg
Cecilia Huerta	María Aura
Nicole Bazaine	Giselle Audirac
Diego "Saba" Madero	Andrés Almeida
Alejandro "Jano" Montes de Oca	Juan Carlos Remolina
Leodegaria "Leo" Victoria	Liboria Rodriguez
Jesús "Chuy" Carranza	Silverio Palacios
Mabel Juárez de Carranza	Andrea López
Christian Carranza	Amaury Sérbulo

Two best friends, spending their last summer together before attending college, convince a beautiful young woman to accompany them on a car trip to an upspoilt Mexcian beach, hoping the journey will lead to sex. Oscar nominee for original screenplay.

Maribel Verdú, Diego Luna, Gael García Bernal

PAULINE & PAULETTE

(**SONY CLASSICS**) Producer, Dominique Janne; Director, Lieven Debrauwer; Screenplay, Lieven Debrauwer, Jacques Boon; Photography, Michel Van Laer; Art Director, Hilde Duyck; Costumes, Erna Siebens; Editor, Philippe Ravoet; Music, Frederic Devreese; Belgian-French-Dutch, 2001; Dolby; Color; Rated PG; 78 minutes; American release date: March 15, 2002

CAST

Pauline	Dora van der Groen
Paulette	Ann Petersen
Cecile	Rosemarie Bergmans
Albert	Idwig Stephane
Martha	Julienne De Bruyn
The Butcher's Wife	Camilia Blereau
Director of the Home	François Beukelaers
Notary	Nand Buyl
Butcher	Herman Coessens
Marie Jose	Magda Cnudde
Marcella	Jenny Tanghe
Funeral Director	Jef Demets
Stage Director	Michel Bauwens
Soprano	Christine Termonia
Count	Koen Crucke
Taxi Driver	Bouli
Prompter	Rita Maddens
Waitress in Tea Room	Freddie Shermann
Client in Tea Shop	Jocelyne Verdier
Girls in Shoeshop	Kiki De Paepe
Frank	Luc Nuyens
Ladies in Institution	Ingrid De Vos, Machteld Ramoudt
Singing Voice	Paulette Maria Verhaert

When her beloved sister Martha dies, mentally handicapped senior citizen Pauline is left at the mercy of her two other sisters, neither of whom is eager to take care of her, until they realize Martha's will has dictated that very request.

© Sony Classics

Ann Petersen, Dora van der Groen

Ricardo Darín, Norma Aleandro, Héctor Alterio

Natalia Verbeke, Gimena Nóbile

SON OF THE BRIDE

(**SONY CLASSICS**) Producers, Fernando Blanco, Pablo Bossi, Jorge Estrada Mora, Gerardo Herrero, Mariela Besuievdsky; Executive Producer, Juan Pablo Galli; Director, Juan José Campanella; General Producer, Adrián Suar; Photography, Daniel Shulman; Designer, Juan Vera; Costumes, Osvaldo Esperón; Music, Angel Illaramendi; Editor, Camilo Antolini; Casting, Valeria Pivato; from Tornasol Films; Argentine-Spanish; Dolby; Color; Rated R; 124 minutes; American release date: March 22, 2002

CAST

Rafael Belvedere	Ricardo Darín
Nino Belvedere	Héctor Alterio
Norma Belvedere	Norma Aleandro
Juan Carlos	Eduardo Blanco
Nati	Natalia Verbeke
Vicky	Gimena Nóbile
Sandra	Claudia Fontán
Nacho	David Masajnik
Francesco	Atilio Pozzobón
Daniel	Salo Pasik

A minor heart attack causes disenchanted restaurant manager Rafael Belvedere to reassess his life and focus on the possibilty of bringing his estranged family together. This film received an Oscar nomination for foreign language film (2001).

© Sony Classics

THE PIANO TEACHER

Benoît Magimel, Isabelle Huppert

(KINO) Producers, Veit Heiduschka, Marin Kamitz, Alain Sarde; Director/Screenplay, Michael Haneke; Based on the novel by Elfriede Jelinek; Photography, Christian Berger; Designer, Christoph Kanter; Costumes, Annette Beaufaÿs; Editors, Monika Willi, Nadine Muse; Music, Martin Achenbach; a Wega-Film, MK2, Les Films Alain Sarde and Arte France Cinema co-production with the participation of Canal+, Arte/BR, CBC, ÖF1, WFF, ORF, and Eurimages; Austrian-French, 2000; Dolby; Color; Not rated; 130 minutes; American release date: March 29, 2002

CAST

Erika Kohut	Isabelle Huppert
Walter Klemmer	Benoît Magimel
The Mother	Annie Girardot
Anna Schober	Anna Sigalevitch
Mrs. Schober	Susanne Lothar
Dr. Blonskij	Udo Samel

A lonely middle-aged piano teacher begins an affair with a student, using him to explore her darkest sadomasochistic fantasies.

© Kino

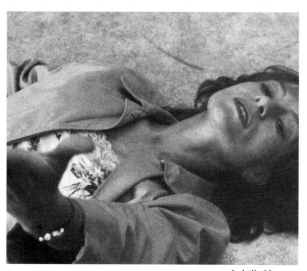

Isabelle Huppert

Benoît Magimel

Isabelle Huppert, Benoît Magimel

TIME OUT

(THINKFILM) Producer, Caroline Benjo; Executive Producer, Barbara Lettelier; Director, Laurent Cantet; Screenplay, Robin Campillo, Laurent Cantet; Photography, Pierre Milon; Art Director, Romain Denis; Costumes, Elizabeth Mehu; Editor, Robin Campillo; Music, Jocelyn Pook; Casting, Stephane Batut, Constance Demontoy; Director of Production, Elise Voitey; a Haut et Court presentation; French, 2001; Dolby; Color; Rated PG-13; 130 minutes; American release date: March 29, 2002

CAST

Vincent	Aurelien Recoing
Muriel	Karin Viard
Jean-Michel	Serge Livrozet
Father	Jean-Pierre Mangeot
Mother	Monique Mangeot
Julien	Nicolas Kalsch
Alice	Marie Cantet
Félix	Félix Cantet
Stan	Olivier Lejoubioux
Nono	Maxime Sassier
Jeanne	Elisabeth Joinet
Jaffrey	Nigel Palmer
Fred	Christopher Charles
Philippe	Didier Perez
Human Resources Director	Philippe Jouannet
Laetitia	Pauline de Laubie
Eati	Jamila Abdallah
Luc	Didier Folques
Valerie	Sophie Cabaille
Patrick	Pascal Maugein
Warehouse Customer	Jacques Gillot
Security Guard	Thierry Fernandez
Jeffrey's Wife	Elisabeth Lalanne
Jeffrey's Daughter	Lola Rhode
Julie	Manon Lepage
Jeffrey's Secretary	Maryline Merat
Fred's Director	Philippe Maynial

Finding himself recently unemployed, Vincent fabricates a new job in order to convince his family and friends that he is still at work, a deception that becomes increasingly elaborate and desperate.

© ThinkFilm

Aurelien Recoing

Aurelien Recoing

Karin Viard, Aurelien Recoing

Aurelien Recoing

CRUSH

(SONY CLASSICS) Producer, Lee Thomas; Director/Screenplay, John McKay; Photography, Henry Braham; Designer, Amanda MacArthur; Costumes, Jill Taylor; Line Producer, Fiona Morham; Editor, Anne Sopel; Music, Kevin Sargent; Casting, Michelle Guish; a FilmFour presentation in association with Film Council, Senator Film and Industry Entertainment of a Pipedream Pictures production; British; Dolby; Panavision; Color; Rated R; 115 minutes; American release date: April 3, 2002

CAST

Kate	Andie MacDowell
Janine	Imelda Staunton
Molly	Anna Chancellor
Jed	Kenny Doughty
Gerald	Bill Paterson
Pam	Caroline Holdaway
Brendan	Joe Roberts
Young Police Constable	Josh Cole
Sergeant	Gary Powell
Kate's Frenchman	Christian Burgess
Bishop	Morris Perry
Lady Governor	Richenda Carey
Hearty Governor	Roger Booth
Little Cremation Man	Derek Deadman
Mr. Yacht	Andrew Bicknell
Mr. Horse	Jeremy Gittins
Mr. Bundesbank	Tim Walker
Mr. Sensitive	Louis Hammond
Boring Martin	John Voce
Minicab Driver	Anthony Renshaw
Stationer	Mathilda Thorpe

and Sarah Rickman, Eve Rose Cooper (Assistants), Claire Nicholson, Elizabeth Hurran (Nurses), David Nicholls (Bill), James Vaughn (Mr. Unspeakable Lying Bastard), Louise Gold (Eleanor), Lauren Stone (Smoking School Girl), Maureen Bennett (Parent), Kevin Sargent (Teacher), Rosie Scanlon Jones (Little Girl in Garden)

Kate finds her friendship with her two other single friends, Janine and Molly, in jeopardy when she begins dating a much younger man.

© Sony Classics

Andie MacDowell, Christian Burgess

Kenny Doughty, Andie MacDowell

Andie MacDowell, Kenny Doughty

Imelda Staunton, Andie MacDowell, Anna Chancellor

LUCKY BREAK

(PARAMOUNT/MIRAMAX) Producers, Barnaby Thompson, Peter Cattaneo; Executive Producers, Paul Webster, Hanno Huth; Director, Peter Cattaneo; Screenplay, Ronan Bennett; Photography, Alwin Küchler; Designer, Max Gottlieb; Costumes, Ffion Elinor; Editor, David Gamble; Hair/Make-Up Designer, Veronica Brebner; Music, Anne Dudley; *Nelson: The Musical* book & lyrics, Stephen Fry; Co-Producers, Lesley Stewart, Elinor Day; Choreographer, Nicky Hinkley; Casting, Janey Fothergill; a FilmFour presentation in asscociation with Senator Film of a Fragile Films-Lucky Break production; British-German, 2001; Dolby; Super 35 Widescreen; Color; Rated PG-13; 107 minutes; American release date: April 5, 2002

CAST

Jimmy Hands	James Nesbitt
Annabel Sweep	Olivia Williams
Cliff Gumbell	Timothy Spall
Roger Chamberlain	Bill Nighy
Rudy Guscott	Lennie James
Perry	Ron Cook
John Toombes	Frank Harper
Darren	Raymond Waring
Graham Mortimer	Christopher Plummer
Paul	Julian Barratt
Officer Barratt	Peter Wight
Amy	Celia Imrie
Ward	Peter McNamara
Kenny	Andy Linden
Old Bill	Ram John Holder
Mad Lenny	John Pierce Jones
Arthur	Desmond McNamara
Wayne	Ofo Uhiara
Officer Phillips	Brian Abbot

and Annette Bentley (Julie), William Howe (Ritchie), John Drew (Security Officer), Sean McKenzie (Perry's Assistant), Georgie Glen (Audience Member)

Facing twelve years behind bars, smalltime crook Jimmy Hands comes up with the plan of staging a musical in order to cover his escape from prison.

James Nesbitt, Frank Harper

Charles Berling, Emmanuelle Béart

LES DESTINÉES

(WELLSPRING) Producer, Bruno Pesery; Co-Producers, Jean-Louis Porchet, Gérard Ruey; Director, Olivier Assayas; Screenplay, Jacques Fieschi, Olivier Assayas; Based on the novel by Jacques Chardonne; Line Producer, Jean-Yves Asselin; Photography, Eric Gautier; Set Designer, Katia Wyszkop; Costumes, Anaïs Romand; Editor, Luc Barnier; Casting, Antoinette Boulat; Arena Films—TF1 Films Productions—Cab Productions with the participation of Canal+—Cofimage 11—Arcade; French-Swiss, 2000; Dolby; Scope; Color; Not rated; 174 minutes; American release date: April 5, 2002

CAST

Pauline	Emmanuelle Béart
Jean Barnery	Charles Berling
Nathalie Barnery	Isabelle Huppert
Philippe Pommerel	Olivier Perrier
Julie Desca	Dominique Reymond
Louise Desca	Alexandra London
Paul Desca	André Marcon
Marcelle	Julie Depardieu
Arthur Pommerel	Louis-Do de Lencquesaing
Mrs. Arthur Pommerel	Valérie Bonneton
Vouzelles	Pascal Bongard
Guy Barney	Didier Flamand
Frédéric Barnery	Jean-Baptiste Malartre
Bavouzet	Nicolas Pignon
Fernande	Catherine Mouchet
Aline	Mia Hansen-Løve
Dominique	Sophie Aubry

and Victor Garrivier (Pasteur Sabatier), Jérôme Huguet (René Fayet), Mathieu Genet (Max Barnery), Rémi Martin (Dahlias), Roger Dumas (Pauline's Boss), Saki Reid (Miss Howard), Claire Hammond (Madame Ducros), Pierre Saternaer (Factory Engineer), Jocelyne Desverchère (Célesinte), Patricia Dinev (Solange), Christian Drillaud (Surgeon), Circé Lethem (Anna), Maryline Even (Bridge Player), Christophe Jazinski (Théodore), Barnaby Southcombe (Marcelle's Escort), Joséphine Firino-Martell (Aline, 5 years old), Alexandre Marcos (Max, 4 years old), Grégory Marcos (Max, 6 years old)

Having moved to Switzerland with his new wife after a scandalous divorce, Jean is summoned back to Limoges to run the family porcelain business.

HUMAN NATURE

(FINE LINE FEATURES) Producers, Anthony Bregman, Ted Hope, Spike Jonze, Charlie Kaufman; Director, Michel Gondry; Screenplay, Charlie Kaufman; Co-Producer, Julie Fong; Photography, Tim Maurice-Jones; Designer, K.K. Barrett; Costumes, Nancy Steiner; Editor, Russell Icke; Music, Graeme Revell; Music Supervisor, Tracy McKnight; Casting, Jeanne McCarthy; a Studiocanal presentation of a Good Machine production in association with Beverly Detroit Studios and Partizan; French-U.S.; Dolby; Color; Rated R; 96 minutes; Release date: April 12, 2002

Rhys Ifans

CAST

Nathan Bronfman . . . . .Tim Robbins
Lila Jute . . . . .Patricia Arquette
Puff . . . . .Rhys Ifans
Gabrielle . . . . .Miranda Otto
Louise . . . . .Rosie Perez
Nathan's Father . . . . .Robert Forster
Nathan's Mother . . . . .Mary Kay Place
Police Detectives . . . . . . .Ken Magee, Sy Richardson, David Warshofsky
Young Lila . . . . .Hilary Duff
Doctor . . . . .Stanley DeSantis
Frank . . . . .Peter Dinklage
Puff's Father . . . . .Toby Huss
Congressman . . . . .Bobby Harwell, Daryl Anderson
Young Puff . . . . .Bobby Pyle
Young Nathan . . . . .Chase Bebak
Wendall the Therapist .Miguel Sandoval
Wayne Bronfman . . . . .Anthony Winsick
Bistro Waitress . . . . .Mary Portser
Aversion Therapy Model . . . . .Laura Grady Peterson
Chester's Waitress . . . . .Angela Little
Stripper . . . . .Deborah Ferrari
Lecture Host . . . . .Jeremy Kramer
Puff's Mother . . . . .Nancy Lenehan

Nathan Bronfman, a repressed behavorist, attempts to refine the beastial impulses of a wild man raised in the jungles, despite the objections of Nathan's assistant, Lila, who hides her hormonal disorder that causes hair to grow all over her body.

© Fine Line Features

Tim Robbins, Patricia Arquette

Tim Robbins, Patricia Arquette

Rhys Ifans, Miranda Otto

THE CAT'S MEOW

(LIONS GATE) Producers, Kim Bieber, Carol Lewis, Dieter Meyer, Julie Baines; Executive Producers, Wieland Schulz-Keil, Michael Paseornek; Director, Peter Bogdanovich; Screenplay, Steven Peros, based on his play; Co-Producer, Ernie Barbarash; Photography, Bruno Delbonnel; Designer, Jean-Vincent Puzos; Costumes, Caroline de Vivaise; Line Producer, Martin Hagemann; Casting, Sarah Beardsall, Beth Bowling; a CP Medien & Dan Films presentation of a Bieber+Lewis production; German-British, 2001; Dolby; Color; Rated PG-13; 112 minutes; American release date: April 12, 2002

CAST

Marion Davies	Kirsten Dunst
William Randolph Hearst	Edward Herrmann
Charlie Chaplin	Eddie Izzard
Thomas Ince	Cary Elwes
Elinor Glyn	Joanna Lumley
Louella Parsons	Jennifer Tilly
Margaret Livingston	Claudia Harrison
Joseph Willicombe	Ronan Vibert
George Thomas	Victor Slezak
Didi	Claudie Blakley
Celia	Chiara Schoras
Mrs. Barham	Ingrid Lacey
Mr. Barham	John C. Vennema
Dr. Daniel Carson Goodman	James Laurenson
Kono	Yuki Iwamoto
Mr. Cannonball	Hendrik Arnst

A drama speculating on what might have happened aboard William Randolph Hearst's yacht during a two day voyage in 1924 when movie producer Thomas Ince ended up dead.

© Lions Gate

Kirsten Dunst

Jennifer Tilly

Kirsten Dunst, Eddie Izzard

Fiona Shaw

TRIUMPH OF LOVE

(PARAMOUNT CLASSICS) Producer, Bernardo Bertolucci; Executive Producers, Massimo Cortesi, Jeremy Thomas, Thomas Schühly, Reinhard Klooss; Director, Clare Peploe; Screenplay, Clare Peploe, Marilyn Goldin, Bernardo Bertolucci; Adapted from the play Le Triomphe de l'amour by Marivaux, based onthe version by Martin Crimp, first produced by the Almeida Theatre Company; Photography, Fabio Cianchetti; Designer, Ben Van Os; Costumes, Metka Kosak; Music, Jason Osborn; Editor, Jacopo Quadri; Associate Producer, Stephan Mallmann; Casting, Nina Gold, Shaila Rubin; a Fiction s.r.l. and Recorded Pictures Company presentation, in association with Medusa Film s.p.a. and Odeon Pictures; Italian-British, 2001; Dolby; Color; Rated PG-13; 107 minutes; American release date: April 17, 2002

CAST

The Princess/Phocion/Aspasie . . . . .Mira Sorvino
Leontine . . . . .Fiona Shaw
Agis . . . . .Jay Rodan
Hermidas . . . . .Rachael Stirling
Harlequin . . . . .Ignazio Oliva
Dimas . . . . .Luis Molteni
Hermocrates . . . . .Ben Kingsley
Coachman . . . . .Carlo Antonione

Finding out that the man she is in love with has been taught by his mentor to hate women, a princess disguises herself as a boy.

© Paramount Classics

Mira Sorvino

Ben Kingsley

Mira Sorvino, Jay Rodan

ENIGMA

Kate Winslet

Dougray Scott, Saffron Burrows

(MANHATTAN PICTURES) Producers, Lorne Michaels, Mick Jagger; Executive Producers, Victoria Pearman, Guy East, Nigel Sinclair, Hanno Huth, Michael White; Director, Michael Apted; Screenplay, Tom Stoppard; Based on the novel by Robert Harris; Co-Executive Producers, Robbert Aarts, Thomas Garvin; Co-Producer, David Brown; Photography, Seamus McGarvey; Designer, John Beard; Costumes, Shirley Russell; Editor, Rick Shaine; Music, John Barry; Make-up and Hair Design, Jenny Shircore; Casting, Mary Selway, Amanda Mackey-Johnson, Cathy Sandrich; an Intermedia Films and Senator Entertainment presentation in association with Meespierson Film CV; a Jagged Films/Broadway Video production; British-German-U.S., 2001; Dolby; Panavision; Color; Rated R; 119 minutes; American release date: April 19, 2002

CAST

Tom Jericho . . . . .Dougray Scott
Hester Wallace . . . . .Kate Winslet
Claire Romilly . . . . .Saffron Burrows
Wigram . . . . .Jeremy Northam
Puck . . . . .Nikolaj Coster-Waldau
Logie . . . . .Tom Hollander
Leveret . . . . .Donald Sumpter
Cave . . . . .Matthew MacFadyen
Baxter . . . . .Richard Leaf
Proudfoot . . . . .Ian Felce
Pinker . . . . .Bohdan Poraj
Kingcome . . . . .Paul Rattray
De Brooke . . . . .Richard Katz
Upjohn . . . . .Tom Fisher
Skynner . . . . .Robert Pugh
Admiral Towbridge . . . . .Corin Redgrave
Villiers . . . . .Nicholas Rowe
and Angus MacInnes (Commander Hammerbeck), Mary MacLeod (Mrs. Armstrong), Michael Troughton (Mermagen), Edward Hardwicke (Heaviside), Anne-Marie Duff (Kay), Tim Bentinck (U-Boat Commander), Rosie Thomson (Duty Clerk), Emma Buckley (Land Army Girl), Mirjam De Rooij (Lady Lodger), Adrian Preater (RAF Corporal), Edward Woodall (Bletchley Brain), Hywel Simons (Lodger), Emma Davies (Pamela), Martin Glyn Murray (RAF Officer)

Top code breaker Tom Jericho is called on to help unravel the newly revamped Nazi communication system just around the same time Claire, the woman with whom he is in love, suddenly disappears.

© Manhattan Pictures

Dougray Scott, Kate Winslet

Dougray Scott, Jeremy Northam

NINE QUEENS

(SONY CLASSICS) Producer, Pablo Bossi; Director/Screenplay, Fabian Bielinsky; Photography, Marcelo Camorino; Art Director, Marcelo Salviola; Costumes, Monica Toschi; Editor, Sergio Zottola; Music, Cesar Lerner; a Patagonik Film Group Ind. — Audiovisuales Argentinas — Kodak Argentina — JZ y asociados — FX Sound in association with Naya Films S.A.; Argentine, 2000; Dolby; Color; Rated R; 115 minutes; American release: April 19, 2002

CAST

Juan	Gastón Pauls
Marcos	Ricardo Darín
Valeria	Leticia Bredice
Federico	Tomás Fonzi
Convenice Store Employees	Graciela Tenembaum, Maria Mercedes Villagara
Convenice Store Manager	Gabriel Correra
Aunt	Pochi Ducasse
Bar Waiter	Luis Armesto
Bar Manager	Ernesto Arias
Woman in Elevator	Amancay Espindola
Vender	Isaac Fajm
Anibal	Jorge Noya
Sandler	Oscar Nuñez
Vidal Gandolfo	Ignasi Abadal
Man on Cell Phone	Carlos Lanari
Texano	Roberto Rey
Mrs. Sandler	Celia Juarez
Washington	Alejandro Awada
D'Agostino	Antonio Ugo
Stamp Expert	Leon Dyzen
Berta	Elsa Berenguer
Amante Berta	Carlos Falcone
Ramiro	Ricardo Diaz Mourelle

and Ulises Celestino (Botones), Norberto Arcusin (Official), Gabriel Molinelli (Cárdenas), Emanuel Mercado (Boy), Claudio Rissi (Spanish Voice)

A pair of small-time con men, Juan and Marcos, team up to sell a forged set of valuable rare stamps, known as The Nine Queens.

Leticia Bredice, Tomás Fonzi, Ricardo Darín

Ricardo Darín, Gastón Pauls

Ricardo Darín, Gastón Pauls, Leticia Bredice

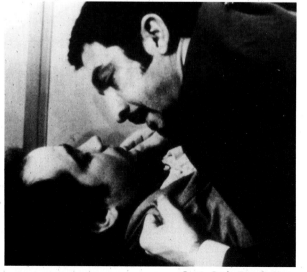

Gastón Pauls, Ricardo Darín

MURDEROUS MAIDS

(RIALTO) Producers, Laurent Pétin, Michèle Pétin; Director, Jean-Pierre Denis; Screenplay, Jean-Pierre Denis, Michèle Pétin; Based on the novel *L'affaire Papin* by Paulette Houdyer; Photography, Jean-Marc Fabre; Desiger, Bernard Vézat; Costumes, Sylvie de Segonaz; Editor, Marie-Hélène Dozo; Casting, Jeanne Biras; a co-production of ARP Sélection, Le Studio Canal+; French, 2000; Dolby; Super 35 Widescreen; Color; Not rated; 94 minutes; American release date: April 19, 2002

CAST

Christine Papin	Sylvie Testud
Léa Papin	Julie-Marie Parmentier
Clémence	Isabelle Renauld
The Veteran	François Levantal
Mme. Lincelan	Dominique Labourier
Mr. Lincelan	Jean-Gabriel Nordmann
Geneviève Lincelan	Marie Donnio
Alberta	Lily Boulogne
Madame 4	Blanche Raynal

The true story of how sister domestics, Christine and Léa Papin, wound up murdering their employer and her daughter in 1933 Le Mans, France. This story was previously dramatized in the 1975 American Film Theatre presentation of *The Maids*, starring Glenda Jackson and Susannah York.

© Rialto

Sylvie Testud, Julie-Marie Parmentier

Julie-Marie Parmentier, Sylvie Testud, Isabelle Renauld

Marianne Denicourt, Daniel Auteuil, Isild Le Besco

SADE

(EMPIRE) Producer, Patrick Godeau; Director, Benoît Jacquot; Screenplay, Jacques Fieschi, Bernard Minoret; Photography, Benoît Delhomme; Designer, Sylvain Chauvelot; Costumes, Christian Gasc; Editor, Luc Barnier; Line Producer, Françoise Galfré; an Alicéleo/TF1 Films Production co-produciton in association with Cofimage 11; French; Color; Not rated; 100 minutes; American release date: April 26, 2002

CAST

Marquis de Sade	Daniel Auteuil
Sensible (Marie-Constance Quesnet)	Marianne Denicourt
Madame Santero	Jeanne Balibar
Fournier	Grégoire Colin
Emilie	Isild Le Besco
Viscount de Lancris	Jean-Pierre Cassel
Coignard	Philippe Duquesne
evalier de Coublier	Vincent Branchet
Président de Maussane	Raymond Gérome
Augustin	Jalil Lespert
Madame de Lancris	Dominique Raymond
Renée de Sade	Sylvie Testud
Latour	François Levantal
Madame d'Amblet	Frédérique Tirmont
Monsieur Santero	Daniel Martin
Duchess Villars-Brancas	Monique Couturier
Robespierre	Scali Delpeyrat
Charles	Léo Le Bévillon

In 1794 France the Marquis de Sade, agitator and author, finds himself enduring prison at Picpus, a life made bearable through the devotion of his former mistress, Sensible.

© Empire

RAIN

(FIREWORKS) Producer, Philippa Campbell; Executive Producer, Robin Scholes; Director/Screenplay, Christine Jeffs; Based on the novel by Kirsty Gunn; Editor, Photography/Associate Producer, John Toon; Art Director/Costumes, Kirsty Cameron; Music, Neil Finn, Edmund McWilliams; Editor, Paul Maxwell; Line Producer, Judith Trye; Casting, Diana Rowan; a Rose Road and Communicado in association with the New Zealand Film Commission presentation; New Zealand, 2001; Dolby; Color; Not rated; 92 minutes; American release date: April 26, 2002

CAST

Janey	Alicia Fulford-Wierzbicki
Kate	Sarah Peirse
Cady	Marton Csokas
Ed	Alistair Browning
Jim	Aaron Murphy

During a summer vacation at an isolated seaside town, thirteen-year-old Janey watches as her mother drifts into an affair with a photographer.

© Fireworks

Alicia Fulford-Wierzbicki

Aaron Murphy

Koji Yakusho, Misa Shimizu

Koji Yakusho, Misa Shimizu

WARM WATER UNDER A RED BRIDGE

(COWBOY PICTURES) Producer, Hisa Iino; Executive Producer, Masaya Nakamura; Director, Shohei Imamura; Screenplay, Motofumi Tomikawa, Daisuke Tengan, Shohei Imamura; Based on the book by Yo Henmi; Photography, Shigeru Kamatsuhara; Set Designer, Hisao Inagaki; Editor, Hajime Okayasu; Music, Shinichiro Ikebe; from Code Red; Japanese, 2001; Dolby; Color; Not rated; 119 minutes; American release date: May 3, 2002

CAST

Yosuke Sasano	Koji Yakusho
Saeko Aizawa	Misa Shimizu
Mitsu Aizawa	Mitsuko Baisho
Gen	Mansaku Fuwa
Taro	Kazuo Kitamura
Masayuki Uomi	Isao Natsuyagi
Shintaro Uomi	Yukiya Kitamura
Miki Tagami	Hijiri Kojima

and Yoshie Negishi (Tomoko Sasano), Sumiko Sakamoto (Masako Yamada), Taka Gatarukanaru (Taizo Tachibana), Mickey Curtis (Nobuyiki), Kazuo Nakamura (Takao Yamada)

Out-of-work Yosuke journeys to a small town in search of a golden Buddha, a quest that leads him to Saeko, a beautiful woman who, when sexually aroused, secretes gallons of water.

© Cowboy Pictures

Aasif Mandvi, James Fox

THE MYSTIC MASSEUR

(THINKFILM) Producers, Mayeem Hafizka, Richard Hawley; Executive Producers, Paul Bradley, Lawrence Duprey; Director, Ismail Merchant; Screenplay, Caryl Phillips; Based on the novel by V.S. Naipaul; Photography, Ernie Vincze; Designer, Lucy Richardson; Costumes, Michael O'Connor; Editor, Roberto Silvi; Music, Richard Robbins, Zakir Hussain; a Merchant Ivory Productions presentation in association with Pritish Nandy Communications and Video Associate Ltd.; French-U.S.; Dolby; Color; Rated PG; 117 minutes; American release date: May 3, 2002

CAST

Ganesh Ransumair	Aasif Mandvi
Ramlogan	Om Puri
Partap	Jimi Mistry
Leela	Ayesha Dharker
Auntie	Zohra Segal
Mr. Stewart	James Fox
Basdeo	Rez Kempton
Beharry	Sanjeev Bhaskar
Suruj Mooma	Sakina Jaffrey

Ganesh Ransumair, a schoolteacher in Trinidad, returns to his country village to handle the burial of his father and decides to stay there to fulfill his dream of becoming a writer.

© ThinkFilm

Kulbhushan Kharbanda, Javed Khan, Rachel Shelley

LAGAAN: ONCE UPON A TIME IN INDIA

(SONY CLASSICS) Producer, Aamir Khan; Director/Screenplay, Ashutosh Gowariker; Photography, Anil Mehta; Designer, Nitin Chandrakant Desai; Costumes, Bhanu Athaiya; Music, A.R. Rahman; Lyricst, Javed Akhtar; Editor, Ballu Saluja; Screenplay, Kumar Dave, Sanjay Dayma; Dialogue, K.P. Saxena; Casting, Danielle Roffe, Uma da Cunha, Ashutosh Gowariker; Indian, 2001; Dolby; Color; Rated PG; 225 minutes; American release date: May 8, 2002

CAST

Bhuvan	Aamir Khan
Gauri	Gracy Singh
Elizabeth Russell	Rachel Shelley
Capt. Andrew Russell	Paul Blackthorne
Yashodamai	Suhasini Mulay
Rajah Puran Singh	Kulbhushan Kharbanda
Bhura	Raghuveer Yadav
Mukhiya	Rajendra Gupta
Guran	Rajesh Vivek
Ishwar	Sri Vallabh Vyas
Ramsingh	Javed Khan
Ismail	Raj Zutshi
Arjan	Akhilendra Mishra
Deva	Pradeep Rawat
Goli	Daya Shankar Padey
Lakha	Yashpal Sharma
Bagha	Amin Hajee
Kachra	Aditya Lakhia
Shambukaka	A.K. Hangal
Col. Boyer	John Rowe
Maj. Warren	David Gant
Maj. Cooton	Jeremy Child
Lt. Smith	Ben Nealon
Narrator	Shri Amitabh Bachchan

In 1893 India, during the British occupation, an outraged citizen, Bhuvan, rallies his other villagers to oppose the land tax a tyrannical captain has imposed on their town, prompting the captain to suggest a cricket match to settle the dispute.

© Sony Classics

Aamir Khan, Gracy Singh

THE LADY AND THE DUKE

(SONY CLASSICS) Producer, Françoise Etchegarary; Executive Producers, François Ivernel, Romain Le Grand, Léonard Glowinski; Director, Eric Rohmer; Photography, Diane Baratier; Art Director, Antoine Fontaine; Paintings, Jean-Baptiste Marot; Costumes, Pierre-Jean Larroque; Editor, Mary Stephen; Associate Producers, Pierre Rissient, Pierre Cottrell, Roland Pellegrino, Dieter Meyer; French, 2001; Dolby; Color; Rated PG-13; 125 minutes; American release date: May 10, 2002

CAST

Grace Elliott	Lucy Russell
Le Duc d'Orléans	Jean-Claude Dreyfus
Dumouriez	François Marthouret
Champcenetz	Leonard Cobiant
Nanon	Caroline Morin
Duc de Biron	Alain Libolt
Madame Meyler	Héléna Dubiel
Section Miromesnil— Officer	Laurent Le Doyen
Section Miromesnil— President	Georges Benoît
Section Miromesnil— Aide	Serge Wolfsperger

and Daniel Tarrare (Justin the Doorman), Charlotte Very (Pulcherie the Cook), Rosette (Fanchette), Marie Riviere (Madame Laurent), Michel Demierre (Chabot), Serge Renko (Vergniaud), Christian Ameri (Guadet), Eric Viellard (Osselin), François-Marie Banier (Robespierre), Henry Ambert (Meudon City Hall Clerk), Charles Borg, Claude Koener, Jean-Paul Rouvray (Vaugirard Gate Officers), Axel Colombel, Gérard Martin (Carmes Convent, Passerbys), Gérard Baume (Bouelvard Saint-Martin Man), Michel Dupuy (Rue de Lancry Doorman), Joël Templeur (Versailles Patrol Officer), Bruno Flender, Thierry Bois (Guards, Soldiers), William Darlin (Guard, Drunk), Anne-Marie Jabraud (Madame de Gramont), Isabelle Auroy (Madame du Châtelet), Jean-Louis Valero (Street Singer)

During the French Revolution, a beautiful English woman begins an affair with Philippe, a cousin of King Louis XVI, who nevertheless supports the cause of the people.

© Sony Classics

Lucy Russell (left)

Jean-Claude Dreyfus, Lucy Russell

Ronit Elkabetz, Lior Loui Ashkenazi

LATE MARRIAGE

(MAGNOLIA PICTURES) Producers, Marek Rozenbaum, Edgar Tenembaum; Director/Screenplay, Dover Kosashvili; Photography, Dani Schneor; Set Designer, Avi Fahima; Costumes, Maya Barsky; Editor, Yael Perlov; Executive Producer, Udi Yerushalmy; Music, Joseph Bardanashvili; Centre National de la Cinematographie/Israeli Film Fund/Keshet Broadcasting (Tel Aviv)/Morgane Production/The Fund for the Promotion of Israeli Film/Transfax Film Productions/ARTE France Cinema; French-Israeli, 2001; Dolby; Color; Not rated; 102 minutes; American release date: May 17, 2002

CAST

Zaza	Lior Loui Ashkenazi
Judith	Ronit Elkabetz
Yasha	Moni Moshonov
Lili	Lili Kosashvili
Ilana	Aya Steinovits Laor
Magouly	Rozina Cambus
Simon	Simon Chen
Madona	Sapir Kugman
Luba	Dina Doron
Otary	Leonid Kanevsky
Margalit	Livia Chachmon Ayaliy
Bessik	Eli Turi
Lali	Maria Ovanov

and Orit Buchnik Sher, Reuen Dayan, Rivka Gur, Ana Feinstein, Zuri Botrashvilli, Nana Dvir, Bachur Gene, Michael Mushonov, Rotem Zoler, Liza Turikashvilli, Nethanel Bitan

In the Georgian emigré community of Tel Aviv, 31-year-old, unmarried Zaza defies his parents wishes by falling in love with a 34-year-old Moroccan single mother.

© Magnolia Pictures

THE IMPORTANCE OF BEING EARNEST

(MIRAMAX) Producer, Barnaby Thompson; Executive Producer, Uri Fruchtmann; Director/Screenplay, Oliver Parker; Based on the play by Oscar Wilde; Co-Producer, David Brown; Photography, Tony Pierce-Roberts; Designer, Luciana Arrighi; Costumes, Maurizio Millenotti; Make-up/Hair Designer, Peter King; Editor, Guy Bensley; Music, Charlie Mole; Casting, Celestia Fox; an Ealing Studios presentation in association with Film Council and Newmarket Capital Group of a Fragile Film; British; Dolby; Panavision; Color; Rated PG; 97 minutes; American release date: May 22, 2002

CAST

Algernon Moncrieff . . . . .Rupert Everett
Jack Worthing . . . . .Colin Firth
Cecily Cardew . . . . .Reese Witherspoon
Gwendolyn Fairfax . . . . .Frances O'Connor
Lady Bracknell . . . . .Judi Dench
Reverend Chasuble . . . . .Tom Wilkinson
Miss Prism . . . . .Anna Massey
Lane . . . . .Edward Fox
Merriman . . . . .Patrick Godfrey
Grisby . . . . .Charles Kay
Pew Opener . . . . .Cyril Shaps
Dowager . . . . .Marsha Fitzalan
Young Lady Bracknell . . . . .Finty Williams
Young Lord Bracknell . . . . .Guy Bensley
Duchess of Devonshire .Christina Robert
Girls in Gambling Club . . . . .Kiera Chaplin, Alexandra Kobi
and Suzie Boyle, Kate Coyne, Bernadette Iglich, Polli Redston, Elaine Tyler-Hall, Gilliam Winn, Holly Collins, Kit Dickinson, Suzanne Thomas (Dancers), Charlie Mole, Darrell Kok, Judd Procter, Martin Knowles (Musical Butlers)

Jack Worthing's hopes of marrying Gwendolyn Fairfax are halted by her mother, Lady Bracknell, when Jack's inauspicious beginnings come to light. Previous film adaptations of the Wilde play include the 1952 British film, released in the U.S. by Universal-International, and starring Michael Redgrave (Jack), Dorothy Tutin (Cecily), Joan Greenwood (Gwendolyn), Michael Denison (Algernon), Edith Evans (Lady Bracknell), and Margaret Rutherford (Prism).

© Miramax

Rupert Everett, Colin Firth

Frances O'Connor, Colin Firth, Rupert Everett, Reese Witherspoon

Reese Witherspoon, Rupert Everett

Rupert Everett, Judi Dench, Reese Witherspoon

ELLING

(FIRST LOOK) Producer, Dag Alveberg; Director, Peter Næss; Screenplay, Axel Hellstenius; Based on the novel *Brødre I Blodet* by Ingvar Ambjørnsen; Photography, Svein Krøvel; Designer, Harald Egede-Nissen; Music, Lars Lillo Stenberg; Editor, Inge-Lise Langfeldt; Line Producer, Synnøve Hørsdal; Costumes, Aslaug Konradsdottir; Casting, Jannecke Bervell, Harald Dal; Produced by Maipo Films OG TV Produksjon in association with Audiovisuelt Produksjonsfond and Nordisk Film-OG TV Fond; Norwegian; Color; Rated R: 89 minutes; American release date: May 29, 2002

CAST

Elling ....Per Christian Ellefsen
Kjell Bjarne ....Sven Nordin
Reidun Nordsletten ....Marit Pia Jacobsen
Frank Åsli ....Jørgen Langhelle
Alfons Jørgensen ....Per Christensen
Gunn ....Hilde Olausson
Hauger ....Ola Otnes
and Eli-Anne Linnestad (Johanne), Cecilie Mosli (Cecilie Kornes), Joachim Rafaelsen (Haakon Willum), Per Gørvel (Eriksen), Knud Dahl (Waiter at Bar), Knut Haugmark (Porter)

Shy, neurotic Elling and his state home roommate, hulking, sex-obsessed Kjell Bjarne, are released from their facility and forced to cope with the real world for the first time.

© First Look

Sven Nordin, Per Christian Ellefsen

Per Christensen, Per Christian Ellefsen,
Marit Pia Jacobsen, Sven Nordin

Doug Allen, Paul Bettany

GANGSTER NO. 1

(IFC FILMS) Producers, Norma Heyman, Jonathan Cavendish; Executive Producer, Peter Bowles; Director, Paul McGuigan; Screenplay, Johnny Ferguson; Photography, Peter Sova; Designer, Richard Bridgland; Costumes, Jany Temine; Editor, Andrew Hulme; Music, John Dankworth; Co-Producers, Nicky Kentish Barnes, Ulrich Felsberg; Casting, Jina Jay; a BSkyB, British Screen, Film Four, Filmboard Berlin-Brandenburg, Little Bbird Ltd., NFH Prods., Pagoda Film, Road Movies Filmproduktion; British-German-Irish, 2000; Dolby; Color; Rated R; 105 minutes; American release date: June 14, 2002

CAST

Gangster 55 ....Malcolm McDowell
Freddie Mays ....David Thewlis
Young Gangster ....Paul Bettany
Karen ....Saffron Burrows
Tommy ....Kenneth Cranham
Lennie Taylor ....Jamie Foreman
Roland ....Razaaq Adoti
Mad John ....Doug Allen
Eddie Miller ....Eddie Marsan
Fat Charlie ....David Kennedy
Maxie King ....Andrew Lincoln
and Cavan Clerkin (Billy), Johnny Harris (Derek), Anton Valensi (Trevor), Alex McSweeney (Bloke in Tailor's), Martin Wimbush (Judge), Binky Baker (Dodgy Geezer), Martyn Read (Rough Diamond), Johnnie Guld (Scarey), Don McCorkindale (Smashing Bloke), Ralph Collis (Stocky), Charles Anderson (Brute), Arthur Nightingale (Toilet Attendant), Jack Pierce (Jack the Lad), Emma Griffiths Malin (Julie), Gary McCormack (Giggler Bennett), Sean Chapman (Bent Cop), Georgina Bull (Fat Charlie's Girl), Jo-Anne Nighy, Simone Bowkett (Roland's Girls), Caroline Pegg (Flo), Mark Montgomerie (Thug, Car #1), Dave Ould (Eric), Lisa Ellis (Waitress), Simon Marc (Freddie's Attacker), Tony Denham (Club Manager), Nadine Leonard (Mel), Jo McInnes (Lesley), Lorraine Stanley (Attacker's Friend), Wayne Matthews, Tony Bowers, Danny Webster (Youths), Ian Boo Khoo (Gambler)

In 1960s London, a psychopathic young gangster comes to work for underworld boss Freddie Mays, with the intention of deposing him and taking over the operations.

© IFC Films

THE FAST RUNNER (ATANARJUAT)

(LOT 47) Producers, Zacharias Kunuk, Norman Cohn, Paul Apak Angilirq; Producer (National Film Board of Canada), Germaine Ying Gee Wong; Executive Producer (NFB), Sally Bochner; Director, Zacharias Kunuk; Screenplay, Paul Apak Angilirq; Photography, Norman Cohn; Art Director, James Ungalaaq; Costumes, Micheline Ammaq, Atuat Akkitirq; Music, Chris Crilly; Editors, Zacharias Kunuk, Norman Cohn, Marie-Christine Sarda; an Igloolik Isuma Productions presentation in co-production with National Film Board of Canada; Canadian; Color; Rated R; 172 minutes; American release date: June 7, 2002

CAST

Atanarjuat	Natar Ungalaaq
Atuat	Sylvia Ivalu
Oki	Peter-Henry Arnatsiaq
Puja	Lucy Tulugarjuk
Panikpak	Madeline Ivalu
Qualitalik	Pauloosie Qulitalik
Sauri	Eugene Ipkarnak
Amaqjuaq	Pakkak Innukshuk

and Neeve Irngaut (Uluriaq), Abraham Ulayuruluk (Tungajuaq), Apayata Kotierk (Kumaglak), Mary Qulitalik (Niriunia), Luke Taqqaugaq (Pittiulak), Alex Uttak (Pakak)

When two brothers dare to challenge an evil shaman, one of them is killed, forcing the other to escape over a sea of ice.

© Lot 47

Natar Ungalaaq, Pakak Innukshuk

Natar Ungalaaq

Lucy Tulugarjuk, Neeve Irnguat, Sylvia Ivalu

Sylvia Ivalu

THE EMPEROR'S NEW CLOTHES

(PARAMOUNT CLASSICS) Producer, Uberto Pasolini; Executive Producers, Paul Webster, Hanno Huth, Roberto Cicutto; Director, Alan Taylor; Screenplay, Kevin Molony, Alan Taylor, Herbie Wave; Adapted from the novel *The Death of Napoleon* by Simon Leys; Co-Producers, Polly Leys, Marco Valerio Pugini, James Wilson; Photography, Alessio Gelsini Torresi; Designer, Andrea Crisanti; Costumes, Sergio Ballo; Editor, Masahiro Hirakubo; Music, Rachel Portman; Casting, Leo Davis; a FilmFour and Redwave presentation in association with Mikado Films and Senator Film of a Redwave production; British-Italian-German; Dolby; Color; Rated PG; 107 minutes; American release date: June 14, 2002

CAST

Napoleon/Eugene	Ian Holm
Pumpkin	Iben Hjejle
Dr. Lambert	Tim McInnerny
Gerard	Tom Watson
Montholon	Nigel Terry
Bertrand	Hugh Bonneville
Antommarchi	Murray Melvin
Marchand	Eddie Marsan
Bommel	Clive Russell
Captain Nicholls	Bob Mason
Leaud	Trevor Cooper
Maurice	Chris Langham
Dr. Quinton	Russell Dixon
Papa Nicholas	George Harris
Adele Raffin	Hayley Carmichael
Bosun	Niall O'Brien

and Philip McGough (English Tourist), Tim Barlow (Bargee), Tony Vogel (British Sergeant), Russell Tovey (Recruit), John McGlynn (Gendarme), Clive Mendus (Senior Orderly), Ashley Artus (Junior Orderly), Roger Frost (Bookseller), Tom Hunsinger (Customer), Matthew Sim (Ticket Seller), Phil Hearne (Man), Moya Brady (Woman), Caterina Venturini (Barmaid), Stefano Gragnani (Bailiff), Hervé Ducroux (Brest Contact), Giovanni Gianasso (Philippe), Francesco Guzzo (Sentry at Garrison), Sergio Ballo (Truchaut), Piero Lorenzo Ferrero (Tailor)

The exiled Napoleon trades places with a lookalike in order to return to Paris and plan his return to the throne, only to find out that no one believes who he is and he must fend for himself as a commoner.

© Paramount Classics

Ian Holm

Iben Hjejle

Ian Holm, Iben Hjejle

Ian Holm

Viveka Seldahl, Sven Wollter

A SONG FOR MARTIN

(FIRST LOOK) Producers, Bille August, Lars Kolvig, Michael Obel; Director/Screenplay, Bille August; Based on the novel *Boken om E* by Ulla Isaksson; Photography, Jorgen Persson; Art Director, Anna Asp; Costumes, Katarina Kvist; Editor, Janus Billieskov-Jansen; Music, Stefan Nilsson; a Moonlight Filmproduction, Svenska Filmopaniet production; Danish-Swedish; Dolby; Color; Rated PG-13; 78 minutes; American release date: June 28, 2002

CAST

Martin Fischer	Sven Wollter
Barbara Hartman	Viveka Seldahl
Biderman	Reine Brynolfsson
Karin	Linda Källgren
Elisabeth	Lisa Werlinder
Phillip	Peter Engman
Erik	Klas Dahlstedt
Susanne	Lo Wahl
Dr. Gierlich	Kristina Tornqvist
Sara	Jonna Ekdahl
Doctor	Jonas Falk
Henrik	Dag Malmberg
TV Reporter	Helena Stalnert
Christian	Jesper Toss

Violinist Barbara Hartman finds her happy marriage to composer-conductor Martin Fischer shattered when it is discovered that he is suffering from Alzheimer's disease.

READ MY LIPS

(MAGNOLIA) Producers, Jean-Louis Livi, Philippe Carcassonne; Executive Producer, Bernard Marescot; Director, Jacques Audiard; Screenplay, Jacques Audiard, Tonino Benacquista; Photography, Mathieu Vadepied; Set Designer, Michel Barthelemy; Costumes, Virginie Montel; Editor, Juliette Welfing; Music, Alexandre Desplat; Line Producer, Jean-Louis Nieuwbourg; Casting, Richard Rousseau; a co-production of Sedif Cine B, Pathe Image, France 2 Cinema, with the participation of Canal+ and CNC; French, 2001; Dolby; Super 35 Widescreen; Color; Not rated; 115 minutes; American release date: July 5, 2002

CAST

Paul Angeli	Vincent Cassel
Carla Bhem	Emmanuelle Devos
Marchand	Olivier Gourmet
Masson	Olivier Perrier
Annie	Olivia Bonamy
Morel	Bernard Alane
Josie Marchand	Cecile Samie
Richard Carambo	David Saracino
Louis Carambo	Christophe Van de Velde
Keller	Pierre Diot
Mammouth	Serge Boutleroff

Carla Bhem, a secretary who feels mistreated and unappreciated by the property development company for which she works, sees a chance for revenge when a new trainee, who happens to be an ex-con and thief, joins the department.

Vincent Cassel, Emmanuelle Devos

Vincent Cassel, Emmanuelle Devos

ME WITHOUT YOU

(GOLDWYN/FIREWORKS) Producer, Finola Dwyer; Executive Producers, Jonathan Olsberg, Stephen Christian; Director, Sandra Goldbacher; Screenplay, Sandra Goldbacher, Laurence Coriat; Photography, Denis Crossan; Designer, Michael Carlin; Costumes, Rosie Hackett; Editor, Michael Ellis; Music, Adrian Johnston; Hair & Make-Up, Christine Blundell; Line Producer, Paul Ritchie; Co-Producers, Torsten Leschly, Judy Counihan, Ulrich Felsberg; Casting, Linda Todd, Jill Trevellick, Kathleen Mackie; a Fireworks Pictures, Samuel Goldwyn Films, Momentum Pictures, Road Movies, and the Isle of Man Film Commission presentation with the participation British Screen and BskyB, a Dakota Films Production in association with Finola Dwyer Productions and WAVEpictures; British-German; Dolby; Color; Rated R; 107 minutes; American release date: July 5, 2002

Michelle Williams

CAST

Holly	Michelle Williams
Marina	Anna Friel
Daniel	Kyle MacLachlan
Linda	Trudie Styler
Nat	Oliver Milburn
Isabel	Marianne Denicourt
Carl	Steve John Shepherd
Max	Allan Corduner
Judith	Deborah Findlay
Young Holly	Ella Jones
Young Marina	Anna Popplewell
Young Nat	Cameron Powrie
Ray	Nicky Henson
Carolyn	Hannah Bourne
Craig	Russell Mabey
Tim	Blake Ritson
Paul	Francis Lee
Sophie	Eve Cooper-Rose

and Lee Williams (Ben), Andrew Beck (Stuart), Ariana Fraval (Earnest Girl), Annabel Mullion (Meredith), Adrian Lukis (Leo), Coco Sumner, Natalie Moss (Holly and Marina's Children)

Holly and Marina, two young girls of the London suburbs, make a pact to be friends, a vow that is constantly challenged by the insecure, unpredictable Marina's need to make Holly feel inferior.

© Goldwyn/Fireworks

Michelle Williams, Anna Friel

Anna Friel, Michelle Williams

Kyle MacLachlan, Anna Friel

SONGS FROM THE SECOND FLOOR

(NEW YORKER) Producer, Lisa Alwert; Executive Producer, Philippe Bober; Director/Screenplay, Roy Andersson; Photography, István Borbás, Jesper Klevenås; Costumes, Leontine Arvidsson; Music, Benny Andersson; Associate Producers, Johan Mardell, Sanne Glaesel; Produced by Roy Andersson Filmproduktion AB; Swedish-French-Danish, 2000; Dolby; Color; Not rated; 98 minutes; American release date: July 5, 2002

CAST

Karl	Lars Nordh
Stefan	Stefan Larsson
Pelle	Torbjörn Fahlström
Lasse	Sten Andersson
Magician	Lucio Vucina
Mia	Hanna Eriksson
Tomas	Peter Roth
Uffe	Tommy Johansson
Sven	Sture Olsson
Economist	Jöran Mueller
Supreme Commander	Hasse Söderholm
Psychologist	Eva Stenfelt
Immigrant	Rolando Nunez
Colonel	Klas Gösta Olsson
Anna	Helene Mathiasson
Volunteer	Per Jörnelius
Hanged Boy	Fredrik Sjögren
Crazy Man	Stephen Whitton
Patient	Nils-Åke Eriksson
Pelle's Friend	Tylar Gustavsson

In a nameless European city a series of strange and illogical events create a vast mental breakdown for its inhabitants.

© New Yorker Films

Lucio Vucina, Per Jörnelius

Torbjörn Fahlström, Tylar Gustavsson

MY WIFE IS AN ACTRESS

(SONY CLASSICS) Producer, Claude Berri; Executive Producer, Pierre Grunstein; Director/Screenplay, Yvan Attal; Photography, Remy Chevrin; Designer, Katia Wyszkop; Costumes, Jacqueline Bouchard; Editor, Jennifer Auger; Music, Brad Mehldau; Line Producer, Nicole Firn; Casting, Gerard Moulevrier; a Katharina/Renn Productions/TF1 Films Productions co-production with the participation of Canal+ and of the CNC; French, 2001; Dolby; Color; Rated R; 93 minutes; American release date: July 12, 2002

CAST

Charlotte	Charlotte Gainsbourg
Yvan	Yvan Attal
John	Terence Stamp
Nathalie	Noemie Lvovsky
Vincent	Laurent Bateau
Géraldine	Ludivine Sagnier
David	Keith Allen
Georges	Lionel Abelanski
David's Assistant	Jo McInnes

and Valérie Leboutte (Young Sexy Girl), Annette Hazanavicius (Yvan's Mother), Jean Abelanski (Yvan's Father), Marie Denarnaud (Colette), Jean Rachid (Blaise), Cécile Guignet (Lisette), Pascal Reneric (Merlin), Edith Perret (Theater Teacher), Aurélie Babled (Grimace Girl), Raphaëlle Moussafir (Girl Who Cries), Gilles Lellouche (Policeman)

An insanely jealous sports writer tests the fidelity of his wife, a popular actress currently making a movie opposite a suave international star.

© Sony Classics

Yvan Attal, Terence Stamp, Charlotte Gainsbourg

REIGN OF FIRE

(TOUCHSTONE) Producers, Richard D. Zanuck, Lili Fini Zanuck, Gary Barber, Roger Birnbaum; Executive Producer, Jonathan Glickman; Director, Rob Bowman; Screenplay, Gregg Chabot, Kevin Peterka, Matt Greenberg; Story, Gregg Chabot, Kevin Peterka; Photography, Adrian Biddle; Designer, Wolf Kroeger; Costumes, Joan Bergin; Editor, Thom Noble; Music, Edward Shearmur; Co-Producers, Dean Zanuck, Derek Evans, Rebekah Rudd, Morgan O'Sullivan, Chris Chrisafis; Visual Effects and Animation, The Secret Lab; Casting, Marcia Ross, Priscilla John; a Spyglass Entertainment presentation of a Zanuck Company production, a Barber/Birnbaum production; a British-Irish co-production; Dolby; Panavision; Technicolor; Rated PG-13; 105 minutes; Release date: July 12, 2002

CAST

Quinn . . . . .Christian Bale
Denton Van Zan . . . . .Matthew McConaughey
Alex . . . . .Izabella Scorupco
Creedy . . . . .Gerard Butler
Jared Wilkie . . . . .Scott James Moutter
Eddie Stax . . . . .David Kennedy
Ajay . . . . .Alexander Siddig
Barlow . . . . .Ned Dennehy
Devon . . . . .Rory Keenan
Gideon . . . . .Terence Maynard
Goosh . . . . .Doug Cockle
Burke . . . . .Randall Carlton
Mead . . . . .Chris Kelly
Young Quinn . . . . .Ben Thornton
Karen Abercromby . . . . .Alice Krige
Stuart . . . . .Malcolm Douglas
Jess . . . . .Dessie Gallagher
and Martin Linnane, Denis Conway (Moles), Duncan Keegan (Michael), Laura Pyper (Lin), Bernard Berts Folan, Brian McGuinness, Barry Barnes (Construction Workers), David Herlihy (Oliver), Gerry O'Brien (Jerry), Paddy Foy (Paddy), Anne Maria McAuley (Rose), Maree Duffy (Rachel), Alex Meacock (Alvarez), David Garrick (Jefferson), Andy Godbold (Piscatella)

In the future, when the world has been overtaken by dragons, Quinn and his ragtag group of survivors team with a volatile American and his team of hunters to kill the beasts and save mankind.

© Touchstone

Dragons over London

Izabella Scorupco, Matthew McConaughey

Gerard Butler, Christian Bale

Christian Bale, Izabella Scorupco, Matthew McConaughey

Hayato Ichihara

THE CROCODILE HUNTER: COLLISION COURSE

(MGM) Producers, Arnold Rifkin, Judi Bailey, John Stainton; Director/Story, John Stainton; Screenplay, Holly Goldberg Sloan; Photography, David Burr; Designer, Jon Dowding; Costumes, Jean Turnbull; Editors, Suresh Ayyar, Bob Blasall; Music, Mark McDuff; Casting, Alison Barrett; Stunts, Chris Anderson; a Best Picture Show Company/Cheynne Enterprises Production; Australian; Dolby; Super 35 Widescreen; Color; Rated PG; 90 minutes; Release date: July 12, 2002

CAST

Himself . . . . .Steve Irwin
Herself . . . . .Terri Irwin
Brozzie Drewitt . . . . .Magda Szubanski
Sam Flynn . . . . .David Wenham
Vaughan Archer . . . . .Lachy Hulme
Ron Buckwhiler . . . . .Aden Young
Robert Wheeler . . . . .Kenneth Ransom
Jo Buckley . . . . .Kate Beahan
and Steve Bastoni (Deputy Director Reynolds), Steve Vidler (Deputy Director Ansell), Alyson Standen (Anne Milking), Alex Ruiz, David Franklin (CIA Agents), Robert Coleby (Dr. Weinberger), Kevin Hides (Dr. Krug), Christopher Morris, Todd Levi (Canberra Space Technicians)

The CIA mistakenly believes that wildlife crusader Steve Irwin and his wife Terri have stolen the confidential contents of a government spy satellite that has crashed somewhere in the crocodile-infested area of Far North Queensland.

© MGM

Steve Irwin

ALL ABOUT LILY CHOU-CHOU

(COWBOY) Director/Screenplay, Shunji Iwai; Photography, Noboru Shinoda; Art Director, Noboru Ishida; Editor, Shunji Iwai; Costumes, Hiromi Shintani; Associate Producer, Koko Maeda; Line Producer, Naoki Hashimoto; Music, Takeshi Kobayashi; a Rockwell Eyes presentation; Japanese, 2001; Dolby; Color; Not rated; 147 minutes; American release date: July 12, 2002

CAST

Yuichi Hasumi . . . . .Hayato Ichihara
Shusuke Hoshino . . . . .Shugo Oshinari
Yoko Kuno . . . . .Ayumi Ito
Shiori Tsuda . . . . .Yu Aoi
Tabito Takao . . . . .Takao Osawa
Shimabukuro . . . . .Miwako Ichikawa
Izumi Hoshino . . . . .Izumi Inamori
Sumika Kanzaki . . . . .Kazusa Matsuda
Kentaro Sasaki . . . . .Takahito Hosoyamada
Tadono . . . . .Tomohiro Kaku
Kyota Shimizu . . . . .Hideyuki Kasahara
Hitoshi Terawaki . . . . .Ryo Katsuji
Kanda . . . . .Isamu Minami
Ryoka Sasano . . . . .Mana Kodama
Izawa . . . . .Ben Anri
and Chiyo Abe (Yuichi Hasumi's Mother), Yoji Tanaka (Kondo, Gym Teacher), Mayuko Yoshioka (Osanai, Home Room Teacher)

A lonely, taunted 14-year-old boy finds solace in the music of pop star Lily Chou-Chou, organizing an internet chat room for fans.

© Cowboy

Terri Irwin, Steve Irwin

SEX AND LUCIA

(PALM PICTURES) Producers, Fernando Bovaira, Enrique López Lavigne; Executive Producer, Anna Cassina; Director/Screenplay, Julio Medem; Photography, Kiko de la Rica; Designer, Montse Sanz; Costumes, Estibaliz Markiegui; Editors, Iván Aledo, El Igloo PC S.L.; Music, Alberto Iglesias; Casting, Mara-Mara S.I.; an Alicia Produce production for Sogecine with the participation of Canal+España and the participation of Televisión Espanola and Studio Canal France; Spanish-French, 2001; Dolby; Widescreen; Color; Not rated; 128 minutes; American release date: July 12, 2002

CAST

Lucia	Paz Vega
Lorenzo	Tristán Ulloa
Elena	Najwa Nimri
Carlos/Antonio	Daniel Freire
Pepe	Javier Cámara
Belén	Elena Anaya
Luna	Silvia Llanos
Manuela	Diana Suárez
Chief	Juan Fernández

and Charo Zapardiel (Midwife), Maria Álvarez (Nurse), Javier Coromina (Vendor in Refreshments Kiosk), Arsenio León (Zúñiga, Footballer), Alesandra Álvarez (Luna, aged 1), David Bulnes (Porno Actor)

Believing her writer boyfriend Lorenzo to be dead, Lucia retreats to the island where the pair had carried on a passionate affair.

© Palm Pictures

Paz Vega, Tristán Ulloa

Elena Anaya

Paz Vega

Tristán Ulloa, Javier Cámara

HAPPY TIMES

(SONY CLASSICS) Producers, Zhao Yu, Yang Qinglong, Zhou Ping, Zhang Weiping; Executive Producers, Edward R. Pressman, Terrence Malick, Wang Wei; Director, Zhang Yimou; Screenplay, Gai Zi; Co-Producer, Erin O'Rourke; Based on novella *Shifu, You'll Do Anything for a Laugh* by Mo Yan; Photography, Hou Yong; Art Director, Cao Jiuping; Costumes, Tong Huarniao; Music, San Bao; Editor, Zhai Ru; a Guangxi Film Studios, Zhu Hai Guo Gi Enterprises Development Company and Beijing New Picture Distribution Company production; Chinese, 2000; Dolby; Color; Rated PG; 106 minutes; American release date: July 26, 2002

CAST

Zhao	Zhao Benshan
Wu Ying	Dong Jie
Stepmother	Dong Lihua
Little Fu	Fu Biao
Li	Li Xuejian
Wu Ying'Stepbrother	Leng Qibin
Old Niu	Niu Ben
Aunty Liu	Gong Jinghua
Lao Zhang	Zhang Hongjie
Lao Bai	Zhao Bingkun

A retired factory worker decides at last to end his bachelorhood by marrying a divorcee only to realize that he does not have sufficient funds for a suitable wedding ceremony.

© Sony Classics

Zhao Benshan, Dong Jie

Zhao Benshan, Dong Lihua

Jacques Dutronc, Isabelle Huppert

MERCI POUR LE CHOCOLAT

(FIRST RUN FEATURES/EMPIRE PICTURES) a.k.a *Nightcap*; Producer, Marin Karmitz; Executive Producer, Jean-Louis Porchet; Director, Claude Chabrol; Screenplay, Caroline Eliacheff, Claude Chabrol; Based on the novel *The Chocolate Cobweb* by Charlotte Armstrong; Photography, Renato Berta; Designer, Yvan Niclass; Costumes, Elisabeth Tavernier; Editor, Monique Fardoulis; Music, Matthieu Chabrol; a co-production of MK2 Productions, CAB Productions, France 2 Cinéma, Télévision Suisse Romande, YMC Productions, with the participation of Canal+, the Office Fédéral de la Culture (DFI), Suisse Succés Cinéma, TELECLUB; French-Swiss, 2000; Dolby; Color; Not rated; 99 minutes; American release date: July 31, 2002

CAST

Marie-Claire Muller-Polonski	Isabelle Huppert
André Polonski	Jacques Dutronc
Jeanne Pollet	Anna Mouglalis
Guillaume Polonski	Rodolphe Pauly
Louise Pollet	Brigitte Catillon
Dufreigne	Michel Robin
Axel	Mathieu Simonet

Guillaume, the son of a famed concert pianist, finds his insecurity about his own talent at the keyboard even further in question with the arrival of another pianist, Jeanne, who claims she was switched at birth with the boy.

© First Run Features/Empire Pictures

24 HOUR PARTY PEOPLE

(UNITED ARTISTS) Producer, Andrew Eaton; Director, Michael Winterbottom; Screenplay, Frank Cottrell Boyce; Executive Producer, Henry Normal; Photography, Robby Müller; Designer, Mark Tidesley; Costumes, Natalie Ward, Stephen Noble; Editor, Trevor Waite; Line Producer, Robert How; Co-Producer, Gina Carter; Music Supervisor, Liz Gallacher; Special Consultant, Tony Wilson; Casting, Wendy Brazington; Presented in association with The Film Consortium, Film Council, and FilmFour; a Revolution Films Production in association with Baby Cow Films; Dolby; Color; Rated R; 117 minutes; American release date: August 9, 2002

CAST

Tony Wilson ....Steve Coogan
Bez ....Chris Coghill
Rob Gretton ....Paddy Considine
Shaunn Ryder ....Danny Cunningham
Ian Curtis ....Sean Harris
Lindsey Wilson ....Shirley Henderson
Alan Erasmus ....Lennie James
Peter Hook (Hooky) ....Ralf Little
Paul Ryder ....Paul Popplewell
Martin Hannett ....Andy Serkis
Bernard Sumner ....John Simm
Charles ....John Thomson
and Nigel Pivaro (Actor at Granada), Martin Hancock (Howard), Mark Windows (Johnny Rotten), Dave Gorman (John the Postman), Ron Cook (Derek), Raymond Waring (Vini), Peter Kay (Don Tonay), Mark E. Smith (Punter), Naomi Radcliffe (Twitchy Girl), Tim Horrocks (Steve), Rob Brydon (Ryan Letts), Howard Devoto (Cleaner), Collette Cooper (Sadie), Tracy Cunliffe (Other Girl in Nosh Van), Enzo Cilenti (Saville), Duncan Whitworth (Jez), Michael Mitchello Jnr. (Simon), Claire Lever (Assistant), Neil Bell (Aspiring Singer), Aidan Cross (Goth), Simon Pegg (Journalist), Elizabeth Kelly (Ian's Gran), Darren Tighe (Mike Pickering), Anna Tyborczyk (Gillian), Peter Gunn (Farmer), Dan Hope (Mark), Nick Clarke (Gaz), Margi Clarke (Actor in Corridor), Mani (Sound Engineer), Smug Roberts, Clint Boon (Railway Guards), Toby Salaman (Sir Keith Joseph), Conrad Murray (Bailey Brother), Martin Coogan (Chris Nagle), Rowetta (Herself), Kieran O'Brien (Nathan), Kate Magowan (Yvette), Paul Ryder (Pel), Roger Kennedy (Doorman Sam), Sean Cernow (Little Pel), Fiona Allen (Cloakroom Girl), Helen Schlesinger (Hilary), Joshua McNicholas (Oliver), Anthony H. Wilson (Studio Director), Keith Allen (Roger Ames), Dino, Mr. A Bowser, Gary Roberts (Wise Guys)

Television host Tony Wilson recounts how he helped cultivate the punk music movement by nuturing various bands and setting up his own record label.

© United Artists

Peter Kay, Steve Coogan, Shirley Henderson, Lennie James

John Simm, Ralf Little, Paddy Considine

Steve Coogan, Shirley Henderson

Sean Harris, Tim Horrocks, John Simm, Ralf Little

I'M GOING HOME

(MILESTONE) Producer, Paulo Branco; Director/Screenplay, Manoel de Oliveira; Photography, Sabine Lancelin; Designer, Yves Fournier; Costumes, Isabel Branco; Editor, Valérie Loiseleux; Co-Produced by Madragoa Filmes (Portugal), Gemini Films (France) and France2 Cinema, with the participation of Centre National de la Cinematographie, Canal+, ICAM (Instituto do Cinema, Audiovisual e Multimedia), RTP (Radiotelevisão Portuguesa); Portuguese-French, 2001; Dolby; Color; Not rated; 90 minutes; American release date: August 14, 2002

CAST

Gilbert Valence . . . . .Michel Piccoli
Marguerite . . . . .Catherine Deneuve
John Crawford, Film Director . . . . .John Malkovich
George . . . . .Antoine Chappey
Sylvia . . . . .Leonor Baldaque
Marie . . . . .Leonor Silveira
Guard . . . . .Ricardo Trêpa
Doctor . . . . .Jean-Michel Arnold
Ferdinand . . . . .Adrien de Van
Ariel . . . . .Sylvie Testud
and Isabel Ruth (Milkmaid), Andrew Wale (Stephen), Robert Dauney (Haines), Jean Koeltgen (Serge, Gilbert's Grandson), Mauricette Gourdon (Guilhermine, The Housekeeper), Vania (Organ-Grinder), Jacques Parsi (Friend of the Agent), Armel Monod (Second Friend of the Agent), Jean Chicot (Waiter), Christian Ameri (Bistro Patron), Bruno Guillot (Street Thug), Bernard Sanchez (Bistro Patron carrying Le Figaro), Jean-Luc Horvais (Bistro Patron carrying Le Monde), Nathalie Guéraud (Agent's Secretary), Madame Duteil (School Director), Catherine Trembloy (Saleswoman at Art Store), Vina Hiridjee, Caroline Lavallée (Autograph Seekers), Emmanuelle Fèvre (Make-up Woman), Philippe Magin (Hairdresser)

A fatal car accident leaves French actor Gilbert Valence with only his young grandson in his life, causing the aging thespian to confront his own mortality.

© Milestone

THE LAST KISS

(THINKFILM) Producer, Domenico Procacci; Director/Screenplay, Gabriele Muccino; Photography, Marcello Montarsi; Designer, Eugenia F. di Napoli; Costumes, Nicoletta Ercole; Music, Paolo Buonvino; Editor, Claudio Di Mauro; Casting, Francesco Vedovati; a Fandango production in collaboration with Medusa Film; Italian, 2001; Dolby; Widescreen; Color; Rated R; 115 minutes; American release date: August 16, 2002

CAST

Carlo . . . . .Stefano Accorsi
Giulia . . . . .Giovanna Mezzogiorno
Anna . . . . .Stefania Sandrelli
Alberto . . . . .Marco Cocci
Marco . . . . .Pierfrancesco Favino
Livia . . . . .Sabrina Impacciatore
Arianna . . . . .Regina Orioli
Adriano . . . . .Giorgio Pasotti
and Daniela Piazza (Veronica), Claudio Santamaria (Paolo), Martina Stella (Francesca), Luigi Diberti (Emilio), Piero Natoli (Michele)

Carlo and his lover Anna, expecting a child, refuse to get married for fear that this level of commitment will spell the end of their passion. Instead they find themselves pursuing outside lovers to fulfill their fantasies one last time.

© ThinkFilm

John Malkovich

Jean Koeltgen, Michel Piccoli

Stefano Accorsi, Giovanna Mezzogiorno

MOSTLY MARTHA

Sergio Castellitto, Martina Gedeck

Martina Gedeck, Sergio Castellitto

(PARAMOUNT CLASSICS) Producers, Karl Baumgartner, Christoph Friedel; Co-Producers, Heinz Stussak, Marcel Hoehn, Carlo Degli Esposti; Director/Screenplay, Sandra Nettelbeck; Photography, Michael Bertl; Designer, Thomas Freudenthal; Costumes, Bettina Helmi; Editor, Mona Bräuer; Casting, Heta Mantscheff; a Bavaria Film International presentation of a Pandora Film Produktion GmbH, Cologne production in co-production with Prisma Film, Vienna T&C Film AG, Zürich Palomar, Rome in association with SWR, WDR, ARTE, ORF, SF DRS/ SRG SSR idée suisse, Teleclub (Switzerland), Rai Cinema; German-Swiss; Dolby; Color; Rated PG; 107 minutes; American release date: August 16, 2002

CAST

Martha	Martina Gedeck
Mario	Sergio Castellitto
Lina	Maxime Foerste
Frida	Sibylle Canonica
Lea	Katja Studt
Bernadette	Idil Üner
Jan	Oliver Broumis
Carlos	Antonio Wannek
Therapist	August Zirner
Sam	Ulrich Thomsen
Mr. Steinberg	Gerhard Garbers
Mrs. Steinberg	Angela Schmidt
Giuseppe Lorenzo	Diego Ribon
Loud Patron	W.D. Sprenger
His Date	Victoria von Trauttmannsdorf
Jean	Jerome Ducournau
Kitchen Helper	Adrian Stein
Bartender	Rocco Dressel

and Leonhard Mazohl (Waiter), Dietrich Adam (Doctor), Katrin Hansmeier (Babysitter), Michael Wittenborn (Teacher), Alexandra Flögel (Sam's Daughter), Oskar Helmi (Sam's Son), Gunnar Titzmann (Policeman), Jophi Ries (Dissatisfied Patron), Regula Grauwiller (His Girlfriend), Maria Fuchs (Girlfriend)

Martha, an uptight chef at an upscale Hamburg restaurant, devotes her life exclusively to food preparation until she is forced to take care of her 8-year-old niece.

© Paramount Classics

276
Martina Gedeck, Katja Studt, Sergio Castellitto

Martina Gedeck, Maxime Foerste, Katja Studt, Sergio Castellitto

HOW I KILLED MY FATHER

Michel Bouquet, Natacha Régnier, Charles Berling

Charles Berling, Michel Bouquet

(NEW YORKER) Producer, Philippe Carcassonne; Director, Anne Fontaine; Screenplay, Jacques Fieschi, Anne Fontaine; Photography, Jean-Marc Fabre; Set Designer, Sylvain Chauvelot; Costumes, Corinne Jorry; Editor, Guy Lecorne; Music, Jocelyn Pook; Line Producer, Frederic Sauvagnac; a Ciné B — Cinéa — France 2 Cinéma — P.H.F. Films Franco-Spanish co-production, with the friendly participation of François Berléand; French-Spanish; Dolby; Color; Not rated; 98 minutes; American release date: August 23, 2002

CAST

Maurice . . . . .Michel Bouquet
Jean-Luc . . . . .Charles Berling
Isa . . . . .Natacha Régnier
Patrick . . . . .Stéphane Guillon
Myriem . . . . .Amira Casar
Jean-Toussaint . . . . .Hubert Koundé
Lætitia . . . . .Karole Rocher
The Prostitute . . . . .Marie Micla
Patient . . . . .Nicole Evans
Homeless Guy/Elderly Patient . . . . .Philippe Lehembre
Isa's Father . . . . .Pierre Londiche
Cyril . . . . .Jean-Christophe Lemberton
Isa's Mother . . . . .Manoëlle Gaillard
and Etienne Louvet (Myriem's Son), Claude Kœner (The Official), Thierry De Carbonnières (Guest at the Reception), Nathalie Mathis (Magali), Emmanuel Booz (The Manager)

Forty-year-old Jean-Luc is dismayed when his long estranged father comes back into his life.

© New Yorker Films

MAD LOVE

(SONY CLASSICS) Producer, Enrique Cerezo; Director/Screenplay, Vicente Aranda; Photography, Paco Femenía; Set Designer, Miguel Chang; Costumes, Javier Artiñano; Editor, Teresa Font; Line Producer, Carlos Bernases; Eurimages/Canal+; Spanish; Dolby; Color; Rated R; 117 minutes; American release date: August 30, 2002

CAST

Joan . . . . .Pilar López de Ayala
Philip . . . . .Daniele Liotti
Aixa . . . . .Manuela Arcuri
Álvari de Estuñiga . . . . .Eloy Azorín
Elvira . . . . .Rosana Pastor
De Vere . . . . .Giuliano Gemma
Admiral . . . . .Roberto Álvarez
Inés . . . . .Carolina Bona
Don Juan Manuel . . . . .Chema de Miguel
Marquis of Villena . . . . .Andrés Lima
Captain Corrales . . . . .Guillermo Toledo
Marliano . . . . .Cipriano Lodosa
Queen Isabella . . . . .Susy Sánchez
King Ferdinand . . . . .Héctor Colomé
Hernán . . . . .Jorge Monge
Mucama . . . . .Sol Abad
and Cristina Arranz (Ana), Cristina Perales (Maria), Maria Ballesteros (Catalina), Sonia Madrid (Brigitte), Cristina Solano (Analfabeta)

Princess Joan is sent to Flanders for an arranged marriage between herself and Philip the Handsome, a forced union that turns into a mutual and uncontrollable passion.

Pilar López de Ayala

© Sony Classics

Bruno Putzulu

IN PRAISE OF LOVE

(MANHATTAN PICTURES) Producers, Alain Sarde, Ruth Waldburger; Director/Screenplay, Jean-Luc Godard; Photography, Christophe Pollock, Julien Hirsch; a co-production of Studio Canal, DFI, Studio Image 7, LTC VDM SIS, NSM SON TEST, Peripheria; French-Swiss, 2001; Dolby; Color/black and white; Not rated; 98 minutes; American release date: September 6, 2002

CAST

Edgar . . . . .Bruno Putzulu
Elle . . . . .Cécile Camp
Grandfather . . . . .Jean Davy
Grandmother . . . . .Françoise Verny
Servant . . . . .Philipp Lyrette
Eglantine . . . . .Audrey Klebaner
Perceval . . . . .Jeremy Lippman
Mr. Rosenthal . . . . .Claude Baignères
Forlani, Esq. . . . . .Remo Forlani
and Mark Hunter (US Journalist), Bruno Mesrine (Magician), Djelloul Beghoura (Algerian Man), Violeta Ferrer, Valérie Ortlieb (Women), Serge Spira (Homeless), Stéphanie Jaubert (Young Woman), Jean Lacouture (Historian), Jean-Henri Roger (City Hall Bureaucrat), Lemmy Constantine (US Assistant), William Doherty (US Civil Servant)

A self-involved filmmaker sets about casting his next project, a reflection on the four stages of love.

© Manhattan Pictures

278   Benoît Magimel, Juliette Binoche

THE CHILDREN OF THE CENTURY

(EMPIRE) Producers, Diane Kurys, Alain Sarde; Executive Producers, Robert Benmussa, Christine Gozlan; Director, Diane Kurys; Screenplay, Murray Head, Diane Kurys, François-Olivier Rousseau; Photography, Vilko Filac; Designer, Bernard Vézat; Music, Luis Bacalov; Editor, Joële Van Effenterre; Casting, Gérard Moulévrier; a co-production of Alexandre Films, Conseil General de l'Indre, FilmFour, France 2 Cinema, Le Studio Canal+, Les Films Alain Sarde, Procirep, Studio Images 5; French, 1999; Dolby; Color; Rated R; 107 minutes; American release date: September 13, 2002

CAST

George Sand . . . . .Juliette Binoche
Alfred de Musset . . . . .Benoît Magimel
Pietro Pagello . . . . .Stefano Dionisi
François Buloz . . . . .Robin Renucci
Marie Dorval . . . . .Karin Viard
Aimée d'Alton . . . . .Isabelle Carré
Gustave Planche . . . . .Patrick Chesnais
Alfred Tattet . . . . .Arnaud Giovaninetti
and Denis Podalydès (Sainte-Beuve), Olivier Foubert (Paul de Musset),Marie-France Mignal (Mem. de Musset), Michel Robin (Larive), Ludivine Sagnier (Hermine de Musset), Victoire (Victoire Thivisol), Julien Léal (Maurice), Pascal Ternisien (Boucoiran), Jean-Claude de Goros (Capo de Feuillide), Mathias Mégard (Delacroix), Robert Plagnol (Jules Sandeau), Yvette Petit (Dressmaker), Massimo De Rossi (Danieli Director), Pascale Oudot (Julie), Philippe Morier-Genoud (Latouche), Olivier Claverie (Pinson), Alika Del Sol (Pretty Half-Caste), Edith Perret (Dowager at Ball), Marie-Thérèse Arène (2nd Dowager), Yacha Kurys, Blandine Ardant Conversi (Children at Luxembourg), Pablo Amaro (Italian Nun), Fabiana Gastaldello (Italian Nun), Thierry de Peretti (Achille Deveria), Tony Gaultier (Porter), Sylvie Herbert (Concierge), Franck Amiach (Buloz Employee), Grégory Reznik (Tattet's Valet), Serge Ridoux (Tortoni's Waiter), Jean-Noël Fenwick (Dashing Dancer), Philippe Mangione (Waffle Seller), Antoni Saint-Aubin (Swarthy Young Man), Olivier Meidinger (Austrian Soldier), Segorene Bonnet, Michelle Guetta (Preening Women), Delphine Quentin (Russian Girl)

The true story of the tumultuous love affair between writers George Sand and Alfred de Musset.

© Empire

Juliette Binoche, Benoît Magimel

ALIAS BETTY

Mathilde Seigner, Luck Mervil

Sandrine Kiberlain

Edouard Baer, Luck Mervil

(WELLSPRING) Producers, Annie Miller, Yves Marmion; Director/Screenplay, Claude Miller; Based on the novel *The Tree of Hands* by Ruth Rendell; Photography, Christophe Pollock; Art Director, Jean-Pierre Kohut Svelko; Editor, Véronique Lange; Co-Producer, Nicole Robert; French-Canadian, 2001; Dolby; Color; Not rated; 101 minutes; American release date: September 13, 2002

CAST

Betty Fisher	Sandrine Kiberlain
Margot Fisher	Nicole Garcia
Carole Novacki	Mathilda Seigner
François Diembele	Luck Mervil
Alex Basato	Édouard Baer
Édouard	Stéphane Freiss
René l'Arménien	Yves Jacques
Doctor Castang	Roschdy Zem
José Novacki	Alexis Chatrian
Milo	Michaël Abiteboul
Joseph Fisher	Arthur Setbon
Madame Barsky	Consuelo de Haviland
Monsieur Barsky	Pascal Bonitzer
Martinaud	Yves Verhoeven

When novelist Betty loses her young son in an accident, her mother takes it upon herself to kidnap a small child in hopes of bringing Betty out of her depression.

© Wellspring

DAS EXPERIMENT

(SAMUEL GOLDWYN) Producers, Norbert Preuss, Marc Conrad, Fritz Wildfeuer; Director, Oliver Hirschbiegel; Screenplay, Mario Giordano, Christoph Darnstädt, Don Bohlinger; Based on the novel *Black Box* by Mario Giordano; Photography, Rainer Klausmann; Art Director, Andrea Kessler; Prison Design, Uli Hanisch; Costumes, Claudia Bobsin; Music, Alexander van Bubenheim; Editor, Hans Funck; Co-Producer, Benjamin Herrmann; Line Producer, Philip Evenkamp; German 2001; Dolby; Color; Not rated; 113 minutes; American release date: September 18, 2002

CAST

THE PRISONERS:
Tarek Fahd, Prisoner Nr. 77 . . . . .Moritz Bleibtreu
Steinhoff, Prisoner Nr. 38 . . . . .Christian Berkel
Schütte, Prisoner Nr. 82 . . . . .Oliver Stokowski
Joe, Prisoner Nr. 69 . . . . .Wotan Wilke Möhring
and Stephan Szask (Prisoner Nr. 53), Polat Dal (Prisoner Nr. 40), Danny Richter (Prisoner Nr. 21), Ralf Müller (Prisoner Nr. 15), Markus Rudolf (Prisoner Nr. 74), Peter Fieseler (Prisoner Nr. 11), Thorsten J.H. Dersch (Prisoner Nr. 86), Sven Grefer (Prisoner Nr. 94)
THE GUARDS:
Berus . . . . .Justus von Dohnànyi
Kamps . . . . .Nicki von Tempelhoff
Eckert . . . . .Timo Dierkes
and Antoine Monot, Jr. (Bosch), Lars Gärtner (Renzel), Jacek Klimontko (Gläser), Markus Klauk (Stock), Ralph Püttmann (Amandy)
THE SCIENTISTS:
Professor Dr. Klaus Thon . . . . .Edgar Selge
Dr. Jutta Grimm . . . . .Andrea Sawatzki
Lars . . . . .Philipp Hochmair
The Others:
Dora . . . . .Maren Eggert
Ziegler . . . . .André Jung
Hans . . . . .Uwe Rohde

Twenty finalists are chosen for an experiment in which they are divided into prisoners and guards and asked to adhere to these roles for fourteen days.

Edgar Selge, Andrea Sawatzki

HIS SECRET LIFE

(STRAND) Producers, Tilde Corsi, Gianni Romoli; Director, Ferzan Ozpetek; Screenplay, Gianni Romoli, Ferzan Ozpetek; Photography, Pasquale Mari; Set Designer, Bruno Cesari; Costumes, Catia Dottori; Editor, Patrizio Marone; Music, Andrea Guerra; a Les Films Balenciaga, R&C Produzioni production; French-Italian, 2001; Dolby; Color; Not rated; 105 minutes; American release date: September 20, 2002

CAST

Antonia . . . . .Margherita Buy
Michele . . . . .Stefano Accorsi
Serra . . . . .Serra Yilmaz
Massimo . . . . .Andrea Renzi
Ernesto . . . . .Gabriel Garko
Veronica . . . . .Erica Blanc
and Rosaria De Cicco (Luisella), Filippo Nigro (Riccardo), Luca Calvani (Sandro), Lucrezia Valia (Mara), Koray Candemir (Emir), Barbara Folchitto (Infermiera), Carmine Recano (Israele), Edilberta Caviteno Bahia (Nora), Leonardo Di Gioia (Giulo), Giorgio Gobbi (Paziente Laboratorio), Marilena Paci (Marilena)

When her beloved husband of ten years, Massimo, is killed in a car accident, Antonia goes into a state of grief until she discovers that he had a male lover for seven years.

Moritz Bleibtreu

Stefano Accorsi

INVINCIBLE

(FINE LINE FEATURES) Producers, Gary Bart, Werner Herzog, Christine Ruppert; Director/Screenplay, Werner Herzog; Photography, Peter Zeitlinger; Designer, Ulrich Bergfelder; Costumes, Jany Temime; Music, Hans Zimmer, Klaus Badelt; Editor, Joe Bini; a Werner Herzog Filmproduktion/TATFILM Production in association with Little Bird and Jan Bart Production in co-production with WDR, DR, Arte; German-British, 2001; Dolby; Color; Rated PG-13; 127 minutes; American release date: September 20, 2002

Jouko Ahola (center)

Jouko Ahola, Anna Gourari

Anna Gourari, Tim Roth

Tim Roth

CAST

Hanussen	Tim Roth
Zishe	Jouko Ahola
Marta Farra	Anna Gourari
Master of Ceremonies	Max Raabe
Benjamin	Jacob Wein
Landwehr	Gustav Peter Wöhler
Count Helldorf	Udo Kier
Rabbi Edelmann	Herbert Golder
Yitzak Breitbart	Gary Bart
Mother Breitbart	Renate Kroßner
Gershon	Ben-Tzion Hershberg
Rebecca	Rebecca Wein
Raphael	Raphael Wein
Daniel	Daniel Wein
Chana	Chana Wein
Innkeeper	Guntis Pilsums
Ringleader	Thorsten Hammann
Rowdy	Jurgis Krasons
Circus Director	Klaus Stiglmeier
Colossus of Rhodos	James Reeves
Carter's Man	Ulrich Bergfelder
Laughing Man	Jakov Rafalson
Delilah	Ieva Aleksandrova
Magician	Rudolph Herzog
Rothschild	Les Bubb
Hedda Christansen	Tina Bordihn
Mrs. Holm	Sylvia Vas
Mr. Peters	Hans-Jürgen Schmiebusch
Stormtrooper	Joachim Paul Assböck
Himmler	Alexander Duda
Goebbels	Klaus Haindl
Judge	Hark Bohm

and Anthony Bramall (Conductor), André Hennicke (Detective), Ilga Martinsone (Woman), Valerijs Iskevic (Young Man), Juris Strenga (Teacher), Grigorij Kravec (Woodcutter), James Mitchell (Doctor), Milena Gulbe (Nurse).

An impoverished strongman leaves his village in eastern Poland and becomes a hero of the Jewish people while performing in vaudeville in 1930s Berlin, thereby making him an enemy of the rising Nazi regime.

8 WOMEN

(FOCUS FEATURES) Producer, Olivier Delbosc, Marc Missonnier; Director/Screenplay, François Ozon; Adapted from the play *8 Femmes* by Robert Thomas; Photography, Jeanne Lapoirie; Set Designer, Arnaud De Moleron; Costumes, Pascaline Chavanne; Editor, Laurence Bawedin; Line Producer, Christine De Jekel; Music, Krishna Levy; Songs by various; Choreographer, Sébastien Charles; Casting, Antoinette Boulat; a Fidelite Productions presentation; a co-production with France 2 Cinema and Mars Films in association with Gimages 5 and BIM Distribuzione with the participation of Canal+ and Centre National de la Cinematographie; French; Dolby; Color; Rated R; 103 minutes; American release date: September 20, 2002

Ludivine Sagnier, Virginie Ledoyen

CAST

Gaby, the Mother . . . . .Catherine Deneuve
Augustine, Gaby's Sister . . . . .Isabelle Huppert
Louise, the Chambermaid . . . . .Emmanuelle Béart
Pierrette, the Victim's Sister . . . . .Fanny Ardant
Suzon, Gaby's Older Daughter . . . . .Virginie Ledoyen
Mamy, the Grandmother .Danielle Darrieux
Catherine, Gaby's Younger Daughter . . . . .Ludivine Sagnier
Madame Chanel, the Housekeeper . . . . .Firmine Richard

Eight women gather at a snowbound country estate for the holiday season only to find that the beloved family patriarch has been murdered.

© Focus Features

Isabelle Huppert, Emmanuelle Béart

Isabelle Huppert

Catherine Deneuve, Ludivine Sagnier, Virginie Ledoyen, Danielle Darrieux, Isabelle Huppert, Firmine Richard, Emmanuelle Béart, Fanny Ardant

Catherine Deneuve

HEAVEN

(MIRAMAX) Producers, Anthony Minghella, William Horberg, Maria Köpf, Stefan Arndt, Frédérique Dumas; Executive Producers, Harvey Weinstein, Agnès Mentré, Sydney Pollack; Director, Tom Tykwer; Screenplay, Krzysztof Kieslowski, Krzysztof Piesiewicz; Based on the trilogy *Heaven, Hell and Purgatory* by Krzysztof Kieslowski, Krzysztof Piesiewicz; Photography, Frank Griebe; Designer, Uli Hanisch; Costumes, Monika Jacobs; Line Producers, Stefan Schieder, Mario Cotone, Marco Guidone; Casting, Shaila Rubin; a X-Filme Creative Pool production in collaboration with Mirage Enterprises and Noé Productions; German-U.S.-French, 2001; Dolby; Color; Rated R; 97 minutes; American release date: October 4, 2002

CAST

Phillippa	Cate Blanchett
Filippo	Giovanni Ribisi
Filippo's Father	Remo Girone
Maggiore Pini	Mattia Sbragia
The Public Prosecutor	Alberto Di Stasio
Marco Vendice	Stefano Santospago
Ariel	Alessandro Sperduti
The Inspector	Giovanni Vettorazzo
The Lieutenant	Gianfranco Barra
Chief Guard	Vincent Riotta
Regina	Stefania Rocca
Doctor	Mauro Marino
Vendice's Secretary	Stefania Orsola Garello

and Fausto Lombardi (Father in High Rise), Giorgia Coppa (Older Daughter), Julienne Liberto (Young Daughter), Mathilde De Sanctis (Janitor), Roberto D'Alessandro (Milk Van Driver), Masha Strago (Woman in Milk Van), Sergio Sivori (Helicopter Pilot), Shaila Rubin (Pharmacist), Luciano Bartoli, Marco Merlini (Technicians in Soundproof Room), Natalia Magni, Teresa Piergentilli (Cleaning Women), Massimilliano Giusti (Policeman Chasing Ariel), Federico Torre (Policeman in Crowded Street), Andrea DiGirolamo, Beppe Loconsole (Special Forces Police)

After accidentally killing four innocent people with a bomb intended for a drug dealer, Phillippa is arrested and interrogated, only to have a young translator assist her in escaping so she can carry out her original goal.

© Miramax

Giovanni Ribisi, Cate Blanchett

Giovanni Ribisi, Cate Blanchett

Cate Blanchett

Cate Blanchett, Giovanni Ribisi

283

BLOODY SUNDAY

(PARAMOUNT CLASSICS) Producer, Mark Redhead; Executive Producers, Pippa Cross, Arthur Lappin, Jim Sheridan, Paul Trijbits, Tristan Whalley; Executive Producer for Bord Scannán na hÉireann/The Irish Film Board; Director/Screenplay, Paul Greengrass; Photography, Ivan Strasberg; Designer, John Paul Kelly; Costumes, Dinah Collin; Editor, Clare Douglas; Music, Dominic Muldowney; Co-Producers, Don Mullan, Paul Myler; Casting, John and Ros Hubbard; a Portman Film presentation in association with Granada, Film Council and Bord Scannán na Héireann/The Irish Film Board of a Granada Film/Hell's Kitchen production; Irish; Dolby; Color; Rated R; 107 minutes; American release date: October 4, 2002

CAST

Ivan Cooper . . . . James Nesbitt
Kevin McCorry . . . . Allan Gildea
Eamonn McCann . . . . Gerard Crossan
Bernadette Devlin . . . . Mary Moulds
Bridget Bond . . . . Carmel McCallion
Major General Ford . . . . Tim Pigott-Smith
Brigadier MacLellan . . . . Nicholas Farrell
Major Steele . . . . Chris Villiers
Colonel Tugwell . . . . James Hewitt
Gerry Donaghy . . . . Declan Duddy
Gerry's Girl . . . . Edel Frazer
Mary Donaghy . . . . Joanne Lindsay
Soldier 027 . . . . Mike Edwards
Para F . . . . Gerry Hammond
Para G . . . . Jason Stammers
Para H . . . . Ken Williams
Para E . . . . Bryan Watts
Colonel Wilford . . . . Simon Mann
Major Loden . . . . Rhidian Bridge
Jim . . . . Jonathan O'Donnel
Dennis . . . . David Rogers
Hugh . . . . Sean O'Kane
Tommy . . . . Thomas McEleney
Bogside Woman . . . . Deirdre Irvine
Mr. O'Keefe . . . . Gerry Newton
Lieutenant 119 . . . . Ross MacDonald
CSM . . . . Jim Alexander
Officer at Barrier 12 . . . . James Scott
Mrs. Hegarty . . . . Grainne Costello
Bogside Priest . . . . Don Mullan
O/C Provos . . . . David Pearse
Briefer . . . . Charles Oakden
Frances . . . . Kathy Kiera Clarke
Chief Supt. Lagan . . . . Gerard McSorley
Brigade Net . . . . Bruce Alexander, Jason Muir
        Tim Clark, Matt Ashenden, Daryl Auckland
Peggy Deery . . . . Rita Hamill
Willie McKinney . . . . Robert O'Connor
Barney McGuigan . . . . Kevin McCallion
Jim Wray . . . . James McLaughlin
Officer at Barrier 14 . . . . Graham Harrison
RUC Man . . . . Oliver Maguire
and Darren Healey (303 Man), Simon Emberley (Lieutenant N), Raymond Cullen (Father Daly), Tony Bates (Doctor Swords), Kevin Meehan (Hospital Administrator), Mark Redhead (Journalist), Ian Dray (SIB Officer)

A docu-drama about the events leading up to the massacre of 13 civil rights protestors in the Northern Ireland town of Derry on January 30, 1972.

© Paramount Classics

James Nesbitt

James Nesbitt (right)

James Nesbitt

SAFE CONDUCT

(EMPIRE) Executive Producers, Alain Sarde, Frederic Bourboulon; Director, Bertrand Tavernier; Screenplay, Bertrand Tavernier, Jean Cosmos; Associate Producer, Christine Gozlan; Photography, Alaine Choquart; Costumes, Valerie Pozzo di Borgo; Editor, Sophie Brunet; Line Producers, Francois Hamel, Agnes Le Pont; from Studio Canal; French; Dolby; Super 35 Widescreen; Color; Not rated; 170 minutes; American release date: October 11, 2002

CAST

Jean Devaivre	Jacques Gamblin
Jean Aurenche	Denis Podalydes
Olga	Marie Gillain
Simone Devaivre	Marie Desgranges
Suzanne Raymond	Charlotte Kady
Reine Sorignal	Maria Pitarresi
Doctor Greven	Christian Berkel
Jean-Paul Le Chanois	Ged Marlon
Maurice Tourneur	Philippe Morier-Genoud
Charles Spaak	Laurent Schilling

and Richard Pottier (Richard Sammel), Olivier Gourmet (Roger Richebé), Philippe Saïd (Pierre Nord), Liliane Rovère (Mémaine)

Two members of the flim industry, Devaivre, an assistant director, and Aurenche a writer, do their part to fight the Nazi menace during World War II, the former by joining the Resistance, the latter by refusing to participate in propaganda films.

© Empire

Jacques Gamblin, Marie Desgranges

THE TRANSPORTER

(20TH CENTURY FOX) Producers, Luc Besson, Steven Chasman; Director, Corey Yuen; Screenplay, Luc Besson, Robert Mark Kamen; Artistic Director, Louis Leterrier; Photography, Pierre Morel; Designer, Hugues Tissandier; Editor, Nicolas Trembasiewicz; Music, Stanley Clarke; Casting, Nathalie Cheron; a Euroacorp Production in co-production with TF1 Films Production in association with Current Entertainment and Canal+; French; Dolby; Color; Rated PG-13; 92 minutes; American release date: October 11, 2002

Jason Statham, Shu Qi

CAST

Frank Martin	Jason Statham
Lai	Shu Qi
Wall Street	Matt Schulze
Tarconi	François Berléand
Mr. Kwai	Ric Young
Leader	Doug Rand
Boss	Didier Saint Melin
Thugs	Tonio Descanvelle, Laurent Desponds, Matthieu Albertini
Pilot	Vincent Nemeth
Little Thug	Jean-Yves Billien
Giant Thug	Jean Marie Paris
Newscaster	Adrian Dearnell

and Alfred Lot, Christian Gazio (Cops), Audrey Hamm (Secretary), Sebastien Migneau (Wheel Man), Laurent Jumeaucourt (Young Thug), Frederic Vallet (Tractor Trailer Driver), Stephan Gudju (Thug 1, Wall Street), Sandrine Rigaux (Nurse), Cameron Watson (Official)

A mercenary transporter, who makes it his policy never to question his mission, is given a package to deliver to a man known as Wall Street, only to realize that he is in possession of a beautiful, gagged woman.

© 20th Century Fox

Jason Statham (center)

Madonna, Adriano Giannini

Jeanne Tripplehorn, Madonna

SWEPT AWAY

(SCREEN GEMS) Producer, Matthew Vaughn; Director/Screenplay, Guy Ritchie; Based on the screenplay by Lina Wertmuller; Photography, Alex Barber; Designer, Russell de Rozario; Costumes, Arianne Phillips; Editor, Eddie Hamilton; Music, Michel Colombier; Co-Producers, Adam Bohling, David Reid; Presented in association with Ska Films and CODI SpA; British; Dolby; Color; Rated R; 89 minutes; American release date: October 11, 2002

CAST

Amber . . . . .Madonna
Giuseppe . . . . .Adriano Giannini
Marina . . . . .Jeanne Tripplehorn
Tony . . . . .Bruce Greenwood
Debi . . . . .Elizabeth Banks
Michael . . . . .David Thornton
Todd . . . . .Michael Beattie
Captain . . . . .Yorgo Voyagis
and Lorenzo Ciompi (Rich Man), Shavawn Marie Gordon (Shop Assistant), Beatrice Luzzi (Rich Lady), Francis Pardeilhan (Tony's Assistant), Ricardo Perna (Crew Member), Rosa Pianeta (Receptionist), Andrea Ragatzu (Bell Boy), Patrizio Rispo (Burly Captain), George Yiasoumi (Chef)

Rich and spoiled Amber, on a Mediterranean cruise with her husband and a group of friends, finds herself marooned on a deserted island with the boat's first mate, whom she had mistreated when he was under her employ. Remake of the film *Swept Away... by an unusual destiny in the blue sea of August*, which played in the United States in 1975. The star of that film, Giancarlo Giannini, is the father of this film's star, Adriano Giannini.

TAKE CARE OF MY CAT

(KINO) Producer, Oh Gi-min; Director/Screenplay, Jeong Jae-eun; Photography, Choi Young-hwan; Art Director, Kim Jin-chui; Costumes, Koh Hye-young, Yoo Young-sook; Editor, Lee Hyun-mee; Music, M&F; a Masulpiri Production presented by iPictures, Terasource Venture Captial in association with Korea Film Commission, Intz. com; South Korean, 2001; Dolby; Color; Not rated; 112 minutes; American release date: October 18, 2002

CAST

Tae-hee . . . . .Bae Doo-na
Hae-joo . . . . .Lee Yo-won
Ji-Young . . . . .Ok Ji-young
Bi-ryu . . . . .Lee Eun-shil
Ohn-jo . . . . .Lee Eun-joo
Chan-yong . . . . .Oh Tae-kyung

The growing disconnection between five friends in their post-high school period is reflected in their unwillingness to take care of a stray kitten, who is passed from one young woman to another.

© Kino

Ok Ji-young

ON GUARD

(EMIPRE) Producer, Patrick Godeau; Executive Producer, Françoise Galfré; Director, Philippe de Broca; Screenplay, Philippe de Broca, Jean Cosmos; Based on the novel *Le Bossu* by Paul Féval; Photography, Jean-François Robin; Art Director, Bernard Vezat; Costumes, Christian Gasc; Editor, Henri Lange; Music, Philippe Sarde; Casting, Catherine Deserbais, Lissa Pillu; Produced by Alicéléo, Cecchi Gori Group Tiger Cinematografica, Center National de la Cinématographie, Cofimage, DA Films, Le Studio Canal+, TF1 Films, Gemini Filmproduktions GmbH, Prima; French, 1998; Dolby; Panavision; Color; Not rated; 128 minutes; American release date: October 18, 2002

CAST

Lagardère (The Hunchback) . . . . .Daniel Auteuil
Gonzague . . . . .Fabrice Luchini
Nevers . . . . .Vincent Perez
Aurore . . . . .Marie Gillain
Philippe d'Orléans . . . . .Philippe Noiret
Peyrolles . . . . .Yann Collette
Cocardasse . . . . .Jean-François Stévenin
Passepoil . . . . .Didier Pain
Blanche . . . . .Claire Nebout
Esope . . . . .Charlie Nelson
Caylus . . . . .Jacques Sereys
Paolo . . . . .Renato Scarpa
Orvella . . . . .Ludovica Tinghi

Lagardère, a foundling raised to be a fencing master, swears vengeance on the dastardly Gonzague, who has murdered his cousin, the Duke de Nevers, in order to inherit his fortune.

© Empire

Fabrice Luchini

Marie Gillain, Daniel Auteuil

Marie Gillain

Vincent Perez

FOOD OF LOVE

(TLA RELEASING) Producers, Ventura Pons; Executive Producers, Michael Smeaton, Thomas Spieker; Director/Screenplay, Ventura Pons; Based on the novella *The Page Turner* by David Leavitt; Photography, Mario Montero; Designer, Aintza Serra; Costumes, Maria Gil; Music, Carles Cases; Editor, Pere Abadal; Associate Producers, Gemma Folch, Monika Ganzenmüller, Petra Schepeler; Casting, Pep Armengol, Leo Davis; a 42nd Street Productions S.L., Els Films de la Rambla S.A., FFP Media Entertainment, TVC, Televisión Española, Via Digital production; Spanish-German; Dolby; Color; Not rated; 112 minutes; American release date: October 25, 2002

Kevin Bishop

CAST

Pamela	Juliet Stevenson
Richard	Paul Rhys
Joseph	Allan Corduner
Paul	Kevin Bishop
Novotna	Geraldine McEwan
Tushi	Leslie Charles
Izzy	Craig Hill
Diane	Pamela Field
Teddy	Naim Thomas
Waiter	Mingo Ràfols
Receptionist	Roger Coma
Gypsy	Pepa López
Hector	Mauricio Cruz
Hustler	Manu Fullola
Alden	Carlos Castañón
Azenon	Hernán González
Students	Brenda Roque, Helenika Hellevig
Carolyn	Sue Flack
Enid	Marianne Choquet
Boyfriend	Jack McKusay

An aspiring young music student becomes a page-turner for a world famous pianist who ends up becoming the lad's lover.

© TLA Releasing

Manu Fullola

Kevin Bishop, Paul Rhys

Allan Corduner, Kevin Bishop

Juliet Stevenson, Kevin Bishop

Kevin Bishop

ALL OR NOTHING

(UNITED ARTISTS) Producers, Alain Sarde, Simon Channing Williams; Director/Screenplay, Mike Leigh; Photography, Dick Pope; Designer, Eve Stewart; Costumes, Jacqueline Durran; Music, Andrew Dickson; Executive Producer, Pierre Edelman; Line Producer, Georgina Lowe; Make-up & Hair Designer, Christine Blundell; Casting, Nina Gold; a Simon Channing Williams production, presented in association with Alain Sarde, Thinman Films; British-French; Dolby; Color; Rated R; 128 minutes; American release date: October 25, 2002

CAST

Phil	Timothy Spall
Penny	Lesley Manville
Rachel	Alison Garland
Rory	James Corden
Maureen	Ruth Sheen
Carol	Marion Bailey
Ron	Paul Jesson
Sid	Sam Kelly
Cécile	Kathryn Hunter
Samantha	Sally Hawkins
Donna	Helen Coker
Craig	Ben Crompton
Dr. Griffiths	Robert Wilfort
Neville	Gary McDonald
Dinah	Diveen Henry
Old Lady	Jean Ainslie
Passengers	Badi Uzzaman, Parvez Qadir
Nutter	Russell Mabey

and Thomas Brown-Lowe, Oliver Golding, Henri McCarthy, Ben Wattley (Small Boys), Leo Bill (Young Man), Peter Stockbridge (Man with Flowers), Brian Bovell (Garage Owner), Daniel Mays (Jason), Timothy Bateson (Harold), Michele Austin (Care Worker), Alex Kelly (Neurotic Woman), Alan Williams (Drunk), Peter Yardley (MC), Dawn Davis (Singer), Emma Lowndes, Maxine Peake (Party-Girls), Matt Bardock, Mark Benton (Men at Bar), Dorothy Atkinson, Heather Craney, Martin Savage (Silent Passengers), Joe Tucker (Fare Dodger), Edna Doré (Martha), Georgie Fitch (Ange), Tracy O'Flaherty (Michelle), Di Botcher (Supervisor Nurse), Valerie Hunkins (Doctor), Daniel Ryan (Crash Driver)

A look at the lives of a disparate group of struggling inhabitants of a drab South London housing complex.

© United Artists

Ruth Sheen, Marion Bailey, Lesley Manville

Sally Hawkins, Ben Crompton

Lesley Manville, Timothy Spall

Ruth Sheen, Helen Coker

FEMME FATALE

(WARNER BROS.) Producers, Tarak Ben Ammar, Marina Gefter; Executive Producer, Mark Lombardo; Director/Screenplay, Brian DePalma; Photography, Thierry Arbogast; Designer, Anne Pritchard; Music, Ryuichi Sakamoto; Editor, Bill Pankow; Associate Producer, Chris Soldo; a Tarak Ben Ammar presentation of a Quinta Communications production; Dolby; Color; Rated R; 110 minutes; American release date: November 6, 2002

CAST

Laure/Lily	Rebecca Romijn-Stamos
Nicolas Bardo	Antonio Banderas
Watts	Peter Coyote
Black Tie	Eriq Ebouaney
Racine	Edouard Montoute
Veronica	Rie Rasmussen
Serra	Thierry Fremont
Shiff	Gregg Henry
Stanfield Phillips	Fiona Curzon
Pierre/Bartender	Daniel Milgram
Seated Guard	Jean-Marc Mineo
Cannes Commentator	Jean Chatel
Bodyguards	Stephane Petit, Olivier Follet
Irma	Eva Darlan
Louis	Jean-Marie Frin

and Philippe Guegan (Bespectacled Man), Denis Hecker (TV Moderator), Laurence Breheret (Flight Attendant), Salvatore Ingoglia (Truck Driver), Matthew Geczy (Embassy Guard), Laurence Martin (Nathalie), Jo Prestia (Napoleon), David Belle (French Policeman), Francoise Michaud (Woman with Blind Man), Alain Figlarz (Sex Shop Man), Bart De Palma (Power Room Guard), Valerie Maes (The Blonde: Restroom, Bridge & Cafe), David Cuny (Groom Hotel Sheraton), Eric Fesais (Policeman), Bertrand Merignac (Photographer), Dan Herzberg, Sam Olivier, Pascal Ondicolberry, Gerard Renault (Surveillance Room Guards), Jaoquina Balaunde (Woman in Panic), Ugne Andrikonyte (Festival Guest), Faco Hanela (Poster Man), Marie Foulquie, Regis Quennesson (Tourists), Matilde Tancredi, Pascale Jacquemot (Mediums on TV Show), Serge Gonnin (Thierry), Aurelie Pauker (Brigitte), Sandrine Bonnaire, Regis Wargnier, Beata Sonczuk-Ben Ammar, Yves Marmion, Ada Marmion, Leonardo De La Fuente, Stephen Van Nukerk, Driki van Zyl, Pascal Silvestre, Henri Ernst, Olivier Albou, Stephen van Nietert, Emilie Chatel, Dorothee Grosjean, Chloe Cremont, Justine Renard (Special Guests, Cannes Film Festival)

Rebecca Romijn-Stamos

Antonio Banderas

Laure Ash attempts to leave behind her life of crime, only to find that her new identity as the wife of a high profile politician has been accidentally exposed by a voyeuristic ex-paparazzo admirer.

© Warner Bros.

Antonio Banderas, Rebecca Romijn-Stamos

Antonio Banderas, Rebecca Romijn-Stamos

THE WAY HOME...

(PARAMOUNT CLASSICS) Producers, Woo-Hyun Hwang, Jae-Woo Hwang; Executive Producer, Seung-Bum Kim; Director/Screenplay, Jeong-Hywang Lee; Photography, Hong-Shik Yoon; Designer, Jum-Hee Shin; Editors, Sang-Beom Kim, Jae-Beom Kim; Music, Dae-Hong Kim, Yang-Hee Kim; a CJ Entertainment presentation in association with Tube Entertainment of a Tube Pictures production; South Korean; Dolby; Color; Rated PG; 80 minutes; American release date: November 15, 2002

CAST

Grandmother . . . . .Eul-Boon Kim
Sang-woo . . . . .Seung-Ho Yoo
Cheol-e . . . . .Kyung-Hoon Min
Hae-Yeon . . . . .Eun-Kyung Yim
Mother . . . . .Hyo-Hee Dong
Bicycle Grandfather . . . . .Chooh-Hoe Lee
and Dong-Jiwol Lee (Marketplace Mom and Pop Store Grandmother), Sang-Kee Yoo (Gas Station Uncle), Jae-Keun Yoon (Shoe Store Owner), Baek-Cheon Ko (Elderly Man Giving Directions), Young-Ja Shin, Kyu-Ho Cho (Momo Pop Store Owners), Kyung-Mo park (Ironware Store Owner), Byun-Moo Ahn (Bus Driver), Seok-Woo Han (Choco-Pie Kid), Jeong-Ae Kim (Chinese Restaurant Owner), Haw-Sang Yoon (Elderly Man Pulling Cow), Ki-Joon Nam (Rear-Car Elderly Man)

After his mother loses her job, young Sang-woo is sent to live with his simple grandmother in her peasant village, where a surprising bond forms between these two contrary people.

Seung-Ho Yoo, Eul-Boon Kim

Eul-Boon Kim, Seung-Ho Yoo

Edouard Baer, Audrey Tautou

GOD IS GREAT, I'M NOT

(EMPIRE) Producers, Alain Sarde, Georges Benayoun; Director, Pascale Bailly; Screenplay, Pascale Bailly, Alain Tasma; Line Producers, Françoise Guglielmi, Christine Gozlan; Designer, Denis Mercier; Costumes, Khadija Zeggal; Casting, Stephane Foenkinos, Brigitte Moidon; Produced by Les Films Alain Sarde, Dacia Films; co-produced by Canal+ and Centre Nationale de la Cinematographie; French, 2001; Dolby; Color; Not rated; 100 minutes; American release date: November 11, 2002

CAST

Michèle . . . . .Audrey Tautou
François . . . . .Edouard Baer
Valérie . . . . .Julie Depardieu
Evelyne . . . . .Catherine Jacob
Jean . . . . .Philippe Laudenbach
Florence . . . . .Cathy Verney
Régine . . . . .Anna Koch
Simon . . . . .Max Tzwangue
Bertrand . . . . .Mathieu Demy
Ali . . . . .Atmen Kelif
Laetitia . . . . .Nelly Camara
Joseph . . . . .Jean Reichman
Jessica . . . . .Nathalie Levy-Lang
The First Patient . . . . .Thierry Neuvic
The Rabbi . . . . .Edwin Gerard
The Cop . . . . .Philippe Guyral
Serge . . . . .Laurent Natrella
Cécile . . . . .Saskia Mulder
Friends from Judaism Lessons . . . . . . .Nathalie Zemirou, Carole Zarka
Model on the Terrace . . . . .Valérie Dashwood

A desperately unhappy 20-year-old girl turns to religion to help her find salvation, ultimately meeting a Jewish veterinarian.

ARARAT

(MIRAMAX) Producers, Robert Lantos, Atom Egoyan; Co-Producer, Sandra Cunningham; Director/Screenplay, Atom Egoyan; Photography, Paul Sarossy; Designer, Phillip Barker; Costumes, Beth Pasternak; Editor, Susan Shipton; Music, Mychael Danna; Associate Producers, Simone Urdl, Julia Rosenberg; an Alliance Atlantis and Serendipity Point Films presentation in association with Ego Film Arts of a Robert Lantos production; Canadian; Dolby; Color; Rated R; 116 minutes; American release date: November 15, 2002

CAST

Raffi	David Alpay
Ani	Arsinee Khanjian
David	Christopher Plummer
Edward Saroyan	Charles Aznavour
Celia	Marie-Josee Croze
Rouben	Eric Bogosian
Philip	Brent Carver
Martin/Clarence Ussher	Bruce Greenwood
Ali/Jevdet Bay	Elias Koteas
Arshile Gorky	Simon Abkarian
Shushan Gorky	Lousnak Abdalain
The Photographer	Raoul Bhaneja
Young Gorky	Garen Boyajian
Dinner Guest/Wailing Mother	Setta Keshishian

and Shant Srabian (Dinner Guest #3/Doctor #1), Max Morrow (Tony), Christie MacFadyen (Janet), Dawn Roach (Customs Officer), Haig Sarkissian (Sevan), Gina Wilkinson (Art Teacher), Arshile Egoyan (Child at Gallery), Kevork Arslanian, Vic Keshishian, Arthur Hagopian, George Kharlakian, Shant Kabrielian (Armenian Fighters), Varazh Stephen (Doctor #2), Samir Ainadi (Turkish Officer), Carlo Essagian (Turkish Soldier), Rose Sarkisyan (Translator), Chris Gillett (Celia's Father), Jean Yoon (Third Assistant Director), Shahan Bulat-Matossian (Wounded Teen Patient), Manuel Ishkhanian (Teen Patient's Brother), Susan Raymond (German Woman), Lorna Noura Kevorkian, Mandyf Nissani, Manal Elmasri, Roberta Angelica, Andrea Loren, Araxie Keshishian (Armenian Brides), Linda Gizirian (Rape Victim), Nicole Anoush Strang (Girl Under Cart), Erica Ehm (Journalist)

The slaughter of millions of Turkish-Armenians during World War I becomes the controversial subject of a film on which both Ani and her son are working, bringing up tensions between the two.

© Miramax

Arsinee Khanjian, Charles Aznavour

David Alpay

Christopher Plummer

Christopher Plummer, David Alpay

EL CRIMEN DEL PADRE AMARO
(THE CRIME OF FATHER AMARO)

(SAMUEL GOLDWYN FILMS) Producers, Alfredo Ripstein, Daniel Birman Ripstein; Executive Producer, Laura Imperiale; Associate Producer, Atahualpa Lichy, Scot Evans, Claudia Becker; Co-Producer, José María Morales; Director, Carlos Carrera; Screenplay, Vicente Leñero; Based on the novel by Eça de Queirós; Photography, Guillermo Granillo; Art Director, Carmen Giménez Cacho; Editor, Óscar Figueroa; Music, Rosino Serrano; Casting, Sandra León Becker; an Alfredo Ripstein, Daniel Birman Ripstein, Alameda Films, Wanda Vision, Blu Films, Fondo Para la Producción Cinematográfica de Calidad, Instituto Mexicano de Cinematografía, Cinecolor México,. Cinecolor Argentina, Videocolor Argentina, Gobierno de Estado de Veracruz-Llave with the support of Programa Ibermedia presentation; Mexican-Spanish-Argentina-French; Dolby; Color; Rated R; 118 minutes; American release date: November 15, 2003

Ernesto Gómez Cruz, Gael García Bernal

Gael García Bernal, Ana Claudia Talancón

CAST

Father Amaro . . . . .Gael García Bernal
Father Benito . . . . .Sancho Gracia
Amelia . . . . .Ana Claudia Talancón
Father Natalio . . . . .Damián Alcázar
Augustina Sanjuanera . . . . .Angélica Aragón
Dionisia . . . . .Luisa Huertas
Bishop . . . . .Ernesto Gómez Cruz
Martín . . . . .Gastón Melo
Rubén de la Rosa . . . . .Andrés Montiel
Doc . . . . .Gerardo Moscoso
Old Man . . . . .Alfredo Gonzáles
The Mayor . . . . .Pedro Armendáriz, Jr.
Amparita, Mayor's Wife . . . . .Verónica Langer
and Lorenzo de Rodas (Don Paco de la Rosa), Roger Nevares (Father Galván), Fernando Becerril (Galarza), Jorge Zárate (Father Mauro), Rosa María Castillo (Chepina), Blanca Loaria (Getsemaní), Juan Ignacio Aranda (Chato Aguilar), Martín Zapata (MP Agent), Dagoberto Gama (Lucas), Rogelio Rojas (Photographer), Jorge Castillo (Matías), Mario Figueroa (Chente), Enrique Vásquez, Cristo Yánez (Assailants), Marina Vera (Head Assailant), Leticia Valenzuela (Doctor), Raúl Azkenazi (Hueso), Carmen Giménez Cacho (Mother Hada), Roberto Linares (Tiburón), Víctor Hernández (Guaraura), Isidra Morales (Dionisia's Friend), Ines Cuspinera (Chato Baby's Godmother) Martha Posternak (Chato Aguilar's Wife), José Luis Caballero (Chato Baby's Godfather), Vanesa Barba (Chato Baby), Paloma Cobos (Pleading MP), Enrique Gilardi, Jamie Cancino, Pablo Hoyos, Daniel Posterman, Dino Demichelis (Drug Friends)

A recently ordained priest arrives in a Mexican village to help an elderly priest establish a medical clinic and finds himself involved in a forbidden relationship with a 16-year-old girl. This film received an Oscar nomination for foreign language film.

Gael García Bernal

293

DIE ANOTHER DAY

(UNITED ARTISTS) Producers, Michael G. Wilson, Barbara Broccoli; Executive Producer, Anthony Waye; Director, Lee Tamahori; Screenplay, Neal Purvis, Robert Wade; Co-Producer, Callum McDougall; Photography, David Tattersall; Designer, Peter Lamont; Costumes, Lindy Hemming; Editor, Christian Wagner; Music, David Arnold; Title song by David Arnold/performed by Madonna; Visual Effects Supervisor, Mara Bryan; 2nd Unit Director, Vic Armstrong; Casting, Debbie McWilliams; an Albert R. Broccoli's Eon Productions presentation; British-U.S.; Dolby; Panavision; Deluxe color; Rated PG-13; 133 minutes; American release date: November 22, 2002

Toby Stephens, Rosamund Pike, Madonna, Pierce Brosnan

Pierce Brosnan, Halle Berry

CAST

James Bond	Pierce Brosnan
Jinx	Halle Berry
Gustav Graves	Toby Stephens
Miranda Frost	Rosamund Pike
Zao	Rick Yune
General Moon	Kenneth Tsang
Colonel Moon	Will Yun Lee
Raoul	Emilio Echevarria
Moneypenny	Samantha Bond
Charles Robinson	Colin Salmon
Vlad	Michael Gorevoy
Mr. Kil	Lawrence Makoare
Q	John Cleese
M	Judi Dench
Falco	Michael Madsen
Snooty Desk Clerk	Ben Wee
Hotel Manager	Ho Yi
Peaceful	Rachel Grant
Creep	Ian Pirie
Dr. Alvarez	Simón Andreu
Van Bierk	Mark Dymond
Air Hostess	Deborah Moore
Concierge	Oliver Skeete
Old Man in Cigar Factory	Joaquin Martinez
General Chandler	Michael G. Wilson
General Han	Daryl Kwan
General Li	Vincent Wong
General Dong	Stuart Ong
Cuban Waiter	Manolo Caro
Korean Scorpion Guard	Tymarah
Doctor	Paul Darrow
Medic	Lucas Hare
Nurse	Cristina Contes
Verity	Madonna

and Stewart Scudamore, Bill Nash, James Wallace, Ami Chorlton (Buckingham Palace Reporters)

British agent James Bond goes on the trail of millionaire Gustav Graves, whose flamboyant Icarus Project is somehow connected to the diamonds renegade North Korean Colonel Moon had been using to buy arms. The 20th official James Bond adventure released by United Artists, and the fourth to star Pierce Brosnan in the part. Returning to their roles from the previous Bond film, *The World Is Not Enough*, are Brosnan, Judi Dench, John Cleese, and Samantha Bond.

Rick Yune

Pierce Brosnan, Toby Stephens

Halle Berry

Pierce Brosnan

Pierce Brosnan, Judi Dench

Halle Berry, Pierce Brosnan

Pierce Brosnan

TALK TO HER

(SONY CLASSICS) Executive Producer, Agustín Almodóvar; Director/Screenplay, Pedro Almodóvar; Director of Production, Esther García; Photography, Javier Aguirresarobe; Costumes, Sonia Grande; Music, Alberto Iglesias; Editor, José Salcedo; Associate Producer, Michel Ruben; Art Director, Antxon Gómez; Casting, Sara Bilbatua; an El Deseo S.A. presentation with the collaboration of A3Tv and Via Digital; Spanish; Dolby; Color; Rated R; 112 minutes; American release date: November 22, 2002

Rosario Flores (center)

Rosario Flores, Adolfo Fernández

Leonor Watling, Rosario Flores

CAST

Benigno	Javier Cámara
Marco	Darío Grandinetti
Alicia	Leonor Watling
Lydia	Rosario Flores
Katarina, the Dance Teacher	Geraldine Chaplin
Rosa	Mariola Fuentes
Matilde	Lola Dueñas
Nurse A	Beatriz Santiago
Amparo	Paz Vega
Alfredo	Fele Martínez
Niño de Valencia	Adolfo Fernández
Ángela	Elena Anaya
TV Host	Loles León
Niño de Valencia's Agent	José Sancho
Lydia's Sister	Ana Fernández
Lydia's Assistant	Angel Infantes "Yiyo"
Lydia's Sister Husband	Carlos García Cambero
Himself	Gaetano Veloso
Musicians	Jacques Morelenbaum, Jorge Helder, Pedro Sá
Nurse B	Mamen Segovia
Doctor	Roberto Álvarez
Alicia's Father	Helio Pedregal
Psychiatrist's Receptionist	Adela Donamaría
Head Nurse	Carmen Machi
Priest	Agustín Almodóvar
Alfredo Mother	Sonia Grande
Hospital Director	Joserra Cadiñanos
Nurse	Ismael Martínez
Hospital Receptionist	Lola García
Public Officials	Esther García, Carlos Miguel Miguel
Concierge	Chus Lampreave
Lawyer	Michel Rubin
Prison Director	Juan Fernández
Themselves	Pina Bausch, Malou Airaudo
Swimmer	Fernando Iglesias
Ben	Ben Lindbergh
Dance Academy Employee Lawyer's	Ana Sanz
Receptionist	Yuyi Beringola
Pianist	Víctor Matos

Two men form a special bond while tending to women, both of whom are in a coma.

Academy Award winner for Best Original Screenplay. This film received an additional Oscar nomination for director.

Javier Conde, Rosario Flores

Javier Cámara

Geraldine Chaplin, Leonor Watling

Rosario Flores, Darío Grandinetti

Javier Cámara, Darío Grandinetti

Leonor Watling, Geraldine Chaplin

Javier Cámara

O FANTASMA

(PICTURE THIS! ENTERTAINMENT) Producer, Amândio Coroado; Director, João Pedro Rodrigues; Screenplay, João Pedro Rodrigues, José Neves, Paulo Rebelo, Alexandre Melo; Photography, Rui Poças; Designer/Costumes, João Rui Guerra da Mata; Line Producer, Vita Lains; Editors, Paulo Rebelo João Pedro Rodrigues; a Rosa Filmes presentation; Portuguese, 2000; Dolby; Super 35 Widescreen; Color; Not rated; 90 minutes; American release date: November 22, 2002

CAST
Sérgio . . . . .Ricardo Meneses
Fátima . . . . .Beatriz Torcato
João . . . . .André Barbosa
Virgílio . . . . .Eurico Vieira

An aimless young garbage collector, who lives for anonymous sexual encounters, finds himself becoming obsessed with a motor-bike riding stranger.

Ricardo Meneses (right)

Ricardo Meneses

Garry McDonald, Kenneth Branagh

RABBIT-PROOF FENCE

(MIRAMAX) Producers, Phillip Noyce, Christine Olsen, John Winter; Executive Producers, David Elfick, Jeremy Thomas, Kathleen McLaughlin; Director, Phillip Noyce; Screenplay, Christine Olsen; Based on the book *Follow the Rabbit-Proof Fence* by Doris Pilkington Garimara; Photography, Christopher Doyle; Designer/Costumes, Roger Ford; Editors, John Scott, Veronika Jenet; Music, Peter Gabriel; Casting, Christine King; a HanWay and Australian Film Finance Corporation presentation of a Rumbalara Films, Olsen Levy production in association with Showtime Australia; Australian-British; Dolby; Super 35 Widescreen; Color; Rated PG; 94 minutes; American release date: November 29, 2002

CAST
Molly Craig . . . . .Everlyn Sampi
Daisy Craig . . . . .Tianna Sansbury
Gracie Fields . . . . .Laura Monaghan
Moodoo . . . . .David Gulpilil
Molly's Mother . . . . .Ningali Lawford
Molly's Grandmother .Myarn Lawford
Mavis . . . . .Deborah Mailman
Constable Riggs . . . . .Jason Clarke
A.O. Neville . . . . .Kenneth Branagh
Nina, Dormitory Boss . . . . .Natasha Wanganeen
Mr. Neal . . . . .Garry McDonald
Police Inspector . . . . .Roy Billing
Miss Jessop . . . . .Celine O'Leary
Matron . . . . .Kate Roberts
and Tracy Monaghan (Moodoo's Daughter), Tamara Flanagan (Olive, Escaped Girl), David Ngoombujarra (Kangaroo Hunter), Anthony Hayes (The Fence Builder), Andrew S. Gilbert (Depot Manager), Sheryl Carter (Gracie's Mother), Trevor Jamieson (Moore River Policeman), Heath Bergerson (Wiluna Liar), Edwina Bishop (First Farm Mother), Kerilee Meuris (Farm Daughter), Andrew Martin (Car Driving Policeman), Ken Radley (Fence Worker), Don Barker (Mr. Evans), Carmel Johnson (Mrs. Evans), David Buchanan (Policeman at Railway), Richard Carter (Policeman at Evans' Farmhouse), Fiona Gregory (Jigalong Mother), Reggie Wanganeen (Tommy Grant), Glenys Sampi (Woman in Queue), Kizzy Flanagan, Antonia Sampi (Dormitory Girls), Maurice Kelly (Aboriginal Hunter), Janganpa Group (Jigalong Extras), Elsie Thomas, Rosie Goodji, Jewess James (Singing Women at Jigalong)

The true story of how three Aboriginal girls, per government orders, were forcibly removed from their families for servant duty and sent south where they escaped and walked 1,200 miles to get back home, using a rabbit-proof fence as their guide.

RUSSIAN ARK

(WELLSPRING) Director/Visual Concept and Principal Image Design, Alexander Sokurov; Screenplay, Anatoly Nikiforov, Alexander Sokurov; Dialogue, Boris Khaimsky, Alexander Sokurov; Photography/Steadicam Operator, Tilman Büttner; Art Directors, Yelena Zhukova, Natalia Kochergina; Costumes, Lidiya Kriukova, Tamara Seferyan, Maria Grishanova; Music, Sergey Yevtushenko; Russian-German; Color; Not rated; 96 minutes; American release date: December 13, 2002

Sergey Dreiden

Sergey Dreiden

Sergey Dreiden (left)

CAST

The Marquis, a 19th-century Diplomat . . . . .Sergey Dreiden
Catherine the Great . . . . .Maria Kuznetsova
The Spy . . . . .Leonid Mozgovoy
Orbeli . . . . .David Giorgobiani
Boris Piotrovsky . . . . .Alexander Chaban
Talented Boy . . . . .Artem Strelnikov
Peter the Great . . . . .Maxim Sergeyv
Catherine the First . . . . .Natalia Nikulenko
First Lady . . . . .Yelena Rufanova
Second Lady . . . . .Yelena Spiridonova
Themselves . . . . . .Mikhail Piotrovsky, Lev Yeliseyev, Oleg Khmelnitsky, Alla Osipenko, Tamara Kurenkova
Nicholas I . . . . .Yuliy Zhurin
Alexandra Fedrovna, Wife of Nicolas I . . . . .Svetlana Svirko
First Cavalier . . . . .Konstantin Anisimov
Second Cavalier . . . . .Alexey Barabash
Third Cavalier . . . . .Ilia Shakunov
Fourth Cavalier . . . . .Alexander Kulikov
and Anna Aleksahina (Alexandra Fyodorovna, Wife of Nicolas II), Vladimir Baranov (Nicholas II), Boris Smolkin (Chancellor Nesselrode), Alexander Razbash (A Museum Official)

A unseen artist finds himself in the Hermitage at St. Petersburg, journeying from room to room, following another displaced figure, a Marquis, as they discuss and experience random moments of Russian history. This entire film is done in one uninterrupted take.

EVELYN

Sophie Vavasseur, Pierce Brosnan, Niall Beagan, Hugh Macdonagh

Pierce Brosnan, Aidan Quinn, Stephen Rea

300   Stephen Rea, Pierce Brosnan, Aidan Quinn

(UNITED ARTISTS) Producers, Pierce Brosnan, Beau St. Clair, Michael Ohoven; Executive Producers, Eberhard Kayser, Mario Ohoven, Kieran Corrigan, Simon Bosanquet; Director, Bruce Beresford; Screenplay/Co-Producer, Paul Pender; Photography, André Fleuren; Designer, John Stoddart; Costumes, Joan Bergin; Editor, Humphrey Dixon; Music, Stephen Endelman; Line Producer, Kevan Barker; Associate Producer, Cynthia A. Palormo; Casting, John and Ros Hubbard; an Irish Dreamtime and CineEvelyn production, presented in association with First Look Media and Cinerenta; Distributed by MGM Distribution Co.; Irish-British-U.S.; Dolby; Panavision; Color; Rated PG; 94 minutes; American release date: December 13, 2002

CAST

Desmond Doyle	Pierce Brosnan
Nick Barron	Aidan Quinn
Bernadette Beattie	Julianna Margulies
Michael Beattie	Stephen Rea
Senior Counsel Mr. Wolfe	John Lynch
Evelyn Doyle	Sophie Vavasseur
Tom Connolly	Alan Bates
Dermot Doyle	Niall Beagan
Maurice Doyle	Hugh MacDonagh
Charlotte Doyle	Mairead Devlin
Henry Doyle	Frank Kelly
Mrs. Daisley	Claire Mullan
Inspector Logan	Alvaro Lucchesi
District Judge	Garrett Keogh
Brother Eustace	Daithi O'Suilleabhain
Sister Brigid	Andrea Irvine
Sister Theresa	Marian Quinn
Sister Felicity	Karen Ardiff
Father O'Malley	Bosco Hogan
Fergal	Des Braiden
Mary	Sorcha Herlihy
Annette Farrell	Lauren Carpenter
Lauren	Lauren O'Connell

and Hugh Grogan, Peter Fowl (Pub Musicians), Gail Fitzpatrick (Miss Gilhooly), Pat McGrath (Gamekeeper), Mark Lambert (Minister of Education), Conor Evans (Justice Ferris), Eamon Rohan (Justice Hall), Alan Barry (Justice McLaughlin), Brian McGrath (Hugh Canning), Mick Nolan (Honest Owen O'Leary), Luke Hayden (Irish Times Reporter), Don Foley (Justice Lynch), Bill Golding (Justice Daley), Sally (Slippery Sam)

The true story of how Desmond Doyle fought the Irish courts in order to regain custody of his children, after the authorities put them in orphanages, claiming he was incapable of raising them himself.

© United Artists

Pierce Brosnan, Julianne Margulies, Aidan Quinn

INTACTO

(**LIONS GATE**) Executive Producers, Fernando Bovaira, Enrique López Lavigne; Director, Juan Carlos Fresnadillo; Screenplay, Juan Carlos Fresnadillo, Andrés Koppel; Photography, Xavier Giménez; Designer, César Macarrón; Costumes, Tatiana Hernández; Editor, Nacho Ruiz Capillas; Music, Lucio Godoy; Casting, Sara Bilbatúa; a Sogecine production for Telecinco with the participation of Canal+Spain and the collaboration of Tenerife Film Commission; Spanish, 2001; Dolby; Super 35 Widescreen; Color; Rated R; 108 minutes; American release date: December 13, 2002

CAST

Tomás Sanz	Leonardo Sbaraglia
Federico	Eusebio Poncela
Sara	Mónica López
Alejandro	Antonio Dechent
Samuel Berg	Max von Sydow
Horacio	Guillermo Toledo
Sara's Husband	Alber Ponte
Sara's Daughter	Andrea San Vicente
Captives	Jesús Noguero, Ramón Serrada
Nurse	Marisa Lull
Gerard	Luis Mesonero Jiménez
Inspector	Pedro Beitia
Manager	Jaime Losada
Woman Captive	Susana Lazaro
Bodyguard	Iván Aledo
Ana	Paz Gómez
Claudia	Marta Gil
Man with Slicked Back Hair	Pere Eugeni Font
Pivote	Ramón Esquinas
Redhead	Chema de Miguel
Casino Boss	Cesar Castillo
Gamblers	Flora Alvaro, Jose Olmo
Tall Gambler	Luis de León
Losing Gambler in Casino	Francisco Sotelo
Airport Employee	Patricia Castro
Policeman	Paco Churruca
Young Policeman	Adria Raluy
Older Policeman	Fernando Albizu
Blond Policeman	Mauricio Bautista
Custody Policemen	Pablo Portillo, Santiago Martinez

Max von Sydow, Eusebio Poncela, Leonardo Sbaraglia

Leonardo Sbaraglia (left), Monica Lopez (right)

Federico helps bank robber Tomás Sanz escape from police custody and teaches him the art of absorbing the luck of others.

© Lions Gate

Leonardo Sbaraglia, Eusebio Poncela

Leonardo Sbaraglia, Max von Sydow

MORVERN CALLAR

(COWBOY) Producers, Robyn Slovo, Charles Pattinson, George Faber; Executive Producers, Andras Hamori, Seaton McLean, David M. Thompson, Barbara McKissack, Lenny Crooks; Director, Lynne Ramsay; Screenplay, Lynne Ramsay, Liana Dognini; Based on the novel by Alan Warner; Photography, Alwin Kuchler; Designer, Jane Morton; Costumes, Sarah Blenkinsop; Editor, Lucia Zucchetti; Casting, Des Hamilton; an Alliance Atlantis and BBC Films presentation in association with Film Council, Scottish Screen and Glasgow Film Fund of a Company Pictures production; British-Canadian-Scottish, 2001; Dolby; Color; Not rated; 98 minutes; American release date: December 20, 2002

Samantha Morton (right)

Samatha Morton

Kathleen McDermott, Samantha Morton

CAST

Morvern Callar . . . . .Samantha Morton
Lanna . . . . .Kathleen McDermott
Boy in Room 1022 . . . . .Raife Patrick Burchell
Dazzer . . . . .Dan Cadan
Tequila Sheila . . . . .Carolyn Calder
Welcoming Courier . . . . .Steven Cardwell
Guy with Hat's Mate . . . . .Bryan Dick
Gypsy Taxi Driver . . . . .El Carrette
Overdose . . . . .Andrew Flannigan
Him . . . . .Des Hamilton
Sick Girl/Bikini Girl . . . . .Mette Karlsvik
Green Boys . . . . .Andrew Knowles, Matthew Townsend
Red Hanna . . . . .Duncan McHardy
Couris Jean . . . . .Ruby Milton
and Paul Popplewell (Guy with Hat), Mischa Richter (Rick, the American Courier), Vito Rocco (Swimming Pool Courier), Danny Schofeld (Dave), Andrew Townley (Creeping Jesus), Yolanda Vazquez (Spanish Mother), Dolly Wells (Susan), Jim Wilson (Tom Boddington)

After finding her boyfriend's corpse, Morvern Callar disregards the instructions in his suicide note, taking money from his account to have a holiday in Spain with her friend Lanna.

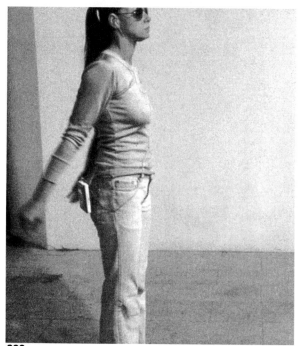

Samatha Morton

© Cowboy

SPIDER

(SONY CLASSICS) Producers, David Cronenberg, Samuel Hadida, Catherine Bailey; Executive Producers, Luc Roeg, Charles Finch, Martin Katz, Jane Barclay, Sharon Harel, Hannah Leader, Zygi Kamasa, Simon Franks, Victor Hadida; Director, David Cronenberg; Screenplay, Patrick McGrath, based on his novel; Photography, Peter Suschitzky; Designer, Andrew Sanders; Costumes, Denise Cronenberg; Editor, Ronald Sanders; Music, Howard Shore; Casting, Suzanne Smith; a Capitol Films and Artists Independent Network presentation in association with Odeon Films and Media Suits, of a Catherine Bailey/Davis Films/Artists Independent Network/Grosvenor Park production; Canadian-British; Dolby; Color; Rated R; 98 minutes; American release date: December 20, 2002

CAST

Dennis "Spider" Cleg	Ralph Fiennes
Mrs. Cleg/Yvonne/Mrs. Wilkinson	Miranda Richardson
Bill Cleg	Gabriel Byrne
Mrs. Wilkinson	Lynn Redgrave
Terrence	John Neville
Boy Spider	Bradley Hall
Freddy	Gary Reineke
John	Philip Craig
Bob	Cliff Saunders
Nora	Tara Ellis
Gladys	Sara Stockbridge
Ernie	Arthur Whycrow
Barmaid	Nicola Duffett
Large Man	Jake Nightingale
Flashing Yvonne	Alison Egan
Toothless Jack	Donald Ewer
Cook	Joan Heney

and Peter Elliott, Alec Stockwell, Scott McCord, Frank Blanch (Residents), Rachel Taggart, Olivia Imogen Harris (Young Woman and Child)

Dennis Cleg, released from a mental institution after twenty years, arrives in 1980 London to retrace the events that led up to his hospitalization.

© Sony Classics

Miranda Richardson, Bradley Hall

John Neville, Ralph Fiennes

Miranda Richardson

Gabriel Byrne, Miranda Richardson

THE PIANIST

Adrien Brody

Maureen Lipman, Julia Rayner, Adrien Brody, Ed Stoppard,
Frank Finlay, Jessica Kate Meyer

(FOCUS) Producers, Roman Polanski, Robert Benmussa, Alain Sarde; Executive Producers, Lew Rywin, Henning Molfenter, Timothy Burrill; Director, Roman Polanski; Screenplay, Ronald Harwood; Based on the book by Wladyslaw Szpilman; Photography, Pawel Edelman; Designer, Allan Starski; Costumes, Anna Sheppard; Editor, Hervé De Luze; Music, Wojciech Kilar; Co-Producer, Gene Gutowski; Associate Producer, Rainer Schaper; Casting, Celestia Fox; an Alain Sarde and Robert Benmussa presentation, of a co-production of R.P. Productions, Heritage Films, Studio Babelsberg, Runteam Ltd. with the participation of Canal+ and StudioCanal Telewizja Polska, Canal+ Poland, Agencja Produkcji Filmowej, Filmboard Berlin, Brandenburg (FBB), Filmfernsehfonds Bayern (FFF), Filmforderungsanstalt (FFA); French-Polish-German-British; Dolby; Color; Rated R; 149 minutes; American release date: December 27, 2002

CAST

Wladyslaw Szpilman	Adrien Brody
Captain Wilm Hosenfeld	Thomas Kretschmann
Mr. Szpilman	Frank Finlay
Mrs. Szpilman	Maureen Lipman
Dorota	Emilia Fox
Henryk Szpilman	Ed Stoppard
Regina Szpilman	Julia Rayner
Halina Szpilman	Jessica Kate Meyer
Jurek	Michael Zebrowski
SS Officer Who Slaps Father	Wanja Mues
Mr. Lipa	Richard Ridings
Feather Woman	Nomi Sharron
Man Waiting to Cross	Anthony Milner
Street Musicians	Lucie Skeaping, Roddy Skeaping, Ben Harlan
Schutzpolizei	Thomas Lawincky, Joachim Paul Assböck
Itzak Heller	Roy Smiles
Yehuda	Paul Bradley
Majorek	Daniel Caltagirone
Benek	Andrzej Blumenfeld
Child at the Wall	Darian Wawer
Customers with Coins	Zbigniew Zamachowski, Lejb Fogelman
SS Officer	Detlev von Wangenheim
Rubinstein	Popek
Woman With Soup	Zofia Czerwinska
The Soup Snatcher	Emilio Fernandez
Schultz	Udo Kroschwald
SS Shooting the Woman	Uwe Rathsam
Wailing Woman	Katarzyna Bargielowska
Woman With Child	Maja Ostaszewska
Dr. Erlich	John Bennett
Mr. Grün	Cyril Shaps

and Wojciech Smolarz (Boy with Sweets), Lech Mackiewicz (Fellow Worker), Ruth Platt (Janina), Frank Michael Köbe (SS Shooting Benek), Torsten Flach (Zig Zag), Peter Rappenglück (SS Making a Speech), Ronan Vibert (Janina's Husband), Krzysztof Pieczynski (Gebczynski), Katarzyna Figura (Neighbor), Valentine Pelka (Dorota's Husband), Andrew Tiernan (Szalas), Tom Strauss (Dr. Luczak), Cezary Kosinski (Lednicki)

The true story of how concert pianist Wladyslaw Szpilman managed to evade the Nazis after they took control of Warsaw.

2002 Academy Award winner for Best Actor (Adrien Brody), Best Director, and Best Adapted Screenplay. This film received additional Oscar nominations for picture, cinematography, editing, and costume design.

© Focus Films

Thomas Kretschmann, Adrien Brody

Adrien Brody

Adrien Brody

Thomas Kretschmann

Adrien Brody

Adrien Brody

Frank Finlay, Jessica Kate Meyer, Ed Stoppard,
Maureen Lipman, Julia Rayner, Adrien Brody

MAX

(LIONS GATE) Producer, Andras Hamori; Executive Producers, Jonathan Debin, Tom Ortenberg, Francois Ivernel, Cameron McCracken; Director/Screenplay, Menno Meyjes; Co-Producers, Andrea Albert, Damon Bryant; Associate Producers, Sidney Blumenthal, John Cusack, Lacia Kornylo; Photography, Lajos Koltai; Designer, Ben Van Os; Costumes, Dien Van Straalen; Music, Dan Jones; Casting, Nina Gould; Canadian-German-Hungarian-British; Dolby; Color; Rated R; 106 minutes; American release date: December 27, 2002

CAST

Max Rothman	John Cusack
Adolf Hitler	Noah Taylor
Liselore Von Peltz	Leelee Sobieski
Nina Rothman	Molly Parker
Captain Mayr	Ulrich Thomsen
Max's Father	David Horovitch
Max's Mother	Janet Suzman
NCO	András Stohl
Nina's Father	John Grillo
Nina's Mother	Anna Nygh
Nina's Brother	Krisztián Kolovratnik
David Cohn	Peter Capaldi
Hildegard	Julia Vysotskaia
Mr. Epp	János Kulka
Mrs. Epp	Katalin Pálfy

John Cusack, Molly Parker

and Kevin McKidd (George Grosz), Heather Cameron (Ada Rothman), Joel Pitts (Paul Rothman), Tamás Lengyel (Franz), Attila Árpa (Wilhelm), Daisy Haggard (Heidi), Gábor Harsay (Waiter), Paul Rattray (Hans), Derek Hagen (Fritz), Caroleen Feeney (Saleslady), Mike Kelly (Herr Wulf), Ben O'Brian (Herr Eichinger), Ágnes Becsei (Singing Girl), Tibor Solténszky (Antique Dealer), Kerric MacDonald (Heckler in Courtyard), Matt Devere (Freikorps Thug), Judit Hernádi (Frau Schmidt), Kerry Shale (Dr. Levi), Heather Hermant (Mrs. Levi), László Borbély (Erich), Péter Linka (Soldier in Courtyard), László Görög (Someone in Crowd), Andor Timár (Ritter von Lieberfelt), János Radó (Organizer), Tamás Puskás (Sidewalk Cafe Owner), Rabbi Robert Frölich (Rabbi), Róbertné Bánky, Miklós Dörögi, Marianna Kovács, Péter Bognár, István Erdös (Puppeteers)

In 1920s Berlin, Max Rothman, a Jewish art dealer, takes an interest in an anti-social, temperamental aspiring painter named Adolf Hitler.

© Lions Gate

Noah Taylor

John Cusack

John Cusack

EISENSTEIN

(INDEPENDENT/FILM FORUM) Producers, Martin Paul-Hus, Regine Schmid; Executive Producer, Wolfram Tichy; Director/Screenplay, Renny Bartlett; Co-Producer, Tom Lasica; Photography, Alexei Rodionov; Designer, Susanne Dieringer; Costumes, Tatyana Poddubnaya; Editor, Wiebke von Carolsfeld; Music, Alexander Balanescu; Casting, Sarah Bird; Produced by Vif Filmproduktion GmbH & Co., Zweite KG and Amérique Film in association with TiMe Film-und TV-Produktions GmbH with the suport SODEC, Telefilm Canada; German-Canadian, 2000; Color; Not rated; 100 minutes; American release date: January 2, 2002. CAST: Simon McBurney (Sergei Eisenstein), Raymond Coulthard (Grisha), Jacqueline McKenzie (Pera), Jonathan Hyde (Meyerhold), Barnaby Kay (Andrej), Leni Parker (Anya), Sonya Walger (Zina), Andrea Mason (Elena), Tim McMullan (Rak), Ian Bartholomew (Pinkov), Daniel MacIvor (Stalker), Rolf Saxon (US Producer), Louis Hammond (Non-Proletarian Actor), Bernard Hill (The Voice of Stalin)

ESCAPE TO LIFE:
THE ERIKA AND KLAUS MANN STORY

(CINEMA GUILD) Producer, Thomas Kufus; Co-Producer, Greta Schiller; Directors/Screenplay, Andrea Weiss, Wieland Speck;' Photography, Uli Fischer, Ann T. Rossetti, Nuala Campbell; Designer, Johannes Weinand, Bader El Hindi; Music, John Eacott; Editors, Andrea Weiss, Priscilla Swann; Costumes, Gabriele Keuneke, Ivan Ingerman; Narrators, Vanessa Redgrave, Corin Redgrave; a Jezebel Films/Zero Film production; German-British, 2001; Color; Not rated; 85 minutes; American release date: January 11, 2002. Docudrama charting the tumultuous lives of the gay offspring of German writer Thomas Mann; featuring Conny Appenzeller, Albrecht Becker, Sol Bondy, Thomas Bronner, Michael Callahan, Dorothee von Diepenbroick, Cora Frost, Christoph Eichhorn.

THE FAREWELL

(NEW YORKER) Producers, Gesche Carstens, Henryk Romanowski, Jan Schütte; Director, Jan Schütte; Screenplay, Klaus Pohl; Photography, Edward Klosinski; Designer, Katharina Wöppermann; Editor, Renate Merck; Music, John Cale; a co-production of Novoskop, Film GmbH, Berlin with WDR, ORB, SWR, ARTE and Studio Babelsberg Independents/Arthur Hofer; German, 2000; Dolby; Color; Not rated; 91 minutes; American release date: January 16, 2002. CAST: Josef Bierbichler (Bertolt Brecht), Monica Bleibtreu (Helen Weigel), Jeanette Hain (Käthe Reichel), Elfriede Irrall (Elisabeth Hauptmann), Margit Rogall (Ruth Berlau), Samuel Fintzi (Wolfgang Harich), Rena Zednikowa (Isot Kilian), Birgit Minichmayr (Barbara Brecht), Tilman Günther, Sawomir Holland, Piotr Kryska (Stasi Officers), Paul Herwig (Manfred Weckwerth), Claudius Freyer (Peter Palitzsch), Emanuel Spitzy (Pioneer). Ulrich Matthes (Wolfgang Harig)

Simon McBurney, Raymond Coulthard in
Eisenstein © Independent / Film Forum

Klaus and Erika Mann in *Escape to Life:
The Erika and Klaus Mann Story* © Cinema Guild

PLASTIC PEOPLE OF THE UNIVERSE

(KINO) Director/Screenplay, Jana Chytilová; Photography, Miroslav Vranek; Editor, Jiri Brozek; a production of Czech TV, Video 57; Czech, 2001; Color; Not rated; 74 minutes; American release date: January 18, 2002. Documentary, featuring Mejla Hlavsa, Vratislav Brabenec, Josef Janicek, Jiri Kabes, Joe Karafiat, Jan Brabec, Lou Reed, Gary Lucas, Ivan M. Jirous, Pavel Zajicek, Dana Nemcova, Martin Bezouska, Egon Bondy, Otakar Motejl, Vaclav Havel, Karel Stome, Pavel Landovsk, Frantisek Stárek, Kveta Princová, Jan Velát (Themselves)

BEYOND THE OCEAN

(ANTHOLOGY FILM ARCHIVES) Producers, Rebecca Feig, Isen Robbins, Ursula Wolschlager; Director, Tony Pemberton; Screenplay, Alexis Brunner, Tony Pemberton; Line Producer, Justin Kelly; Photography, Philip Robertson, Ted Sappington; Designers, Martin Lang, Chelsea Maruskin; Costumes, Christina Darch, Eduard Galkin; Editor, Svetlana Guralskaya; a co-production of Go East Productions and Intrinsic Value Films; Russian, 2000; Dolby; Color; Not rated; 89 minutes; American release date: January 24, 2002. CAST: Dasha Volga (Adult Pitsee), Tatyana Kamina (Young Pitsee), Rita Kamina (Pitsee, 4 year old), Rik Nagel (Alex "Sasha" Kuznetsova), Sage (Dogwalker), Tatyana Kuznetsova (Grandmother Mohi), Donovan Barton (Uncle Alyosha), Camille Gaston (Bike Messenger), Peter von Berg (Seva), Aleksei Khardikov (Father), Yelena Antimova (Irena), Alexandr Tutin (Angry Drunk), Igor Filippov (Mother's Love), Misha Mudrov, Sasha Salminov (Fighting Boys), Catherine Donaldson (Customer at Icon Store), Craig Lechner (Dude at Club), Amanda Vogel (Dude's Partner), Pani Bronya (Babushka), Ursula Wolschlager (Foot Artist), Aldo Hernandez (Throb Background DJ), Robert Bruton (Waiter at Club), Tony Pemberton (Deadman)

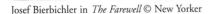

Josef Bierbichler in *The Farewell* © New Yorker

WAYDOWNTOWN

(LOT 47 FILMS) Producer, Shirley Vercruysse; Director, Gary Bruns; Screenplay, Gary Burns, James Martin; Photography, Patrick McLaughlin; Editor, Mark Lemmon; Music, John Abram; an Alliance Atlantis presentation of an Odeon Films presentation of a Burns Film production; Canadian; Color; Not rated; 87 minutes; American release date: January 25, 2002. CAST: Fabrizio Filippo (Tom), Don McKellar (Brad), Marya Delver (Sandra West), Tammy Isbell (Kathy), Gordon Currie (Curt Schwin), Tobias Godson (Randy), Jennifer Clement (Vicki), James McBurney (Phil), Nick Cleary (James), Brian Stollery (Birks Clerk), Michelle Beaudoin (Anise), Judith Buchan (Mrs. Drysdale), Mike Eberly (Superhero), Derek Flores (Paul), Harris Hart (Mr. Mather), Xantha Radley (June), Jack Rich (Secretary), Dan Willmott (Julian), John Markey (Pizza Guy)

Tima in *Metropolis* © TriStar

METROPOLIS

(TRISTAR) Director, Rintaro; Screenplay, Katsuhiro Otomo; Based on the comic by Osamu Tezuka; Character Design/Chief Key-Animation Supervisor, Yasuhiro Nakura; Key-Animation Supervisors, Shigeo Akahori, Kunihiko Sakurai, Shigeru Fujita; Art Director/CGI Art Director, Shuichi Hirata; CGI Technical Director, Tsuneo Maeda; Music, Toshiyuki Honda; Animation Studio, Madhouse; a Metropolis Committe production; Color; Rated PG-13; 107 minutes; American release date: January 25, 2002. ENGLISH VOICE CAST: Brianne Siddale (Kenichi), Rebecca Olkewski (Tima), Dave Whittenberg (Rock), Scott Weinger (Atlas), Tony Pope (Shunsaku Ban), Dave Mallow (Pero), Sy Prescott (Dr. Laughton)

Don McKellar, Fabrizio Filippo in *Waydowntown* © Lot 47

MAY DAY: MAYHEM

(INDEPENDENT) Producer, Gábor Garami; Director, Róbert Koltai; Screenplay, Róbert Koltai, Gábor Nógrádi; Photography, Tibor Máthé; Designer, Peter Horgas; Costumes, Györgyi Szakács; Editor, Mari Miklós; Hungarian, 2001; Color; Not rated; 91 minutes; American release date: January 25, 2002. CAST: Róbert Koltai (Csocsó), Gábor Máté (Antal Pék), Ildikó Tóth (Rózsika), Attila Králik (Zsoltika Pék), Ferenc Zenthe (Tata), Sándor Gáspár (Lt.-Col. Dezsõ Gubinyi), Adél Kováts (Lidike), András Stohl (Veréb), Judit Pogány (Piroska), András Kern (Tömõ), Juli Básti (Beke's Wife), Zoltán Benkóczy (Baka), Beáta Borsos (Évike)

HEY, HAPPY!

(BIG DADDY BEER GUTS) Producers, Laura Nichalchyshyn, Noam Gonick; Director/Screenplay, Noam Gonick; Photography, Paul Suderman; Designer, Simon Hughes; Costumes, Billy Martin; Editor, Bruce Little; Music Supervisor, Chris Robinson; Dolby; CinemaScope; Color; Canadian, 2001; Not rated; 75 minutes; American release date: January 25, 2002. CAST: Jeremie Yuen (DJ Sabu), Craig Aftanas (Happy), Clayton Godson (Spanky O'Niel), Johnny Simone (Ricky G), Dita Vendetta (Darnel), Chelsey Perfanick (Chelsea), Sylvia Dueck (Sylvia), Lola Wong (Lola)

Hey, Happy! © Big Daddy Beer Guts

MAELSTROM

(ARROW) Producers, Roger Frappier, Luc Vandal; Director/Screenplay, Denis Villeneuve; Photography, Andre Turpin; Art Director, Sylvain Gingras; Costumes, Denis Sperdouklis; Editor, Richard Comeau; Casting, Lucie Robitaille; Canadian, 2000; Dolby; Color; Not rated; 83 minutes; American release date: January 25, 2002. CAST: Marie-Josee Croze (Bibi Champagne), Jean-Nicolas Verreault (Evian), Stephanie Morgenstern (Claire Gunderson), Pierre Lebeau (Voice of the Fish), Marc Gelinas (Stranger in the Subway), Klimbo (Head-Annstein Karlsen), Bobby Beshro (Philippe Champagne), Virginie Dubois (Sara), Marie-France Lambert (Marie-Jeanne Sirois, L'Avenir), Sylvie Moreau (Photographer), Clermont Jolicouer (Jean "The One Night Stand"), John Dunn-Hill (Owner of the Fish Market), Robin Aubert (Fireman)

ESCAFLOWNE

(BANDAI ENTERTAINMENT) Producers, Masuo Udeda, Minoru Takanashi, Masahiko Minami, Toyoyuki Yokohama; Director, Kazuki Akane; Creators, Hajime Yatate, Shoji Kawamori; Screenplay, Ryota Yamaguchi, Kazuki Akane; Music, Yoko Kanno, Hajime Mizoguchi; Character Design & Animation Director, Nobuteru Yuuki; Animation Director, Hiroshi Ohsaka; Mechanical Design, Kimotoshi Yamane; a Sunrise production, association with Bones productions; Japanese; Color; Rated R; 98 minutes; American release date: January 25, 2002.

Marie-Josee Croze in *Maelstrom* © Arrow

Escaflowne © Bandai Entertainment

TRICKY LIFE

(WANDA VISION) Producers, Stefan Schmitz, Hubert Toint; Director, Beatriz Flores Silva; Screenplay, Beatriz Flores Silva, János Kovácsi; Based on the novel *El Huevo de la Serpiente* by Maria Urruzola; Photography, Francisco Gózon; Editor, Daniel Márquez; Music, Carlos Da Silveira; a Bavaria Film International presentation of a co-production of BFS Productions, Saga Film, Avalon Productions S.L., ICAIC; Urugan-Argentine-Cuban-Spanish-Belgian; Dolby; Color; Not rated; 100 minutes; American release date: January 25, 2002. CAST: Agustin Abreu (Nicolas), Nelson Albano (Don Eusebio), Hugo Blandamuro (El Gordo), Roberto Bornes (Agent Fernandez), Andrea Fantoni (Lulú), Marisa Girardi (Tita), Fermi Hererro (El Gigante), José Linuesa (Marcelo), Augusto Mazzarelli (Garcia), Mariana Santángelo (Elisa), Silvestre (Plácido el Cara), Rodrigo Speranza (Marcos), Enrique Vidal (Agent Prada)

LONERS

(INDEPENDENT) Producer, David Ondricek; Executive Producers, Radek Auer, Robert Vicek; Director, David Ondricek; Screenplay, Petr Zelenka; Story, Olga Dabrowska, Petr Zelenka; Photography, Richard Rericha; Designer, Radek Hanák; Costumes, Katka Coufalikova; Editor, Michal Lánsky; Music, Jan P. Muchow; Casting, Sona Tichacková, Ivan Vorlícek; a co-production of CinemArt, Czech TV, E-motion Film, Lucky Man Films, Milk & Honey; Czech, 2000; Dolby; Color; Not rated; 103 minutes; American release date: February 1, 2002. CAST: Jitka Schneiderová (Hanka), Sasa Rasilov (Petr), Labina Mitevska (Vesna), Ivan Trojan (Ondrej), Jiri Machácek (Jakub), Mikulás Kren (Robert), Dana Sedlakova (Lenka), Hana Maciuchová (Hanka's Mother), Frantisek Nemec (Hanka's Father), Emma Cerná (Robert's Mother), Tatiana Vilhelmová (Prostitute), Zdenek Suchy (Drug Dealer), David Matásek (Radio Owner), Petr Kasnar (Magician), Pavla Drtinová (Girl in Bar), Markéta Simácková, Karolína Simácková (Ondrej & Lenka's Daughters), Petr Janis (Stranger Customer), Zdena Sperkova (Robert's Sister)

TALIESIN JONES

(IMPACT ENTERTAINMENT) a.k.a. *The Testimony of Taliesin Jones*; Producers, Louise Claire Clark, Ben Goddard, Helena Mackenzie, Kevin Marcy; Executive Producer, Michael Ryan; Director, Martin Duffy; Screenplay, Maureen Tilyou; Based on the novel by Rhidian Brook; Photography, Tony Imi; Designer, Hayden Pearce; Costumes, Ffion Elinor; Music, Mark Thomas; Editor, Jonathan Rudd; a Snake River production; British-U.S., 2000; Color; Rated PG; 90 minutes; American release date: February 1, 2002. CAST: Jonathan Pryce (Da), Ian Bannen (Billy), Griff Rhys Jones (Caesar), Geraldine James (Mum), Matthew Rhys (Jonathon), John-Paul Macleod (Taliesin), Robert Pugh (Handicott), Rhys Tucker (Hooper), Boyd Clack (Toni), Sophie Sherrington (Julie Dyer), Mark Bishop (Luc Daniels), Anwen Williams (Mrs. Willis)

Han Suk-Kyu, Choi Min-Sik in *Shiri* © Goldwyn

SHIRI

(GOLDWYN) Director, Je-guy Kang; Screenplay, Je-guy Kang, Je-hyun Park, Un-hak Baik, Yun-su Chun; Photography, Sung-Bok Kim; Designer, Sang-Man Oh; Editor, Gok-ji Park; Music, Dong-jun Lee; Special Effects, Do-ahn Jung; Line Producers, Kwan-hak Lee, Moo-lim Byun; a SamSung Entertainment Group presentation of a Kang JeGyu Films production; South Korean, 1999; Dolby; Color; Rated R; 124 minutes; American release date: February 8, 2002. CAST: Suk-kyu Han (Jung-won Ryu), Kang-ho Song (Jung-gil Lee), Min-sik Choi (Mu-sik Park), Yun-jin Kim (Myung-hyun Lee), Ju-sang Yun (Jung-suk Ko), Yong-woo Park (Sung-sik Er), Eun-sook Park (Bang-hee Lee), Duck-hyun Cho (Won-doo Lee), Jong-moon Park (Won-sik Bae), Jin-o Jungh (Yong-snag Park), Su-ro Kim (Hyun-chui Ahn), Sang-mi Kim (Soo), Myung-chul Nam (Ho Kwan), Ho-kyun Son (Bong-joo Lim), Duck-sung Kur (Doctor Min), Suk-ju Kim (Autopsy Surgeon), Jin-soo Jung (President), Young-tae Song (Instructor), Ki-san Park (Chul-min Jang), Jung-min Kim (Bong-suk Kim), Ji-yeul Park (Director of National Defense Institute)

Mark Rylance in *Much Ado About Something* © Films Transit Intl.

MUCH ADO ABOUT SOMETHING

(FILMS TRANSIT INTL.) Producers, Michael Rubbo, Penelope McDonald; Director/Screenplay/Photography, Michael Rubbo; Editor, Jane St. Vincent Welsh; Music, Christopher Gordon; an Australian Film Finance Corporation presentation of The Helpful Eye and Chili Films production; Australian, 2001; Color; Not rated; 94 minutes; American release date: February 13, 2002. Documentary about the 400-year-old controversy surrounding the authenticity of William Shakespeare's writings. With John Mitchell and Mark Rylance.

MEAN MACHINE

(PARAMOUNT CLASSICS) Producer, Matthew Vaughn; Executive Producers, Guy Ritchie, Albert S. Ruddy, Cynthia Pett-Dante; Director, Barry Skolnick; Screenplay, Charlie Fletcher, Chris Baker, Andrew Day; Based on the film *The Longest Yard*, screenplay by Tracy Keenan Wynn, from a story by Albert S. Ruddy; Co-Producer, Georgia Masters; Photography, Alex Barber; Designer, Russell De Rozario; Costumes, Stephanie Collie; Editors, Eddie Hamilton, Dayn Williams; Music, John Murphy; Casting, Gary Davy; a Matthew Vaughn Production in association with Ruddy/Morgan Productions and Brad Grey Pictures; British-U.S.; Dolby; Color; Rated R; 99 minutes; American release date: February 22, 2002. CAST: Vinnie Jones (Danny Meehan), David Kelly (Doc), David Hemmings (Governor), Ralph Brown (Burton), Vas Blackwood (Massive), Robbie Gee (Trojan), Geoff Bell (Ratchett), John Forgeham (Sykes), Sally Phillips (Tracey), Jason Flemyng (Bob Likely), Danny Dyer (Billy the Limpet), Jason Statham (Monk), Martin Wimbush (Z), David Reid, David Cropman (Barmen), Tim Perrin, Paul Mari (Policemen), Nick Moss (Hayter), Stephen Walters (Nitro), Andrew Grainger (Ketch), Jake Abraham (Bob Carter), Geoff Innocent (Bald Friend), Joseph Rye (Walker), Jamie Sives (Chiv), Omid Djalili (Raj), Chopper (Jerome), Adam Fogerty (Mouse), Rocky Marshall (Cigs), J.J. Connolly (Barry the Bookie), Stephen Bent (Referee), Perry Digweed (Marsden), Charlie Hartfield, Nevin Saraya (Prisoners, Footballers), Wally Downes (Physiotherapist), Marc Alexander, Peter Downes, Paul Fishenden, Brian Gayles, Danny Hibert, Mark Lovell (Guards, Footballers), Marc Egan (Nick)

YELLOW ASPHALT

(NEW YORKER) Producer/Director/Screenplay, Danny Vereté; Photography, Yoram Millo; Designers, David Gaon, Halil Jahalin; Editors, Rachel Yagil, Anna Finkelstein, Zak Hana; Music, Yves Touati; Israeli, 2000; Color; Not rated; 87 minutes; American release date: March 13, 2002. CAST: *Black Spot*: Zevik Raz (1st Driver), Moshe Ivgi (2nd Driver); *Here Is Not There*: Tatjana Blacher (Tamam Um Razala), Abed Zuabi (Sliman); *Red Roofs*: Motti Katz (Shmuel), Raeda Adon (Suhilla), Sami Samir (Abed), Hagit Keler (Anat)

Vinnie Jones in *Mean Machine* © Paramount Classics

Abed Zuabi, Tatjana Blacher in *Yellow Asphalt* © New Yorker

PROMISES

(COWBOY PICTURES) Producers/Directors/Screenplay, Justine Shapiro, B.Z. Goldberg; Co-Director/Editor, Carlos Bolado; Photography, Yoram Millo, Ilan Buchbinder; Executive Producer, Janet Cole; Consulting Writer/Researcher, Stephen Most; Produced in association with the Independent Television Service (ITVS) with partial funding proivded by the Corporation for Public Broadcasting; Israeli-U.S., 2001; Dolby; Color; Not rated; 106 minutes; American release date: March 15, 2002. Documentary in which seven Israeli and Palestinian children talk about what it is like to live in fear in Jerusalem.

VERY ANNIE MARY

(EMPIRE) Producers, Graham Broadbent, Damian Jones; Director/Screenplay, Sara Sugarman; Photography, Barry Ackroyd; Designer, Alice Normington; Costumes, Caroline Harris; Editor, Robin Sales; Music, Stephen Warbeck; Produced by Dragon Pictures, co-produced by FilmFour Ltd., The Arts Council of Wales, The Arts Council of England; British-French, 2001; Dolby; Color; Not rated; 105 minutes; American release date: March 29, 2002. CAST: Rachel Griffiths (Annie Mary), Jonathan Pryce (Father), Ioan Gruffudd (Hob), Matthew Rhys (Nob), Ruth Madoc (Mrs. Ifans), Kenneth Griffith (Minister), Rhys Miles Thomas (Colin), Joanna Page (Bethan Bevan), Grafton Radcliffe (Mayor), Josh Richards (Mr. Bevan), Jill Richards (Mrs. Roberts), Gwenyth Petty (Harmonium Player), Mary Hopkin, Maureen Rees, Stevie Parry, Iris Griffiths, Mari Gravell (Chapel Women), Rhodri Hugh (Mervin), Llyr Evans (Ginger Gravedigger), Rachel Isaac (Estate Agent), Ray Gravell (Frank, the Bookie), Melissa Vincent (Betting Shop Assistant), Lynn Hunter (Mrs. Thomas), Donna Edwards (Mrs. Bevan), Michele McTernan (Mother), Jennifer Pascoe (Young Annie Mary), Rhian Grundy (Kelly, Bracket), Wendy Phillips (Megan, Hinge), Anna Mountford (Blodwyn, Minge), Gwenllian Davies (Gwenllian, Twinge), Cerys Matthews (Nerys), Glan Davies (Stage Manger), Llinos Daniel (Braccy Nurse), Binda Singh (Doctor), Crisian Hunnam (District Nurse), Marged Esli (Midwelly Hall Cook), Peggy Mason (Peggy), Ruth Jones (Complaining Customer), Carys Williams (Miss Hughes), Marlene Griffiths (Dinnerlady), David Devereaux (Philip), Morgan Hopkin (Big Fat Walloper), Wayne Cater (Competition Judge), Colin Price (Cardiff Bookie), Simon Holt (Sports Commentator), Meriel Andrews (Singing Voice of Annie Mary)

Yarko, Faraj in *Promises* © Cowboy Pictures

Rhys Miles Thomas, Rachel Griffiths in *Very Annie Mary* © Empire

AMBUSH

(FILM KITCHEN) Producers, Ilkka Matila, Marko Rohr; Director, Olli Saarela; Screenplay, Olli Saarela, Antti Turri; Based on the novel by Antti Turri; Photography, Kjell Lagerroos; Art Director, Pertti Hilkamo; Costumes, Anu Pirila; Music, Tuomas Kantelinen; Editors, Jukka Nykanen, Olli Soinio; a co-production of Matila & Rohr Productions Oy, SVT Drama, Yleisradio (YLE); Finnish; Dolby; Color; Not rated; 123 minutes; American release date: April 5, 2002. CAST: Peter Franzen (Eero Perkola), Irina Bjorklund (Kaarina Vainikainen), Kari Heiskanen (Jussi Lukkari), Taisto Reimaluoto (Unto Saarinen), Kari Vaananen (Tauno Snicker), Tommi Eronen (Simo Krappinen), Pekka Heikkinen (Evert Ronkko), Pekka Huotari (Martii Raassina), Tero Jartti (Moilanen), Rauno Juvonen (Hamalainen), Arttu Kapulainen (Ville Snicker), Matti Laitinen (Knihti), Petri Manninen (Ahti Heikkinen), Kristo Salminen (Kukkonen), Kari-Pekka Toivonen (Leinonen), Maria Jarvenhelmi (Sinikka Kauppila), Minna Pirla (Marja Louhela), Ilkka Heiskanen (Lt. Passivirta), Kai Lehtinen (Major Kivkari), Robert Enckell (Capt. Rautakorpi), Jari Nissinen (2nd Lt. Torko), Jevgeni Haukka (Wounded Russian)

THE KOMEDIANT

(NEW YORKER) Producers, Amir Harel, Arnon Goldfinger, Oshra Schwartz; Director, Arnon Goldfinger; Screenplay, Oshra Schwartz; Photography, Yoram Millo; Editor, Einat Glaser-Zarhin; Zebra Productions Ltd.; Israeli, 1999; Color; Not rated; 85 minutes; Release date: April 5, 2002. Documentary on the Bursteins, legendary performers of the Yiddish stage; featuring Mike Burstyn, Lillian Lux, Susan Burstein-Roth, Fyvush Finkel, Shifra Lerer, Israel Becker, Mina Bern

Susan Burstein-Roth in *The Komediant* © New Yorker

KARMEN GEI

(CALIFORNIA NEWSREEL) Producer, Richard Sandler; Director/Screenplay, Joseph Gaï Ramaka; Photography, Bertrand Chatry; Designer, Nikos Meletopoulos; Costumes, Mame Faueye Ba; Editor, Hélène Girard; Music, David Murray; a Euripide Productions, Zagarianka, Les Ateliers de l'Arche, Matarnka Inc., ARTE France Cinema — Canal+ Horizons production; French-Canadian, 2001; Color; Not rated; 84 minutes; American release date: April 10, 2002. CAST: Djeïnaba Diop Gaï (Karmen Geï), Magaye Niang (Lamine Diop), Stéphanie Biddle (Angelique), Thierno Ndiaye Dos (Old Samba), Djeynaba Niang (Ma Penda), El Hadji Ndiaye (Massigi), Aïssatou Diop (Majguene), Widemir Normil (Divisional), Yandé Codou Sene (Singer on the Beach), Dieye Madieye (Mansour), Ibrahima Khalil Paye (Sidar/Police Laye), Marie-Augustine Diatta (Prison Officer in Chief), Coly Mbaye (Inspector Tali), Abasse Wade (Informer Calki), Patricia Gomis (Marie-Madeleine), Seune Sene (Maty Sene), Fatou Sow (Jaga), Mayanne Mboup (Diba), Doudou N'Diaye Rose (Doudoud N'diaye), Kader Oussamatou (Bidew), Ndeye Thiaba Diop (Waitress Mama Gec), Samba Cisse (Bus Driver), Joséphine Bessene (Prison Officer), Joseph Couly Bouschanzi (Policeman at the Police Station), Elian Wilfrid Mayila (Policeman Boxère), Philippe Cosson (Priest), Oumi Samb (Oumi), Abdoulaye Gnaga N'Diaye (Fosco the Saxo), Mor Ba (Tidjiane), Ndèye Maguette Niang (Dancer Upukal), Malick Niasse (Molasson), Anna Bob (Fishmonger).

GIRLS CAN'T SWIM

(WELLSPRING) Producers, Philippe Jacquier (Sépia Production); Co-Producer, Yvonn Crenn (YMC Production); Director, Anne-Sophie Birot; Screenplay, Anne-Sophie Birot, Christophe Honoré; Photography, Nathalie Durand; Art Director, Yvon Moreno; Music, Ernest Chausson; Editor, Pascale Chavance; French, 2000; Dolby; Color; Not rated; 101 minutes; American release date: April 19, 2002. CAST: Isild Le Besco (Gwen), Karen Alyx (Lise), Pascale Bussières (Céline), Pascal Elso (Alain), Marie Rivière (Anne-Marie), Yelda Reynaud (Solange), Sandrine Blancke (Vivianne), Julien Cottereau (Fredo), Dominique Lacarrière (Rose)

Djeïnaba Diop Gaï in *Karmen Gei* © California Newsreel

Anne Boyd in *Facing the Music* © Film Australia

Fhi Fan, Keiko Takahashi in *Uzumaki* © Viz Films/Tidepoint

FACING THE MUSIC

(FILM AUSTRALIA) Producers/Directors, Bob Connolly, Robin Anderson; Photography, Bob Connolly; Editor, Ray Thomas; Executive Producer for Film Australia, Stefan Moore; Produced in association with Arundel Films, the Australian Broadcasting Corporation and Channel Four (UK); Australian-British, 2001; Color; not rated; 89 minutes; American release date: April 24, 2002. Documentary on composer Anne Boyd, a leading figure in the music department at the University of Sydney, as her department faces a budget crunch.

UZUMAKI

(VIZ FILMS/TIDEPOINT) Producer, Sumiji Miyake; Executive Producers, Mitsuru Kurosawa, Toyoyuki Yokohama; Director, Higuchinsky; Screenplay, Takao Nitta; Based on the manga by Junji Ito; Photography, Gen Kobayashi; Designer, Hiroshi Hayashida; Japanese, 2000; Color; Not rated; 90 minutes; American release date: May 1, 2002. CAST: Eriko Hatsune (Kirie Goshima), Fhi Fan (Shuichi Saito), Hinako Saeki (Kyoko Sekino), Shin Eun Kyung (Chie Maruyama), Keiko Takahashi (Yukie Saito), Ren Osugi (Toshio Saito)

Isild Le Besco, Karen Alyx in *Girls Can't Swim* © Wellspring

DEAR FIDEL

(COLIFILMS) Producers, Wilfried Huismann, Yvonne Ruocco, Detlef Ziegert; Director/Screenplay, Wilfried Huismann; Photography, Reinhard Gossmann; Music, Klaus Doldinger; German, 2000; Color; Not rated; 90 minutes; American release date: May 1, 2002. Documentary on Marita Lorenz, the daughter of a German sea captain, who claimed to be the mistress of Fidel Castro.

A GRIN WITHOUT A CAT

(FIRST RUN ICARUS) Director/Screenplay/Editor, Chris Marker; Music, Luciano Berio; produced by ISKRA, INA, and DOVIDIS; English Voices, Jim Broadbent, Robert Kramer, Cyril Cusack; French, 1977, 1993; Color; Not rated; 179 minutes; American release date: May 1, 2002. Documentary chronicling political conflicts of the 1960s and 70s, updated in 1993 to include the demise of the Soviet Union.

ABC AFRICA

(NEW YORKER) Director/Editor, Abbas Kiarostami; Photography, Seifollah Samadian; In collaboration with IFAD; Iranian, 2001; Dolby; Color; Not rated; 84 minutes; Release date: May 3, 2002. Documentary about the devastating effects AIDS and civil war have had on Uganda.

Fidel Castro in *A Grin Without a Cat* © First Run Icarus

Orphaned boy in *ABC Africa* © New Yorker

Gabriel in *Diamonds and Rust* © First Run/Icarus

Lei Huang, Chao-te Yin in *Fleeing by Night* © Strand

FLEEING BY NIGHT

(STRAND) Producers, Li-kong Hsu, Shi-hao Chang; Executive Producers, Li-kong Hau, Shun-ching Chiu; Director, Li-kong Hsu, Chi Yin; Screenplay, Hui-ling Wang, Ming-xia Wang; Photography, Cheng-hui Tsai; Costumes, Jien-hua Tzou; Editor, Po-wen Chen; Music, Chris Babida; a Zoom Hunt International, Central Motion Picture and Broadband Films presentation; Taiwanese, 2000; Dolby; Color; Not rated; 123 minutes; American release date: May 3, 2002. CAST: Rene Liu (Wei Ing'er), Lei Huang (Hsu Shao-dung), Chao-te Yin (Lin Chung), Li-jen Tai (Huang Zilei), Ah-leh Gua (Wei's Mother)

DIAMONDS AND RUST

(FIRST RUN ICARUS) Producers/Directors, Adi Barash, Ruth Shatz; Photography, Adi Barash; Editor, Ruth Shatz; a New Israel Foundation for Cinema and Television Production; Israeli); Color; Not rated; 73 minutes; American release date: May 8, 2002. Documentary about life on the *Spirit of Namibia*, a diamond mining vessel.

JANICE BEARD

(EMPIRE) Producers, Judy Counihan, Jonathan Olsberg; Co-Producer, Torsten Leschly; Director, Clare Kilner; Screenplay, Ben Hopkins, Clare Kilner; Photography, Richard Greatrex, Peter Thwaites; Designer, Sophie Becher; Editor, Mary Finlay; a co-production of Arts Council of England, Dakota Films, Film Consortium, FilmFour, WAVEpictures; British, 1999; Dolby; Color; Not rated; 81 minutes; American release date: May 10, 2002. CAST: Eileen Walsh (Janice Beard), Patsy Kensit (Julia), Rhys Ifans (Sean), Sandra Voe (Mimi), David O'Hara (O'Brien), Frances Grey (Violet), Zita Sattar (Jane), Amelia Curtis (June), Mossie Smith (Dolores), Sarah McVicar (Tracy), Eddie Marsan (Mr. Tense), Perry Fenwick (Mr. Button), Maynard Eziashi (Clive Morley), Robbie Barnett (Janice's Father), Jean Murphy (Midwife), Bill Leadbitter (Doctor), Ella Stanley (Baby Janice), Amy Lynch (Young Janice), Laura Lumley (Young Violet), Mary Ann O'Donoghue (1st Office Woman), Evelyn Voight (Trolley Lady), Richard Morant (Boss), Ronnie Fox (Stallholder), Steve English (Guard), Gawn Grainger (Browne), Clive Merrison (Tobo), Joseph Deery (Baby Sean), Paul Jones (Young Sean), James Greene (Michael), Peter Quince (Barman), Elder Sanchez (Alonso), Andrew Havitt (Piers), Ken Drury (McHeath), Jonathan Hackett (Hartley), John McArdle (Pyesek), Quentin Willson (Himself), Smart Pendred (Policeman), Anna Copley (Sean's Mother), Peter Copley (Sean's Father), Carlton Jarvis (Crash Team Doctor)

BLACKWOODS

(THINKFILM) Producer, Shawn Williamson; Executive Producers, Philip Selkirk, James Shavick; Director, Uwe Boll; Screenplay, Robert Dean Klein; Photography, Mathias Neumann; Designer, Jason Sutherland; Music, Reinhard Besser; Casting, Katy Wallin, Maureen Webb; Boll Films, Cinemedia, Shavick Entertainment, Taunus Film-Produktions GmbH; Canadian-German; Color; Rated R; 90 minutes; American release date: May 10, 2002. CAST: Patrick Muldoon (Matth Sullivan), Keegan Connor Tracy (Dawn/Molly), Will Sanderson (Jim), Michael Paré (Sheriff William Harding), Clint Howard (Gregg the Motel Clerk), Anthony Harrison (Tall Man/Dr. Kelly), Matthew Walker (Pa Franklin), Janet Wright (Ma Franklin), Sean Campbell (Jack Franklin), Ben Derrick (John Franklin), Michael Eklund (Billy Franklin), Samantha Ferris (Beth the Waitress), Patricia Dahlquist (Mrs. Sullivan), Kate Robbins (Paula the Housekeeper), Nathaniel DeVeaux (E.R. Doctor), Heather Feeney (E.R. Nurse), Sarah Deakins (Sarah, Matt's Date), Bill Ferguson (Trucker)

Thomas Miller-El in *The Back of the World* © UIP

Fatoumata Diawara in *Sia, the Dream of the Python* © ArtMattan

NINA HAGEN = PUNK + GLORY

(INDEPENDENT) Producer/Director/Editor, Peter Sempel; Screenplay, Tamara Goldsworthy; Photography, Frank Blasberg, Claus Bosch-Dos Santos, Jörg Grönitz, Jonas Scholz, Peter Sempel; Music, FM Einheit, Nina Hagen; Black SUN Flower Filmproduction; German, 1999; Color; Not rated; 108 minutes; American release date: May 15, 2002. Documentary on German punk rocker Nina Hagen, featuring Nina Hagen, Angelyne, Blixa Bargeld, Herman Brood, George Clinton, Thomas D, Samuel Fuller, Cosma Shiva Hagen, Eva Maria Hagen, Otis Hagen, Anthony Kiedis, Udo Kier, Lemmy, Jonas Mekas, Nam June Paik, Dee Dee Ramone, Wim Wenders

THE BACK OF THE WORLD

(UIP) Producers, Gusa Alonso-Pimentel, Bibiana Bergia; Director, Javier Corcuera; Screenplay, Elias Querejeta, Fernando León de Aranoa, Javier Corcuera; Photography, Jordi Abusada; Editors, Iván Fernández, Nacho Ruiz-Capillas; Associate Producer, Jaume Roures (Mediapro); an Elías Querejeta; Spanish; Color; Not rated; 89 minutes; American release date: May 22, 2002. Documentary on three different stories of injustice: a child laborer in Peru, an exiled Kurdish activist, and a Texas man who has been sitting on death row since 1986.

SIA, THE DREAM OF THE PYTHON

(ARTMATTAN) Producers, Claude Gilaizeau, Elisabeth Lopez, Sylvie Maigne; Director, Dani Kouyaté; Screenplay, Moussa Diagana; Adaptation, Dani Kouyaté; Based on the play *La Légende du Wagudu vue par Sia Yatabéré* by Moussa Diagana; Photography, Robert Millie; Designer, Papa Kouyaté; Costumes, Judith Hentz, Ester Marty Kouyaté, Massiri-So, Abdou Ouolos; Editor, Zoé Durouchoux; Music, Daniel Rousseau, Fanny Touré; Les Productions de la Lanterne, Sahélis Productions; French-Burkina Faso; Stereo; Color; Not rated; 96 minutes; American release date: May 24, 2002. CAST: Fatoumata Diawara (Sia), Sotigui Kouyaté (Wakhané), Balla Habib Dembélé (Le Griot), Hamadoun Kassogué (Kerfa), Ibrahim Baba Cissé (Mamadi), Kardigué Laïco Traoré (Kaya Maghan), Marietou Kouyaté (Empress), Fily Traoré (Kélétigui), Kary Coulibaly (Hairdresser), Abdoulaye Komboudri (Coward), Ahmed Kadio (Prince), Djeneba Diawara (Sia's Mother), Toumansé Coulibaly (Sia's Father)

NIJINSKY: THE DIARIES OF VASLAV NIJINSKY

(WELLSPRING) Producers, Paul Cox, Aanya Whitehead; Executive Producers, Kevin Lucas, William T. Marshall; Director, Paul Cox; Based on the diary *Cahiers* by Vaslav Nijinsky; Photography, Paul Cox, Hans Sonneveld; Choreographer/Dance Supervisor, Alida Chase; Music, Paul Grabowsky; Costumes, Jilly Hickey; an Illumination Films and MusicArtsDance Films presentation; Dolby; Color; Not rated; 95 minutes; American release date: May 29, 2002. Documentary on dancer Vaslav Nijinsky, with passages from his diary read by Derek Jacobi; featuring Delia Silvan, Chris Haywood, Vicki Attard, David McAllister, Csaba Buday, and the Leigh Warren & Dancers company

Rehane Abrahams, Ayesha Meer Krige in *Mama Africa* © Wellspring

Lee Ross, Charlotte Brittain in *Secret Society* © First Run Features

David McAllister, Vicki Attard in
Nijinsky: The Diaries of Vaslav Nijinsky © Wellspring

SECRET SOCIETY

(FIRST RUN FEATURES) Producers, Vesna Jovanoska, David Pupkewitz; Co-Producers, Ralph Stephan Dietrich, Erwin W. Dietrich, Malcolm Kohll; Director, Imogen Kimmel; Screenplay Catriona McGowan, Imogen Kimmel; Based on an original idea by Catriona McGowan; Photography, Glynn Speeckaert; Designer, Eddy Andres; Costumes, Suzannah Buxton, Nigel Egerton; Editor, Katharina Schmidt; Music, Paul Heard; Casting, Carrie Hilton; a Vesna Jovanoska/David Pupewitz production, an ena Film/Focus Films production, in co-production with WDR and ARTE and Ascot Film and Television Productions in association with CLT-UFA International, Isle of Man Film Commission; Germany-U.K., 2000; Dolby; Color; Not rated; 89 minutes; American release date: June 7, 2002. CAST: Charlotte Brittain (Daisy), Lee Ross (Ken), Annette Badland (Marlene), James Hooton (Billy), Charles Dale (Paul), Lisa Riley (Beth Trailor), Rachel Smith (Sue), Sharon Duce (Janice), Kate Fitzgerald (Mrs. Selby); Women Sumo Wrestlers: Clare Cathcart (Pigmy Hippo), Sharon D. Clarke (Typhoon), Troy Jackson (Woolly Mammoth), Jackie D. Broad (She Elephant), Joann Condon (Giant Butterfly), Donna Combe (Mighty Walrus), Alison Garland (Polar Bear), Mikyla Dodd (Sea Cow), Iliana Flade (Big White Orca), Morag Siller (Raging Bull), Alice Wilson (Sea Squid); Japanese Sumo Wrestlers: Takeshi Nara (Tateishi), Noriaki Iwaya (Volcano), Taiyo Ichinome (Pig Panda), Masaru Kudo (Monsoon), Akimori Nakagawa (Big Oak), Takahito Toinaga (Kirishima); Syd Hoare (Referee), Finetime Fonteyne (Mr. Brough), Peter Hugo-Daly (Barry), Willie Ross (Mr. Swanley), Janice Small (Mrs. Swanley), Jason Moore (Fat Boy), Tim Murphy (Razor), Rachel Fielding (TV Reporter), Liam Barr (Hammer), Sharon Holland (Hospital Nurse), Clare Van D'Osier (Police Woman), Toby Longworth (Video Earth Woman), Lisa Riley, Miriam Wiesemann, Ilka Schirner (Amazon Women); Jürgen Jansen (Husband)

MAMA AFRICA

(WELLSPRING) Presented by Queen Latifah, from Big World Cinema; South African; Dolby; Color; Not rated; 89 minutes; American release date: June 7, 2002. *Uno's World*: Producer, Joel Phiri; Director, Bridget Pickering; Photography, Lionel Cousin; Editor, Jackie Le Cordeur; from Ice Media; CAST: Sophie David (Uno), Elia Jack Nakalemo (Jose), Muhindua Kaura (Kaura), Esi Shimming-Chase (Stella), Adama Mhone (Desiree), Sacha Olivier (Tricia), Judy Matjila (Vivian), Agene Eichab (Farmer Hans), Dalton Ashikoto (Dex), Florence Naobes (2-4 Months Old Baby), Dalha Haifene (Mother). *Hang Time*: Producer, Simon Onwurah; Director, Ngozi Onwurah; Photography, Alwin Kuchler; Editor, Liz Webber; from Non-Aligned Films; CAST: Brian Biragi (Kwame), Brian Bovell (Olu), Elizabeth Mathebula (Mama), Hija Lindsay-Parkinson (Chiddy), Seputla Sebogodi (Daddy), Yinka Dare (Young Dad/Boxer), Arthur Leope (Moussa), George Bisa (Coach), Neo Muyanga (Musician), David Mello, Teboho Fokane (Robbers), Bentley Nkomonde, Lehlohlonolo Makoko (Policemen), Sbusiso Ngwenya (Uche), Sifiso Moyo (Tiki), Itumeleng Mathebula (Iffy). *Raya*: Producers, Steven Markovitz, Platon Trakoshis; Director, Zulfah Otto-Sallies; Photography, Michael Brierley; Designer, Tom Hannam; Editor, Jackie Le Cordeur; CAST: Rehane Abrahams (Raya), Ayesha Meer Krige (Madeegah), Denise Newman (Salaama), Oscar Petersen (Joe), Eudoia Samson (Jenny), Peter Butler (Neighbor), Graham Weir (Drug Dealer), Ivan D. Lucas (Restaurant Owner), Sylvia Esau (Warden)

Migel Del Morales in *Cuba Feliz* © Empire Pictures

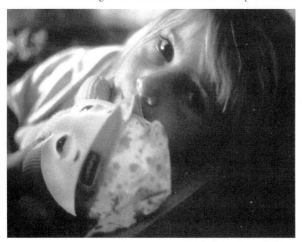

Cathy Hinderchild in *Skin of Man, Heart of Beast*
© Leisure Time Features/Kimstim

Liu Ye in *Lan Yu* © Strand

THE LEGEND OF BHAGAT SINGH

(TIPS FILMS) Director, Rajkumar Santoshi; Co-Executive Producers, Kumar Taurani, Ramesh S. Taurani; Photography, Anand K.V.; Music, A.R. Rahman; Indian; Dolby; Color; Rated PG; 155 minutes; American release date: June 7, 2002. CAST: Ajay Devgan (Bhagat Singh), Santosh (Rajguru), Sushant Singh (Sukhdev), Raj Babbar (Kishen Singh), Farida Jalal (Mother), Akhilendra Mishra (Chandrashekhar Azad), Amrita Rao (The Girl)

CUBA FELIZ

(EMPIRE PICTURES) Producers, Alain Rozanes, Pascal Verroust, Jacques Debs; Director/Photography, Karim Dridi; Screenplay, Pascal Letellier, Karim Dridi; Editor, Lise Beaulieu; Produced by ADR Productions; Co-produced by Le Studio Canal Plus, El Movimieno Nacional de Video de Cuba, Canal+, CNC; Spanish, 1997; Dolby; Color; Not rated; 90 minutes; Release date: June 12, 2002. Documentary on traveling musician Miguel Del Morales ("El Gallo"), featuring Miguel Del Morales, Pepin Vaillant, Mirta Gonzales, Anibal Avila, Alberto Pablo, Admandito Machado, Candido Fabre, Mario Sanchez Martinez, Zaïda Reyte, Gilberto Mendez, Alejandro Almenares, Los Cubanos Jubilados, Paisan Mallet, Eulises Sanchez, Carlo Boromeo Planchez

FREEZE ME

(MEDIA BLASTERS) Producers, Takashi Ishii, Nobuaki Nagae, Taketo Niitsu; Director/Screenplay, Takashi Ishii; Photography, Yasushi Sasakibara; Designer, Teru Yamazaki; Music, Goro Yasukawa; produced by KSS Inc., Nikkatsu Corporation; Japanese, 2000; Color; Not rated; 101 minutes; American release date: June 14, 2002. CAST: Harumi Inoue (Chihiro), Shingo Tsurumi (Kojima), Kazuki Kitamura (Hirokawa), Shunsuke Matsuoka (Nogami), Naoto Takenaka (Baba)

SKIN OF MAN, HEART OF BEAST

(LEISURE TIME FEATURES/KIMSTIM) Director, Hélène Angel; Screenplay, Hélène Angel, Agnès de Sacy, Jean-Claude Janer; Photography, Isabelle Razavet; Editors, Laurent Rouan, Eric Renault; Music, Philippe Miller; a Why Not Production-Arte France Cinema co-production; French, 1999; Color; not rated; 97 minutes; American release date: June 21, 2002. CAST: Serge Riaboukine (Franky), Barnard Blancan (Coco), Pascal Cervo (Alex), Maaike Jansen (Marthe), Cathy Hinderchild (Aurelie), Virginie Guinand (Christelle)

LAN YU

(STRAND) Producer, Zhang Yongning; Director, Stanley Kwan; Screenplay, Jimmy Ngai; Basedon the internet novel *Beijing Story* written anonymously by "Beijing Comrade"; Executive Producer, Jian Qin; Associate Producers, Yi Feng, Zhou Bin; Photography, Yang Tao; Designer/Editor, William Chang; Music, Zhang Yadong; a Yongning Creation Workshop production; Hong Kong, 2001; Color; Not rated; 86 minutes; American release date: July 3, 2002. CAST: Hu Jun (Chen Handong), Liu Ye (Lan Yu), Su Jin (Jingping), Li Huatong (Liu Zheng), Lu Fang (Yongdong, Handong's Sister), Zhang Yongning (Daning, Her Husband), Li Shuang (Weidong, Handong's Brother), Zhao Minfen (Mrs. Chen, Handong's Mother), Zhang Fan (Jian'er, The College Athlete)

TATTOO BAR

(ARTMATTAN) Producer, Jordi Rediu; Director/Screenplay, Jo Sol; Photography, Angel Luis Fernandez; Set Designer, Deliaadroer; Tattoos, Pury Arroyo; Editor, Julia Ju Aniz; Music, Lol; Costumes, Annick Celine; Casting, Gala Garbo, Wilson Casting; Spanish; Color; Not rated; 90 minutes; American release date: July 5, 2002. CAST: Alexis Valdes (Mariel), Mercedes Ortega (Simona), Paulina Galvez (Bug), Miguel Molina (Francis), Elsa Pataky (Blanca), Juan Marquez (Fly), Gabriella Roy (Joany), Carlos Lasarte (Enrique)

TOSCA

(AVATAR) Producers, Daniel Toscan Du Plantier; Director, Benoit Jacquot; Screenplay, Benoit Jacquot, from the libretto of Puccini's Opera; Co-Producers, Douglas Cummins, Alessandro Verdecchi, Alfred Hurmer, Frédéric Sichler; Music, Giacomo Puccini; Photography, Romain Winding; Set Designer, Sylvain Chauvelot; Costumes, Christian Gasc; Costumes, Laurence Guindollet; Editor, Luc Barnier; a Euripide Prods. (Paris)- Veradia Film (Rome)- Integral Film (Berlin)- Axiom Films (London) co-production, in association with French-Italian-German-British, 2001; Dolby; Color; Not rated; 120 minutes; American release date: July 12, 2002. CAST: Angela Gheorghiu (Floria Tosca), Roberto Alagna (Mario Cavaradossi), Ruggero Raimondi (Baron Scarpia), David Cangelosi (Spoletta), Sorin Coliban (Sciarrone), Enrico Fissore (Le Sacristain), Maurizio Muraro (Angelotti), Gwynne Howell (Le Geôlier), James Savage-Hanford (Le Pâtre)

Roberto Alagna, Angela Gheorghiu in *Tosca* © Avatar

Judi Dench, Jeremy Irons in *Langrishe Go Down* © Castle Hill

Perumal in *Ayurveda: The Art of Being* © Kino

LANGRISHE GO DOWN

(CASTLE HILL) Executive Producer, Max Rosenberg; Director, David Hugh Jones; Screenplay (Teleplay), Harold Pinter; Based on the novel by Aidan Higgins; Photography, Elmer Cossey; Music, Carl Davis; Editor, Chris Wimble; a BBC production; British; 1978; Color; Not rated; 105 minutes; American release date: July 12, 2002. CAST: Jeremy Irons (Otto Beck), Judi Dench (Imogen Langrishe), Annette Crosbie (Helen Langrishe), Susan Williamson (Lily), Harold Pinter (Barry Shannon), Margaret Whiting (Maureen Layde). (Note: This film premiered on BBC2 Television in 1978 as part of *Play of the Week*)

AYURVEDA: THE ART OF BEING

(KINO) Producer, Christoph Friedel; Director/Screenplay/Editor, Pan Nalin; Photography, Serge Guez; Music, Cyril Morin; Indian; Color; Not rated; 102 minutes; American release date: July 17, 2002. Documentary on the practice of the ancient holistic medicine called Ayurveda.

WHAT TO DO IN CASE OF FIRE

(DEUTSCHE COLUMBIA) Producers, Jakob Claussen, Thomas Wöbke; Director, Gregor Schnitzler; Screenplay, Stefan Dahnert, Anne Wild; Photography, Andreas Berger; Designer, Albrecht Konrad; Costumes, Ivana Milos; Music, Stephen Zacharias; Editor, Hansjörg Weissbrich; Line Producer, Uli Putz; Casting, Nessie Nesslauer; a Claussen+Wöbke Filmproduktion production; German; Dolby; Color; Rated R; 101 minutes; American release date: July 19, 2002. CAST: Til Schweiger (Tim), Martin Feifel (Hotte), Sebastian Blomberg (Maik), Nadja Uhl (Nele), Matthias Matschke (Terror), Doris Schretzmayer (Flo), Klaus Löwitsch (Manowsky), Devid Striesow (Henkel), Barbara Philipp (Pritt), Jamie Schuricht (Melli), Aykut Kayacik (Bülent), Hubert Mulzer (Police Chief), Oliver Mommsen (Konrad), This Maag (Shmitz), Johanna von Halem (Agency Assistant), Sandra Nedeleff (Real Estate Agent), Tim-Owe Georgi (Undersecretary of State), Johanna Rudolph (Painter)

SCARLET DIVA

(MEDIA BLASTERS) Producers, Claudio Argento, Dario Argento; Executive Producers, Gianluca Curti, Adriana Chiesa DiPalma, John Sirabella; Director/Screenplay, Asia Argento; Photography, Frederic Fasano; Designer, Alessandro Rosa; Costumes, Susy Mattolini; Music, John Hughes; Editors, Anna Rosa Napoli, Scott Marchfield, Kahlid Mills; an Opera Film production; Italian, 2001; Dolby; Color; Not; rated; 90 minutes; American release date: August 9, 2002. CAST: Asia Argento (Anna Battista), Jean Shepard (Kirk Vaines), Herbert Fritsch (Aaron Ulrich), Gianluca Arcopinto (Dr. Pascuccia), Joe Coleman (Mr. Paar), Francesca d'Aloja (Margherita), Vera Gemma (Veronica Lanza), Justinian Kfoury (J-Bird), Daria Nicolodi (Anna's Mother), Schoolly D. (Hash-Man), Selen (Quelou), Alessandro Villari (Maid), Leo Gullotta (Dr. Vessi), Paolo Bonacelli (Swiss Journalist), Vanessa Crane (Luke Ford), David D'Ingeo (Adam), Jeff Alexander (Tyrone), David Brandon (Director), Robert Sommer (Cesare, the Actor), Gloria Pirrocco (Anna as a Child), Leonardo Servadio (Alioscia as a Child), Deborah Restante (Simona), Massimo De Lorenzo (Drunk), Giovanna Papa (Fast Food Woman), Taiyo Yamanouchi (Japanese Man), Angelica Di Majo (Piercing Girl)

Nassim Abdi in *Secret Ballot* © Sony Classics

Rupert Graves, Lucia Culkova in *All My Loved Ones* © Northern Arts

SECRET BALLOT

(SONY CLASSICS) Producers, Marco Muller, Babak Payami; Executive Producer, Hooshangh Payami; Director/Screenplay, Babak Payami; Photography, Farzad Jadat; Designer, Mandana Masoudi; Costumes, Faride Harajl; Music, Mike Galasso; Editor, Babak Karimi; a Fabrica, Payam, Rai Cinemafiction, Sharmshir, Televisione Svizzera Italiana production; Italian-Canadian-Swiss-Iranian, 2001; Dolby; Color; Rated G; 123 minutes; American release date: August 9, 2002. CAST: Nassim Abdi (Girl), Cyrus Abidi (Soldier), Youssef Habashi, Farrokh Shojaii, Gholbahar Janghali

ALL MY LOVED ONES

(NORTHERN ARTS) Producers, Jiri Bartoska, Rudolf Biermann; Executive Producers, Sting, Veronika Marczuk-Pazura; Director, Matej Minac; Screenplay, Jiri Hubac; Photography, Dodo Simonoc; Art Director, Martin Kurel; Music, Janusz Stoklosa; Editor, Patrik Pass; a Czech TV, In Film production; Czech-Polish, 2000; Dolby; Color; Not rated; 91 minutes; American release date: August 16, 2002. CAST: Rupert Graves (Nicholas Winton), Josef Abrhám (Jakub Silberstein), Jiri Bartoska (Samuel), Libuse Safránková (Irma), Hanna Dunowska (Eva Marie), Krzysztof Kolberger (Leo), Krzysztof Kowalewski (Rous), Marián Labuda (Spitzer), Agnieszka Wagner (Anna), Grazyna Wolszczak (Angelika), Ondrej Vetchy (Max), Tereza Brodská (Hedviga), Brano Holicek (David), Lucia Culkova (Sosa), Andrzej Deskur (Robert), Jiri LáBus (Marcel), Jiří Menzel (Stein), Martin Zbrozek (Violinist)

Til Schweiger in *What to Do in Case of Fire* © Columbia

SATIN ROUGE

(ZEITGEIST) Producers, Alain Rozanes, Pascal Verroust, Dora Bouchoucha Fourati; Director/Screenplay, Raja Amari; Photography, Diane Baratier; Set Designer, Kaïs Rostom; Costumes, Magdalena Garcia Caniz; Editor, Pauline Dairou; Music, Nawfel El Manaa; an ADR Productions, Nomadis Images, Arte France Cinema, l'Agence Nationale de Promotion de l'Audiovisuel-Tunisie; French-Tunisian; Dolby; Color; Not rated; 100 minutes; American release date: August 23, 2002. CAST: Hiam Abbas (Lilia), Hend El Fahem (Salma), Maher Kamoun (Chokri), Monia Hichri (Folla), Faouzia Badr (The Neighbor), Nadra Lamloum (Hela), Abou Moez El Fazaa (The Boss), Salah Miled (Béchir)

THE ISLE

(EMPIRE) Executive Producer, Lee Eun; Director/Screenplay/Art Director, Kim Ki-Duk; Photography, Whang Suh-Shik; Costumes/Makeup, Joo Eun-Jung; Editor, Kyung Min-Ho; Music, Jeon Sang-Yoon; Korean, 2000; Color; Not rated; 89 minutes; American release date: August 23, 2002. CAST: Suh Jung (Hee-Jin), Kim Yoo-Suk (Hyun-Shik), Park Sung-Hee (Eun-A), Cho Jae-Hyung (Mang-Chee), Jang Hang-Sun (Middle-aged Man)

*CORPUS CALLOSUM

(MICHAEL SNOW ARTWORKS) Producer/Director/Screenplay/Design, Michael Snow; Photography, Robbi Hinds, Haralad Bachmann; Special Effects Supervisor, Greg Hermanovic; Senior Animator, Rob del Ciancio; On-Line Editor, Paul Cormack; Canadian; Color; Not rated; 93 minutes; Release date: August 28, 2002. CAST: Kim Plate, Greg Hermanovic, John Massey, Joanne Tod, John Penner, Tom Sherman.

Corpus Callosum © Michael Snow Artworks

Hiam Abbas in *Satin Rouge* © Zeitgeist

Natascha McElhone, Stephen Dorff in *Feardotcom* © Warner Bros.

AGNI VARSHA: THE FIRE AND THE RAIN

(CINEBELLA ENTERTAINMENT) Executive Producers, Meeta Khanna, Seema Sawhney; Director, Arjun Sajnani; Screenplay, Anil Mehta, T. Jayshree, Arjun Sajnani, Atul Tiwari; Photography, Anil Mehta; Art Director, Shashi Adappa; Costumes, Rukmini Krishnan, Leena Singh; Music, Taufiq Qureshi, Sandesh Shandilya; Editor, Jabeen Merchant; iDream productions; Indian; Dolby; Color; Not rated; 126 minutes; American release date: August 30, 2002. CAST: Jackie Shroff (Paravasu), Raveena Tandon (Vishakha), Milind Soman (Arvasu), Sonali Kulkarni (Nittilai), Nagarjuna (Yavakri), Prabhudeva (Rakshasa), Mohan Agashe (Raibhya), Amitabh Bachchan (Indra), Raghuvir Yadav (Actor Manager), Zul Vellani (Andhaka), Gopal Piplani (Junior Courtier), Ashfaq Rauf (King), Kumar Iyengar (Senior Courtier), Tarun Kapoor (Courtier), Veena Sajnani (Actor Manager's Wife), Sandeep B.G. (Vishwa), G. Shankar Rao (Nittilai's Father), Sameem Rizvi (Nittali's Brother), Deepti Sudhendra (Siddhi), G. Shankar Rao (Nittilai's Father), Lakshmi Krishnamurthy (Nittilai's Aunt), Pradeesh (Nittilai's Husband), Deepti Bhatnagar (Dancer)

FEARDOTCOM

(WARNER BROS.) Producers, Moshe Diamant, Limor Diamant; Executive Producers, Elie Samaha, Andrew Stevens, David Saunders, Mark Damon, Rudy Cohen, Frank Hübner, Romain Schroeder; Director, William Malone; Screenplay, Josephine Coyle; Story, Moshe Diamant; Photography, Christian Sebaldt; Designer, Jerome Latour; Music, Nicholas Pike; Co-Producer, Jan Fantl; an MDP Worldwide presentation of an Apollomedia/Fear.com Productions/Carousel Film Company co-production with the support of Film Fund Luxembourg; U.K.-German-Luxembourg; Dolby; Super 35 Widescreen; Technicolor; Rated R; 100 minutes; American release date: August 30, 2002. CAST: Stephen Dorff (Mike Reilly), Natascha McElhone (Terry Huston), Stephen Rea (Alistair Pratt), Udo Kier (Polidori), Amelia Curtis (Denise), Jeffrey Combs (Styles), Nigel Terry (Turnbull), Gesine Cukrowski (Jeannine), Michael Sarrazin (Frank Bryant), Jana Güttgemanns (Little Girl), Anna Thalbach (Kate), Siobhan Flynn (Thana Brinkman), Evie Garratt (Albino Woman), Lex Kreps (Tenant), Joan McBride (Mrs. Richardson), Isabelle Van Waes (Victim), Derek Kueter (Officer #1), Elizabeth McKechnie (Alice Turnbull), Arnita Swanson (Barlow), Gordon Peters (Rooney), Nils Brunkhorst (Prisoner), Sven Pippig (Henry), Anja Van Greuningen (Ashley), Anjelika Khrohova (Ashley's Mother), Sigal Diamant (Nurse), Matthias Schweighöfer (Dieter Schrader), Birthe Wolter (Nina Blank), Frances Potasnik, Mascha Litterscheid (Nurses), Dean Gregory (Maintenance Man #1), Chris Bearner (Warehouse Attendant), Emma Campbell (Goth-Chick), Kwasi Songhi (Young Detective), Astrid Skuyat (Alistair's Victim)

THE PINOCHET CASE

(FIRST RUN/ICARUS) Producer, Yves Jeanneau; Director/Screenplay, Patricio Guzmán; Photography, Jacques Bouquin; Editor, Claudio Martinez; a co-production of Les Films d'Ici, Pathé Télévision, Renn Productions, Les Films de La Passerelle, R.T.B.FG., Benece Paco Poch, Patricio Guzmán Producciones; French-Spanish-Belgian; Color; Not rated; 110 minutes; American release date: September 11, 2002. Documentary on the case against former Chilean military dictator Gen. Augusto Pinochet for human rights abuses.

QUITTING

(SONY CLASSICS) Producer, Peter Loehr; Executive Producer, Sam Dunn; Director, Zhang Yang; Screenplay, Zhang Yang, Huo Xin; Photography, Wang Yu, Cheng Shouqi; Art Director, An Bin; Editor, Yang Hong Yu; Music, Zhang Yadong; from Imar Films; Chinese; Dolby; Color; Rated R; 112 minutes; American release date: September 13, 2002. CAST: Jia Hongsheng (Himself), Jia Fengsen (Hongsheng's Father), Chai Xiurong (Hongsheng's Mother), Wang Tong (Hongsheng's Sister), Shun Xing (Jia's Roommate), Li Jie (Hongsheng's Musician Friend), Zhang Yang (Director), An Bin (Art Director), Yuo Baoshan, Du Chunxia, Chen Liang, Zheng Pin, Bai Yuhong, Zhao Zuan (Doctors and Nurses), Hao Chunqiu, Cui Jingjia, Zhao Jiuli, Liu Tianran, Lu Wei, Liu Wu, Jiao Zhongsheng, Wei Liyuan (Patients)

Augusto Pinochet, Ricardo Izurieta Caffarena in
The Pinochet Case © First Run/Icarus

Jia Hongsheng in *Quitting* © Sony Classics

Paul Gross, Peter Outerbridge, Jed Rees, James Allodi in
Men with Brooms © Artisan

MEN WITH BROOMS

(ARTISAN) Producer, Robert Lantos; Co-Producer, Julia Rosenberg; Director, Paul Gross; Screenplay, Paul Gross, John Krizane, Paul Quarrington; Photography, Paul Best; Designer, Paul D. Austerberry; Costumes, Noreen Landry; Editor, Susan Maggi; Music, Paul Gross, Jack Lenz, The Tragically Hip; Casting, Deirdre Bowen; a Serendipity Point Films, Whizbang Films Inc. production; Canadian; Dolby; Deluxe color; Rated R; 102 minutes; Release date: September 20, 2002. CAST: Paul Gross (Chris Cutter), Connor Price (Brandon Foley), Leslie Nielsen (Gordon Cutter), Kari Matchett (Linda Bucyk), Molly Parker (Amy Foley), Michelle Nolden (Julie Foley), Peter Outerbridge (James Lennox), Jed Rees (Eddie Strombeck), Polly Shannon (Joanne), James Allodi (Neil Bucyk); The Tragically Hip: Gord Downie, Johnny Fay, Gord Sinclair, Bobby Baker, Paul Langlois (Curlers, Team Kingston), Tim Post (Freisen), Bob Bainborough (Greg Guinness), Greg Bryk (Alexander "The Juggernaut" Yount), George Buza (Stuckmore), James B. Douglas (Donald Foley), David G. Fremlin (Drunk Piper), Barbara Gordon (Mrs. Foley), Mike "Nug" Nahrgang (Nug McTeague), Victoria Snow (Officer Darte), Jane Spidell (Lily Strombeck), Beau Starr (Scott Blendick), Michael Stevens (Bartender), Timm Zemanek (Marvin Feigler)

THE LONELY AFFAIR OF THE HEART

(PATHFINDER) Producer, Tetsutomo Kosugi; Executive Producers, Ryuichi Suzuki, Junichi Suzuki; Director, Junichi Suzuki; Screenplay, Masaru Baba; Japanese; Dolby; Black and white/color; Not rated; 89 minutes; American release date: September 27, 2002. CAST: Rumi Sakakibara (Orie), Kazuya Takahashi (Young Man), Masakane Yonekura (Shiraki)

BIGGIE AND TUPAC

(LIONS GATE) Producer, Michele D'Acosta; Director, Nick Broomfield; Photography, Joan Churchill; Editors, Jaime Estrada-Torres, Mark Atkins; Music, Christian Henson; a Lafayette Film produced for Channel 4; British; Dolby; Color; Not rated; 108 minutes; American release date: September 27, 2002. Documentary on the fatal shootings of hip-hop performers Tupac Shakur and Biggie Smalls, featuring Nick Broomfield, Russell Poole, David Hicken, Billy Garland, Voletta Wallace, Mopreme, Kevin Hackle, Reggie Wright Sr., Frank Alexander, Sonia Flores, Marshall Bigtower, Sonia Flores, Marshall Bigtower, Don Seabold, Mark Hyland, Lil' Cease, Marion "Suge" Knight

SHANGHAI GHETTO

(MENEMSHA) Producers/Directors/Editors, Dana Janklowicz-Mann, Amir Mann; Photography, Amir Mann; Music, Sujin Nam; Narrator, Martin Landau; Dolby; Color/black and white; Not rated; 95 minutes; American release date: September 27, 2002. Documentary on Jews who fled Europe during World War II for the safety of Shanghai; featuring Alfred (Laco) Kohn, Harold Janklowicz, I. Betty Grebenschikoff, Sigmund Tobias, Evelyn Pike Rubin

HERA PURPLE

(PATHFINDER) Director/Screenplay, Kil-chae Jeong; Photography, Eung-Hwi Heo; Editor, Ki-hyeong Jo; Music, Richard Chung; Jeong Kil-chae productions; South Korean, 2001; Dolby; Color; Not rated; 93 minutes; American release date: September 27, 2002. CAST: Se-chang Lee (Lee Eung-ju), Chang Kim (Lee Hye-rim), Ho-seong Lee (Kim Jeong-wook), Chun-bae Uhm (Priest), Seok-cheon Hong (Inspector)

PANTALEÓN Y LAS VISITADORAS
(CAPTAIN PANTOJA AND THE SPECIAL SERVICES)

(VENEVISION INTERNATIONAL) Producer, José Enrique Crousillat; Executive Producers, Mariela Besuievski, Gustavo Sánchez; Director, Francisco J. Lombardi; Screenplay, Enrique Moncloa, Giovanna Pollarolo; Based on the novel by Mario Vargas Llosa; Photography, Teo Delgado; Art Directors, Alfredo Rojas, Alejandro Rossi; Music, Bingen Mendizábal; Editor, Danielle Fillios; Casting, Ricard Velásquez; an América Producciones, Inca Films S.A., Tornasol Films S.A. production; Spanish-Peruvian, 2000; Dolby; Color; Rated R; 137 minutes; American release date: September 27, 2002. CAST: Angie Cepeda (Olga Arellano), Salvador del Solar (Capt. Pantaleón Pantoja), Pilar Bardem (Chuchupe), Mónica Sánchez (Pochita), Tatiana Astengo (Pechuga), Norka Ramírez (Vanessa), Patty Cabrera (Lalita), Maricielo Effio (Salomé)

Shanghai Ghetto © Menemsha

Tupac Shakur, Biggie Smalls in Biggie and Tupac © Lions Gate

Pokémon 4ever © Miramax

WASABI

(TRISTAR) Producer/Screenplay, Luc Besson; Executive Producers, Shohei Kotaki, Kanjiro Sakura; Director, Gérard Krawczyk; Photography, Gérard Sterin; Designer, Jacques Bufnoir, Jean-Jacques Gernolle; Costumes, Agnès; Music, Julien Schultheis, Eric Serra; Editor, Yann Hervé; Casting, Swan Pham; a Europa Corp., K2, LeStudio Canal+, Leeloo Productions, Samitose Productions, TF1 Films Productions, Tokyo Broadcasting System, Victor Company of Japan presentation; French-Japanese; Dolby; Widescreen; Technicolor; Rated R; 94 minutes; American release date: September 27, 2002. CAST: Jean Reno (Hubert Fiorentini), Ryoko Hirosue (Yumi Yoshimodo), Michel Muller (Maurice "Momo"), Carole Bouquet (Sofia), Ludovic Berthillot (Jean-Baptiste 1), Yan Epstein (Jean-Baptiste 2), Michel Scourneau (Van Eyck), Christian Sinniger (The Squale), Jean-Marc Montalto (Olivier), Alexandre Brik (Irène), Fabio Zeononi (Josy), Véronique Balme (Betty), Jacques Bondoux (Del Rio), Yoshi Oida (Takanawa), Haruhiko Hirata (Ishibashi), Osamu Tsuruya, Akihiko Nishida (Customs Officers), Elodie Frenck (Banque de la Trinite Secretary), Anthony Decadi (Prefect's Son), Dorothée Brière (Air Hostess), Yuki Sakai (Miko), Karine Stoffer (Dancer), Yuji Yamashita, Takashi Ishii (Rebes), Makiko Ishii (Ishibashi's Secretary)

ROAD

(MEDIA PARTNERS) Producer, Ram Gopal Varma; Executive Producers, A.V.S. Raju, P.T. Giridhar Rao, Ram Gopal Varma, Suman Varma; Director, Rajat Mukherjee; Screenplay, Rajnish Thakur; Photography, Sudeep Chatterjee; Art Director, Sunil Nigvekar; Editor, Chandan Arora; Indian; Color; Not rated; 134 minutes; American release date: September 27, 2002. CAST: Manoj Bajpai (Babu), Vivek Oberoi (Arvind), Antara Mali (Lakshmi), Sayaji Shinde (Inspector Singh), Makrand Deshpande (Inderpal), Rajpal Yadav (Bhanwar Singh), Vijay Raaz (Villager on the Road), Ganesh Yadav (Bungalow Watchman), Raj Zutshi (Ishan Bhai), Rajnish Thakur (Hotel Receptionist), Mithilesh Chaturvedi (Old Man), Vidya Phadnis (Old Lady), Ganesh Acharya, Koena Mitra (Dancers)

POKÉMON 4EVER

(MIRAMAX) Producers, Choji Yoshikawa, Yukako Matsusako, Takemoto Mori; English Adaptation Producer, Kathy Borland; Executive Producers, Masakazu Kubo, Takashi Kawaguchi, Alfred R. Kahn, Norman J. Grossfeld; Director, Kunihiko Yuyama; English Adaptation Director, Jim Malone; Screenplay, Hideki Sonoda; English Adaptation Screenplay, Michael Haigney; Created by Satoshi Tajiri; Photography, Hisao Shirai; Art Directors, Katsuyoshi Kanemura, Katsumi Takao; Editors, Jay Film, Toshio Henmi, Yutaka Ito, Wins, Yumiko Fuse, Yukiko Nojiri; Music, Shinji Miyazaki; Animation Supervisor, Yoichi Kotabe; Animation Directors, Akihiro Tamagawa, Sayuri Ichiishi, Tokuhiro Matsubara, Yuji Ikeda, Yuko Inoue, Chisato Ikehira, Masaru Fukumoto; Digital Effects, Betelgeuse Productions; Special Effects Animator, Noriyuki Ota; a Pokemon USA presentation of a Pikachu Project 2002-Shogakukan production in association with 4Kids Entertainment; Japanese; Dolby; Imagica Color; Rated G; 79 minutes; American release date: October 11, 2002. VOICE CAST: Veronica Taylor (Ash Ketchum), Rachael Lillis (Misty Williams/Jesse of Team Rocket), Eric Stuart (Brock Harrison/James Morgan of Team Rocket), Addie Blaustein (Meowth), Ikue Ootani (Pikachu), Tara Jayne (Sammy), Stan Hart (Professor Oak)

UNDER THE MOONLIGHT

(INDEPENDENT) Producer, Manouchehr Mohammadi; Director/Screenplay, Seyyed Reza Mir-Karimi; Photography, Hamid Khozui-Abyaneh; Music, Mohammad Reza Aligholi; Designer, Rez Torabi; Editor, Nazanin Mofakham; Iranian, 2001; Color; Not rated; 96 minutes; American release date: October 18, 2002. CAST: Hossein Parastar (Sayyed Hassan), Hamed Rajabali (Jojeh), Mehran Rajabi (Principal), Shaghayegh Dehghan (Jojeh's Sister), Mahmud Nazar-Alian, Fereshteh Sadr-Orafai, Ashar Heidari

THE HAPPINESS OF THE KATAKURIS

(VITAGRAPH) Producers, Hirotsugu Yoshida, Tetsuo Sasho; Director, Takashi Miike; Screenplay, Kikumi Yamagishi; Photography, Akio Nomura; Designer, Yasuo Kamata; Editor, Yasushi Shimamura; Music, Koji Endo; Japanese; Dolby; Color; Not rated; 113 minutes; American release date: October 18, 2002. CAST: Naomi Nishida (Shizue Katakuri), Kenji Sawada (Masao Katakuri), Keiko Matsuzaka (Terue Katakuri), Shinji Takeda (Masayuki Katakuri), Tetsuro Tanba (Jinpei Katakuri), Naoto Takenaka (Miyake, the Policeman), Kiyoshiro Imawano (Richard)

Kenji Sawada, Tetsuro Tanba, Keiko Matsuzaka in *The Happiness of the Katakuris* © Vitagraph

Samuel L. Jackson, Robert Carlyle in *Formula 51* © Screen Gems

FORMULA 51

(SCREEN GEMS) a.k.a *The 51st State*; Producers, Andras Hamori, Seaton McLean, Jonathan Debin, David Pupkewitz, Malcolm Kohll; Executive Producers, Samuel L. Jackson, Eli Selden, Julie Yorn, Stephanie Davis; Director, Ronny Yu; Screenplay, Stel Pavlou; Co-Producer, Mark Aldridge; Photography, Poon Hang Sang; Designer, Alan MacDonald; Costumes, Kate Carin; Music, Headrillaz; Music Supervisors, Abi Leland, Dan Rose; Editor, David Wu; Casting, Nina Gold; an Alliance Atlantis presentation in association with the Film Consortium and Film Council, of a Focus Films/Fifty First Films/Alliance Atlantis production; British-Canadian, 2001; Dolby; Super 35 Widescreen; Color; Rated R; 92 minutes; American release date: October 18, 2002. CAST: Samuel L. Jackson (Elmo McElroy), Robert Carlyle (Felix DeSouza), Emily Mortimer (Dakota), Sean Pertwee (Det. Virgil Kane), Ricky Tomlinson (Leopold Durant), Rhys Ifans (Iki), Meat Loaf (The Lizard), Jake Abraham (Konnoko), Ade (Omar), Marc Anwar (Pharmacist), Paul Barber (Frederick), Barbara Barnes (Boy's Mother), Nick Bartlett (Trevor), Paul Broughton (Anfield Commissionaire), Joan Campion (Hotel Maid), Robert Fyfe (Hector Douglas McElroy), Christopher Hunter (Lawrence), Junix Inocian (Mr. Ho-Fat), Robert Jezek (Priest), Anna Keaveney (Shirley DeSouza), Angus MacInnes (Pudsey Smith), Mac McDonald (Mr. Davidson), Sonny Muslim (Child in Plane), Terry O'Neill (Deck Hand), Michael J. Reynolds (Mr. Escobar), James Roach (Grimtooth), Michael Starke (Arthur), Aaron Swartz (Mr. Yuri), Stephen Walters (Blowfish), David Webber (Mr. Jones), Nigel Whitmey (LA Highway Patrol)

David Wenham in *The Bank* © Cinema Guild

THE BANK

(CINEMA GUILD) Producer, John Maynard; Director/Screenplay, Robert Connolly; Photography, Tristan Milani; Designer, Luigi Pittorino; Costumes, Annie Marshall; Music, Alan John; Editor, Nick Meyers; Casting, Jane Norris; an Arenafilm, Showtime Australia production; Australian-Italian, 2001; Dolby; Color; Not rated; 103 minutes; American release date: October 25, 2002. CAST: David Wenham (Paul/Jim Doyle), Anthony LaPaglia (Simon O'Reilly), Sibylla Budd (Michelle Roberts), Steve Rodgers (Wayne Davis), Mitchell Butel (Stephen), Mandy McElhinney (Diane Davis), Greg Stone (Vincent), Kazuhiro Muroyama (Toshio), Andrew Bayly (Mr. Johnson), Thomas Blackburne (Young Jim), Sharon Oppy (Teacher), Robert Van Mackelenberg (Chairman), Jeff Keogh (Christopher), Matt Norman (Limo Driver), Ian Bliss, Peter Barron (Executives), Holly Myers (Yvonne), Tanja Bulatovic (Computer Lab Tech), Peta Doodson (Librarian), Vincent Gil (Sheriff), Tim Aris (Police Detective), Stephen Leeder (Billy), Emily Lumbers (Monica), Sue Jones (Bank Barrister), Maureen Edwards (Supreme Court Judge), Bruce Myles (ben), Lance Anderson (Jim's Father), Aris Gounaris (Immigration Officer)

ALL THE QUEEN'S MEN

(STRAND) Producers, Zachary Feuer, Gabrielle Kelly, Marco Weber; Executive Producer, Rainer Virnich; Line Producer, Miggel; Director, Stefan Ruzowitzky; Screenplay, David Schneider; Story, Digby Wolfe, Joseph Manduke, June Roberts; Co-Producer, Danny Krausz, György Marosi; Photography, Wedigo von Schultzendorff; Designer, Frank Bollinger; Costumes, Nicole Fischnaller; Casting, Celestia Fox; an Atlantic Streamline presentation in coproduction with Dor Film, Constantin Film, B.A. Film, and Phoenix Film of a Marco Weber production; German-Austrian-Hungarian-U.S., 2001; Dolby; Widescreen; Color; Not rated; 105 minutes; American release: October 25, 2002. CAST: Matt LeBlanc (Steven O'Rourke), Eddie Izzard (Tony Parker), James Cosmo (Archie), Nicolette Krebitz (Romy), Udo Kier (Gen. Lansdorf), David Birkin (Johnno), Oliver Korittke (Franz), Karl Markovics (Liebl), Edward Fox (Col. Aiken)

ONE GIRL AGAINST THE MAFIA:
DIARY OF A SICILIAN REBEL

(INDEPENDENT) Producers, Marco Amenta, Florent Marcie; Director/Screenplay, Marco Amenta; Photography, Sergio Salvati, Enrico Lucidi; Editors, Timothy Miller, Xavier Barthelemy; Italian, 1998; Color; Not rated; 60 minutes; American release date: November 6, 2002. Documentary on Rita Atria, who testafied against the Mafia after her father and brother were murdered; featuring Piera Aiello, Alessandra Camassa, Carmelo Canale, Mario Blunda, Vito Santangelo, Salvatore Girgenti, Antonio Di Giorgi

Michelle Reis in *The City of Lost Souls* © Vitagraph

Seiichi Tanabe in *Hush!* © Strand

THE CITY OF LOST SOULS

(VITAGRAPH) Producers, Kazunari Hasiguchi, Toshiki Kimura; Executive Producer, Yasuyoshi Tokuma; Director, Takashi Miike; Screenplay, Ichiro Ruy; Based on the novel by Seishu Hase; Photography, Naosuke Imaizumi; Designer, Akira Ishige; Music, Koji Endo; Editor, Yasushi Shimamura; Casting, Donna Brower; a Daiei Motion Picture Company, Tohokashinsha Film Company, Tokuma Shoten, Tokyo FM Broadcasting Company production; Japanese, 2000; Color; Not rated; 103 minutes; American release date: November 6, 2002. CAST: Teah (Mario), Michelle Reis (Kei), Patricia Manterola (Lucia), Mitsuhiro Oikawa (Ko), Koji Kikkawa (Fushimi), Anatoli Krasnov (Khodoloskii), Sebastian DeVicente (Ricardo), Terence Yin (Riku), Atsushi Okuno (Carlos), Akira Emoto (Kuwatat), Eugene Nomura (Yamazaki), Marcio Rosario (Sanchez), Ryushi Mizukami (Ide)

HUSH!

(STRAND) Producer, Tetsujiro Yamagami; Director/Screenplay/Editor, Ryosuke Hashiguchi; Photography, Shogo Ueno; Designer, Fumio Ogawa; Costumes, Masae Miyamoto; Music, Bobby McFerrin; Casting, Shiro Kido, Naohiko Ueda; Japanese, 2001; Color; Not rated; 135 minutes; American release date: November 8, 2002. CAST: Kazuya Takahashi (Naoya), Seiichi Tanabe (Katsuhiro), Reiko Kataoka (Asako), Yoko Akino (Yoko Kurtia), Manami Fuji (Katsumi), Ken Mitsuishi (Shoji Kurita), Tsugumi (Emi Nagata), Tetsu Sawaki (Makoto)

Matt LeBlanc, David Birkin, James Cosmo, Eddie Izzard in
All the Queen's Men © Strand

ETOILES: DANCERS OF THE PARIS OPERA BALLET

(FIRST RUN FEATURES) Producers, Frederic Bourboulon, Agnes Le Pont; Executive Producer, Agathe Berman; Director/Screenplay, Nils Tavernier; Photography, Dominique Le Rigoleur, Nils Tavernier; Black & White Still Photography, Vincent Tessier; Editor, Florence Ricard; a Little Bear production, in association with Gaia Films, with support from Canal+, Centre National de la Cinematographie; French, 2000; Dolby; Color; Not rated; 100 minutes; American release date: November 8, 2002. Documentary on the Paris Opera Ballet, featuring Maurice Bejart, Jiri Kylian, Marie-Agnes Gillot, Elisabeth Platel.

BÁNK BÁN

(BUNYIK ENTERTAINMENT) Producer, András Wermer; Director, Csaba Káel; Screenplay, Gábor Mészöly; Based on the play by Béni Egresi, from the novel by József Katona; Photography, Vilmos Zsigmond; Designer, Attila Csikós; Costumes, Rita Velich; Editor, Thomas Ernst; Music, Ferenc Erkel; Casting, Gyorgy Lörinczy; Hungarian, 2001; Dolby; Color; Not rated; 118 minutes; American release date: November 15, 2002. CAST: Kolos Kováts (Endre the Second), Eva Marton (Gertrúd the Queen), Andra Rost (Melinda), Dénes Gulyás (Otto), Attila Kiss B. (Bánk Bán), Sándor Sólymon-Nagy (Petur Bán), Attila Réti (Biberach), Lajos Miller (Tiborc)

POWER AND TERROR:
NOAM CHOMSKY IN OUR TIMES

(FIRST RUN FEATURES) Producer, Tetsujiro Yamagami; Director, John Junkerman; Photography, Koshiro Otsu; Editors, John Junkerman, Takeshi Hata; Associate Producer, Mayu Ogawa; Music, Kiyoshiro Imawano; Japanese; Color; Not rated; 74 minutes; American release date: November 22, 2002. Documentary in which political philosopher Noam Chomsky presents his theories and analysis on the September 11, 2001 terrorist attacks.

RIVERS AND TIDES:
ANDY GOLDSWORTHY WORKING WITH TIME

(ROXIE RELEASING) Producer, Annedore v. Donop; Co-Producers, Trevor Davies, Leslie Hills; Director/Photography/Editor, Thomas Riedelsheimer; Music, Fred Frith; German, 2000; Dolby; Color; Not rated; 90 minutes; American release date: November 20, 2002. Documentary on British earthworks artist Andy Goldsworthy.

Noam Chomsky in *Power and Terror: Noam Chomsky in Our Times*
© First Run Features

Andy Goldsworthy in *Rivers and Tides:*
Andy Goldsworthy Working with Time © Roxie Releasing

BOLLYWOOD/HOLLYWOOD

(MOGREL MEDIA) Producer, David Hamilton; Executive Producers, Camelia Frieberg, Ajay Virmani; Line Producer, Mehernaz Lentin; Director/Screenplay, Deepa Mehta; Photography, Douglas Koch; Designer, Tamara Deverell; Costumes, Anne Dixon, Ritu Kumar; Editor, Barry Farrell; Music, Sandeep Chowta; a co-production of Bollywood/Hollywood Productions, Different Tree Same Wood; Canadian; Dolby; Color; Not rated; 103 minutes; American release date: November 22, 2002. CAST: Rahul Khanna (Rahul Seth), Lisa Ray (Sue Singh), Moushumi Chatterjee (Mummy ji), Dina Pathak (Grandma ji), Kulbhushan Kharbanda (Mr. Singh), Ranjit Chowdhry (Rocky), Jessica Paré (Kimberly), Leesa Gaspari (Lucy), Arjun Lombardi-Singh (Go), Rishma Malik (Twinky), Jazz Mann (Bobby)

Etoiles: Dancers of the Paris Opera Ballet © First Run Features

Maria Chen in *Dead or Alive: Final* © Kino

EXTREME OPS

(PARAMOUNT) Producers, Moshe Diamant, Jan Fantl; Executive Producers, Romain Schroeder, Rudy Cohen, Mark Damon, Davis Sanders; Director, Christian Duguay; Screenplay, Michael Zaidan; Story, Timothy Scott Bogart, Mark Mullin; Photography, Hannes Hubach; Designer, Philip Harrison; Costumes, Maria Schicker; Editors, Clive Barrett, Sylvain Lebel; Music, Normand Corbeil, Stanislas Syrewicz; Special Effects, Stephane Landry, Uli Nefzer; Stunts, Tom Delmar; a MDP Worldwide, Diamant Cohen Prods. presentation of an Apollomedia/Extreme Prods. production in association with the Carousel Picture Co; German-Luxembourg-U.S.; Dolby; Super 35 Widescreen; Technicolor; Rated PG-13; 93 minutes; American release date: November 27, 2002. CAST: Devon Sawa (Will), Rupert Graves (Jeffrey), Rufus Sewell (Ian), Bridgette Wilson-Sampras (Chloe), Heino Ferch (Mark), Joe Absolom (Silo), Jean-Pierre Castaldi (Zoran), Klaus Lowitsch (Slobovan Pavle), Jana Pallaske (Kittie), Heinrich Schmieder (Goran), Liliana Komorowska (Yana)

DEAD OR ALIVE: FINAL

(KINO) Producers, Makoto Okada (Toei Video), Yoshihiro Masuda (Daiei); Executive Producers, Mitsuru Kurosawa, Tsutomu Tsuchikawa; Director, Takashi Miike; Screenplay, Hitoshi Ishikawa, Yoshinobu Kamo, Ichiro Ryu; Photography, Kazunari Tanaka; Editor, Shuuwa Kogen; Music, Kôji Endô; Japanese, 2001; Dolby; Color; Not rated; 90 minutes; American release date: November 29, 2002. CAST: Show Aikawa (Ryo), Riki Takeuchi (Honda), Maria Chen (Michelle), Richard Cheung (Dictator Woo), Tony Ho (Ho), Josie Ho (Jyun), Terence Yin (Fong), Kenneth Low (Fuyuki)

MASSOUD, THE AFGHAN

(NEW YORKER) Producer/Director/Screenplay/Photography, Christophe de Ponfilly; Editors, Tatiana Andrews, Jean-François Giré; Music, Anita Vallero; Co-Produced by La Sept ARTE, Interscoop; French, 1998; Color; Not rated; 90 minutes; American release date: December 4, 2002. Documentary on Northern Alliance leader Ahmed Shah Massoud's battle against the Taliban.

MY KINGDOM

(FIRST LOOK) Producers, Neal Weisman, Gabriele Bacher; Executive Producers, William Turner, Nadine Mellor; Line Producer, Anthony Waye; Director, Don Boyd; Screenplay, Nick Davies, Don Boyd; Photography, Dewald Aukema; Designer, Luana Hanson; Costumes, Mary-Jane Reyner; Editor, Adam Ross; Music, Simon Fisher-Turner, Deirdre Gribbin; Casting, Judi Hayfield; Close Grip Films Ltd., Primary Pictures, Sky Pictures; British-Italian, 2001; Dolby; Color; Not rated; 117 minutes; American release date: December 6, 2002. CAST: Richard Harris (Sandeman), Lynn Redgrave (Mandy), Tom Bell (Quick), Emma Catherwood (Jo), Aidan Gillen (Puttnam), Louise Lombard (Kath), Paul McGann (Dean), Jimi Mistry (Jug), Reece Noi (The Boy), Lorraine Pilkington (Tracy), Colin Salmon (The Chair), James Foy (Animal), James McMartin (Mineral), Danny Lawrence (Tigger), Gerard Starkey (Minder), Sasha Johnston Manning (Soprano), Seamus O'Neill (Snowy), Chris Armstrong, Ingi Thor Jonsson (Dutch Farmers), Otis Graham (Delroy), David Yip (Merv), Kieran O'Brien (Photographer), Jack Marsden (Billy the Whizz), Amer Nazir (Mutt), Mushi Noor (Jef), Carl Learmond (Rudi), Anthony Dorrs (Skunk), Steve Foster (Toffee), Oscar James (Desmond), Sylvia Gatril (Brothl Receptionist), Sharon Byatt (Annie), Desmond Bayliss (John the Dog), Kelly Murphy (Karen), Leanne Burrows (Miss Joy)

Rupert Graves in *Extreme Ops* © Paramount

Richard Harris, Carl Learmond in *My Kingdom* © Overseas Film Group

Ahmed Shah Massoud in *Massoud, the Afghan*
© New Yorker

BLACKBOARDS

(LEISURE TIME/KIMSTIM) Executive Producer, Mohammad Ahmadi; Director, Samira Makhmalbaf; Screenplay, Samira Makhmalbaf, Mohsen Makhmaldbaf; Photography, Ebrahim Ghafouri; Editor, Mohsen Makhmalbaf; Music, Mohammad-Reza Darvishi; a Makhmalbaf Film House in association with Fabrice Cinema/Radiotelevisione Italiana/T-Mark production; Iranian-Italian-Japanese, 2000; Color; Not rated; 86 minutes; American release date: December 6, 2002. CAST: Saeed Mohamadi (Saïd), Behnaz Jafari (Halaleh), Bahman Ghobadi (Reeboir), Mohamad Karim Rahmati (Father), Rafat Moradi (Ribvar), Mayas Rostami (The Young Boy), Saman Akbari (Group Leader), Ahmad Bahrami (Marriage Registrar), Mohamad Moradi (Matchmaker), Karim Moradi (Old Man), Hassan Mohamadi (Child), Rasool Mohamadi (The Boy Porter), Somaye Veisee (Little Girl)

PRISONER OF PARADISE

(ALLIANCE ATLANTIS) Producers, Malcolm Clarke, Karl-Eberhard Schaefer; Directors, Malcolm Clarke, Stuart Sender; Screenplay, Malcolm Clarke; Executive Producers, Jake Eberts, Stuart Sender; Photography, Michael Hammon; Music, Luc St. Pierre; Editors, Glenn Berman, Susan Shanks; Media Verite & Cafe Productions; Canadian-U.S.-German-British; Black and white/color; Not rated; American release date: December 11, 2002. Documentary on how actor-filmmaker Kurt Gerron, a German Jew, was forced to make a pro-Nazi documentary, *The Fuhrer Gives a City to the Jews*, to give the impression to the world that nothing of a heinous nature was going on at Thereseinenstadt concentration camp.

EL BOLA

(FILM MOVEMENT) Executive Producer, José Antonio Félez; Director, Achero Mañas; Screenplay, Achero Mañas, Verónica Fernández; Photography, Juan Carlos Gómez; Designer, Daniel Goldstein, Ricardo Steinberg; Costumes, Mar Bardavío; Music, Eduardo Arbide; Editor, Nacho Ruiz Capillas; a Televisión Española (TVE), Tesela Producciones Cinematográficas S.R.L., Vía Digital; Spanish, 2000; Dolby; Color; Not rated; 88 minutes; American release date: December 13, 2002. CAST: Juan José Ballesta (Pablo, El Bola), Pablo Galán (Alfredo), Alberto Jiménez (José, Father of Alfredo), Manuel Morón (Mariano, Father of El Bola), Ana Wagener (Laura), Nieve de Medina (Marisa), Gloria Muñoz (Aurora, Mother of El Bola), Omar Muñoz (Juan), Soledad Osorio (Grandmother of El Bola)

DEVILS ON THE DOORSTEP

(COWBOY) Producer/Director, Jiang Wen; Screenplay, You Fengwei, Shi Jianquan, Shu Ping, Jiang Wen; Inspired by the novella *Shengcun* by You Fengwei; Photography, Gu Changwei; Music, Cui Jian, Liu Xing, Li Haiying; Editors, Zhang Yifan, Folmer Weisinger; an Asian Union Film & Entertainment, Beijing Zhongbo-Times Film Planning, CMC Xiandai Trade Co., China Film Co-Production Corporation, Huyai Brothers Advertising production; Chinese, 2001; Dolby; Black and white; Not rated; 140 minutes; American release date: December 18, 2002. CAST: Jiang Wen (Ma Dasan), Jiang Hongbo (Yu'er), Kagawa Teruyuki (Hanaya Kosaburo, The Prisoner), Yuan Ding (Dong Hanchen, The Translator), Cong Zhijun (Grandfather), Xi Zi (Liu Wang), Li Haibin (Me), Sawada Kenya (Inokichi Sakatsuka), Cai Weidong (Er Bozi), Lianmei Chen (Aunt), Miyaji Yoshimoto (Koji Nonomura), Chen Qiang ("One Stroke" Liu), Wu David (Major Gao)

SMOKERS ONLY
(VAGÓN FUMADOR)

(STRAND) Executive Producer, Martín De Arbelaiz; Director, Verónica Chen; Photography, Nicolás Theodossiou; Art Director, Julián D'Angiolillo; Music, Pablo Siriani; Editor, Verónica Chen; Argentine, 2001; Not rated; 87 minutes; American release: December 20, 2002. CAST: Cecilia Bengolea (Reni), Leonardo Brezicki (Andrés), Carlos Issa (Charly), Fernando Moumdjian (El Armenio), Juan Martín Ibero (Juanma), Adrián Fondari (Hotel Client), Pablo Razuk (Band Manager/ Banelco Client), Fabián Talín (Car Client), Adrián Blaco (Male Stripper)

PINOCCHIO

(MIRAMAX) Producers, Gianluigi Braschi, Nicoletta Braschi, Elda Ferri; Executive Producer, Mario Cotone; Director, Roberto Benigni; Screenplay, Vincenzo Cerami, Roberto Benigni; Based on the book *Le Avventure di Pinocchio* (*The Adventures of Pinocchio*) by Carlo Collodi; Photography, Dante Spinotti; Designer/Costumes, Danilo Donati; Editor, Simona Paggi; Music, Nicola Piovani; Visual Effects Supervisor, Rob Hodgson; a Medusa Film, Mario & Cecchi Gori presentation, in association with Miramax Films of a Melampo Cinematografica production; Italian; Dolby; Panavision; Technicolor; Rated G; 100 minutes; American release date: December 25, 2002. CAST: Roberto Benigni (Pinocchio), Nicoletta Braschi (Blue Fairy), Mino Bellei (Medoro), Carlo Giuffre (Geppetto), Kim Rossi Stuart (Leonardo), Peppe Barra (The Talking Cricket), Franco Javarone (Fire Eater), Max Cavallari (The Cat), Bruno Arena (The Fox), Luis Molteni (Butter Man), Alessandro Bergonzoni (Ring Master), Corrado Pani (The Judge), Vincenzo Cerami (Man with the Mustache), Giorgio Ariani (Host of the Red Crown), Tomasso Bianco (Pulcinella), Giorgio Noe (Boy); U.S. VOICE CAST: Breckin Meyer (Pinocchio), Glenn Close (Blue Fairy), Eric Idle (Medoro), David Suchet (Geppetto/Narrator), John Cleese (Talking Cricket), Kevin James (Fire Eater), Eddie Griffin (The Cat), Cheech Marin (The Fox), Regis Philbin (Ringmaster), James Belushi (Farmer), Queen Latifah (Dove), Topher Grace (Leonardo), Erik Bergmann (Butter Man)

Leonardo Brezicki, Pablo Razuk in *Smokers Only* © Strand

Roberto Benigni in *Pinocchio* © Miramax

BIOGRAPHICAL DATA

Jane Adams

Jennifer Aniston

Hank Azaria

Cate Blanchett

Edward Burns

Jackie Chan

AAMES, WILLIE: (William Upton): Los Angeles, CA, July 15, 1960.

AARON, CAROLINE: Richmond, VA, Aug. 7, 1954. Catholic U.

ABBOTT, DIAHNNE: NYC, 1945.

ABBOTT, JOHN: London, June 5, 1905.

ABRAHAM, F. MURRAY: Pittsburgh, PA, Oct. 24, 1939. UTx.

ACKLAND, JOSS: London, Feb. 29, 1928.

ADAMS, BROOKE: NYC, Feb. 8, 1949. Dalton.

ADAMS, CATLIN: Los Angeles, Oct. 11, 1950.

ADAMS, DON: NYC, Apr. 13, 1926.

ADAMS, EDIE (Elizabeth Edith Enke): Kingston, PA, Apr. 16, 1927. Juilliard, Columbia.

ADAMS, JANE: Washington, DC, Apr. 1, 1965.

ADAMS, JOEY LAUREN: Little Rock, AR, Jan. 6, 1971.

ADAMS, JULIE (Betty May): Waterloo, IA, Oct. 17, 1926. Little Rock, Jr. College.

ADAMS, MASON: NYC, Feb. 26, 1919. UWi.

ADAMS, MAUD (Maud Wikstrom): Lulea, Sweden, Feb. 12, 1945.

ADJANI, ISABELLE: Germany, June 27, 1955.

AFFLECK, BEN: Berkeley, CA, Aug. 15, 1972.

AFFLECK, CASEY: Falmouth, MA, Aug. 12, 1975.

AGUTTER, JENNY: Taunton, England, Dec. 20, 1952.

AIELLO, DANNY: NYC, June 20, 1933.

AIMEE, ANOUK (Dreyfus): Paris, France, Apr. 27, 1934. Bauer Therond.

AKERS, KAREN: NYC, Oct. 13, 1945, Hunter College.

ALBERGHETTI, ANNA MARIA: Pesaro, Italy, May 15, 1936.

ALBERT, EDDIE (Eddie Albert Heimberger): Rock Island, IL, Apr. 22, 1908. U of Minn.

ALBERT, EDWARD: Los Angeles, Feb. 20. 1951. UCLA.

ALBRIGHT, LOLA: Akron, OH, July 20, 1925.

ALDA, ALAN: NYC, Jan. 28, 1936. Fordham.

ALEANDRO, NORMA: Buenos Aires, Dec. 6, 1936.

ALEJANDRO, MIGUEL: NYC, Feb. 21, 1958.

ALEXANDER, JANE (Quigley): Boston, MA, Oct. 28, 1939. Sarah Lawrence.

ALEXANDER, JASON (Jay Greenspan): Newark, NJ, Sept. 23, 1959. Boston U.

ALICE, MARY: Indianola, MS, Dec. 3, 1941.

ALLEN, DEBBIE (Deborah): Houston, TX, Jan. 16, 1950. Howard U.

ALLEN, JOAN: Rochelle, IL, Aug. 20, 1956. EastIllU.

ALLEN, KAREN: Carrollton, IL, Oct. 5, 1951. UMd.

ALLEN, NANCY: NYC, June 24, 1950.

ALLEN, TIM: Denver, CO, June 13, 1953. W. MI. Univ.

ALLEN, WOODY (Allan Stewart Konigsberg): Brooklyn, Dec. 1, 1935.

ALLEY, KIRSTIE: Wichita, KS, Jan. 12, 1955.

ALLYSON, JUNE (Ella Geisman): Westchester, NY, Oct. 7, 1917.

ALONSO, MARIA CONCHITA: Cuba, June 29, 1957.

ALT, CAROL: Queens, NY, Dec. 1, 1960. HofstraU.

ALVARADO, TRINI: NYC, Jan. 10, 1967.

AMBROSE, LAUREN: New Haven, CT, Feb. 20, 1978.

AMIS, SUZY: Oklahoma City, OK, Jan. 5, 1958. Actors Studio.

AMOS, JOHN: Newark, NJ, Dec. 27, 1940. Colo. U.

ANDERSON, ANTHONY: Los Angeles, Aug. 15, 1970.

ANDERSON, GILLIAN: Chicago, IL, Aug. 9, 1968. DePaul U.

ANDERSON, KEVIN: Waukeegan, IL, Jan. 13, 1960.

ANDERSON, LONI: St. Paul, MN, Aug. 5, 1946.

ANDERSON, MELISSA SUE: Berkeley, CA, Sept. 26, 1962.

ANDERSON, MELODY: Edmonton, Canada, 1955. Carlton U.

ANDERSON, MICHAEL, JR.: London, England, Aug. 6, 1943.

ANDERSON, RICHARD DEAN: Minneapolis, MN, Jan. 23, 1950.

ANDERSSON, BIBI: Stockholm, Sweden, Nov. 11, 1935. Royal Dramatic Sch.

ANDES, KEITH: Ocean City, NJ, July 12, 1920. Temple U., Oxford.

ANDRESS, URSULA: Bern, Switzerland, Mar. 19, 1936.

ANDREWS, ANTHONY: London, Dec. 1, 1948.

ANDREWS, JULIE (Julia Elizabeth Wells): Surrey, England, Oct. 1, 1935.

ANGLIM, PHILIP: San Francisco, CA, Feb. 11, 1953.

ANISTON, JENNIFER: Sherman Oaks, CA, Feb. 11, 1969.

ANN-MARGRET (Olsson): Valsjobyn, Sweden, Apr. 28, 1941. Northwestern U.

ANSARA, MICHAEL: Lowell, MA, Apr. 15, 1922. Pasadena Playhouse.

ANSPACH, SUSAN: NYC, Nov. 23, 1945.

ANTHONY, LYSETTE: London, 1963.

ANTHONY, TONY: Clarksburg, WV, Oct. 16, 1937. Carnegie Tech.

ANTON, SUSAN: Yucaipa, CA, Oct. 12, 1950. Bernardino College.

ANTONELLI, LAURA: Pola, Italy, Nov. 28, 1941.

ANWAR, GABRIELLE: Lalehaam, England, Feb. 4, 1970.

APPLEGATE, CHRISTINA: Hollywood CA, Nov. 25, 1972.

ARCHER, ANNE: Los Angeles, Aug. 25, 1947.

ARCHER, JOHN (Ralph Bowman): Osceola, NB, May 8, 1915. USC.

ARDANT, FANNY: Monte Carlo, Mar 22, 1949.

ARKIN, ADAM: Brooklyn, NY, Aug. 19, 1956.

ARKIN, ALAN: NYC, Mar. 26, 1934. LACC.

ARMSTRONG, BESS: Baltimore, MD, Dec. 11, 1953.

ARNAZ, DESI, JR.: Los Angeles, Jan. 19, 1953.

ARNAZ, LUCIE: Hollywood, July 17, 1951.

ARNESS, JAMES (Aurness): Minneapolis, MN, May 26, 1923. Beloit College.

ARQUETTE, DAVID: Winchester, VA, Sept. 8, 1971.

ARQUETTE, PATRICIA: NYC, Apr. 8, 1968.

ARQUETTE, ROSANNA: NYC, Aug. 10, 1959.

ARTHUR, BEATRICE (Frankel): NYC, May 13, 1924. New School.

ASHER, JANE: London, Apr. 5, 1946.

ASHLEY, ELIZABETH (Elizabeth Ann Cole): Ocala, FL, Aug. 30, 1939.

ASHTON, JOHN: Springfield, MA, Feb. 22, 1948. USC.

ASNER, EDWARD: Kansas City, KS, Nov. 15, 1929.

ASSANTE, ARMAND: NYC, Oct. 4, 1949. AADA.

ASTIN, JOHN: Baltimore, MD, Mar. 30, 1930. U Minn.

ASTIN, MacKENZIE: Los Angeles, May 12, 1973.

ASTIN, SEAN: Santa Monica, Feb. 25, 1971.

ATHERTON, WILLIAM: Orange, CT, July 30, 1947. Carnegie Tech.

ATKINS, CHRISTOPHER: Rye, NY, Feb. 21, 1961.

ATKINS, EILEEN: London, June 16, 1934.

ATKINSON, ROWAN: England, Jan. 6, 1955. Oxford.

ATTENBOROUGH, RICHARD: Cambridge, England, Aug. 29, 1923. RADA.

AUBERJONOIS, RENE: NYC, June 1, 1940. Carnegie Tech.

AUDRAN, STEPHANE: Versailles, France, Nov. 8, 1932.

AUGER, CLAUDINE: Paris, France, Apr. 26, 1942. Dramatic Cons.

AULIN, EWA: Stockholm, Sweden, Feb. 14, 1950.

AUTEUIL, DANIEL: Alger, Algeria, Jan. 24, 1950.

AVALON, FRANKIE (Francis Thomas Avallone): Philadelphia, PA, Sept. 18, 1939.

AYKROYD, DAN: Ottawa, Canada, July 1, 1952.

AZARIA, HANK: Forest Hills, NY, Apr. 25, 1964. AADA, Tufts Univ.

AZNAVOUR, CHARLES (Varenagh Aznourian): Paris, France, May 22, 1924.

AZZARA, CANDICE: Brooklyn, NY, May 18, 1947.

BACALL, LAUREN (Betty Perske): NYC, Sept. 16, 1924. AADA.

BACH, BARBARA: Queens, NY, Aug. 27, 1946.

BACH, CATHERINE: Warren, OH, Mar. 1, 1954.

BACKER, BRIAN: NYC, Dec. 5, 1956. Neighborhood Playhouse.

BACON, KEVIN: Philadelphia, PA, July 8, 1958.

BAIN, BARBARA: Chicago, IL, Sept. 13, 1934. U Ill.

BAIO, SCOTT: Brooklyn, NY, Sept. 22, 1961.

BAKER, BLANCHE: NYC, Dec. 20, 1956.

BAKER, CARROLL: Johnstown, PA, May 28, 1931. St. Petersburg, Jr. College.

BAKER, DIANE: Hollywood, CA, Feb. 25, 1938. USC.

BAKER, JOE DON: Groesbeck, TX, Feb.12, 1936.

BAKER, KATHY: Midland, TX, June 8, 1950. UC Berkley.

BAKULA, SCOTT: St. Louis, MO, Oct. 9, 1955. KansasU.

BALABAN, BOB: Chicago, IL, Aug. 16, 1945. Colgate.

BALDWIN, ADAM: Chicago, IL, Feb. 27, 1962.

BALDWIN, ALEC: Massapequa, NY, Apr. 3, 1958. NYU.

BADLWIN, DANIEL: Massapequa, NY, Oct. 5, 1960.

BALDWIN, STEPHEN: Massapequa, NY, 1966.

BALDWIN, WILLIAM: Massapequa, NY, Feb. 21, 1963.

BALE, CHRISTIAN: Pembrokeshire, West Wales, Jan. 30, 1974.

BALK, FAIRUZA: Point Reyes, CA, May 21, 1974.

BALLARD, KAYE: Cleveland, OH, Nov. 20, 1926.

BANCROFT, ANNE (Anna Maria Italiano): Bronx, NY, Sept. 17, 1931. AADA.

BANDERAS, ANTONIO: Malaga, Spain, Aug. 10, 1960.

BANERJEE, VICTOR: Calcutta, India, Oct. 15, 1946.

BANES, LISA: Chagrin Falls, OH, July 9, 1955. Juilliard.

BARANSKI, CHRISTINE: Buffalo, NY, May 2, 1952. Juilliard.

BARBEAU, ADRIENNE: Sacramento, CA, June 11, 1945. Foothill College.

BARDEM, JAVIER: Gran Canaria, Spain, May 1, 1969.

BARDOT, BRIGITTE: Paris, France, Sept. 28, 1934.

BARKIN, ELLEN: Bronx, NY, Apr. 16, 1954. Hunter College.

BARNES, CHRISTOPHER DANIEL: Portland, ME, Nov. 7, 1972.

BARR, JEAN-MARC: San Diego, CA, Sept. 1960.

BARRAULT, JEAN-LOUIS: Vesinet, France, Sept. 8, 1910.

BARRAULT, MARIE-CHRISTINE: Paris, France, Mar. 21, 1944.

BARREN, KEITH: Mexborough, England, Aug. 8, 1936. Sheffield Playhouse.

BARRETT, MAJEL (Hudec): Columbus, OH, Feb. 23, 1939. Western Reserve U.

BARRIE, BARBARA: Chicago, IL, May 23, 1931.

BARRY, GENE (Eugene Klass): NYC, June 14, 1919.

BARRY, NEILL: NYC, Nov. 29, 1965.

BARRYMORE, DREW: Los Angeles, Feb. 22, 1975.

BARRYMORE, JOHN DREW: Beverly Hills, CA, June 4, 1932. St. John's Military Academy.

BARYSHNIKOV, MIKHAIL: Riga, Latvia, Jan. 27, 1948.

BASINGER, KIM: Athens, GA, Dec. 8, 1953. Neighborhood Playhouse.

BASSETT, ANGELA: NYC, Aug. 16, 1958.

BATEMAN, JASON: Rye, NY, Jan. 14, 1969.

BATEMAN, JUSTINE: Rye, NY, Feb. 19, 1966.

BATES, ALAN: Allestree, Derbyshire, England, Feb. 17, 1934. RADA.

BATES, JEANNE: San Francisco, CA, May 21, 1918. RADA.

BATES, KATHY: Memphis, TN, June 28, 1948. S. Methodist U.

BAUER, STEVEN (Steven Rocky Echevarria): Havana, Cuba, Dec. 2, 1956. U Miami.

BAXTER, KEITH: South Wales, England, Apr. 29, 1933. RADA.

BAXTER, MEREDITH: Los Angeles, June 21, 1947. Intelochen Acad.

BAYE, NATHALIE: Mainevile, France, July 6, 1948.

BEACH, ADAM: Winnipeg, Canada, Nov. 11, 1972.

BEACHAM, STEPHANIE: Casablanca, Morocco, Feb. 28, 1947.

BEALS, JENNIFER: Chicago, IL, Dec. 19, 1963.

BEAN, ORSON (Dallas Burrows): Burlington, VT, July 22, 1928.

BEAN, SEAN: Sheffield, Yorkshire, England, Apr. 17, 1958.

BÉART, EMMANUELLE: Gassin, France, Aug. 14, 1965.

BEATTY, NED: Louisville, KY, July 6, 1937.

BEATTY, WARREN: Richmond, VA, Mar. 30, 1937.

BECK, JOHN: Chicago, IL, Jan. 28, 1943.

BECK, MICHAEL: Memphis, TN, Feb. 4, 1949. Millsap College.

BECKINSALE, KATE: England, July 26, 1974.

BEDELIA, BONNIE: NYC, Mar. 25, 1946. Hunter College.

BEGLEY, ED, JR.: NYC, Sept. 16, 1949.

BELAFONTE, HARRY: NYC, Mar. 1, 1927.

BEL GEDDES, BARBARA: NYC, Oct. 31, 1922.

BELL, TOM: Liverpool, England, Aug. 2, 1933.

BELLER, KATHLEEN: NYC, Feb. 10, 1957.

BELLWOOD, PAMELA (King): Scarsdale, NY, June 26, 1951.

BELMONDO, JEAN PAUL: Paris, France, Apr. 9, 1933.

BELUSHI, JAMES: Chicago, IL, June 15, 1954.

BELZER, RICHARD: Bridgeport, CT, Aug. 4, 1944.

BENEDICT, DIRK (Niewoehner): White Sulphur Springs, MT, March 1, 1945. Whitman College.

BENEDICT, PAUL: Silver City, NM, Sept. 17, 1938.

BENIGNI, ROBERTO: Tuscany, Italy, Oct. 27, 1952.

BENING, ANNETTE: Topeka, KS, May 29, 1958. SFSt. U.

BENJAMIN, RICHARD: NYC, May 22, 1938. Northwestern U.

BENNENT, DAVID: Lausanne, Sept. 9, 1966.

BENNETT, ALAN: Leeds, England, May 9, 1934. Oxford.

BENNETT, BRUCE (Herman Brix): Tacoma, WA, May 19, 1909. U Wash.

BENNETT, HYWEL: Garnant, So. Wales, Apr. 8, 1944.

BENSON, ROBBY: Dallas, TX, Jan. 21, 1957.

BENTLEY, WES: Jonesboro, AR, Sept. 4, 1978.

BERENGER, TOM: Chicago, IL, May 31, 1950, U Mo.

BERENSON, MARISA: NYC, Feb. 15, 1947.

BERG, PETER: NYC, March 11, 1964. Malcalester College.

BERGEN, CANDICE: Los Angeles, May 9, 1946. U PA.

BERGEN, POLLY: Knoxville, TN, July 14, 1930. Compton, Jr. College.

BERGER, HELMUT: Salzburg, Austria, May 29, 1942.

BERGER, SENTA: Vienna, Austria, May 13, 1941. Vienna Sch. of Acting.

BERGER, WILLIAM: Austria, Jan. 20, 1928. Columbia.

BERGERAC, JACQUES: Biarritz, France, May 26, 1927. Paris U.

BERGIN, PATRICK: Dublin, Feb. 4, 1951.

BERKLEY, ELIZABETH: Detroit, MI, July 28, 1972.

BERKOFF, STEVEN: London, England, Aug. 3, 1937.

BERLIN, JEANNIE: Los Angeles, Nov. 1, 1949.

BERLINGER, WARREN: Brooklyn, Aug. 31, 1937. Columbia.

BERNAL, GAEL GARCÍA: Guadalajara, Mexico, Oct. 30, 1978.

BERNHARD, SANDRA: Flint, MI, June 6, 1955.

BERNSEN, CORBIN: Los Angeles, Sept. 7, 1954. UCLA.

BERRI, CLAUDE (Langmann): Paris, France, July 1, 1934.

BERRIDGE, ELIZABETH: Westchester, NY, May 2, 1962. Strasberg Inst.

BERRY, HALLE: Cleveland, OH, Aug. 14, 1968.
BERRY, KEN: Moline, IL, Nov. 3, 1933.
BERTINELLI, VALERIE: Wilmington, DE, Apr. 23, 1960.
BEST, JAMES: Corydon, IN, July 26, 1926.
BETTGER, LYLE: Philadelphia, PA, Feb. 13, 1915. AADA.
BEY, TURHAN: Vienna, Austria, Mar. 30, 1921.
BEYMER, RICHARD: Avoca, IA, Feb. 21, 1939.
BIALIK, MAYIM: San Diego, CA, Dec. 12, 1975.
BIEHN, MICHAEL: Anniston, AL, July 31, 1956.
BIGGERSTAFF, SEAN: Glasgow, Mar. 15, 1983.
BIGGS, JASON: Pompton Plains, NJ, May 12, 1978.
BIKEL, THEODORE: Vienna, May 2, 1924. RADA.
BILLINGSLEY, PETER: NYC, Apr. 16, 1972.
BINOCHE, JULIETTE: Paris, France, Mar. 9, 1964.
BIRCH, THORA: Los Angeles, Mar. 11, 1982.
BIRKIN, JANE: London, Dec. 14, 1947.
BIRNEY, DAVID: Washington, DC, Apr. 23, 1939. Dartmouth, UCLA.
BIRNEY, REED: Alexandria, VA, Sept. 11, 1954. Boston U.
BISHOP, JOEY (Joseph Abraham Gotlieb): Bronx, NY, Feb. 3, 1918.
BISHOP, JULIE (Jacqueline Wells): Denver, CO, Aug. 30, 1917. Westlake School.
BISHOP, KEVIN: Kent, Eng., Sept. 18, 1980.
BISSET, JACQUELINE: Waybridge, England, Sept. 13, 1944.
BLACK, JACK: Edmonton, Alberta, Canada, Apr. 7, 1969.
BLACK, KAREN (Ziegler): Park Ridge, IL, July 1, 1942. Northwestern.
BLACK, LUCAS: Danville, AL, Nov. 29, 1982.
BLACKMAN, HONOR: London, Aug. 22, 1926.
BLADES, RUBEN: Panama City, July 16, 1948. Harvard.
BLAIR, BETSY (Betsy Boger): NYC, Dec. 11, 1923.
BLAIR, JANET (Martha Jane Lafferty): Blair, PA, Apr. 23, 1921.
BLAIR, LINDA: Westport, CT, Jan. 22, 1959.
BLAIR, SELMA: Southfield, MI, June 23, 1972.
BLAKE, ROBERT (Michael Gubitosi): Nutley, NJ, Sept. 18, 1933.
BLAKELY, SUSAN: Frankfurt, Germany, Sept. 7, 1950. U TX.
BLAKLEY, RONEE: Stanley, ID, 1946. Stanford U.
BLANCHETT, CATE: Melbourne, Australia, May 14, 1969.
BLETHYN, BRENDA: Ramsgate, Kent, Eng., Feb. 20, 1946.
BLOOM, CLAIRE: London, Feb. 15, 1931. Badminton School.
BLOOM, ORLANDO: Canterbury, Eng., Jan. 13, 1977.
BLOOM, VERNA: Lynn, MA, Aug. 7, 1939. Boston U.
BLOUNT, LISA: Fayettville, AK, July 1, 1957. UAk.
BLUM, MARK: Newark, NJ, May 14, 1950. UMinn.
BLYTH, ANN: Mt. Kisco, NY, Aug. 16, 1928. New Waybum Dramatic School.
BOCHNER, HART: Toronto, Canada, Oct. 3, 1956. U San Diego.
BOCHNER, LLOYD: Toronto, Canada, July 29, 1924.
BOGOSIAN, ERIC: Woburn, MA, Apr. 24, 1953. Oberlin College.
BOHRINGER, RICHARD: Paris, France, Jan. 16, 1941.
BOLKAN, FLORINDA (Florinda Soares Bulcao): Ceara, Brazil, Feb. 15, 1941.
BOLOGNA, JOSEPH: Brooklyn, NY, Dec. 30, 1938. Brown U.
BOND, DEREK: Glasgow, Scotland, Jan. 26, 1920. Askes School.
BONET, LISA: San Francisco, CA, Nov. 16, 1967.
BONHAM-CARTER, HELENA: London, England, May 26, 1966.
BOONE, PAT: Jacksonville, FL, June 1, 1934. Columbia U.
BOOTHE, JAMES: Croydon, England, Dec.19, 1930.
BOOTHE, POWERS: Snyder, TX, June 1, 1949. So. Methodist U.
BORGNINE, ERNEST (Borgnino): Hamden, CT, Jan. 24, 1917. Randall School.
BOSCO, PHILIP: Jersey City, NJ, Sept. 26, 1930. CatholicU.
BOSLEY, TOM: Chicago, IL, Oct. 1, 1927. DePaul U.
BOSTWICK, BARRY: San Mateo, CA, Feb. 24, 1945. NYU.
BOTTOMS, JOSEPH: Santa Barbara, CA, Aug. 30, 1954.
BOTTOMS, SAM: Santa Barbara, CA, Oct. 17, 1955.
BOTTOMS, TIMOTHY: Santa Barbara, CA, Aug. 30, 1951.
BOULTING, INGRID: Transvaal, So. Africa, 1947.

BOUTSIKARIS, DENNIS: Newark, NJ, Dec. 21, 1952. CatholicU.
BOWIE, DAVID (David Robert Jones): Brixton, South London, England, Jan. 8, 1947.
BOWKER, JUDI: Shawford, England, Apr. 6, 1954.
BOXLEITNER, BRUCE: Elgin, IL, May 12, 1950.
BOYD, BILLY: Glasgow, Scotland, Aug. 28, 1968.
BOYLE, LARA FLYNN: Davenport, IA, Mar. 24, 1970.
BOYLE, PETER: Philadelphia, PA, Oct. 18, 1933. LaSalle College.
BRACCO, LORRAINE: Brooklyn, NY, 1955.
BRADFORD, JESSE: Norwalk, CT, May 27, 1979.
BRAEDEN, ERIC (Hans Gudegast): Kiel, Germany, Apr. 3, 1942.
BRAGA, SONIA: Maringa, Brazil, June 8, 1950.
BRANAGH, KENNETH: Belfast, No. Ireland, Dec. 10, 1960.
BRANDAUER, KLAUS MARIA: Altaussee, Austria, June 22, 1944.
BRANDIS, JONATHAN: CT, Apr. 13, 1976.
BRANDO, JOCELYN: San Francisco, Nov. 18, 1919. Lake Forest College, AADA.
BRANDO, MARLON: Omaha, NB, Apr. 3, 1924. New School.
BRANDON, CLARK: NYC, Dec. 13, 1958.
BRANDON, MICHAEL (Feldman): Brooklyn, NY, Apr. 20, 1945.
BRANTLEY, BETSY: Rutherfordton, NC, Sept. 20, 1955. London Central Sch. of Drama.
BRATT, BENJAMIN: San Francisco, Dec. 16, 1963.
BRENNAN, EILEEN: Los Angeles, CA, Sept. 3, 1935. AADA.
BRENNEMAN, AMY: Glastonbury, CT, June 22, 1964.
BRIALY, JEAN-CLAUDE: Aumale, Algeria, 1933. Strasbourg Cons.
BRIDGES, BEAU: Los Angeles, Dec. 9, 1941. UCLA.
BRIDGES, JEFF: Los Angeles, Dec. 4, 1949.
BRIMLEY, WILFORD: Salt Lake City, UT, Sept. 27, 1934.
BRINKLEY, CHRISTIE: Malibu, CA, Feb. 2, 1954.
BRITT, MAY (Maybritt Wilkins): Sweden, Mar. 22, 1936.
BRITTANY, MORGAN (Suzanne Cupito): Los Angeles, Dec. 5, 1950.
BRITTON, TONY: Birmingham, England, June 9, 1924.
BROADBENT, JIM: Lincoln, England, May 24, 1959.
BRODERICK, MATTHEW: NYC, Mar. 21, 1962.
BRODY, ADRIEN: NYC, Dec. 23, 1976.
BROLIN, JAMES: Los Angeles, July 18, 1940. UCLA.
BROLIN, JOSH: Los Angeles, Feb. 12, 1968.
BROMFIELD, JOHN (Farron Bromfield): South Bend, IN, June 11, 1922. St. Mary's College.
BRON, ELEANOR: Stanmore, England, Mar. 14, 1934.
BRONSON, CHARLES (Buchinsky): Ehrenfield, PA, Nov. 3, 1920.
BROOKES, JACQUELINE: Montclair, NJ, July 24, 1930. RADA.
BROOKS, ALBERT (Einstein): Los Angeles, July 22, 1947.
BROOKS, MEL (Melvyn Kaminski): Brooklyn, NY, June 28, 1926.
BROSNAN, PIERCE: County Meath, Ireland. May 16, 1952.
BROWN, BLAIR: Washington, DC, Apr. 23, 1947. Pine Manor.
BROWN, BRYAN: Panania, Australia, June 23, 1947.
BROWN, GARY (Christian Brando): Hollywood, CA, 1958.
BROWN, GEORG STANFORD: Havana, Cuba, June 24, 1943. AMDA.
BROWN, JAMES: Desdemona, TX, Mar. 22, 1920. Baylor U.
BROWN, JIM: St. Simons Island, NY, Feb. 17, 1935. Syracuse U.
BROWNE, LESLIE: NYC, 1958.
BROWNE, ROSCOE LEE: Woodbury, NJ, May 2, 1925.
BUCHHOLZ, HORST: Berlin, Germany, Dec. 4, 1933. Ludwig Dramatic School.
BUCKLEY, BETTY: Big Spring, TX, July 3, 1947. TxCU.
BUJOLD, GENEVIEVE: Montreal, Canada, July 1, 1942.
BULLOCK, SANDRA: Arlington, VA, July 26, 1964.
BURGHOFF, GARY: Bristol, CT, May 24, 1943.
BURGI, RICHARD: Montclair, NJ, July 30, 1958.
BURKE, PAUL: New Orleans, July 21, 1926. Pasadena Playhouse.
BURNETT, CAROL: San Antonio, TX, Apr. 26, 1933. UCLA.
BURNS, CATHERINE: NYC, Sept. 25, 1945. AADA.
BURNS, EDWARD: Valley Stream, NY, Jan. 28, 1969.
BURROWS, DARREN E.: Winfield, KS, Sept. 12, 1966.

Russell Crowe

Penelope Cruz

Alan Cumming

Robert De Niro

Kirsten Dunst

Colin Firth

BURROWS, SAFFRON: London, Jan. 1, 1973.

BURSTYN, ELLEN (Edna Rae Gillhooly): Detroit, MI, Dec. 7, 1932.

BURTON, LeVAR: Los Angeles, CA, Feb. 16, 1958. UCLA.

BUSCEMI, STEVE: Brooklyn, NY, Dec. 13, 1957.

BUSEY, GARY: Goose Creek, TX, June 29, 1944.

BUSFIELD, TIMOTHY: Lansing, MI, June 12, 1957. E. Tenn. St. U.

BUTTONS, RED (Aaron Chwatt): NYC, Feb. 5, 1919.

BUZZI, RUTH: Westerly, RI, July 24, 1936. Pasadena Playhouse.

BYGRAVES, MAX: London, Oct. 16, 1922. St. Joseph's School.

BYRNE, DAVID: Dumbarton, Scotland, May 14, 1952.

BYRNE, GABRIEL: Dublin, Ireland, May 12, 1950.

BYRNES, EDD: NYC, July 30, 1933.

CAAN, JAMES: Bronx, NY, Mar. 26,1939.

CAESAR, SID: Yonkers, NY, Sept. 8, 1922.

CAGE, NICOLAS (Coppola): Long Beach, CA, Jan.7, 1964.

CAIN, DEAN (Dean Tanaka): Mt. Clemens, MI, July 31, 1966.

CAINE, MICHAEL (Maurice Micklewhite): London, Mar. 14, 1933.

CAINE, SHAKIRA (Baksh): Guyana, Feb. 23, 1947. Indian Trust College.

CALLAN, MICHAEL (Martin Calinieff): Philadelphia, Nov. 22, 1935.

CALLOW, SIMON: London, June 15, 1949. Queens U.

CAMERON, KIRK: Panorama City, CA, Oct. 12, 1970.

CAMP, COLLEEN: San Francisco, CA, 1953.

CAMPBELL, BILL: Chicago, IL, July 7, 1959.

CAMPBELL, GLEN: Delight, AR, Apr. 22, 1935.

CAMPBELL, NEVE: Guelph, Ontario, Canada, Oct. 3, 1973.

CAMPBELL, TISHA: Oklahoma City, OK, Oct. 13, 1968.

CANALE, GIANNA MARIA: Reggio Calabria, Italy, Sept. 12, 1927.

CANNON, DYAN (Samille Diane Friesen): Tacoma, WA, Jan. 4, 1937.

CAPERS, VIRGINIA: Sumter, SC, Sept. 25, 1925. Juilliard.

CAPSHAW, KATE: Ft. Worth, TX, Nov. 3, 1953. UMo.

CARA, IRENE: NYC, Mar. 18, 1958.

CARDINALE, CLAUDIA: Tunis, N. Africa. Apr. 15, 1939. College Paul Cambon.

CAREY, HARRY, JR.: Saugus, CA, May 16, 1921. Black Fox Military Academy.

CAREY, PHILIP: Hackensack, NJ, July 15, 1925. U Miami.

CARIOU, LEN: Winnipeg, Canada, Sept. 30, 1939.

CARLIN, GEORGE: NYC, May 12, 1938.

CARLYLE, ROBERT: Glasgow, Scotland, Apr. 14, 1961.

CARMEN, JULIE: Mt. Vernon, NY, Apr. 4, 1954.

CARMICHAEL, IAN: Hull, England, June 18, 1920. Scarborough College.

CARNE, JUDY (Joyce Botterill): Northampton, England, 1939. Bush-Davis Theatre School.

CARNEY, ART: Mt. Vernon, NY, Nov. 4, 1918.

CARON, LESLIE: Paris, France, July 1, 1931. Nat'l Conservatory, Paris.

CARPENTER, CARLETON: Bennington, VT, July 10, 1926. Northwestern.

CARRADINE, DAVID: Hollywood, Dec. 8, 1936. San Francisco State.

CARRADINE, KEITH: San Mateo, CA, Aug. 8, 1950. Colo. State U.

CARRADINE, ROBERT: San Mateo, CA, Mar. 24, 1954.

CARREL, DANY: Tourane, Indochina, Sept. 20, 1936. Marseilles Cons.

CARRERA, BARBARA: Managua, Nicaragua, Dec. 31, 1945.

CARRERE, TIA (Althea Janairo): Honolulu, HI, Jan. 2, 1965.

CARREY, JIM: Jacksons Point, Ontario, Canada, Jan. 17, 1962.

CARRIERE, MATHIEU: Hannover, West Germany, Aug. 2, 1950.

CARROLL, DIAHANN (Johnson): NYC, July 17, 1935. NYU.

CARROLL, PAT: Shreveport, LA, May 5, 1927. Catholic U.

CARSON, JOHN DAVID: California, Mar. 6, 1952. Valley College.

CARSON, JOHNNY: Corning, IA, Oct. 23, 1925. U of Neb.

CARSTEN, PETER (Ransenthaler): Weissenberg, Bavaria, Apr. 30, 1929. Munich Akademie.

CARTER, NELL: Birmingham, AL, Sept. 13, 1948.

CARTWRIGHT, VERONICA: Bristol, England, Apr 20, 1949.

CARUSO, DAVID: Forest Hills, NY, Jan. 7, 1956.

CARVEY, DANA: Missoula, MT, Apr. 2, 1955. SFST.CoI.

CASELLA, MAX: Washington D.C, June 6, 1967.

CASEY, BERNIE: Wyco, WV, June 8, 1939.

CASSAVETES, NICK: NYC, 1959, Syracuse U, AADA.

CASSEL, JEAN-PIERRE: Paris, France, Oct. 27, 1932.

CASSEL, SEYMOUR: Detroit, MI, Jan. 22, 1935.

CASSEL, VINCENT: Paris, Nov. 23, 1966.

CASSIDY, DAVID: NYC, Apr. 12, 1950.

CASSIDY, JOANNA: Camden, NJ, Aug. 2, 1944. Syracuse U.

CASSIDY, PATRICK: Los Angeles, CA, Jan. 4, 1961.

CATES, PHOEBE: NYC, July 16, 1962.

CATTRALL, KIM: Liverpool, England, Aug. 21, 1956. AADA.

CAULFIELD, MAXWELL: Glasgow, Scotland, Nov. 23, 1959.

CAVANI, LILIANA: Bologna, Italy, Jan. 12, 1937. U Bologna.

CAVETT, DICK: Gibbon, NE, Nov. 19, 1936.

CAVIEZEL, JIM: Mt. Vernon, WA, Sept. 26, 1968.

CHAKIRIS, GEORGE: Norwood, OH, Sept. 16, 1933.

CHAMBERLAIN, RICHARD: Beverly Hills, CA, March 31, 1935. Pomona.

CHAMPION, MARGE (Marjorie Belcher): Los Angeles, Sept. 2, 1923.

CHAN, JACKIE: Hong Kong, Apr. 7, 1954.

CHANNING, CAROL: Seattle, WA, Jan. 31, 1921. Bennington.

CHANNING, STOCKARD (Susan Stockard): NYC, Feb. 13, 1944. Radcliffe.

CHAPIN, MILES: NYC, Dec. 6, 1954. HB Studio.

CHAPLIN, BEN: London, July 31, 1970.

CHAPLIN, GERALDINE: Santa Monica, CA, July 31, 1944. Royal Ballet.

CHAPLIN, SYDNEY: Los Angeles, Mar. 31, 1926. Lawrenceville.

CHARISSE, CYD (Tula Ellice Finklea): Amarillo, TX, Mar. 3, 1922. Hollywood Professional School.

CHARLES, JOSH: Baltimore, MD, Sept. 15, 1971.

CHARLES, WALTER: East Strousburg, PA, Apr. 4, 1945. Boston U.

CHASE, CHEVY (Cornelius Crane Chase): NYC, Oct. 8, 1943.

CHAVES, RICHARD: Jacksonville, FL, Oct. 9, 1951. Occidental College.

CHAYKIN, MAURY: Canada, July 27, 1954.

CHEADLE, DON: Kansas City, MO, Nov. 29, 1964.

CHEN, JOAN (Chen Chung): Shanghai, Apr. 26, 1961. CalState.

CHER (Cherilyn Sarkisian): El Centro, CA, May 20, 1946.

CHILES, LOIS: Alice, TX, Apr. 15, 1947.

CHONG, RAE DAWN: Vancouver, Canada, Feb. 28, 1962.

CHONG, THOMAS: Edmonton, Alberta, Canada, May 24, 1938.

CHRISTIAN, LINDA (Blanca Rosa Welter): Tampico, Mexico, Nov. 13, 1923.

CHRISTIE, JULIE: Chukua, Assam, India, Apr. 14, 1941.

CHRISTOPHER, DENNIS (Carrelli): Philadelphia, PA, Dec. 2, 1955. Temple U.

CHRISTOPHER, JORDAN: Youngstown, OH, Oct. 23, 1940. Kent State.

CILENTO, DIANE: Queensland, Australia, Oct. 5, 1933. AADA.

CLARK, CANDY: Norman, OK, June 20, 1947.

CLARK, DICK: Mt. Vernon, NY, Nov. 30, 1929. Syracuse U.

CLARK, MATT: Washington, DC, Nov. 25, 1936.

CLARK, PETULA: Epsom, England, Nov. 15, 1932.

CLARK, SUSAN: Sarnid, Ont., Canada, Mar. 8, 1943. RADA.

CLARKSON, PATRICIA: New Orleans, Dec. 29, 1959.

CLAY, ANDREW DICE (Andrew Silverstein): Brooklyn, NY, Sept. 29, 1957. Kingsborough College.

CLAYBURGH, JILL: NYC, Apr. 30, 1944. Sarah Lawrence.

CLEESE, JOHN: Weston-Super-Mare, England, Oct. 27, 1939, Cambridge.

CLOSE, GLENN: Greenwich, CT, Mar. 19, 1947. William & Mary College.

CODY, KATHLEEN: Bronx, NY, Oct. 30, 1953.

COFFEY, SCOTT: HI, May 1, 1967.

COLE, GEORGE: London, Apr. 22, 1925.

COLEMAN, DABNEY: Austin, TX, Jan. 3, 1932.

COLEMAN, GARY: Zion, IL, Feb. 8, 1968.

COLEMAN, JACK: Easton, PA, Feb. 21, 1958. Duke U.

COLIN, MARGARET: NYC, May 26, 1957.

COLLET, CHRISTOPHER: NYC, Mar. 13, 1968. Strasberg Inst.

COLLETTE, TONI: Sydney, Australia, Nov. 1, 1972.

COLLINS, JOAN: London, May 21, 1933. Francis Holland School.

COLLINS, PAULINE: Devon, England, Sept. 3, 1940.

COLLINS, STEPHEN: Des Moines, IA, Oct. 1, 1947. Amherst.

COLON, MIRIAM: Ponce, PR., 1945. UPR.

COLTRANE, ROBBIE: Ruthergien, Scotland, Mar. 30, 1950.

COMBS, SEAN "PUFFY": NYC, Nov. 4, 1969.

COMER, ANJANETTE: Dawson, TX, Aug. 7, 1942. Baylor, Tex. U.

CONANT, OLIVER: NYC, Nov. 15, 1955. Dalton.

CONAWAY, JEFF: NYC, Oct. 5, 1950. NYU.

CONNELLY, JENNIFER: NYC, Dec. 12, 1970.

CONNERY, JASON: London, Jan. 11, 1963.

CONNERY, SEAN: Edinburgh, Scotland, Aug. 25, 1930.

CONNICK, HARRY, JR.: New Orleans, LA, Sept. 11, 1967.

CONNOLLY, BILLY: Glasgow, Scotland, Nov. 24, 1942.

CONNORS, MIKE (Krekor Ohanian): Fresno, CA, Aug. 15, 1925. UCLA.

CONRAD, ROBERT (Conrad Robert Falk): Chicago, IL, Mar. 1, 1935. Northwestern U.

CONSTANTINE, MICHAEL: Reading, PA, May 22, 1927.

CONTI, TOM: Paisley, Scotland, Nov. 22, 1941.

CONVERSE, FRANK: St. Louis, MO, May 22, 1938. Carnegie Tech.

CONWAY, GARY: Boston, Feb. 4, 1936.

CONWAY, KEVIN: NYC, May 29, 1942.

CONWAY, TIM (Thomas Daniel): Willoughby, OH, Dec. 15, 1933. Bowling Green State.

COOGAN, KEITH (Keith Mitchell Franklin): Palm Springs, CA, Jan. 13, 1970.

COOK, RACHAEL LEIGH: Minneapolis, MN, Oct. 4, 1979.

COOPER, BEN: Hartford, CT, Sept. 30, 1930. Columbia U.

COOPER, CHRIS: Kansas City, MO, July 9, 1951. UMo.

COOPER, JACKIE: Los Angeles, Sept. 15, 1921.

COPELAND, JOAN: NYC, June 1, 1922. Brooklyn College, RADA.

CORBETT, GRETCHEN: Portland, OR, Aug. 13, 1947. Carnegie Tech.

CORBETT, JOHN: Wheeling, WV, May 9, 1961.

CORBIN, BARRY: Dawson County, TX, Oct. 16, 1940. Texas Tech. U.

CORCORAN, DONNA: Quincy, MA, Sept. 29, 1942.

CORD, ALEX (Viespi): Floral Park, NY, Aug. 3, 1931. NYU, Actors Studio.

CORDAY, MARA (Marilyn Watts): Santa Monica, CA, Jan. 3, 1932.

CORNTHWAITE, ROBERT: St. Helens, OR, Apr. 28, 1917. USC.

CORRI, ADRIENNE: Glasgow, Scot., Nov. 13, 1933. RADA.

CORT, BUD (Walter Edward Cox): New Rochelle, NY, Mar. 29, 1950. NYU.

CORTESA, VALENTINA: Milan, Italy, Jan. 1, 1924.

COSBY, BILL: Philadelphia, PA, July 12, 1937. Temple U.

COSTER, NICOLAS: London, Dec. 3, 1934. Neighborhood Playhouse.

COSTNER, KEVIN: Lynwood, CA, Jan. 18, 1955. CalStaU.

COURTENAY, TOM: Hull, England, Feb. 25, 1937. RADA.

COURTLAND, JEROME: Knoxville, TN, Dec. 27, 1926.

COX, BRIAN: Dundee, Scotland, June 1, 1946. LAMDA.

COX, COURTENEY: Birmingham, AL, June 15, 1964.

COX, RONNY: Cloudcroft, NM, Aug. 23, 1938.

COYOTE, PETER (Cohon): NYC, Oct. 10, 1941.

CRAIG, DANIEL: Chester, England, 1968.

CRAIG, MICHAEL: Poona, India, Jan. 27, 1929.

CRAIN, JEANNE: Barstow, CA, May 25, 1925.

CRAVEN, GEMMA: Dublin, Ireland, June 1, 1950.

CRAWFORD, MICHAEL (Dumbel-Smith): Salisbury, England, Jan. 19, 1942.

CREMER, BRUNO: Saint-Mande, Val-de-Varne, France, Oct. 6, 1929.

CRENNA, RICHARD: Los Angeles, Nov. 30, 1926. USC.

CRISTAL, LINDA (Victoria Moya): Buenos Aires, Feb. 25, 1934.

CROMWELL, JAMES: Los Angeles, CA, Jan. 27, 1940.

CRONYN, HUME (Blake): Ontario, Canada, July 18, 1911.

CROSBY, DENISE: Hollywood, CA, Nov. 24, 1957.

CROSBY, HARRY: Los Angeles, CA, Aug. 8, 1958.

CROSBY, MARY FRANCES: Los Angeles, CA, Sept. 14, 1959.

CROSS, BEN: London, Dec. 16, 1947. RADA.

CROSS, MURPHY (Mary Jane): Laurelton, MD, June 22, 1950.

CROUSE, LINDSAY: NYC, May 12, 1948. Radcliffe.

CROWE, RUSSELL: New Zealand, Apr. 7, 1964.

CROWLEY, PAT: Olyphant, PA, Sept. 17, 1932.

CRUDUP, BILLY: Manhasset, NY, July 8, 1968. UNC/Chapel Hill.

CRUISE, TOM (T. C. Mapother, IV): July 3, 1962, Syracuse, NY.

CRUZ, PENÉLOPE (P.C. Sanchez): Madrid, Spain, Apr. 28, 1974.

CRYER, JON: NYC, Apr. 16, 1965, RADA.

CRYSTAL, BILLY: Long Beach, NY, Mar. 14, 1947. Marshall U.

CULKIN, KIERAN: NYC, Sept. 30, 1982.

CULKIN, MACAULAY: NYC, Aug. 26, 1980.

CULKIN, RORY: NYC, July 21, 1989.

CULLUM, JOHN: Knoxville, TN, Mar. 2, 1930. U Tenn.

CULLUM, JOHN DAVID: NYC, Mar. 1, 1966.

CULP, ROBERT: Oakland, CA, Aug. 16, 1930. U Wash.

CUMMING, ALAN: Perthshire, Scotland, Jan. 27, 1965.

CUMMINGS, CONSTANCE: Seattle, WA, May 15, 1910.

CUMMINGS, QUINN: Hollywood, Aug. 13, 1967.

CUMMINS, PEGGY: Prestatyn, N. Wales, Dec. 18, 1926. Alexandra School.

CURRY, TIM: Cheshire, England, Apr. 19, 1946. Birmingham U.

CURTIN, JANE: Cambridge, MA, Sept. 6, 1947.

CURTIS, JAMIE LEE: Los Angeles, CA, Nov. 22, 1958.

CURTIS, TONY (Bernard Schwartz): NYC, June 3, 1924.

CUSACK, JOAN: Evanston, IL, Oct. 11, 1962.

CUSACK, JOHN: Chicago, IL, June 28, 1966.

CUSACK, SINEAD: Dalkey, Ireland, Feb. 18, 1948.

DAFOE, WILLEM: Appleton, WI, July 22, 1955.

DAHL, ARLENE: Minneapolis, Aug. 11, 1928. U Minn.
DALE, JIM: Rothwell, England, Aug. 15, 1935.
DALLESANDRO, JOE: Pensacola, FL, Dec. 31, 1948.
DALTON, TIMOTHY: Colwyn Bay, Wales, Mar. 21, 1946. RADA.
DALTREY, ROGER: London, Mar. 1, 1944.
DALY, TIM: NYC, Mar. 1, 1956. Bennington College.
DALY, TYNE: Madison, WI, Feb. 21, 1947. AMDA.
DAMON, MATT: Cambridge, MA, Oct. 8, 1970.
DAMONE, VIC (Vito Farinola): Brooklyn, NY, June 12, 1928.
DANCE, CHARLES: Plymouth, England, Oct. 10, 1946.
DANES, CLAIRE: New York, NY, Apr. 12, 1979.
D'ANGELO, BEVERLY: Columbus, OH, Nov. 15, 1953.
DANGERFIELD, RODNEY (Jacob Cohen): Babylon, NY, Nov. 22, 1921.
DANIELS, JEFF: Athens, GA, Feb. 19, 1955. EMichSt.
DANIELS, WILLIAM: Brooklyn, NY, Mar. 31, 1927. Northwestern.
DANNER, BLYTHE: Philadelphia, PA, Feb. 3, 1944. Bard College.
DANNING, SYBIL (Sybille Johanna Danninger): Vienna, Austria, May 4, 1949.
DANSON, TED: San Diego, CA, Dec. 29, 1947. Stanford, Carnegie Tech.
DANTE, MICHAEL (Ralph Vitti): Stamford, CT, 1935. U Miami.
DANZA, TONY: Brooklyn, NY, Apr. 21, 1951. UDubuque.
D'ARBANVILLE-QUINN, PATTI: NYC, May 25, 1951.
DARBY, KIM (Deborah Zerby): North Hollywood, CA, July 8, 1948.
DARCEL, DENISE (Denise Billecard): Paris, France, Sept. 8, 1925. U Dijon.
DARREN, JAMES: Philadelphia, PA, June 8, 1936. Stella Adler School.
DARRIEUX, DANIELLE: Bordeaux, France, May 1, 1917. Lycee LaTour.
DAVENPORT, NIGEL: Cambridge, England, May 23, 1928. Trinity College.
DAVID, KEITH: NYC, June 4, 1954. Juilliard.
DAVIDOVICH, LOLITA: Toronto, Ontario, Canada, July 15, 1961.
DAVIDSON, JAYE: Riverside, CA, 1968.
DAVIDSON, JOHN: Pittsburgh, Dec. 13, 1941. Denison U.
DAVIES, JEREMY (Boring): Rockford, IA, Oct. 28, 1969.
DAVIS, CLIFTON: Chicago, IL, Oct. 4, 1945. Oakwood College.
DAVIS, GEENA: Wareham, MA, Jan. 21, 1957.
DAVIS, HOPE: Tenafly, NJ, Mar. 23, 1964.
DAVIS, JUDY: Perth, Australia, Apr. 23, 1955.
DAVIS, MAC: Lubbock, TX, Jan. 21,1942.
DAVIS, NANCY (Anne Frances Robbins): NYC, July 6, 1921. Smith College.
DAVIS, OSSIE: Cogdell, GA, Dec. 18, 1917. Howard U.
DAVIS, SAMMI: Kidderminster, Worcestershire, England, June 21, 1964.
DAVISON, BRUCE: Philadelphia, PA, June 28, 1946.
DAWBER, PAM: Detroit, MI, Oct. 18, 1954.
DAY, DORIS (Doris Kappelhoff): Cincinnati, Apr. 3, 1924.
DAY, LARAINE (Johnson): Roosevelt, UT, Oct. 13, 1917.
DAY-LEWIS, DANIEL: London, Apr. 29, 1957. Bristol Old Vic.
DAYAN, ASSI: Israel, Nov. 23, 1945. U Jerusalem.
DEAKINS, LUCY: NYC, 1971.
DEAN, JIMMY: Plainview, TX, Aug. 10, 1928.
DEAN, LOREN: Las Vegas, NV, July 31, 1969.
DeCARLO, YVONNE (Peggy Yvonne Middleton): Vancouver, B.C., Canada, Sept. 1, 1922. Vancouver School of Drama.
DEE, FRANCES: Los Angeles, Nov. 26, 1907. Chicago U.
DEE, JOEY (Joseph Di Nicola): Passaic, NJ, June 11, 1940. Patterson State College.
DEE, RUBY: Cleveland, OH, Oct. 27, 1924. Hunter College.
DEE, SANDRA (Alexandra Zuck): Bayonne, NJ, Apr. 23, 1942.
DeGENERES, ELLEN: New Orleans, LA, Jan. 26, 1958.
DeHAVEN, GLORIA: Los Angeles, July 23, 1923.

DeHAVILLAND, OLIVIA: Tokyo, Japan, July 1, 1916. Notre Dame Convent School.
DELAIR, SUZY (Suzanne Delaire): Paris, France, Dec. 31, 1916.
DELANY, DANA: NYC, March 13, 1956. Wesleyan U.
DELON, ALAIN: Sceaux, France, Nov. 8, 1935.
DELORME, DANIELE: Paris, France, Oct. 9, 1926. Sorbonne.
DELPY, JULIE: Paris. Dec, 21, 1969.
DEL TORO, BENICIO: Santurce, Puerto Rico, Feb. 19, 1967.
DeLUISE, DOM: Brooklyn, NY, Aug. 1, 1933. Tufts College.
DeLUISE, PETER: NYC, Nov. 6, 1966.
DEMONGEOT, MYLENE: Nice, France, Sept. 29, 1938.
DeMORNAY, REBECCA: Los Angeles, Aug. 29, 1962. Strasberg Inst.
DEMPSEY, PATRICK: Lewiston, ME, Jan. 13, 1966.
DeMUNN, JEFFREY: Buffalo, NY, Apr. 25, 1947. Union College.
DENCH, JUDI: York, England, Dec. 9, 1934.
DENEUVE, CATHERINE: Paris, France, Oct. 22, 1943.
De NIRO, ROBERT: NYC, Aug. 17, 1943. Stella Adler.
DENNEHY, BRIAN: Bridgeport, CT, Jul. 9, 1938. Columbia.
DENVER, BOB: New Rochelle, NY, Jan. 9, 1935.
DEPARDIEU, GÉRARD: Chateauroux, France, Dec. 27, 1948.
DEPP, JOHNNY: Owensboro, KY, June 9, 1963.
DEREK, BO (Mary Cathleen Collins): Long Beach, CA, Nov. 20, 1956.
DERN, BRUCE: Chicago, IL, June 4, 1936. UPA.
DERN, LAURA: Los Angeles, Feb. 10, 1967.
DeSALVO, ANNE: Philadelphia, Apr. 3, 1949.
DESCHANEL, ZOOEY: Los Angeles, Jan. 17, 1980.
DEVANE, WILLIAM: Albany, NY, Sept. 5, 1939.
DeVITO, DANNY: Asbury Park, NJ, Nov. 17, 1944.
DEY, SUSAN: Pekin, IL, Dec. 10, 1953.
DeYOUNG, CLIFF: Los Angeles, CA, Feb. 12, 1945. Cal State.
DIAMOND, NEIL: NYC, Jan. 24, 1941. NYU.
DIAZ, CAMERON: Long Beach, CA, Aug. 30, 1972.
DiCAPRIO, LEONARDO: Hollywood, CA, Nov.11, 1974.
DICKINSON, ANGIE (Angeline Brown): Kulm, ND, Sept. 30, 1932. Glendale College.
DIESEL, VIN (Mark Vincent): NYC, July 18, 1967.
DIGGS, TAYE (Scott Diggs): Rochester, NY, Jan. 2, 1972.
DILLER, PHYLLIS (Driver): Lima, OH, July 17, 1917. Bluffton College.
DILLMAN, BRADFORD: San Francisco, Apr. 14, 1930. Yale.
DILLON, KEVIN: Mamaroneck, NY, Aug. 19, 1965.
DILLON, MATT: Larchmont, NY, Feb. 18, 1964. AADA.
DILLON, MELINDA: Hope, AR, Oct. 13, 1939. Goodman Theatre School.
DIXON, DONNA: Alexandria, VA, July 20, 1957.
DOBSON, KEVIN: NYC, Mar. 18, 1944.
DOBSON, TAMARA: Baltimore, MD, May 14, 1947. MD Inst. of Art.
DOHERTY, SHANNEN: Memphis, TN, Apr. 12, 1971.
DOLAN, MICHAEL: Oklahoma City, OK, June 21, 1965.
DONAT, PETER: Nova Scotia, Jan. 20, 1928. Yale.
DONNELLY, DONAL: Bradford, England, July 6, 1931.
D'ONOFRIO, VINCENT: Brooklyn, NY, June 30, 1959.
DONOHOE, AMANDA: London, June 29 1962.
DONOVAN, MARTIN: Reseda, CA, Aug. 19, 1957.
DONOVAN, TATE: NYC, Sept. 25, 1963.
DOOHAN, JAMES: Vancouver, BC, Mar. 3, 1920. Neighborhood Playhouse.
DOOLEY, PAUL: Parkersburg WV, Feb. 22, 1928. U WV.
DORFF, STEPHEN: Atlanta, GA, July 29, 1973.
DOUG, DOUG E. (Douglas Bourne): Brooklyn, NY, Jan. 7, 1970.
DOUGLAS, DONNA (Dorothy Bourgeois): Baywood, LA, Sept. 26, 1935.
DOUGLAS, ILLEANA: MA, July 25, 1965.
DOUGLAS, KIRK (Issur Danielovitch): Amsterdam, NY, Dec. 9, 1916. St. Lawrence U.
DOUGLAS, MICHAEL: New Brunswick, NJ, Sept. 25, 1944. U Cal.
DOUGLASS, ROBYN: Sendai, Japan, June 21, 1953. UCDavis.

DOURIF, BRAD: Huntington, WV, Mar. 18, 1950. Marshall U.

DOWN, LESLEY-ANNE: London, Mar. 17, 1954.

DOWNEY, ROBERT, JR.: NYC, Apr. 4, 1965.

DRAKE, BETSY: Paris, France, Sept. 11, 1923.

DRESCHER, FRAN: Queens, NY, Sept. 30, 1957.

DREW, ELLEN (formerly Terry Ray): Kansas City, MO, Nov. 23, 1915.

DREYFUSS, RICHARD: Brooklyn, NY, Oct. 19, 1947.

DRILLINGER, BRIAN: Brooklyn, NY, June 27, 1960. SUNY/Purchase.

DRIVER, MINNIE (Amelia Driver): London, Jan. 31, 1971.

DUCHOVNY, DAVID: NYC, Aug. 7, 1960. Yale.

DUDIKOFF, MICHAEL: Torrance, CA, Oct. 8, 1954.

DUGAN, DENNIS: Wheaton, IL, Sept. 5, 1946.

DUKAKIS, OLYMPIA: Lowell, MA, June 20, 1931.

DUKE, BILL: Poughkeepsie, NY, Feb. 26, 1943. NYU.

DUKE, PATTY (Anna Marie): NYC, Dec. 14, 1946.

DULLEA, KEIR: Cleveland, NJ, May 30, 1936. SF State College.

DUNAWAY, FAYE: Bascom, FL, Jan. 14, 1941. Fla. U.

DUNCAN, SANDY: Henderson, TX, Feb. 20, 1946. Len Morris College.

DUNNE, GRIFFIN: NYC, June 8, 1955. Neighborhood Playhouse.

DUNST, KIRSTEN: Point Pleasant, NJ, Apr. 30, 1982.

DUPEREY, ANNY: Paris, France, June 28, 1947.

DURBIN, DEANNA (Edna): Winnipeg, Canada, Dec. 4, 1921.

DURNING, CHARLES S.: Highland Falls, NY, Feb. 28, 1923. NYU.

DUSHKU, ELIZA: Boston, Dec. 30, 1980.

DUSSOLLIER, ANDRÉ: Annecy, France, Feb. 17, 1946.

DUTTON, CHARLES: Baltimore, MD, Jan. 30, 1951. Yale.

DUVALL, ROBERT: San Diego, CA, Jan. 5, 1931. Principia College.

DUVALL, SHELLEY: Houston, TX, July 7, 1949.

DYSART, RICHARD: Brighton, ME, Mar. 30, 1929.

DZUNDZA, GEORGE: Rosenheim, Germ., July 19, 1945.

EASTON, ROBERT: Milwaukee, WI, Nov. 23, 1930. U Texas.

EASTWOOD, CLINT: San Francisco, May 31, 1931. LACC.

EATON, SHIRLEY: London, 1937. Aida Foster School.

EBSEN, BUDDY (Christian, Jr.): Belleville, IL, Apr. 2, 1910. U Fla.

ECKEMYR, AGNETA: Karlsborg, Sweden, July 2. Actors Studio.

EDELMAN, GREGG: Chicago, IL, Sept. 12, 1958. Northwestern U.

EDEN, BARBARA (Huffman): Tucson, AZ, Aug. 23, 1934.

EDWARDS, ANTHONY: Santa Barbara, CA, July 19, 1962. RADA.

EDWARDS, LUKE: Nevada City, CA, Mar. 24, 1980.

EGGAR, SAMANTHA: London, Mar. 5, 1939.

EICHHORN, LISA: Reading, PA, Feb. 4, 1952. Queens Ont. U RADA.

EIKENBERRY, JILL: New Haven, CT, Jan. 21, 1947.

EILBER, JANET: Detroit, MI, July 27, 1951. Juilliard.

EKBERG, ANITA: Malmo, Sweden, Sept. 29, 1931.

EKLAND, BRITT: Stockholm, Sweden, Oct. 6, 1942.

ELDARD, RON: Long Island, NY, Feb. 20, 1965.

ELFMAN, JENNA (Jennifer Mary Batula): Los Angeles, Sept. 30, 1971.

ELIZONDO, HECTOR: NYC, Dec. 22, 1936.

ELLIOTT, ALISON: San Francisco, CA, May 19, 1970.

ELLIOTT, CHRIS: NYC, May 31, 1960.

ELLIOTT, PATRICIA: Gunnison, CO, July 21, 1942. UCol.

ELLIOTT, SAM: Sacramento, CA, Aug. 9, 1944. U Ore.

ELWES, CARY: London, Oct. 26, 1962.

ELY, RON (Ronald Pierce): Hereford, TX, June 21, 1938.

EMBRY, ETHAN (Ethan Randall): Huntington Beach, CA, June 13, 1978.

ENGLUND, ROBERT: Glendale, CA, June 6, 1949.

EPPS, OMAR: Brooklyn, July 23, 1973.

ERBE, KATHRYN: Newton, MA, July 2, 1966.

ERDMAN, RICHARD: Enid, OK, June 1, 1925.

ERICSON, JOHN: Dusseldorf, Ger., Sept. 25, 1926. AADA.

ERMEY, R. LEE (Ronald): Emporia, KS, Mar. 24, 1944.

ESMOND, CARL (Willy Eichberger): Vienna, June 14, 1906. U Vienna.

ESPOSITO, GIANCARLO: Copenhagen, Denmark, Apr. 26, 1958.

ESTEVEZ, EMILIO: NYC, May 12, 1962.

ESTRADA, ERIK: NYC, Mar. 16, 1949.

EVANS, JOSH: NYC, Jan. 16, 1971.

EVANS, LINDA (Evanstad): Hartford, CT, Nov. 18, 1942.

EVERETT, CHAD (Ray Cramton): South Bend, IN, June 11, 1936.

EVERETT, RUPERT: Norfolk, England, 1959.

EVIGAN, GREG: South Amboy, NJ, Oct. 14, 1953.

FABARES, SHELLEY: Los Angeles, Jan. 19, 1944.

FABIAN (Fabian Forte): Philadelphia, Feb. 6, 1943.

FABRAY, NANETTE (Ruby Nanette Fabares): San Diego, Oct. 27, 1920.

FAHEY, JEFF: Olean, NY, Nov. 29, 1956.

FAIRCHILD, MORGAN (Patsy McClenny): Dallas, TX, Feb. 3, 1950. UCLA.

FALCO, EDIE: Brooklyn, July 5, 1963.

FALK, PETER: NYC, Sept. 16, 1927. New School.

FARENTINO, JAMES: Brooklyn, NY, Feb. 24, 1938. AADA.

FARGAS, ANTONIO: Bronx, NY, Aug. 14, 1946.

FARINA, DENNIS: Chicago, IL, Feb. 29, 1944.

FARINA, SANDY (Sandra Feldman): Newark, NJ, 1955.

FARR, FELICIA: Westchester, NY, Oct. 4. 1932. Penn State College.

FARRELL, COLIN: Castleknock, Ireland, Mar. 31, 1976.

FARROW, MIA (Maria): Los Angeles, Feb. 9, 1945.

FAULKNER, GRAHAM: London, Sept. 26, 1947. Webber-Douglas.

FAVREAU, JON: Queens, NY, Oct. 16, 1966.

FAWCETT, FARRAH: Corpus Christie, TX, Feb. 2, 1947. TexU.

FEINSTEIN, ALAN: NYC, Sept. 8, 1941.

FELDMAN, COREY: Encino, CA, July 16, 1971.

FELDON, BARBARA (Hall): Pittsburgh, Mar. 12, 1941. Carnegie Tech.

FELDSHUH, TOVAH: NYC, Dec. 27, 1953, Sarah Lawrence College.

FELLOWS, EDITH: Boston, May 20, 1923.

FENN, SHERILYN: Detroit, MI, Feb. 1, 1965.

FERRELL, CONCHATA: Charleston, WV, Mar. 28, 1943. Marshall U.

FERRELL, WILL: Irvine, CA, July 16, 1968.

FERRER, MEL: Elbeton, NJ, Aug. 25, 1912. Princeton U.

FERRER, MIGUEL: Santa Monica, CA, Feb. 7, 1954.

FERRIS, BARBARA: London, 1943.

FIEDLER, JOHN: Plateville, WI, Feb. 3, 1925.

FIELD, SALLY: Pasadena, CA, Nov. 6, 1946.

FIELD, SHIRLEY-ANNE: London, June 27, 1938.

FIELD, TODD (William Todd Field): Pomona, CA, Feb. 24, 1964.

FIENNES, JOSEPH: Salisbury, Wiltshire, England, May 27, 1970.

FIENNES, RALPH: Suffolk, England, Dec. 22, 1962. RADA.

FIERSTEIN, HARVEY: Brooklyn, NY, June 6, 1954. Pratt Inst.

FINCH, JON: Caterham, England, Mar. 2, 1941.

FINLAY, FRANK: Farnworth, England, Aug. 6, 1926.

FINNEY, ALBERT: Salford, Lancashire, England, May 9, 1936. RADA.

FIORENTINO, LINDA: Philadelphia, PA, Mar. 9, 1960.

FIRTH, COLIN: Grayshott, Hampshire, England, Sept. 10, 1960.

FIRTH, PETER: Bradford, England, Oct. 27, 1953.

FISHBURNE, LAURENCE: Augusta, GA, July 30, 1961.

FISHER, CARRIE: Los Angeles, CA, Oct. 21, 1956. London Central School of Drama.

FISHER, EDDIE: Philadelphia, PA, Aug. 10, 1928.

FISHER, FRANCES: Milford-on-the-Sea, Eng., May 11, 1952.

FITZGERALD, GERALDINE: Dublin, Ireland, Nov. 24, 1914. Dublin Art School.

FITZGERALD, TARA: London, Sept. 17, 1968.

FLAGG, FANNIE: Birmingham, AL, Sept. 21, 1944. UAl.

FLANAGAN, FIONNULA: Dublin, Dec. 10, 1941.

FLANNERY, SUSAN: Jersey City, NJ, July 31, 1943.

FLEMING, RHONDA (Marilyn Louis): Los Angeles, Aug. 10, 1922.

FLEMYNG, ROBERT: Liverpool, England, Jan. 3, 1912. Haileybury College.

FLETCHER, LOUISE: Birmingham, AL, July 22 1934.

FLOCKHART, CALISTA: Stockton, IL, Nov. 11, Rutgers U.

FOCH, NINA: Leyden, Holland, Apr. 20, 1924.

FOLEY, DAVE: Toronto, Canada, Jan. 4, 1963.

FOLLOWS, MEGAN: Toronto, Canada, Mar. 14, 1968.
FONDA, BRIDGET: Los Angeles, Jan. 27, 1964.
FONDA, JANE: NYC, Dec. 21, 1937. Vassar.
FONDA, PETER: NYC, Feb. 23, 1939. U Omaha.
FONTAINE, JOAN: Tokyo, Japan, Oct. 22, 1917.
FOOTE, HALLIE: NYC, 1953. UNH.
FORD, GLENN (Gwyllyn Samuel Newton Ford): Quebec, Canada, May 1, 1916.
FORD, HARRISON: Chicago, IL, July 13, 1942. Ripon College.
FOREST, MARK (Lou Degni): Brooklyn, NY, Jan. 1933.
FORLANI, CLAIRE: London, July 1, 1972.
FORREST, FREDERIC: Waxahachie, TX, Dec. 23, 1936.
FORREST, STEVE: Huntsville, TX, Sept. 29, 1924. UCLA.
FORSLUND, CONNIE: San Diego, CA, June 19, 1950. NYU.
FORSTER, ROBERT (Foster, Jr.): Rochester, NY, July 13, 1941. Rochester U.
FORSYTHE, JOHN (Freund): Penn's Grove, NJ, Jan. 29, 1918.
FORSYTHE, WILLIAM: Brooklyn, NY, June 7, 1955.
FOSSEY, BRIGITTE: Tourcoing, France, Mar. 11, 1947.
FOSTER, BEN: Boston, MA, Oct. 29, 1980.
FOSTER, JODIE (Ariane Munker): Bronx, NY, Nov. 19, 1962. Yale.
FOSTER, MEG: Reading, PA, May 14, 1948.
FOX, EDWARD: London, Apr. 13, 1937. RADA.
FOX, JAMES: London, May 19, 1939.
FOX, MICHAEL J.: Vancouver, BC, June 9, 1961.
FOX, VIVICA A.: Indianapolis, July 30, 1964.
FOXWORTH, ROBERT: Houston, TX, Nov. 1, 1941. Carnegie Tech.
FRAIN, JAMES: Leeds, England, Mar. 14, 1969.
FRAKES, JONATHAN: Bethlehem, PA, Aug. 19, 1952. Harvard.
FRANCIOSA, ANTHONY (Papaleo): NYC, Oct. 25, 1928.
FRANCIS, ANNE: Ossining, NY, Sept. 16, 1932.
FRANCIS, ARLENE (Arlene Kazanjian): Boston, Oct. 20, 1908. Finch School.
FRANCIS, CONNIE (Constance Franconero): Newark, NJ, Dec. 12, 1938.
FRANCKS, DON: Vancouver, Canada, Feb. 28, 1932.
FRANKLIN, PAMELA: Tokyo, Feb. 4, 1950.
FRANZ, ARTHUR: Perth Amboy, NJ, Feb. 29, 1920. Blue Ridge College.
FRANZ, DENNIS: Chicago, IL, Oct. 28, 1944.
FRASER, BRENDAN: Indianapolis, IN, Dec. 3, 1968.
FRAZIER, SHEILA: NYC, Nov. 13, 1948.
FRECHETTE, PETER: Warwick, RI, Oct. 1956. URI.
FREEMAN, AL, JR.: San Antonio, TX, Mar. 21, 1934. CCLA.
FREEMAN, MONA: Baltimore, MD, June 9, 1926.
FREEMAN, MORGAN: Memphis, TN, June 1, 1937. LACC.
FREWER, MATT: Washington, DC, Jan. 4, 1958, Old Vic.
FRICKER, BRENDA: Dublin, Ireland, Feb. 17, 1945.
FRIELS, COLIN: Glasgow, Sept. 25, 1952.
FRY, STEPHEN: Hampstead, London, Eng., Aug. 24, 1957.
FULLER, PENNY: Durham, NC, 1940. Northwestern U.
FUNICELLO, ANNETTE: Utica, NY, Oct. 22, 1942.
FURLONG, EDWARD: Glendale, CA, Aug. 2, 1977.
FURNEAUX, YVONNE: Lille, France, 1928. Oxford U.
GABLE, JOHN CLARK: Los Angeles, Mar. 20, 1961. Santa Monica College.
GABOR, ZSA ZSA (Sari Gabor): Budapest, Hungary, Feb. 6, 1918.
GAIL, MAX: Derfoil, MI, Apr. 5, 1943.
GAINES, BOYD: Atlanta, GA, May 11, 1953. Juilliard.
GALECKI, JOHNNY: Bree, Belgium, Apr. 30, 1975.
GALLAGHER, PETER: NYC, Aug. 19, 1955. Tufts U.
GALLIGAN, ZACH: NYC, Feb. 14, 1963. ColumbiaU.
GALLO, VINCENT: Buffalo, NY, Apr. 11, 1961.
GAM, RITA: Pittsburgh, PA, Apr. 2, 1928.

GAMBLE, MASON: Chicago, IL, Jan. 16, 1986.
GAMBON, MICHAEL: Dublin, Ireland, Oct. 19, 1940.
GANDOLFINI, JAMES: Westwood, NJ, Sept. 18, 1961.
GANZ, BRUNO: Zurich, Switzerland, Mar. 22, 1941.
GARBER, VICTOR: Montreal, Canada, Mar. 16, 1949.
GARCIA, ADAM: Wahroonga, New So. Wales, Australia, June 1, 1973.
GARCIA, ANDY: Havana, Cuba, Apr. 12, 1956. FlaInt.
GARFIELD, ALLEN (Allen Goorwitz): Newark, NJ, Nov. 22, 1939. Actors Studio.
GARFUNKEL, ART: NYC, Nov. 5, 1941.
GARLAND, BEVERLY: Santa Cruz, CA, Oct. 17, 1926. Glendale College.
GARNER, JAMES (James Baumgarner): Norman, OK, Apr. 7, 1928. Okla. U.
GARNER, JENNIFER: Houston, TX, Apr. 17, 1972.
GAROFALO, JANEANE: Newton, NJ, Sept. 28, 1964.
GARR, TERI: Lakewood, OH, Dec. 11, 1949.
GARRETT, BETTY: St. Joseph, MO, May 23, 1919. Annie Wright Seminary.
GARRISON, SEAN: NYC, Oct. 19, 1937.
GARY, LORRAINE: NYC, Aug. 16, 1937.
GAVIN, JOHN: Los Angeles, Apr. 8, 1935. Stanford U.
GAYLORD, MITCH: Van Nuys, CA, Mar. 10, 1961. UCLA.
GAYNOR, MITZI (Francesca Marlene Von Gerber): Chicago, IL, Sept. 4, 1930.
GAZZARA, BEN: NYC, Aug. 28, 1930. Actors Studio.
GEARY, ANTHONY: Coalsville, UT, May 29, 1947. UUt.
GEDRICK, JASON: Chicago, IL, Feb. 7, 1965. Drake U.
GEESON, JUDY: Arundel, England, Sept. 10, 1948. Corona.
GELLAR, SARAH MICHELLE: NYC, Apr. 14, 1977.
GEOFFREYS, STEPHEN (Miller): Cincinnati, OH, Nov. 22, 1959. NYU.
GEORGE, SUSAN: West London, England, July 26, 1950.
GERARD, GIL: Little Rock, AR, Jan. 23, 1940.
GERE, RICHARD: Philadelphia, PA, Aug. 29, 1949. U Mass.
GERROLL, DANIEL: London, Oct. 16, 1951. Central.
GERSHON, GINA: Los Angeles, June 10, 1962.
GERTZ, JAMI: Chicago, IL, Oct. 28, 1965.
GETTY, BALTHAZAR: Los Angeles, CA, Jan. 22, 1975.
GETTY, ESTELLE: NYC, July 25, 1923. New School.
GHOLSON, JULIE: Birmingham, AL, June 4, 1958.
GHOSTLEY, ALICE: Eve, MO, Aug. 14, 1926. Okla U.
GIAMATTI, PAUL: NYC, June 6, 1967.
GIANNINI, GIANCARLO: Spezia, Italy, Aug. 1, 1942. Rome Acad. of Drama.
GIBB, CYNTHIA: Bennington, VT, Dec. 14, 1963.
GIBSON, HENRY: Germantown, PA, Sept. 21, 1935.
GIBSON, MEL: Peekskill, NY, Jan. 3, 1956. NIDA.
GIBSON, THOMAS: Charleston, SC, July 3, 1962.
GIFT, ROLAND: Birmingham, England, May 28 1962.
GILBERT, MELISSA: Los Angeles, CA, May 8, 1964.
GILES, NANCY: NYC, July 17, 1960, Oberlin College.
GILLETTE, ANITA: Baltimore, MD, Aug. 16, 1938.
GILLIAM, TERRY: Minneapolis, MN, Nov. 22, 1940.
GILLIS, ANN (Alma O'Connor): Little Rock, AR, Feb. 12, 1927.
GINTY, ROBERT: NYC, Nov. 14, 1948. Yale.
GIRARDOT, ANNIE: Paris, France, Oct. 25, 1931.
GISH, ANNABETH: Albuquerque, NM, Mar. 13, 1971. DukeU.
GIVENS, ROBIN: NYC, Nov. 27, 1964.
GLASER, PAUL MICHAEL: Boston, MA, Mar. 25, 1943. Boston U.
GLASS, RON: Evansville, IN, July 10, 1945.
GLEASON, JOANNA: Winnipeg, Canada, June 2, 1950. UCLA.
GLEASON, PAUL: Jersey City, NJ, May 4, 1944.
GLENN, SCOTT: Pittsburgh, PA, Jan. 26, 1942. William and Mary College.
GLOVER, CRISPIN: NYC, Sept 20, 1964.

Adam Garcia

Andy Garcia

Gene Hackman

Josh Hartnett

Teri Hatcher

Ethan Hawke

GLOVER, DANNY: San Francisco, CA, July 22, 1947. SFStateCol.
GLOVER, JOHN: Kingston, NY, Aug. 7, 1944.
GLYNN,CARLIN: Cleveland, Oh, Feb. 19, 1940. Actors Studio.
GOLDBERG, WHOOPI (Caryn Johnson): NYC, Nov. 13, 1949.
GOLDBLUM, JEFF: Pittsburgh, PA, Oct. 22, 1952. Neighborhood Playhouse.
GOLDEN, ANNIE: Brooklyn, NY, Oct. 19, 1951.
GOLDSTEIN, JENETTE: Beverly Hills, CA, 1960.
GOLDTHWAIT, BOB: Syracuse, NY, May 1, 1962.
GOLDWYN, TONY: Los Angeles, May 20, 1960. LAMDA.
GOLINO, VALERIA: Naples, Italy, Oct. 22, 1966.
GONZALES-GONZALEZ, PEDRO: Aguilares, TX, Dec. 21, 1926.
GONZALEZ, CORDELIA: Aug. 11, 1958, San Juan, PR. UPR.
GOODALL, CAROLINE: London, Nov. 13, 1959. BristolU.
GOODING, CUBA, JR.: Bronx, N.Y., Jan. 2, 1968.
GOODMAN, DODY: Columbus, OH, Oct. 28, 1915.
GOODMAN, JOHN: St. Louis, MO, June 20, 1952.
GORDON, KEITH: NYC, Feb. 3, 1961.
GORDON-LEVITT, JOSEPH: Los Angeles, Feb. 17, 1981.
GORSHIN, FRANK: Pittsburgh, PA, Apr. 5, 1933.
GORTNER, MARJOE: Long Beach, CA, Jan. 14, 1944.
GOSS, LUKE: London, Sept. 28, 1968.
GOSSETT, LOUIS, JR.: Brooklyn, NY, May 27, 1936. NYU.
GOULD, ELLIOTT (Goldstein): Brooklyn, NY, Aug. 29, 1938. Columbia U.
GOULD, HAROLD: Schenectady, NY, Dec. 10, 1923. Cornell.
GOULD, JASON: NYC, Dec. 29, 1966.
GOULET, ROBERT: Lawrence, MA, Nov. 26, 1933. Edmonton.
GRAF, DAVID: Lancaster, OH, Apr. 16, 1950. OhStateU.
GRAFF, TODD: NYC, Oct. 22, 1959. SUNY/ Purchase.
GRAHAM, HEATHER: Milwaukee, WI, Jan. 29, 1970.
GRANGER, FARLEY: San Jose, CA, July 1, 1925.
GRANT, DAVID MARSHALL: Westport, CT, June 21, 1955. Yale.
GRANT, HUGH: London, Sept. 9, 1960. Oxford.
GRANT, KATHRYN (Olive Grandstaff): Houston, TX, Nov. 25, 1933. UCLA.
GRANT, LEE: NYC, Oct. 31, 1927. Juilliard.
GRANT, RICHARD E: Mbabane, Swaziland, May 5, 1957. Cape Town U.
GRAVES, PETER (Aurness): Minneapolis, Mar. 18, 1926. U Minn.
GRAVES, RUPERT: Weston-Super-Mare, England, June 30, 1963.
GRAY, COLEEN (Doris Jensen): Staplehurst, NB, Oct. 23, 1922. Hamline.
GRAY, LINDA: Santa Monica, CA, Sept. 12, 1940.
GRAY, SPALDING: Barrington, RI, June 5, 1941.
GRAYSON, KATHRYN (Zelma Hedrick): Winston-Salem, NC, Feb. 9, 1922.
GREEN, KERRI: Fort Lee, NJ, Jan. 14, 1967. Vassar.
GREEN, SETH: Philadelphia, PA, Feb. 8, 1974.
GREENE, ELLEN: NYC, Feb. 22, 1950. Ryder College.
GREENE, GRAHAM: Six Nations Reserve, Ontario, June 22, 1952.
GREENWOOD, BRUCE: Quebec, Canada, Aug. 12, 1956.

GREER, MICHAEL: Galesburg, IL, Apr. 20, 1943.
GREIST, KIM: Stamford, CT, May 12, 1958.
GREY, JENNIFER: NYC, Mar. 26, 1960.
GREY, JOEL (Katz): Cleveland, OH, Apr. 11, 1932.
GREY, VIRGINIA: Los Angeles, Mar. 22, 1917.
GRIECO, RICHARD: Watertown, NY, Mar. 23, 1965.
GRIEM, HELMUT: Hamburg, Germany, Apr. 6, 1932. HamburgU.
GRIER, DAVID ALAN: Detroit, MI, June 30, 1955. Yale.
GRIER, PAM: Winston-Salem, NC, May 26, 1949.
GRIFFIN, EDDIE: Kansas City, MO, July 15, 1968.
GRIFFITH, ANDY: Mt. Airy, NC, June 1, 1926. UNC.
GRIFFITH, MELANIE: NYC, Aug. 9, 1957. Pierce Col.
GRIFFITH, THOMAS IAN: Hartford, CT, Mar. 18, 1962.
GRIFFITHS, RACHEL: Melbourne, Australia, 1968.
GRIFFITHS, RICHARD: Tornaby-on-Tees, England, July 31, 1947.
GRIMES, GARY: San Francisco, June 2, 1955.
GRIMES, SCOTT: Lowell, MA, July 9, 1971.
GRIMES, TAMMY: Lynn, MA, Jan. 30, 1934. Stephens College.
GRIZZARD, GEORGE: Roanoke Rapids, NC, Apr. 1, 1928. UNC.
GRODIN, CHARLES: Pittsburgh, PA, Apr. 21, 1935.
GROH, DAVID: NYC, May 21, 1939. Brown U, LAMDA.
GROSS, MARY: Chicago, IL, Mar. 25, 1953.
GROSS, MICHAEL: Chicago, IL, June 21, 1947.
GRUFFUD, IOAN: Cardiff, Wales, Oct. 6, 1973.
GUEST, CHRISTOPHER: NYC, Feb. 5, 1948.
GUEST, LANCE: Saratoga, CA, July 21, 1960. UCLA.
GUILLAUME, ROBERT (Williams): St. Louis, MO, Nov. 30, 1937.
GULAGER, CLU: Holdenville, OK, Nov. 16 1928.
GUTTENBERG, STEVE: Massapequa, NY, Aug. 24, 1958. UCLA.
GUY, JASMINE: Boston, Mar. 10, 1964.
GYLLENHAAL, JAKE: Los Angeles, Dec. 19, 1980.
GYLLENHAAL, MAGGIE: Los Angeles, Nov. 16, 1977.
HAAS, LUKAS: West Hollywood, CA, Apr. 16, 1976.
HACK, SHELLEY: Greenwich, CT, July 6, 1952.
HACKETT, BUDDY (Leonard Hacker): Brooklyn, NY, Aug. 31, 1924.
HACKMAN, GENE: San Bernardino, CA, Jan. 30, 1930.
HAGERTY, JULIE: Cincinnati, OH, June 15, 1955. Juilliard.
HAGMAN, LARRY (Hageman): Weatherford, TX, Sept. 21, 1931. Bard.
HAID, CHARLES: San Francisco, June 2, 1943. CarnegieTech.
HAIM, COREY: Toronto, Canada, Dec. 23, 1972.
HALE, BARBARA: DeKalb, IL, Apr. 18, 1922. Chicago Academy of Fine Arts.
HALEY, JACKIE EARLE: Northridge, CA, July 14, 1961.
HALL, ALBERT: Boothton, AL, Nov. 10, 1937. Columbia.
HALL, ANTHONY MICHAEL: Boston, MA, Apr. 14, 1968.
HALL, ARSENIO: Cleveland, OH, Feb. 12, 1959.
HAMEL, VERONICA: Philadelphia, PA, Nov. 20, 1943.
HAMILL, MARK: Oakland, CA, Sept. 25, 1952. LACC.
HAMILTON, GEORGE: Memphis, TN, Aug. 12, 1939. Hackley.
HAMILTON, LINDA: Salisbury, MD, Sept. 26, 1956.
HAMLIN, HARRY: Pasadena, CA, Oct. 30, 1951.
HAMPSHIRE, SUSAN: London, May 12, 1941.

HAMPTON, JAMES: Oklahoma City, OK, July 9, 1936. NTexasStU.

HAN, MAGGIE: Providence, RI, 1959.

HANDLER, EVAN: NYC, Jan. 10, 1961. Juillard.

HANKS, COLIN: Sacramento, CA, Nov. 24, 1977.

HANKS, TOM: Concord, CA, Jul. 9, 1956. CalStateU.

HANNAH, DARYL: Chicago, IL, Dec. 3, 1960. UCLA.

HANNAH, PAGE: Chicago, IL, Apr. 13, 1964.

HARDEN, MARCIA GAY: LaJolla, CA, Aug. 14, 1959.

HARDIN, TY (Orison Whipple Hungerford, II): NYC, June 1, 1930.

HAREWOOD, DORIAN: Dayton, OH, Aug. 6, 1950. U Cinn.

HARMON, MARK: Los Angeles, CA, Sept. 2, 1951. UCLA.

HARPER, JESSICA: Chicago, IL, Oct. 10, 1949.

HARPER, TESS: Mammoth Spring, AK, 1952. SWMoState.

HARPER, VALERIE: Suffern, NY, Aug. 22, 1940.

HARRELSON, WOODY: Midland, TX, July 23, 1961. Hanover College.

HARRINGTON, PAT: NYC, Aug. 13, 1929. Fordham U.

HARRIS, BARBARA (Sandra Markowitz): Evanston, IL, July 25, 1935.

HARRIS, ED: Tenafly, NJ, Nov. 28, 1950. Columbia.

HARRIS, JULIE: Grosse Point, MI, Dec. 2, 1925. Yale Drama School.

HARRIS, MEL (Mary Ellen): Bethlehem, PA, 1957. Columbia.

HARRIS, NEIL PATRICK: Albuquerque, NM, June 15, 1973.

HARRIS, ROSEMARY: Ashby, England, Sept. 19, 1930. RADA.

HARRISON, GREGORY: Catalina Island, CA, May 31, 1950. Actors Studio.

HARRISON, NOEL: London, Jan. 29, 1936.

HARROLD, KATHRYN: Tazewell, VA, Aug. 2, 1950. Mills College.

HARRY, DEBORAH: Miami, IL, July 1, 1945.

HART, IAN: Liverpool, England, Oct. 8, 1964.

HART, ROXANNE: Trenton, NJ, July 27, 1952, Princeton.

HARTLEY, MARIETTE: NYC, June 21, 1941.

HARTMAN, DAVID: Pawtucket, RI, May 19, 1935. Duke U.

HARTNETT, JOSH: San Francisco, July 21, 1978.

HASSETT, MARILYN: Los Angeles, CA, Dec. 17, 1947.

HATCHER, TERI: Sunnyvale, CA, Dec. 8, 1964.

HATOSY, SHAWN: Fredrick, MD, Dec. 29, 1975.

HAUER, RUTGER: Amsterdam, Holland, Jan. 23, 1944.

HAUSER, COLE: Santa Barbara, CA, Mar. 22, 1975.

HASUER, WINGS (Gerald Dwight Hauser): Hollywood, CA, Dec. 12, 1947.

HAVER, JUNE: Rock Island, IL, June 10, 1926.

HAVOC, JUNE (Hovick): Seattle, WA, Nov. 8, 1916.

HAWKE, ETHAN: Austin, TX, Nov. 6, 1970.

HAWN, GOLDIE: Washington, DC, Nov. 21, 1945.

HAYEK, SALMA: Coatzacoalcos, Veracruz, Mexico, Sept. 2, 1968.

HAYES, ISAAC: Covington, TN, Aug. 20, 1942.

HAYS, ROBERT: Bethesda, MD, July 24, 1947, SD State College.

HAYSBERT, DENNIS: San Mateo, CA, June 2, 1954.

HEADLY, GLENNE: New London, CT, Mar. 13, 1955. AmCollege.

HEALD, ANTHONY: New Rochelle, NY, Aug. 25, 1944. MIStateU.

HEARD, JOHN: Washington, DC, Mar. 7, 1946. Clark U.

HEATHERTON, JOEY: NYC, Sept. 14, 1944.

HECHE, ANNE: Aurora, OH, May 25, 1969.

HEDAYA, DAN: Brooklyn, NY, July 24, 1940.

HEDISON, DAVID: Providence, RI, May 20, 1929. Brown U.

HEDREN, TIPPI (Natalie): Lafayette, MN, Jan. 19, 1931.

HEGYES, ROBERT: Metuchen, NJ, May 7, 1951.

HELMOND, KATHERINE: Galveston, TX, July 5, 1934.

HEMINGWAY, MARIEL: Ketchum, ID, Nov. 22, 1961.

HEMMINGS, DAVID: Guilford, England, Nov. 18, 1941.

HEMSLEY, SHERMAN: Philadelphia, PA, Feb. 1, 1938.

HENDERSON, FLORENCE: Dale, IN, Feb. 14, 1934.

HENDRY, GLORIA: Winter Have, FL, Mar. 3, 1949.

HENNER, MARILU: Chicago, IL, Apr. 6, 1952.

HENRIKSEN, LANCE: NYC, May 5, 1940.

HENRY, BUCK (Henry Zuckerman): NYC, Dec. 9, 1930. Dartmouth.

HENRY, JUSTIN: Rye, NY, May 25, 1971.

HENSTRIDGE, NATASHA: Springdale, Newfoundland, Canada, Aug. 15, 1974.

HEPBURN, KATHARINE: Hartford, CT, May 12, 1907. Bryn Mawr.

HERRMANN, EDWARD: Washington, DC, July 21, 1943. Bucknell, LAMDA.

HERSHEY, BARBARA (Herzstein): Hollywood, CA, Feb. 5, 1948.

HESSEMAN. HOWARD: Lebanon, OR, Feb. 27, 1940.

HESTON, CHARLTON: Evanston, IL, Oct. 4, 1922. Northwestern U.

HEWITT, JENNIFER LOVE: Waco, TX, Feb. 21, 1979.

HEWITT, MARTIN: Claremont, CA, Feb. 19, 1958. AADA.

HEYWOOD, ANNE (Violet Pretty): Birmingham, England, Dec. 11, 1932.

HICKMAN, DARRYL: Hollywood, CA, July 28, 1933. Loyola U.

HICKMAN, DWAYNE: Los Angeles, May 18, 1934. Loyola U.

HICKS, CATHERINE: NYC, Aug. 6, 1951. Notre Dame.

HIGGINS, ANTHONY (Corlan): Cork City, Ireland, May 9, 1947. Birmingham Sch. of Dramatic Arts.

HIGGINS, MICHAEL: Brooklyn, NY, Jan. 20, 1921. AmThWing.

HILL, ARTHUR: Saskatchewan, Canada, Aug. 1, 1922. U Brit. College.

HILL, BERNARD: Manchester, England, Dec. 17, 1944.

HILL, STEVEN: Seattle, WA, Feb. 24, 1922. U Wash.

HILL, TERRENCE (Mario Girotti): Venice, Italy, Mar. 29, 1941. U Rome.

HILLER, WENDY: Bramhall, Cheshire, England, Aug. 15, 1912. Winceby House School.

HILLERMAN, JOHN: Denison, TX, Dec. 20, 1932.

HINDS, CIARAN: Belfast, No. Ireland, Feb. 9, 1953.

HINES, GREGORY: NYC, Feb.14, 1946.

HINGLE, PAT: Denver, CO, July 19, 1923. Tex. U.

HIRSCH, EMILE: Topanga Canyon, CA, Mar. 13, 1985.

HIRSCH, JUDD: NYC, Mar. 15, 1935. AADA.

HOBEL, MARA: NYC, June 18, 1971.

HODGE, PATRICIA: Lincolnshire, England, Sept. 29, 1946. LAMDA.

HOFFMAN, DUSTIN: Los Angeles, Aug. 8, 1937. Pasadena Playhouse.

HOFFMAN, PHILIP SEYMOUR: Fairport, NY, July 23, 1967.

HOGAN, JONATHAN: Chicago, IL, June 13, 1951.

HOGAN, PAUL: Lightning Ridge, Australia, Oct. 8, 1939.

HOLBROOK, HAL (Harold): Cleveland, OH, Feb. 17, 1925. Denison.

HOLLIMAN, EARL: Tennass Swamp, Delhi, LA, Sept. 11, 1928. UCLA.

HOLM, CELESTE: NYC, Apr. 29, 1919.

HOLM, IAN: Ilford, Essex, England, Sept. 12, 1931. RADA.

HOLMES, KATIE: Toledo, OH, Dec. 18, 1978.

HOMEIER, SKIP (George Vincent Homeier): Chicago, IL, Oct. 5, 1930. UCLA.

HOOKS, ROBERT: Washington, DC, Apr. 18, 1937. Temple.

HOPE, BOB (Leslie Townes Hope): London, May 26, 1903.

HOPKINS, ANTHONY: Port Talbot, So. Wales, Dec. 31, 1937. RADA.

HOPPER, DENNIS: Dodge City, KS, May 17, 1936.

HORNE, LENA: Brooklyn, NY, June 30, 1917.

HORROCKS, JANE: Rossendale Valley, England, Jan. 18, 1964.

HORSLEY, LEE: Muleshoe, TX, May 15, 1955.

HORTON, ROBERT: Los Angeles, July 29, 1924. UCLA.

HOSKINS, BOB: Bury St. Edmunds, England, Oct. 26, 1942.

HOUGHTON, KATHARINE: Hartford, CT, Mar. 10, 1945. Sarah Lawrence.

HOUSER, JERRY: Los Angeles, July 14, 1952. Valley, Jr. College.

HOWARD, ARLISS: Independence, MO, 1955. Columbia College.

HOWARD, KEN: El Centro, CA, Mar. 28, 1944. Yale.

HOWARD, RON: Duncan, OK, Mar. 1, 1954. USC.

HOWELL, C. THOMAS: Los Angeles, Dec. 7, 1966.

HOWELLS, URSULA: London, Sept. 17, 1922.

HOWES, SALLY ANN: London, July 20, 1930.

HOWLAND, BETH: Boston, MA, May 28, 1941.

HUBLEY, SEASON: NYC, May 14, 1951.

David Hemmings

Anthony Hopkins

Ice Cube

Mathieu Kassovitz

Chris Kattan

Ben Kingsley

HUDDLESTON, DAVID: Vinton, VA, Sept. 17, 1930.

HUDSON, ERNIE: Benton Harbor, MI, Dec. 17, 1945.

HUDSON, KATE: Los Angeles, Apr. 19, 1979.

HUGHES, BARNARD: Bedford Hills, NY, July 16, 1915. Manhattan College.

HUGHES, KATHLEEN (Betty von Gerkan): Hollywood, CA, Nov. 14, 1928. UCLA.

HULCE, TOM: Plymouth, MI, Dec. 6, 1953. N.C. Sch. of Arts.

HUNNICUT, GAYLE: Ft. Worth, TX, Feb. 6, 1943. UCLA.

HUNT, HELEN: Los Angeles, June 15, 1963.

HUNT, LINDA: Morristown, NJ, Apr. 1945. Goodman Theatre.

HUNT, MARSHA: Chicago, IL, Oct. 17, 1917.

HUNTER, HOLLY: Atlanta, GA, Mar. 20, 1958. Carnegie-Mellon.

HUNTER, TAB (Arthur Gelien): NYC, July 11, 1931.

HUPPERT, ISABELLE: Paris, France, Mar. 16, 1955.

HURLEY, ELIZABETH: Hampshire, Eng., June 10, 1965.

HURT, JOHN: Lincolnshire, England, Jan. 22, 1940.

HURT, MARY BETH (Supinger): Marshalltown, IA, Sept. 26, 1948. NYU.

HURT, WILLIAM: Washington, DC, Mar. 20, 1950. Tufts, Juilliard.

HUSSEY, RUTH: Providence, RI, Oct. 30, 1917. U Mich.

HUSTON, ANJELICA: Santa Monica, CA, July 9, 1951.

HUTTON, BETTY (Betty Thornberg): Battle Creek, MI, Feb. 26, 1921.

HUTTON, LAUREN (Mary): Charleston, SC, Nov. 17, 1943. Newcomb College.

HUTTON, TIMOTHY: Malibu, CA, Aug. 16, 1960.

HYER, MARTHA: Fort Worth, TX, Aug. 10, 1924. Northwestern U.

ICE CUBE (O'Shea Jackson): Los Angeles, June 15, 1969.

IDLE, ERIC: South Shields, Durham, England, Mar. 29, 1943. Cambridge.

INGELS, MARTY: Brooklyn, NY, Mar. 9, 1936.

IRELAND, KATHY: Santa Barbara, CA, Mar. 8, 1963.

IRONS, JEREMY: Cowes, England, Sept. 19, 1948. Old Vic.

IRONSIDE, MICHAEL: Toronto, Canada, Feb. 12, 1950.

IRVING, AMY: Palo Alto, CA, Sept. 10, 1953. LADA.

IRWIN, BILL: Santa Monica, CA, Apr. 11, 1950.

ISAAK, CHRIS: Stockton, CA, June 26, 1956. UofPacific.

IVANEK, ZELJKO: Lujubljana, Yugo., Aug. 15, 1957. Yale, LAMDA.

IVEY, JUDITH: El Paso, TX, Sept. 4, 1951.

IZZARD, EDDIE: Aden, Yemen, Feb. 7, 1962.

JACKSON, ANNE: Alleghany, PA, Sept. 3, 1926. Neighborhood Playhouse.

JACKSON, GLENDA: Hoylake, Cheshire, England, May 9, 1936. RADA.

JACKSON, JANET: Gary, IN, May 16, 1966.

JACKSON, KATE: Birmingham, AL, Oct. 29, 1948. AADA.

JACKSON, MICHAEL: Gary, IN, Aug. 29, 1958.

JACKSON, SAMUEL L.: Atlanta, Dec. 21, 1948.

JACKSON, VICTORIA: Miami, FL, Aug. 2, 1958.

JACOBI, DEREK: Leytonstone, London, Oct. 22, 1938. Cambridge.

JACOBI, LOU: Toronto, Canada, Dec. 28, 1913.

JACOBS, LAWRENCE-HILTON: Virgin Islands, Sept. 14, 1953.

JACOBY, SCOTT: Chicago, IL, Nov. 19, 1956.

JAGGER, MICK: Dartford, Kent, England, July 26, 1943.

JAMES, CLIFTON: NYC, May 29, 1921. Ore. U.

JANNEY, ALLISON: Dayton, OH, Nov. 20, 1960. RADA.

JARMAN, CLAUDE, JR.: Nashville, TN, Sept. 27, 1934.

JASON, RICK: NYC, May 21, 1926. AADA.

JEAN, GLORIA (Gloria Jean Schoonover): Buffalo, NY, Apr. 14, 1927.

JEFFREYS, ANNE (Carmichael): Goldsboro, NC, Jan. 26, 1923. Anderson College.

JEFFRIES, LIONEL: London, June 10, 1926. RADA.

JERGENS, ADELE: Brooklyn, NY, Nov. 26, 1922.

JETER, MICHAEL: Lawrenceburg, TN, Aug. 26, 1952. Memphis St.U.

JILLIAN, ANN (Nauseda): Cambridge, MA, Jan. 29, 1951.

JOHANSEN, DAVID: Staten Island, NY, Jan. 9, 1950.

JOHN, ELTON (Reginald Dwight): Middlesex, England, Mar. 25, 1947. RAM.

JOHNS, GLYNIS: Durban, S. Africa, Oct. 5, 1923.

JOHNSON, DON: Galena, MO, Dec. 15, 1950. UKan.

JOHNSON, PAGE: Welch, WV, Aug. 25, 1930. Ithaca.

JOHNSON, RAFER: Hillsboro, TX, Aug. 18, 1935. UCLA.

JOHNSON, RICHARD: Essex, England, July 30, 1927. RADA.

JOHNSON, ROBIN: Brooklyn, NY, May 29, 1964.

JOHNSON, VAN: Newport, RI, Aug. 28, 1916.

JOLIE, ANGELINA (Angelina Jolie Voight): Los Angeles, June 4, 1975.

JONES, CHRISTOPHER: Jackson, TN, Aug. 18, 1941. Actors Studio.

JONES, DEAN: Decatur, AL, Jan. 25, 1931. Actors Studio.

JONES, GRACE: Spanishtown, Jamaica, May 19, 1952.

JONES, JACK: Bel-Air, CA, Jan. 14, 1938.

JONES, JAMES EARL: Arkabutla, MS, Jan. 17, 1931. U Mich.

JONES, JEFFREY: Buffalo, NY, Sept. 28, 1947. LAMDA.

JONES, JENNIFER (Phyllis Isley): Tulsa, OK, Mar. 2, 1919. AADA.

JONES, L.Q. (Justice Ellis McQueen): Aug 19, 1927.

JONES, ORLANDO: Mobile, AL, Apr. 10, 1968.

JONES, SAM J.: Chicago, IL, Aug. 12, 1954.

JONES, SHIRLEY: Smithton, PA, March 31, 1934.

JONES, TERRY: Colwyn Bay, Wales, Feb. 1, 1942.

JONES, TOMMY LEE: San Saba, TX, Sept. 15, 1946. Harvard.

JOURDAN, LOUIS: Marseilles, France, June 19, 1920.

JOVOVICH, MILLA: Kiev, Ukraine, Dec. 17, 1975.

JOY, ROBERT: Montreal, Canada, Aug. 17, 1951. Oxford.

JUDD, ASHLEY: Los Angeles, CA, Apr. 19, 1968.

KACZMAREK, JANE: Milwaukee, WI, Dec. 21, 1955.

KANE, CAROL: Cleveland, OH, June 18, 1952.

KAPLAN, MARVIN: Brooklyn, NY, Jan. 24, 1924.

KAPOOR, SHASHI: Calcutta, India, Mar. 18, 1938.

KAPRISKY, VALERIE (Cheres): Paris, France, Aug. 19, 1962.

KARRAS, ALEX: Gary, IN, July 15, 1935.

KARTHEISER, VINCENT: Minneapolis, MN, May 5, 1979.

KASSOVITZ, MATHIEU: Paris, Aug. 3, 1967.

KATT, WILLIAM: Los Angeles, CA, Feb. 16, 1955.

KATTAN, CHRIS: Mt. Baldy, CA, Oct. 19, 1970.

KAUFMANN, CHRISTINE: Lansdorf, Graz, Austria, Jan. 11, 1945.

KAVNER, JULIE: Burbank, CA, Sept. 7, 1951. UCLA.

KAZAN, LAINIE (Levine): Brooklyn, NY, May 15, 1942.

KAZURINSKY, TIM: Johnstown, PA, March 3, 1950.

KEACH, STACY: Savannah, GA, June 2, 1941. U Cal., Yale.

KEATON, DIANE (Hall): Los Angeles, CA, Jan. 5, 1946. Neighborhood Playhouse.

KEATON, MICHAEL: Coraopolis, PA, Sept. 9, 1951. KentStateU.

KEEGAN, ANDREW: Los Angeles, Jan. 29, 1979.

KEEL, HOWARD (Harold Leek): Gillespie, IL, Apr. 13, 1919.

KEENER, CATHERINE: Miami, FL, Mar. 26, 1960.

KEESLAR, MATT: Grand Rapids, MI, Oct. 15, 1972.

KEITEL, HARVEY: Brooklyn, NY, May 13, 1939.

KEITH, DAVID: Knoxville, TN, May 8, 1954. UTN.

KELLER, MARTHE: Basel, Switzerland, 1945. Munich Stanislavsky Sch.

KELLERMAN, SALLY: Long Beach, CA, June 2, 1936. Actors Studio West.

KELLY, MOIRA: Queens, NY, Mar. 6, 1968.

KEMP, JEREMY (Wacker): Chesterfield, England, Feb. 3, 1935. Central Sch.

KENNEDY, GEORGE: NYC, Feb. 18, 1925.

KENNEDY, LEON ISAAC: Cleveland, OH, 1949.

KENSIT, PATSY: London, Mar. 4, 1968.

KERR, DEBORAH: Helensburg, Scotland, Sept. 30, 1921. Smale Ballet School.

KERR, JOHN: NYC, Nov. 15, 1931. Harvard, Columbia.

KERWIN, BRIAN: Chicago, IL, Oct. 25, 1949.

KEYES, EVELYN: Port Arthur, TX, Nov. 20, 1919.

KIDDER, MARGOT: Yellow Knife, Canada, Oct. 17, 1948. UBC.

KIDMAN, NICOLE: Hawaii, June 20, 1967.

KIEL, RICHARD: Detroit, MI, Sept. 13, 1939.

KIER, UDO: Koeln, Germany, Oct. 14, 1944.

KILMER, VAL: Los Angeles, Dec. 31, 1959. Juilliard.

KINCAID, ARON (Norman Neale Williams, III): Los Angeles, June 15, 1943. UCLA.

KING, ALAN (Irwin Kniberg): Brooklyn, NY, Dec. 26, 1927.

KING, PERRY: Alliance, OH, Apr. 30, 1948. Yale.

KINGSLEY, BEN (Krishna Bhanji): Snaiton, Yorkshire, England, Dec. 31, 1943.

KINNEAR, GREG: Logansport, IN, June 17, 1963.

KINSKI, NASTASSJA: Berlin, Ger., Jan. 24, 1960.

KIRBY, BRUNO: NYC, Apr. 28, 1949.

KIRK, TOMMY: Louisville, KY, Dec.10 1941.

KIRKLAND, SALLY: NYC, Oct. 31, 1944. Actors Studio.

KITT, EARTHA: North, SC, Jan. 26, 1928.

KLEIN, CHRIS: Hinsdale, IL, March 14, 1979.

KLEIN, ROBERT: NYC, Feb. 8, 1942. Alfred U.

KLINE, KEVIN: St. Louis, MO, Oct. 24, 1947. Juilliard.

KLUGMAN, JACK: Philadelphia, PA, Apr. 27, 1922. Carnegie Tech.

KNIGHT, MICHAEL E.: Princeton, NJ, May 7, 1959.

KNIGHT, SHIRLEY: Goessel, KS, July 5, 1937. Wichita U.

KNOX, ELYSE: Hartford, CT, Dec. 14, 1917. Traphagen School.

KOENIG, WALTER: Chicago, IL, Sept. 14, 1936. UCLA.

KOHNER, SUSAN: Los Angeles, Nov. 11, 1936. U Calif.

KORMAN, HARVEY: Chicago, IL, Feb. 15, 1927. Goodman.

KORSMO, CHARLIE: Minneapolis, MN, July, 20, 1978.

KOTEAS, ELIAS: Montreal, Quebec, Canada, 1961. AADA.

KOTTO, YAPHET: NYC, Nov. 15, 1937.

KOZAK, HARLEY JANE: Wilkes-Barre, PA, Jan. 28, 1957. NYU.

KRABBE, JEROEN: Amsterdam, The Netherlands, Dec. 5, 1944.

KRETSCHMANN, THOMAS: Dessau, E. Germany, Sept. 8, 1962.

KREUGER, KURT: St. Moritz, Switzerland, July 23, 1917. U London.

KRIGE, ALICE: Upington, So. Africa, June 28, 1955.

KRISTEL, SYLVIA: Amsterdam, The Netherlands, Sept. 28, 1952.

KRISTOFFERSON, KRIS: Brownsville, TX, June 22, 1936, Pomona College.

KRUGER, HARDY: Berlin, Germany, April 12, 1928.

KRUMHOLTZ, DAVID: NYC, May 15, 1978.

KUDROW, LISA: Encino, CA, July 30, 1963.

KURTZ, SWOOSIE: Omaha, NE, Sept. 6, 1944.

KUTCHER, ASHTON (Christopher Ashton Kutcher.): Cedar Rapids, IA, Feb. 7, 1978.

KWAN, NANCY: Hong Kong, May 19, 1939. Royal Ballet.

LaBELLE, PATTI: Philadelphia, PA, May 24, 1944.

LACY, JERRY: Sioux City, IA, Mar. 27, 1936. LACC.

LADD, CHERYL (Stoppelmoor): Huron, SD. July 12, 1951.

LADD, DIANE (Ladner): Meridian, MS, Nov. 29, 1932. Tulane U.

LAHTI, CHRISTINE: Detroit, MI, Apr. 4, 1950. U Mich.

LAKE, RICKI: NYC, Sept. 21, 1968.

LAMAS, LORENZO: Los Angeles, Jan. 28, 1958.

LAMBERT, CHRISTOPHER: NYC, Mar. 29, 1958.

LANDAU, MARTIN: Brooklyn, NY, June 20, 1931. Actors Studio.

LANDRUM, TERI: Enid, OK, 1960.

LANE, ABBE: Brooklyn, NY, Dec. 14, 1935.

LANE, DIANE: NYC, Jan. 22, 1963.

LANE, NATHAN: Jersey City, NJ, Feb. 3, 1956.

LANG, STEPHEN: NYC, July 11, 1952. Swarthmore College.

LANGE, HOPE: Redding Ridge, CT, Nov. 28, 1931. Reed College.

LANGE, JESSICA: Cloquet, MN, Apr. 20, 1949. U Minn.

LANGELLA, FRANK: Bayonne, NJ, Jan. 1, 1940. SyracuseU.

LANSBURY, ANGELA: London, Oct. 16, 1925. London Academy of Music.

LaPAGLIA, ANTHONY: Adelaide, Australia. Jan 31, 1959.

LARROQUETTE, JOHN: New Orleans, LA, Nov. 25, 1947.

LASSER, LOUISE: NYC, Apr. 11, 1939. Brandeis U.

LATIFAH, QUEEN (Dana Owens): East Orange, NJ, 1970.

LAUGHLIN, JOHN: Memphis, TN, Apr. 3.

LAUGHLIN, TOM: Minneapolis, MN, 1938.

LAUPER, CYNDI: Astoria, Queens, NYC, June 20, 1953.

LAURE, CAROLE: Montreal, Canada, Aug. 5, 1951.

LAURIE, HUGH: Oxford, Eng., June 11, 1959.

LAURIE, PIPER (Rosetta Jacobs): Detroit, MI, Jan. 22, 1932.

LAUTER, ED: Long Beach, NY, Oct. 30, 1940.

LAVIN, LINDA: Portland, ME, Oct. 15 1939.

LAW, JOHN PHILLIP: Hollywood, CA, Sept. 7, 1937. Neighborhood Playhouse, U Hawaii.

LAW, JUDE: Lewisham, Eng., Dec. 29, 1972.

LAWRENCE, BARBARA: Carnegie, OK, Feb. 24, 1930. UCLA.

LAWRENCE, CAROL (Laraia): Melrose Park, IL, Sept. 5, 1935.

LAWRENCE, MARTIN: Frankfurt, Germany, Apr. 16, 1965.

LAWRENCE, VICKI: Inglewood, CA, Mar. 26, 1949.

LAWSON, LEIGH: Atherston, England, July 21, 1945. RADA.

LEACHMAN, CLORIS: Des Moines, IA, Apr. 30, 1930. Northwestern U.

LEARY, DENIS: Boston, MA, Aug. 18, 1957.

LÉAUD, JEAN-PIERRE: Paris, France, May 5, 1944.

LeBLANC, MATT: Newton, MA, July 25, 1967.

LEDGER, HEATH: Perth, Australia, Apr. 4, 1979.

LEE, CHRISTOPHER: London, May 27, 1922. Wellington College.

LEE, JASON: Huntington Beach, CA, Apr. 25, 1970.

LEE, MARK: Sydney, Australia, 1958.

LEE, MICHELE (Dusiak): Los Angeles, June 24, 1942. LACC.

LEE, SHERYL: Augsburg, Germany, Arp. 22, 1967.

LEE, SPIKE (Shelton Lee): Atlanta, GA, Mar. 20, 1957.

LEGROS, JAMES: Minneapolis, MN, Apr. 27, 1962.

LEGUIZAMO, JOHN: Columbia, July 22, 1965. NYU.

LEIBMAN, RON: NYC, Oct. 11, 1937. Ohio Wesleyan.

LEIGH, JANET (Jeanette Helen Morrison): Merced, CA, July 6, 1926. ColofPacific.

LEIGH, JENNIFER JASON: Los Angeles, Feb. 5, 1962.

Hugh Laurie   Robert Sean Leonard   Jet Li   LL Cool J   Jennifer Lopez   Andie MacDowell

Le MAT, PAUL: Rahway, NJ, Sept. 22, 1945.
LEMMON, CHRIS: Los Angeles, Jan. 22, 1954.
LENO, JAY: New Rochelle, NY, Apr. 28, 1950. Emerson College.
LENZ, KAY: Los Angeles, Mar. 4, 1953.
LENZ, RICK: Springfield, IL, Nov. 21, 1939. U Mich.
LEONARD, ROBERT SEAN: Westwood, NJ, Feb. 28, 1969.
LEONI, TÉA (Elizabeth Tea Pantaleoni): NYC, Feb. 25, 1966.
LERNER, MICHAEL: Brooklyn, NY, June 22, 1941.
LESLIE, JOAN (Joan Brodell): Detroit, Jan. 26, 1925. St. Benedict's.
LESTER, MARK: Oxford, England, July 11, 1958.
LETO, JARED: Bossier City, LA, Dec. 26, 1971.
LEVELS, CALVIN: Cleveland. OH, Sept. 30, 1954. CCC.
LEVIN, RACHEL (Rachel Chagall): NYC, Nov. 24, 1954. Goddard College.
LEVINE, JERRY: New Brunswick, NJ, Mar. 12, 1957, Boston U.
LEVY, EUGENE: Hamilton, Canada, Dec. 17, 1946. McMasterU.
LEWIS, CHARLOTTE: London, Aug.7, 1967.
LEWIS, GEOFFREY: San Diego, CA, Jan. 1, 1935.
LEWIS, JERRY (Joseph Levitch): Newark, NJ, Mar. 16, 1926.
LEWIS, JULIETTE: Los Angeles CA, June 21, 1973.
LI, JET: Beijing, China, Apr. 26, 1963.
LIGON, TOM: New Orleans, LA, Sept. 10, 1945.
LILLARD, MATTHEW: Lansing, MI, Jan. 24, 1970.
LINCOLN, ABBEY (Anna Marie Woolridge): Chicago, IL, Aug. 6, 1930.
LINDEN, HAL: Bronx, NY, Mar. 20, 1931. City College of NY.
LINDO, DELROY: London, Nov. 18, 1952.
LINDSAY, ROBERT: Ilketson, Derbyshire, England, Dec. 13, 1951, RADA.
LINN-BAKER, MARK: St. Louis, MO, June 17, 1954, Yale.
LINNEY, LAURA: New York, NY, Feb. 5, 1964.
LIOTTA, RAY: Newark, NJ, Dec. 18, 1955. UMiami.
LISI, VIRNA: Rome, Nov. 8, 1937.
LITHGOW, JOHN: Rochester, NY, Oct. 19, 1945. Harvard.
LIU, LUCY: Queens, NY, Dec. 2, 1967.
LL COOL J (James Todd Smith): Queens, NY, Jan. 14, 1968.
LLOYD, CHRISTOPHER: Stamford, CT, Oct. 22, 1938.
LLOYD, EMILY: London, Sept. 29, 1970.
LOCKE, SONDRA: Shelbyville, TN, May, 28, 1947.
LOCKHART, JUNE: NYC, June 25, 1925. Westlake School.
LOCKWOOD, GARY: Van Nuys, CA, Feb. 21, 1937.
LOGGIA, ROBERT: Staten Island, NY, Jan. 3, 1930. UMo.
LOHMAN, ALISON: Palm Springs, CA, Sept. 18, 1979.
LOLLOBRIGIDA, GINA: Subiaco, Italy, July 4, 1927. Rome Academy of Fine Arts.
LOM, HERBERT: Prague, Czechoslovakia, Jan. 9, 1917. Prague U.
LOMEZ, CELINE: Montreal, Canada, May 11, 1953.
LONE, JOHN: Hong Kong, Oct 13, 1952. AADA.
LONG, NIA: Brooklyn, NY, Oct. 30, 1970.
LONG, SHELLEY: Ft. Wayne, IN, Aug. 23, 1949. Northwestern U.
LOPEZ, JENNIFER: Bronx, NY, July 24, 1970.
LOPEZ, PERRY: NYC, July 22, 1931. NYU.

LORDS, TRACY (Nora Louise Kuzma): Steubenville, OH, May 7, 1968.
LOREN, SOPHIA (Sophia Scicolone): Rome, Italy, Sept. 20, 1934.
LOUIS-DREYFUS, JULIA: NYC, Jan. 13, 1961.
LOUISE, TINA (Blacker): NYC, Feb. 11, 1934, Miami U.
LOVE, COURTNEY (Love Michelle Harrison): San Francisco, July 9, 1965.
LOVETT, LYLE: Klein, TX, Nov. 1, 1957.
LOVITZ, JON: Tarzana, CA, July 21, 1957.
LOWE, CHAD: Dayton, OH, Jan. 15, 1968.
LOWE, ROB: Charlottesville, VA, Mar. 17, 1964.
LÖWITSCH, KLAUS: Berlin, Apr. 8, 1936, Vienna Academy.
LUCAS, LISA: Arizona, 1961.
LUCKINBILL, LAURENCE: Fort Smith, AK, Nov. 21, 1934.
LUFT, LORNA: Los Angeles, Nov. 21, 1952.
LUKE, DEREK: Jersey City, NJ, Apr. 24, 1974.
LULU (Marie Lawrie): Glasgow, Scotland, Nov. 3, 1948.
LUNA, BARBARA: NYC, Mar. 2, 1939.
LUNA, DIEGO: Mexico City, Dec. 29, 1979.
LUNDGREN, DOLPH: Stockolm, Sweden, Nov. 3, 1959. Royal Inst.
LuPONE, PATTI: Northport, NY, Apr. 21, 1949, Juilliard.
LYDON, JAMES: Harrington Park, NJ, May 30, 1923.
LYNCH, KELLY: Minneapolis, MN, Jan. 31, 1959.
LYNLEY, CAROL (Jones): NYC, Feb. 13, 1942.
LYON, SUE: Davenport, IA, July 10, 1946.
LYONNE, NATASHA (Braunstein): NYC, Apr. 4, 1979.
MacARTHUR, JAMES: Los Angeles, Dec. 8, 1937. Harvard.
MACCHIO, RALPH: Huntington, NY, Nov. 4, 1961.
MacCORKINDALE, SIMON: Cambridge, England, Feb. 12, 1953.
MACDONALD, KELLY: Glasgow, Feb. 23, 1976.
MacDOWELL, ANDIE (Rose Anderson MacDowell): Gaffney, SC, Apr. 21, 1958.
MacFADYEN, ANGUS: Scotland, Oct. 21, 1963.
MacGINNIS, NIALL: Dublin, Ireland, Mar. 29, 1913. Dublin U.
MacGRAW, ALI: NYC, Apr. 1, 1938. Wellesley.
MacLACHLAN, KYLE: Yakima, WA, Feb. 22, 1959. UWa.
MacLAINE, SHIRLEY (Beaty): Richmond, VA, Apr. 24, 1934.
MacLEOD, GAVIN: Mt. Kisco, NY, Feb. 28, 1931.
MacNAUGHTON, ROBERT: NYC, Dec. 19, 1966.
MACNEE, PATRICK: London, Feb. 1922.
MacNICOL, PETER: Dallas, TX, Apr. 10, 1954. UMN.
MacPHERSON, ELLE: Sydney, Australia, 1965.
MacVITTIE, BRUCE: Providence, RI, Oct. 14, 1956. BostonU.
MACY, W. H. (William): Miami, FL, Mar. 13, 1950. Goddard College.
MADIGAN, AMY: Chicago, IL, Sept. 11, 1950. Marquette U.
MADONNA (Madonna Louise Veronica Cicone): Bay City, MI, Aug. 16, 1958. UMi.
MADSEN, MICHAEL: Chicago, IL, Sept. 25, 1958.
MADSEN, VIRGINIA: Winnetka, IL, Sept. 11, 1963.
MAGNUSON, ANN: Charleston, WV, Jan. 4, 1956.
MAGUIRE, TOBEY: Santa Monica, CA, June 27, 1975.
MAHARIS, GEORGE: Astoria, NY, Sept. 1, 1928. Actors Studio.

Sophie Marceau

Ewan McGregor

Helen Mirren

Julianne Moore

Rita Moreno

Carrie-Anne Moss

MAHONEY, JOHN: Manchester, England, June 20, 1940, WUIll.

MAILER, STEPHEN: NYC, Mar. 10, 1966. NYU.

MAJORS, LEE: Wyandotte, MI, Apr. 23, 1940. E. Ky. State College.

MAKEPEACE, CHRIS: Toronto, Canada, Apr. 22, 1964.

MAKO (Mako Iwamatsu): Kobe, Japan, Dec. 10, 1933. Pratt.

MALDEN, KARL (Mladen Sekulovich): Gary, IN, Mar. 22, 1914.

MALKOVICH, JOHN: Christopher, IL, Dec. 9, 1953, IllStateU.

MALONE, DOROTHY: Chicago, IL, Jan. 30, 1925.

MANN, TERRENCE: KY, 1945. NCSchl Arts.

MANOFF, DINAH: NYC, Jan. 25, 1958. CalArts.

MANTEGNA, JOE: Chicago, IL, Nov. 13, 1947. Goodman Theatre.

MANZ, LINDA: NYC, 1961.

MARAIS, JEAN: Cherbourg, France, Dec. 11, 1913, St. Germain.

MARCEAU, SOPHIE (Maupu): Paris, Nov. 17, 1966.

MARCOVICCI, ANDREA: NYC, Nov. 18, 1948.

MARGULIES, JULIANNA: Spring Valley, NY, June 8, 1966.

MARIN, CHEECH (Richard): Los Angeles, July 13, 1946.

MARIN, JACQUES: Paris, France, Sept. 9, 1919. Conservatoire National.

MARINARO, ED: NYC, Mar. 31, 1950. Cornell.

MARS, KENNETH: Chicago, IL, Apr. 14, 1936.

MARSDEN, JAMES: Stillwater, OK, Sept. 18, 1973.

MARSH, JEAN: London, England, July 1, 1934.

MARSHALL, KEN: NYC, June 27, 1950. Juilliard.

MARSHALL, PENNY: Bronx, NY, Oct. 15, 1942. UN. Mex.

MARSHALL, WILLIAM: Gary, IN, Aug. 19, 1924. NYU.

MARTIN, ANDREA: Portland, ME, Jan. 15, 1947.

MARTIN, DICK: Battle Creek, MI Jan. 30, 1923.

MARTIN, GEORGE N.: NYC, Aug. 15, 1929.

MARTIN, MILLICENT: Romford, England, June 8, 1934.

MARTIN, PAMELA SUE: Westport, CT, Jan. 15, 1953.

MARTIN, STEVE: Waco, TX, Aug. 14, 1945. UCLA.

MARTIN, TONY (Alfred Norris): Oakland, CA, Dec. 25, 1913. St. Mary's College.

MASON, MARSHA: St. Louis, MO, Apr. 3, 1942. Webster College.

MASSEN, OSA: Copenhagen, Denmark, Jan. 13, 1916.

MASTERS, BEN: Corvallis, OR, May 6, 1947. UOr.

MASTERSON, MARY STUART: Los Angeles, June 28, 1966, NYU.

MASTERSON, PETER: Angleton, TX, June 1, 1934. Rice U.

MASTRANTONIO, MARY ELIZABETH: Chicago, IL, Nov. 17, 1958. UIll.

MASUR, RICHARD: NYC, Nov. 20, 1948.

MATHESON, TIM: Glendale, CA, Dec. 31, 1947. CalState.

MATHIS, SAMANTHA: NYC, May 12, 1970.

MATLIN, MARLEE: Morton Grove, IL, Aug. 24, 1965.

MATTHEWS, BRIAN: Philadelphia, Jan. 24. 1953. St. Olaf.

MAY, ELAINE (Berlin): Philadelphia, Apr. 21, 1932.

MAYO, VIRGINIA (Virginia Clara Jones): St. Louis, MO, Nov. 30, 1920.

MAYRON, MELANIE: Philadelphia, PA, Oct. 20, 1952. AADA.

MAZURSKY, PAUL: Brooklyn, NY, Apr. 25, 1930. Bklyn College.

MAZZELLO, JOSEPH: Rhinebeck, NY, Sept. 21, 1983.

McCALLUM, DAVID: Scotland, Sept. 19, 1933. Chapman College.

McCAMBRIDGE, MERCEDES: Jolliet, IL, Mar. 17, 1918. Mundelein College.

McCARTHY, ANDREW: NYC, Nov. 29, 1962, NYU.

McCARTHY, KEVIN: Seattle, WA, Feb. 15, 1914. Minn. U.

McCARTNEY, PAUL: Liverpool, England, June 18, 1942.

McCLANAHAN, RUE: Healdton, OK, Feb. 21, 1934.

McCLORY, SEAN: Dublin, Ireland, Mar. 8, 1924. U Galway.

McCLURE, MARC: San Mateo, CA, Mar. 31, 1957.

McCLURG, EDIE: Kansas City, MO, July 23, 1950.

McCORMACK, CATHERINE: Alton, Hampshire, Eng., Jan. 1, 1972.

McCOWEN, ALEC: Tunbridge Wells, England, May 26, 1925. RADA.

McCRANE, PAUL: Philadelphia, PA, Jan. 19. 1961.

McCRARY, DARIUS: Walnut, CA, May 1, 1976.

McDERMOTT, DYLAN: Waterbury, CT, Oct. 26, 1962. Neighborhood Playhouse.

McDONALD, CHRISTOPHER: NYC, Feb. 15, 1955.

McDONNELL, MARY: Wilkes Barre, PA, Apr. 28, 1952.

McDORMAND, FRANCES: Illinois, June 23, 1957.

McDOWELL, MALCOLM (Taylor): Leeds, England, June 19, 1943. LAMDA.

McELHONE, NATASCHA (Natasha Taylor): London, Mar. 23, 1971.

McENERY, PETER: Walsall, England, Feb. 21, 1940.

McENTIRE, REBA: McAlester, OK, Mar. 28, 1955. SoutheasternStU.

McGAVIN, DARREN: Spokane, WA, May 7, 1922. College of Pacific.

McGILL, EVERETT: Miami Beach, FL, Oct. 21, 1945.

McGILLIS, KELLY: Newport Beach, CA, July 9, 1957. Juilliard.

McGINLEY, JOHN C.: NYC, Aug. 3, 1959. NYU.

McGOOHAN, PATRICK: NYC, Mar. 19, 1928.

McGOVERN, ELIZABETH: Evanston, IL. July 18, 1961. Juilliard.

McGOVERN, MAUREEN: Youngstown, OH, July 27, 1949.

McGREGOR, EWAN: Perth, Scotland, March 31, 1971.

McGUIRE, BIFF: New Haven, CT, Oct. 25. 1926. Mass. Stale College.

McHATTIE, STEPHEN: Antigonish, NS, Feb. 3. Acadia U AADA.

McKEAN, MICHAEL: NYC, Oct. 17, 1947.

McKEE, LONETTE: Detroit, MI, July 22, 1955.

McKELLEN, IAN: Burnley, England, May 25, 1939.

McKENNA, VIRGINIA: London, June 7, 1931.

McKEON, DOUG: Pompton Plains, NJ, June 10, 1966.

McKUEN, ROD: Oakland, CA, Apr. 29, 1933.

McLERIE, ALLYN ANN: Grand Mere, Canada, Dec. 1, 1926.

McMAHON, ED: Detroit, MI, Mar. 6, 1923.

McNAIR, BARBARA: Chicago, IL, Mar. 4, 1939. UCLA.

McNAMARA, WILLIAM: Dallas, TX, Mar. 31, 1965.

McNICHOL, KRISTY: Los Angeles. CA, Sept. 11, 1962.

McQUEEN, ARMELIA: North Carolina, Jan. 6, 1952. Bklyn Consv.

McQUEEN, CHAD: Los Angeles, CA, Dec. 28, 1960. Actors Studio.

McRANEY, GERALD: Collins, MS, Aug. 19, 1948.

McSHANE, IAN: Blackburn, England, Sept. 29, 1942. RADA.

McTEER, JANET: York, England, May 8, 1961.

MEADOWS, JAYNE (formerly Jayne Cotter): Wuchang, China, Sept. 27, 1924. St. Margaret's.

MEANEY, COLM: Dublin, May 30, 1953.

MEARA, ANNE: Brooklyn, NY, Sept. 20, 1929.

MEAT LOAF (Marvin Lee Aday): Dallas, TX, Sept. 27, 1947.

MEDWIN, MICHAEL: London, 1925. Instut Fischer.

MEKKA, EDDIE: Worcester, MA, June 14, 1952. Boston Cons.

MELATO, MARIANGELA: Milan, Italy, Sept. 18, 1941. Milan Theatre Acad.

MEREDITH, LEE (Judi Lee Sauls): Oct. 22, 1947. AADA.

MERKERSON, S. EPATHA: Saganaw, MI, Nov. 28, 1952. Wayne St. Univ.

MERRILL, DINA (Nedinia Hutton): NYC, Dec. 29, 1925. AADA.

MESSING, DEBRA: Brooklyn, NY, Aug. 15, 1968.

METCALF, LAURIE: Edwardsville, IL, June 16, 1955., IIIStU.

METZLER, JIM: Oneonda, NY, June 23, 1955. Dartmouth.

MEYER, BRECKIN: Minneapolis, May 7, 1974.

MICHELL, KEITH: Adelaide, Australia, Dec. 1, 1926.

MIDLER, BETTE: Honolulu, HI, Dec. 1, 1945.

MILANO, ALYSSA: Brooklyn, NY, Dec. 19, 1972.

MILES, JOANNA: Nice, France, Mar. 6, 1940.

MILES, SARAH: Ingatestone, England, Dec. 31, 1941. RADA.

MILES, SYLVIA: NYC, Sept. 9, 1934. Actors Studio.

MILES, VERA (Ralston): Boise City, OK, Aug. 23, 1929. UCLA.

MILLER, ANN (Lucille Ann Collier): Chireno, TX, Apr. 12, 1919. Lawler Professional School.

MILLER, BARRY: Los Angeles, CA, Feb. 6, 1958.

MILLER, DICK: NYC, Dec. 25, 1928.

MILLER, JONNY LEE: Surrey, England, Nov. 15, 1972.

MILLER, LINDA: NYC, Sept. 16, 1942. Catholic U.

MILLER, PENELOPE ANN: Santa Monica, CA, Jan. 13, 1964.

MILLER, REBECCA: Roxbury, CT, 1962. Yale.

MILLS, DONNA: Chicago, IL, Dec. 11, 1945. UIl.

MILLS, HAYLEY: London, Apr. 18, 1946. Elmhurst School.

MILLS, JOHN: Suffolk, England, Feb. 22, 1908.

MILLS, JULIET: London, Nov. 21, 1941.

MILNER, MARTIN: Detroit, MI, Dec. 28, 1931.

MIMIEUX, YVETTE: Los Angeles, CA, Jan. 8, 1941. Hollywood High.

MINNELLI, LIZA: Los Angeles, Mar. 19, l946.

MIOU-MIOU (Sylvette Henry): Paris, France, Feb. 22, 1950.

MIRREN, HELEN (Ilynea Mironoff): London, July 26, 1946.

MITCHELL, JAMES: Sacramento, CA, Feb. 29, 1920. LACC.

MITCHELL, JOHN CAMERON: El Paso, TX, Apr. 21, 1963. NorthwesternU.

MITCHUM, JAMES: Los Angeles, CA, May 8, 1941.

MODINE, MATTHEW: Loma Linda, CA, Mar. 22, 1959.

MOFFAT, DONALD: Plymouth, England, Dec. 26, 1930. RADA.

MOFFETT, D. W.: Highland Park, IL, Oct. 26, 1954. Stanford U.

MOHR, JAY: New Jersey, Aug. 23, 1971.

MOKAE, ZAKES: Johannesburg, So. Africa, Aug. 5, 1935. RADA.

MOLINA, ALFRED: London, May 24, 1953. Guildhall.

MOLL, RICHARD: Pasadena, CA, Jan. 13, 1943.

MONAGHAN, DOMINIC: Berlin, Dec. 8, 1976.

MONK, DEBRA: Middletown, OH, Feb. 27, 1949.

MONTALBAN, RICARDO: Mexico City, Nov. 25, 1920.

MONTENEGRO, FERNADA (Arlete Pinheiro): Rio de Janeiro, Brazil, 1929.

MONTGOMERY, BELINDA: Winnipeg, Canada, July 23, 1950.

MOODY, RON: London, Jan. 8, 1924. London U.

MOOR, BILL: Toledo, OH, July 13, 1931. Northwestern.

MOORE, CONSTANCE: Sioux City, IA, Jan. 18, 1919.

MOORE, DEMI (Guines): Roswell, NM, Nov. 11, 1962.

MOORE, DICK: Los Angeles, Sept. 12, 1925.

MOORE, JULIANNE (Julie Anne Smith): Fayetteville, NC, Dec. 30, 1960.

MOORE, KIERON: County Cork, Ireland, 1925. St. Mary's College.

MOORE, MANDY: Nashua, NH, Apr. 10, 1984.

MOORE, MARY TYLER: Brooklyn, NY, Dec. 29, 1936.

MOORE, ROGER: London, Oct. 14, 1927. RADA.

MOORE, TERRY (Helen Koford): Los Angeles, Jan. 7, 1929.

MORALES, ESAI: Brooklyn, NY, Oct. 1, 1962.

MORANIS, RICK: Toronto, Canada, Apr. 18, 1954.

MOREAU, JEANNE: Paris, France, Jan. 23, 1928.

MORENO, RITA (Rosita Alverio): Humacao, P.R., Dec. 11, 1931.

MORGAN, HARRY (HENRY) (Harry Bratsburg): Detroit, Apr. 10, 1915. U Chicago.

MORGAN, MICHELE (Simone Roussel): Paris, France, Feb. 29, 1920. Paris Dramatic School.

MORIARTY, CATHY: Bronx, NY, Nov. 29, 1960.

MORIARTY, MICHAEL: Detroit, MI, Apr. 5, 1941. Dartmouth.

MORISON, PATRICIA: NYC, Mar. 19, 1915.

MORITA, NORIYUKI "PAT": Isleton, CA, June 28, 1932.

MORRIS, GARRETT: New Orleans, LA, Feb. 1, 1937.

MORRIS, HOWARD: NYC, Sept. 4, 1919. NYU.

MORROW, ROB: New Rochelle, NY, Sept. 21, 1962.

MORSE, DAVID: Hamilton, MA, Oct. 11, 1953.

MORSE, ROBERT: Newton, MA, May 18, 1931.

MORTENSEN, VIGGO: New York, NY, Oct. 20, 1958.

MORTON, JOE: NYC, Oct. 18, 1947. Hofstra U.

MORTON, SAMANTHA: Nottingham, England, 1977.

MOSES, WILLIAM: Los Angeles, Nov. 17, 1959.

MOSS, CARRIE-ANNE: Vancouver, BC, Canada, Aug. 21, 1967.

MOSTEL, JOSH: NYC, Dec. 21, 1946. Brandeis U.

MOUCHET, CATHERINE: Paris, France, 1959. Ntl. Consv.

MUELLER-STAHL, ARMIN: Tilsit, East Prussia, Dec. 17, 1930.

MULDAUR, DIANA: NYC, Aug. 19, 1938. Sweet Briar College.

MULGREW, KATE: Dubuque, IA, Apr. 29, 1955. NYU.

MULHERN, MATT: Philadelphia, PA, July 21, 1960. Rutgers Univ.

MULL, MARTIN: N. Ridgefield, OH, Aug. 18, 1941. RISch. of Design.

MULRONEY, DERMOT: Alexandria, VA, Oct. 31, 1963. Northwestern.

MUMY, BILL (Charles William Mumy, Jr.): San Gabriel, CA, Feb. 1, 1954.

MUNIZ, FRANKIE: Ridgewood, NJ, Dec. 5, 1985.

MURPHY, BRITTANY: Atlanta, GA, Nov. 10, 1977.

MURPHY, DONNA: Queens, NY, March 7, 1958.

MURPHY, EDDIE: Brooklyn, NY, Apr. 3, 1961.

MURPHY, MICHAEL: Los Angeles, CA, May 5, 1938. UAz.

MURRAY, BILL: Wilmette, IL, Sept. 21, 1950. Regis College.

MURRAY, DON: Hollywood, CA, July 31, 1929.

MUSANTE, TONY: Bridgeport, CT, June 30, 1936. Oberlin College.

MYERS, MIKE: Scarborough, Canada, May 25, 1963.

NABORS, JIM: Sylacauga, GA, June 12, 1932.

NADER, MICHAEL: Los Angeles, CA, 1945.

NAMATH, JOE: Beaver Falls, PA, May 31, 1943. UAla.

NAUGHTON, DAVID: Hartford, CT, Feb. 13, 1951.

NAUGHTON, JAMES: Middletown, CT, Dec. 6, 1945.

NEAL, PATRICIA: Packard, KY, Jan. 20, 1926. Northwestern U.

NEESOM, LIAM: Ballymena, Northern Ireland, June 7, 1952.

NEFF, HILDEGARDE (Hildegard Knef): Ulm, Germany, Dec. 28, 1925. Berlin Art Acad.

NEILL, SAM: No. Ireland, Sept. 14, 1947. U Canterbury.

NELLIGAN, KATE: London, Ont., Canada, Mar. 16, 1951. U Toronto.

NELSON, BARRY (Robert Nielsen): Oakland, CA, Apr. 16, 1920.

NELSON, CRAIG T.: Spokane, WA, Apr. 4, 1946.

NELSON, DAVID: NYC, Oct. 24, 1936. USC.

NELSON, JUDD: Portland, ME, Nov. 28, 1959, Haverford College.

NELSON, LORI (Dixie Kay Nelson): Santa Fe, NM, Aug. 15, 1933.

NELSON, TIM BLAKE: Tulsa, OK, 1964.

NELSON, TRACY: Santa Monica, CA, Oct. 25, 1963.

NELSON, WILLIE: Abbott, TX, Apr. 30, 1933.

NEMEC, CORIN: Little Rock, AK, Nov. 5, 1971.

NERO, FRANCO (Francisco Spartanero): Parma, Italy, Nov. 23, 1941.
NESMITH, MICHAEL: Houston, TX, Dec. 30, 1942.
NETTLETON, LOIS: Oak Park, IL, 1931. Actors Studio.
NEUWIRTH, BEBE: Princeton, NJ, Dec. 31, 1958.
NEWHART, BOB: Chicago, IL, Sept. 5, 1929. Loyola U.
NEWMAN, BARRY: Boston, MA, Nov. 7, 1938. Brandeis U.
NEWMAN, LARAINE: Los Angeles, Mar. 2, 1952.
NEWMAN, NANETTE: Northampton, England, 1934.
NEWMAN, PAUL: Cleveland, OH, Jan. 26, 1925. Yale.
NEWMAR, JULIE (Newmeyer): Los Angeles, Aug. 16, 1933.
NEWTON, THANDIE: Zambia, Nov. 16, 1972.
NEWTON-JOHN, OLIVIA: Cambridge, England, Sept. 26, 1948.
NGUYEN, DUSTIN: Saigon, Vietnam, Sept. 17, 1962.
NICHOLAS, DENISE: Detroit, MI, July 12, 1945.
NICHOLAS, PAUL: Peterborough, Cambridge, Eng., Dec. 3, 1945.
NICHOLS, NICHELLE: Robbins, IL, Dec. 28, 1933.
NICHOLSON, JACK: Neptune, NJ, Apr. 22, 1937.
NICKERSON, DENISE: NYC, Apr. 1, 1959.
NICOL, ALEX: Ossining, NY, Jan. 20, 1919. Actors Studio.
NIELSEN, BRIGITTE: Denmark, July 15, 1963.
NIELSEN, CONNIE: Elling, Denmark, July 3, 1965.
NIELSEN, LESLIE: Regina, Saskatchewan. Canada, Feb. 11, 1926. Neighborhood Playhouse.
NIMOY, LEONARD: Boston, MA, Mar. 26, 1931. Boston College, Antioch College.
NIXON, CYNTHIA: NYC, Apr. 9, 1966. Columbia U.
NOBLE, JAMES: Dallas, TX, Mar. 5, 1922, SMU.
NOIRET, PHILIPPE: Lille, France, Oct. 1, 1930.
NOLAN, KATHLEEN: St. Louis, MO, Sept. 27, 1933. Neighborhood Playhouse.
NOLTE, NICK: Omaha, NE, Feb. 8, 1940. Pasadena City College.
NORRIS, BRUCE: Houston, TX, May 16, 1960. Northwestern.
NORRIS, CHRISTOPHER: NYC, Oct. 7, 1943. Lincoln Square Acad.
NORRIS, CHUCK (Carlos Ray): Ryan, OK,Mar. 10, 1940.
NORTH, HEATHER: Pasadena, CA, Dec. 13, 1950. Actors Workshop.
NORTH, SHEREE (Dawn Bethel): Los Angeles. Jan. 17, 1933. Hollywood High.
NORTHAM, JEREMY: Cambridge, Eng., Dec. 1, 1961.
NORTON, EDWARD: Boston, MA, Aug. 18, 1969.
NORTON, KEN: Jacksonville, Il, Aug. 9, 1945.
NOSEWORTHY, JACK: Lynn, MA, Dec. 21, 1969.
NOURI, MICHAEL: Washington, DC, Dec. 9, 1945.
NOVAK, KIM (Marilyn Novak): Chicago, IL, Feb. 13, 1933. LACC.
NOVELLO, DON: Ashtabula, OH, Jan. 1, 1943. UDayton.
NUYEN, FRANCE (Vannga): Marseilles, France, July 31, 1939. Beaux Arts School.
O'BRIAN, HUGH (Hugh J. Krampe): Rochester, N,. Apr. 19, 1928. Cincinnati U.
O'BRIEN, CLAY: Ray, AZ, May 6, 1961.
O'BRIEN, MARGARET (Angela Maxine O'Brien): Los Angeles, Jan. 15, 1937.
O'CONNELL, JERRY (Jeremiah O'Connell): New York, NY, Feb. 17, 1974.
O'CONNOR, CARROLL: Bronx, NY, Aug. 2, 1924. Dublin National Univ.
O'CONNOR, DONALD: Chicago, IL, Aug. 28, 1925.
O'CONNOR, GLYNNIS: NYC, Nov. 19, 1955. NYSU.
O'DONNELL, CHRIS: Winetka, IL, June 27, 1970.
O'DONNELL, ROSIE: Commack, NY, March 21, 1961.
O'HARA, CATHERINE: Toronto, Canada, Mar. 4, 1954.
O'HARA, MAUREEN (Maureen Fitzsimons): Dublin, Ireland, Aug. 17, 1920.
O'HERLIHY, DAN: Wexford, Ireland, May 1, 1919. National U.
O'KEEFE, MICHAEL: Larchmont, NY, Apr. 24, 1955. NYU, AADA.

OLDMAN, GARY: New Cross, South London, England, Mar. 21, 1958.
OLIN, KEN: Chicago, IL, July 30, 1954. UPa.
OLIN, LENA: Stockholm, Sweden, Mar. 22, 1955.
OLMOS, EDWARD JAMES: Los Angeles, Feb. 24, 1947. CSLA.
O'LOUGHLIN, GERALD S.: NYC, Dec. 23, 1921. U Rochester.
OLSON, JAMES: Evanston, IL, Oct. 8, 1930.
OLSON, NANCY: Milwaukee, WI, July 14, 1928. UCLA.
OLYPHANT, TIMOTHY: HI, May 20, 1968.
O'NEAL, GRIFFIN:Los Angeles, 1965.
O'NEAL, RON: Utica, NY, Sept. 1, 1937. Ohio State.
O'NEAL, RYAN: Los Angeles, Apr. 20, 1941.
O'NEAL, TATUM: Los Angeles, Nov. 5, 1963.
O'NEIL, TRICIA: Shreveport, LA, Mar. 11, 1945. Baylor U.
O'NEILL, ED: Youngstown, OH, Apr. 12, 1946.
O'NEILL, JENNIFER: Rio de Janeiro, Feb. 20, 1949. Neighborhood Playhouse.
ONTKEAN, MICHAEL: Vancouver, B.C., Canada, Jan. 24, 1946.
O'QUINN, TERRY: Newbury, MI, July 15, 1952.
ORBACH, JERRY: Bronx, NY, Oct. 20, 1935.
ORMOND, JULIA: Epsom, England, Jan. 4, 1965.
O'SHEA, MILO: Dublin, Ireland, June 2, 1926.
OSMENT, HALEY JOEL: Los Angeles, Apr. 10, 1988.
O'TOOLE, ANNETTE (Toole): Houston, TX, Apr. 1, 1953. UCLA.
O'TOOLE, PETER: Connemara, Ireland, Aug. 2, 1932. RADA.
OVERALL, PARK: Nashville, TN, Mar. 15, 1957. Tusculum College.
OWEN, CLIVE: Keresley, Eng., Oct. 3, 1964.
OZ, FRANK (Oznowicz): Hereford, England, May 25, 1944.
PACINO, AL: NYC, Apr. 25, 1940.
PACULA, JOANNA: Tamaszow Lubelski, Poland, Jan. 2, 1957. Polish Natl. Theatre Sch.
PAGET, DEBRA (Debralee Griffin): Denver, Aug. 19, 1933.
PAIGE, JANIS (Donna Mae Jaden): Tacoma, WA, Sept. 16, 1922.
PALANCE, JACK (Walter Palanuik): Lattimer, PA, Feb. 18, 1920. UNC.
PALIN, MICHAEL: Sheffield, Yorkshire, England, May 5, 1943, Oxford.
PALMER, BETSY: East Chicago, IN, Nov. 1, 1926. DePaul U.
PALMER, GREGG (Palmer Lee): San Francisco, Jan. 25, 1927. U Utah.
PALMINTERI, CHAZZ (Calogero Lorenzo Palminteri): New York, NY, May 15, 1952.
PALTROW, GWYNETH: Los Angeles, Sept. 28, 1973.
PAMPANINI, SILVANA: Rome, Sept. 25, 1925.
PANEBIANCO, RICHARD: NYC, 1971.
PANKIN, STUART: Philadelphia, Apr. 8, 1946.
PANTOLIANO, JOE: Jersey City, NJ, Sept. 12, 1954.
PAPAS, IRENE: Chiliomodion, Greece, Mar. 9, 1929.
PAQUIN, ANNA: Winnipeg, Manitoba, Canada, July, 24, 1982.
PARE, MICHAEL: Brooklyn, NY, Oct. 9, 1959.
PARKER, COREY: NYC, July 8, 1965. NYU.
PARKER, ELEANOR: Cedarville, OH, June 26, 1922. Pasadena Playhouse.
PARKER, FESS: Fort Worth, TX, Aug. 16, 1925. USC.
PARKER, JAMESON: Baltimore, MD, Nov. l8, 1947. Beloit College.
PARKER, JEAN (Mae Green): Deer Lodge, MT, Aug. 11, 1912.
PARKER, MARY-LOUISE: Ft. Jackson, SC, Aug. 2, 1964. Bard College.
PARKER, NATHANIEL: London, May 18, 1962.
PARKER, SARAH JESSICA: Nelsonville, OH, Mar. 25, 1965.
PARKER, SUZY (Cecelia Parker): San Antonio, TX, Oct. 28, 1933.
PARKER, TREY: Auburn, AL, May 30, 1972.
PARKINS, BARBARA: Vancouver, Canada, May 22, 1943.
PARKS, MICHAEL: Corona, CA, Apr. 4, 1938.
PARSONS, ESTELLE: Lynn, MA, Nov. 20, 1927. Boston U.
PARTON, DOLLY: Sevierville, TN, Jan. 19, 1946.
PATINKIN, MANDY: Chicago, IL, Nov. 30, 1952. Juilliard.
PATRIC, JASON: NYC, June 17, 1966.
PATRICK, ROBERT: Marietta, GA, Nov. 5, 1958.
PATTERSON, LEE: Vancouver, Canada, Mar. 31, 1929. Ontario College.
PATTON, WILL: Charleston, SC, June 14, 1954.

Sam Neill

Mekhi Phifer

Ryan Phillippe

Freddie Prinze Jr.

Jonathan Pryce

Daniel Radcliffe

PAULIK, JOHAN: Prague, Czech., 1975.

PAVAN, MARISA (Marisa Pierangeli): Cagliari, Sardinia, June 19, 1932. Torquado Tasso College.

PAXTON, BILL: Fort Worth, TX, May. 17, 1955.

PAYMER, DAVID: Long Island, NY, Aug. 30, 1954.

PAYS, AMANDA: Berkshire, England, June 6, 1959.

PEACH, MARY: Durban, S. Africa, Oct. 20, 1934.

PEARCE, GUY: Ely, England, Oct. 5, 1967.

PEARSON, BEATRICE: Dennison, TX, July 27, 1920.

PECK, GREGORY: La Jolla, CA, Apr. 5, 1916. U Calif.

PEET, AMANDA: NYC, Jan. 11, 1972.

PEÑA, ELIZABETH: Cuba, Sept. 23, 1961.

PENDLETON, AUSTIN: Warren, OH, Mar. 27, 1940. Yale U.

PENHALL, BRUCE: Balboa, CA, Aug. 17, 1960.

PENN, SEAN: Burbank, CA, Aug. 17, 1960.

PEPPER, BARRY: Campbell River, BC, Canada, Apr. 4, 1970.

PEREZ, JOSE: NYC, 1940.

PEREZ, ROSIE: Brooklyn, NY, Sept. 6, 1964.

PERKINS, ELIZABETH: Queens, NY, Nov. 18, 1960. Goodman School.

PERKINS, MILLIE: Passaic, NJ, May 12, 1938.

PERLMAN, RHEA: Brooklyn, NY, Mar. 31, 1948.

PERLMAN, RON: NYC, Apr. 13, 1950. UMn.

PERREAU, GIGI (Ghislaine): Los Angeles, Feb. 6, 1941.

PERRINE, VALERIE: Galveston, TX, Sept. 3, 1943. U Ariz.

PERRY, LUKE (Coy Luther Perry, III): Fredricktown, OH, Oct. 11, 1966.

PESCI, JOE: Newark, NJ. Feb. 9, 1943.

PESCOW, DONNA: Brooklyn, NY, Mar. 24, 1954.

PETERS, BERNADETTE (Lazzara): Jamaica, NY, Feb. 28, 1948.

PETERS, BROCK: NYC, July 2, 1927. CCNY.

PETERSEN, PAUL: Glendale, CA, Sept. 23, 1945. Valley College.

PETERSEN, WILLIAM: Chicago, IL, Feb. 21, 1953.

PETERSON, CASSANDRA: Colorado Springs, CO, Sept. 17, 1951.

PETTET, JOANNA: London, Nov. 16, 1944. Neighborhood Playhouse.

PETTY, LORI: Chattanooga, TN, Mar. 23, 1963.

PFEIFFER, MICHELLE: Santa Ana, CA, Apr. 29, 1958.

PHIFER, MEKHI: NYC, Dec. 12, 1975.

PHILLIPPE, RYAN (Matthew Phillippe): New Castle, DE, Sept. 10, 1975.

PHILLIPS, LOU DIAMOND: Phillipines, Feb. 17, 1962, UTx.

PHILLIPS, MacKENZIE: Alexandria, VA, Nov. 10, 1959.

PHILLIPS, MICHELLE (Holly Gilliam): Long Beach, CA, June 4, 1944.

PHILLIPS, SIAN: Bettws, Wales, May 14, 1934. UWales.

PHOENIX, JOAQUIN: Puerto Rico, Oct. 28, 1974.

PICARDO, ROBERT: Philadelphia, PA, Oct. 27, 1953. Yale.

PICERNI, PAUL: NYC, Dec. 1, 1922. Loyola U.

PIDGEON, REBECCA: Cambridge, MA, 1963.

PIERCE, DAVID HYDE: Saratoga Springs, NY, Apr. 3, 1959.

PIGOTT-SMITH, TIM: Rugby, England, May 13, 1946.

PINCHOT, BRONSON: NYC, May 20, 1959. Yale.

PINE, PHILLIP: Hanford, CA, July 16, 1920. Actors' Lab.

PISCOPO, JOE: Passaic. NJ, June 17, 1951.

PISIER, MARIE-FRANCE: Vietnam, May 10, 1944. U Paris.

PITILLO, MARIA: Mahwah, NJ, 1965.

PITT, BRAD (William Bradley Pitt): Shawnee, OK, Dec. 18, 1963.

PIVEN, JEREMY: NYC, July 26, 1965.

PLACE, MARY KAY: Tulsa OK, Sept. 23, 1947. U Tulsa.

PLATT, OLIVER: Windsor, Ontario, Can., Oct. 10, 1960.

PLAYTEN, ALICE: NYC, Aug. 28, 1947. NYU.

PLESHETTE, SUZANNE: NYC, Jan. 31, 1937. Syracuse U.

PLIMPTON, MARTHA: NYC, Nov. 16, 1970.

PLOWRIGHT, JOAN: Scunthorpe, Brigg, Lincolnshire, England, Oct. 28, 1929. Old Vic.

PLUMB, EVE: Burbank, CA, Apr. 29, 1958.

PLUMMER, AMANDA: NYC, Mar. 23, 1957. Middlebury College.

PLUMMER, CHRISTOPHER: Toronto, Canada, Dec. 13, 1927.

PODESTA, ROSSANA: Tripoli, June 20, 1934.

POITIER, SIDNEY: Miami, FL, Feb. 27, 1927.

POLANSKI, ROMAN: Paris, France, Aug. 18, 1933.

POLITO, JON: Philadelphia, PA, Dec. 29, 1950. Villanova U.

POLITO, LINA: Naples, Italy, Aug. 11, 1954.

POLLACK, SYDNEY: South Bend, IN, July 1, 1934.

POLLAK, KEVIN: San Francisco, Oct. 30, 1958.

POLLAN, TRACY: NYC, June 22, 1960.

POLLARD, MICHAEL J.: Passaic, NJ, May 30, 1939.

POLLEY, SARAH: Toronto, Ontario, Can., Jan. 8, 1979.

PORTMAN, NATALIE: Jerusalem, June 9, 1981.

POSEY, PARKER: Baltimore, MD, Nov. 8, 1968.

POSTLETHWAITE, PETE: London, Feb. 7, 1945.

POTENTE, FRANKA: Dulmen, Germany, July 22, 1974.

POTTER, MONICA: Cleveland, OH, June 30, 1971.

POTTS, ANNIE: Nashville, TN, Oct. 28, 1952. Stephens College.

POWELL, JANE (Suzanne Burce): Portland, OR, Apr. 1, 1928.

POWELL, ROBERT: Salford, England, June 1, 1944. Manchester U.

POWER, TARYN: Los Angeles, CA, Sept. 13, 1953.

POWER, TYRONE, IV: Los Angeles, CA, Jan. 22, 1959.

POWERS, MALA (Mary Ellen): San Francisco, CA, Dec. 29, 1921. UCLA.

POWERS, STEFANIE (Federkiewicz): Hollywood, CA, Oct. 12, 1942.

PRENTISS, PAULA (Paula Ragusa): San Antonio, TX, Mar. 4, 1939. Northwestern U.

PRESLE, MICHELINE (Micheline Chassagne): Paris, France, Aug. 22, 1922. Rouleau Drama School.

PRESLEY, PRISCILLA: Brooklyn, NY, May 24, 1945.

PRESNELL, HARVE: Modesto, CA, Sept. 14, 1933. USC.

PRESTON, KELLY: Honolulu, HI, Oct. 13, 1962. USC.

PRESTON, WILLIAM: Columbia, PA, Aug. 26, 1921. PaStateU.

PRICE, LONNY: NYC, Mar. 9, 1959. Juilliard.

PRIESTLEY, JASON: Vancouver, Canada, Aug, 28, 1969.

PRIMUS, BARRY: NYC, Feb. 16, 1938. CCNY.

PRINCE (P. Rogers Nelson): Minneapolis, MN, June 7, 1958.

PRINCIPAL, VICTORIA: Fukuoka, Japan, Jan. 3, 1945. Dade, Jr. College.

PRINZE, JR., FREDDIE: Los Angeles, March 8, 1976.

345

Charlotte Rampling

Robert Redford

Carl Reiner

Julia Roberts

Jada Pinkett Smith

Maggie Smith

PROCHNOW, JURGEN: Berlin, June 10, 1941.
PROSKY, ROBERT: Philadelphia, PA, Dec. 13, 1930.
PROVAL, DAVID: Brooklyn, NY, May 20, 1942.
PROVINE, DOROTHY: Deadwood, SD, Jan. 20, 1937. U Wash.
PRYCE, JONATHAN: Wales, UK, June 1, 1947, RADA.
PRYOR, RICHARD: Peoria, IL, Dec. 1, 1940.
PULLMAN, BILL: Delphi, NY, Dec. 17, 1954. SUNY/Oneonta, UMass.
PURCELL, LEE: Cherry Point, NC, June 15, 1947. Stephens.
PURDOM, EDMUND: Welwyn Garden City, England, Dec. 19, 1924. St. Ignatius College.
QUAID, DENNIS: Houston, TX, Apr. 9, 1954.
QUAID, RANDY: Houston, TX, Oct. 1, 1950. UHouston.
QUINLAN, KATHLEEN: Mill Valley, CA, Nov. 19, 1954.
QUINN, AIDAN: Chicago, IL, Mar. 8, 1959.
RADCLIFFE, DANIEL: London, July 23, 1989.
RAFFERTY, FRANCES: Sioux City, IA, June 16, 1922. UCLA.
RAFFIN, DEBORAH: Los Angeles, Mar. 13, 1953. Valley College.
RAGSDALE, WILLIAM: El Dorado, AK, Jan. 19, 1961. Hendrix College.
RAILSBACK, STEVE: Dallas, TX, 1948.
RAINER, LUISE: Vienna, Austria, Jan. 12, 1910.
RALSTON, VERA (Vera Helena Hruba): Prague, Czech., July 12, 1919.
RAMIS, HAROLD: Chicago, IL, Nov. 21, 1944. WashingtonU.
RAMPLING, CHARLOTTE: Surmer, England, Feb. 5, 1946. U Madrid.
RAMSEY, LOGAN: Long Beach, CA, Mar. 21, 1921. St. Joseph.
RANDALL, TONY (Leonard Rosenberg): Tulsa, OK, Feb. 26, 1920. Northwestern U.
RANDELL, RON: Sydney, Australia, Oct. 8, 1920. St. Mary's College.
RAPAPORT, MICHAEL: March 20, 1970.
RAPP, ANTHONY: Chicago, Oct. 26, 1971.
RASCHE, DAVID: St. Louis, MO, Aug. 7, 1944.
REA, STEPHEN: Belfast, No. Ireland, Oct. 31, 1949.
REAGAN, RONALD: Tampico, IL, Feb. 6, 1911. Eureka College.
REASON, REX: Berlin, Ger., Nov. 30, 1928. Pasadena Playhouse.
REDDY, HELEN: Melbourne, Australia, Oct. 25, 1942.
REDFORD, ROBERT: Santa Monica, CA, Aug. 18, 1937. AADA.
REDGRAVE, CORIN: London, July 16, 1939.
REDGRAVE, LYNN: London, Mar. 8, 1943.
REDGRAVE, VANESSA: London, Jan. 30, 1937.
REDMAN, JOYCE: County Mayo, Ireland, 1919. RADA.
REED, PAMELA: Tacoma, WA, Apr. 2, 1949.
REEMS, HARRY (Herbert Streicher): Bronx, NY, 1947. U Pittsburgh.
REES, ROGER: Aberystwyth, Wales, May 5, 1944.
REESE, DELLA: Detroit, MI, July 6, 1932.
REEVE, CHRISTOPHER: NYC, Sept. 25, 1952. Cornell, Juilliard.
REEVES, KEANU: Beiruit, Lebanon, Sept. 2, 1964.
REGEHR, DUNCAN: Lethbridge, Canada, Oct. 5, 1952.
REID, ELLIOTT: NYC, Jan. 16, 1920.
REID, TIM: Norfolk, VA, Dec, 19, 1944.

REILLY, CHARLES NELSON: NYC, Jan. 13, 1931. UCt.
REILLY, JOHN C.: Chicago, IL, May 24, 1965.
REINER, CARL: NYC, Mar. 20, 1922. Georgetown.
REINER, ROB: NYC, Mar. 6, 1947. UCLA.
REINHOLD, JUDGE (Edward Ernest, Jr.): Wilmington, DE, May 21, 1957. NCSchool of Arts.
REINKING, ANN: Seattle, WA, Nov. 10, 1949.
REISER, PAUL: NYC, Mar. 30, 1957.
REMAR, JAMES: Boston, MA, Dec. 31, 1953. Neighborhood Playhouse.
RENFRO, BRAD: Knoxville, TN, July 25, 1982.
RENO, JEAN (Juan Moreno): Casablanca, Morocco, July 30, 1948.
REUBENS, PAUL (Paul Reubenfeld): Peekskill, NY, Aug. 27, 1952.
REVILL, CLIVE: Wellington, NZ, Apr. 18, 1930.
REY, ANTONIA: Havana, Cuba, Oct. 12, 1927.
REYNOLDS, BURT: Waycross, GA, Feb. 11, 1935. Fla. State U.
REYNOLDS, DEBBIE (Mary Frances Reynolds): El Paso, TX, Apr. 1, 1932.
RHAMES, VING (Irving Rhames): NYC, May 12, 1959.
RHOADES, BARBARA: Poughkeepsie, NY, Mar. 23, 1947.
RHODES, CYNTHIA: Nashville, TN, Nov. 21, 1956.
RHYS, PAUL: Neath, Wales, Dec. 19, 1963.
RHYS-DAVIES, JOHN: Salisbury, England, May 5, 1944.
RHYS-MEYERS, JONATHAN: Cork, Ireland, July 27, 1977.
RIBISI, GIOVANNI: Los Angeles, CA, Dec. 17, 1974.
RICCI, CHRISTINA: Santa Monica, CA, Feb. 12, 1980.
RICHARD, CLIFF (Harry Webb): India, Oct. 14, 1940.
RICHARDS, DENISE: Downers Grove, IL, Feb. 17, 1972.
RICHARDS, MICHAEL: Culver City, CA, July 14, 1949.
RICHARDSON, JOELY: London, Jan. 9, 1965.
RICHARDSON, MIRANDA: Southport, England, Mar. 3, 1958.
RICHARDSON, NATASHA: London, May 11, 1963.
RICKLES, DON: NYC, May 8, 1926. AADA.
RICKMAN, ALAN: Hammersmith, England, Feb. 21, 1946.
RIEGERT, PETER: NYC, Apr. 11, 1947. U Buffalo.
RIFKIN, RON: NYC, Oct. 31, 1939.
RIGG, DIANA: Doncaster, England, July 20, 1938. RADA.
RILEY, JOHN C.: Chicago, May 24, 1965.
RINGWALD, MOLLY: Rosewood, CA, Feb. 16, 1968.
RITTER, JOHN: Burbank, CA, Sept. 17, 1948. US. Cal.
RIVERS, JOAN (Molinsky): Brooklyn, NY, NY, June 8, 1933.
ROACHE, LINUS: Manchester, England, 1964.
ROBARDS, SAM: NYC, Dec. 16, 1963.
ROBBINS, TIM: NYC, Oct. 16, 1958. UCLA.
ROBERTS, ERIC: Biloxi, MS, Apr. 18, 1956. RADA.
ROBERTS, JULIA: Atlanta, GA, Oct. 28, 1967.
ROBERTS, RALPH: Salisbury, NC, Aug. 17, 1922. UNC.
ROBERTS, TANYA (Leigh): Bronx, NY, Oct. 15, 1954.
ROBERTS, TONY: NYC, Oct. 22, 1939. Northwestern U.
ROBERTSON, CLIFF: La Jolla, CA, Sept. 9, 1925. Antioch College.
ROBERTSON, DALE: Oklahoma City, July 14, 1923.
ROBINSON, CHRIS: West Palm Beach, FL, Nov. 5, 1938. LACC.
ROBINSON, JAY: NYC, Apr. 14, 1930.

ROBINSON, ROGER: Seattle, WA, May 2, 1940. USC.
ROCHEFORT, JEAN: Paris, France, 1930.
ROCK, CHRIS: Brooklyn, NY, Feb. 7, 1966.
ROCKWELL, SAM: Daly City, CA, Nov. 5, 1968.
RODRIGUEZ, MICHELLE: Bexar County, TX, July 12, 1978.
ROGERS, MIMI: Coral Gables, FL, Jan. 27, 1956.
ROGERS, WAYNE: Birmingham, AL, Apr. 7, 1933. Princeton.
ROMIJN-STAMOS, REBECCA: Berkeley, CA, Nov. 6, 1972.
RONSTADT, LINDA: Tucson, AZ, July 15, 1946.
ROOKER, MICHAEL: Jasper, AL, Apr. 6, 1955.
ROONEY, MICKEY (Joe Yule, Jr.): Brooklyn, NY, Sept. 23, 1920.
ROSE, REVA: Chicago, IL, July 30, 1940. Goodman.
ROSEANNE (Barr): Salt Lake City, UT, Nov. 3, 1952.
ROSS, DIANA: Detroit, MI, Mar. 26, 1944.
ROSS, JUSTIN: Brooklyn, NY, Dec. 15, 1954.
ROSS, KATHARINE: Hollywood, Jan. 29, 1943. Santa Rosa College.
ROSSELLINI, ISABELLA: Rome, June 18, 1952.
ROSSOVICH, RICK: Palo Alto, CA, Aug. 28, 1957.
ROTH, TIM: London, May 14, 1961.
ROUNDTREE, RICHARD: New Rochelle, NY, Sept. 7, 1942. Southern Ill.
ROURKE, MICKEY (Philip Andre Rourke, Jr.): Schenectady, NY, Sept. 16, 1956.
ROWE, NICHOLAS: London, Nov. 22, 1966, Eton.
ROWLANDS, GENA: Cambria, WI, June 19, 1934.
RUBIN, ANDREW: New Bedford, MA, June 22, 1946. AADA.
RUBINEK, SAUL: Fohrenwold, Germany, July 2, 1948.
RUBINSTEIN, JOHN: Los Angeles, CA, Dec. 8, 1946. UCLA.
RUCK, ALAN: Cleveland, OH, July 1, 1960.
RUCKER, BO: Tampa, FL, Aug. 17, 1948.
RUDD, PAUL: Boston, MA, May 15, 1940.
RUDD, PAUL: Passaic, NJ, Apr. 6, 1969.
RUDNER, RITA: Miami, FL, Sept. 17, 1955.
RUEHL, MERCEDES: Queens, NY, Feb. 28, 1948.
RULE, JANICE: Cincinnati, OH, Aug. 15, 1931.
RUPERT, MICHAEL: Denver, CO, Oct. 23, 1951. Pasadena Playhouse.
RUSH, BARBARA: Denver, CO, Jan. 4, 1927. U Calif.
RUSH, GEOFFREY: Toowoomba, Queensland, Australia, July 6, 1951. Univ. of Queensland.
RUSSELL, JANE: Bemidji, MI, June 21, 1921. Max Reinhardt School.
RUSSELL, KURT: Springfield, MA, Mar. 17, 1951.
RUSSELL, THERESA (Paup): San Diego, CA, Mar. 20, 1957.
RUSSO, JAMES: NYC, Apr. 23, 1953.
RUSSO, RENE: Burbank, CA, Feb. 17, 1954.
RUTHERFORD, ANN: Toronto, Canada, Nov. 2, 1920.
RYAN, JOHN P.: NYC, July 30, 1936. CCNY.
RYAN, MEG: Fairfield, CT, Nov. 19, 1961. NYU.
RYAN, TIM (Meineslschmidt): Staten Island, NY, 1958. Rutgers U.
RYDER, WINONA (Horowitz): Winona, MN, Oct. 29, 1971.
SACCHI, ROBERT: Bronx, NY, 1941. NYU.
SÄGEBRECHT, MARIANNE: Starnberg, Bavaria, Aug. 27, 1945.
SAINT, EVA MARIE: Newark, NJ, July 4, 1924. Bowling Green State U.
SAINT JAMES, SUSAN (Suzie Jane Miller): Los Angeles, Aug. 14, 1946. Conn. College.
ST. JOHN, BETTA: Hawthorne, CA, Nov. 26, 1929.
ST. JOHN, JILL (Jill Oppenheim): Los Angeles, Aug. 19, 1940.
SALA, JOHN: Los Angeles, CA, Oct. 5, 1962.
SALDANA, THERESA: Brooklyn, NY, Aug. 20, 1954.
SALINGER, MATT: Windsor, VT, Feb. 13, 1960. Princeton, Columbia.
SALT, JENNIFER: Los Angeles, Sept. 4, 1944. Sarah Lawrence College.
SAMMS, EMMA: London, Aug. 28, 1960.
SAN GIACOMO, LAURA: Orange, NJ, Nov. 14, 1961.
SANDERS, JAY O.: Austin, TX, Apr. 16, 1953.
SANDLER, ADAM: Bronx, NY, Sept. 9, 1966. NYU.
SANDS, JULIAN: Yorkshire, England, Jan 15, 1958.
SANDS, TOMMY: Chicago, IL, Aug. 27, 1937.

SAN JUAN, OLGA: NYC, Mar. 16, 1927.
SARA, MIA (Sarapocciello): Brooklyn, NY, June 19, 1967.
SARANDON, CHRIS: Beckley, WV, July 24, 1942. U WVa., Catholic U.
SARANDON, SUSAN (Tomalin): NYC, Oct. 4, 1946. Catholic U.
SARRAZIN, MICHAEL: Quebec City, Canada, May 22, 1940.
SAVAGE, FRED: Highland Park, IL, July 9, 1976.
SAVAGE, JOHN (Youngs): Long Island, NY, Aug. 25, 1949. AADA.
SAVIOLA, CAMILLE: Bronx, NY, July 16, 1950.
SAVOY, TERESA ANN: London, July 18, 1955.
SAWA, DEVON: Vancouver, BC, Canada, Sept. 7, 1978.
SAXON, JOHN (Carmen Orrico): Brooklyn, NY, Aug. 5, 1935.
SBARGE, RAPHAEL: NYC, Feb. 12, 1964.
SCACCHI, GRETA: Milan, Italy, Feb. 18, 1960.
SCALIA, JACK: Brooklyn, NY, Nov. 10, 1951.
SCARWID, DIANA: Savannah, GA, Aug. 27, 1955, AADA. Pace U.
SCHEIDER, ROY: Orange, NJ, Nov. 10, 1932. Franklin-Marshall.
SCHEINE, RAYNOR: Emporia, VA, Nov. 10. VaCommonwealthU.
SCHELL, MARIA: Vienna, Jan. 15, 1926.
SCHELL, MAXIMILIAN: Vienna, Dec. 8, 1930.
SCHLATTER, CHARLIE: Englewood, NJ, May 1, 1966. Ithaca College.
SCHNEIDER, JOHN: Mt. Kisco, NY, Apr. 8, 1960.
SCHNEIDER, MARIA: Paris, France, Mar. 27, 1952.
SCHREIBER, LIEV: San Francisco, CA, Oct. 4, 1967.
SCHRODER, RICK: Staten Island, NY, Apr. 13, 1970.
SCHUCK, JOHN: Boston, MA, Feb. 4, 1940.
SCHULTZ, DWIGHT: Milwaukee, WI, Nov. 10, 1938. MarquetteU.
SCHWARTZMAN, JASON: Los Angeles, June 26, 1980.
SCHWARZENEGGER, ARNOLD: Austria, July 30, 1947.
SCHWIMMER, DAVID: Queens, NY, Nov. 12, 1966.
SCHYGULLA, HANNA: Katlowitz, Germany, Dec. 25, 1943.
SCIORRA, ANNABELLA: NYC, Mar. 24, 1964.
SCOFIELD, PAUL: Hurstpierpoint, England, Jan. 21, 1922. London Mask Theatre School.
SCOGGINS, TRACY: Galveston, TX, Nov. 13, 1959.
SCOLARI, PETER: Scarsdale, NY, Sept. 12, 1956. NYCC.
SCOTT, CAMPBELL: South Salem, NY, July 19, 1962. Lawrence.
SCOTT, DEBRALEE: Elizabeth, NJ, Apr. 2, 1953.
SCOTT, GORDON (Gordon M. Werschkul): Portland, OR, Aug. 3, 1927. Oregon U.
SCOTT, LIZABETH (Emma Matso): Scranton, PA, Sept. 29, 1922.
SCOTT, MARTHA: Jamesport, MO, Sept. 22, 1914. U Mich.
SCOTT THOMAS, KRISTIN: Redruth, Cornwall, Eng., May 24, 1960.
SEAGAL, STEVEN: Detroit, MI, Apr. 10, 1951.
SEARS, HEATHER: London, Sept. 28, 1935.
SEDGWICK, KYRA: NYC, Aug. 19, 1965. USC.
SEGAL, GEORGE: NYC, Feb. 13, 1934. Columbia.
SELBY, DAVID: Morganstown, WV, Feb. 5, 1941. UWV.
SELLARS, ELIZABETH: Glasgow, Scotland, May 6, 1923.
SELLECK, TOM: Detroit, MI, Jan. 29, 1945. USCal.
SERBEDZIJA, RADE: Bunic, Yugoslavia, July 27, 1946.
SERNAS, JACQUES: Lithuania, July 30, 1925.
SERRAULT, MICHEL: Brunoy, France. Jan. 24, 1928. Paris Consv.
SETH, ROSHAN: New Delhi, India. Aug. 17, 1942.
SEWELL, RUFUS: Twickenham, Eng., Oct. 29, 1967.
SEYMOUR, JANE (Joyce Frankenberg): Hillingdon, England, Feb. 15, 1952.
SHALHOUB, TONY: Green Bay, WI, Oct. 9, 1953.
SHANDLING, GARRY: Chicago, IL, Nov. 29, 1949.
SHARIF, OMAR (Michel Shalhoub): Alexandria, Egypt, Apr. 10, 1932. Victoria College.
SHATNER, WILLIAM: Montreal, Canada, Mar. 22, 1931. McGill U.
SHAVER, HELEN: St. Thomas, Ontario, Canada, Feb. 24, 1951.
SHAW, FIONA: Cork, Ireland, July 10, 1955. RADA.
SHAW, STAN: Chicago, IL, 1952.
SHAWN, WALLACE: NYC, Nov. 12, 1943. Harvard.
SHEA, JOHN: North Conway, NH, Apr. 14, 1949. Bates, Yale. **347**

SHEARER, HARRY: Los Angeles, Dec. 23, 1943. UCLA.
SHEARER, MOIRA: Dunfermline, Scotland, Jan. 17, 1926. London Theatre School.
SHEEDY, ALLY: NYC, June 13, 1962. USC.
SHEEN, CHARLIE (Carlos Irwin Estevez): Santa Monica, CA, Sept. 3, 1965.
SHEEN, MARTIN (Ramon Estevez): Dayton, OH, Aug. 3, 1940.
SHEFFER, CRAIG: York, PA, Apr. 23, 1960. E. StroudsbergU.
SHEFFIELD, JOHN: Pasadena, CA, Apr. 11, 1931. UCLA.
SHELLEY, CAROL: London, England, Aug. 16, 1939.
SHEPARD, SAM (Rogers): Ft. Sheridan, IL, Nov. 5, 1943.
SHEPHERD, CYBILL: Memphis, TN, Feb. 18, 1950. Hunter, NYU.
SHER, ANTONY: England, June 14, 1949.
SHERIDAN, JAMEY: Pasadena, CA, July 12, 1951.
SHIELDS, BROOKE: NYC, May 31, 1965.
SHIRE, TALIA: Lake Success, NY, Apr. 25, 1946. Yale.
SHORT, MARTIN: Toronto, Canada, Mar. 26, 1950. McMasterU.
SHUE, ELISABETH: S. Orange, NJ, Oct. 6, 1963. Harvard.
SIEMASZKO, CASEY: Chicago, IL, March 17, 1961.
SIKKING, JAMES B.: Los Angeles, Mar. 5, 1934.
SILVA, HENRY: Brooklyn, NY, 1928.
SILVER, RON: NYC, July 2, 1946. SUNY.
SILVERMAN, JONATHAN: Los Angeles, CA, Aug. 5, 1966. USC.
SILVERSTONE, ALICIA: San Francisco, CA, Oct. 4, 1976.
SILVERSTONE, BEN: London, Eng, Apr. 9, 1979.
SIMMONS, JEAN: London, Jan. 31, 1929. Aida Foster School.
SIMON, PAUL: Newark, NJ, Nov. 5, 1942.
SIMON, SIMONE: Bethune, France, Apr. 23, 1910.
SIMPSON, O. J. (Orenthal James): San Francisco, CA, July 9, 1947. UCLA.
SINBAD (David Adkins): Benton Harbor, MI, Nov. 10, 1956.
SINCLAIR, JOHN (Gianluigi Loffredo): Rome, Italy, 1946.
SINDEN, DONALD: Plymouth, England, Oct. 9, 1923. Webber-Douglas.
SINGER, LORI: Corpus Christi, TX, May 6, 1962. Juilliard.
SINISE, GARY: Chicago, Mar. 17. 1955.
SIZEMORE, TOM: Detroit, MI, Sept. 29, 1964.
SKARSGÅRD, STELLAN: Gothenburg, Vastergotland, Sweden, June 13, 1951.
SKERRITT, TOM: Detroit, MI, Aug. 25, 1933. Wayne State U.
SKYE, IONE (Leitch): London, England, Sept. 4, 1971.
SLATER, CHRISTIAN: NYC, Aug. 18, 1969.
SLATER, HELEN: NYC, Dec. 15, 1965.
SMITH, CHARLES MARTIN: Los Angeles, CA, Oct. 30, 1953. CalState U.
SMITH, JACLYN: Houston, TX, Oct. 26, 1947.
SMITH, JADA PINKETT: Baltimore, MD, Sept. 18, 1971.
SMITH, KERR: Exton, PA, Mar. 9, 1972.
SMITH, KEVIN: Red Bank, NJ, Aug. 2, 1970.
SMITH, KURTWOOD: New Lisbon, WI, Jul. 3, 1942.
SMITH, LANE: Memphis, TN, Apr. 29, 1936.
SMITH, LEWIS: Chattanooga, TN, 1958. Actors Studio.
SMITH, LOIS: Topeka, KS, Nov. 3, 1930. U Wash.
SMITH, MAGGIE: Ilford, England, Dec. 28, 1934.
SMITH, ROGER: South Gate, CA, Dec. 18, 1932. U Ariz.
SMITH, WILL: Philadelphia, PA, Sept. 25, 1968.
SMITHERS, WILLIAM: Richmond, VA, July 10, 1927. Catholic U.
SMITS, JIMMY: Brooklyn, NY, July 9, 1955. Cornell U.
SNIPES, WESLEY: NYC, July 31, 1963. SUNY/Purchase.
SNODGRESS, CARRIE: Chicago, IL, Oct. 27, 1946. UNI.
SOBIEKSI, LEELEE (Liliane Sobieski): NYC, June 10, 1982.
SOLOMON, BRUCE: NYC, 1944. U Miami, Wayne State U.
SOMERS, SUZANNE (Mahoney): San Bruno, CA, Oct. 16, 1946. Lone Mt. College.

SOMMER, ELKE (Schletz): Berlin, Germany, Nov. 5, 1940.
SOMMER, JOSEF: Greifswald, Germany, June 26, 1934.
SORDI, ALBERTO: Rome, Italy, June 15, 1920.
SORVINO, MIRA: Tenafly, NJ, Sept. 28, 1967.
SORVINO, PAUL: NYC, Apr. 13, 1939. AMDA.
SOTO, TALISA (Miriam Soto): Brooklyn, NY, Mar. 27, 1967.
SOUL, DAVID: Chicago, IL, Aug. 28, 1943.
SPACEK, SISSY: Quitman, TX, Dec. 25, 1949. Actors Studio.
SPACEY, KEVIN: So. Orange, NJ, July 26, 1959. Juilliard.
SPADE, DAVID: Birmingham, MS, July 22, 1964.
SPADER, JAMES: Buzzards Bay, MA, Feb. 7, 1960.
SPALL, TIMOTHY: London, Feb. 27, 1957.
SPANO, VINCENT: Brooklyn, NY, Oct. 18, 1962.
SPENSER, JEREMY: London, July 16, 1937.
SPINELLA, STEPHEN: Naples, Italy, Oct. 11, 1956. NYU.
SPRINGFIELD, RICK (Richard Spring Thorpe): Sydney, Australia, Aug. 23, 1949.
STACK, ROBERT: Los Angeles, Jan. 13, 1919. USC.
STADLEN, LEWIS J.: Brooklyn, NY, Mar. 7, 1947. Neighborhood Playhouse.
STAHL, NICK: Dallas, TX, Dec. 5, 1979.
STALLONE, FRANK: NYC, July 30, 1950.
STALLONE, SYLVESTER: NYC, July 6, 1946. U Miami.
STAMP, TERENCE: London, July 23, 1939.
STANFORD, AARON: Westford, MA, Dec. 18, 1977.
STANG, ARNOLD: Chelsea, MA, Sept. 28, 1925.
STANTON, HARRY DEAN: Lexington, KY, July 14, 1926.
STAPLETON, JEAN: NYC, Jan. 19, 1923.
STAPLETON, MAUREEN: Troy, NY, June 21, 1925.
STARR, RINGO (Richard Starkey): Liverpool, England, July 7, 1940.
STAUNTON, IMELDA: UK, Jan. 9, 1956.
STEELE, BARBARA: England, Dec. 29, 1937.
STEELE, TOMMY: London, Dec. 17, 1936.
STEENBURGEN, MARY: Newport, AR, Feb. 8, 1953. Neighborhood Playhouse.
STERLING, JAN (Jane Sterling Adriance): NYC, Apr. 3, 1923. Fay Compton School.
STERLING, ROBERT (William Sterling Hart): Newcastle, PA, Nov. 13, 1917. UPittsburgh.
STERN, DANIEL: Bethesda, MD, Aug. 28, 1957.
STERNHAGEN, FRANCES: Washington, DC, Jan. 13, 1932.
STEVENS, ANDREW: Memphis, TN, June 10, 1955.
STEVENS, CONNIE (Concetta Ann Ingolia): Brooklyn, NY, Aug. 8, 1938. Hollywood Professional School.
STEVENS, FISHER: Chicago, IL, Nov. 27, 1963. NYU.
STEVENS, STELLA (Estelle Eggleston): Hot Coffee, MS, Oct. 1, 1936.
STEVENSON, JULIET: Essex, Eng., Oct. 30, 1956.
STEVENSON, PARKER: Philadelphia, PA, June 4, 1953. Princeton.
STEWART, ALEXANDRA: Montreal, Canada, June 10, 1939. Louvre.
STEWART, ELAINE (Elsy Steinberg): Montclair, NJ, May 31, 1929.
STEWART, FRENCH (Milton French Stewart): Albuquerque, NM, Feb. 20, 1964.
STEWART, JON (Jonathan Stewart Liebowitz): Trenton, NJ, Nov. 28, 1962.
STEWART, MARTHA (Martha Haworth): Bardwell, KY, Oct. 7, 1922.
STEWART, PATRICK: Mirfield, England, July 13, 1940.
STIERS, DAVID OGDEN: Peoria, IL, Oct. 31, 1942.
STILES, JULIA: NYC, Mar. 28, 1981.
STILLER, BEN: NYC, Nov. 30, 1965.
STILLER, JERRY: NYC, June 8, 1931.
STING (Gordon Matthew Sumner): Wallsend, England, Oct. 2, 1951.
STOCKWELL, DEAN: Hollywood, Mar. 5, 1935.
STOCKWELL, JOHN (John Samuels, IV): Galveston, TX, Mar. 25, 1961. Harvard.
STOLTZ, ERIC: Whittier, CA, Sept. 30, 1961. USC.

Timothy Spall

Julia Stiles

Tilda Swinton

Audrey Tautou

Uma Thurman

Marisa Tomei

STONE, DEE WALLACE (Deanna Bowers): Kansas City, MO, Dec. 14, 1948. UKS.
STORM, GALE (Josephine Cottle): Bloomington, TX, Apr. 5, 1922.
STOWE, MADELEINE: Eagle Rock, CA, Aug. 18, 1958.
STRASSMAN, MARCIA: New Jersey, Apr. 28, 1948.
STRATHAIRN, DAVID: San Francisco, Jan. 26, 1949.
STRAUSS, PETER: NYC, Feb. 20, 1947.
STREEP, MERYL (Mary Louise): Summit, NJ, June 22, 1949 Vassar, Yale.
STREISAND, BARBRA: Brooklyn, NY, Apr. 24, 1942.
STRITCH, ELAINE: Detroit, MI, Feb. 2, 1925. Drama Workshop.
STROUD, DON: Honolulu, HI, Sept. 1, 1937.
STRUTHERS, SALLY: Portland, OR, July 28, 1948. Pasadena Playhouse.
STUDI, WES (Wesley Studie): Nofire Hollow, OK, Dec. 17, 1947.
SUMMER, DONNA (LaDonna Gaines): Boston, MA, Dec. 31, 1948.
SUTHERLAND, DONALD: St. John, New Brunswick, Canada, July 17, 1935. U Toronto.
SUTHERLAND, KIEFER: Los Angeles, CA, Dec. 18, 1966.
SUVARI, MENA: Newport, RI, Feb. 9, 1979.
SVENSON, BO: Goreborg, Sweden, Feb. 13, 1941. UCLA.
SWANK, HILARY: Bellingham, WA, July 30, 1974.
SWAYZE, PATRICK: Houston, TX, Aug. 18, 1952.
SWEENEY, D. B. (Daniel Bernard Sweeney): Shoreham, NY, Nov. 14, 1961.
SWINTON, TILDA: London, Nov. 5, 1960.
SWIT, LORETTA: Passaic, NJ, Nov. 4, 1937, AADA.
SYLVESTER, WILLIAM: Oakland, CA, Jan. 31, 1922. RADA.
SYMONDS, ROBERT: Bistow, AK, Dec. 1, 1926. TexU.
SYMS, SYLVIA: London, June 1, 1934. Convent School.
SZARABAJKA, KEITH: Oak Park, IL, Dec. 2, 1952. UChicago.
T, MR. (Lawrence Tero): Chicago, IL, May 21, 1952.
TABORI, KRISTOFFER (Siegel): Los Angeles, Aug. 4, 1952.
TAKEI, GEORGE: Los Angeles, CA, Apr. 20, 1939. UCLA.
TALBOT, NITA: NYC, Aug. 8, 1930. Irvine Studio School.
TAMBLYN, RUSS: Los Angeles, Dec. 30, 1934.
TARANTINO, QUENTIN: Knoxville, TN, Mar. 27, 1963.
TATE, LARENZ: Chicago, IL, Sept. 8, 1975.
TAUTOU, AUDREY: Beaumont, France, Aug. 9, 1978.
TAYLOR, ELIZABETH: London, Feb. 27, 1932. Byron House School.
TAYLOR, LILI: Glencoe, IL, Feb. 20, 1967.
TAYLOR, NOAH: London, Sept. 4, 1969.
TAYLOR, RENEE: NYC, Mar. 19, 1935.
TAYLOR, ROD (Robert): Sydney, Aust., Jan. 11, 1929.
TAYLOR-YOUNG, LEIGH: Washington, DC, Jan. 25, 1945. Northwestern.
TEEFY, MAUREEN: Minneapolis, MN, Oct. 26, 1953, Juilliard.
TEMPLE, SHIRLEY: Santa Monica, CA, Apr. 23, 1927.
TENNANT, VICTORIA: London, England, Sept. 30, 1950.
TENNEY, JON: Princeton, NJ, Dec. 16, 1961.
TERZIEFF, LAURENT: Paris, France, June 25, 1935.
TEWES, LAUREN: Braddock, PA, Oct. 26, 1954.

THACKER, RUSS: Washington, DC, June 23, 1946. Montgomery College.
THAXTER, PHYLLIS: Portland, ME, Nov. 20, 1921. St. Genevieve.
THELEN, JODI: St. Cloud, MN, 1963.
THERON, CHARLIZE: Benoni, So. Africa, Aug. 7, 1975.
THEWLIS, DAVID: Blackpool, Eng., 1963.
THOMAS, HENRY: San Antonio, TX, Sept. 8, 1971.
THOMAS, JAY: New Orleans, July 12, 1948.
THOMAS, JONATHAN TAYLOR (Weiss): Bethlehem, PA, Sept. 8, 1981.
THOMAS, MARLO (Margaret): Detroit, Nov. 21, 1938. USC.
THOMAS, PHILIP MICHAEL: Columbus, OH, May 26, 1949. Oakwood College.
THOMAS, RICHARD: NYC, June 13, 1951. Columbia.
THOMPSON, EMMA: London, England, Apr.15, 1959. Cambridge.
THOMPSON, FRED DALTON: Sheffield, AL, Aug. 19, 1942.
THOMPSON, JACK (John Payne): Sydney, Australia, Aug. 31, 1940.
THOMPSON, LEA: Rochester, MN, May 31, 1961.
THOMPSON, REX: NYC, Dec. 14, 1942.
THOMPSON, SADA: Des Moines, IA, Sept. 27, 1929. Carnegie Tech.
THORNTON, BILLY BOB: Hot Spring, AR, Aug. 4, 1955.
THORSON, LINDA: Toronto, Canada, June 18, 1947. RADA.
THULIN, INGRID: Solleftea, Sweden, Jan. 27, 1929. Royal Drama Theatre.
THURMAN, UMA: Boston, MA, Apr. 29, 1970.
TICOTIN, RACHEL: Bronx, NY, Nov. 1, 1958.
TIERNEY, LAWRENCE: Brooklyn, NY, Mar. 15, 1919. Manhattan College.
TIFFIN, PAMELA (Wonso): Oklahoma City, OK, Oct. 13, 1942.
TIGHE, KEVIN: Los Angeles, Aug. 13, 1944.
TILLY, JENNIFER: Los Angeles, CA, Sept. 16, 1958.
TILLY, MEG: Texada, Canada, Feb. 14, 1960.
TOBOLOWSKY, STEPHEN: Dallas, TX, May 30, 1951. So. Methodist U.
TODD, BEVERLY: Chicago, IL, July 1, 1946.
TODD, RICHARD: Dublin, Ireland, June 11, 1919. Shrewsbury School.
TOLKAN, JAMES: Calumet, MI, June 20, 1931.
TOMEI, MARISA: Brooklyn, NY, Dec. 4, 1964. NYU.
TOMLIN, LILY: Detroit, MI, Sept. 1, 1939. Wayne State U.
TOPOL (Chaim Topol): Tel-Aviv, Israel, Sept. 9, 1935.
TORN, RIP: Temple, TX, Feb. 6, 1931. UTex.
TORRES, LIZ: NYC, Sept. 27, 1947. NYU.
TOTTER, AUDREY: Joliet, IL, Dec. 20, 1918.
TOWSEND, ROBERT: Chicago, IL, Feb. 6, 1957.
TOWNSEND, STUART: Dublin, Dec. 15, 1972.
TRAVANTI, DANIEL J.: Kenosha, WI, Mar. 7, 1940.
TRAVIS, NANCY: Astoria, NY, Sept. 21, 1961.
TRAVOLTA, JOEY: Englewood, NJ, Oct. 14, 1950.
TRAVOLTA, JOHN: Englewood, NJ, Feb. 18, 1954.
TREMAYNE, LES: London, Apr. 16, 1913. Northwestern, Columbia, UCLA.
TRINTIGNANT, JEAN-LOUIS: Pont-St. Esprit, France, Dec. 11, 1930. DullinBalachova Drama School.

Stanley Tucci

Paul Walker

Emily Watson

Dianne Wiest

Kate Winslet

Renée Zellweger

TRIPPLEHORN, JEANNE: Tulsa, OK, June 10, 1963.

TSOPEI, CORINNA: Athens, Greece, June 21, 1944.

TUBB, BARRY: Snyder, TX, 1963. AmConsv Th.

TUCCI, STANLEY: Katonah, NY, Jan. 11, 1960.

TUCKER, CHRIS: Decatur, GA, Aug. 31, 1972.

TUCKER, JONATHAN: Boston, May 31, 1982.

TUCKER, MICHAEL: Baltimore, MD, Feb. 6, 1944.

TUNE, TOMMY: Wichita Falls, TX, Feb. 28, 1939.

TUNNEY, ROBIN: Chicago, June 19, 1972.

TURNER, JANINE (Gauntt): Lincoln, NE, Dec. 6, 1963.

TURNER, KATHLEEN: Springfield, MO, June 19, 1954. UMd.

TURNER, TINA (Anna Mae Bullock): Nutbush, TN, Nov. 26, 1938.

TURTURRO, JOHN: Brooklyn, NY, Feb. 28, 1957. Yale.

TUSHINGHAM, RITA: Liverpool, England, Mar. 14, 1940.

TWIGGY (Lesley Hornby): London, Sept. 19, 1949.

TWOMEY, ANNE: Boston, MA, June 7, 1951. Temple U.

TYLER, BEVERLY (Beverly Jean Saul): Scranton, PA, July 5, 1928.

TYLER, LIV: Portland, ME, July 1, 1977.

TYRRELL, SUSAN: San Francisco, Mar. 18, 1945.

TYSON, CATHY: Liverpool, England, June 12, 1965. Royal Shake. Co.

TYSON, CICELY: NYC, Dec. 19, 1933. NYU.

UGGAMS, LESLIE: NYC, May 25, 1943. Juilliard.

ULLMAN, TRACEY: Slough, England, Dec. 30, 1959.

ULLMANN, LIV: Tokyo, Dec. 10, 1938. Webber-Douglas Acad.

ULRICH, SKEET (Bryan Ray Ulrich): North Carolina, Jan. 20, 1969.

UMEKI, MIYOSHI: Otaru, Hokaido, Japan, Apr. 3, 1929.

UNDERWOOD, BLAIR: Tacoma, WA, Aug. 25, 1964. Carnegie-Mellon U.

UNGER, DEBORAH KARA: Victoria, British Columbia, May 12, 1966.

USTINOV, PETER: London, Apr. 16, 1921. Westminster School.

VACCARO, BRENDA: Brooklyn, NY, Nov. 18, 1939. Neighborhood Playhouse.

VALLI, ALIDA: Pola, Italy, May 31, 1921. Academy of Drama.

VAN ARK, JOAN: NYC, June 16, 1943. Yale.

VAN DAMME, JEAN-CLAUDE (J-C Vorenberg): Brussels, Belgium, Apr. 1, 1960.

VAN DE VEN, MONIQUE: Zeeland, Netherlands, July 28, 1952.

VAN DER BEEK, JAMES: Chesire, CT, March 8, 1977.

VAN DEVERE, TRISH (Patricia Dressel): Englewood Cliffs, NJ, Mar. 9, 1945. Ohio Wesleyan.

VAN DIEN, CASPER: Ridgefield, NJ, Dec. 18, 1968.

VAN DOREN, MAMIE (Joan Lucile Olander): Rowena SD, Feb. 6, 1933.

VAN DYKE, DICK: West Plains, MO, Dec. 13, 1925.

VANITY (Denise Katrina Smith): Niagara, Ont., Can, Jan. 4, 1959.

VAN PALLANDT, NINA: Copenhagen, Denmark, July 15, 1932.

VAN PATTEN, DICK: NYC, Dec. 9, 1928.

VAN PATTEN, JOYCE: NYC, Mar. 9, 1934.

VAN PEEBLES, MARIO: NYC, Jan. 15, 1958. Columbia U.

VAN PEEBLES, MELVIN: Chicago, IL, Aug. 21, 1932.

VANCE, COURTNEY B.: Detroit, MI, Mar. 12, 1960.

VARDALOS, NIA: Winnipeg, Manitoba, Can., Sept. 24, 1962.

VAUGHN, ROBERT: NYC, Nov. 22, 1932. USC.

VAUGHN, VINCE: Minneapolis, MN, Mar. 28, 1970.

VEGA, ISELA: Hermosillo, Mexico, Nov. 5, 1940.

VELJOHNSON, REGINALD: NYC, Aug. 16, 1952.

VENNERA, CHICK: Herkimer, NY, Mar. 27, 1952. Pasadena Playhouse.

VENORA, DIANE: Hartford, CT, 1952. Juilliard.

VEREEN, BEN: Miami, FL, Oct. 10, 1946.

VERNON, JOHN: Montreal, Canada, Feb. 24, 1932.

VICTOR, JAMES (Lincoln Rafael Peralta Diaz): Santiago, D.R., July 27, 1939. Haaren HS/NYC.

VINCENT, JAN-MICHAEL: Denver, CO, July 15, 1944. Ventura.

VIOLET, ULTRA (Isabelle Collin-Dufresne): Grenoble, France, Sept. 6, 1935.

VITALE, MILLY: Rome, Italy, July 16, 1928. Lycee Chateaubriand.

VOHS, JOAN: St. Albans, NY, July 30, 1931.

VOIGHT, JON: Yonkers, NY, Dec. 29, 1938. Catholic U.

VON BARGEN, DANIEL: Cincinnati, OH, June 5, 1950. Purdue.

VON DOHLEN, LENNY: Augusta, GA, Dec. 22, 1958. UTex.

VON SYDOW, MAX: Lund, Sweden, July 10, 1929. Royal Drama Theatre.

WAGNER, LINDSAY: Los Angeles, June 22. 1949.

WAGNER, NATASHA GREGSON: Los Angeles, CA, Sept. 29, 1970.

WAGNER, ROBERT: Detroit, Feb. 10, 1930.

WAHL, KEN: Chicago, IL, Feb. 14, 1953.

WAITE, GENEVIEVE: South Africa, 1949.

WAITE, RALPH: White Plains, NY, June 22, 1929. Yale.

WAITS, TOM: Pomona, CA, Dec. 7, 1949.

WALKEN, CHRISTOPHER: Astoria, NY, Mar. 31, 1943. Hofstra.

WALKER, CLINT: Hartfold, IL, May 30, 1927. USC.

WALKER, PAUL: Glendale, CA, Sept. 12, 1973.

WALLACH, ELI: Brooklyn, NY, Dec. 7, 1915. CCNY, U Tex.

WALLACH, ROBERTA: NYC, Aug. 2, 1955.

WALLIS, SHANI: London, Apr. 5, 1941.

WALSH, M. EMMET: Ogdensburg, NY, Mar. 22, 1935. Clarkson College, AADA.

WALTER, JESSICA: Brooklyn, NY, Jan. 31, 1944 Neighborhood Playhouse.

WALTER, TRACEY: Jersey City, NJ, Nov. 25, 1942.

WALTERS, JULIE: London, Feb. 22, 1950.

WALTON, EMMA: London, Nov. 1962. Brown U.

WANAMAKER, ZOË: NYC, May 13, 1949.

WARD, BURT (Gervis): Los Angeles, July 6, 1945.

WARD, FRED: San Diego, CA, Dec. 30, 1942.

WARD, RACHEL: London, Sept. 12, 1957.

WARD, SELA: Meridian, MS, July 11, 1956.

WARD, SIMON: London, Oct. 19, 1941.

WARDEN, JACK (Lebzelter): Newark, NJ, Sept. 18, 1920.

WARNER, DAVID: Manchester, England, July 29, 1941. RADA.

WARNER, MALCOLM-JAMAL: Jersey City, NJ, Aug. 18, 1970.

WARREN, JENNIFER: NYC, Aug. 12, 1941. U Wisc.

WARREN, LESLEY ANN: NYC, Aug. 16, 1946.

WARREN, MICHAEL: South Bend, IN, Mar. 5, 1946. UCLA.

WARRICK, RUTH: St. Joseph, MO, June 29, 1915. U Mo.

WASHINGTON, DENZEL: Mt. Vernon, NY, Dec. 28, 1954. Fordham.

WASSON, CRAIG: Ontario, OR, Mar. 15, 1954. UOre.

WATERSTON, SAM: Cambridge, MA, Nov. 15, 1940. Yale.

WATSON, EMILY: London, Jan. 14, 1967.

WATSON, EMMA: Oxford, England, Apr. 15, 1990.

WATTS, NAOMI: Shoreham, Eng., Sept. 28, 1968.

WAYANS, DAMON: NYC, Sept. 4, 1960.

WAYANS, KEENEN, IVORY: NYC, June 8, 1958. Tuskegee Inst.

WAYNE, PATRICK: Los Angeles, July 15, 1939. Loyola.

WEATHERS, CARL: New Orleans, LA, Jan. 14, 1948. Long Beach CC.

WEAVER, DENNIS: Joplin, MO, June 4, 1924. U Okla.

WEAVER, FRITZ: Pittsburgh, PA, Jan. 19, 1926.

WEAVER, SIGOURNEY (Susan): NYC, Oct. 8, 1949. Stanford, Yale.

WEAVING, HUGO: Nigeria, Apr. 4, 1960. NIDA.

WEBER, STEVEN: Queens, NY, March 4, 1961.

WEDGEWORTH, ANN: Abilene, TX, Jan. 21, 1935. U Tex.

WEISZ, RACHEL: London, Mar. 7, 1971.

WELCH, RAQUEL (Tejada): Chicago, IL, Sept. 5, 1940.

WELD, TUESDAY (Susan): NYC, Aug. 27, 1943. Hollywood Professional School.

WELDON, JOAN: San Francisco, Aug. 5, 1933. San Francisco Conservatory.

WELLER, PETER: Stevens Point, WI, June 24, 1947. AmThWing.

WENDT, GEORGE: Chicago, IL, Oct. 17, 1948.

WEST, ADAM (William Anderson): Walla Walla, WA, Sept. 19, 1929.

WEST, SHANE: Baton Rouge, LA, June 10, 1978.

WETTIG, PATRICIA: Cincinatti, OH, Dec. 4, 1951. TempleU.

WHALEY, FRANK: Syracuse, NY, July 20, 1963. SUNY/Albany.

WHALLEY-KILMER, JOANNE: Manchester, England, Aug. 25, 1964.

WHEATON, WIL: Burbank, CA, July 29, 1972.

WHITAKER, FOREST: Longview, TX, July 15, 1961.

WHITAKER, JOHNNY: Van Nuys, CA, Dec. 13, 1959.

WHITE, BETTY: Oak Park, IL, Jan. 17, 1922.

WHITE, CHARLES: Perth Amboy, NJ, Aug. 29, 1920. Rutgers U.

WHITELAW, BILLIE: Coventry, England, June 6, 1932.

WHITMAN, STUART: San Francisco, Feb. 1, 1929. CCLA.

WHITMORE, JAMES: White Plains, NY, Oct. 1, 1921. Yale.

WHITNEY, GRACE LEE: Detroit, MI, Apr. 1, 1930.

WHITTON, MARGARET: Philadelphia, PA, Nov. 30, 1950.

WIDDOES, KATHLEEN: Wilmington, DE, Mar. 21, 1939.

WIDMARK, RICHARD: Sunrise, MN, Dec. 26, 1914. Lake Forest.

WIEST, DIANNE: Kansas City, MO, Mar. 28, 1948. UMd.

WILBY. JAMES: Burma, Feb. 20, 1958.

WILCOX, COLIN: Highlands, NC, Feb. 4, 1937. U Tenn.

WILDER, GENE (Jerome Silberman): Milwaukee, WI, June 11, 1935. Uiowa.

WILKINSON, TOM: Leeds, England, Dec. 12, 1948. Univ.of Kent.

WILLARD, FRED: Shaker Heights, OH, Sept. 18, 1939.

WILLIAMS, BILLY DEE: NYC, Apr. 6, 1937.

WILLIAMS, CARA (Bernice Kamiat): Brooklyn, NY, June 29, 1925.

WILLIAMS, CINDY: Van Nuys, CA, Aug. 22, 1947. KACC.

WILLIAMS, CLARENCE, III: NYC, Aug. 21, 1939.

WILLIAMS, ESTHER: Los Angeles, Aug. 8, 1921.

WILLIAMS, JOBETH: Houston, TX, Dec 6, 1948. Brown U.

WILLIAMS, MICHELLE: Kalispell, MT, Sept. 9, 1980.

WILLIAMS, OLIVIA: London, Jan. 1, 1968.

WILLIAMS, PAUL: Omaha, NE, Sept. 19, 1940.

WILLIAMS, ROBIN: Chicago, IL, July 21, 1951. Juilliard.

WILLIAMS, TREAT (Richard): Rowayton, CT, Dec. 1, 1951.

WILLIAMS, VANESSA L.: Tarrytown, NY, Mar. 18, 1963.

WILLIAMSON, FRED: Gary, IN, Mar. 5, 1938. Northwestern.

WILLIAMSON, NICOL: Hamilton, Scotland, Sept. 14, 1938.

WILLIS, BRUCE: Penns Grove, NJ, Mar. 19, 1955.

WILLISON, WALTER: Monterey Park, CA, June 24, 1947.

WILSON, DEMOND: NYC, Oct. 13, 1946. Hunter College.

WILSON, ELIZABETH: Grand Rapids, MI, Apr. 4, 1925.

WILSON, LAMBERT: Neuilly-sur-Seine, France, Aug. 3, 1958.

WILSON, LUKE: Dallas, TX, Sept. 21, 1971.

WILSON, OWEN: Dallas, TX, Nov. 18, 1968.

WILSON, SCOTT: Atlanta, GA, Mar. 29, 1942.

WINCOTT, JEFF: Toronto, Canada, May 8, 1957.

WINCOTT, MICHAEL: Toronto, Canada, Jan. 6, 1959. Juilliard.

WINDOM, WILLIAM: NYC, Sept. 28, 1923. Williams College.

WINFIELD, PAUL: Los Angeles, May 22, 1940. UCLA.

WINFREY, OPRAH: Kosciusko, MS, Jan. 29, 1954. TnStateU.

WINGER, DEBRA: Cleveland, OH, May 17, 1955. Cal State.

WINKLER, HENRY: NYC, Oct. 30, 1945. Yale.

WINN, KITTY: Washington, D.C., Feb, 21, 1944. Boston U.

WINNINGHAM, MARE: Phoenix, AZ, May 6, 1959.

WINSLET, KATE: Reading, Eng., Oct. 5, 1975.

WINSLOW, MICHAEL: Spokane, WA, Sept. 6, 1960.

WINTER, ALEX: London, July 17, 1965. NYU.

WINTERS, JONATHAN: Dayton, OH, Nov. 11, 1925. Kenyon College.

WINTERS, SHELLEY (Shirley Schrift): St. Louis, Aug. 18, 1922. Wayne U.

WITHERS, GOOGIE: Karachi, India, Mar. 12, 1917. Italia Conti.

WITHERS, JANE: Atlanta, GA, Apr. 12, 1926.

WITHERSPOON, REESE (Laura Jean Reese Witherspoon): Nashville, TN, Mar. 22, 1976.

WOLF, SCOTT: Newton, MA, June 4, 1968.

WONG, B.D.: San Francisco, Oct. 24,1962.

WONG, RUSSELL: Troy, NY, Mar. 1, 1963. SantaMonica College.

WOOD, ELIJAH: Cedar Rapids, IA, Jan 28, 1981.

WOODARD, ALFRE: Tulsa, OK, Nov. 2, 1953. Boston U.

WOODLAWN, HOLLY (Harold Ajzenberg): Juana Diaz, PR, 1947.

WOODS, JAMES: Vernal, UT, Apr. 18, 1947. MIT.

WOODWARD, EDWARD: Croyden, Surrey, England, June 1, 1930.

WOODWARD, JOANNE: Thomasville, GA, Feb. 27, 1930. Neighborhood Playhouse.

WORONOV, MARY: Brooklyn, NY, Dec. 8, 1946. Cornell.

WRAY, FAY: Alberta, Canada, Sept. 15, 1907.

WRIGHT, AMY: Chicago, IL, Apr. 15, 1950.

WRIGHT, MAX: Detroit, MI, Aug. 2, 1943. WayneStateU.

WRIGHT, ROBIN: Dallas, TX, Apr. 8, 1966.

WRIGHT, TERESA: NYC, Oct. 27, 1918.

WUHL, ROBERT: Union City, NJ, Oct. 9, 1951. UHouston.

WYATT, JANE: NYC, Aug. 10, 1910. Barnard College.

WYLE, NOAH: Los Angeles, June 2, 1971.

WYMAN, JANE (Sarah Jane Fulks): St. Joseph, MO, Jan. 4, 1914.

WYMORE, PATRICE: Miltonvale, KS, Dec. 17, 1926.

WYNN, MAY (Donna Lee Hickey): NYC, Jan. 8, 1930.

WYNTER, DANA (Dagmar): London, June 8. 1927. Rhodes U.

YORK, MICHAEL: Fulmer, England, Mar. 27, 1942. Oxford.

YORK, SUSANNAH: London, Jan. 9, 1941. RADA.

YOUNG, ALAN (Angus): North Shield, England, Nov. 19, 1919.

YOUNG, BURT: Queens, NY, Apr. 30, 1940.

YOUNG, CHRIS: Chambersburg, PA, Apr. 28, 1971.

YOUNG, SEAN: Louisville, KY, Nov. 20, 1959. Interlochen.

YULIN, HARRIS: Los Angeles, Nov. 5, 1937.

YUN-FAT, CHOW: Lamma Island, Hong Kong, May 18, 1955.

ZACHARIAS, ANN: Stockholm, Sweden, Sweden, 1956.

ZADORA, PIA: Hoboken, NJ, May 4, 1954.

ZELLWEGER, RENÉE: Katy, TX, Apr. 25, 1969.

ZERBE, ANTHONY: Long Beach, CA, May 20, 1939.

ZETA-JONES, CATHERINE: Swansea, Wales, Sept. 25, 1969.

ZIMBALIST, EFREM, JR.: NYC, Nov.30, 1918. Yale.

ZUNIGA, DAPHNE: Berkeley, CA, Oct.28, 1963. UCLA.

OBITUARIES - 2002

John Agar

Parley Baer

Milton Berle

Eddie Bracken

Michael Bryant

Phyllis Calvert

JOHN AGAR, 81, Chicago-born screen and television actor, died of emphysema on April 7, 2002 in Burbank, CA. He made his movie debut in 1948 in director John Ford's *Fort Apache*, opposite his wife (1946-49), Shirley Temple. This was followed by such films as *She Wore a Yellow Ribbon, Sands of Iwo Jima, Adventure in Baltimore, Along the Great Divide, The Magic Carpet, The Rocket Man, Shield for Murder, Revenge of the Creature, Tarantula, The Mole People, Joe Butterfly, The Brain from Planet Arous, Attack of the Puppet People, Raymie, Stage to Thunder Rock, Women of the Prehistoric Planet, The St. Valentine's Day Massacre, The Undefeated, Chisum, King Kong* (1976), and *Miracle Mile*. He is survived by a daughter (from his marriage to Temple), two sons, four grandchildren, and two brothers.

SHELDON ALLMAN, 77, Chicago-born actor-composer, who wrote the theme for the animated cartoon "George of the Jungle," died of heart failure on Jan. 22, 2002 in Culver City, CA. As an actor he was seen in such movies as *Hud, The Sons of Katie Elder, Nevada Smith,* and *In Cold Blood*.

PARLEY BAER, 88, Salt Lake City-born screen, stage and television character player, died of complications from a stroke on Nov. 22, 2002. He appeared in such movies as *Union Station, People Will Talk, Elopement, Away All Boats, The Young Lions, The FBI Story, Cash McCall, Bedtime Story, Those Calloways, Fluffy, Where Were You When the Lights Went Out?,* and *Last of the Dogmen*. On television his voice was familiar as the Keebler elf. He is survived by two daughters and three grandchildren.

MILTON BERLE (Milton Berlinger), 93, New York City-born comedian-actor, one of the pioneering entertainers of the early days of television, who earned the nickname "Uncle Miltie," died in his sleep at his home in Los Angeles on March 27, 2002. He started as a child actor, appearing in support of Charlie Chaplin in *Tillie's Punctured Romance,* then moved on to nightclubs and Broadway as an adult performer. He made his big splash on the small screen with "Texaco Star Theatre" which ran from 1948 to 1954. On the big screen he was seen in such motion pictures as *New Faces of 1937, Sun Valley Serenade, Over My Dead Body, Always Leave Them Laughing, The Bellboy, Let's Make Love, It's a Mad Mad Mad Mad World, The Loved One, The Oscar, The Happening, Who's Minding the Mint?, Can Hieronymus Merkin Ever Forget Mercy Humppe and Find True Happiness?, Lepke, Won Ton Ton, The Dog Who Saved Hollywood, The Muppet Movie,* and *Pee-wee's Big Adventure.* Survived by his third wife and his daughter.

BILLIE BIRD, 94, Idaho-born screen and television character actress, died of Alzheimer's disease on Nov. 27, 2002 in Granada Hills, CA. She was seen in such films as *Darling How Could You!, Somebody Loves Me, Half a Hero, Blue Denim, Barefoot in the Park, The Odd Couple, Getting Straight, Sixteen Candles, Ernest Saves Christmas, Home Alone,* and *Dennis the Menace.*

MARGARET BOOTH, 104, Los Angeles-born film editor whose seven-decade career in the industry brought her a special Oscar from the Motion Picture Academy in 1977, died on Oct. 28, 2002 in Los Angeles of complications from a stroke. Her credits include such movies as *Memory Lane, Strange Interlude, Dancing Lady, The Barretts of Wimpole Street* (1934), *Mutiny on the Bounty* (Oscar nomination), *Camille, A Yank at Oxford, The Red Badge of Courage, Funny Girl, The Owl and the Pussycat, Fat City, The Sunshine Boys, Murder by Death,* and *Annie.* Survived by a cousin.

EDDIE BRACKEN, 87, New York City-born screen, stage, and television actor, best known for his starring roles in the Preston Sturges classics *The Miracle of Morgan's Creek* and *Hail the Conquering Hero,* died of complications from surgery on Nov. 14, 2002 in Montclair, NJ. His other films include *Too Many Girls, Life With Henry, Caught in the Draft, Reaching for the Sun, The Fleet's In, Sweater Girl, Star Spangled Rhythm, Happy Go Lucky, Bring on the Girls, Duffy's Tavern, Out of This World, Summer Stock, We're Not Married, About Face, National Lampoon's Vacation, Oscar,* and *Rookie of the Year.* His wife of 63 years, actress Connie Nickerson, had passed away in August of that year. He is survived by his five children, nine grandchildren, and two great-grandchildren.

MARY BRIAN (Louise Byrdie Dantzler), 96, Texas-born screen actress who appeared in such notable films of the early sound era as *The Virginian, The Royal Family of Broadway,* and *The Front Page,* died on Dec. 30, 2002 in Del Mar, CA. Among her other films were *Beau Geste* (1926), *Behind the Front, Harold Teen, River of Romance, Man on the Flying Trapeze, Shadows of Sing Sing, College Rhythm,* and *Navy Blues.* She married film editor George Tomasini in 1947, the same year she made her last motion picture, *Dragnet.* Survived by her godson.

MICHAEL BRYANT, 74, London-born screen and stage character actor died on April 25, 2002 at his home in Richmond, Surrey, England. He could be seen in such movies as *A Night to Remember* (1958), *The Mind Benders, The Deadly Affair, Goodbye Mr. Chips* (1969), *Nicholas and Alexandra* (as Lenin), *The Ruling Class, Gandhi,* and *Hamlet* (1996). He is survived by his second wife, and four children from his first marriage.

PHYLLIS CALVERT (Phyllis Bickle), 87, British leading lady of such popular Gainsborough Studios melodramas as *The Man in Gray* and *Fanny by Gaslight,* died of natural causes on Oct. 8, 2002 in London. Her other credits include *Kipps, Madonna of the Seven Moons, They Were Sisters, Appointment With Danger, Mandy, Mr. Denning Drives North, Indiscreet, The Battle of the Villa Fiorita, Oh! What a Lovely War,* and *Mrs. Dalloway.* She is survived by a son, daughter, and a grandson.

KATRIN CARTLIDGE, 41, London-born actress, best known for her roles in the Mike Leigh films *Naked* and *Career Girls,* died of septicemia resulting from pneumonia on Sept. 7, 2002 in London. She was seen in such other pictures as *Before the Rain, Breaking the Waves, Claire Dolan,* and *No Man's Land.* She is survived by her parents, a brother, a sister, and her partner.

James Coburn

Jeff Corey

Keene Curtis

Maurice Denham

Brad Dexter

John Frankenheimer

ROSEMARY CLOONEY, 74, Kentucky-born singer of such 1950s novelty hits as "Come on-a My House" and "Mambo Italiana," who later gained a following as an acclaimed cabaret performer and pop-jazz song stylist, died of complications from lung cancer at her Beverly Hills home on June 29, 2002. She appeared in the films *The Stars Are Singing, Here Come the Girls, Red Garters, White Christmas, Deep in My Heart* (opposite then-husband Jose Ferrer), and *Radioland Murders*. She is survived by her second husband; her five children from her marriage to Ferrer, including actor Miguel Ferrer; 10 grandchildren; her brother, television commentator Nick Clooney (father of actor George Clooney); and her sister.

JOE COBB, 85, Oklahoma-born child actor, who was one of the earliest stars of the "Our Gang" shorts, died in Santa Ana, CA, on May 21, 2002. Among the shorts in which he could be seen were "The Big Show," "A Pleasant Journey," "Lodge Night," "Stage Fright," "No Noise," "Tire Trouble," "It's a Bear," and "Cradle Robbers." Survivors include a sister.

JAMES COBURN, 74, Nebraska born-screen and television actor, whose rugged devil-may-car charm was seen in such films as *Our Man Flint, Waterhole #3,* and *The President's Analyst,* died of cardiac arrest at Cedars-Sinai Hospital in Los Angeles on Nov. 18, 2002. Following his 1959 debut in *Ride Lonesome* he was seen such pictures as *The Magnificent Seven, Hell Is for Heroes, The Great Escape, Charade, The Americanization of Emily, Major Dundee, A High Wind in Jamaica, The Loved One, What Did You Do in the War Daddy?, Dead Heat on a Merry-Go-Round, In Like Flint, Candy, Last of the Mobile Hot Shots, Duck You Sucker (A Fistful of Dynamite), The Carey Treatment, The Last of Sheila, Pat Garrett and Billy the Kid, Harry in Your Pocket, Bite the Bullet, Hard Times* (1975), *Midway, Cross of Iron, The Muppet Movie, Goldengirl, Loving Couples, Looker, Hudson Hawk, Maverick, The Nutty Professor* (1996), *Affliction* (for which he won the Academy Award as Best Supporting Actor of 1998), *Monsters Inc.* (voice), and *The Man From Elysian Fields.* He is survived by his wife, two children, and two grandchildren.

HERMAN COHEN, 76, Detroit-born producer-writer of such low budget horror films as *I Was a Teenage Werewolf, I Was a Teenage Frankenstein,* and *How to Make a Monster,* died at Cedars-Sinai Medical Center in Los Angeles on June 2, 2002. He had been suffering from throat cancer. His other credits include *Black Zoo, Konga, A Study in Terror, Berserk!,* and *Trog.* He is survived by a brother and a sister.

JEFF COREY, 88, Brooklyn-born character actor whose long career was interrupted in the 1950s when he was blacklisted for his past association with the Communist party and thereby became a noted drama teacher, died on Aug. 16, 2002 in Los Angeles. His many credits include *All That Money Can Buy, The Reluctant Dragon, Roxie Hart, The Moon Is Down, My Friend Flicka, The Killers* (1946), *The Gangster, Unconquered, Wake of the Red Witch, Joan of Arc, Home of the Brave, The Outriders, The Next Voice You Hear, Bright Leaf, Fourteen Hours, The Balcony, Lady in a Cage, The Cincinnati Kid, Mickey One, Seconds, In Cold Blood, The Boston Strangler, True Grit, Butch Cassidy and the Sundance Kid, Getting Straight, Little Big Man, The Last Tycoon, Oh God!, Conan the Destroyer, Bird on a Wire, Ruby Cairo,* and *Color of Night.* Survived by his wife of 64 years, three daughters, and six grandchildren.

KEENE CURTIS, 79, Salt Lake City-born screen, stage, and television actor, died of complications from Alzheimer's disease on Oct. 13, 2002 in Bountiful, UT. In addition to his Tony Award-winning role in *The Rothschilds* and his recurring role on "Cheers," he was seen in such movies as *American Hot Wax, Heaven Can Wait* (1978), and *Rabbit Test.* No immediate survivors.

TED DEMME, 38, film director died of a heart attack while playing basketball in Santa Monica, CA, on Jan. 13, 2002. His feature credits include *The Ref, Beautiful Girls, Life,* and *Blow.* He was the nephew of director Jonathan Demme.

MAURICE DENHAM (William Maurice Denham), 92, British character player died in London on July 24, 2002 of natural causes. He could be seen in such films as *Oliver Twist* (1948), *Miranda, The Blue Lagoon* (1949), *Man With a Million, 23 Paces to Baker Street, All at Sea (Barnacle Bill), Curse of the Demon, Our Man in Havana, Sink the Bismarck!, The Mark, Damn the Defiant! (H.M.S. Defiant), Operation Crossbow, Nicholas & Alexandra, Sunday Bloody Sunday, Julia,* and *84 Charing Cross Road.* Survived by two sons and a daughter.

ANDRE DE TOTH (Sasvrai Farkasfalvi Tothfalusi Toth Endre Anral Mihaly), 89 or 92, Hungary-born director-writer, best known for helming the most noted of all the 1950s 3-D features, *House of Wax,* died of an aneurysm on Oct. 27, 2002 at his home in Burbank, CA. His other films include *Passport to Suez, Dark Waters, Slattery's Hurricane, Pitfall, Springfield Rifle, Crime Wave, Last of the Comanches, The Stranger Wore a Gun, The Indian Fighter, Monkey on My Back, Day of the Outlaw, The Mongols,* and *Play Dirty.* He earned his sole Oscar nomination for co-writing the script for *The Gunfighter.* He was married (1944 to 1952) to actress Veronica Lake, whom he directed in the film *Ramrod.* Survivors include his seventh wife and an unspecified number of his 19 children.

Cliff Gorman

Dolores Gray

James Gregory

Carrie Hamilton

Richard Harris

Signe Hasso

BRAD DEXTER (Boris Milanovich), 85, Nevada-born screen and television actor, best known for playing one of *The Magnificent Seven*, died on Dec. 12, 2002 in Rancho Mirage, CA, of emphysema. His other films include *The Asphalt Jungle, Macao, The Oklahoman, Taras Bulba, Bus Riley's Back in Town, Von Ryan's Express,* and *Blindfold*. He also received producer credit on the films *The Naked Runner* and *The Lawyer*.

JOHN ENTWISTLE, 57, British bass player for the popular rock group The Who, died on June 27, 2002 of a heart attack in Las Vegas, NV, where he and the other surviving members of the band were about to embark on a tour. With The Who he could be seen in the films *Monterey Pop, Woodstock, Tommy* (for which he helped collaborate on several songs as well), and *The Kids Are Alright*. Survived by a son.

SUSAN FLEMING, 94, New York City-born actress, best known for playing W.C. Fields' daughter in the satire *Million Dollar Legs*, died in Rancho Mirage, CA, of a heart attack on Dec. 22, 2002. She could also be seen in such movies as *Men Are Like That, A Dangerous Affair, Charlie Chan's Courage, Navy Wife, Gold Diggers of 1937,* and *God's Country and the Woman*. She retired from acting shortly after marrying Harpo Marx in 1936. They remained wed until his death in 1964.

JOHN FRANKENHEIMER, 72, New York City-born director, whose credits include such classic 1960s dramas as *The Manchurian Candidate, Birdman of Alcatraz,* and *Seven Days in May*, died of a massive stroke from complications after spinal surgery on July 6, 2002 in Los Angeles. Following a career of directing on television, he made his theatrical debut with *The Young Stranger*, followed by such credits as *All Fall Down, The Train, Seconds, Grand Prix, The Fixer, The Gypsy Moths, I Walk the Line, Black Sunday, 52 Pick-Up, The Island of Dr. Moreau, Ronin,* and *Reindeer Games*. He is survived by his wife of 41 years, Evans Evans, two daughters, a grandson, his sister, and his brother.

LEONARD GERSHE, 79, New York City-born screen and stage writer, who earned an Oscar nomination for his script for *Funny Face* (for which he also collaborated on two songs with Roger Edens), died of complications from a stroke on March 9, 2002 in Beverly Hills, CA. He adapted his best known play, *Butterflies Are Free*, to the screen in 1972. Survived by a brother and a sister.

SIDNEY GLAZIER, 86, Philadelphia-born movie producer whose best-known credit is the classic 1968 Mel Brooks' comedy *The Producers*, died in Bennington, VT, on Dec. 14, 2002. His other movies include *Take the Money and Run, The Twelve Chairs, Quackser Fortune Has a Cousin in the Bronx,* and *Glen and Randa*. He is survived by his brother, and a daughter.

CLIFF GORMAN, 65, Queens-born screen, stage, and television actor, who played the flamboyantly gay Emory in *The Boys in the Band* (repeating his Obie Award-winning role from the original Off-Broadway production), died of leukemia on Sept. 5, 2002 at his home in Manhattan. He could be seen in such other movies as *Justine, Cops and Robbers, Rosebud, An Unmarried Woman, All That Jazz, Angel, Night and the City* (1992), and *Ghost Dog: The Way of the Samurai*. On Broadway he won a Tony Award for his starring role in *Lenny*. Survived by his wife.

TERESA GRAVES, 53, Houston-born actress, who appeared on the series "Rowan & Martin's Laugh-In" and "Get Christie Love!," died on Oct. 10, 2002 after a fire in her home in Los Angeles. Her movies include *Black Eye, That Man Bolt,* and *Vampira*. She left show business in 1983 to concentrate on religion. No reported survivors.

DOLORES GRAY, 78, Chicago-born actress-singer of screen and stage died of a heart attack on June 26, 2002 in her Manhattan apartment. Following her Tony Award-winning performance in the Broadway show *Carnival in Flanders* (in which she introduced "Here's That Rainy Day"), she was signed to a contract by MGM, appearing in four films, *It's Always Fair Weather, Kismet, The Opposite Sex,* and *Designing Woman*. Survived by her stepdaughter.

JAMES GREGORY, 90, Bronx-born screen, stage, and television actor, died of natural causes on Sept. 16, 2002 at his home in Sedona, AZ. His motion picture credits include *The Young Stranger, Onionhead, Hey Boy! Hey Girl!, Two Weeks in Another Town, The Manchurian Candidate, Captain Newman M.D., Twilight of Honor, The Sons of Katie Elder, The Silencers, Clambake, The Love God?, Beneath the Planet of the Apes, Million Dollar Duck,* and *The Main Event*. On television he was best known for playing Inspector Luger on "Barney Miller." He is survived by his wife of 58 years.

CARRIE HAMILTON, 38, actress-writer died in Los Angeles on Jan. 21, 2002 of cancer. In addition to acting in such films as *Tokyo Pop, Shag,* and *Cool World*, she co-wrote the play *Hollywood Arms* with her mother, actress Carol Burnett. Along with Burnett, she is survived by her two sisters.

LIONEL HAMPTON, 94, Kentucky-born vibraphone player who became on of the leading figures of the swing era, died of complications of old age and a recent heart attack on Aug. 31, 2002 in Manhattan. He appeared as himself in such motion pictures as *Pennies from Heaven* (1936), *Hollywood Hotel, A Song Is Born, The Benny Goodman Story, Mister Rock and Roll,* and *Listen Up: The Lives of Quincy Jones*.

George Roy Hill

Kim Hunter

Katy Jurado

John Justin

Hildegard Knef

Jack Kruschen

JONATHAN HARRIS, 87, New York City-born character actor, best known for playing the pompous Dr. Zachary Smith on the 1960s series "Lost in Space," died of a blood clot on Nov. 3, 2002 in Los Angeles. His movie credits include *Botany Bay* and *The Big Fisherman*, plus voice work in *A Bug's Life* and *Toy Story 2*. Survived by his wife of 64 years, a son, two grandchildren, and two sisters.

RICHARD HARRIS, 72, Ireland-born screen, stage, and television actor, who earned Oscar nominations for his work in *This Sporting Life* and *The Field*, died of lymphatic cancer on Oct. 25, 2002 in London. During the 1960s the dynamic and unpredictable actor became one of the major British imports of the decade and his long list of films came to include such titles as *The Wreck of the Mary Deare, The Night Fighters (A Terrible Beauty), The Long and the Short and the Tall (The Jungle Fighters), Mutiny on the Bounty* (1962), *Red Desert, Major Dundee, The Heroes of Telemark, Hawaii, The Bible, Caprice, Camelot, The Molly Maguires, A Man Called Horse, Cromwell, Man in the Wilderness, The Hero (Broomfield;* which he also directed and co-wrote), *Juggernaut, Robin and Marian, The Cassandra Crossing, Orca, The Wild Geese, Tarzan the Ape Man* (1981), *Mack the Knife, Patriot Games, Unforgiven, Wrestling Ernest Hemingway, Cry the Beloved Country* (1995), *Trojan Eddie, Gladiator, Harry Potter and the Sorcerer's Stone, The Count of Monte Cristo* (2002), and *Harry Potter and the Chamber of Secrets.* Survived by his three sons from his first marriage, including actor Jared Harris.

SIGNE HASSO (Signe Larsson), 91, Swedish actress, who appeared in such notable 1940s films as *The House on 92nd Street* and *A Double Life*, died in Los Angeles on June 7, 2002. Among her other credits are *Assignment in Brittany, The Seventh Cross, Johnny Angel, A Scandal in Paris, Where There's Life, To the Ends of the Earth, Crisis, Picture Mommy Dead, The Black Bird,* and *I Never Promised You a Rose Garden.* Survived, by a sister and three nieces.

GEORGE ROY HILL, 81, Minneapolis-born director who won the Academy Award for his work on the 1973 Best Picture winner *The Sting*, died of complications from Parkinson's disease on Dec. 27, 2002 at his Manhattan apartment. His other film credits are *Period of Adjustment* (his debut, in 1962), *Toys in the Attic, The World of Henry Orient, Hawaii, Thoroughly Modern Millie, Butch Cassidy and the Sundance Kid* (for which he earned an Oscar nomination), *Slaughterhouse Five, The Great Waldo Pepper* (also producer and story), *Slap Shot, A Little Romance, The World According to Garp* (also producer and actor), *The Little Drummer Girl,* and *Funny Farm.* He is survived by two sons, two daughters, and 12 grandchildren.

PETER R. HUNT, 77, British film editor and director, best known for helming the 1969 James Bond adventure *On Her Majesty's Secret Service,* died of heart failure on Aug. 14, 2002 in Santa Monica, CA. As an editor he worked on such movies as *Sink the Bismarck!, Damn the Defiant! (H.M.S. Defiant), Dr. No, From Russia With Love, Goldfinger,* and *The Ipcress Files,* while his directorial credits include *Gold, Shout at the Devil, Death Hunt,* and *Assassination.* Survived by his son and a brother.

KIM HUNTER (Janet Cole), 79, Detroit-born screen, stage, and television actress, best known for her Oscar-winning portrayal of Stella Kowalski in the classic 1951 film *A Streetcar Named Desire* (repeating her role from the Broadway original), died of a heart attack in her Manhattan apartment on Sept. 11, 2002. Following her 1943 debut in the thriller *The Seventh Victim,* she appeared in such movies as *Tender Comrade, You Came Along, Stairway to Heaven (A Matter of Life and Death), Deadline U.S.A., Anything Can Happen, Storm Center, The Young Stranger, Lilith, Planet of the Apes* (as simian Dr. Zira, a role she repeated in two sequels), *The Swimmer, Two Evil Eyes, Midnight in the Garden of Good and Evil,* and *A Price Above Rubies.* She is survived by her daughter, a son, and six grandchildren.

CHUCK JONES, 89, Spokane-born animator and director, best known for his work on the Warner Bros. Looney Tunes and Merry Melodies shorts, died of congestive heart failure on Feb. 22, 2002 at his home in Corona del Mar, CA. Joining Warners in 1933, he became one of the key animators who brought to life such classic characters as Bugs Bunny, Daffy Duck, and Porky Pig. He himself came up with such creations as Road Runner, Wile E. Coyote, Pepe Le Pew, and Marvin Martian. He won the Academy Award for the 1965 short "The Dot and the Line" and received a special Oscar in 1996. His feature credits include directing and producing *The Phantom Tollbooth* and making cameos in *Gremlins* and *Innerspace.* Survived by his second wife, a stepson, a stepdaughter, three grand-children, three step-grandchildren, and six great-grandchildren.

KATY JURADO, 78, Mexican actress, best known for her role as Gary Cooper's former mistress in the classic western *High Noon*, died on July 5, 2002 in Cuernavaca, Mexico, after suffering from lung and heart ailments. After a career in Mexican films she made her American debut in 1951 in *Bullfighter and the Lady*, followed by such credits as *Arrowhead, Broken Lance* (for which she earned an Oscar nomination in the supporting category), *The Racers, Trial, Trapeze, Dragoon Wells Massacre, The Badlanders* (acting opposite Ernest Borgnine to whom she was briefly married), *One-Eyed Jacks, Barabbas, Smoky, A Covenant With Death, Stay Away Joe, Pat Garrett and Billy the Kid, Under the Volcano,* and *The Hi-Lo Country.* Survived by her daughter, several grandchildren, and a brother.

Peggy Lee

Buddy Lester

Linda Lovelace

Nobu McCarthy

Bill McCutcheon

Leo McKern

JOHN JUSTIN (John Justinian de Ledesma), 85, British actor, best known for playing Prince Ahmad in the 1940 version of *The Thief of Bagdad*, died on Nov. 29, 2002. Among his other credits are *The Angel With the Trumpet, Breaking the Sound Barrier, Melba, King of the Khyber Rifles, Crest of the Wave (Seagulls Over Sorrento), Safari, Island in the Sun, The Golden Salamander, Savage Messiah, Lisztomania, Valentino* (1977), and *Trenchcoat*. Survived by his third wife, and three daughters from his marriage to actress Barbara Murray.

WARD KIMBALL, 88, Minneapolis-born Walt Disney animator, one of the studio's fabled "nine old men," died of natural causes on July 8, 2002 in San Gabriel, CA. He worked as animator or directing animator on such Disney films as *Snow White and the 7 Dwarfs, Pinocchio* (he is credited with creating Jiminy Cricket), *Fantasia, The Three Caballeros, Cinderella, Peter Pan,* and *Mary Poppins.* He also headed the group responsible for the Oscar-winning short subjects "Toot, Whistle, Plunk and Boom" and "It's Tough to Be a Bird." He is survived by his wife of 77 years, three children, five grandchildren, and two great-grandchildren.

HILDEGARD KNEF, 76, German actress-singer-writer, died of a lung infection on Feb. 1, 2002 in Berlin. Following World War II she acted in such films as *Die Morder sind unter uns (Muderers Among Us)* and *Die Sunderin (The Sinner),* then came to the United States where she was seen in *Decision Before Dawn, Diplomatic Courier, The Snows of Kilimanjaro,* and *Night Without Sleep.* Her later credits include *Holiday for Henrietta, The Man Between, Svengali, Port of Desire, Subway in the Sky, The Three Penny Opera, And So to Bed, The Lost Continent,* and *Fedora.* Survived by her daughter and third husband.

JACK KRUSCHEN, 80, Canada-born character actor, best known for his Oscar-nominated role as Dr. Dreyfuss in the Academy Award-winning classic *The Apartment,* died of natural causes on Apr. 2, 2002. His other movies include *The War of the Worlds, It Should Happen to You, Tennessee Champ, The Night Holds Terror, The Benny Goodman Story, Julie, Reform School Girl, The Decks Ran Red, The Gazebo, The Bellboy, The Last Voyage, Studs Lonigan, Lover Come Back, Cape Fear* (1962), *The Unsinkable Molly Brown, Caprice, Freebie and the Bean,* and *'Til There Was You.* Survived by his wife, his children, and grandchildren.

PEGGY LEE (Norma Deloris Egstrom), 81, North Dakota-born singer, songwriter, and actress, whose inimitable sultry vocals turned such songs as "Why Don't You Do That Right?," "Mañana," "Fever," and "Is That All There Is?" into classic recordings, died of a heart attack at her home in Los Angeles on Jan. 21, 2002. She appeared in the films *The Powers Girl, Stage Door Canteen, Mr. Music, The Jazz Singer* (1952; which featured the song "It's a Good Day" which she co-wrote with Dave Barbour, to whom she was married, 1943-51), and *Pete Kelly's Blues* (for which she received an Oscar nomination). Her voice was also heard in the 1955 Disney animated film *Lady and the Tramp.* Ms. Lee, whose five marriages included those to actors Brad Dexter and Dewey Martin, is survived by a daughter from her marriage to Barbour.

ROSETTA LeNOIRE (Rosetta Burton), 90, New York City-born screen, stage, and television actress, died of natural causes on March 17, 2002 in Teaneck, NJ. In addition to appearing as Mother Winslow on the TV series "Family Matters," she was seen in such motion pictures as *Anna Lucasta, The Sunshine Boys, Daniel, The Brother from Another Planet, Moscow on the Hudson,* and *Brewster's Millions* (1985). She is survived by her son, her sister, her two brothers, two grandchildren, and two great-grandchildren.

BUDDY LESTER, 85, Chicago-born comedian-turned-character actor, whose roles included playing one of the heist participants in the 1960 version of *Ocean's Eleven,* died in Los Angeles on Oct. 4, 2002, of cancer. He could be seen in such other pictures as *The Gene Krupa Story, The Ladies Man, Sergeants 3, The Nutty Professor* (1963), *The Patsy, The Big Mouth,* and *Hardly Working.* He is survived by a daughter, a son, four grandchildren, and three great grandchildren.

LINDA LOVELACE (Linda Boreman), 53, Bronx born actress, who starred in perhaps the most famous of all pornographic films, *Deep Throat,* died on April 22, 2002 in Denver from injuries from a car accident on April 3. She later denounced her past, writing a book about her experiences, *Ordeal,* in 1980. She is survived by her son and daughter from her second marriage, a sister, and three grandchildren.

JAMES LUISI, 73, New York-born basketball player-turned-actor, best known for his role as Lt. Chapman on the television series "The Rockford Files," died of cancer in Los Angeles on June 7, 2002. Among his feature films were *Ben, I Escaped from Devil's Island, Norma Rae, Fade to Black, Star 80,* and *Murphy's Law.* Survived by his wife, a daughter, two grandchildren, and his brother.

LUCILLE LUND, 89, film actress of the 1930s died on Feb. 15, 2002 at her home in Rolling Hills, CA. Her credits include *Saturday's Millions, The Black Cat* (1934), *Kiss and Makeup, Blake of Scotland Yard. Broadway Melody of 1936, Panic on the Air, The Devil Is Driving,* and *There's That Woman Again.* No reported survivors.

SIHUNG LUNG (Hsiung Lang), 72, Taiwanese actor who appeared in the Ang Lee films *Pushing Hands, The Wedding Banquet, Eat Drink Man Woman,* and *Crouching Tiger, Hidden Dragon,* died of liver failure on May 2, 2002 in Taipei. He is survived by his wife and a daughter.

IAN MacNAUGHTON, 76, British actor-turned-director, best known for directing the series "Monty Python's Flying Circus," died in Munich on Dec. 10, 2002 after being injured in a car accident. His acting credits include *Rob Roy the Highland Rogue* and *X the Unknown.* Survived by his two children.

Marvin Mirisch

Dudley Moore

George Nader

Joel Oliansky

Bibi Osterwald

Bruce Paltrow

ALAN MANSON, 83, screen, stage, and television actor, died in New York on Mar. 5, 2002 of natural causes. He could be seen in such movies as *This Is the Army, Cop Hater, The Rain People, Let's Scare Jessica to Death, Bang the Drum Slowly, The Doors,* and *The Cemetery Club.* Survived by his wife and his brother.

NOBU McCARTHY (Nobu Atsumi), 67, Ottawa-born actress who became the artistic director of the first Asian American theatre company, East West Players, died after collapsing on a movie set on Apr. 6, 2002 in Londrina, Brazil. Following her 1958 film debut in *The Geisha Boy,* she appeared in such movies *The Hunters, Wake Me When It's Over, Walk Like a Dragon, The Karate Kid Part II,* and *Pacific Heights.* She is survived by two children from her first marriage and by three brothers.

BILL McCUTCHEON, 77, Kentucky-born character player of screen, stage, and television, perhaps most recognizable as "Uncle Wally" on the educational series "Sesame Street," died in Ridgewood, NJ, on Jan. 9, 2002 after a long illness. His film credits include *Santa Claus Conquers the Martians, Viva Max!, The Stoolie, W.W. and the Dixie Dancekings, Hot Stuff, Steel Magnolias, Family Business, Tune in Tomorrow...,* and *Mr. Destiny.* Survived by his wife, his son, two daughters, and five grandchildren.

LEO McKERN, 82, Sydney-born character actor, whose best known roles include playing the cultist Clang in the Beatles film *Help!* and prosecutor Cromwell in the Oscar-winning *A Man for All Seasons,* died on July 23, 2002 in Bath, England after a long illness. His other films include *Murder in the Cathedral* (debut, 1952), *Time Without Pity, A Tale of Two Cities* (1958), *The Mouse That Roared, Scent of Mystery, Mr. Topaze (I Like Money), The Day the Earth Caught Fire, A Jolly Bad Fellow, King and Country, The Amorous Adventures of Moll Flanders, The Shoes of the Fisherman, Ryan's Daughter* (as Ryan), *The Adventure of Sherlock Holmes' Smarter Brother, The Omen, Candleshoe, The Blue Lagoon* (1980), *The French Lieutenant's Woman, Ladyhawke,* and *Traveling North.* On television he was best known as the star of the series "Rumpole of the Bailey." He is survived by his wife, and two daughters, one of whom, Abigail McKern, appeared with her father in the "Rumpole" series.

SPIKE MILLIGAN (Terence Alan Milligan), 83, British comedian-character actor, best known for starring in and writing the influential U.K. radio series "The Goon Show" (with Peter Sellers, Harry Secombe, and Michael Bentine), died of kidney failure at his home in Sussex, England on Feb. 27, 2002. His motion picture credits include *Penny Points to Paradise, Down Among the Z Men* (which he also wrote), *Postman's Knock, The Magic Christian, The Bed Sitting Room* (and writer), *Alice's Adventures in Wonderland, The Adventures of Barry McKenzie, The Three Musketeers* (1974), *The Great McGonagall* (and writer), *Ghost in the Noonday Sun* (and writer), *The Last Remake of Beau Geste, Life of Brian, History of the World Part 1,* and *Yellowbeard.* Survived by his third wife, as well as a son and three daughters from his previous marriages.

MARVIN MIRISCH, 84, New York City-born motion picture executive, who along with his brothers Walter and Harold, formed the Mirisch Company and were responsible for the three Academy Award winners for best picture, *The Apartment, West Side Story,* and *In the Heat of the Night,* died of a heart attack on Nov. 17, 2002 in Los Angeles. Among his other credits were *The Great Escape, The Pink Panther,* and *The Russians Are Coming! The Russians Are Coming!* He is survived by his brother Walter; his wife of 60 years, his son, his two daughters, and six grandchildren.

DUDLEY MOORE, 66, British comedian-actor-pianist, who earned an Oscar nomination for playing the perpetually soused millionaire in the 1981 comedy hit *Arthur,* died of pneumonia as a complication of progressive supranuclear palsy, at his home in Plainfield, NJ, on March 27, 2002. First known as a member of the satirical quartet "Beyond the Fringe," he and another member, Peter Cook, split from the group and worked as a team for a period, appearing in such films as *The Wrong Box, The Bed Sitting Room,* and *Those Daring Young Men in Their Jaunty Jalopies.* As a solo performer Moore was seen in such pictures as *30 Is a Dangerous Age Cynthia* (for which he also wrote the music), *Foul Play, 10, Wholly Moses, Six Weeks, Lovesick, Romantic Comedy, Unfaithfully Yours, Micki + Maude, Santa Claus, Like Father Like Son, Crazy People,* and *Blame It on the Bellboy.* He is survived by his sister, and his two sons.

PEGGY MORAN (Marie Jeanette Moran), 84, Iowa-born actress of the 1940s, died on Oct. 25, 2002 in Camarillo, CA, of complications from injuries sustained in an auto accident. Her films include *Girls' School, Ninotchka, The Mummy's Hand, Oh Johnny How You Can Love, One Night in the Tropics, Horror Island, Rhythm in the Saddle, Drums of the Congo, Seven Sweethearts,* and *King of the Cowboys.* She retired in 1942 after marrying director Henry Koster (who died in 1988). She is survived by a son and a stepson.

GEORGE NADER, 80, Pasadena-born screen and television actor died on Feb. 4, 2002 in Woodland Hills, CA, of cardiac pulminary failure. His film credits include *The Prowler, Phone Call from a Stranger, Robot Monster, Carnival Story, Six Bridges to Cross, Lady Godiva, The Second Greatest Sex, Away All Boats, The Unguarded Moment, Four Girls in Town, Joe Butterfly, The Female Animal, The Human Duplicators,* and *House of 1000 Dolls.* He directed-produced the film *Walk by the Sea* and later published the gay-themed crime novel "Crome." No reported survivors.

JOEL OLIANSKY, 66, writer-director responsible for the 1980 film *The Competition,* died on July 20, 2002 in Los Angeles. He wrote the films *The Todd Killings* and *Bird,* and several television productions. Survived by his sister and two children.

Harold Russell

Avery Schreiber

Rod Steiger

Guy Stockwell

Ray Stricklyn

Richard Sylbert

BIBI OSTERWALD (Margaret Osterwald), 83, New Jersey-born screen, stage, and television character actress, died on Jan. 2, 2002 in Burbank, CA. Among her motion picture credits are *Parrish, The World of Henry Orient, A Fine Madness, The Tiger Makes Out, Bank Shot, Moving, Angie,* and *As Good as It Gets.* Survived by her husband, a son, and two granddaughters.

LA WAND PAGE, 81, Cleveland-born film and television actress, best known for playing Aunt Esther on the sit-com "Sanford and Son," died of complications from diabetes on Sept. 14, 2002 in Los Angeles. Her movies include *Shakes the Clown* and *Friday.* A daughter and a sister survive her.

BRUCE PALTROW, 58, Brooklyn-born producer-director, best known for the television series "The White Shadow" and "St. Elsewhere," died in Rome on Oct. 3, 2002, from a recurrence of pneumonia and complications of throat cancer. In addition to his television work he directed the theatrical features *A Little Sex* and *Duets,* which featured his daughter, actress Gwyneth Paltrow. He is survived by her, his wife, actress Blythe Danner, his son, his mother, a brother, and two sisters.

DENNIS PATRICK (Dennis Patrick Harrison), 84, Philadelphia-born screen, stage and television character actor, perhaps best known to movie audiences for his starring role as conservative dad Bill Compton in the 1970 drama *Joe,* died of smoke inhalation in a fire that swept his Hollywood home on Oct. 13, 2002. Among his other films were *Daddy's Gone A-Hunting, Dear Dead Delilah, Chances Are,* and *The Air Up There.* On television he was known for his roles on the serials *Dark Shadows* and *Dallas.* He had been married to actress Barbara Cason from 1970 until her death in 1990.

BILL PEET (William Bartlett Peed), 87, Indiana-born Disney animator-writer, died on May 11, 2002 in Studio City, CA. He contributed to such animated features as *Dumbo, Song of the South, Cinderella, Sleeping Beauty, 101 Dalmatians, The Sword in the Stone,* and *The Jungle Book.* Survived by his wife, his son, and three grandchildren.

JULIA PHILLIPS, 57, New York City-born film producer, who became the first woman in that field to win an Academy Award, for co-producing *The Sting,* died of cancer in West Hollywood, CA, on January 1, 2002. Her other credits include *Steelyard Blues, Taxi Driver* (for which she earned an Oscar nomination), and *Close Encounters of the Third Kind.* She later published a best-selling memoir, *You'll Never Eat Lunch in This Town Again,* lambasting the Hollywood community. She is survived by her daughter, her brother, and her son-in-law.

ERNEST PINTOFF, 70, Connecticut-born filmmaker, who received an Academy Award for his 1963 short subject "The Critic," died in Woodland Hills, CA, of complications from a stroke on Jan. 12, 2002. His feature credits include *Harvey Middleman: Fireman* (which he also wrote), *Who Killed Mary What's 'Er Name?, Blade* (also writer), *Jaguar Lives!,* and *St. Helens.* Survived by his wife, a son, a daughter, and three grandsons.

DEAN RIESNER, 83, New York City-born screenwriter, who received a special Academy Award for directing and writing the all-bird feature *Bill and Coo,* died on Aug. 18, 2002 at his home in Los Angeles. He acted in such movies as *The Pilgrim* and *Young Man With a Horn,* while his screenwriting credit include *The Helen Morgan Story, Paris Holiday, Coogan's Bluff, Dirty Harry, Charlie Varrick,* and *The Enforcer.* No immediate survivors.

MATT ROBINSON, 65, actor-writer, best known for playing Gordon on "Sesame Street," died on Aug. 5, 2002 at his home in Los Angeles. He had been suffering from Parkinson's disease for some twenty years. He also wrote and produced the films *Save the Children* and *Amazing Grace,* in addition to writing for such series as "Sanford and Son" and "The Cosby Show." Survived by his daughter, actress Holly Robinson Peete, a son, and five grandchildren.

TED ROSS, 68, screen, stage, and television character actor, best known for his Tony Award-winning portrayal of the Cowardly Lion in the musical *The Wiz* (a part he later recreated in the 1978 motion picture adaptation), died on Sept. 3, 2002 in Dayton, OH. He had suffered a stroke four years earlier. Among his other film credits were *Arthur, Ragtime, Police Academy, Stealing Home,* and *The Fisher King.* No reported survivors.

HAROLD RUSSELL, 88, Nova Scotia-born actor, who received the 1946 Academy Award for his performance as the World War II vet who much adjust to civilian life after losing both his hands, in *The Best Years of Our Lives,* died on Jan. 29, 2002 at a nursing home in Needham, MA. An actual amputee, he also received an honorary Academy Award that same year "for bringing hope and courage to his fellow veterans" and later became an activist in rights for disabled veterans. He founded the World Veterans Foundation and returned to appear in one more theatrical feature, *Inside Moves,* in 1980. Survivors include his daughter, a son, four grandchildren, and seven great-grandchildren.

EDGAR SCHERICK, 78, New York-born movie and television producer, died of complications of leukemia on Dec. 3, 2002 in Los Angeles. His theatrical features include *Take the Money and Run, The Heartbreak Kid, Sleuth,* and *The Stepford Wives.*

J. Lee Thompson

Kenneth Tobey

Robert Urich

Raf Vallone

Billy Wilder

Irene Worth

AVERY SCHREIBER, 66, Chicago-born film, stage, and television actor, best known for his comedic teaming with Jack Burns, died of a heart attack in Los Angeles on January 7, 2002. He was seen in such motion pictures as *Don't Drink the Water, Swashbuckler, The Last Remake of Beau Geste, Scavenger Hunt, Caveman, Robin Hood: Men in Tights,* and *Dracula: Dead and Loving It.* Survivors include his wife.

GEORGE SIDNEY, 85, Queens-born director, best known for such classic MGM musicals as *Annie Get Your Gun, Show Boat,* and *Kiss Me Kate,* died of complications from lymphoma on May 5, 2002 at his home in Las Vegas. A former child actor he moved on to directing short subjects for Metro, winning Oscars for "Quick 'n a Wink" and "Of Pups and Puzzles," before making his move into features with *Thousands Cheer* in 1943. His other films include *Bathing Beauty, Anchors Aweigh, The Harvey Girls, Cass Timberlane, The Three Musketeers* (1948), *Scaramouche, Jupiter's Darling, The Eddy Duchin Story, Pal Joey, Who Was That Lady?, Pepe, Bye Bye Birdie, Viva Las Vegas,* and *Half a Sixpence.* Survived by his third wife and his stepson.

DARWOOD SMITH, 72, Colorado-born child actor, who, as the bespectacled "Waldo Kaye," appeared in several "Our Gang" comedies, died on May 15, 2002 in Riverside, CA, after being struck by a passing truck while on his daily walk. He could also be seen in the features *Heroes of the Saddle, Best Foot Forward,* and *My Reputation,* and later became a pastor at several California churches. No reported survivors.

ROD STEIGER, 77, Long Island-born screen, stage, and television actor, who won an Academy Award for playing Southern Sheriff Bill Gillespie in the 1967 Best Picture Oscar-winner *In the Heat of the Night,* died on July 9, 2002 in Los Angeles, after being hospitalized with pneumonia and kidney failure. Following his 1951 debut in *Teresa,* he was seen in such movies as *On the Waterfront* (Oscar nomination), *The Big Knife, Oklahoma!, The Court-Martial of Billy Mitchell, Jubal, The Harder They Fall, Run of the Arrow, The Unholy Wife, Cry Terror!, Al Capone, Seven Thieves, 13 West Street, The Mark, The Longest Day, The Pawnbroker* (Oscar nomination), *The Loved One, Doctor Zhivago, No Way to Treat a Lady, The Sergeant, The Illustrated Man, Three Into Two Won't Go, Waterloo, Happy Birthday Wanda June, Duck You Sucker (A Fistful of Dynamite), Lucky Luciano, Hennessy, W.C. Fields and Me, F.I.S.T., The Amityville Horror, Lion of the Desert, Cattle Annie and Little Britches, The Chosen, American Gothic, The January Man, Ballad of the Sad Cafe, Guilty as Charged, Mars Attacks!, Shiloh, Crazy in Alabama, The Hurricane* (1999), and *Poolhall Junkies.* He is survived by wife fifth wife, his daughter from his marriage to actress Claire Bloom, and his son from his fourth marriage.

MEL STEWART, 72, screen and television character actor died in Pacifica, CA, on Feb. 24, 2002 of Alzheimer's disease. His film credits include *Steelyard Blues, Newman's Law,* and *Made in America.* Survived by his wife, a daughter, and a brother.

GUY STOCKWELL, 67, Hollywood-born actor, best known for playing the title role in the 1966 version of *Beau Geste,* died in Prescott, AZ, on Feb. 6, 2002. Under contract to Universal he appeared in such other films as *The War Lord, Blindfold, The Plainsman* (1966), *And Now Miguel, The King's Pirate, Tobruk, Banning,* and *Airport 1975.* Survived by his daughter; two sons; a brother, actor Dean Stockwell; and two grandchildren.

RAY STRICKLYN, 73, Houston-born screen, stage, and television actor of the 1950s, died of emphysema on May 14, 2002 at his home in Los Angeles. He was seen in such films as *The Catered Affair, The Last Wagon, The Return of Dracula, Ten North Frederick, The Remarkable Mr. Pennypacker, The Big Fisherman, Young Jesse James, The Lost World* (1960), *The Plunderers,* and *Track of Thunder.* He later wrote and starred in the one-man show *Confessions of a Nightingale,* playing Tennessee Williams. Survived by his sister, and his companion, stage director David Galligan.

MARY STUART, 76, soap opera star of the series "Search for Tomorrow" and "Guiding Light," died at her New York home on Feb. 28, 2002 after a stroke. She had been ill with gastric cancer and bone cancer. She had roles in such feature films as *The Girl from Jones Beach, Adventures of Don Juan,* and *This Time for Keep.* Survived by her third husband, a daughter and a son, and two grandchildren.

RICHARD SYLBERT, 73, Brooklyn-born set-designer who won Academy Awards for his work on *Who's Afraid of Virginia Woolf?* and *Dick Tracy,* died of cancer on March 23, 2002 in Woodland Hills, CA. He received additional Oscar nominations for *Chinatown, Shampoo, Reds,* and *The Cotton Club.* Starting in 1975 he spent three years as vice president in charge of production for Paramount Pictures. He is survived by his brother, designer Paul Sylbert; his wife, three sons, and two daughters.

RON TAYLOR, 49, Texas-born screen, television, and stage actor, best known for supplying the voice of the monstrous plant "Audrey II" in the original Off-Broadway production of the hit musical *Little Shop of Horrors,* died of heart failure on Jan. 15, 2002 at his home in Los Angeles. He appeared in such films as *Who's That Girl, Dead Heat, The Mighty Quinn, Downtown, Heart Condition, A Rage in Harlem,* and *Amos & Andrew.* He is survived by his wife, his parents, two sisters, and a son.

J. LEE THOMPSON, 88, British film director-producer-writer, who received an Oscar nomination for directing the 1961 adventure *The Guns of Navarone*, died of congestive heart failure at his summer home in Sooke, British Columbia, Canada, on Aug. 30, 2002. Among his other directorial credits are *The Yellow Balloon* (also writer), *An Alligator Named Daisy, Ice Cold in Alex, Tiger Bay, Northwest Frontier (Flame Over India), I Aim at the Stars, Cape Fear* (1962), *Taras Bulba, Kings of the Sun, What a Way to Go!, John Goldfarb Please Come Home, Return from the Ashes* (and producer), *Eye of the Devil, Mackenna's Gold, The Chairman, Brotherly Love (Country Dance), Conquest of the Planet of the Apes, Huckleberry Finn* (1974), *The Reincarnation of Peter Proud, St. Ives, The Greek Tycoon, 10 to Midnight* (and co-writer), *The Evil That Men Do, King Solomon's Mines* (1985), and *Murphy's Law*. Survived by his wife, a daughter, and a granddaughter.

KENNETH TOBEY, 83, Oakland-born actor, best known for starring in the classic sci-fi film *The Thing From Another World*, died of natural causes on Dec. 22, 2002 in Rancho Mirage, CA. His many other films include *I Was a Male War Bride, Twelve O'Clock High, The Gunfighter, Up Front, Angel Face, The Beast from 20000 Fathoms, The Bigamist, The Steel Cage, It Came from Beneath the Sea, The Steel Jungle, The Man in the Gray Flannel Suit, The Great Locomotive Chase, The Search for Bridey Murphy, The Wings of Eagles, The Vampire, Cry Terror!, X-15, Marlowe, Billy Jack, Ben, Walking Tall, Dirty Mary Crazy Larry, Baby Blue Marine, Hero at Large, Airplane!, Strange Invaders, Gremlins, Innerspace,* and *Honey I Blew Up the Kid.*

MICHAEL TODD, JR., 72, Los Angeles-born motion picture producer died of lung cancer on May 5, 2002 at his home in County Carlow, Ireland. Following the death of his father, Mike Todd, he took over his production company and came up with the 1960 Smell-O-Vision feature *Scent of Mystery*, in which odors were released in the theatre to coincide with events on screen. His only other production credit was on the film *The Bell Jar*. Survived by his second wife, his six children from his first wife, and his half-sister, Liza, the daughter of Elizabeth Taylor.

ROBERT URICH, 55, Ohio-born screen and television actor, best known for starring in the series "Vega$" and "Spenser: For Hire," died of cancer on Apr. 16, 2002 in Thousand Oaks, CA. His motion picture credits include *Magnum Force, Endangered Species, The Ice Pirates,* and *Turk 182!* Survived by his wife, his mother, three children, two brothers, and a sister.

RAF VALLONE, 86, Italian actor, who became a star after appearing in the 1948 film *Bitter Rice*, died on Oct. 31, 2002 in Rome. His many other films include *Passionate Summer, Therese Raquin (The Adulteress), No Escape, The Sins of Rose Bernd, Two Women, El Cid, A View from the Bridge, Phaedra, The Cardinal, Nevada Smith, Kiss the Girls and Make Them Die, The Italian Job* (1969), *The Kremlin Letter, A Gunfight, Rosebud, The Other Side of Midnight, The Greek Tycoon, An Almost Perfect Affair, Lion of the Desert, A Time to Die,* and *The Godfather Part 3*. Survived by his wife, actress Elena Varzi, a son, and a daughter.

WILLIAM WARFIELD, 82, Arkansas-born singer, best known to movie audiences for singing "Old Man River" in the 1951 adaptation of *Show Boat*, died on Aug. 25, 2002 in Chicago from a broken neck suffered in a fall a month earlier. On stage he was most closely associated with performing the lead in several versions of *Porgy and Bess*, of which he made a notable recording with his wife (1952-72), Leontyne Pryce. Survived by two brothers.

BILLY WILDER, 95, Austro-Hungarian-born director-writer-producer, one of Hollywood greatest filmmakers, who won a total of six Academy Awards for his work, died at his home in Beverly Hills on March 27, 2002. He had been suffering from pneumonia. Starting in Germany as a writer he eventually co-directed one film in Europe, *Mauvaise Graine*, before coming to the United States where he received script credit on such productions as *Music in the Air, Bluebeard's Eighth Wife, Midnight, Ninotchka* (Oscar nomination), *Arise My Love, Ball of Fire* (Oscar nomination), and *Hold Back the Dawn* (Oscar nomination). In 1942 he turned to directing with *The Major and the Minor*, continuing as his own screenwriter, always in collaboration. His other credits as director-writer are *Five Graves to Cairo, Double Indemnity* (Oscar nominations for dir. & wr.), *The Lost Weekend* (Academy Award winner for Best Director and Best Screenplay, in collaboration with Charles Brackett), *The Emperor Waltz, A Foreign Affair* (Oscar nomination for wr.), *Sunset Blvd.* (Academy Award winner for Best Story and Screenplay, in collaboration with Charles Brackett and D.M. Marshman, Jr.; nomination for dir.), *The Seven Year Itch, The Spirit of St. Louis, Witness for the Prosecution* (Oscar nomination for dir.), *The Front Page* (1974), and *Buddy Buddy*. He served as director-writer and producer for *Ace in the Hole (The Big Carnival), Stalag 17* (Oscar nomination for dir.), *Sabrina* (Oscar nomination for dir. & wr.), *Love in the Afternoon, Some Like It Hot* (Oscar nominations for dir. & wr.), *The Apartment* (Academy Award winner for Best Director, Best Story and Screenplay—Written Directly for the Screen, in collaboration with I.A.L. Diamond, and Best Picture), *One Two Three, Irma La Douce, Kiss Me Stupid, The Fortune Cookie* (Oscar nomination for wr.), *The Private Life of Sherlock Holmes, Avanti!,* and *Fedora*. He is survived by his second wife and his daughter from his first marriage.

IRENE WORTH (Harriet Abrams), 85, Nebraska-born actress, who won Tony Awards for her work in *Tiny Alice, Sweet Bird of Youth*, and *Lost in Yonkers*, died on March 10, 2002 in New York after suffering a stroke at a post office near her apartment. Although essentially a stage actress, she appeared in some films including *One Night With You, The Secret People, Seven Seas to Calais, Rich Kids, Deathtrap, Just the Ticket,* and *Onegin*. Survived by her sister and brother.

INDEX

A

Aaliyah, 24
Aames, Willie, 329
Aaron, Caroline, 192, 193, 197, 329
Aaron, Hank, 178
Aarts, Robbert, 257
Abad, Sol, 277
Abadal, Ignasi, 258
Abadal, Pere, 288
Abadie, William, 55
Abagnale, Frank W., 164
Abandon, 205, 214
Abandon Pictures, 18
Abarico, Erwin, 142
Abatemarco, Tony, 39
Abbas, Hiam, 319
Abbati, Stefano, 242
Abbot, Brian, 253
Abbott, Abdul Malik, 172
Abbott, Christie, 187
Abbott, David, 211
Abbott, Diahnne, 329
Abbott, John, 329
Abbott, Matthew, 30
Abbott, Scott, 24
ABC Africa, 313
Abdalain, Lousnak, 292
Abdallah, Jamila, 251
Abdi, Nassim, 318
Abdul, Paula, 89
Abe, Chiyo, 271
Abelanski, Jean, 269
Abelanski, Lionel, 269
Abell, Tim, 26
Abellon, Alejandro, 133
Abernathy, Louisa, 60
Abidi, Cyrus, 318
Abiteboul, Michaël, 279
Abkarian, Simon, 129, 292
Abma, Marie, 143
Aboriginal Peoples Television Network, 201
Abou-Samah, Michel "Gish," 66
About a Boy, 58–59, 234

About Schmidt, 152–53, 228, 231, 233
Abraham, F. Murray, 182, 329
Abraham, Jake, 310, 322
Abraham, Marc, 115, 116, 141
Abraham, Peter, 195x
Abrahams, Doug, 24
Abrahams, Jon, 211
Abrahams, Rehane, 315, 316
Abram, John, 308
Abramoff, Robert, 173
Abrams, Abiola Wendy, 189
Abrams, Peter, 179
Abrams, Tony R., 192
Abrell, Brad, 80
Abreu, Agustin, 309
Abrhám, Josef, 318
ABS-CBN Entertainment, 173
Absolom, Joe, 325
Abubo, Megan, 96
Abunuwara, Kim, 178
Abusada, Jordi, 314
Accorsi, Stefano, 242, 275, 280
Acharya, Ganesh, 321
Achenbach, Martin, 250
Acheson, James, 52
Acker, Amy, 164
Ackerman, Anne, 209
Ackerman, Josh, 179
Ackerman, Peter, 32
Ackerman, Roy, 109
Ackerman, Thomas, 12
Ackert, David, 176
Ackland, Joss, 85, 329
Ackles, Alan, 196
Ackroyd, Barry, 311
Acogny, George, 163
Acord, Lance, 72, 148
Acosta, Lina, 123
Acovone, Jay, 17
Acuña, Jason "Wee Man," 206
Adachi, Jeff, 179
Adachi, Leanne, 133
Adam, Christian, 237

Adam, Dietrich, 276
Adam, Paul, 61
Adams, Allen, 134
Adams, Amy, 164, 192, 196
Adams, Brooke, 329
Adams, Bryan, 61
Adams, Caitlin, 329
Adams, Denae, 177
Adams, Don, 329
Adams, Eddie, 86
Adams, Edie, 329
Adams, Enid-Raye, 65
Adams, Evan, 187
Adams, Granville, 146
Adams, Hayden, 30
Adams, Jane, 11, 329
Adams, Jay, 49
Adams, J.B., 136
Adams, Joey Lauren, 181, 329
Adams, Julie, 329
Adams, Lillian, 42
Adams, Lloyd, 162
Adams, Mason, 329
Adams, Maud, 329
Adams, Orny, 117
Adams, Steve, 170
Adams, Tacey, 210
Adam Sandler's Eight Crazy Nights, 144, 234
Adam's Fall, 205
Adamson, Christopher, 241
Adappa, Shashi, 319
Adaptation., 148–49, 226, 228, 231
Aday, Marvin Lee, 343
Addessi, A. Charles, 173
Addessi, Charles, II, 173
Addessi, Charles A., 173
Addison, Heidi, 176
Addy, Mark, 28
Ade, 322
Ade, Melyssa, 184
Adefarasin, Remi, 58
Adjani, Isabelle, 329
Adler, Gilbert, 128
Adler, Justin, 198
Adler, Mark, 202

Adler, Richard, 140
Adon, Raeda, 310
Adoti, Razaq, 264
ADR Productions, 316, 319
Adsit, Scott, 78
Adventures of Pluto Nash, The, 196
Affleck, Ben, 33, 44, 45, 66, 329
Affleck, Casey, 329
Affleck, Rab, 160
Aftanas, Craig, 308
Afterman, Peter, 154
Agamanolis, Christina, 191
Agar, John, 355
Agashe, Mohan, 319
Ager, Nikita, 125
Aghdashloo, Shohreh, 176
Agnès, 321
Agnew, Ian, 160
Agni Varsha: The Fire and the Rain, 319
Aguado, Ken, 50, 201
Aguero, Sergio, 248
Aguirresarobe, Javier, 296
Agutter, Jenny, 329
Ahern, Lloyd, 99
Ahlf, Al, 89
Ahluwalia, Polly, 209
Ahmad, Maher, 128
Ahmadi, Mohammad, 326
Ahn, Byun-Moo, 291
Ahola, Jouko, 281
Ahrenberg, Staffan, 142
Ai, Catherine, 185
Aibel, Douglas, 90, 182
Aidem, Betsy, 136
Aiello, Danny, 329
Aiello, Piera, 323
Aihara, Hironori, 222
Aihara, Kazumi, 211
Aikawa, Show, 325
Aiken, Daniel, 109
Aiken, Liam, 82, 208
Aikman, Chuck, 209
Aimée, Anouk, 29, 329

Ainadi, Samir, 292
Ainge, Danny, 174
Ainge, Michelle, 174
Ainslie, Jean, 289
Airaudo, Malou, 296
Aird, Holly, 97
Airlie, Andrew, 106
Airoldi, Conchita, 199
Ajaye, Franklyn, 24
Ákadóttir, Margarét, 34
Akahori, Shigeo, 308
Akane, Kazuki, 309
Akbari, Saman, 326
Akerman, Jeremy, 85
Akers, Karen, 329
Akhtar, Javed, 261
Akin, Philip, 66
Akinfemi, Bayo, 109
Akinnouye-Agbaje, Adewale, 71
Akino, Yoko, 323
Akins, Francis, 143
Akkad, Moustapha, 194
Akkitirq, Atuat, 265
Alachiotis, Nick, 65
Alagna, Roberto, 317
Alaina, 120
Alameda Films, 293
Alan, Jordan, 176
Alane, Bernard, 267
Alarcon, Sergio, 211
Alban, Carlo, 197
Albanese, Alba, 186
Albano, Anthony, 204
Albano, Nelson, 309
Albarran, Gerardo, 17
Alberg, Tom, 210
Alberghetti, Anna Maria, 329
Albert, Andrea, 306
Albert, Eddie, 329
Albert, Edward, 329
Albert, Kenny, 190
Albert, Steve, 132
Albert, Trevor, 192
Alberti, Maryse, 154
Alberti, Sole, 48
Albertini, Matthieu, 285
Albizu, Fernando, 301
Albou, Olivier, 290
Albright, Lola, 329

Anderson, Richard Dean, 329
Anderson, Robin, 312
Anderson, Sam, 174
Anderson, Seth, 197
Anderson, Stanley, 27, 52, 100, 115
Anderson, Timothy G., 86
Anderson, Tron, 172
Anderson, Vera, 199
Anderson, William, 103
Anderson-Bazzoli, Christopher, 176
Andersson, Benny, 269
Andersson, Bibi, 329
Andersson, Roy, 269
Andersson, Sten, 269
Andes, Keith, 329
Andeson, Tracy, 211
Ando, Masashi, 222
Andolong, Sandy, 173
Andre, Charles, 200
Andrei, Damir, 175
Andres, Barbara, 64
Andres, Eddy, 315
Andress, Ursula, 329
Andretta, Lindsay, 136, 137
Andreu, Simón, 294
Andrew, Beanie, 181
Andrew, Karen, 128, 219
Andrew, Mane Rich, 154
Andrews, Anthony, 329
Andrews, David, 15
Andrews, Jason, 118
Andrews, Julie, 329
Andrews, Leasi, 89
Andrews, Meriel, 311
Andrews, Michael, 11
Andrews, Naveen, 175
Andrews, Peter, 89, 144
Andrews, Rusty, 204
Andrews, Tatiana, 325
Andrick, Virl, 136
Andrikonyte, Ugne, 290
Andronache, Gabi, 193
Andronica, James, 204
Androsky, Carol, 100
Andrus, Mark, 68
Anello, Frank, 38
Angarano, Erica, 197
Angarano, Michael, 197
Angel, Hélène, 316
Angel, Jack, 76, 145, 222
Angel, Nick, 58
Angelella, Dominic, 116
Angelica, Roberta, 292
Angell, Vincent, 26

Angelyne, 314
Angencja Produkcji Filmowej, 304
Angilirq, Paul Apak, 265
Anglim, Philip, 329
Anglin, Florence, 79
Anglin, Karin, 203
Angus, Kristi, 181, 184
Anichkin, Harry, 122
Anisimov, Konstantin, 299
Aniston, Jennifer, 92, 329
Aniz, Julia Ju, 317
Ankrom, Herbert, 42
Annabelle, Ron, 22
Annesley, Imogen, 24
Ann-Margret, 329
Anri, Ben, 271
Ansara, Michael, 329
Anspach, Susan, 329
Ant, 183
Antaki, Joseph, 66
Antarctic, 188
Anthology Film Archives, 199, 307
Anthony, Bryan, 42
Anthony, Jasmine Jessica, 164
Anthony, Kevin, 197
Anthony, Lysette, 329
Anthony, Robert C., 187
Anthony, Tanya, 170
Anthony, Tony, 329
Antidote Films Intl., 204
Antimova, Yelena, 307
Ant Man Bee, 196
Antoine, Benz, 182
Antoine, Geoffrey, 128
Antolini, Camilo, 249
Anton, George, 85
Anton, Scott Michael, 247
Anton, Susan, 329
Antonelli, Laura, 329
Antoni, Mark De Gli, 67
Antonia Company, 186
Antonic, Dragan, 247
Antonio, Jim, 164
Antonione, Carlo, 256
Antonioni, Marty, 203
Antoon, Jason, 66, 74, 163
Antwone Fisher, 159, 216
Anuik, Marika, 183
Anvar, Hedia, 206
Anwar, Gabrielle, 329
Anwar, Marc, 322
Aoi, Yu, 271
AOP Production, 49

Aparo, Michael, 181
Apel, Peter, 130
Apgar, Jen, 112
Apicella, John, 41
Apicella, Stephen, 202
Apollomedia, 319, 325
Appel, Deena, 86
Appel, Peter, 52, 84
Appenzeller, Conny, 307
Appleby, Shiri, 102
Applegate, Christina, 42, 329
Applegate, Royce D., 35
Appleyard, Leslie, 11
Apps, Greg, 24
April, Renée, 170
Apsion, Annabelle, 58
Apted, Michael, 60, 257
Apter, Josh, 189
Aquila, Deborah, 20, 50, 98
Aquilino, Frank, 84, 147
Aquino, Amy, 121
Aquino, Asa, 96
Aquino, Michael, 11
Aquirre, Carmen, 133
Arad, Avi, 34, 52
Aragón, Angélica, 293
Aranda, Juan Ignacio, 293
Aranda, Vicente, 277
Aranha, Ray, 151
Ararat, 292
Arbelaiz, Martí de, 326
Arbide, Eduardo, 326
Arbogast, Thierry, 290
Arbour, France, 66
Arbusto, Nicole, 210
Arcade, 253
Arcand, Nathaniel, 201
Archer, Anne, 329
Archer, Caleb, 44
Archer, John, 329
Arcidi, Anthony, 182
Arcieri, Leila, 94
Arc Light Films, 240
Arcopinto, Gianluca, 318
Arcoraci, Vene, 74
Arcuri, Manuela, 277
Arcusin, Norberto, 258
ARD, 204
Ard, Ken, 219
Ardant, Fanny, 282, 329
Arden, Murielle, 55
Ardezzone, Chuck, 60
Ardiff, Karen, 300
Arena, Bruno, 326
Arenafilm, 323
Arena Films, 253

Arenas Entertainment, 146
Arend, Geoffrey, 21
Arène, Marie-Thérèse, 278
Arevalo, Robert, 180
Argento, Asia, 94, 318
Argento, Claudio, 318
Argento, Dario, 318
Argiro, Vinny, 184
Argo, Victor, 209
Argoud-Morrisey, Karen, 61
Argyll Film Partners, 211
Ari, Robert, 30
Ariani, Giorgio, 326
Arias, Ernesto, 258
Arias, Yancey, 28
Arieff, Rachel, 39
Aris, Jonathan, 243
Aris, Tim, 323
Arita, Maria, 196
Arkin, Adam, 329
Arkin, Alan, 64, 329
Arkin, Anthony, 51, 202
Arkin, Matthew, 38
Arkin, Tony, 210
Arkoosh, John, 188
Arlen, Alice, 131
Armendáriz, Pedro, Jr., 293
Armengol, Pep, 288
Armesto, Luis, 258
Armian, Neda, 129
Armisen, Fred, 81, 195
Armnas, Adrian, 89
Armour, Duff, 211
Armstrong, Alun, 247
Armstrong, Andrew James, 39
Armstrong, Bess, 329
Armstrong, Charlotte, 273
Armstrong, Chris, 325
Armstrong, Craig, 142
Armstrong, Curtis, 179
Armstrong, David, 208
Armstrong, Dido, 19
Armstrong, Dwight, 39
Armstrong, Matthew, 178
Armstrong, Naomi Young, 104
Armstrong, Rami, 19
Armstrong, Su, 24
Armstrong, Vic, 294
Armstrong, Xander, 243
Arnatsiaq, Peter-Henry, 265
Arnaud, Virginie, 237

Arnaz, Desi, Jr., 329
Arnaz, Lucie, 329
Arndt, Denis, 99
Arndt, Stefan, 283
Arness, James, 329
Arngrímsdóttir, Anna Kristín, 34
Arnold, David, 44, 60, 294
Arnold, Evan, 52
Arnold, Jean-Michel, 275
Arnold, Jeanne, 112
Arnold, Tom, 204
Arnold, William, 118, 174
Arnost, Stacy, 208
Arnott, David, 175
Arnst, Hendrik, 255
Aronofsky, Darren, 122
Aronson, Lety, 51
Arora, Chandan, 321
Arora, Jas, 244
Árpa, Attila, 306
Arpad Production, 21
ARP Sélection, 259
Arquette, David, 122, 194, 329
Arquette, Patricia, 254, 329
Arquette, Richmond, 200
Arquette, Rosanna, 23, 329
Arranz, Cristina, 277
Arrick, Rose, 195
Arrighi, Luciana, 97, 263
Arrival, 204
Arrow, 180, 309
Arrow, David, 103
Arroyave, Karina, 146
Arroyo, Pury, 317
Arslanian, Kevork, 292
ARTE, 276, 281, 307, 315
ARTE France Cinema, 250, 262, 312, 316, 319
Arteta, Miguel, 92
ARTE-Zeta Prods., 109
Arthur, Beatrice, 329
Arthur, Brooks, 144
Arthur, Michael, 183
Arthur Hofer Productions, 307
Artiñano, Javier, 277
Artisan, 114, 130, 140, 179, 180, 234, 320

Boisvert, Léopold, 175
Bokal, Nikki, 60
Bokelberg, Oliver, 189
Boken om E, 267
Bokhour, Ray, 44
Bola, El, 326
Bolado, Carlos, 311
Boland, Mary-Clay, 175
Bolar, Woody, 104
Bolding, Shelley, 175
Boling, Vincent, 100
Bolkan, Florinda, 331
Boll, Uwe, 314
Boll Films, 314
Bollinger, Frank, 323
Bollywood/Hollywood, 324
Bologna, Joseph, 204, 331
Bolster, Thomas, 30
Bolt, Anna, 33
Bolt, Jeremy, 33
Bolton, Buddy, 79, 89, 205
Bomba, David J., 68
Bona, Carolina, 277
Bonacelli, Paolo, 318
Bonamy, Olivia, 267
Bond, Bradford, 187
Bond, Chelsea Lee, 42
Bond, Derek, 331
Bond, Greg, 173
Bond, Samantha, 294
Bondelli, Roger, 12, 195
Bondoux, Jacques, 321
Bondy, Egon, 307
Bondy, Sol, 307
Bones, Hank, 182
Bones Productions, 309
Bonet, Lisa, 331
Boneza, Jenn, 96
Bonfils, Khan, 57
Bongard, Pascal, 253
Bonham-Carter, Helena, 331
Bonifacio, Charlie, 21
Bonilla, Daryl, 211
Bonitzer, Pascal, 279
Bonnaire, Sandrine, 290
Bonneau, Father, 44
Bonnekamp, Ulli, 188
Bonnet, Segorene, 278
Bonneton, Valérie, 253
Bonnevie, Dina, 173
Bonneville, Hugh, 266
Bonnot, Françoise, 126
Bono, Joseph, 147
Bonsangue, Frank, 147
Bonucci, Silvia, 242

Boom: The Sound of Eviction, 211
Boon, Clint, 274
Boon, Jacques, 249
Boone, Fontella, 197
Boone, Pat, 331
Boorem, Mika, 96
Boortz, Jeffery, 67
Booth, Margaret, 355
Booth, Roger, 252
Booth, Ron, 173
Boothe, James, 331
Boothe, Powers, 43, 331
Booz, Emmanuel, 237, 277
Booz, Manu, 71
Boragno, Jade, 132
Borbás, István, 269
Borbély, László, 306
Bordihn, Tina, 281
Bordoff, Shawn, 183
Bórd Scannán na hÉireann, 246, 284
Borg, Charles, 262
Borg, Dominique, 237
Borge, Frederikke, 55
Borghi, Vanni, 199
Borgnine, Ernest, 331
Borland, Kathy, 322
Borman, Moritz, 85, 142
Born, Justin, 211
Bornes, Roberto, 309
Bornt, Tom, 118
Boromeo Planchez, Carlo, 316
Borowiecki, Ben, 138
Borstal Boy, 246
Borstein, Alex, 31
Borucka, Zofia, 201
Boryea, Jay, 101
Bosanquet, Simon, 300
Bosch-Dos Santos, Clas, 314
Bosco, Mario, 198
Bosco, Philip, 205, 331
Bosek, Gary, 140
Bosley, Tom, 331
Bosmajian, Harlan, 78, 176, 189
Boss, Alan, 203
Bossi, Pablo, 249, 258
Bossu, Le, 287
Bostick, Michael, 25
Bostwick, Barry, 331
Bosworth, Kate, 96, 120
Botcher, Di, 289
Botrashvilli, Zuri, 262
Botticelli, Michelle, 122
Bottoms, Joseph, 331
Bottoms, Sam, 206, 331

Bottoms, Timothy, 331
Botwick, Terry, 114
Bouchard, Jacqueline, 269
Bouchet, Barbara, 160
Bouchez, Elodie, 188
Bouchner, Vitezslav, 94
Bougere, Teagle F., 163
Bouich, Mohamed, 107
Boulat, Antoinette, 93, 253, 282
Boulogne, Lily, 259
Boulting, Ingrid, 331
Bouquet, Carole, 321
Bouquet, Michel, 277
Bouquin, Jacques, 320
Bourboulon, Frederic, 285, 324
Bourdieu, Emmanuel, 245
Bouril, Amy, 52
Bourke, Charlotte, 30, 69, 176, 208
Bourne, Hannah, 268
Bourne, Michael, 198
Bourne, Timothy M., 150
Bourne Identity, The, 71, 233
Bournelis, Zoe, 180
Bouschanzi, Joseph Couly, 312
Boutiba, Fouad, 191
Boutilier, Kate, 163
Boutleroff, Serge, 267
Boutsikaris, Dennis, 331
Bova, Anthony Vincent, 141
Bovaira, Fernando, 272, 301
Bovell, Brian, 289, 316
Bowden, Tom'ya, 191
Bowen, Deirdre, 320
Bowen, Julie, 197
Bower, Humphrey, 24
Bower, Tom, 41
Bowers, Bill, 163
Bowers, Cheryl Lynn, 125
Bowers, David, 57
Bowers, George, 88
Bowers, Marjorie, 108
Bowers, Patricia, 128, 150, 209
Bowers, Tony, 264
Bowers, William T., 209
Bowie, Angela, 140
Bowie, David, 331
Bowker, Judi, 331
Bowles, Peter, 264

Bowlett, Simone, 264
Bowling, Beth, 255
Bowling For Columbine, 220–21
Bowling for Soup, 19
Bowman, James, 195
Bowman, Rob, 270
Bowman, Steven, 186
Boxhead Revolution, 196
Boxing Cat Films, 133
Boxleitner, Bruce, 331
Boyajian, Garen, 292
Boyar, Lombardo, 100, 204
Boyce, David, 12
Boyce, Frank Cottrell, 274
Boyce, Teejay, 94
Boyd, Alexandra, 163
Boyd, Anne, 312
Boyd, Billy, 156, 157, 331
Boyd, Don, 325
Boyd, Jim, 187
Boyd, Joshua, 164
Boyd, Lynda, 132
Boyd, Michael T., 26
Boyd, Pauline, 169
Boyd, Philip S., 76
Boyd, Tanya, 181
Boyens, Philippa, 156
Boyer, Katy, 74
Boylan, Grace Duffie, 16
Boyle, John, 191
Boyle, Lara Flynn, 80, 331
Boyle, Peter, 166, 196, 331
Boyle, Sharon, 192
Boyle, Steven, 57
Boyle, Suzie, 263
Boz, 99
Bozilovic, Ivana, 179
Bozman, Ron, 44
Bozulich, Carla, 206
Brabec, Jan, 307
Brabenec, Vratislav, 307
Braccini, Dennis, 71
Bracco, Lorraine, 331
Brace, John, 60
Brace, Tony, 245
Brache, Denia, 209
Bracho, Diana, 248
Bracken, Eddie, 355
Brackman, Jessica, 176
Bradford, Daniel, 92
Bradford, Jesse, 39, 102, 331
Bradford, Richard, 111

Brad Grey Pictures, 101, 310
Bradley, David, 138, 168
Bradley, Ellen, 172
Bradley, Paul, 261, 304
Bradley, Shawn, 174
Bradshaw, Joan, 82
Brady, Derrex, 100
Brady, Jonathan, 207
Brady, Lisa, 154
Brady, Moya, 266
Brady, Paul, 188
Brady, Tom, 154
Brady, William, 79
Brad Zions Films, 30
Braeden, Eric, 331
Braga, Sonia, 146, 331
Braham, Henry, 252
Braiden, Des, 300
Brainard, Tom, 182
Bramall, Anthony, 281
Branagh, Kenneth, 24, 138, 298, 331
Branca, Julius, 191
Brancato, Chris, 199
Brancato, Lillo, 196, 209
Branch, Michelle, 154
Branch, Vanessa, 22
Branchet, Vincent, 259
Branco, Isabel, 275
Branco, Paulo, 275
Brand, Larry, 194
Brand, Steven, 48
Brandauer, Klaus Maria, 331
Brandis, Jonathan, 20, 331
Brandl, Oliver, 146
Brando, Jocelyn, 331
Brando, Marlon, 331
Brandon, Chad, 181
Brandon, Clark, 331
Brandon, David, 318
Brandon, Mark, 24, 211
Brandon, Michael, 331
Brandt, Gibby, 125
Brandt, Victor, 133
Brangan, Felicity, 97
Brangle, Tom, 189
Bransford, Jennifer, 197
Brantley, Betsy, 331
Brantley, Erin, 150
Braquet, Jean-Claude, 237
Braschi, Gianluigi, 326
Braschi, Nicoletta, 326
Brass, Steffani, 199
Brassard, Jean, 175
Bratt, Benjamin, 205, 331

Curtis, Jamie Lee, 194, 333
Curtis, Keene, 356
Curtis, Mickey, 260
Curtis, Pauline, 319
Curtis, Stephanie, 152
Curtis, Thomas, 112, 204
Curtis, Tommy, 115
Curtis, Tony, 333
Curto, Vinnie, 199
Curzon, Fiona, 290
Cusack, Cyril, 313
Cusack, Joan, 333
Cusack, John, 148, 306, 333
Cusack, Sinead, 333
Cuspinera, Ines, 293
Cut Chemist and Numark of Jurassic 5, 176
Cuthbert, Neil, 196
Cutler, Miriam, 197
Cygan, John, 145
Cymerman, Henryk, 211
Cyze, Bobby, 132
Czarnecki, Jim, 169, 220
Czech TV, 307, 309, 318
Czerwinska, Zofia, 304
Czuchry, Matt, 194

D

Dabas, Parvin, 244
Dabrowska, Olga, 309
Dacascos, Mark, 237
Dacia Films, 291
D'Acosta, Michele, 320
da Cunha, Uma, 244
Dadras, Thomas, 194
Daehn, Werner, 94
DA Films, 287
Dafoe, Willem, 52, 53, 125, 333
Dague, Shelley, 180
Dahan, Magali, 188
Dahl, Arlene, 334
Dahl, Knud, 264
Dahlen, Michael, 80
Dahlgren, Tom, 110
Dahling, Lisa, 12
Dahlquist, Patricia, 314
Dahlstedt, Klas, 267
Dahm, Erica, 190
Dahm, Jaclyn, 190
Dahm, Nicole, 190
Dahmer, 191
Dahnert, Stefan, 318
Daiei Motion Picture Company, 323

Daigle, Suzette, 128
Daily, E.G., 80
Daimer, Michelle, 101
Dairou, Pauline, 319
Dakota Films, 246, 268, 314
Dakoyannis, Jamie, 180
Dal, Harald, 264
Dal, Polat, 280
Daldry, Stephen, 166
Dale, Alan, 155
Dale, Charles, 315
Dale, Emily, 138
Dale, J. Miles, 181
Dale, Jim, 334
Dale, Peter, 140
Daleo, Joseph, III, 173
Daleo, Joseph, Jr., 173
D'Alessandro, Kary, 183
D'Alessandro, Roberto, 283
D'Alessio, Joe, 173
Dalian, Susan, 99
Dallago, Rick, 96
Dallas, Keith, 132
Dallas, Walter, 140
Dallasandro, Joe, 334
Dallimore, Stevie Ray, 136
Dallison, Lorna, 58
d'Aloja, Francesca, 318
Dalrymple, Chris, 194
Dalton, Kristen, 78
Dalton, Sarah, 177
Dalton, Timothy, 334
Daltrey, Roger, 334
Daly, Beth, 67
Daly, Peter Hugo, 160
Daly, Tim, 334
Daly, Tyne, 334
Damian, Pedro, 17
D'Amico, Kirk, 92, 179
d'Amico, Suso Cecchi, 114
Damon, Mark, 319, 325
Damon, Matt, 33, 61, 71, 170, 334
Damon, Una, 172
Damone, Vic, 334
Dampf, Ethan, 17
Dana, Jonathan, 140
Danaux, Marine, 129
Danbury, Betsy, 192
Danby, Noah, 109
Dance, Charles, 334
Danco, Eleonora, 242
Dancy, Patrick, 100
Dane, Dana, 119
Danes, Claire, 103, 166, 167, 334

Danes, Perry, 96
Danese, Shera, 22
Danetti, Theodor, 193
Dan Films, 255
D'Angelo, Beverly, 334
D'Angelo, Carr, 154
Danger, Amy, 108
Dangerfield, Rodney, 210, 334
D'Angerio, Joe, 99
Dangerous Lives of Altar Boys, The, 72, 215
D'Angiolillo, Julián, 326
Danie, 158
Daniel, Gregg, 179
Daniel, Llinos, 311
Daniel, Sean, 48
Danielle, Lisa, 52
Daniels, Anthony, 57
Daniels, Erin, 98
Daniels, Jeff, 95, 166, 167, 334
Daniels, Liba, 180
Daniels, William, 334
Danish Film Institute, 239
Danitz, Brian, 220
Danker, Jonathan, 164
Dankworth, John, 264
Danna, Jeff, 88, 122, 185
Danna, Mychael, 154, 159, 185, 244, 292
Danner, Blythe, 334
Danner, Harry, 179
Danning, Sybil, 334
Dano, Paul, 141
Danson, Ted, 334
Dante, Michael, 334
Dante, Peter, 79, 144
Dantès, Edmond, 151
Danza, Tony, 334
Daphtary, Ranjit, 179
Dar, Fuman, 67
Darabont, Frank, 50
Daraiseh, Ammar, 67
D'Arbanville-Quinn, Patti, 143, 334
D'Arbeloff, Eric, 78
Darby, Kim, 334
Darcel, Denise, 334
Darch, Christina, 307
Darcy, Alison, 66
Dare, Eric, 199
Dare, Yinka, 316
Darga, Christopher, 31, 88
Darigo, Sal, 197
Darín, Ricardo, 249, 258
Daring, Mason, 73

Dark, Alice Elliott, 188
Dark Castle Entertainment, 128
Darkwoods, 50
Darlan, Eva, 290
Darlin, William, 262
Darling, David, 190
Darling, Jennifer, 76, 145, 222
Darlow, Cynthia, 158
Darlow, David, 82
Darmody, Don, 101
Darmon, Virginie, 237
Darnstädt, Christoph, 280
Darren, James, 334
Darrieux, Danielle, 282, 334
Darrow, Paul, 294
Darvishi, Mohammad-Reza, 326
Das, Vasundhara, 244
Das Experiment, 280
Dash (Dog), 12
Dash, Bobby, 172
Dash, Damon, 128, 172
Dashwood, Valérie, 291
Da Silveira, Carlos, 309
Dass, Ram, 176
Datig, Fred, 164
Dauchy, Derek, 94
Dauda, Raven, 128
Daugherty, Josh, 26
Daughter From Danang, 207
Daughton, James, 177
Dauney, Robert, 275
Daurio, Ken, 133
Dauterive, Mitchell, 17
Davao, Ricky, 173
Dave, Kumar, 261
Davenport, Amy, 196
Davenport, Lucy, 160
Davenport, Nigel, 334
Davey, Annette, 188
Davey, Bruce, 26
Davey, John, 174
Davi, Robert, 154, 210
David, Elvin "Chopper," 71
David, Keith, 104, 334
David, Lorena, 180
David, Sophie, 316
David Entertainment, 183
David Foster Productions, 20
David Kirschner Production, 43
David Ladd Films, 20

Davidoff, Irina, 79
Davidovich, Lolita, 334
Davidson, Alan, 43
Davidson, Boaz, 99
Davidson, Daniel, 109
Davidson, Jaye, 334
Davidson, Jeremy, 70
Davidson, John, 334
Davidson, Kristen, 52
Davidson, Selina Lewis, 202
Davidson, Tommy, 190
Davidtz, Embeth, 141
Davies, Emma, 257
Davies, Freeman, 99
Davies, Glan, 311
Davies, Gwenllian, 311
Davies, Jeremy, 108, 144, 188, 334
Davies, Lucy, 168
Davies, Nick, 325
Davies, Oliver Ford, 57
Davies, Peter, 67
Davies, Trevor, 324
Davila, John B., 178
Davis, Aaron Amara, 188
Davis, Alice, 192
Davis, Andrew, 17
Davis, Andrew Z., 115
Davis, Ayo, 201
Davis, Carl, 317
Davis, Clifton, 334
Davis, Craig, 28
Davis, Dane A., 145
Davis, Dawn, 289
Davis, Deanna, 190
Davis, DeRay, 104
Davis, Don, 200
Davis, Edgar L., 43
Davis, Elliot, 27, 121
Davis, Frances E., 15
Davis, G. Paul, 148
Davis, Geena, 84, 334
Davis, Hope, 152, 334
Davis, Jeff, 70
Davis, Jim, 109
Davis, John, 183, 198
Davis, John M., 181
Davis, Jonathan, 24
Davis, Josie, 212
Davis, Judy, 334
Davis, Julie, 197
Davis, Karen, 67
Davis, Kyle, 19, 164
Davis, Leo, 245, 266, 288
Davis, Mac, 334
Davis, Matt, 122
Davis, Matthew, 96

Elise, Kimberly, 22
Elizondo, Hector, 335
Elk, William Joseph, III, 187
Elkabetz, Ronit, 262
Elkayem, Ellory, 194
Elkin, Ilona, 170
Elkin, Michelle, 86
Ellefsen, Per Christian, 264
Ellenbogen, Michael, 178
Elling, 264
Ellingsen, María, 34
Elliot, Martha, 191
Elliot, Ronnie W., Sr., 100
Elliot, Shawn, 64
Elliott, Alison, 335
Elliott, Beverly, 133
Elliott, Chris, 335
Elliott, Jeremy, 174, 200
Elliott, Joel, 31
Elliott, Michael, 81, 119
Elliott, Patricia, 335
Elliott, Paul, 140
Elliott, Peter, 303
Elliott, Sam, 26, 335
Elliott, Ted, 145
Elliott, William, 65
Ellis, Aunjanue, 65, 78
Ellis, Brett Easton, 120
Ellis, Chris, 164, 169
Ellis, Elaine M., 186
Ellis, Greg, 211
Ellis, Jason, 94
Ellis, Lisa, 264
Ellis, Madine, 154
Ellis, Marc, 89, 144
Ellis, Michael, 268
Ellis, Mike, 178
Ellis, Ray, 144
Ellis, Robert, 35
Ellis, Tara, 303
Ellison, Michael, 140
Ellsen, Isabel, 247
Ellsworth, Chuck, 122
El Manaa, Nawfel, 319
Elmasri, Manal, 292
Elmes, Frederick, 14, 106
Elmiger, Suzy, 181
Elmore, Karen, 81
El Movimieno Nacional de Video de Cuba, 316
Elouahabi, Nabil, 66
El Razzac, Abdul Salaam, 134
Elrod, Carson, 30

Elsen, John, 212
Els Films de la Rambla S.A., 288
Elso, Pascal, 312
Elswit, Robert, 172
Elswitt, Robert, 118
Elvira Films, 193
Elvira's Haunted Hills, 193
Elwes, Cary, 255, 335
Ely, Kiara Nicole, 150
Ely, Ron, 335
Elyashkevich, Dimitry, 206
Emanuel, Stuart, 180
Emberley, Simon, 284
Embry, Ethan, 112, 211, 335
Emerson, Michael, 55
Emerson, Russ, 176
Emery, Lisa, 55, 130
Emery, Margaret, 60
Emilio, Andy, 162
Eminem, 134, 135
Emmerich, Noah, 70
Emmerich, Roland, 194
Emmerich, Toby, 29, 34, 86, 140
Emmet Furla Films, 162
Emmett, Randall, 162, 209
Emond, Linda, 101
E-motion Film, 309
Emoto, Akira, 323
Emperor's Club, The, 141, 215
Emperor's New Clothes, The, 266
Empire, 146
Empire Pictures, 245, 259, 273, 278, 285, 287, 291, 311, 314, 316, 319
ena Film, 315
Enckell, Robert, 311
Endelman, Stephen, 300
Endo, Koji, 322, 323, 325
Endoso, Michael, 186
Eng, Sofia, 189
Engblom, Skip, 49
Engel, Georgia B., 42
Engelman, Robert, 69
Engelman, Tom, 211
Engfehr, Kurt, 220
Engfer, Dave, 98
England, Dave, 206
Engleberg, Jacob, 168
Engler, Bruce, 194
Engler, Kosha, 116

English, Mitch, 174
English, Steve, 314
Englund, Robert, 335
Engman, Peter, 267
Enigma, 257
Ennis, Glenn, 132
Ennis, John, 194
Enoch, Alfred, 138
Enos, Ken, 189
Enos, Lisa, 189
Enough, 60, 234
Ensign, Michael, 144, 170
Entertainment Highway, 182
Entitled Entertainment, 64
Entwistle, John, 357
Eon Productions, 294
Epiphany Films, 182
Epps, Ben, 102, 181
Epps, Mike, 29, 140
Epps, Omar, 40, 335
Epsilon, 190
Epstein, Brad, 58
Epstein, Jesse, 188
Epstein, Peter, 183
Epstein, Robert J., 189
Epstein, Scottie, 181
Epstein, Yan, 321
Equilibrium, 146
Erb, Stephanie, 124
Erbe, Kathryn, 335
Erby, Kyle, 209
Ercole, Nicoletta, 275
Erdman, Richard, 335
Erdös, István, 306
Eric, James, 16
Erickson, C.O., 70
Erickson, Sage, 96
Erickson, Yvonne, 13, 72
Ericson, John, 335
Erikson, Anne, 140
Eriksson, Hanna, 269
Eriksson, Nils-Åke, 269
Erkel, Ferenc, 324
Ermey, R. Lee, 50, 185, 335
Ernades, Jack, 200
Ernst, Donald W., 222
Ernst, Henri, 290
Ernst, Robert, 61
Ernst, Thomas, 324
Eronen, Tommi, 311
Errico, Melissa, 183
Erskine, Howard, 51
Erwin, Mike, 187
Esau, Sylvia, 316
Escaflowne, 309
Escamilla, Mike, 94

Escape to Life: The Erika and Klaus Mann Story, 307
Escarpeta, Arlen, 41
Esco, Willie, 172
Escobar, Daniel, 88
Escobar, Elsie, 11, 192
Escoffier, Jean-Yves, 97
Escott, Mike, 78
Eshelman, Melinda, 177
Eshkol, Galit, 238
Eskwad, 237
Esli, Marged, 311
Esmond, Carl, 335
Esperón, Osvaldo, 249
Espindola, Amancay, 258
Espinosa, Axuce, 193
Espinosa, Teresa, 154
Espinozaé, Diego, 126
Esposito, Anthony, 182
Esposito, Giancarlo, 335
Esposito, Jennifer, 89, 114
Esquinas, Ramón, 301
Esquire, 101
Essagian, Carlo, 292
Essandoh, Ato, 130
Estabrooks, Nicole, 247
Esteban, Michelle, 183
Estes, Charles, 141
Estes, Larry, 187
Estevez, Emilio, 335
Esther Kahn, 245
Estrada, Erik, 179, 335
Estrada Mora, Jorge, 249
Estrada-Torres, Jaime, 320
E.T.: The Extra-Terrestrial (reissue), 234
Etchegarary, Françoise, 262
Et la-bas, quelle heure est-il?, 238
Etoiles: Dancers of the Paris Opera Ballet, 324
Etter, John, 148
Ettinger, Cynthia, 43
Eul, Reeny, 116
Eurimages, 250, 277
Euripide Productions, 312, 317
Europa Corp., 285, 321
Eusebio, Johnny, 173
Eusebio, Jonathan, 28
Euston, Jennifer, 84
Euvrard, Benjamin, 129
Evans, Ashley, 69
Evans, Bridget, 178

Evans, Chad, 179
Evans, Colin, 22
Evans, Conor, 300
Evans, Derek, 270
Evans, Evan, 176, 180
Evans, Jay, 178
Evans, Josh, 335
Evans, Kate, 243
Evans, Leesa, 69
Evans, Linda, 335
Evans, Llyr, 311
Evans, Na'Tasha Marie, 159
Evans, Nicole, 277
Evans, Noelle, 120
Evans, Pamela, 136
Evans, Quincy, 120
Evans, Rick, 42
Evans, Robert, 88
Evans, Scot, 293
Evans, Stephen, 170
Evans, Venida, 119, 201
Eve, 94, 104
Eve, Trevor, 97
Evelator Pictures, 202
Evelyn, 300
Even, Maryline, 253
Evenkamp, Philip, 280
Everett, Chad, 335
Everett, Rupert, 163, 263, 335
Everett, Tom, 94, 201
Evermore, J.D., 35
Everton, Deborah, 39
Evigan, Greg, 335
Evigan, Vanessa, 177
Ewanuick, Fred, 24, 133
Ewer, Donald, 303
Ewing, Blake, 192
Ewing, Joel, 164
Excel Entertainment Group, 200
Execution of Wanda Jean, The, 198
Exile Productions, 210
Exodus Entertainment, 180
Experiment, Das, 280
Extreme Ops, 325
Extreme Productions, 325
Eyre, Chris, 201
Eziashi, Maynard, 314
Ezra, Rachel, 50

F

Fabares, Shelley, 335
Faber, George, 302

Faber, Matthew, 180
Fabian, 335
Fabray, Nanette, 335
Fabre, Candido, 316
Fabre, Jean-Marc, 259, 277
Fabrica, 318
Fabrice Cinema, 326
Face, 147
Facinelli, Peter, 48
Facing the Music, 312
Fafard, Andrée, 196
Fagan, Bob, 203
Fagan, Joan, 177
Fahey, Jeff, 335
Fahey, Philip B., 115
Fahima, Avi, 262
Fahlström, Torbjörn, 269
Fahrenkrog-Petersen, Uwe, 103
Faia, Renee, 210
Failla, Paul D., 49, 55
Failma, Roel, 28
Fairbank, Christopher, 122
Fairchild, Mark, 151
Fairchild, Morgan, 179, 335
Fairfax, Sarah, 179
Faison, Donald, 16
Faison, Frankie, 31, 64, 115, 188
Fajm, Isaac, 258
Falco, Edie, 73, 335
Falcone, Carlos, 258
Falcone, Frank, 47
Falk, Jonas, 267
Falk, Peter, 99, 335
Falk, Ronald, 57
Fallon, John, 205
Falls, Pat, 16
FallsApart Productions, 187
Fam, Ghia, 185
Family Fundamentals, 202
Famuyima, Rick, 119
Fan, Fhi, 312
Fanaro, Barry, 80
Fancher, Cynthia, 179
Fancy, Richard, 110
Fandango, 275
Fann, Stacey A., 150
Fanning, Dakota, 106, 112, 204
Fanning, Neil, 69
Fantl, Jan, 319, 325
Fantl, Nicole, 24
Fantoni, Andrea, 309
Faraday, Tim, 160

Faragallah, Ramsey, 51
Faraj, 311
Farber, Daniel, 11, 177
Farber, Stacey, 162
Farcy, Bernard, 237
Fardoulis, Monique, 273
Farentino, James, 335
Farewell, The, 307
Far From Heaven, 136–37, 229
Fargas, Antonio, 335
Fargnoli, Marco, 188
Farhat, Jon, 25
Farid, Zaid, 31
Farina, Dennis, 40, 199, 335
Farina, Sandy, 335
Faris, Anna, 154
Farkas, Andrew, 18
Farley, Bob, 184
Farley, John, 144
Farley, Kevin, 144
Farley, Kevin P., 185
Farmer, Cyrus, 101
Farmer, Evan, 86
Farmer, Gary, 148, 201
Farmer, Orran, 209
Farmer, Todd, 184
Farmiga, Vera, 207
Farnham, Robert, 24
Farokhnezad, Hamid, 199
Farr, Felicia, 335
Farr, Shonda, 19
Farrar, Scott, 74
Farré, Jean-Paul, 237
Farrell, Ali, 203, 218
Farrell, Barry, 324
Farrell, Colin, 20, 74, 335
Farrell, Nicholas, 284
Farrell, Peggy, 190
Farrell, Victoria, 182
Farren, Dan, 196
Farris, Susie, 30, 202
Farrow, Mia, 335
Fasano, Felicia, 104, 122, 162, 181, 192
Fasano, Frederic, 318
Fason, Mark, 178
Fast Runner, The, 265
Father and Daughter, 163
Fatone, Joey, 47
Fattell, Louis, 147
Fattori, Laura, 160
Faulcon, Kent, 25, 144
Faulconbridge, Scott, 205
Faulkner, Graham, 335

Faulkner, Jack Bowden, 179
Faulkner, Mary, 174
Fauser, Mark, 207
Faust, Isis, 182
Faust, Lauren, 80
Favino, Pierfrancesco, 275
Favreau, Jon, 192, 335
Fawcett, Farrah, 335
Fawcett, Rupert, 245
Faxon, Nat, 11, 174
Fay, Johnny, 320
Fay, Meagan, 88, 89
Fay, William, 194
Faye, Denise, 219
Fear.com Productions, 319
Feardotcom, 319
Fearn, Scott, 138
Featherly, Susan, 199
Featherman, Gregg, 33
Featherstone, Angela, 189
Febre, Louis, 102
Fechter, Lori, 198
Federman, Wayne, 207
Feeley, Stella, 241
Feeney, Caroleen, 189, 306
Feeney, Heather, 314
Fegarotti, Flaminia, 160
Fegley, Michael, 178
Fehlberg, Mega, 219
Feick, Fritz, 210
Feifel, Martin, 318
Feifer, Michael, 200
Feig, Erik, 174
Feig, Paul, 199
Feig, Rebecca, 307
Feigen, Richard, 202
Feinstein, Alan, 335
Feinstein, Ana, 262
Felce, Ian, 257
Felder, Nora, 88
Felder-Shaw, Hannah, 125
Feldman, Alex, 191
Feldman, Ben, 30
Feldman, Corey, 335
Feldman, Edward S., 85
Feldman, Tibor, 30, 60, 189
Feldon, Barbara, 335
Feldscher, Paul, 107
Feldschuh, Carolyn, 44
Feldshuh, Tovah, 30, 335
Félez, José Antonio, 326
Felice, Lina, 162

Felix, Paul, 76
Feliz, Suzanne Leonard, 38
Fellner, Eric, 27, 58
Fellner, Steve, 163
Felloni, Elena, 199
Fellows, Edith, 335
Felsberg, Ulrich, 264, 268
Felt, Jan Broberg, 197
Feltch, John, 84
Felton, Tom, 138, 139
Femenía, Paco, 277
Femme Fatale, 290
Femme Infidèle, La, 54
Feneira, Marlida, 170
Fenelon, Carol, 134
Feniksi, 129
Fenn, Sherilyn, 335
Fenton, George, 112
Fenton, Mike, 210, 211
Fenwick, Jean-Noël, 278
Fenwick, Perry, 314
Feore, Colm, 66, 219
Ferch, Heino, 325
Ferdman, Oleg, 175
Ferguson, Alex, 186
Ferguson, Bill, 314
Ferguson, J. Don, 190
Ferguson, Johnny, 264
Ferguson, Katrina, 191
Ferguson, Larry, 175
Ferguson, Lisa, 219
Ferguson, Lou, 151
Ferguson, Myles, 182
Ferguson, Sharon, 86
Ferland, Jodelle Micah, 211
Ferlito, Vanessa, 158
Fernández, Adolfo, 296
Fernández, Ana, 296
Fernandez, Angel Luis, 317
Fernandez, Emilio, 304
Fernandez, Frank, 204
Fernandez, Giselle, 154
Fernández, Iván, 314
Fernández, Juan, 272, 296
Fernandez, Louise, 188
Fernandez, Thierry, 251
Fernández, Verónica, 326
Ferrabee, Gillian, 205
Ferrara, Abel, 209
Ferrara, David, 181
Ferrara, Frank, 175
Ferrari, Deborah, 254
Ferrari, Giacomo, 199
Ferrell, Bill, 67

Ferrell, Conchata, 79, 335
Ferrell, Will, 335
Ferrer, Mel, 335
Ferrer, Miguel, 73, 335
Ferrer, Violeta, 278
Ferrera, America, 123, 215
Ferrero, Piero Lorenzo, 266
Ferretti, Dante, 160
Ferretti, Robert A., 194
Ferri, Elda, 326
Ferri, Linda, 242
Ferrigno, Lou, 185
Ferrin, Ingrid, 133
Ferrini, Carolyn, 205
Ferris, Barbara, 335
Ferris, Pam, 38
Ferris, Samantha, 314
Ferry, April, 43
Ferry, Dawn, 177
Ferry, Dawn R., 177
Fesais, Eric, 290
Fessenden, Larry, 175, 178
Festival in Cannes, 29
Feuer, Howard, 46
Feuer, Zachary, 323
Feuerstein, Mark, 163, 205
Féval, Paul, 287
Fèvre, Emmanuelle, 275
Fewell, Shaina, 179
Fey, Dan, 21
FFP Media Entertainment, 288
FGM Entertainment, 181
FHE Pictures, 114
Fichtner, William, 146
Fickes, Colin, 130
Fiction s.r.l., 256
Fidel, 204
Fidélité Productions, 282
Fiedler, John, 335
Fiedler, Shannon, 163
Field, Chantille, 180
Field, JJ, 85
Field, Pamela, 288
Field, Sally, 335
Field, Shirley Anne, 335
Field, Ted, 211
Field, Todd, 335
Fielding, Rachel, 315
Fields, Anne E., 42
Fields, Strawberry, 24
Fiennes, Joseph, 335
Fiennes, Ralph, 115, 151, 303, 335

Hiatt, John, 88
Hibert, Danny, 310
Hichri, Monia, 319
Hicken, David, 320
Hickenlooper, George, 111
Hickey, Cameron, 205
Hickey, Jilly, 315
Hickey, John Benjamin, 44
Hickey, Tom, 97
Hickman, Camille, 21
Hickman, Darryl, 338
Hickman, Dwayne, 338
Hickox, Emma E., 15, 96
Hicks, Catherine, 338
Hicks, Chuck, 124
Hicks, Ed, 23
Hicks, Richard, 103, 190
Hidalgo, Mary, 145
Hides, Kevin, 271
Hiep Thi Le, 185
Hieu, Joseph, 26
Higginbotham, Marty, 82
Higgins, Aidan, 317
Higgins, Anthony, 338
Higgins, Doug, 200
Higgins, Douglas, 211
Higgins, John Michael, 179
Higgins, Michael, 86, 102, 338
Higgs, Andrew, 118
High Crimes, 41, 234
Hightower, Tennison, 78
Highway Films, 88
Higuchi, Kerri, 60, 177
Higuchinsky, 312
Hildreth, Mark, 211
Hildreth, Thomas, 191
Hilkamo, Pertti, 311
Hill, Aaliyyah, 119
Hill, Amy, 16, 76
Hill, Arthur, 338
Hill, Bernard, 48, 156, 307, 338
Hill, Billy, 168
Hill, Colin, 160
Hill, Craig, 288
Hill, Dennis M., 179
Hill, George Roy, 358
Hill, Prudence, 208
Hill, Steven, 338
Hill, T. Aszur, 76
Hill, Teresa, 179
Hill, Terrence, 338
Hill, Tony, 74
Hill, Walter, 99

Hiller, Randi, 48, 96
Hiller, Wendy, 338
Hillerman, John, 338
Hillier, James, 107
Hillman, Lisa Anne, 110
Hills, Leslie, 324
Hilmarsson, Björn Ingi, 34
Hilow, Mike, 48
Hilton, Carrie, 315
Hilton, Robert, 203
Hiltz, Nicole, 86
Himelstein, Aaron, 86
Himmelstein, David, 67
Hinderchild, Cathy, 316
Hinderer, Gym, 170
Hinds, Ciarán, 66, 82, 131, 338
Hinds, Robbi, 319
Hinds-Johnson, Marcia, 132
Hines, Celeste, 209
Hines, Gregory, 338
Hines, Suzanne, 29, 140
Hingle, Pat, 338
Hink, Christopher, 192
Hinkle, Marin, 189
Hinkley, Brent, 95, 192
Hinkley, Nicky, 253
Hinkley, Tommy, 170
Hinkson, Gershon, 180
Hinton, Annie, 180
Hinton, Gregory, 183
Hiraizumi, Gina, 211
Hirakubo, Masahiro, 266
Hirata, Haruhiko, 321
Hirata, Shuichi, 308
Hiridjee, Vina, 275
Hirosue, Ryoko, 321
Hirsch, Brandon, 150
Hirsch, Emile, 72, 141, 215, 338
Hirsch, Halee, 205
Hirsch, Judd, 338
Hirsch, Julien, 278
Hirsch, Paul, 196
Hirsch, Peter, 30
Hirsch, Seymour, 109
Hirschbiegel, Oliver, 280
Hirschfeld, Richard E., 151
Hirschfelder, David, 131
Hirschfeld/Liberman, 16
Hirsh, David, 170
Hirshenson, Janet, 204
Hirst, Jeremy, 183
Hisaishi, Joe, 222
Hiser, James, 210
His Secret Life, 280

History Television, 109
Hitchens, Christopher, 109
Hivernet, Delphine, 237
Hixon, Ken, 101
Hjartarson, Jón, 34
Hjejle, Iben, 266
Hjorten, Jacob, 201
Hlady, Gregory, 66
Hlavsa, Melja, 307
Ho, A. Kitman, 131
Ho, Coco, 96
Ho, Jeff, 49
Ho, Josie, 325
Ho, Steven, 89
Ho, Tony, 325
Hoang, Ferdinand, 142
Hoare, Syd, 315
Hobart, Deborah, 68
Hobbs, Johnnie, Jr., 197
Hobbs, Nick, 122
Hobby, Amy, 64, 108, 189
Hobel, Mara, 143, 338
Hoberman, David, 110
Hobgood, Elizabeth, 141
Hoblit, Gregory, 20
Hobson, Greg, 177
Hochmair, Philipp, 280
Hochstin, Keith, 146
Hocke, Bernard, 212
Hoda, Hiro, 89
Hodder, Kane, 184
Hodge, Bryan, 188
Hodge, Mark, 69
Hodge, Mike, 185
Hodge, Patricia, 338
Hodge, Tim, 114
Hodges, Cory, 159
Hodgson, Bryce, 133
Hodgson, Rob, 326
Hodlen, Alexandra, 154
Hoechlin, Tyler, 82, 83
Hoefke, Teresa, 159
Hoehn, Marcel, 276
Hoelck, Anna, 84
Hoelck, Ashley, 84
Hoenig, Dov, 17
Hofflund, Judy, 36
Hofflund/Polone, 36
Hoffman, Alexandra, 110
Hoffman, Ali, 144
Hoffman, Dustin, 88, 110, 338
Hoffman, Gordy, 169
Hoffman, Jackie, 30
Hoffman, Mat, 94
Hoffman, Matt, 199
Hoffman, Max, 144

Hoffman, Michael, 141
Hoffman, Peter, 60
Hoffman, Philip Seymour, 115, 118, 158, 169, 338
Hoffman, Rick, 95
Hoffman, Shawn, 173
Hoffman, Susan, 46, 60
Hoffman/Schroeder, 46
Hoffs, Susanna, 86
Hofmann, Trish, 103, 119, 122
Hofrichter, Suzi, 24
Hogan, Bosco, 300
Hogan, Jonathan, 210, 338
Hogan, Michael, 168
Hogan, Paul, 338
Hogan, Robert, 188
Hogan, Siobhan Fallon, 40
Hogg, Edward, 168
Hogue, Joe, 173
Hogue, Stacy, 24
Hohlweg, Karoline, 24
Holbrook, Ann E., 179
Holbrook, Ashley, 183
Holbrook, Hal, 338
Holcomb, Carey, 81
Holcomb, David, 52
Holdaway, Caroline, 252
Holden, Arthur, 66, 205
Holden, Beau, 35
Holden, Larry, 62
Holden-Ried, Kristen, 85
Holder, Grady, 28
Holder, Nick, 107
Holder, Ram John, 253
Holdsworth, Peter, 142
Holford, Steve, 69
Holicek, Brano, 318
Holland, Agnieszka, 178
Holland, Dick, 160
Holland, Gill, 191, 210
Holland, Mandel, 185
Holland, Matt, 66
Holland, Odell, 185
Holland, Samantha, 245
Holland, Sawomir, 307
Holland, Sharon, 315
Holland, Stephen, 81
Holland, Todd, 144
Hollander, Tom, 97, 257
Hollenberg, Vicki, 193
Holliday, Jennifer, 208
Holliday, Kate, 211
Holliman, Earl, 338
Hollingsworth, Rachel, 151

Hollis, Jeffrey Lee, 206
Holloman, Laurel, 208
Hollowell, Danielle, 65
Holly, Kristen Marie, 52
Holly, Lauren, 222
Hollywood, Holly, 120
Hollywood Ending, 51, 216
Hollywood Partners, 99
Holm, Celeste, 338
Holm, Fred Longberg, 195
Holm, Ian, 245, 266, 338
Holman, Bob, 190
Holme, Katherine, 241
Holmes, Channing Cook, 160
Holmes, Darren, 76
Holmes, David, 138, 147
Holmes, Jamie, 181
Holmes, Katie, 205, 338
Holmes, Lee, 50
Holmes, Peggy, 88
Holmes, Teck, 179
Holmes, Tina, 14
Holness, Karen, 219
Holofcener, Nicole, 78
Holt, James A., 190, 200, 209
Holt, Joe, 136
Holt, Sandrine, 200
Holt, Simon, 311
Holtzman, Eric, 190
Holwick, Matt, 194
Holyoke, John, 191
Hom, 134
Home Box Office, 47
Homeier, Skip, 338
Home Movie, 186
Homer, Dru, 79
Hometown Legend, 173
Homme, Joshua, 72
Honaker, Nancy, 192
Honda, Toshiyuki, 308
Honess, Peter, 138
Honest John, 181
Hong, Seok-cheon, 321
Hong Nhung, 142
Honoré, Christophe, 312
Hood, Brendan William, 211
Hood, Don, 169
Hood, Morag, 186
Hood, Sean, 194
Hooda, Randeep, 244
Hook, Jamie, 191
Hooker, Houston, 16
Hooker, Kanan, 16

Liotta, Ray, 16, 22, 162, 341
Liotti, Daniele, 277
Lipinski, Eugene, 175, 195
Lipman, Maureen, 304–5
Lipman, Nicola, 18
Lipnicki, Jonathan, 81, 84
Lippman, Jeremy, 278
Lippold, Richard, 202
Lipschtick, 30
Lipscomb, Rudee, 197
Lipton, Dina, 187
Lirette, Blake "The Blade," 132
Liroff, Marci, 62
Li Shuang, 240, 317
Lisi, Joe, 203
Lisi, Virna, 341
Lissek, Leon, 245
Lister, Tommy "Tiny," 86
Litfin, Rebekah, 114
Lithgow, John, 11, 341
Littenberg, Susan, 84
Litterscheid, Mascha, 319
Little, Angela, 254
Little, Bruce, 308
Little, Ralf, 274
Little, Ryan, 174
Little, Zarah, 199
Little Altars Everywhere, 68
Little Bear Productions, 324
Little Bird Ltd., 264, 281
Little Red Button, 195
Little Secrets, 197
Littleton, Carol, 129
Little Z Productions, 178
Litwin, Megan, 179
Liu, Alice, 189
Liu, Brenda, 185
Liu, Kerry, 211
Liu, Lucy, 200, 219, 341
Liu, Rene, 313
Liu Jie, 240
Liu Jingyi, 240
Liu Lei, 240
Liu Tianran, 320
Liu Wu, 320
Liu Xing, 326
Liu Ye, 316, 317
LivePlanet, 33, 141
Livers, Karen Kaia, 212

Livi, Jean-Louis, 267
Livingston, Lacy, 89
Livingston, Ron, 16, 148
Livingstone, Sally, 52
Livingstone, Sidney, 58
Li Volzi, Vincenzo, 199
Livrozet, Serge, 251
Lix, Ricky, 181
Li Xuejian, 273
Li Zhenhua, 240
Ljung, David, 176
Llanos, Silvia, 272
LL Cool J, 175, 341
Lleras, Anibal O., 188
Lloyd, Arrowyn, 24
Lloyd, Billy, 124
Lloyd, Christopher, 192, 341
Lloyd, Emily, 341
Lloyd, Eric, 133
Lloyd, Jermaine, 128
Lloyd, John Bedford, 21
Lloyd, Michael, 200, 209
Lo, Eugene, 185
Lo, Mayin, 60
Loaria, Blanca, 293
Loayza, Alan, 100
Lobis, Francine, 182
Lobo, Teesha, 179
Locane, Amy, 108
Locke, Peter, 181
Locke, Sondra, 341
Lockhart, June, 341
Lockhart, Liam, 184
Lockhart, Otis, 140
Lockwood, Gary, 341
Loconsole, Beppe, 283
LoConti, Kate, 205
Lodosa, Cipriano, 277
Lo Duca, Joseph, 237
Loehr, Peter, 320
Loew, Sarah, 11
Lo-Fi Pictures, 189
Loftin, Lennie, 66
Loftus, George, 166
Logan, Christopher, 245
Logan, Daniel, 57
Logan, John, 28, 155
Logan, Robert, 35, 116
Logan, Zoe "Joshua Tree," 183
Logan-Black, Marc, 33
Loggia, Robert, 341
LoGiudice, Gaetano, 147
Logothettis, Stavroula, 47
Logue, Donal, 93
Logue, Karina, 74

Lohman, Alison, 121, 204, 215, 341
Lohmann, Katie, 125, 154, 192
Loiseleux, Valérie, 275
Loizou, Loizos, 245
Lol, 317
Lollobrigida, Gina, 341
Lolos, Dawn, 208
Lom, Herbert, 341
Lombard, Louise, 325
Lombardi, Fausto, 283
Lombardi, Francisco J., 321
Lombardi, Kate, 26
Lombardi, Louis, 154, 186
Lombardi-Singh, Arjun, 324
Lombardo, Mark, 290
Lombardo, Tony, 210
Lombardozzi, Domenick, 207
Lomez, Celine, 341
Lo Nardo, Emanuele, 242
Londiche, Pierre, 277
London, Alexandra, 253
London, Daniel, 40, 74
London, Michael, 27
Lone, John, 341
Lonely Affair of the Heart, The, 320
Lonergan, Kenneth, 160
Loners, 309
Long, Jodi, 154
Long, Justin, 19
Long, Marlon, 196
Long, Nia, 341
Long, Shelley, 341
Long, Tyler, 72
Longest Yard, The, 310
Longfellow Pictures, 141
Longley, James, 195
Long Nhuyen, 185
Longo, Tony, 180, 196
Longstreet, Robert, 68
Longworth, Roby, 315
Lonich, Yugomir, 105
Lonsdale Productions, 24
Looking Through Lilian, 206
Loomis, Margie, 79
Loop, Karen, 43
Looper, Chloe, 76
Loose Screw Films, 201
Lopes, Danny, 74
López, Aida, 126
López, Andrea, 248
Lopez, Carmen, 40

Lopez, Dashia, 146
Lopez, Elisabeth, 315
Lopez, Fernando, 64
Lopez, George, 123, 180, 185
Lopez, Jennifer, 60, 151, 341
Lopez, Josefina, 123
Lopez, Mario, 180
López, Mónica, 301
López, Pepa, 288
Lopez, Perry, 341
Lopez, Priscilla, 151
Lopez, Sal, 105
Lopez, Seidy, 204
López de Ayala, Pilar, 277
López Lavigne, Enrique, 272, 301
López Mercado, Ana, 248
Loquasto, Santo, 51
Lordan, John, 25
Lord of the Rings, The: The Two Towers, 156–57, 233
Lords, Tracy, 341
Loree, Brad, 194
Loren, Andrea, 292
Loren, Sophia, 341
Lorenz, Carsten, 106
Lorenz, Deirdre, 141
Lorenz, Marita, 313
Lorenz, Robert, 95
Lörinczy, Gyorgy, 324
Losada, Jaime, 301
Los Cubanos Jubilados, 316
Lose Yourself, 134
Losick, Vic, 193
Lot, Alfred, 285
Lot 47 Films, 18, 184, 265, 308
Lothar, Susanne, 250
Lotito, Mark, 110
Loud Films, 128
Loughlin, Terry, 190
Loughran, Jonathan, 89, 118, 144
Loughran, Scott, 204
Louie, Jada S., 159
Louis, Adrian C., 201
Louis, Christopher, 191
Louis, Gaspard, 193
Louis-Dreyfus, Julia, 341
Louise, Tina, 341
Louiso, Todd, 169
Loukota, Jan, 34
Loutreuil, Xavier, 237
Louvet, Etienne, 277

Louza, Daveed, 109
Love, Courtney, 106, 341
Love, Faizon, 96
Love, Lisa, 148
Loveheart, C.C., 136
Love in the Time of Money, 207
Lovejoy, Deirdre, 64
Lovelace, Linda, 359
Lovelett, James, 44
Love Liza, 169
Lovell, Mark, 310
Lovely & Amazing, 78
Loventhal, Charlie, 186
Lover, Ed, 99
Lovett, Lyle, 187, 341
Lovino, Pierpaolo, 199
Lovitz, Jon, 144, 341
Low, Eddie James, 42
Low, Jason, 27
Low, Kenneth, 325
Lowe, Chad, 55, 341
Lowe, Crystal, 62, 132
Lowe, Georgina, 289
Lowe, Jennifer Dundas, 44, 69
Lowe, Rob, 341
Lowe, Ron, 195
Lowell, Chip, 206
Lowell, Randy, 89
Lowen, Travis, 204
Lowenthal, Kesley, 112
Low Heights, 199
Löwitsch, Klaus, 318, 325, 341
Lowndes, Emma, 289
Lowry, Hunt, 15, 68, 114, 121
Lowy, Linda, 24, 60
Lu, June Kyoko, 95
Lu, Peggy, 173
Lubert, Claire, 245
Lubezki, Emmanuel, 248
Lubin, Aaron, 203
Lucarelli, Rosanne C., 146
Lucas, Gary, 307
Lucas, George, 56
Lucas, Ivan D., 316
Lucas, Josh, 112, 113, 131
Lucas, Kevin, 315
Lucas, Lisa, 341
Lucasfilm Ltd., 56
Lucchesi, Alvaro, 241, 300
Lucchesi, Gary, 13
Lucci, Fran, 103
Luce, Charlie, 21

Maid in Manhattan, 151, 233
Maier, Charlotte, 163
Maier, Lucia, 193
Maigne, Sylvie, 315
Mailer, Michael, 146, 181
Mailer, Stephen, 342
Mailloux, Hazel, 118
Mailman, Deborah, 298
Mailman, Paul, 179
Maimone, Kasia Walicka, 64
Maipo Films OG TV Produksjon, 264
Maisler, Francine, 52, 84, 100, 115
Mai Thi Kim, 207
Maitland, Matthew, 55
Majestic Film Partners IV, 204
Major, Grant, 156
Majors, Austin, 145
Majors, Lee, 16, 342
Makarov, Vitali, 175
Makatsch, Heike, 33
Makepeace, Chris, 342
Makhmalbaf, Mohsen, 326
Makhmalbaf, Samira, 326
Makhmalbaf Film House, 326
Making and Meaning of "We Are Family," 177
Mako, 342
Makoare, Lawrence, 294
Makoko, Lehlohlonolo, 316
Malamud, Vsevolod, 175
Malanitchev, Dima, 163
Malartre, Jean-Baptiste, 253
Malavarca, Eddie, 199
Malco, Romany, 93, 109, 204
Malcolm, Robyn, 156
Malda, Rob, 176
Malden, Karl, 342
Maldonado, Allen, 140
Maldone, Richard, 147, 173
Malek, David, 197
Malhotra, Vini, 179
Mali, Antara, 321
Malibu Comic, 80
Malick, Terrence, 273
Malick, Wendie, 205
Malicki-Sanchez, Keram, 22

Malík, Jan, 34
Malik, Rishma, 324
Malil, Shelley, 17
Malin, Emma Griffiths, 264
Malina, Judith, 202
Malivoire, Martin, 203
Malkasian, Cathy, 163
Malkovich, John, 148, 202, 203, 275, 342
Mallal, Samir, 205
Mallet, Paisan, 316
Mallmann, Stephan, 256
Mallon, Brian, 160
Mallow, Dave, 308
Malloy, Matt, 44, 136
Malmberg, Dag, 267
Malnati, Will, 33
Malone, Coleen, 124
Malone, Dorothy, 342
Malone, Jena, 72
Malone, Jim, 322
Malone, Mike, 89
Malone, Miracle, 206
Malone, William, 319
Malota, Kristina, 176
Malpaso Production, 95
Malsulpiri Production, 286
Maltes, Nick, 14
Malthe, Natassia, 194
Mama Africa, 315, 316
Mammerella, Enrico, 24
Mañas, Achero, 326
Mancuso, Frank, Jr., 181
Mandalay Pictures, 196
Mandan, Robert, 179
Mandehr, Daniel, 121
Mandel, Holly, 31
Mandel, Howie, 204
Mandell, Scott, 197
Mandil, David, 238
Mandoki, Luis, 106
Mandolin Entertainment, 106
Manduke, Joseph, 323
Mandvi, Aasif, 179, 261
Mandylor, Louis, 47
Manesh, Marshall, 31, 199
Manfredi, Matt, 109
Manfredi, Tina, 208
Manfredini, Harry, 184
Man From Elysian Fields, The, 111
Mangan, Stephen, 243
Manganiello, Joe, 52
Mangeot, Jean-Pierre, 251
Mangeot, Monique, 251

Manghane, DeVonda, 121
Mangione, Philippe, 278
Mangold, James, 42
Mangos, George, 142
Manhardt, Mary, 198
Manhattan, 4
Manhattan Pictures, 257, 278
Mani, 274
Maniaci, Jim, 48
Manifest Film Company, 41, 131
Manis, David, 191
Mankoff, Doug, 64
Mankofsky, Isidore, 182
Mankuma, Blu, 133
Manley, Chris, 191
Manley, Jennifer, 39, 164
Manlove, Richard, 107
Mann, Alex Craig, 29
Mann, Amir, 321
Mann, Erika, 307
Mann, Gabriel, 71, 205
Mann, Jeff, 31
Mann, Klaus, 307
Mann, Leslie, 11, 199
Mann, Margaret Elizabeth, 178
Mann, Monroe, 102
Mann, Simon, 284
Mann, Terrence, 342
Mann, Thomas, 307
Mann, Wesley, 174
Manna From Heaven, 205
Manninen, Petri, 311
Manning, Joe, 24
Manning, Sasha Johnston, 325
Manning, Taryn, 19, 121, 134
Manoff, Dinah, 342
Manon, Christian, 24
Manoux, J.P., 69, 201
Mansell, Carol, 199
Mansell, Clint, 46, 182, 203, 205, 212
Mansfield, David, 68
Manson, Alan, 360
Manson, Marilyn, 33, 220
Manson, Ted, 112
Mantegna, Joe, 342
Mantell, Michael, 108
Manterola, Patricia, 323
Mantscheff, Heta, 276
Manuel, Bernard J., 132
Manuel, Michael, 25
Manulis, John Bard, 179

Manville, Lesley, 289
Manz, Linda, 342
Mao, Caitlin, 74
Mapother, Amy, 102
Mapother, William, 74
Maquignon, Charles, 237
Mara, Kate, 84
Marable, Brian, 140
Marable, Mary Bradley, 159
Marais, Jean, 342
Mara-Mara S.I., 272
Marantz, Andrew, 14
Marasco, Ron, 200
Maravell, Nick, 202
Marc, Christian, 237
Marc, Simon, 264
Marceau, Sophie, 342
Marchfield, Scott, 318
Marchisello, Andrew, 173
Marcie, Florent, 323
Marcon, André, 253
Marcos, Alexandre, 253
Marcos, Grégory, 253
Marcovicci, Andrea, 342
Marcovici, Nadine, 237
Marco Weber Productions, 323
Marcune, Patrick, 147
Marcus, Andrew, 68
Marcus, Coltrane Isaac, 81
Marcus, Gary, 188
Marcus, Jim, 101
Marcus, Michael, 60
Marcus, Paul, 203
Marcy, Kevin, 309
Marczuk-Pazura, Veronika, 318
Mardell, Johan, 269
Mare, Quentin, 143
Mareiniss, Lisa Beth, 184
Mares, Ivan, 34
Marescot, Bernard, 267
Marevan, 180
Margarita Happy Hour, 178
Margera, Bam, 206
Margherita, Tony, 195
Margolyes, Miriam, 138, 139
Margotta, Daniel, 173
Margulies, Julianna, 111, 128, 300, 342
Mari, Pasquale, 280
Mari, Paul, 310
Maria-Guerrini, Orso, 71

Marie, Tina, 206
Marienthal, Eli, 88
Marin, Cheech, 93, 326, 342
Marin, Jacques, 342
Marin, Jasmine, 93
Marin, Mindy, 28, 66, 70, 102, 184, 192
Marinaro, Ed, 342
Marine, Jeanne, 97
Marinelli, Anthony, 111
Marino, Joe, 180
Marino, John, 204
Marino, Mauro, 283
Marino, Roger, 199
Marinoff, Michael, 18
Mario (Dog), 12
Mario & Cecchi Gori, 326
Marioles, Ian, 40
Mariolis, Nicko, 154
Marion, Anetta, 193
Marivaux, Pierre de, 256
Mark, D. Neil, 133
Mark, David, 243
Markbreit, Jerry, 66
Markel, Heidi Jo, 189
Markell, Jodie, 51, 106
Marker, Chris, 313
Markey, Craig, 187
Markey, John, 308
Markey, Patrick, 121
Markham, Kika, 245
Markiegui, Estibaliz, 272
Markland, Bridge, 34
Mark of a Murderer, 101
Markopoulos, Ierotheos, 180
Markovics, Karl, 323
Markovitz, Steven, 316
Markowitz, Barry, 212
Marks, Sara, 88
Marlboro Road Gang, 203
Marley, Christopher, 100
Marlon, Ged, 285
Marlow, Gregory, 136
Marmion, Ada, 290
Marmion, Yves, 279, 290
Marmo, Ronnie, 186
Marner, Richard, 66
Marnika, Dino, 24
Maro, Tania, 184
Marone, Patrizio, 280
Maronna, Michael C., 27, 174
Maropis, Adoni, 48, 67
Marosi, György, 323

Murphy, Shamus, 186
Murphy, Shannon, 42
Murphy, Stephen, 203
Murphy, Tim, 315
Murray, Abigail, 172
Murray, Alexia J., 160
Murray, Bill, 343
Murray, Brian, 145
Murray, Cole, 185, 208
Murray, Conrad, 274
Murray, David, 312
Murray, Devon, 138
Murray, Don, 343
Murray, Maritza, 154
Murray, Rich, 197
Murray, Thomas, 209
Murtaugh, James, 64
Murtaugh, Keith, 246
Musacchia, Rocco, 163
Musante, Tony, 343
Muscal, Michael, 199
Muse, Bob, 23
Muse, Nadine, 250
Muse/Blacklist, 169
Musgrove, Robert, 100
Mushin, Pip, 24
Mushonov, Michael, 262
MusicArtsDance Films, 315
Musker, John, 145
Musky, Jane, 101, 151
Muslim, Sonny, 322
Musooli, Peter "Mus," 12
Musselman, Robert, 183
Mussenden, Roger, 79, 89
Mutafian, Mark, 140
Mutambirwa, Garikayi, 39
Mutant Aliens, 182
Mutombo, Dikembe, 190
Muyanga, Neo, 316
My Big Fat Greek Wedding, 47, 233
Myer, Bart, 16
Myers, Chris, 190
Myers, Duncan, 24
Myers, Dwight "Heavy D," 40
Myers, Holly, 323
Myers, Margo, 183
Myers, Matthew, 189
Myers, Mike, 7, 86, 87, 343
Myers, Ruth, 107, 168
Myers, Stephen R., 193
Myhre, John, 218
My Kingdom, 325

Mykytiuk, Lubomir, 66, 85
Myler, Paul, 246, 284
Myles, Bruce, 24, 323
Mynster, Karen-Lise, 239
Myriad Pictures, 92, 179
Myrin, Arden, 125
Myron, Ben, 207
Myrtle & Glen, 189
Mystic Masseur, The, 261
My Wife Is an Actress, 269

N

Naaktgeboren, Sef, 245
Nabatoff, Diane, 162
Nabili, Teymoore, 208
Nabors, Jim, 343
Nachtwey, James, 190
Nadel, Eric, 35
Nader, George, 360
Nader, Michael, 343
Nadler, Eric, 204
Nadler-Friedman, 204
Naebig, Kurt, 82
Næss, Peter, 264
Nagae, Nobuaki, 316
Nagarjuna, 319
Nagase, Takashi, 211
Nagel, Maryanne, 114
Nagel, Rik, 307
Naggar, Alan, 78
Nahon, Philippe, 93, 237
Nahrgang, Mike "Nug," 109, 320
Naidu, Ajay, 179
Naidu, Sulekha, 209
Naipaul, V. S., 261
Nair, Ishaan, 244
Nair, Mira, 244
Nair, Sahira, 244
Nair, Urvashi, 244
Nair, Vikram, 244
Nakagawa, Akimori, 315
Nakajima, Shu, 211
Nakalemo, Elia Jack, 316
Nakamura, Ivan, 173
Nakamura, Kazuo, 260
Nakamura, Kenji, 50
Nakamura, Masaya, 260
Nakashima, Frank T., 109
Nakura, Yasuhiro, 308
Nalin, Pan, 317
Nall, Benita Krista, 74, 164
Nall, Rashaan, 197

Nam, Ki-Joon, 291
Nam, Myung-chul, 310
Nam, Sujin, 321
Namath, Joe, 343
Name, Billy, 202
Nanu, 180
Naobes, Florence, 316
Naomi, 109
Napier, Charles, 61
Napizia, Paolo, 199
Napoleon, Landon J., 190
Napoli, Anna Rosa, 318
Napoli, Eugenia F. di, 275
Nappo, Tony, 195, 203
Naqoyqatsi, 205
Nara, Takeshi, 315
Narc, 162
Narciso, Alfredo, 154
Narita, Yutaka, 222
Nartay, Daniel Erskine, 71
Nas, 22
Nascarella, Arthur, 203
Nash, Aimee, 24
Nash, Bill, 294
Nash, Jason, 176
Nash, Steve, 81
Nashel, Peter, 109
Nasht, Simon, 208
Nassif, Robin, 194
Nasso, Julius R., 162
Natale, Anthony, 177
Natale, Nazzareno, 160
Natalizio, Peter, 203
Natexis Banques, 237
Nathanson, Jeff, 164
Nation, Karen, 79
National Asian American Telecommunications Association (NAATA), 207
National Film Board of Canada, 265
National Geographic, 85
National Lampoon's Van Wilder, 179
Natividad, Kitten, 184
Natoli, Angelo, 147
Natoli, Piero, 275
Natrella, Laurent, 291
Natsuyagi, Isao, 260
Naude, Nicky, 71, 237
Nauffts, Geoffrey, 55
Naughton, David, 343
Naughton, James, 343
Naughton, Maura, 178
Nauzyciel, Arthur, 238
Nava, Gregory, 126

Naval, Deepti, 209
Navara, Dwane, 175
Navarro, Loló, 126
Navarro, Tony, 178
Navia Nguyen, 142
Navidi, Barry, 23
Nawrocki, Mike, 114
Naya Films S.A., 258
Nayor, Nancy, 197
Nazar-Alian, Mahmud, 322
Nazir, Ahmed, 180
Nazir, Amer, 325
NBA Entertainment, 81
Ndegeocello, Meshell, 140
N'Diaye, Abdoulaye Gnaga, 312
Ndiaye, Anna Diafe, 107
Ndiaye, El Hadji, 312
Ndiaye, Medoune, 107
Neal, Dylan, 27
Neal, Elise, 128, 208
Neal, Patricia, 343
Nealon, Ben, 261
Nealon, Kevin, 89, 117, 144
Neate, Antony, 24
Nebout, Claire, 287
Nebrida, Vincent R., 173
Nedeleff, Sandra, 318
Neece, Allen, 177
Neeson, Liam, 85, 160, 161, 343
Neff, Hildegarde, 343
Nefsky, Malcolm, 22
Nefzer, Uli, 325
Negishi, Toshie, 260
Negri, Federico, 205
Negron, Joel, 94
Negron, Rick, 219
Neill, Roger, 188
Neill, Sam, 343, 345
Neilson, Gary, 200
Neiman, Christopher, 100, 125
Nelligan, Kate, 343
Nelligan, Micaela, 197
Nelly, 197
Nelson, Anne, 154
Nelson, Barry, 343
Nelson, Charlie, 287
Nelson, Craig T., 343
Nelson, David, 343
Nelson, Dee, 110
Nelson, Dillon, 201
Nelson, John, 85
Nelson, Judd, 343

Nelson, Kathy, 67, 94, 146
Nelson, Keith, 105
Nelson, Lori, 343
Nelson, Maria E., 123
Nelson, Mary Beth, 152
Nelson, Novella, 159
Nelson, Peter, 179, 202
Nelson, Phil, 200
Nelson, Roy, 198
Nelson, Steven, 26
Nelson, Tim Blake, 67, 74, 92, 122, 343
Nelson, Traci L., 140
Nelson, Tracy, 343
Nelson, Willie, 88, 343
Nemcova, Dana, 307
Nemec, Corin, 343
Nemec, Frantisek, 309
Nemejovsky, Jan, 20, 67
Nemeth, Stephen, 49
Nemeth, Vincent, 285
Nemoy, Carole Curb, 202
Nepomniaschy, Alex, 162
Nepomuceno, Leo, 159
Neri, Francesca, 17
Nero, Franco, 344
Nes, Nasty, 173
Nesbitt, James, 253, 284
Nesic, Alex, 41
Nesmith, Michael, 344
Nesslauer, Nessie, 318
Nest, Julian, 188
Nettelbeck, Sandra, 276
Nettleton, Lois, 344
Netzley, Heidi Jayne, 82
Neufeld, Mace, 66
Neulight, Joe, 197
Neumann, David, 34
Neumann, Drew, 163
Neumann, Mathias, 314
Neustadt, Ted, 51, 136, 147
Neuvic, Thierry, 291
Neuwirth, Bebe, 84, 344
Nevares, Roger, 293
Never Again, 193
Neves, José, 298
Neville, John, 181, 303
Newberg, Bruce H., 245
New Best Friend, 181
Newborn, Ira, 189
Newbould, Tanya, 115
Newcomb, Virginia, 110
Newell, Jill, 169
Newgren, Greta Danielle, 61